CLINICAL DECISION MAKING™ SERIES

Consulting Editor
Ben Eiseman, M.D.

OBSTETRICAL DECISION MAKING

Second Edition

OBSTETRICAL DECISION MAKING

Second Edition

By the Staff of the Beth Israel Hospital, Boston

Emanuel A. Friedman, M.D., Sc.D.

Professor of Obstetrics and Gynecology
Harvard Medical School

Obstetrician-Gynecologist-in-Chief
Beth Israel Hospital
Boston, Massachusetts

David B. Acker, M.D.

Assistant Professor of Obstetrics and Gynecology
Harvard Medical School

Associate Chief, Department of Obstetrics and Gynecology
Beth Israel Hospital, Boston, Massachusetts

Benjamin P. Sachs, M.B., B.S., D.P.H.

Assistant Professor of Obstetrics and Gynecology
Harvard Medical School

Assistant Professor, Harvard School of Public Health
Director, Section on Maternal-Fetal Medicine
Department of Obstetrics and Gynecology
Beth Israel Hospital, Boston, Massachusetts

1987

B.C. DECKER INC • Toronto • Philadelphia

Publisher

B.C. Decker Inc
3228 South Service Road
Burlington, Ontario   L7N 3H8

B.C. Decker Inc
320 Walnut Street
Suite 400
Philadelphia, Pennsylvania   19106

Sales and Distribution

United States
and Possessions

The C.V. Mosby Company
11830 Westline Industrial Drive
Saint Louis, Missouri   63146

Canada

The C.V. Mosby Company, Ltd.
5240 Finch Avenue East, Unit No. 1
Scarborough, Ontario   M1S 4P2

United Kingdom, Europe
and the Middle East

Blackwell Scientific Publications, Ltd.
Osney Mead, Oxford OX2 OEL, England

Australia

Harcourt Brace Jovanovich
30–52 Smidmore Street
Marrickville, N.S.W. 2204
Australia

Japan

Igaku-Shoin Ltd.
Tokyo International P.O. Box 5063
1-28-36 Hongo, Bunkyo-ku, Tokyo 113, Japan

Asia

Infomed
1932, Fei Ngo Shan
Kowloon, Hong Kong

Obstetrical Decision Making–2   ISBN 1–55664–061–1

Library of Congress catalog card number: 82-70759

10 9 8 7 6 5 4 3 2 1

DAVID B. ACKER, M.D.

Assistant Professor of Obstetrics and Gynecology, Harvard Medical School; Associate Chief, Department of Obstetrics and Gynecology, Beth Israel Hospital, Boston, Massachusetts

CATHERINE T. ALVAREZ, R.N.

Audit and Data Coordinator, Department of Obstetrics and Gynecology, Beth Israel Hospital, Boston, Massachusetts

BALMOOKOOT BALGOBIN, M.D.

Instructor in Obstetrics and Gynecology, Harvard Medical School; Clinical Director, Ambulatory Care Program, Department of Obstetrics and Gynecology, Beth Israel Hospital, Boston, Massachusetts

BERYL R. BENACERRAF, M.D.

Assistant Clinical Professor of Obstetrics and Gynecology and Assistant Professor of Radiology, Harvard Medical School; Consultant in Obstetrics and Gynecology and in Radiology, Department of Obstetrics and Gynecology, Brigham and Women's Hospital, Boston, Massachusetts

JEANETTE BLANK, R.N.

Unit Teacher, Labor and Delivery Unit, Division of Nursing, Beth Israel Hospital, Boston, Massachusetts

MAX BORTEN, M.D.

Associate Professor of Obstetrics and Gynecology, Harvard Medical School; Director, Division of Medical Gynecology, Department of Obstetrics and Gynecology, Beth Israel Hospital, Boston, Massachusetts

LOUIS BURKE, M.D.

Associate Professor of Obstetrics and Gynecology, Harvard Medical School; Director, Colposcopy Unit, Department of Obstetrics and Gynecology, Beth Israel Hospital, Boston, Massachusetts

JEROLD M. CARLSON, M.D., M.P.H.

Instructor in Obstetrics and Gynecology, Harvard Medical School; Director, Geriatric Gynecology Unit, Department of Obstetrics and Gynecology, Beth Israel Hospital, Boston, Massachusetts

DAVID S. CHAPIN, M.D.

Instructor in Obstetrics and Gynecology, Harvard Medical School; Director, Gynecology Service, Department of Obstetrics and Gynecology, Beth Israel Hospital, Boston, Massachusetts

WILLIAM D. COCHRAN, M.D.

Assistant Clinical Professor of Pediatrics, Harvard Medical School; Chief, Joint Program in Neonatology, Beth Israel Hospital, Boston, Massachusetts

EMANUEL A. FRIEDMAN, M.D., Sc.D.

Professor of Obstetrics and Gynecology, Harvard Medical School; Obstetrician-Gynecologist-in-Chief, Department of Obstetrics and Gynecology, Beth Israel Hospital, Boston, Massachusetts

LYNN H. GALEN, M.D.

Instructor in Obstetrics and Gynecology, Harvard Medical School; Associate in Obstetrics and Gynecology, Beth Israel Hospital; and Obstetrician Gynecologist, East Boston Neighborhood Health Center, Boston, Massachusetts.

JEFFREY R. GARBER, M.D.

Clinical Instructor in Medicine, Harvard Medical School; Assistant in Medicine, Department of Medicine, Beth Israel Hospital, Boston, Massachusetts

HENRY KLAPHOLZ, M.D.

Assistant Professor of Obstetrics and Gynecology, Harvard Medical School; Assistant Director, Section on Maternal-Fetal Medicine, Department of Obstetrics and Gynecology, Beth Israel Hospital, Boston, Massachusetts

ERIC D. LICHTER, M.D.

Instructor in Obstetrics and Gynecology, Harvard Medical School; Coordinator, Emergency Unit, Obstetrics and Gynecology, Department of Obstetrics and Gynecology, Beth Israel Hospital, Boston, Massachusetts

TOBY MARDER, R.N., M.S.

Nursing Instructor, Parent Education Unit, Division of Nursing, Beth Israel Hospital, Boston, Massachusetts

MAUREEN J. McRAE, R.N., M.S.

Head Nurse, Labor and Delivery Unit, Division of Nursing, Beth Israel Hospital, Boston, Massachusetts

JANET L. MITCHELL, M.D.

Assistant Professor of Obstetrics and Gynecology, Harvard Medical School; Director, Ambulatory High-Risk Obstetrics Unit, Department of Obstetrics and Gynecology, Beth Israel Hospital, Boston, Massachusetts

NANCY E. ORIOL, M.D.

Instructor in Anesthesia, Harvard Medical School; Director, Section on Obstetrical Anesthesiology, Department of Anesthesiology, Beth Israel Hospital, Boston, Massachusetts

JOHANNA F. PERLMUTTER, M.D.

Assistant Professor of Obstetrics and Gynecology, Harvard Medical School; Director, Section on Human Sexuality, Department of Obstetrics and Gynecology, Beth Israel Hospital, Boston, Massachusetts

HAROLD W. RUBIN, M.D.

Assistant Professor of Obstetrics and Gynecology, Emeritus, Harvard Medical School; Honorary Obstetrician-Gynecologist, Department of Obstetrics and Gynecology, Beth Israel Hospital, Boston, Massachusetts

BENJAMIN P. SACHS, M.B., B.S., D.P.H.

Assistant Professor of Obstetrics and Gynecology, Harvard Medical School; Assistant Professor, Harvard School of Public Health; Director, Section on Maternal-Fetal Medicine, Department of Obstetrics and Gynecology, Beth Israel Hospital, Boston, Massachusetts

MACHELLE M. SEIBEL, M.D.

Associate Professor of Obstetrics and Gynecology, Harvard Medical School; Director, In-Vitro Fertilization Program, Division of Reproductive Endocrinology and Infertility, Department of Obstetrics and Gynecology, Beth Israel Hospital, Boston, Massachusetts

FRANCI SHEEHAN-WEBER, R.N.C., M.S.

Nurse Manager, Women's Health Associates, Ambulatory Care Program, Beth Israel Hospital, Boston, Massachusetts

LENARD R. SIMON, M.D.

Instructor in Obstetrics and Gynecology, Harvard Medical School; Director, Section on Gynecologic Oncology, Department of Obstetrics and Gynecology, Beth Israel Hospital, Boston, Massachusetts

PATRICIA S. STEWART, M.S., M.S.W.

Senior Clinical Social Worker, Department of Social Service and Consultant to Department of Obstetrics and Gynecology, Beth Israel Hospital, Boston, Massachusetts

SUSAN B. WILSON, M.D.

Instructor in Obstetrics and Gynecology, Harvard Medical School; Administrative Coordinator, Ambulatory Care Program, Department of Obstetrics and Gynecology, Beth Israel Hospital, Boston, Massachusetts

PREFACE

In the five years since the first edition of this book was published, obstetrical practices have changed a great deal. This short interval has seen the introduction of such new technology as that for obtaining placental tissue for tissue culture (by chorionic villus biopsy) and fetal blood samples for direct study (by percutaneous umbilical venipuncture) and for applying intrauterine surgical procedures to the fetus affected by hydrocephalus or obstructive uropathy. While these approaches are not yet widely available, or necessarily appropriate for wide use (shunting for hydrocephalus, for example, has not realized its original promise), they indicate the exciting direction of the discipline. Meanwhile, counterbalancing forces are at work to solidify the humanistic trends of recent decades and temper the antitechnology concerns of the public. In this regard, permissive attitudes now pervade obstetrical units where most gravidas and their significant others can essentially dictate their own birthing experience in a warm, nonthreatening, homelike setting with a minimum of interference from hospital personnel, yet have the benefits of safety for themselves and their fetus based on discrete, but astute observations to detect problems as they arise and on the ready ability to mobilize intensive care and aggressive interventive measures when indicated. This balance between comfort and safety, between humanistic concerns for the mother's psychological needs and the technological considerations of surveillance and management of risk situations, has been struck in our collective attempts to respond to real, but conflicting objectives.

This book tries to fill a need, expressed periodically by obstetricians, generalists, residents, and medical students, for a resource in which they can get clear and unambiguous clinical instruction and guidance about how to approach diagnostic and therapeutic problems. As academically oriented clinicians, we are torn between our perceived roles as teachers of facts and principles, on the one hand, and as catalysts of thoughtful generation of creative ideas and innovative approaches. A volume such as this one fulfills the former aim, but it has the potential to run counter to the latter by fixing algorithms in print as if they represented the only approach to a given clinical issue, thereby appearing to divest the reader of the opportunity or option to think for himself or herself. Accordingly, we feel it important to emphasize that, while the recommendations we make here for various decision making sequences are those generally carried out at our institution, we do not believe that they exclude other designs nor are they necessarily better than other valid approaches to evaluation and management. Although we recognize that much of what we do is empirical, based on good outcome results, our general guiding principle is to seek a logical pathway to solving knotty clinical problems, seeking answers to key questions that will clarify diagnostic dilemmas or limit the direction of therapeutic options.

This edition considers a much larger number of clinical and clinically related issues than previously. Not only has the original material been extensively revised and rewritten as time has given us fresh perspectives, but many subjects have been attacked that had not previously been deemed worthy or capable of being displayed in a systemic decision tree format. Those dealing with counseling and medicolegal issues are examples of this expanded scope. We are encouraged to believe that these subjects will enhance the value of this book to a wider readership, emphasizing to all that the practice of medicine, especially as it applies to obstetrics, is much more than focussing on case finding, diagnostic problem solving, and skillful therapeutic interventions.

The editors wish to express appreciation to all contributing authors for their special efforts to comply with the somewhat paradoxical specifications of writing comprehensively, yet concisely without superficiality, to provide the rational bases for each step in decision making. The accomplishments were hard won for each of them, given the considerable difficulty inherent in creating these paradigms. Special thanks are also due to Ms. Audrey Landay whose special word processing and editorial skills greatly facilitated production of this book; we are very grateful. Sincere thanks go to Mrs. Cynthia McCann as well for her fine art work for this edition.

The objectives stated in the first edition still apply, namely, to provide all who care for pregnant women, from midwife to specialist, from student to seasoned practitioner, with a practical and conceptual framework upon which to build their clinical practice activities. Our intention is not to concretize such clinical activities, but rather to foster logical thought about problems, to guide health care providers in more conscious decision analysis by weighing the consequences of decisions in terms of relative benefits and risks, and thereby to improve results for both mother and fetus.

Emanuel A. Friedman, M.D., Sc.D.
Boston

CONTENTS

Decision making in medicine is an art that is difficult to learn and cannot be formally taught except by example and continued exposure. The best doctors, admittedly very rare, weigh benefits and risks consciously. They can rationalize in a clearly logical stepwise and systematic manner how they approach a problem. They parse it into its component compartments, dissect the issues so that they can be examined separately and lucidly, evaluate the several options available for assessment or treatment, and determine the likely results attendant upon each while simultaneously evaluating its fiscal and risk costs. Only when all factors are considered will they then implement a course of action. Many others acquire the same complex skills, but they do not ever appear to achieve that level of scholarly performance that allows communicating them orally or in writing. Their clinical excellence, derived intuitively, cannot be readily passed on to envious colleagues or admiring students.

The algorithms presented here are intended to provide a series of examples related to the spectrum of issues facing health care providers in obstetrics to serve as templates for decision making. Attempts have been made, perhaps with only limited success, to illustrate the logical sequences applicable in these instances. They reflect current practices at our institution and should not be held to be the last word on the subject. Comparisons with the previous edition of this book will show that major changes have been wrought by time, clinical experience, and newly developed research data. While we are confident that decisions made on the basis of the rational arguments are acceptable today, we are equally sure that many will change in time. They are offered, therefore, not so much to mold practice activities, although feedback from readers of the first edition indicates that this has been the case, but to help teach how to apply logical precepts to clinical decision making instead. Once this skill is acquired, the technique can then be more broadly utilized to modify future practices by incorporating newly developed concepts and facts.

To use these paradigms, several entrance keys are available. Each decision tree has a central theme in the form of a diagnostic problem or therapeutic objective to introduce the reader to the range of decisions we are expected to make for our patients. Other approaches include addressing options pertaining to specific symptoms (reduced fetal movement, unremitting vomiting, acute abdominal pain), manifestations (silent cervical dilatation, genital rash, insufficient uterine growth), laboratory observations (leukocytosis, abnormal alpha fetoprotein, low oxygen saturation), family or personal historical information (neural tube defect, multiple pregnancy, translocation carrier), special demographic or actuarial attributes (elderly gravida, drug abuser, socioeconomically indigent), suspected or established diagnoses (bronchial asthma, diabetes mellitus, fetal anomaly), or anticipated operative intervention (induction of labor, intrauterine fetal surgery, pregnancy interruption). Access, once achieved, should lead one along a logical pathway for meaningful evaluation of a given case, ultimately opening onto a rational management program that can generally be expected to yield good outcome results.

QUALITY ASSURANCE

Catherine T. Alvarez, R.N.

A. The commitment to high quality obstetrical care is motivated by a number of driving forces. Foremost is the professional desire to ensure good results in the interest of maternal and fetal well-being. The need to establish and maintain minimal standards of practice is mandated by accrediting agencies. Cost containment pressures may be a stimulus to reduce unnecessary (or marginally indicated) admissions and procedures. Risk-versus-benefit considerations have to be kept in mind at all times, however, to avoid reducing costs (and associated care) to the point at which the patient's welfare is potentially jeopardized.

B. A number of objective indices can be used to identify cases that warrant critical review, including death, major morbidity, and complications. A fully functional audit system should make it possible to examine all major operative cases, concentrating especially on those with documented errors in diagnosis, apparently inappropriate or unacceptable procedures, or serious complications.

C. Institutions without an existing audit procedure or those in which the system does not function adequately should undertake an educational and organizational program to involve relevant physicians, nurses, and administrative personnel to generate understanding, motivation, and cooperation.

D. Without some degree of autonomy and authority, it is unlikely that a quality assurance unit can fulfill its roles of reviewing cases, establishing standards, assessing the quality of care, determining responsibility, reporting deficiencies, collecting data, and publishing reports. Clear statements of objectives and operating principles need to be enunciated. A written policy and procedure manual should be created and updated regularly.

E. As a general guide, continuity of leadership is important, but the entire staff should participate in rotation.

F. A full-time staff is optimal if warranted by the number of cases to be examined. Work space and the necessary operational budget have to be provided to facilitate carrying out the responsibilities to coordinate the daily flow of records and information gathering.

G. A training period with supervision will orient auditors to their tasks. A check list can be devised to ensure smooth operations in regard to reviewing case records for completeness, accuracy, and internal consistency, and for detecting morbidity and complications. Data collection processes can be readily formalized to enable the staff to generate accurate periodic reports as needed.

H. Given specific guidelines, the auditors can identify the cases that the audit committee should review. These will include all with major complications as well as those involving procedures in which the preoperative diagnosis could not be confirmed, normal tissue was removed, or justification was minimal or absent. The committee will review and discuss flagged cases and designate whether they have been managed acceptably, marginally justifiably, or inappropriately.

I. The audit committee should maintain a record of its deliberations to serve as the basis for analysis of its immediate and long range impact, giving periodic information to the staff about recommended practice modifications. Adverse comments about any case are forwarded to the department chairman.

J. The chairman reviews all referred cases with the responsible parties. The justification and rationale are examined; documentation is sought. Recommendations are made for future practice and recorded in the physician's files, as indicated. If the problem is chronic, formal practice constraints or supervision may be required.

K. Institutions should have some formal grievance procedure (usually specified by the hospital bylaws) to give a physician whose privileges have been restricted or removed the opportunity to seek redress by formal review of the process by which the restraint was imposed.

References

Donabedian A. Criteria and standards for quality assessment and monitoring. Qual Rev Bull 12:99, 1986.

Rifkin M, Lynne C, Williams R, Hilsenbeck C. Managing quality assurance activities in a large teaching hospital. Qual Rev Bull 10:418, 1984.

Warner AM. Education for roles and responsibilities in quality assurance. Qual Rev Bull 11:78, 1985.

Warner AM. Education for roles and responsibilities in quality assurance: Physician leadership. Qual Rev Bull 11:111, 1985.

QUALITY ASSURANCE NEED

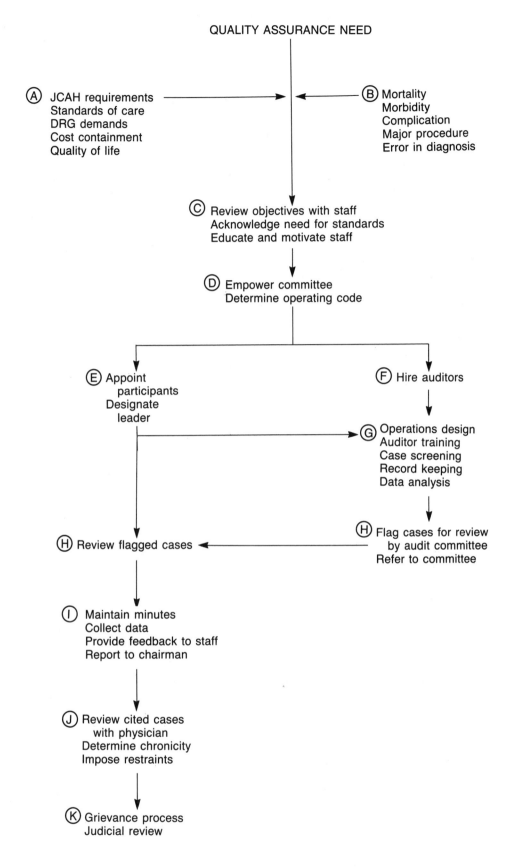

Ⓐ JCAH requirements
Standards of care
DRG demands
Cost containment
Quality of life

Ⓑ Mortality
Morbidity
Complication
Major procedure
Error in diagnosis

Ⓒ Review objectives with staff
Acknowledge need for standards
Educate and motivate staff

Ⓓ Empower committee
Determine operating code

Ⓔ Appoint
participants
Designate
leader

Ⓕ Hire auditors

Ⓖ Operations design
Auditor training
Case screening
Record keeping
Data analysis

Ⓗ Flag cases for review
by audit committee
Refer to committee

Ⓗ Review flagged cases

Ⓘ Maintain minutes
Collect data
Provide feedback to staff
Report to chairman

Ⓙ Review cited cases
with physician
Determine chronicity
Impose restraints

Ⓚ Grievance process
Judicial review

PREGNANCY VERIFICATION

Susan B. Wilson, M.D.

A. Suspicion of pregnancy may arise when a patient presents with amenorrhea, irregular uterine bleeding, or symptoms commonly seen in conjunction with pregnancy, such as breast tenderness, morning sickness, bloating, fatigue, dizziness, urinary frequency, or constipation. Characteristic physical findings include cyanosis of the vaginal mucosa, softening of the cervix, enlargement and softening of the uterine corpus, and dissociation of the corpus from the cervix due to softening of the isthmus. The presence of these findings strongly suggests pregnancy but is not diagnostic; their absence does not rule out pregnancy either.

B. The beta subunit of human chorionic gonadotropin (hCG) should be detectable in blood and urine by nine days after ovulation and fertilization. Levels of hCG increase on the average 113 percent every 48 hours until they peak at eight to 12 weeks. Urine tests vary in sensitivity and may occasionally be falsely positive because of proteinuria, bacteriuria, hematuria, semen, luteinizing hormone peak, or drug ingestion. Low levels relative to the duration of amenorrhea should alert one to the possibility of ectopic pregnancy (p 54).

C. Amenorrhea, menometrorrhagia, or the presence of a pelvic mass requires endocrinologic and ultrasonographic evaluation. Persistent gastrointestinal or central nervous system symptoms deserve evaluation for general medical conditions, if necessary by an internist. Pseudocyesis is worth considering in women who periodically seek evaluation for pregnancy.

D. Doppler ultrasonic auscultation can usually detect fetal heart tones ten to 12 weeks after the last menstrual period. Failure to hear the fetal heart may reflect an error in dating, but it may also indicate fetal death. Other clinical milestones worth noting as pregnancy advances include quickening at 16 to 18 weeks and the detection of fetal heart tones by stethoscopic auscultation at 18 to 20 weeks.

E. Ultrasonography makes it possible to detect a gestational sac by five to seven weeks, when the beta subunit hCG levels exceed 1,800 mU per milliliter. Fetal heart motion is generally seen by 42 days after conception in normal pregnancy by this method. Early ultrasonographic assessment of the crown-rump length is the most accurate means for gestational dating. Landmarks that can be used for establishing the diagnosis of pregnancy and estimating gestational age and expected due date are shown in Figure 1. Ultrasound techniques can also help in evaluating a patient for hydatidiform molar pregnancy, blighted ovum, missed abortion, multiple gestation, and ectopic pregnancy.

References

Lagrew DC, Wilson EA, Jawad ML. Determination of gestational age by serum concentration of human chorionic gonadotropin. Obstet Gynecol 62:37, 1983.

Lyons EA, Levi S. Ultrasound in the first trimester of pregnancy. Radiol Clin North Am 20:259, 1982.

Nyberg DA, Filly RA, Mahony BS, Monroe S, Laing FC, Jeffrey RB. Early gestation: Correlation of hCG level and sonographic identification. Am J Radiol 144:951, 1985.

Sinosich MJ, Grudzinskas JG, Saunders DM. Placental proteins in the diagnosis and evaluation of the "elusive" early pregnancy. Obstet Gynecol Surv 40:273, 1985.

Yosselson-Superstine S. Drug interference with pregnancy tests. Am J Hosp Pharm 41:1098, 1984.

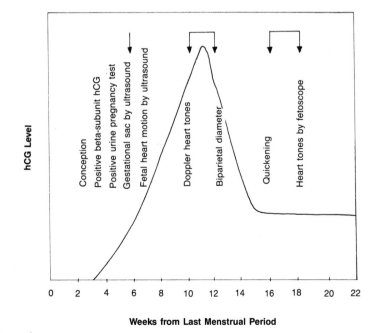

Figure 1 Landmarks for establishing diagnosis of pregnancy and estimating gestational age and expected due date.

SUSPICION OF PREGNANCY

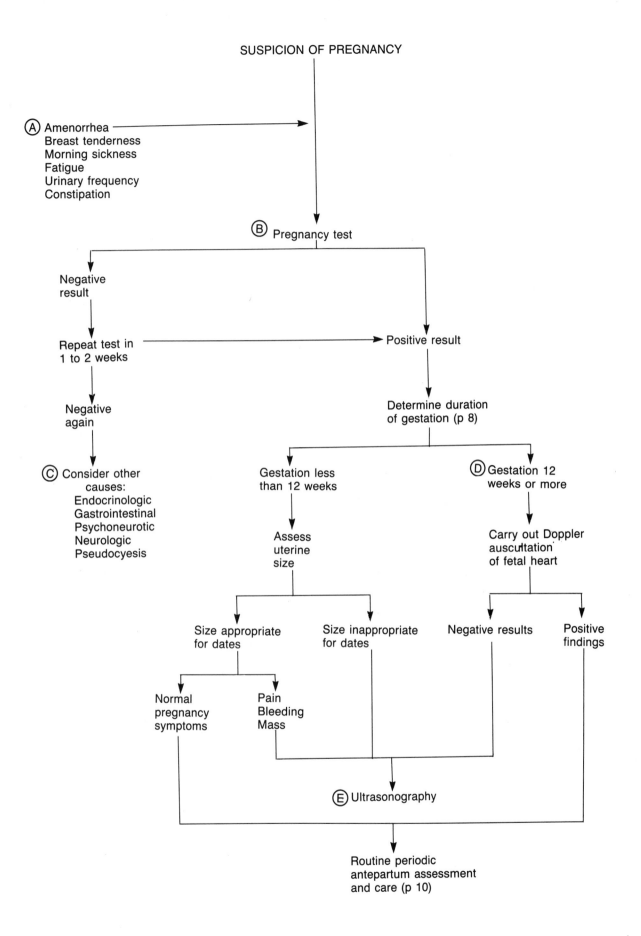

Ⓐ Amenorrhea
  Breast tenderness
  Morning sickness
  Fatigue
  Urinary frequency
  Constipation

Ⓑ Pregnancy test

Negative
result

Repeat test in
1 to 2 weeks

Positive result

Negative
again

Determine duration
of gestation (p 8)

Ⓒ Consider other
    causes:
    Endocrinologic
    Gastrointestinal
    Psychoneurotic
    Neurologic
    Pseudocyesis

Gestation less
than 12 weeks

Ⓓ Gestation 12
   weeks or more

Assess
uterine
size

Carry out Doppler
auscultation
of fetal heart

Size appropriate
for dates

Size inappropriate
for dates

Negative results

Positive
findings

Normal
pregnancy
symptoms

Pain
Bleeding
Mass

Ⓔ Ultrasonography

Routine periodic
antepartum assessment
and care (p 10)

FETAL DEATH DIAGNOSIS

Benjamin P. Sachs, M.B., B.S., D.P.H.

A. In the first trimester and early second trimester, fetal death is often associated with subjective appreciation by the gravida that her pregnancy symptoms have subsided abruptly, especially nausea, breast tenderness, bloating, and urinary frequency. Vaginal staining may occur; it is sometimes characterized by a dark brown to black discharge. Suspect fetal death if uterine growth stops or the uterus feels firm or firmer than previously. Although any of these manifestations may merely represent normal variations or misperceived sensations, the obstetrician must immediately evaluate the patient to confirm or refute the suspicion of fetal demise. Equally important, in advanced pregnancy the symptoms may serve to identify a fetus in distress for whom prompt evaluation and treatment may be lifesaving.

B. Risk factors for early fetal death include debilitating disease, habitual abortion, a chromosomal defect, and acute febrile illness. Clinical conditions associated with late fetal demise include malnutrition, chronic renal disease, Rh isoimmunization, diabetes mellitus, hypertension, abnormal placentation, fetal malformations, infections, asphyxia, and fetomaternal hemorrhage.

C. The presence of a viable fetus can be confirmed by stethoscopic or Doptone auscultation of the fetal heart rate. To be sure that the tones are fetal in origin, the rate must be significantly different from the maternal pulse rate as simultaneously determined by palpation. The fetal heart may be difficult to auscultate or locate, even with an office Doptone unit, if the patient is obese, if polyhydramnios exists, if the fetus is in transverse lie, or the placenta is implanted anteriorly.

D. After the sixth gestational week, an experienced ultrasonographer should be able to discern the fetal pole surrounded by trophoblastic tissue. Its absence can be diagnostic of the blighted ovum, confirming fetal death. Prior to the sixth week, the empty sac may be a normal finding; repeat evaluation is necessary before a definitive diagnosis can be made. After eight weeks, the rhythmically beating fetal heart generally can be visualized. Absence of fetal heart motion confirms fetal demise at this time. Human chorionic gonadotropin levels vary in their relationship to gestational age and may persist for weeks after fetal demise. Therefore, this test is not immediately helpful unless the result is negative. However, if the pregnancy has not been confirmed previously as being implanted within the uterus, the obstetrician must always be alert to the possibility of an ectopic pregnancy (p 54).

E. The absence of fetal heart motion is a critical sign. It confirms the suspicion that the fetus is dead. If the demise is not recent, oligohydramnios and collapse of fetal skull bones may be noted.

F. X-ray study is not recommended as a routine means for assessing these cases. However, if ultrasonography is not satisfactory or available and the patient or physician desires a rapid answer, the benefit of radiography outweighs its theoretical (and negligible) risk. The x-ray signs of fetal demise include overlapping skull bones (Spalding's sign), exaggerated curvature of the fetal spine, and the presence of gas bubbles within the fetal body. These signs often take days to evolve; nonetheless, their presence confirms the suspicion.

References

Laube DW, Schauberger CW. Fetomaternal bleeding as a cause for "unexplained" fetal death. Obstet Gynecol 60:649, 1982.

Meier PR, Manchester DR, Shikes RH, et al. Perinatal autopsy: Its clinical value. Obstet Gynecol 67:369, 1986.

Morrison I, Olsen J. Weight-specific stillbirths and associated causes of death: An analysis of 765 stillbirths. Am J Obstet Gynecol 152:975, 1985.

SUSPICION OF FETAL DEATH

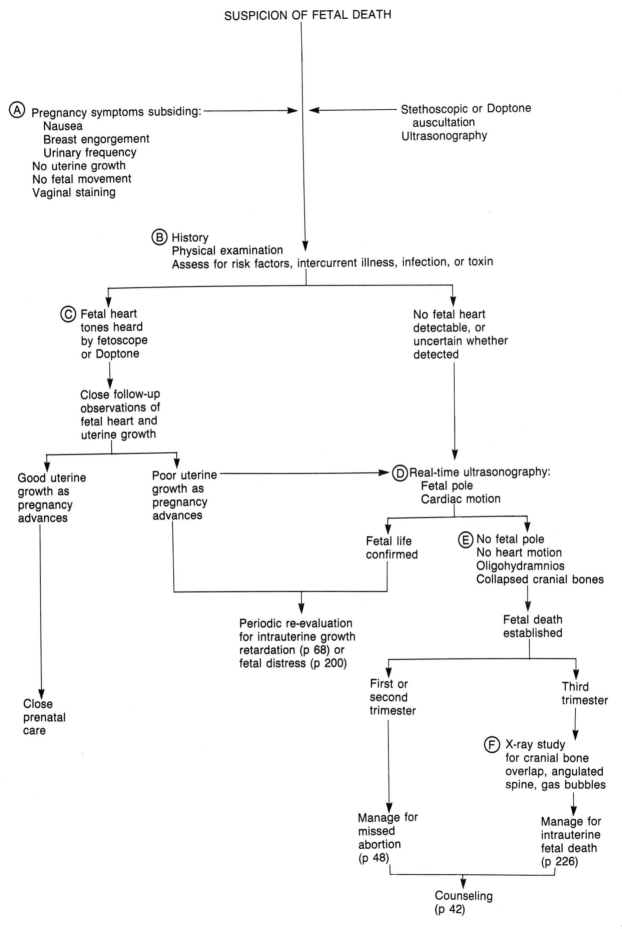

Ⓐ Pregnancy symptoms subsiding:
   Nausea
   Breast engorgement
   Urinary frequency
No uterine growth
No fetal movement
Vaginal staining

Stethoscopic or Doptone
auscultation
Ultrasonography

Ⓑ History
   Physical examination
   Assess for risk factors, intercurrent illness, infection, or toxin

Ⓒ Fetal heart
tones heard
by fetoscope
or Doptone

No fetal heart
detectable, or
uncertain whether
detected

Close follow-up
observations of
fetal heart and
uterine growth

Good uterine
growth as
pregnancy
advances

Poor uterine
growth as
pregnancy
advances

Ⓓ Real-time ultrasonography:
Fetal pole
Cardiac motion

Fetal life
confirmed

Ⓔ No fetal pole
No heart motion
Oligohydramnios
Collapsed cranial bones

Periodic re-evaluation
for intrauterine growth
retardation (p 68) or
fetal distress (p 200)

Fetal death
established

Close
prenatal
care

First or
second
trimester

Third
trimester

Ⓕ X-ray study
for cranial bone
overlap, angulated
spine, gas bubbles

Manage for
missed
abortion
(p 48)

Manage for
intrauterine
fetal death
(p 226)

Counseling
(p 42)

7

DURATION OF GESTATION

Benjamin P. Sachs, M.B., B.S., D.P.H.

A. The classic clinical measurement of gestational age is the duration of time elapsed from the last menstrual period. The expected date of confinement can be calculated using Naegele's rule by adding nine months and seven days to the first day of the last menstrual period. This calculation assumes that ovulation occurs 14 days after the last menstrual period and that the normal gestational duration is 266 days from ovulation and fertilization to term. It is accurate only for women whose menstrual cycles are regular and recur at 28 day intervals. Even among these women, however, it is only reliable to within two weeks.

B. Irregular periods make it inappropriate to use Naegele's rule because the timing of ovulation is so inaccurate. The same generally applies for women whose periods are spaced far apart. Ovulation generally occurs 12 days prior to the next period regardless of the interval between periods. If ovulation symptoms are recognizable (e.g., by the manifestation of mittelschmerz), the expected date of confinement can be calculated by adding eight months

and 23 days (266 days) to that date with a degree of accuracy comparable to that with Naegele's rule.

C. If conception occurs following a single well-timed coital exposure, such as with fertilization by artificial insemination, the timing tends to be fairly reliable. Other information may also be helpful, such as when the pregnancy test first becomes positive (three weeks after conception for tube or slide tests), when the patient first experiences pregnancy symptoms (two to three weeks after conception), when the fetal heart is first detected (eight to ten weeks by ultrasound, 16 weeks by stethoscope), and when quickening occurs (at 16 to 18 weeks).

D. The reliability of real-time ultrasonographic measurement of the biparietal diameter for determination of the gestational age decreases as pregnancy advances (Table 1). During the first trimester, the crown-rump fetal length is a more reliably accurate measurement. The length of the femur may also prove useful.

TABLE 1   Accuracy of Biparietal Diameter Measurement as a Predictor of Gestational Duration

Gestational Age (Weeks)	Variation (Days)
16	±7
17–26	±10–11
27–28	±14
29–40	±21

References

Nielsen JP, Munjanja SP, Whitefield CR. Screening for small for dates fetuses: A controlled trial. Br Med J 289:1179, 1986.

Sabbagha RE (Editor). Diagnostic Ultrasound. Philadelphia: Harper & Row, 1980, p84.

Thurnau GR, Tamura RK, Sabbagha R, Depp OR, Dyer A. Larkin R, Lee T, Laughlin C. Simple estimated fetal weight equation based on real-time ultrasound measurements of fetuses less than 34 weeks' gestation. Am J Obstet Gynecol 145:557, 1983.

DETERMINATION OF
GESTATIONAL AGE

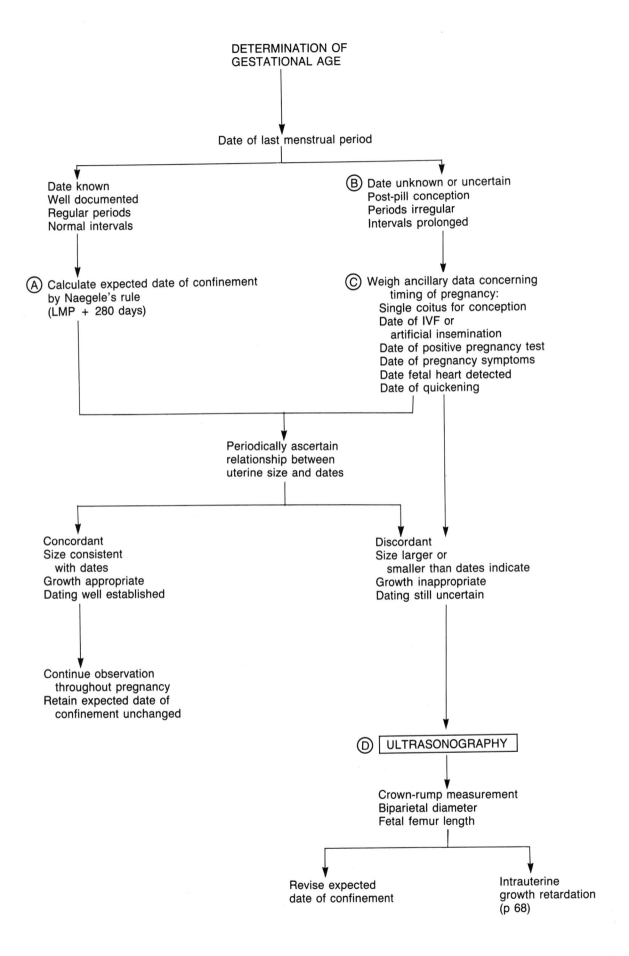

Date of last menstrual period

Date known
Well documented
Regular periods
Normal intervals

Ⓑ Date unknown or uncertain
Post-pill conception
Periods irregular
Intervals prolonged

Ⓐ Calculate expected date of confinement
by Naegele's rule
(LMP + 280 days)

Ⓒ Weigh ancillary data concerning
timing of pregnancy:
Single coitus for conception
Date of IVF or
artificial insemination
Date of positive pregnancy test
Date of pregnancy symptoms
Date fetal heart detected
Date of quickening

Periodically ascertain
relationship between
uterine size and dates

Concordant
Size consistent
with dates
Growth appropriate
Dating well established

Discordant
Size larger or
smaller than dates indicate
Growth inappropriate
Dating still uncertain

Continue observation
throughout pregnancy
Retain expected date of
confinement unchanged

Ⓓ ULTRASONOGRAPHY

Crown-rump measurement
Biparietal diameter
Fetal femur length

Revise expected
date of confinement

Intrauterine
growth retardation
(p 68)

9

ANTEPARTUM ASSESSMENT

Susan B. Wilson, M.D.

A. It is important to delve into each patient's family, social, medical, surgical, and obstetrical history. A family history of diabetes mellitus or hypertension increases the risk of a patient's developing these disorders during pregnancy. Sexually transmitted diseases, such as herpes, condyloma, gonorrhea, syphilis, and chlamydia infection, increase perinatal risks and should be screened for if the patient has a history of such a disorder or presents with symptoms or exposure. Drug, alcohol, or cigarette use warrants thorough counseling and education about fetal effects and associated pregnancy implications.

B. The physical examination should assess obesity and the general nutritional status, concentrating also on thyroid, cardiopulmonary, and orthopedic disorders. A careful pelvic examination must include the cervical appearance and status, uterine size and concordance with dates, and the presence of a pelvic mass and assess pelvic architecture and capacity.

C. Initial laboratory evaluation includes a complete blood count, blood typing and antibody screen, sickle cell preparation (when indicated), rubella titer, tine test for tuberculosis, serology for syphilis, gonorrhea culture, urine culture and analysis, and Papanicolaou smear. A baseline toxoplasmosis titer may be considered if the patient has cats, does gardening, or eats raw meat. An alpha fetoprotein assessment at 16 weeks helps detect a variety of disorders, including neural tube defects and Down syndrome. Screening can be done for predisposition to genetic disorders, including hemoglobinopathies and Tay-Sachs disease. AIDS or teratogenic factors should be investigated before 16 weeks' gestation so that appropriate evaluation and counseling can be done. Chorionic villus biopsy is available at an even earlier gestational age and should be considered for the diagnosis of selected genetic disorders. Glucose tolerance screening is worthwhile in all women over 30 years old as well as in any who have a family history of diabetes or have delivered a large, malformed, or stillborn infant.

D. Specific disease states disclosed by the prenatal evaluations require appropriate management in pregnancy. These include diabetes mellitus, chronic hypertension, renal disease, cardiac disease, and sexually transmitted diseases (p 154). Proteinuria must be evaluated, as well as glycosuria, anemia, and a positive serologic test for syphilis.

E. Antepartum visits should be scheduled monthly until 32 weeks, biweekly until 36 weeks, and weekly thereafter unless more frequent visits are needed. At each follow-up visit, urinalysis is repeated to detect albuminuria and glycosuria. The hematocrit level determination should be repeated at 28 and 36 weeks. An Rh antibody determination is done monthly after 20 weeks in susceptible individuals. A one hour postprandial glucose screening test for gestational diabetes is recommended at 28 weeks. Repeat serology as well as cultures for gonococcus, herpes, and group B beta streptococcus should be considered near term.

F. At each visit, the blood pressure must be checked. The uterine size and weight gain are evaluated. The fetal heart is checked as well. Hyperreflexia and edema are noted, if present. Critical manifestations of potentially serious problems are searched for, such as decreased fetal movement, persistent headaches or visual disturbance, venous and circulatory symptoms, vaginal bleeding, abdominal pain or cramping, and leakage of vaginal fluid.

References

Adams MJ, Windham GC, James LM, Greenberg F, Clayton-Hopkins JA, Reimer CB, Oakley GP. Clinical interpretation of maternal serum alpha-fetoprotein concentrations. Am J Obstet Gynecol 148:241, 1984.

Crattingius S, Axelsson O, Ekulund G, Lindmark G. Smoking, maternal age and fetal growth. Obstet Gynecol 66:449, 1985.

Elias S, Simpson JL, Martin AD, Sabbagha RE, Gerbie AB, Keith LG. Chorionic villus sampling for first trimester prenatal diagnosis: Northwestern University program. Am J Obstet Gynecol 152:204, 1985.

Minkoff H, Mead P. An obstetric approach to prevention of early onset group B beta hemolytic streptococcal sepsis. Am J Obstet Gynecol 154:973, 1986.

Stern J, Berg C, Jones J, Detter JC. A screening protocol for a prenatal population at risk for inherited hemoglobin disorders: Results of its application to a group of southeast Asians and Blacks. Am J Obstet Gynecol 150:333, 1984.

ANTEPARTUM ASSESSMENT

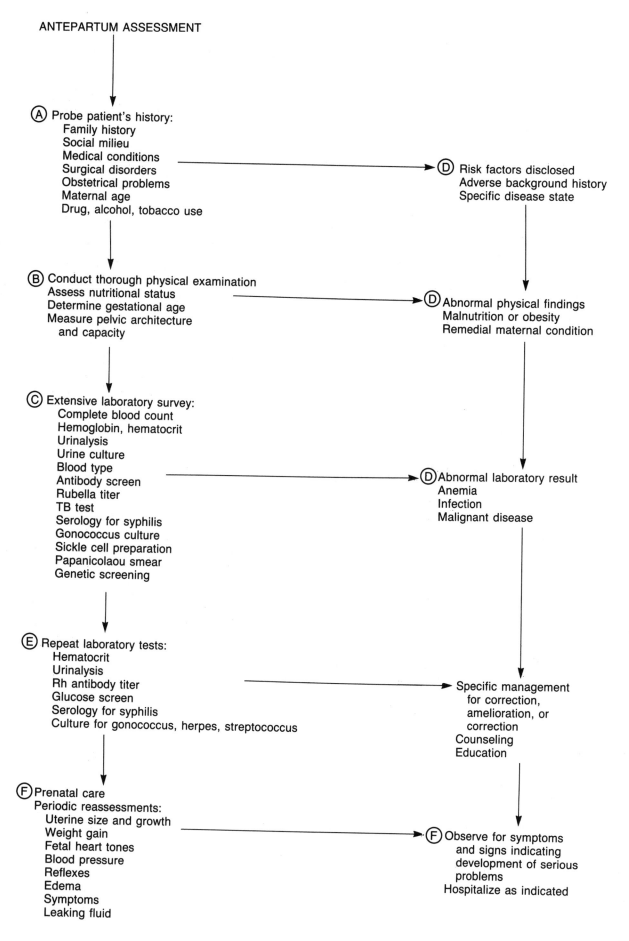

(A) Probe patient's history:
    Family history
    Social milieu
    Medical conditions
    Surgical disorders
    Obstetrical problems
    Maternal age
    Drug, alcohol, tobacco use

(D) Risk factors disclosed
    Adverse background history
    Specific disease state

(B) Conduct thorough physical examination
    Assess nutritional status
    Determine gestational age
    Measure pelvic architecture
      and capacity

(D) Abnormal physical findings
    Malnutrition or obesity
    Remedial maternal condition

(C) Extensive laboratory survey:
    Complete blood count
    Hemoglobin, hematocrit
    Urinalysis
    Urine culture
    Blood type
    Antibody screen
    Rubella titer
    TB test
    Serology for syphilis
    Gonococcus culture
    Sickle cell preparation
    Papanicolaou smear
    Genetic screening

(D) Abnormal laboratory result
    Anemia
    Infection
    Malignant disease

(E) Repeat laboratory tests:
    Hematocrit
    Urinalysis
    Rh antibody titer
    Glucose screen
    Serology for syphilis
    Culture for gonococcus, herpes, streptococcus

Specific management
    for correction,
    amelioration, or
    correction
    Counseling
    Education

(F) Prenatal care
    Periodic reassessments:
      Uterine size and growth
      Weight gain
      Fetal heart tones
      Blood pressure
      Reflexes
      Edema
      Symptoms
      Leaking fluid

(F) Observe for symptoms
    and signs indicating
    development of serious
    problems
    Hospitalize as indicated

NUTRITIONAL EVALUATION

Balmookoot Balgobin, M.D.

A. Be alert to factors that are commonly associated with poor nutrition in pregnancy, such as adolescence (especially under 16 years because of the gravida's own growth needs), prior poor obstetrical outcome, rapid succession of deliveries, heavy smoking, chronic alcoholic intake, drug dependency, low prepregnancy weight (less than 85 percent of the expected standard weight), inadequate weight gain in pregnancy (less than one-half pound gain weekly or an actual weight loss), and intrauterine growth retardation. Physical findings of overt malnutrition or specific nutritional deficiencies should be sought, including rare cutaneous and mucosal changes seen only in the severest cases.

B. There are few good laboratory indices of malnutrition, except anemia and hypoproteinemia. A sickle cell preparation is important in black women. Anemia (see p 112) with blood indices showing microcytic, hypochromic erythrocytes warrants determination of the serum iron level total iron binding capacity, and ferritin level; macrocytosis requires serum and red cell folate levels. Consider other relevant investigations as well, such as the serum vitamin B_{12} concentration, reticulocyte count, electrophoresis, and even a bone marrow smear.

C. Overnutrition leading to morbid obesity does not necessarily mean that the patient is receiving a balanced diet. Unbalanced high carbohydrate, protein deficient diets are not uncommon in some. Appropriate dietary review and counseling are clearly in order. Hypervitaminosis is not without risks. Patients should be counseled to avoid excessive intake of vitamins in the mistaken belief that it will benefit them and their fetus. Excess vitamin A and vitamin D, for example, can lead to toxic reactions and congenital abnormalities.

D. The therapy of anemia (see p 112) should be specific if possible. Give replacement and maintenance oral doses of ferrous sulfate (or an equivalent iron containing product) for iron deficiency anemia in addition to special dietary correction. Parenteral iron administration is seldom required. Similar programs are needed for the less common folate deficiencies. Whereas iron deficiency and folic acid deficiency are usually separate entities, they may coexist with severe nutritional deficiencies.

E. Follow-up includes reassessment of and counseling about diet. Weight gain is an index of caloric intake, but it is not a reliable indicator of an adequate diet. The laboratory and clinical responses to treatment are especially useful. Periodic laboratory studies help determine whether anemia or hypoalbuminemia has been corrected. Intrauterine growth retardation should be searched for (p 68). At delivery, the baby's weight should be noted relative to length and gestational age. Postpartum re-evaluation of the nutritional status is important as well, with advice about pregnancy spacing and contraception (see p 294).

F. Protein malnutrition has a seriously adverse impact on the fetus. It may be manifest in the gravida only by weight loss or inadequate weight gain. Severe hypoalbuminemia results in generalized edema. Inadequate protein stores can be replenished by means of a high protein diet containing at least 2 g per kilogram daily. In rare cases of intense depletion, the intravenous administration of albumin and hyperalimentation may be indicated, but such measures are not without risk. Severe maternal iodine deficiency, once endemic in certain parts of the world, predisposes to fetal cretinism and severe neurologic deficits; it is now easily corrected or avoided by the use of iodized salt. The value of zinc supplementation, however, has not yet been established, although reports suggest an association of low zinc levels with suboptimal growth.

References

Pitkin RM. Assessment of nutritional status of mother, fetus and newborn. Am J Clin Nutr 3:658, 1981.

Prentice AM, Whitehead RG, Watkinson M, Lamb WH, Cole JJ. Prenatal dietary supplementation of African women and birthweight. Lancet 1:489, 1983.

Simmer K, Thompson RPH. Maternal zinc and intrauterine growth retardation. Clin Sci 68:395, 1985.

Taylor DJ, Mallen C, McDougall N, Lind T. Effect of iron supplementation on serum ferritin levels during and after pregnancy. Br J Obstet Gynaecol 89:1011, 1982.

Zlatnik FJ, Burmeister LF. Dietary protein in pregnancy: Effect on anthropometric indices of the newborn. Am J Obstet Gynecol 146:199, 1983.

NUTRITIONAL EVALUATION

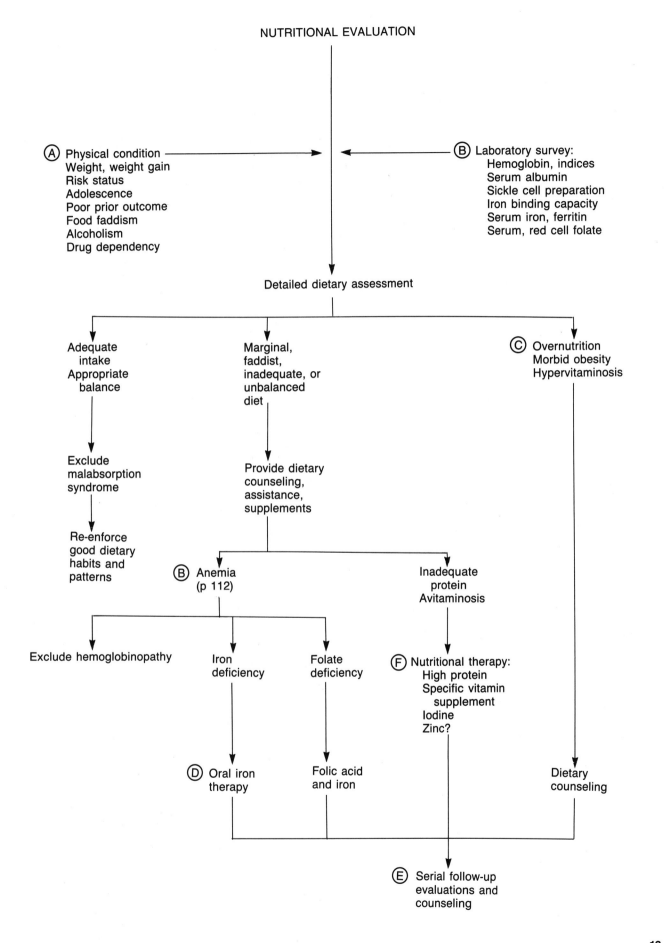

Ⓐ Physical condition
    Weight, weight gain
    Risk status
    Adolescence
    Poor prior outcome
    Food faddism
    Alcoholism
    Drug dependency

Ⓑ Laboratory survey:
    Hemoglobin, indices
    Serum albumin
    Sickle cell preparation
    Iron binding capacity
    Serum iron, ferritin
    Serum, red cell folate

Detailed dietary assessment

Adequate
intake
Appropriate
    balance

Marginal,
faddist,
inadequate, or
unbalanced
diet

Ⓒ Overnutrition
    Morbid obesity
    Hypervitaminosis

Exclude
malabsorption
syndrome

Provide dietary
counseling,
assistance,
supplements

Re-enforce
good dietary
habits and
patterns

Ⓑ Anemia
    (p 112)

Inadequate
protein
Avitaminosis

Exclude hemoglobinopathy

Iron
deficiency

Folate
deficiency

Ⓕ Nutritional therapy:
    High protein
    Specific vitamin
        supplement
    Iodine
    Zinc?

Ⓓ Oral iron
    therapy

Folic acid
and iron

Dietary
counseling

Ⓔ Serial follow-up
    evaluations and
    counseling

WEIGHT GAIN

Susan B. Wilson, M.D.

A. Underweight patients are those weighing under 10 percent less than their ideal body weight at the beginning of pregnancy. Underweight patients with a total weight gain over the course of pregnancy of less than 10 pounds (or more critically, less than 0.5 pound per week in the second half of pregnancy) are at risk for pregnancy complications, such as abruptio placentae, amnionitis, premature labor, and low birth weight infants. They should be evaluated for hyperemesis, manifestations of malnutrition, and malabsorption syndrome, as well as drug, alcohol, and cigarette use. Counseling about dietary needs and practices is essential (p 12).

B. Women with a prepregnancy weight of over 200 pounds are considered to be significantly obese. Obesity increases the maternal risks of pregnancy induced hypertension, gestational diabetes, pyelonephritis, macrosomia, and shoulder dystocia; these women need cesarean section more frequently than other gravidas.

C. Patients who are losing weight should be assessed for dehydration and ketonuria. They must be followed frequently with aggressive nutritional counseling until the weight stabilizes and they begin to gain adequately. Other patients may be followed at the usual prenatal care intervals for office visits. The average weekly weight gain is 0.8 to 1.0 pounds from 13 weeks to term. The overall average weight gained in pregnancy of 24 to 28 pounds is attributed to the fetus (7.5 lb), the placenta (1.4 lb), amniotic fluid (1.8 lb), uterine growth (2.1 lb), breast hypertrophy (0.9 lb), blood volume (2.8 lb), extravascular volume (3.7 lb), and maternal stores (7.4 lb).

D. The gravida who gains poorly in pregnancy (less than 0.5 lb per week) needs a complete history and a thorough physical examination to rule out obstetrical problems such as hyperemesis and medical problems that would predispose to malnutrition or malabsorption. The dietary history and attitudes regarding dietary intake and dieting and its effect on fetal well-being should be explored in depth. Dietary and vitamin supplementation may be called for; in extreme conditions of weight loss, even hyperalimentation may be required.

E. Pregnant women with large weight gain, especially acute weight gain, need careful assessment for edema and the development of pregnancy induced hypertension. Other obstetrical causes of rapid weight gain are multiple gestation, polyhydramnios, and diabetes mellitus, all of which should be carefully evaluated for and managed if found.

References

Garbaciak JA, Richter M, Miller S, Barton J. Maternal weight and pregnancy complications. Am J Obstet Gynecol 152:238, 1985.

Gross TL, Kazzi GM: Effects of maternal malnutrition and obesity on pregnancy outcome. In: Gleicher N (Editor). Principles of Medical Therapy in Pregnancy. New York: Plenum Medical Book Co., 1985.

Naeye RL. Weight gain and the outcome of pregnancy. Am J Obstet Gynecol 135:3, 1979.

Pitkin RM. Obstetrics and gynecology. In: Schneider HA (Editor). Nutritional Support of Medical Practice. 2nd ed. Philadelphia: Harper and Row, 1983.

Rayburn W, Wolk R, Mercer N, Roberts J. Parenteral nutrition in obstetrics and gynecology. Obstet Gynecol Surv 41:200, 1986.

EVALUATE FOR WEIGHT GAIN

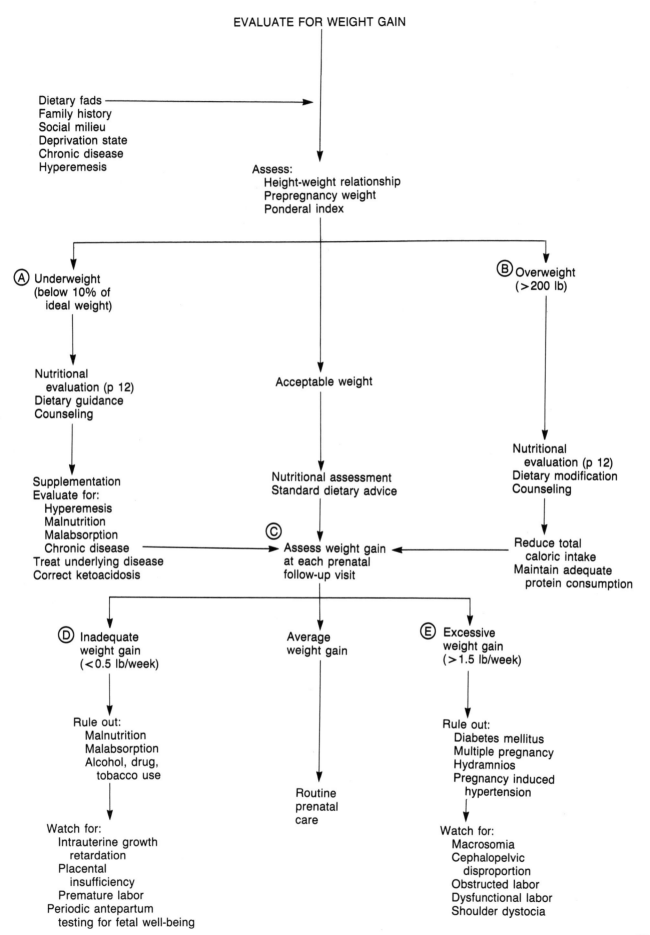

Dietary fads
Family history
Social milieu
Deprivation state
Chronic disease
Hyperemesis

Assess:
  Height-weight relationship
  Prepregnancy weight
  Ponderal index

Ⓐ Underweight
  (below 10% of
  ideal weight)

Ⓑ Overweight
  (>200 lb)

Nutritional
  evaluation (p 12)
Dietary guidance
Counseling

Acceptable weight

Nutritional
  evaluation (p 12)
Dietary modification
Counseling

Supplementation
Evaluate for:
  Hyperemesis
  Malnutrition
  Malabsorption
  Chronic disease
Treat underlying disease
Correct ketoacidosis

Nutritional assessment
Standard dietary advice

Ⓒ Assess weight gain
  at each prenatal
  follow-up visit

Reduce total
  caloric intake
Maintain adequate
  protein consumption

Ⓓ Inadequate
  weight gain
  (<0.5 lb/week)

Average
weight gain

Ⓔ Excessive
  weight gain
  (>1.5 lb/week)

Rule out:
  Malnutrition
  Malabsorption
  Alcohol, drug,
    tobacco use

Routine
prenatal
care

Rule out:
  Diabetes mellitus
  Multiple pregnancy
  Hydramnios
  Pregnancy induced
    hypertension

Watch for:
  Intrauterine growth
    retardation
  Placental
    insufficiency
  Premature labor
  Periodic antepartum
    testing for fetal well-being

Watch for:
  Macrosomia
  Cephalopelvic
    disproportion
  Obstructed labor
  Dysfunctional labor
  Shoulder dystocia

EXERCISE IN PREGNANCY

Johanna F. Perlmutter, M.D.

A. Our knowledge of the effects of work and exercise during pregnancy on the fetus and the mother is very limited. Most current recommendations are intuitive, based on known cardiovascular and neuromuscular changes of pregnancy. Obstetrical personnel are responsible for advising gravidas about the need to avoid overexertion, exhaustion, dehydration, hyperthermia, hypoglycemia, ketoacidosis, and electrolyte imbalance resulting from excessive physical exercise. Women should be taught about warning signs, such as chest pain, dyspnea, palpitations, syncope, exhaustion, uterine cramps and bleeding, back or pelvic pain, and difficulty in walking. Work is acceptable for the uncomplicated gravida provided it is not overtiring or hazardous owing to physical effort or exposure to potentially toxic materials.

B. Screen for risk factors, including anemia, extreme obesity or underweight habitus, or a metabolic, cardiac, or hypertensive condition. Pregnancy complications make exercise hazardous, especially habitual abortion, incompetent cervix, vaginal bleeding, ruptured membranes, malpresentation, multiple pregnancy, intrauterine growth retardation, placenta previa, and prior premature or precipitate labor.

C. Softening of the connective tissue in pregnancy may lead to joint instability. Therefore, care should be taken to avoid activities that may cause physical injury, such as strenuous jumping or bouncing or rapid changes in direction. Even stretching may cause damage if done too vigorously or excessively. Back pain is particularly common during pregnancy. The gravida's center of gravity in the upright posture changes, and there are new stresses on different muscle groups. Use of a simple, gentle exercise, the pelvic tilt, several times a day helps alleviate this discomfort. Standing, sitting, or lying with the feet somewhat apart and knees bent, the patient contracts her abdominal and buttocks muscles and rotates her pelvis forward, holding this position for 10 seconds.

D. In pregnancy the heart rate and cardiac output are high, even at rest. During exercise the heart rate objectives should be set 25 to 30 percent lower than in the nonpregnant state. Exercise programs should be modified accordingly, for example, to set an upper heart rate limit of 140 per minute. Advise anemic women not to exercise vigorously. During exercise, blood flow is diverted to the muscles, theoretically reducing blood flow to the uterus; if flow is diverted sufficiently, fetal hypoxia might result. Animal fetuses are not affected until the uterine blood flow is reduced by half. Excessive exercise may therefore have a potentially adverse effect, especially if the fetoplacental reserve is already reduced. Although not substantiated in humans, it is prudent to advise against vigorous exercise as a general rule, restricting it to no more than 15 minutes daily. Physical activity also increases circulating norepinephrine levels, which may increase the frequency and amplitude of uterine contractions. Thus, women at risk for premature labor should avoid vigorous exercise.

E. After 16 weeks' gestational age, the uterus is capable of compressing the inferior vena cava when a gravida is in the supine position, reducing venous return to the heart. Even without measurable brachial artery hypotension, blood flow to the uterus may be significantly diminished. Therefore, no exercise should be done in the supine position. Moreover, advise changing position slowly, especially from prone to upright, to avoid orthostatic hypotension.

F. The basal body temperature of the pregnant woman is physiologically elevated. Vigorous physical activity further increases the body core temperature to cause hyperthermia (a theoretical teratogenic factor) and dehydration. Insuring hydration is an effective preventive measure if done before and after exercise. Febrile illnesses or hot and humid weather interdicts exercise in pregnancy.

References

Exercise During Pregnancy and the Postnatal Period: ACOG Home Exercise Programs. Washington, DC: American College of Obstetricians and Gynecologists, 1985.

Mamelle N, Laumon B, Lazar P. Prematurity and occupational activity during pregnancy. Am J Epidemiol 119:309, 1984.

Pregnancy, Work and Disability. Technical Bulletin No. 58. Washington, DC: American College of Obstetricians and Gynecologists, 1980.

Zuckerman BS, Frank DA, Hingson R, et al. Impact of maternal work outside the home during pregnancy on neonatal outcome. Pediatrics 77:459, 1986.

INQUIRY CONCERNING WORK OR EXERCISE

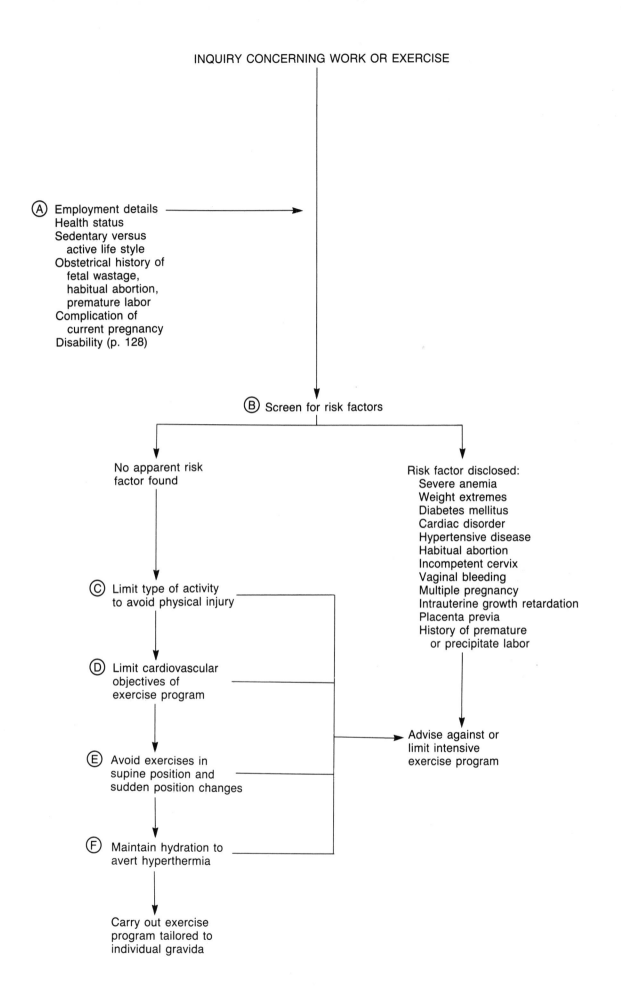

A Employment details
Health status
Sedentary versus
    active life style
Obstetrical history of
    fetal wastage,
    habitual abortion,
    premature labor
Complication of
    current pregnancy
Disability (p. 128)

B Screen for risk factors

No apparent risk
factor found

Risk factor disclosed:
    Severe anemia
    Weight extremes
    Diabetes mellitus
    Cardiac disorder
    Hypertensive disease
    Habitual abortion
    Incompetent cervix
    Vaginal bleeding
    Multiple pregnancy
    Intrauterine growth retardation
    Placenta previa
    History of premature
        or precipitate labor

C Limit type of activity
to avoid physical injury

D Limit cardiovascular
objectives of
exercise program

E Avoid exercises in
supine position and
sudden position changes

F Maintain hydration to
avert hyperthermia

Advise against or
limit intensive
exercise program

Carry out exercise
program tailored to
individual gravida

ADOLESCENT PREGNANCY

Janet L. Mitchell, M.D.

A. Although pregnancy among adolescents remains a societal problem with far-reaching impact on the girl, the offspring, the father of the baby, the respective families, and all who are involved by her pregnancy, there is now evidence that compliance in an organized, integrated prenatal care program greatly reduces untoward obstetrical outcomes heretofore reported to be so common. Adverse long-term impacts on education, employment, health, and economic status may also be reduced or even averted by such concerted effort.

B. The initial assessment should include establishing the gestational age, evaluating the nutritional status, and assessing psychosocial supports. Establishing the gestational age may be difficult (p. 8) because many adolescents enter prenatal care late in gestation, and the last menstrual period may not be accurately recalled. If the patient has not established a regular menstrual cycle, the last menstrual period may not be an appropriate marker; in some instances, pregnancy may even have occurred before the first period. One should also ensure a thorough examination by history, physical, and laboratory means to uncover any underlying medical problems that require attention for care and correction.

C. Successful programs provide consistent care providers, especially nurses or nurse-midwives, to integrate intensive medical surveillance with a comprehensive educational and psychosocial support program. Essential to these programs are components to evaluate and provide education about nutritional services, parenting skills, and contraceptive choices.

D. The adolescent years are characterized by poor nutritional habits. Pregnancy, with its increased nutritional demands, underscores the situation that pregnant teenagers are still adolescents whose own nutritional requirements are often inadequately met and whose deficits will only be enhanced during gestation. Much instructive discussion, informational resource, support, and reenforcement are needed to increase acceptance of nutritional foodstuff, a well balanced, adequate diet, and compliance in taking needed supplemental iron and vitamins.

E. Although many of the poor obstetrical outcomes can be improved with prenatal care, pregnancy induced hypertension and low birth weight remain potentially serious problems because so many pregnant adolescents are primigravid, ethnic minority gravidas of low socioeconomic status. They should be followed assiduously and hospitalized promptly when they develop early manifestations of disorders that threaten them and their fetuses, such as hypertension, poor uterine growth, or premature labor.

References

Baldwin W. Adolescent pregnancy and childbearing: Rates, trends, research findings from the CPR. Springfield, VA: NICHD, National Technical Information Service, 1984.

Elster AB. The effect of maternal age, parity, and prenatal care on perinatal outcome in adolescent mothers. Am J Obstet Gynecol 149:845, 1984.

Loris P, Dewey KG, Poirier-Brode K. Weight gain and dietary intake of pregnant teenagers. J Am Diet Assoc 85:1296, 1985.

Neeson JD, Patterson KA, Mercer RT, May KA. Pregnancy outcome for adolescents receiving prenatal care by nurse practitioners in extended roles. J Adol Health Care 4:94, 1983.

Zuckerman B, Walker DK, Frank D, Chase C. Adolescent pregnancy and parenthood: An update. Adv Develop Behav Ped 7:1, 1986.

PREGNANT TEENAGER

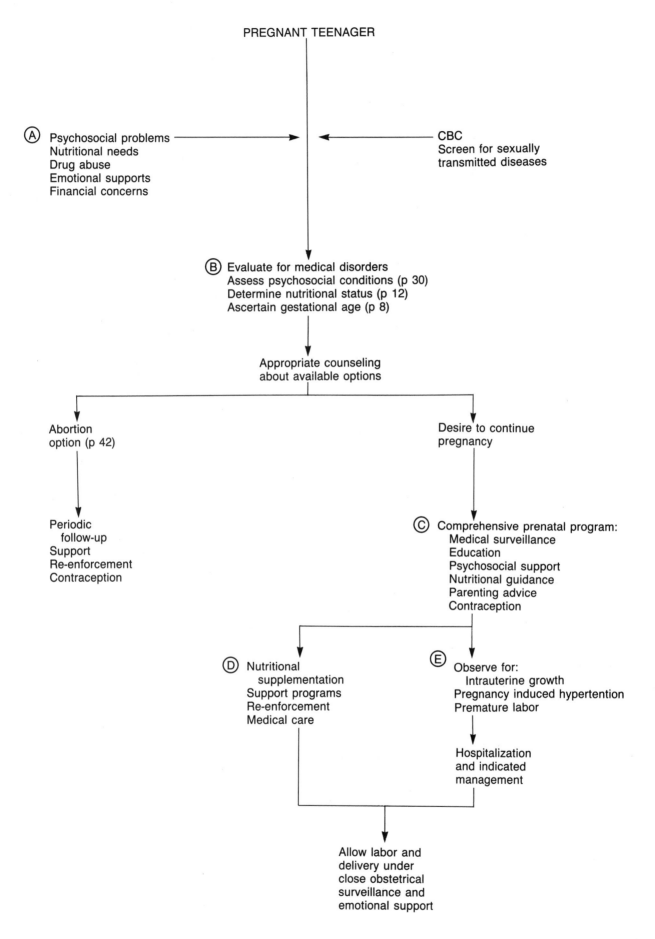

(A) Psychosocial problems ——————→   ←—————— CBC
    Nutritional needs   Screen for sexually
    Drug abuse   transmitted diseases
    Emotional supports
    Financial concerns

(B) Evaluate for medical disorders
    Assess psychosocial conditions (p 30)
    Determine nutritional status (p 12)
    Ascertain gestational age (p 8)

Appropriate counseling
about available options

Abortion   Desire to continue
option (p 42)   pregnancy

Periodic   (C) Comprehensive prenatal program:
follow-up   Medical surveillance
Support   Education
Re-enforcement   Psychosocial support
Contraception   Nutritional guidance
                                                Parenting advice
                                                Contraception

(D) Nutritional   (E) Observe for:
    supplementation   Intrauterine growth
    Support programs   Pregnancy induced hypertention
    Re-enforcement   Premature labor
    Medical care
                                            Hospitalization
                                            and indicated
                                            management

                    Allow labor and
                    delivery under
                    close obstetrical
                    surveillance and
                    emotional support

ELDERLY GRAVIDA

David B. Acker, M.D.

A. Conception after age 35 years may be the result of either voluntary (career choice) or involuntary (infertility) delay; in either case, it imposes stresses on the gravida. The physician should inquire about and be sensitive to special circumstances that surround the pregnancy and the special needs these patients have, particularly as regards anxieties, fears, and misconceptions. Although there is an increased incidence of medical and obstetrical complications among them, the hazards of pregnancy for the healthy mature gravida tend to be exaggerated. They generally do quite well. Factual information and reassurance should be offered.

B. During the first trimester, ultrasonographic evaluation confirms the fetal gestational age and detects the presence of multiple gestational sacs or leiomyomas. Screening tests should be performed for urinary tract infection and diabetes mellitus; chronic hypertension should be diagnosed; obese gravidas should receive nutritional counseling. Advice concerning work and exercise is especially useful.

C. Fetal chromosome abnormalities, open neural tube defects, and cardiac defects (even in the absence of Down syndrome) are increased in older gravidas. The risks and benefits of genetic amniocentesis should be explained (p 74). If accepted, an ultrasonographically guided amniocentesis should be performed at 15 to 16 weeks to obtain amniotic fluid for fetal cell karyotyping and determination of the alpha fetoprotein level. Careful ultrasonographic fetal surveillance is done to detect gross fetal anomalies. Even skilled ultrasonographers may require consultation for evaluation of the fetal heart. If am-

niocentesis is declined, a maternal serum alpha fetoprotein level should be obtained at 16 weeks.

D. The patient should be alerted to the significance and early clinical signs of premature labor, spontaneous rupture of the membranes, passage of meconium stained amniotic fluid, and abruptio placentae. Ultrasonographic examination should be repeated to rule out placenta previa and to confirm appropriate fetal growth.

E. Increased frequencies of intrapartum uteroplacental insufficiency and neonatal depression have been noted in the offspring of older gravidas. Macrosomic fetuses are also more commonly born to older multiparas who are obese, especially if they have gained more than 44 pounds in the course of the pregnancy. Continuous electronic fetal heart rate monitoring should be used for these patients during labor; a pediatrician or other physician skilled in neonatal resuscitation should attend the delivery.

References

Acker DB, Sachs BP. Reproductive outcome of the older gravida. In: Sachs BP, Acker DB (Editors). Clinical Obstetrics: A Public Health Perspective. Littleton, MA: PSG Publishing Co., 1986.

Boyd ME, Usher RH, McLean FH. Fetal macrosomia: Prediction and management. Obstet Gynecol 61:715, 1983.

Kirz DS, Dorchester W, Freeman RK. Advanced maternal age: The mature gravida. Am J Obstet Gynecol 152:7, 1985.

Naeye R. Maternal age, obstetric complications, and the outcome of pregnancy. Obstet Gynecol 61:210, 1983.

GRAVIDA OF 35 YEARS OR MORE

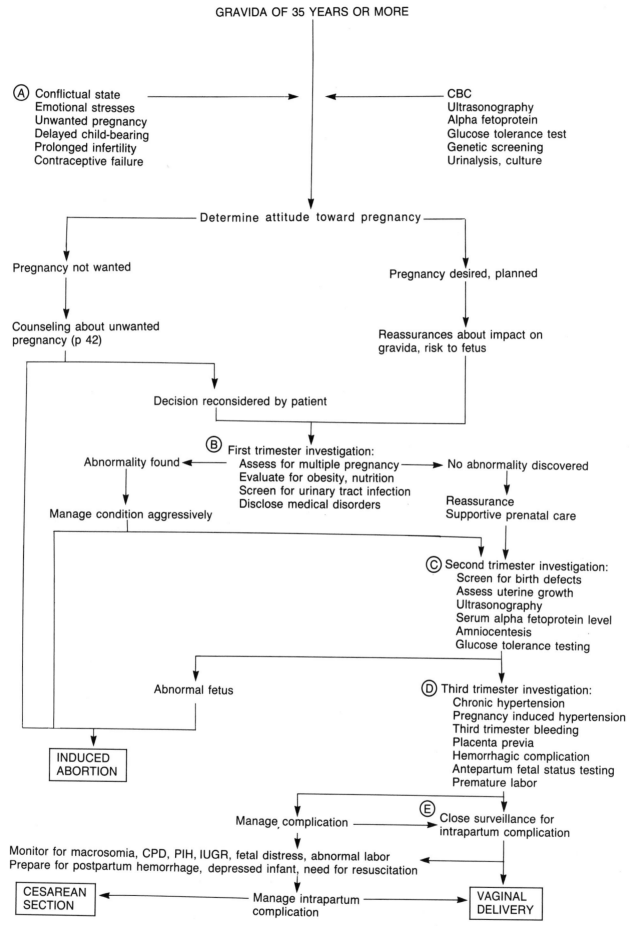

Ⓐ Conflictual state
Emotional stresses
Unwanted pregnancy
Delayed child-bearing
Prolonged infertility
Contraceptive failure

CBC
Ultrasonography
Alpha fetoprotein
Glucose tolerance test
Genetic screening
Urinalysis, culture

Determine attitude toward pregnancy

Pregnancy not wanted

Pregnancy desired, planned

Counseling about unwanted pregnancy (p 42)

Counseling about unwanted pregnancy (p 42)

Reassurances about impact on gravida, risk to fetus

Decision reconsidered by patient

Ⓑ First trimester investigation:
Assess for multiple pregnancy
Evaluate for obesity, nutrition
Screen for urinary tract infection
Disclose medical disorders

Abnormality found

No abnormality discovered

Manage condition aggressively

Reassurance
Supportive prenatal care

Ⓒ Second trimester investigation:
Screen for birth defects
Assess uterine growth
Ultrasonography
Serum alpha fetoprotein level
Amniocentesis
Glucose tolerance testing

Abnormal fetus

Ⓓ Third trimester investigation:
Chronic hypertension
Pregnancy induced hypertension
Third trimester bleeding
Placenta previa
Hemorrhagic complication
Antepartum fetal status testing
Premature labor

INDUCED
ABORTION

Manage complication

Ⓔ Close surveillance for intrapartum complication

Monitor for macrosomia, CPD, PIH, IUGR, fetal distress, abnormal labor
Prepare for postpartum hemorrhage, depressed infant, need for resuscitation

CESAREAN
SECTION

Manage intrapartum complication

VAGINAL
DELIVERY

PSYCHOPROPHYLACTIC PREPARATION

Johanna F. Perlmutter, M.D.
Toby Marder, R.N., M.S.

A. The basic objectives of prelabor classes include providing education and allaying fears by familiarization with labor physiology, hospital routine, facilities, and personnel.

B. Once the patient enters the hospital in labor, we try to establish and reaffirm interpersonal relationships. This is done early in labor, if possible. Spend time reviewing what the patient should expect; explain the facilities again; if any procedures are to be done, go over the details in advance. Try to understand the patient's preferences and needs. Encourage the gravida and her support person to participate in decision making. Allow them time for privacy within the constraints of safety. Keep a sense of humor (but avoid making light of their concerns) and try to allay apprehensions. In early labor, foster ambulation, if appropriate to the patient's condition. To minimize attention to pain and discomfort, the patient should not be asked to time each contraction. Distractions should be encouraged. Breathing patterns should be reviewed in early labor because of the variety of techniques available. The patient should demonstrate those patterns and techniques with which she is familiar. Use of relaxation techniques at this stage of labor should be fostered; encourage slow deep breathing as long as possible, but not hyperventilation. Avoid advancing too quickly to breathing techniques that ought to be reserved for later in labor.

C. In active labor, more support is needed for both the gravida and her support person. Periodically relate the details of progress in labor and provide verbal encouragement. As labor progresses, use various active measures to relieve pain until the one (or ones) best for the patient herself is (are) determined. Try hot compresses to the back, cold compresses to the forehead, and ice chips by mouth. Ensure relaxation between contractions. Maintain a calm, subdued environment with reduced noise and light. Limit the number of people around. Combine breathing patterns as needed—e.g., slow chest breathing as the contraction begins; then a brief period of rapid, shallow breathing at the peak; and slow chest breathing again as the contraction subsides.

D. During transition (near full cervical dilatation), give simple, direct, concrete, and specific instructions. The partner (support person) should become assertive and participate actively. Focus the patient's attention during contractions; increase eye contact; enhance touching; and perform breathing rituals. As labor advances into the second stage, frequent position changes in bed may prove beneficial. Effective pushing can be done with the patient on her back (semisitting to avoid vena caval compression and supine hypotension), on her side, squatting, kneeling, or sitting on a commode, with traditional breath holding and bearing down. An alternative method is "trumpet blowing," which involves slow exhalation breathing during expulsion.

References

El Sherif C, McGrath G, Smyrski JT. Coaching the coach. J Obstet Gynecol Nurs 8:87, 1979.

Howe CL. Physiologic and psychosocial assessment in labor. Nurs Clin North Am 17:49, 1982.

Worthington EL, Martin GA. A laboratory analysis of response to pain after training in three Lamaze techniques. J Psychosom Res 24:106, 1980.

PRENATAL PREPARATION

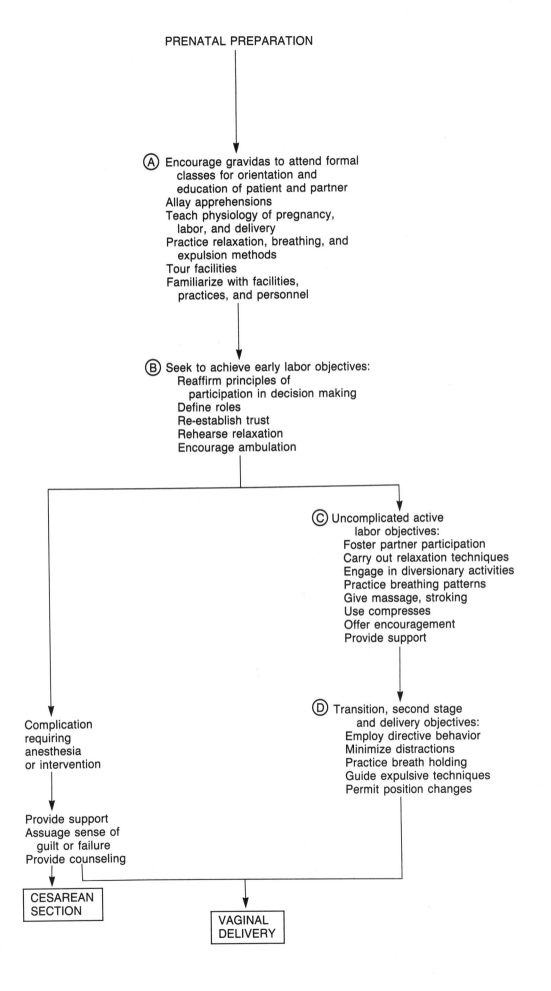

Ⓐ Encourage gravidas to attend formal
    classes for orientation and
    education of patient and partner
  Allay apprehensions
  Teach physiology of pregnancy,
    labor, and delivery
  Practice relaxation, breathing, and
    expulsion methods
  Tour facilities
  Familiarize with facilities,
    practices, and personnel

Ⓑ Seek to achieve early labor objectives:
  Reaffirm principles of
    participation in decision making
  Define roles
  Re-establish trust
  Rehearse relaxation
  Encourage ambulation

Ⓒ Uncomplicated active
    labor objectives:
  Foster partner participation
  Carry out relaxation techniques
  Engage in diversionary activities
  Practice breathing patterns
  Give massage, stroking
  Use compresses
  Offer encouragement
  Provide support

Ⓓ Transition, second stage
    and delivery objectives:
  Employ directive behavior
  Minimize distractions
  Practice breath holding
  Guide expulsive techniques
  Permit position changes

Complication
requiring
anesthesia
or intervention

Provide support
Assuage sense of
  guilt or failure
Provide counseling

CESAREAN
SECTION

VAGINAL
DELIVERY

CLINICAL CEPHALOPELVIMETRY

Henry Klapholz, M.D.

A. Suspect the possibility that cephalopelvic disproportion will occur if the patient is short, chronically malnourished, or suffering a debilitating disease, especially one involving the neuromuscular system. A history of a difficult delivery or an infant damaged at the time of a vaginal birth should raise one's index of suspicion. The same applies for the finding of prenatal glucose intolerance.

B. Assessing fetopelvic relationships is the keystone for many critical decisions related to the conduct of labor. Pelvic architecture and capacity have to be assessed in detail as early in pregnancy as possible (see Fig. 1). The features that flag the patient who may have an inadequate pelvis are: diagonal conjugate <12 cm, narrow subpubic arch, flat sacrum, bi-ischial diameter <8 cm, convergent sidewalls, prominent ischial spines, and sacrospinous ligament <2.5 cm. Screen all antepartum patients to identify those at risk. Re-evaluate late in pregnancy when the pelvic tissues soften for a still better assessment.

C. The intrapartum examination should include a careful review of the pelvic architecture and relate the pelvic capacity to the presenting fetal head size. The presence of any compensatory space should now be apparent. The labor pattern (p 234) is important for identifying fetopelvic disproportion. One must be familiar with the way pelvic architecture affects the course of labor.

D. The abnormal labor patterns of protraction or arrest disorders (p 238 and 240) signify serious risk regardless of one's prior impression of the pelvic shape or capacity. Such patterns often signal a high degree of cephalopelvic disproportion. Clinical pelvimetry demonstrating features of a small or unfavorably shaped pelvis in a patient who has a protraction or arrest disorder indicates a grave prognosis for atraumatic vaginal delivery. These patients probably warrant delivery by cesarean section as opposed to potentially traumatic, difficult vaginal operative procedures that are inherently more dangerous to both mother and fetus.

E. A useful dynamic clinical means for assessing cephalopelvic relationships is to determine the "thrust" of the fetal head in the birth canal. At the height of a uterine contraction augmented by the application of fundal pressure, vaginal palpation of the presenting part demonstrates whether the head is tightly fixed in the pelvis or capable of further descent. Clear evidence of an obstruction tends to confirm the presence of disproportion, whereas advancement of the head in the pelvis rules out an obstruction at that pelvic station. The latter does not necessarily rule out an impediment at a lower station, however.

F. X-ray cephalopelvimetry should be reserved for objective documentation of an obstruction when this diagnosis cannot be made with relative certainty using the dynamic test of pelvic capacity in conjunction with an analysis of the disordered labor pattern. X-ray pelvimetry merely for the purpose of measuring the pelvic dimensions (without simultaneously obtaining fetal head measurements) is not recommended. If techniques are not available for the simultaneous measurement of both fetal and maternal pelvis and for comparing these measurements, it is preferable to bypass this step entirely. A trial of oxytocin may be in order instead with very careful monitoring of both fetal and maternal status to ensure against harm. If oxytocin augmentation does not readily bring about progressive dilatation and descent, one should not persist.

References

Friedman EA, Sachtleben MR. Station of the fetal presenting part. VI. Arrest of descent in multiparas. Obstet Gynecol 47:129, 1976.

Friedman EA, Taylor MB. A modified nomographic aid for cephalopelvimetry. Am J Obstet Gynecol 105:1110, 1969; 106:884, 1970.

Klapholz H. A computerized aid to Ball pelvimetry. Am J Obstet Gynecol 121:1067, 1975.

Parsons MT, Spellacy WN. Prospective randomized study of x-ray pelvimetry in the primigravida. Obstet Gynecol 66:76, 1985.

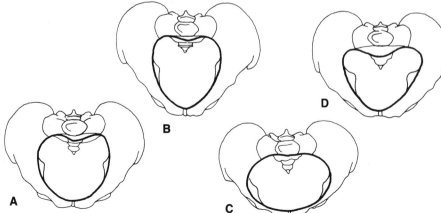

Figure 1 Four typical pelvic types, frontal inlet view, based on shape of inlet: *A,* gynecoid; *B,* anthropoid; *C,* platypelloid; *D,* android.

PELVIC ASSESSMENT

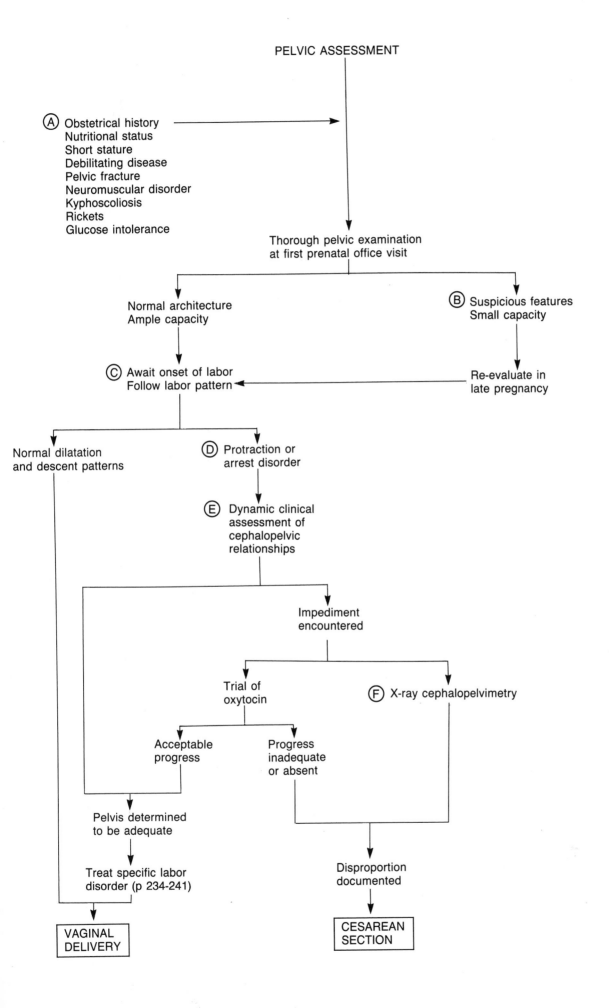

(A) Obstetrical history
Nutritional status
Short stature
Debilitating disease
Pelvic fracture
Neuromuscular disorder
Kyphoscoliosis
Rickets
Glucose intolerance

Thorough pelvic examination
at first prenatal office visit

Normal architecture
Ample capacity

(B) Suspicious features
Small capacity

(C) Await onset of labor
Follow labor pattern

Re-evaluate in
late pregnancy

Normal dilatation
and descent patterns

(D) Protraction or
arrest disorder

(E) Dynamic clinical
assessment of
cephalopelvic
relationships

Impediment
encountered

Trial of
oxytocin

(F) X-ray cephalopelvimetry

Acceptable
progress

Progress
inadequate
or absent

Pelvis determined
to be adequate

Disproportion
documented

Treat specific labor
disorder (p 234-241)

VAGINAL
DELIVERY

CESAREAN
SECTION

SEXUALITY IN PREGNANCY

Johanna F. Perlmutter, M.D.

A. There is no documented association between coitus and premature labor, premature rupture of the membranes, chorioamnionitis, or puerperal infection. However, some sexually transmitted diseases may be associated with abortion or delivery complications (p 154). There is an increased risk of spontaneous abortion from herpes, *Listeria monocytogenes*, and acute viral hepatitis infections. Syphilis may cause abortion on rare occasions as well as stillbirth and congenital syphilis of the newborn. Gonorrhea, group B streptococcus, chlamydia, and mycoplasmas have all been related to neonatal and puerperal infections. There are complications of pregnancy that should restrict sexual activity. Intercourse can introduce infection in a woman with premature rupture of membranes. Orgasm may reinitiate uterine contractions in the woman who has been in premature labor; the protective effect of tocolytic drugs under these circumstances is as yet unknown. Third trimester bleeding, particularly with documented placenta previa, contraindicates sexual activity.

B. Although intercourse is not prohibited in the first trimester, the gravida is often markedly fatigued, with a reduced libido. If vaginal bleeding or spotting occurs, the patient is generally advised to desist from all sexual activity. This recommendation is based on an intuitive approach because of the association of orgasm with uterine contractions. Given that most spontaneous abortions involve blighted ova (p 32), there is doubt that this practice is valid, although it is still adhered to in practice. Almost any form of sexual activity is permissible except blowing air into the vagina during sex play. Maternal deaths have been reported from air embolism. It should be strictly prohibited in pregnancy.

C. During the second trimester, sexual activity is usually unrestricted. Because the gravida feels physically and emotionally better, both her interest and her participation increase. The risks of first trimester spontaneous abortion have passed and those of premature labor in the third trimester have not yet arisen. This interval is perhaps the safest, and there is no reason to limit sexual activity without a substantive reason in the form of an actual or anticipated complication of pregnancy.

D. With the increasing abdominal girth in the third trimester, physical activity of all kinds may be limited by the gravida herself. As term approaches, she tends to tire more easily and libido once again decreases. Although some may be concerned about injury to the mother or fetus during coitus, this fear has no foundation. Instruction in lateral coital positions may prove helpful.

E. Traditionally coitus has been prohibited during pregnancy from six weeks prior to the expected date of confinement until six weeks post partum. Many couples ignore this 12 week proscription against sexual intercourse unless they have been strongly advised on the basis of some high risk problem or find coitus uncomfortable (because of a healing episiotomy or perineal laceration, for example).

F. Most women usually wait four to six weeks after delivery before reinitiating sexual activity. Uterine infection and breakdown of the perineal repair are the principal concerns during this time. Dyspareunia can occur. The episiotomy repair may restrict the introital opening. Manual dilatation and a lubricant are beneficial. Mediolateral episiotomy generally causes more discomfort than a midline incision. This discomfort usually subsides with time, although small neuromas sometimes do develop. If they are unresponsive to conservative therapy, the scar may have to be excised. Anticipatory fear of discomfort can inhibit lubrication, enhancing the pain. The libido is often diminished in lactating women; this is compounded by reduced vaginal lubrication. Water soluble lubricants are usually helpful but not curative. This situation usually improves with time, but it may not return completely until breast feeding is terminated.

References

Klebanoff MA, Nugent RP, Rhoads GG. Coitus during pregnancy: Is it safe? Lancet 2:914, 1984.

Reamy K, White SE. Sexuality in pregnancy and the puerperium: A review. Obstet Gynecol Survey 40:1, 1985.

Robson KM, Brant HA, Kumar R. Maternal sexuality during first pregnancy and after childbirth. Br J Obstet Gynaecol 82:882, 1981.

INQUIRY CONCERNING SEXUAL PRACTICES

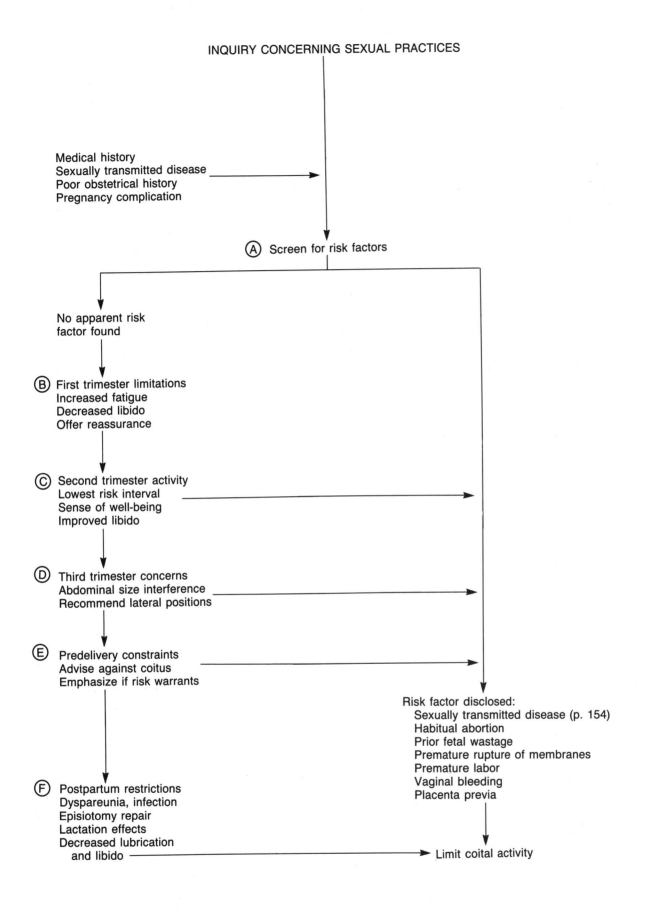

Medical history
Sexually transmitted disease
Poor obstetrical history
Pregnancy complication

(A) Screen for risk factors

No apparent risk
factor found

(B) First trimester limitations
Increased fatigue
Decreased libido
Offer reassurance

(C) Second trimester activity
Lowest risk interval
Sense of well-being
Improved libido

(D) Third trimester concerns
Abdominal size interference
Recommend lateral positions

(E) Predelivery constraints
Advise against coitus
Emphasize if risk warrants

Risk factor disclosed:
   Sexually transmitted disease (p. 154)
   Habitual abortion
   Prior fetal wastage
   Premature rupture of membranes
   Premature labor
   Vaginal bleeding
   Placenta previa

(F) Postpartum restrictions
Dyspareunia, infection
Episiotomy repair
Lactation effects
Decreased lubrication
   and libido

Limit coital activity

IN VITRO FERTILIZATION

Machelle M. Seibel, M.D.

A. Virtually all cases of infertility of various causes may now be appropriately treated by in vitro fertilization techniques. However, the cost is high and is generally not covered by third party insurance carriers. Experienced centers can achieve a 15 to 20 percent pregnancy incidence by this approach.

B. A complete infertility evaluation is mandatory to avoid overlooking conditions amenable to more conventional forms of treatment. Mycoplasma screening is done to preclude potential contamination of the incubator. A semen specimen is frozen prior to initiating a cycle in the event that there is temporary impotence or circumstances that may interfere with obtaining the semen specimen at the appropriate time. Owing to the severe emotional stress associated with in vitro fertilization, all participating couples should be seen and counseled initially by a mental health worker familiar with the procedure.

C. Superovulation to develop multiple follicles for fertilization may be achieved by a number of regimens. Clomiphene citrate and human menopausal gonadotropins (Pergonal, Serono Laboratories, Randolph, MA) either sequentially, simultaneously, or individually are used most often. Occasionally luteinizing hormone releasing hormone or follicle stimulating hormone is also used. One fourth of the cycles initiated have to be cancelled because of suboptimal superovulation prior to oocyte retrieval. Monitoring for the preovulatory luteinizing hormone surge greatly reduces the potential for ovulation to occur prior to oocyte retrieval.

D. Laparoscopic aspiration of oocytes is the predominant technique thus far. Ultrasonographically guided aspiration by way of the transabdominal-transvesical, transurethral-transvesical, or transvaginal route has recently been employed with good success.

E. The retrieved oocytes are incubated with semen under ideal sterile laboratory conditions and studied periodically to determine whether fertilization and cleavage have occurred. Fertilization fails to occur with 15 percent of oocytes. In such cases, careful investigation of the andrologic, embryologic, and ovulation-induction components must be reassessed. Poor semen parameters (number, motility, and morphology) are associated with poor fertilization results. More recent methods of sperm separation suggest that an improved outcome can be expected even with poor semen parameters. Sperm penetration assay is not entirely reliable because false negative results do occur.

F. Once pregnancy is established, the patient can be managed just as any other gravida. However, there is an increased incidence of fetal loss and premature delivery (but not congenital anomalies) with in vitro fertilization conceptions. This warrants special attention as for other high risk conditions. Progesterone is given to help maintain the pregnancy, recognizing that it is of unproven value but probably harm-free.

References

Alper MM, Lee G, Seibel MM, et al. The relationship of semen parameters to fertilization in patients participating in a program of in vitro fertilization. J In Vitro Fertil Embryo Transfer 2:217, 1985.

Edwards RG, Fishel SB, Cohen J, et al. Factors influencing the success of in vitro fertilization for alleviating human infertility. J In Vitro Fertil Embryo Transfer 1:3, 1984.

Jones HW Jr, Jones GS, Andrews MC, et al. The program of in vitro fertilization at Norfolk. Fertil Steril 38:14, 1982.

Taymor ML, Seibel MM, Oskowitz SP, et al. In vitro fertilization and embryo transfer: An individualized approach to ovulation induction. J In Vitro Fertil Embryo Transfer 2:162, 1985.

IN VITRO FERTILIZATION CANDIDATE

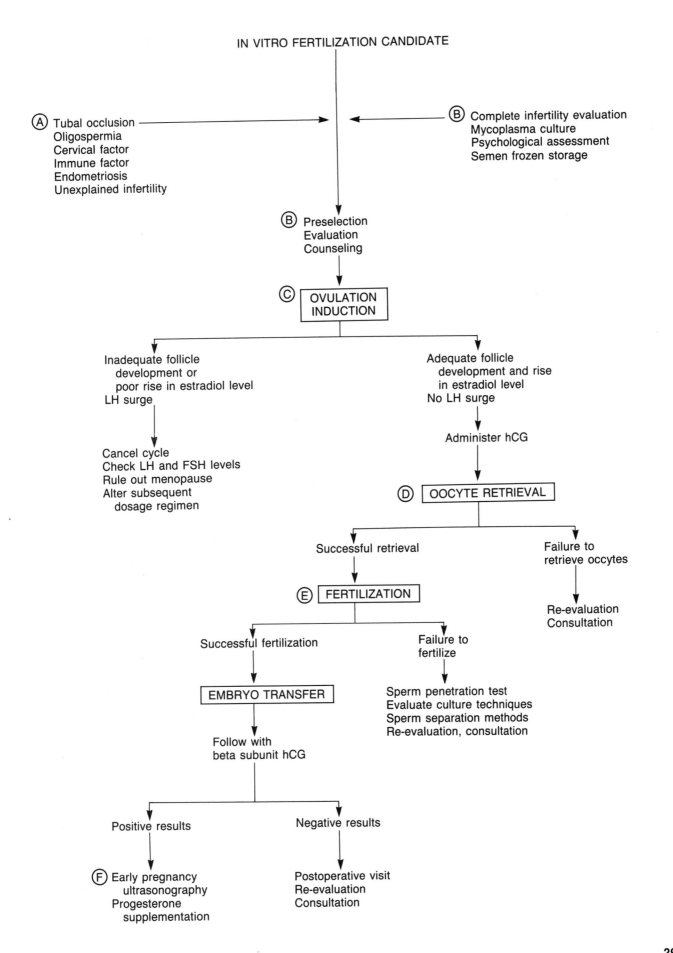

(A) Tubal occlusion
Oligospermia
Cervical factor
Immune factor
Endometriosis
Unexplained infertility

(B) Complete infertility evaluation
Mycoplasma culture
Psychological assessment
Semen frozen storage

(B) Preselection
Evaluation
Counseling

(C) OVULATION INDUCTION

Inadequate follicle
development or
poor rise in estradiol level
LH surge

Adequate follicle
development and rise
in estradiol level
No LH surge

Administer hCG

Cancel cycle
Check LH and FSH levels
Rule out menopause
Alter subsequent
dosage regimen

(D) OOCYTE RETRIEVAL

Successful retrieval

Failure to
retrieve occytes

Re-evaluation
Consultation

(E) FERTILIZATION

Successful fertilization

Failure to
fertilize

EMBRYO TRANSFER

Sperm penetration test
Evaluate culture techniques
Sperm separation methods
Re-evaluation, consultation

Follow with
beta subunit hCG

Positive results

Negative results

(F) Early pregnancy
ultrasonography
Progesterone
supplementation

Postoperative visit
Re-evaluation
Consultation

PSYCHOSOCIAL ASSESSMENT

Patricia S. Stewart, M.S., M.S.W.

A. Emotional trauma is an expected result of some life stresses, including real or anticipated events, for everyone. Certain individuals, however, tend to react in a particularly severe or aberrant fashion. The obstetrician's primary objective is to differentiate between normal grief and a maladaptative reaction. Thus, he or she needs to be alert to gravid women who are at greatest risk, such as those who were victims of child abuse or neglect themselves and those with a history of psychologic impairment, drug dependency, or behavioral problems.

B. The kinds of stressful events that can precipitate a serious depression or maladaptive reaction are many. In some women, ego strength and defenses are so marginal that they are unable to cope with even the stresses of an otherwise uneventful pregnancy, labor, and delivery. By contrast, some events prove so catastrophic that many quite healthy women respond unfavorably. These include a spontaneous abortion and the delivery of a premature (p 174), malformed, or dead baby (p 226). Early consultation with knowledgeable social service or mental health personnel is important.

C. Physicians and nurses should regularly evaluate patients at office visits, during hospitalization, and before and after delivery. Assessment of the mental status entails determining orientation to time, place, and person as well as ensuring alertness, appropriate behavior, and adaptation.

D. Watch for evidence of abnormal mental status, ranging from incapacitating depression to overt psychotic manifestations, including bizarre or extraordinary behavior or speech. If the safety and well-being of the patient or others are involved, urgent referral to a psychiatrist for further diagnostic evaluation and decisions concerning management is indicated. Be especially alert to women whose personal life is chaotic or whose support system is tenuous or nonexistent.

E. Communication, collaboration, and coordination between psychiatric, social service, obstetrical, and pediatric providers are essential. An agreed upon management plan can eliminate mixed or conflicting messages, which can compound a patient's problems.

F. One of the major criteria for hospitalization is concern that the patient's condition may constitute a danger to herself or others. Consider also the risk that may be imposed on the fetus. Hospitalization not only provides custodial care, but it also permits intensive assessment of the patient's mental and emotional status and affords the opportunity to treat her by psychotropic medications, if indicated.

G. Poor prognostic indicators include impaired psychological status or aberrant social functioning, family discord, substance abuse, and the failure to evolve realistic plans for child care. For drug dependent women, denial or minimization of fetal risk, refusal to accept referral to a drug counseling program, and continuation of drug use constitute unfavorable prognostic signs. They warrant delaying discharge until legal mechanisms can be explored to seek protection of the infant.

H. The patient and her family must have ready access to counseling in substantive form, both in free discussion and in writing. They should perceive that health care providers are always available to respond to their needs, answer their questions, and assuage their concerns. In practice, one individual—usually a social worker—serves as principal contact and coordinator.

I. Proper referral and maintenance of follow-up contact are critical aspects of the management of psychosocial problems. Because community sources vary widely, one should determine in advance what is locally available so as to be prepared when the need arises. In addition to public financial aid (welfare), seek out established special needs support groups (e.g., Down syndrome, cerebral palsy, cleft palate, infant loss, sudden infant death syndrome). In addition, there are often pediatric, hospital, community health, and religious support groups for these purposes.

Reference

Friedman R, Gradstein B. Surviving Pregnancy Loss. Boston: Little, Brown, 1982.

PSYCHOSOCIAL ASSESSMENT

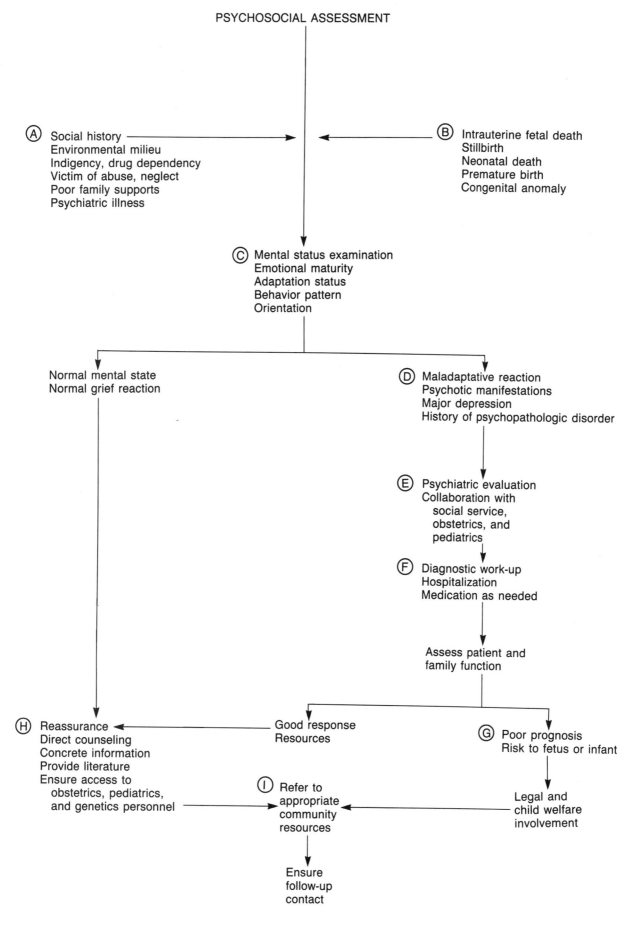

Ⓐ Social history
Environmental milieu
Indigency, drug dependency
Victim of abuse, neglect
Poor family supports
Psychiatric illness

Ⓑ Intrauterine fetal death
Stillbirth
Neonatal death
Premature birth
Congenital anomaly

Ⓒ Mental status examination
Emotional maturity
Adaptation status
Behavior pattern
Orientation

Normal mental state
Normal grief reaction

Ⓓ Maladaptative reaction
Psychotic manifestations
Major depression
History of psychopathologic disorder

Ⓔ Psychiatric evaluation
Collaboration with
social service,
obstetrics, and
pediatrics

Ⓕ Diagnostic work-up
Hospitalization
Medication as needed

Assess patient and
family function

Ⓗ Reassurance
Direct counseling
Concrete information
Provide literature
Ensure access to
obstetrics, pediatrics,
and genetics personnel

Good response
Resources

Ⓖ Poor prognosis
Risk to fetus or infant

Ⓘ Refer to
appropriate
community
resources

Legal and
child welfare
involvement

Ensure
follow-up
contact

THREATENED ABORTION

Max Borten, M.D.

A. While first trimester vaginal bleeding or staining is the usual presenting manifestation of threatened abortion, with or without uterine cramping, approximately 20 percent of all pregnant women experience bleeding or staining without necessarily any apparent adverse effect on themselves or the fetus. The cervix remains closed and no products of conception are expelled. Pregnancy related symptoms continue unchanged. Nonetheless, as many as 50 percent of these gestations progress to spontaneous abortion.

B. If a gestational sac cannot be identified within the uterus by ultrasonography, one must consider that an ectopic pregnancy may exist (p 54). This diagnosis is supported if the uterine corpus is smaller than expected for the duration of the amenorrhea. Careful surveillance and appropriate counseling are essential; hospitalization must be considered if the index of suspicion for ectopic pregnancy warrants it. Observation of the gestational sac in an extrauterine location, while quite infrequent, is clear documentation of ectopic pregnancy.

C. Ultrasonographic verification of an intrauterine gestational sac effectively rules out ectopic pregnancy. Rare exceptions are cases of heterotopic pregnancy with concomitant intrauterine gestation (1 in 10,000 ectopic pregnancies). In cases of threatened abortion, one must try to ascertain whether the conceptus is "blighted" or whether the fetus is present and developing normally. This can be accomplished by repeating the ultrasonographic evaluation after a two-week interval.

D. Prior to eight weeks' gestational age (timing from last menstrual period), ultrasonography is not entirely reliable in determining the fetal status. Fetal heart motion is usually readily seen by eight weeks; it constitutes definitive evidence that the fetus is alive and developing well thus far. Absence of a fetus or failure to detect fetal heart motion prior to eight weeks cannot be confidently interpreted to mean that a fetus is not present or that it is incapable of progressive development. There-

fore, unless vaginal bleeding continues or the patient passes products of conception vaginally, ultrasonographic re-examination is indicated as soon as the pregnancy has advanced beyond the eighth week.

E. The very sensitive and specific radioimmunoassay of the beta subunit of human chorionic gonadotropin is useful in assessing cases of threatened abortion, especially if tests are done serially. During early normal gestation, the quantitative levels rise rapidly; doubling time averages 2.2 days (standard deviation, 1.0 day). Thus, two or more beta subunit human chorionic gonadotropin assays will provide a reliable means for evaluating the pregnancy status and prognosis, especially within the first 30 days of gestation (dating from conception).

F. The use of progestational drugs is not advised. They have been shown to prolong the interval to spontaneous abortion even in cases of blighted ovum without improving the outcome by way of salvage. Bed rest and restricted activity are generally recommended because they are relatively harm-free, but their value is also in doubt. Sexual abstinence reduces the potential for stimulation of uterine contractions from prostaglandin production. Persistent or increased vaginal bleeding usually indicates progression to inevitable abortion.

References

Batzofin JH, Fielding WL, Friedman EA. Effect of vaginal bleeding in early pregnancy outcome. Obstet Gynecol 63:515, 1984.

Eriksen BC, Eik-Nes SH. Prognostic value of ultrasound, hCG and progesterone in threatened abortion. JCU 14:3, 1986.

Hertz JB. Diagnostic procedures in threatened abortion. Obstet Gynecol 64:223, 1984.

Nyberg DA, Laing FC, Filly RA. Threatened abortion: Sonographic distinction of normal and abnormal gestation sacs. Radiology 158:397, 1986.

VAGINAL BLEEDING

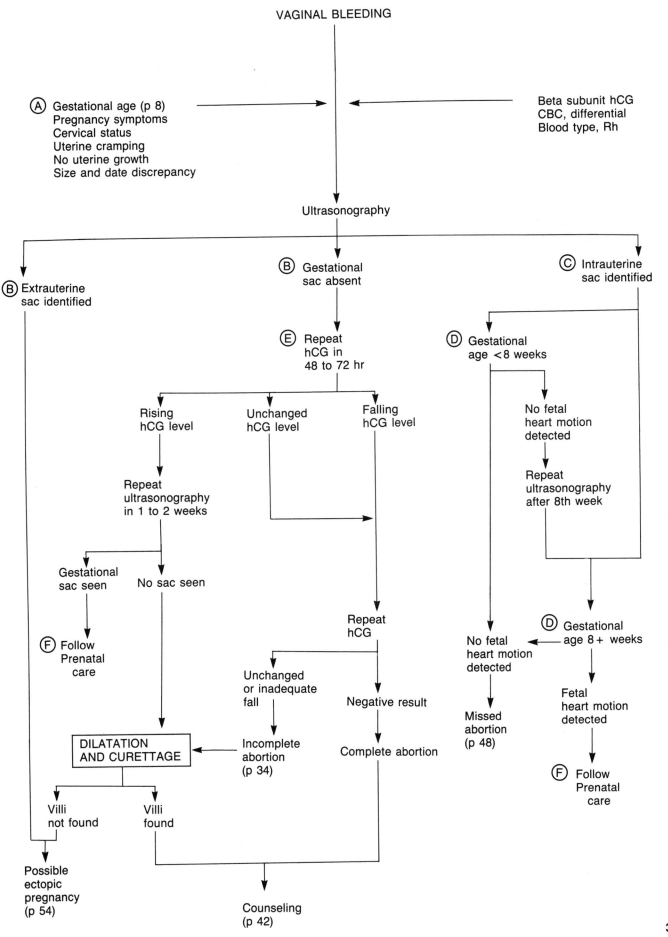

Ⓐ Gestational age (p 8)
Pregnancy symptoms
Cervical status
Uterine cramping
No uterine growth
Size and date discrepancy

Beta subunit hCG
CBC, differential
Blood type, Rh

Ultrasonography

Ⓑ Extrauterine
sac identified

Ⓑ Gestational
sac absent

Ⓒ Intrauterine
sac identified

Ⓔ Repeat
hCG in
48 to 72 hr

Ⓓ Gestational
age <8 weeks

Rising
hCG level

Unchanged
hCG level

Falling
hCG level

No fetal
heart motion
detected

Repeat
ultrasonography
in 1 to 2 weeks

Repeat
ultrasonography
after 8th week

Gestational
sac seen

No sac seen

Repeat
hCG

No fetal
heart motion
detected

Ⓓ Gestational
age 8+ weeks

Ⓕ Follow
Prenatal
care

Unchanged
or inadequate
fall

Negative result

Missed
abortion
(p 48)

Fetal
heart motion
detected

DILATATION
AND CURETTAGE

Incomplete
abortion
(p 34)

Complete abortion

Ⓕ Follow
Prenatal
care

Villi
not found

Villi
found

Possible
ectopic
pregnancy
(p 54)

Counseling
(p 42)

INCOMPLETE ABORTION

Max Borten, M.D.

A. The characteristic clinical symptoms of an incomplete abortion are vaginal bleeding and cramping pelvic pain. Fetal death usually precedes a spontaneous first trimester abortion. However, just because a pregnant woman has pelvic cramps and vaginal bleeding does not necessarily signify that she is experiencing an incomplete abortion. Surgical intervention is not indicated until the diagnosis is confirmed. This is of special concern for infertile patients or other women desirous of retaining the pregnancy; they may show signs of threatened abortion (p 32) without actually passing any tissue vaginally. There may be a normal intrauterine pregnancy present that will continue to term if left undisturbed.

B. The diagnosis becomes progressively more likely with increasingly heavy vaginal bleeding, passage of tissue (especially if the fetus or the fetal sac is identified), and progressive cervical dilatation. The uterine size is observed to be smaller than expected for the gestational age, or it becomes smaller and firmer. Pathologic examination of the tissue is required if products of conception are not identified with the naked eye. A good method to help identify villi is to float the tissue in saline. If frozen section examination is contemplated, the tissue should be transported quickly in a fresh state or immersed in normal saline; formaldehyde or other fixation precludes prompt histologic assessment. Verification of placental or fetal tissue in the material passed by the gravida warrants a procedure for evacuating the uterine cavity, especially if there is any concern that the spontaneous process is not yet complete; if there is any doubt, the uterus should be evacuated.

C. When the diagnosis of incomplete abortion is in doubt, serial determinations of the beta subunit of hCG are helpful for ascertaining whether the pregnancy is salvageable. If the levels fall rapidly to zero, they will also help make the diagnosis of complete abortion (see F, below).

D. Ultrasonography should aid in identifying the fetal sac by about six weeks from the last menstrual period. Similarly, fetal heart motion should be detectable by the eighth week; its absence supports a diagnosis of incomplete abortion or blighted ovum.

E. Sharp curettage risks denuding the deep endometrial surface, with subsequent synechia formation. Suction evacuation is gentler, just as effective, and somewhat safer insofar as the risk of uterine perforation is concerned; it is, therefore, preferable. If the cervix is sufficiently open to accept the passage of a suction curette, no anesthesia is generally needed, or paracervical anesthesia is all that is generally required for the procedure.

F. Complete abortion cases do not require further intervention. Too often, however, spontaneous abortions deemed to be complete are subsequently found not to be. Retained placental tissue is signaled by continued vaginal bleeding and infection, which may not become manifest for days or even weeks. If there is any doubt that the spontaneous abortion process is really complete, proceed with uterine evacuation. A follow-up beta subunit hCG determination is indicated to confirm the presumptive diagnosis of complete abortion. Some gynecologists advocate instrumental evacuation in all cases to ensure that none (or almost none) are missed inadvertently. There is much to be said in support of this practice in terms of both the substantive benefit and the negligible risk of the procedure.

References

Batzer FR, Weiner S, Corson SL. Landmarks during the first forty-two days of gestation demonstrated by the beta-subunit of human chorionic gonadotropin and ultrasound. Am J Obstet Gynecol 146:973, 1983.

Bernard KG, Cooperberg PL. Sonographic differentiation between blighted ovum and early viable pregnancy. Am J Radiol 144:597, 1985.

Corson SL, Batzer FR, Schlaff S. A comparison of serial quantitative serum and urine tests in early pregnancy. J Reprod Med 26:611, 1981.

PAIN AND BLEEDING

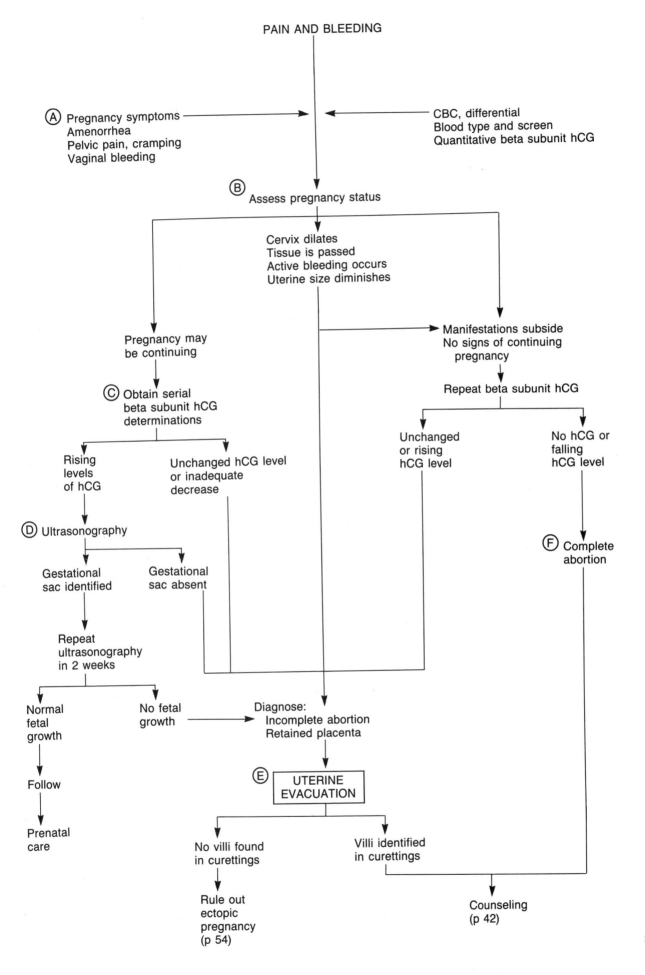

(A) Pregnancy symptoms
Amenorrhea
Pelvic pain, cramping
Vaginal bleeding

CBC, differential
Blood type and screen
Quantitative beta subunit hCG

(B) Assess pregnancy status

Cervix dilates
Tissue is passed
Active bleeding occurs
Uterine size diminishes

Pregnancy may
be continuing

Manifestations subside
No signs of continuing
pregnancy

Repeat beta subunit hCG

(C) Obtain serial
beta subunit hCG
determinations

Rising
levels
of hCG

Unchanged hCG level
or inadequate
decrease

Unchanged
or rising
hCG level

No hCG or
falling
hCG level

(D) Ultrasonography

Gestational
sac identified

Gestational
sac absent

(F) Complete
abortion

Repeat
ultrasonography
in 2 weeks

Normal
fetal
growth

No fetal
growth

Diagnose:
Incomplete abortion
Retained placenta

Follow

(E) UTERINE
EVACUATION

Prenatal
care

No villi found
in curettings

Villi identified
in curettings

Rule out
ectopic
pregnancy
(p 54)

Counseling
(p 42)

SEPTIC ABORTION

Max Borten, M.D.

A. Any pregnant female who develops fever, uterine cramps, and vaginal staining or bleeding should be suspected of having a septic abortion. There may have been instrumentation of the uterine cavity recently, most often for induced abortion (p 44). Pregnancy occurring with an IUD in situ is at special risk of developing sepsis, often with an insidious onset and flulike symptoms. The condition, while gratifyingly rare today, is so serious that it warrants attention and a high index of suspicion.

B. Helpful preliminary information is often obtained by a Gram stain of a smear of cervical secretions. Finding the intracellular Gram negative diplococci of gonorrhea helps avoid surgical intervention. Obtain cervical, blood, and urine cultures before giving antibiotics. Both aerobic and anaerobic studies are important because anaerobes and mixed flora are so common. The results become especially valuable in cases that later prove to be resistant to an aggressive, but conservative nonsurgical management program. Abdominal x-ray studies disclose ileus; films taken with the patient upright may show the presence of air under the diaphragm in cases of bowel perforation. These examinations must be done whenever one suspects that the bowel has been damaged by instrumentation. Ultrasonography is particularly useful for identifying an intrauterine gestational sac, a retained placenta, an adnexal mass, and collections of blood or pus.

C. Assess the patient's risk status to decide between conservative medical management and intensive, expeditious operative intervention. Among the critical risk factors for identifying the patient who is at special risk are a developing shock state (p 268) with cardiovascular instability, coagulopathy, oliguria, hypothermia, and signs of peritonitis, intra-abdominal bleeding, uterine perforation, or bowel injury. A midtrimester septic abortion poses a considerably greater risk than one in the first trimester, even with minimal clinical signs; therefore, even in the absence of other risk indicators, septic abortion in midpregnancy or later should automatically be designated high risk.

D. After antibiotic therapy is begun in the low risk patient, one can justifiably wait until circulating blood levels rise to a therapeutic range and allow the patient's condition to stabilize. The uterus then can be evacuated under optimal anesthesia conditions. Suction is preferable to sharp curettage because there is less chance of uterine perforation or the later development of intrauterine synechiae.

E. The patient with a high risk of septic abortion must be managed aggressively and expeditiously. Uterine evacuation is undertaken if there are no peritoneal signs or any suspicion of uterine or bowel injury. If the uterus is large, prostaglandin or oxytocin stimulation may be useful, if time permits. Operative intervention is usually required at once, however, because of the patient's precarious state.

F. Laparoscopic control helps ensure against uterine perforation during the procedure for transcervical evacuation of the uterine contents. It may also be useful as a guide in evacuating a uterus that has already been perforated, especially if there is no active bleeding.

G. Laparotomy is done to ascertain the extent of intra-abdominal infection, injury, or bleeding when it is clear that the clinical picture demands such intervention. Bleeding from a uterine perforation can be arrested by suturing or, if the damage is extensive or associated with myometrial necrosis or microabscesses, by hysterectomy. Injured bowel must be repaired or resected; a diverting colostomy may prove necessary. Adequate drainage of the infected peritoneal cavity is essential by means of one or more abdominal stab incisions.

References

Cavanagh D, Rao PS, Comas MR. Septic Shock in Obstetrics and Gynecology. Philadelphia: WB Saunders, 1977.

Grimes DA, Cates W Jr, Selik RM. Fatal septic abortion in the United States: 1975–1977. Obstet Gynecol 57:739, 1981.

Rackow EC, Weil MH. Recent trends in diagnosis and management of septic shock. Curr Surg 40:181:1983.

Rivlin ME, Hunt JA. Surgical management of diffuse peritonitis complicating obstetric/gynecologic infections. Obstet Gynecol 67:652, 1986.

Singhal PC, Kher VK, Dhall GI, et al. Conservative vs. surgical management of septic abortion with renal failure. Int J Gynaecol Obstet 20:189, 1982.

FEVER AND BLEEDING

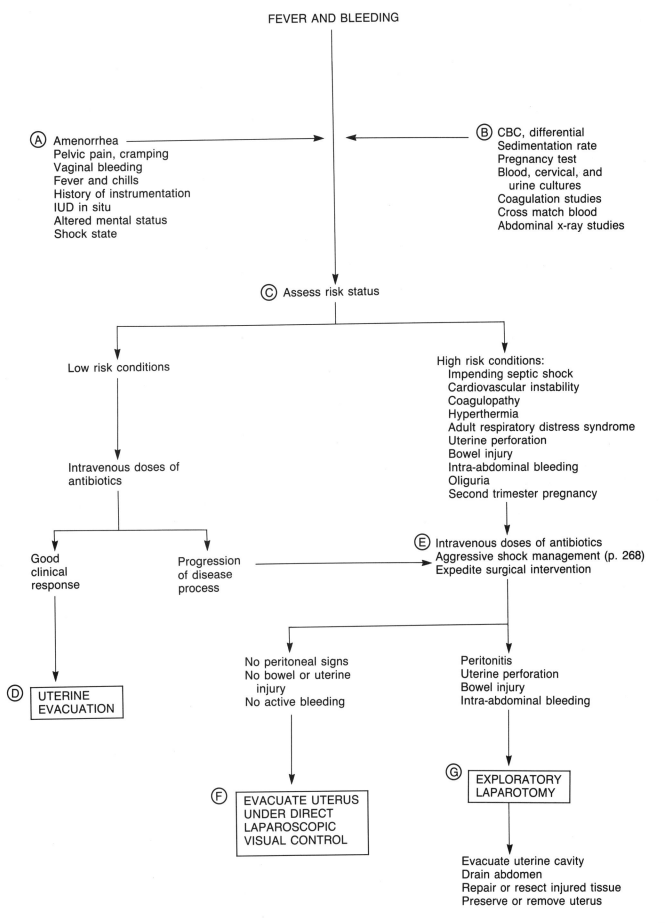

Ⓐ Amenorrhea
Pelvic pain, cramping
Vaginal bleeding
Fever and chills
History of instrumentation
IUD in situ
Altered mental status
Shock state

Ⓑ CBC, differential
Sedimentation rate
Pregnancy test
Blood, cervical, and
    urine cultures
Coagulation studies
Cross match blood
Abdominal x-ray studies

Ⓒ Assess risk status

Low risk conditions

High risk conditions:
    Impending septic shock
    Cardiovascular instability
    Coagulopathy
    Hyperthermia
    Adult respiratory distress syndrome
    Uterine perforation
    Bowel injury
    Intra-abdominal bleeding
    Oliguria
    Second trimester pregnancy

Intravenous doses of
antibiotics

Good
clinical
response

Progression
of disease
process

Ⓔ Intravenous doses of antibiotics
Aggressive shock management (p. 268)
Expedite surgical intervention

Ⓓ UTERINE
EVACUATION

No peritoneal signs
No bowel or uterine
    injury
No active bleeding

Peritonitis
Uterine perforation
Bowel injury
Intra-abdominal bleeding

Ⓕ EVACUATE UTERUS
UNDER DIRECT
LAPAROSCOPIC
VISUAL CONTROL

Ⓖ EXPLORATORY
LAPAROTOMY

Evacuate uterine cavity
Drain abdomen
Repair or resect injured tissue
Preserve or remove uterus

PREGNANCY WITH INTRAUTERINE DEVICE

Johanna F. Perlmutter, M.D.

A. Although few women are having intrauterine devices (IUDs) inserted any longer, many still have them in place. If pregnancy should occur, it may be a serious, life threatening risk. Ultrasonography is useful for verifying the pregnancy and locating the device. The device may have been expelled without the gravida's being aware of it; alternatively, it may have "migrated" to an extrauterine site, thereby presenting no hazard to the current pregnancy, although there may still be a risk to the patient that requires attention at a later date (see H, below).

B. Although the presence of a string at the cervical os usually means that the IUD is within the uterine cavity, it may have perforated into the broad ligament or even the abdominal cavity. Thus, there is still generally a need for ultrasonographic confirmation of its location.

C. The greatest risks of an IUD in situ during pregnancy are sepsis and spontaneous abortion. More than half these patients abort, and the majority of them suffer from infection. The condition may be fatal, especially during the second trimester of the pregnancy. Therefore, induced abortion is a preferable option.

D. For the patient who wishes to retain the pregnancy or for whom abortion is unacceptable, one should try to remove the device by firm, but gentle traction on the exposed string. Bear in mind that the string is liable to break because its tensile strength tends to weaken if the device has been in place for a long time. If removal is successful, abortion occurs in less than 30 percent of the cases. The remaining pregnancies should be able to carry to term with no further problems.

E. If the IUD is within the uterine cavity and the string is not found, it cannot be removed without disturbing the gestation. This leaves either induced abortion or continuing the pregnancy with the IUD in place as the only choices. Of these, abortion is preferable because it offers much less risk to the mother.

F. The patient who chooses to continue the pregnancy with an IUD in place is at increased risk for spontaneous abortion, premature rupture of the membranes, bleeding complications, premature labor, and stillbirth. She may develop potentially fatal sepsis. She must be followed very carefully with frequent visits and examinations for the development of subtle symptoms that may presage fulminating sepsis.

G. Copper containing devices in the peritoneal cavity may cause an intense inflammatory reaction with adhesion formation. An extrauterine IUD may be removed through a laparoscopic approach or by way of a colpotomy or laparotomy incision. The choice and timing depend upon the site and the device. Some fit through a laparoscope, but embedment in the omentum may make them inaccessible or not readily or safely removable. If the device is inert and does not appear to be causing any difficulty, removal can be postponed indefinitely or at least until after delivery; if it is active (containing copper, which can cause an intense inflammatory reaction, or progesterone, which can potentially affect the developing fetus) or causing symptoms, it is best removed promptly by whatever means prove necessary; laparotomy is generally required.

H. About one pregnancy in 20 with an IUD in place will be tubal in location. This high relative incidence reflects the fact that there are fewer intrauterine pregnancies rather than that there is a real increase in ectopic pregnancies. For early diagnosis, one should always have a high index of suspicion (p 54).

References

Foreman H, Stadel BV, Schlesselman S. Intrauterine device usage and fetal loss. Obstet Gynecol 58:669, 1981.

Gentile GP, Siegler A. The misplaced or missing IUD. Obstet Gynecol Surv 32:627, 1977.

McArdle C. Ultrasonic localization of missing intrauterine contraceptive devices. Obstet Gynecol 51:330, 1978.

Perlmutter JF. Pregnancy and the IUD. J Reprod Med 20:133, 1978.

PREGNANCY WITH IUD

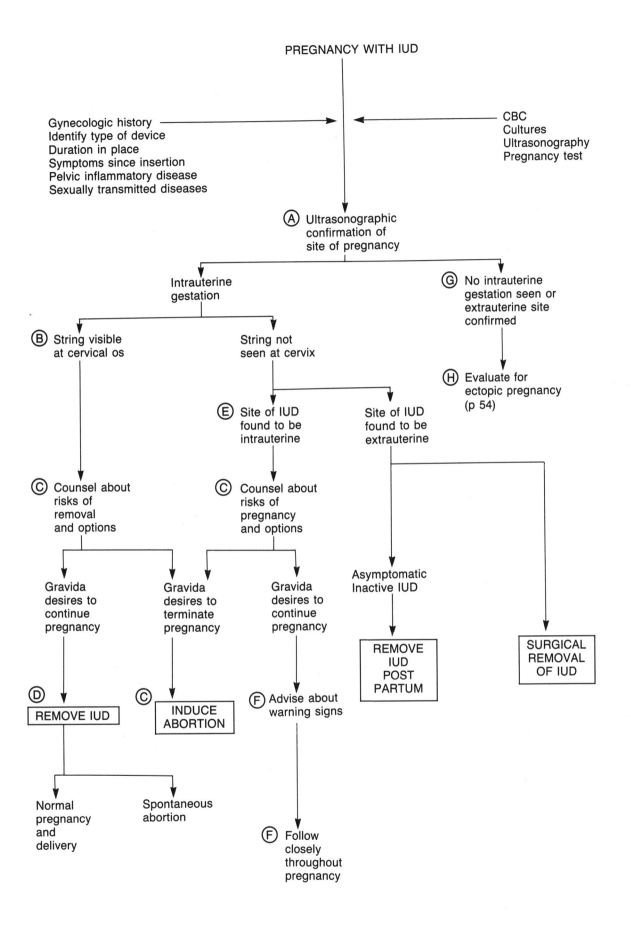

Gynecologic history
Identify type of device
Duration in place
Symptoms since insertion
Pelvic inflammatory disease
Sexually transmitted diseases

CBC
Cultures
Ultrasonography
Pregnancy test

(A) Ultrasonographic confirmation of site of pregnancy

Intrauterine gestation

(G) No intrauterine gestation seen or extrauterine site confirmed

(H) Evaluate for ectopic pregnancy (p 54)

(B) String visible at cervical os

String not seen at cervix

(E) Site of IUD found to be intrauterine

Site of IUD found to be extrauterine

(C) Counsel about risks of removal and options

(C) Counsel about risks of pregnancy and options

Gravida desires to continue pregnancy

Gravida desires to terminate pregnancy

Gravida desires to continue pregnancy

Asymptomatic Inactive IUD

(D) REMOVE IUD

(C) INDUCE ABORTION

(F) Advise about warning signs

REMOVE IUD POST PARTUM

SURGICAL REMOVAL OF IUD

Normal pregnancy and delivery

Spontaneous abortion

(F) Follow closely throughout pregnancy

UNPLANNED PREGNANCY

Johanna F. Perlmutter, M.D.
Patricia S. Stewart, M.S., M.S.W.

A. An unexpected, unplanned, or undesired pregnancy can be a devastating crisis for a woman, especially if her family supports are meager and her emotional structure is impaired. She may feel disconsolate because of the potential impact the pregnancy may have on her education, career plans, or economic situation. She may also feel anxiety, depression, anger, ambivalence, shame, or guilt, although today's societal mores make out-of-wedlock pregnancy less of a stigma than in the past. One must be nonjudgmental at all times. A psychosocial evaluation must be undertaken at the first opportunity to assess her mental status, social history, environmental supports, and current functioning. Determine whether the pregnancy is unwanted or just unplanned. The impact of the unplanned pregnancy may be catastrophic at one extreme or merely an inconvenience at the other. If the former, the gravida needs intensive support and counseling; if the latter, guidance to provide a period of readjustment may be all that is necessary. Psychosocial investigation should probe for major behavioral disorders in the patient's background, seeking information pertaining to impaired psychologic status or social functioning, family discord, substance abuse, and a chaotic life style.

B. Outline options appropriate to the gestational age. Provide information and appropriate referral as well as counseling during decision making. Patient education is needed to ensure that she understands the significance to her of a choice between abortion and carrying the fetus to term for adoption placement or to keep and raise. Ensure that her choice is not based on pressure by her partner or parents (p 42). She must be given ample opportunity to discuss alternatives alone with her physician or social worker. Support and counseling are critical to the decision process. Although the gravida's decision must prevail, it is prudent to involve her partner or a family member in counseling with her permission.

C. The gravida who chooses to carry her pregnancy to term for the purpose of placing the infant for adoption should be referred to a licensed adoption agency for continued counseling and services over the remaining course of gestation. Establish and maintain a strong long term liaison between patient, agency, and physician. Enlist family supports and, if possible, include the father of the baby in the continuing care and planning activities. Anticipate that the gravida will need considerable family support to deal with the pain of separation and loss. Be sure that she is reassessed periodically, especially at delivery before reconfirming her resolve. Follow-up with the agency and health care providers is essential. Continued counseling and support are warranted.

D. The patient who elects to continue the pregnancy and keep her infant should be given the same kind of considered, attentive care provided to others, because she may be equally (or more) vulnerable. Age appropriate education is essential for the anticipated parenting role. Assess and help formulate concrete plans for further academic or work study objectives. Plans should be sufficiently realistic that they have a reasonable chance of succeeding within the constraints of financial, space, and logistic resources available to the gravida, her newborn infant, and her partner or family. Be especially alert to unrealistic plans (or no plans) being made by the immature or psychologically unstable or aberrant gravida. Enlist aid from local agencies to monitor child welfare if there is any doubt in this regard. Adolescents require special attention to their unique pregnancy related problems (p 18), particularly as regards nutrition, parenting skills, and contraception. If the baby is to be kept, it is critical to ensure the availability of pediatric follow-up care as well as some form of surveillance for adequacy of the home environment to enforce compliance with minimally acceptable standards of child care, emotional nurturing, and development.

E. Postpartum counseling, support, education, and reevaluation are important aspects of care to help avoid a recurrence. Contraceptive advice is given with more than the usual degree of thoroughness and emphasis (p 298).

References

Dryfoos V. Contraceptive use, pregnancy intentions and pregnancy outcomes among U.S. women. Fam Plann Perspect 14:81, 1982.

Dryfoos V. A new strategy for preventing unintended teenage childbearing. Fam Plann Perspect 16:193, 1984.

Tietze C. Unintended pregnancies in the United States, 1970–1972. Fam Plann Perspect 11:186, 1979.

Westoff CF. Women's reactions to pregnancy. Fam Plann Perspect 12:135, 1980.

AMBIVALENT PATIENT WITH UNPLANNED PREGNANCY

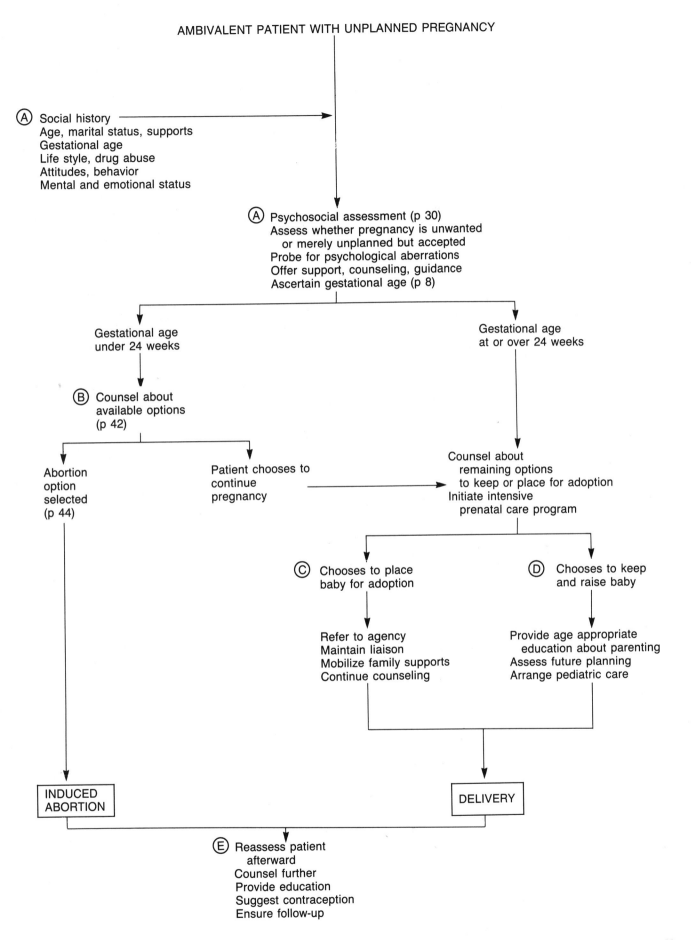

Ⓐ Social history
   Age, marital status, supports
   Gestational age
   Life style, drug abuse
   Attitudes, behavior
   Mental and emotional status

Ⓐ Psychosocial assessment (p 30)
   Assess whether pregnancy is unwanted
     or merely unplanned but accepted
   Probe for psychological aberrations
   Offer support, counseling, guidance
   Ascertain gestational age (p 8)

Gestational age
under 24 weeks

Gestational age
at or over 24 weeks

Ⓑ Counsel about
   available options
   (p 42)

Abortion
option
selected
(p 44)

Patient chooses to
continue
pregnancy

Counsel about
   remaining options
     to keep or place for adoption
   Initiate intensive
     prenatal care program

Ⓒ Chooses to place
   baby for adoption

Ⓓ Chooses to keep
   and raise baby

Refer to agency
Maintain liaison
Mobilize family supports
Continue counseling

Provide age appropriate
  education about parenting
Assess future planning
Arrange pediatric care

INDUCED
ABORTION

DELIVERY

Ⓔ Reassess patient
   afterward
   Counsel further
   Provide education
   Suggest contraception
   Ensure follow-up

ABORTION COUNSELING

Max Borten, M.D.
Patricia S. Stewart, M.S., M.S.W.

A. Whenever a woman requests interruption of an otherwise uncomplicated pregnancy, explore her decision making process. Not infrequently the abortion request is the result of pressure placed on her by her partner or parents. It is important to provide the opportunity for the gravida to discuss her decision with her physician or counselor on a one-to-one basis. Reassurance must be provided that no procedure will be performed against her will. Explore her psychosocial background, ability to function, and supports (p 30). Especially seek to determine whether she is emotionally immature or intellectually impaired.

B. Few women find the decision to terminate a pregnancy easy. Most welcome opportunities for nonjudgmental counseling. They especially need balanced information about options; in the absence of any medicolegal constraints, most gravidas have three options, namely, elective induced abortion (p 44), continuing the pregnancy to term, and either keeping the baby or placing it for adoption or foster care. Intense predecision counseling is essential in addition to follow-up support services. If adoption is the chosen alternative, referral to an appropriate licensed agency is necessary for continuing surveillance and concrete services. If possible, involve the father of the fetus in the decision making. Enlist family supports whenever possible. Establish a good liaison between the patient, the agency, and the obstetrician. Experience has shown that women seeking abortions frequently demonstrate psychological disturbances. However, these are usually transient as a consequence of the short term stresses of the abortion (termed situational anxiety). When feelings of anxiety, depression, anger, and guilt are evaluated, the pattern of response is similar to that of other forms of crisis reaction and crisis resolution.

C. Support and counseling are integral and necessary components of the abortion procedure. Abortion counseling cannot just be limited to the time when the procedure is about to be done. With the patient's consent, it is advisable to include her partner or parents or others whom she considers supportive in the counseling session. This is particularly important in the young adolescent. Counseling can be provided individually or as a group.

D. Although some women may experience adverse psychological sequelae following voluntary termination of pregnancy, the majority do not. In contrast, refusal to provide an abortion to a woman who desires it often results in great psychological distress. Seldom does a woman change her mind and carry a pregnancy to term as a result of having been refused the procedure. More often she will explore alternatives and thereby increase the risks of illegal procedures with undesirable and potentially serious consequences.

E. Ambivalence concerning the decision to undergo an abortion is not unusual. One must keep in mind that ultimately the decision to interrupt a gestation rests primarily with the pregnant woman. To enable her to make an informed and intelligent choice, the counselor must provide written as well as detailed verbal information about the nature of the procedure, its medical risks, and long term effects.

F. Concern for the woman requesting an abortion should not end when the procedure is completed. Although the patient may feel relieved by having resolved her immediate concern, counseling should not be considered complete until she has had an opportunity to verbalize her feelings about her decision and resolve adverse effects, and until contraceptive information has been provided. Concern about the future well-being of the woman becomes the first priority.

References

Beeman PB. Peers, parents, and partners: Determining the needs of the support person in an abortion clinic. J Obstet Gynecol Neonatal Nurs 14:54, 1985.

Handy JA. Psychological and social aspects of induced abortion. Br J Clin Psychol 21:29, 1982.

Landy U. Abortion counselling: A new component of medical care. Clin Obstet Gynaecol 13:33, 1986.

Leppert PC, Pahlka BS. Grieving characteristics after spontaneous abortion: A management approach. Obstet Gynecol 64:119, 1984.

REQUEST FOR PREGNANCY TERMINATION

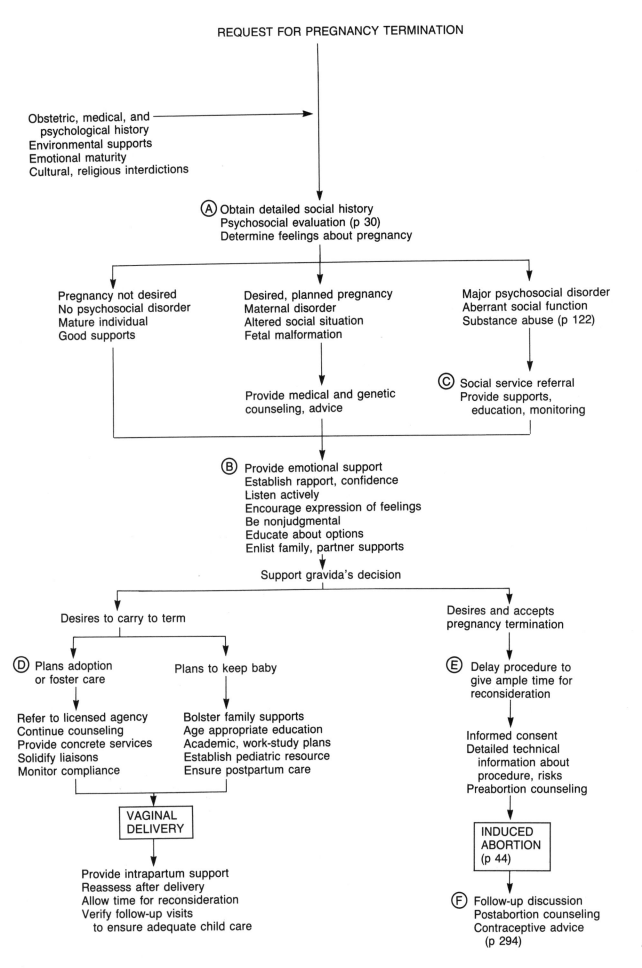

Obstetric, medical, and
   psychological history
Environmental supports
Emotional maturity
Cultural, religious interdictions

Ⓐ Obtain detailed social history
   Psychosocial evaluation (p 30)
   Determine feelings about pregnancy

Pregnancy not desired
No psychosocial disorder
Mature individual
Good supports

Desired, planned pregnancy
Maternal disorder
Altered social situation
Fetal malformation

Major psychosocial disorder
Aberrant social function
Substance abuse (p 122)

Provide medical and genetic
   counseling, advice

Ⓒ Social service referral
   Provide supports,
     education, monitoring

Ⓑ Provide emotional support
   Establish rapport, confidence
   Listen actively
   Encourage expression of feelings
   Be nonjudgmental
   Educate about options
   Enlist family, partner supports

Support gravida's decision

Desires to carry to term

Desires and accepts
pregnancy termination

Ⓓ Plans adoption
   or foster care

Plans to keep baby

Ⓔ Delay procedure to
   give ample time for
   reconsideration

Refer to licensed agency
Continue counseling
Provide concrete services
Solidify liaisons
Monitor compliance

Bolster family supports
Age appropriate education
Academic, work-study plans
Establish pediatric resource
Ensure postpartum care

Informed consent
Detailed technical
   information about
   procedure, risks
Preabortion counseling

VAGINAL
DELIVERY

INDUCED
ABORTION
(p 44)

Provide intrapartum support
Reassess after delivery
Allow time for reconsideration
Verify follow-up visits
   to ensure adequate child care

Ⓕ Follow-up discussion
   Postabortion counseling
   Contraceptive advice
   (p 294)

INDUCED ABORTION

Max Borten, M.D.

A. It is essential for the gravida to be fully informed about alternative resources and options and about the safety and risks of the procedure. Psychosocial assessment and counseling are done at the very first visit (p 30). In addition to the medical history, an in-depth social history including relationships with others, attitudes about abortion, and support systems must be obtained at this time. Preabortion counseling should be open and understanding. No decision should be made by the gravida in haste, under duress, or without adequate time and information. Special attention should be given to feelings of ambivalence, guilt, anger, shame, sadness, and sense of loss. Family supports, if available, should be mobilized. Postoperative contraception must be emphasized. Counseling should also be done prior to the procedure and again during the follow-up visit.

B. One of the first requirements of medical screening is to establish that pregnancy actually exists. This applies especially in women whose period is late by a short time. Patients requesting an abortion must also be screened to uncover any serious medical or psychiatric conditions. Cardiac, metabolic, pulmonary, neurologic, and renal diseases may put the gravida at high risk. Such individuals are best referred to regionalized centers for care. If the patient chooses to continue the pregnancy, intensive prenatal care and counseling are essential.

C. Menstrual extraction is an effective technique for interrupting very early pregnancies (less than seven weeks from the last menstrual period). It is relatively risk-free, but it is associated with a high incidence of failure. Because it is done so early, some women may not actually be pregnant; this means that the procedure was unnecessary. Be alert for an ectopic pregnancy if no villi are found in the uterus. To prevent Rh sensitization, low dose anti-D (Micro-Rhogam) must be administered to Rh negative gravidas.

D. The technique used most often is suction evacuation, generally done under paracervical block anesthesia. For especially anxious patients or those with medical indications, general anesthesia may have to be used. If so, be sure to avoid myometrial relaxing drugs (such as the halogenated compounds) because they can cause uterine atony unresponsive to uterotonic drugs, resulting in excessive blood loss. Most first trimester abortions can be safely performed in free-standing surgical units; however, it is prudent to hospitalize patients with medical, surgical, or anesthetic risk factors. Suitable preoperative evaluation and the availability of adequate staff and facilities are essential for properly dealing with any complications that may arise.

E. Dilatation and evacuation appears to constitute the safest technique for early midtrimester pregnancy interruptions (13 to 17 weeks). The overall incidence of complications with dilatation and evacuation is lower than that reported with the intra-amniotic infusion of hypertonic saline or prostaglandin. Cervical dilatation is facilitated (and made safer) by the preoperative use of laminaria. The use of a paracervical block for dilatation and evacuation appears to be safer and less expensive than general anesthesia. Special care must be taken to ensure complete emptying of the large uterus and to avoid trauma or perforation.

F. The intra-amniotic administration of $PGF_2\alpha$ alone or in combination with hypertonic saline is an effective method in late second trimester abortions. Hypertonic saline, if used to avert a live birth, is limited to no more than 50 ml to avoid acute coagulopathy. Rapid concurrent intravenous administration of a normotonic electrolyte-containing solution (500 cc over 30 minutes) reduces the incidence of systemic side effects. Avoid using prostaglandins in women with a history of bronchial asthma or epilepsy; they can be given intra-amniotic hypertonic saline alone (150 to 200 ml). An intravenous oxytocin infusion, given to accelerate the late abortion process, increases the risk of uterine rupture and cervical lacerations and should, therefore, be avoided.

G. Following delivery of the fetus, add oxytocin to the intravenous solution (20 IU per 1,000 ml) to stimulate uterine contractions. If the placenta is not expelled within two hours after fetal expulsion, suction evacuation is done to reduce the risk of blood loss and infection. Uterine curettage is also needed if the expelled placenta does not appear to be intact.

References

Borten M. Use of combination prostaglandin $F_2\alpha$ and hypertonic saline for midtrimester abortion. Prostaglandins 12:625, 1976.

Fielding WL, Lee SY, Borten M, Friedman EA. Continued pregnancy after failed first trimester abortion. Obstet Gynecol 63:421, 1984.

Grimes DA, Schulz KF, Cates W Jr. Prophylactic antibiotics for curettage abortion. Am J Obstet Gynecol 150:689, 1984.

MacKay HT, Schulz KF, Grimes DA. Safety to local versus general anesthesia for second-trimester dilatation and evacuation abortion. Obstet Gynecol 66:661, 1985.

Stubblefield PG. Surgical techniques of uterine evacuation of first- and second-trimester abortion. Clin Obstet Gynaecol 13:53, 1986.

PREGNANCY CONFIRMED

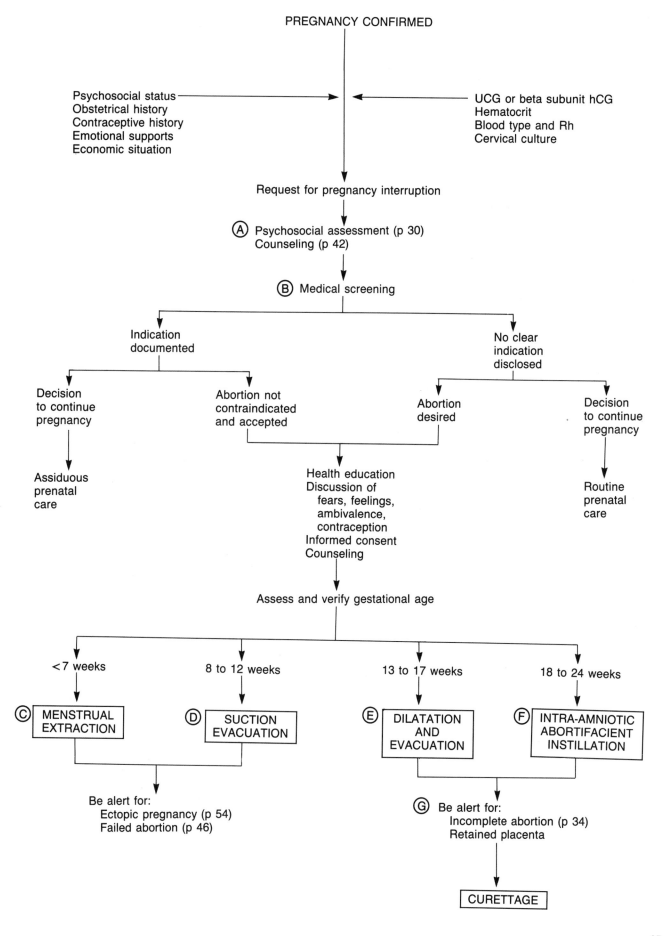

Psychosocial status
Obstetrical history
Contraceptive history
Emotional supports
Economic situation

UCG or beta subunit hCG
Hematocrit
Blood type and Rh
Cervical culture

Request for pregnancy interruption

Ⓐ Psychosocial assessment (p 30)
Counseling (p 42)

Ⓑ Medical screening

Indication documented

No clear indication disclosed

Decision to continue pregnancy

Abortion not contraindicated and accepted

Abortion desired

Decision to continue pregnancy

Assiduous prenatal care

Health education
Discussion of fears, feelings, ambivalence, contraception
Informed consent
Counseling

Routine prenatal care

Assess and verify gestational age

<7 weeks

8 to 12 weeks

13 to 17 weeks

18 to 24 weeks

Ⓒ MENSTRUAL EXTRACTION

Ⓓ SUCTION EVACUATION

Ⓔ DILATATION AND EVACUATION

Ⓕ INTRA-AMNIOTIC ABORTIFACIENT INSTILLATION

Be alert for:
Ectopic pregnancy (p 54)
Failed abortion (p 46)

Ⓖ Be alert for:
Incomplete abortion (p 34)
Retained placenta

CURETTAGE

FAILED ABORTION

Max Borten, M.D.

A. Patients who are at special risk for failure of a first trimester abortion, in whom the pregnancy continues despite the procedure, are those whose pregnancy duration is poorly established (especially when dates and uterine size are discrepant) or whose cervix is stenotic or uterus anomalous so that the operation cannot be done well. Even in well conducted first trimester abortions, however, the procedure may fail. This occurs in less than 1 percent of the cases. The operator should be especially alert to this possibility during the course of the operation. If the curettings are minimal relative to gestational age, evacuation may not be complete. One should note the amount of tissue removed to verify that it is approximately what should be expected for the gestational age. In addition, specific efforts should be made in each case to identify the gestational sac and chorionic villi by floating the material in saline. This can usually be done with the naked eye (or a magnifying loupe or dissecting microscope) with good lighting. Observing fetal parts is definitive. Histologic examination of all specimens is especially valuable for ruling out ectopic pregnancy (p 54), except for the exceedingly rare case of concurrent intrauterine and extrauterine (heterotopic) pregnancy. However, it cannot verify complete evacuation.

B. Persistence of pregnancy-related signs and symptoms beyond 3 to 4 days following the induced abortion should raise one's index of suspicion. Continued vaginal bleeding, unrelieved morning nausea, breast tenderness, chronic fatigue, urinary frequency, and constipation are important manifestations. The patient should be advised to return for prompt re-evaluation under these circumstances. She must be contacted directly and urged to seek care if the pathologic study does not confirm the presence of chorionic villi (because of the risk of ectopic pregnancy).

C. Incomplete evacuation usually results in continued vaginal bleeding, uterine cramping, and in some instances fever and malaise. Continued pregnancy should be suspected if the uterus is enlarging so that it is still appropriate in size for the gestational age and soft in consistency. Re-examination should be done 1 to 2 weeks after the primary abortion procedure to ensure that normal uterine involution is occurring. If not, the possibility of incomplete abortion or continued pregnancy warrants attention.

D. Uterine malformations, especially with gestational implantation in one horn of a double uterus, places the patient at special risk for continued pregnancy. Additional risk factors include marked uterine anteflexion or retroflexion. Pelvic ultrasonography is useful to confirm or rule out an intrauterine gestational sac, retained products of conception, or a congenital anomaly of the uterus.

E. It is essential to provide intensive counseling for these patients. Patients who learn that their pregnancy is still intact sometimes change their minds about terminating it. This is especially the case for women who were ambivalent in the first instance. Prenatal care, moral support, and continued counseling throughout the pregnancy are in order for them.

References

Fielding WL, Lee SY, Borten M, Friedman EA. Continued pregnancy after failed first-trimester abortion. Obstet Gynecol 63:421, 1984.

Jerome M, Armstead JW, Burnhill MS, et al. Early recognition of ectopic pregnancy at a free-standing abortion clinic. Adv Planned Parent 75:144, 1981.

Munsick RA. Clinical test for placenta in 300 consecutive menstrual aspirations. Obstet Gynecol 60:738, 1982.

Rubin GL, Cates W, Gold J, et al. Fatal ectopic pregnancy after attempted legally induced abortion. JAMA 244:1705, 1980.

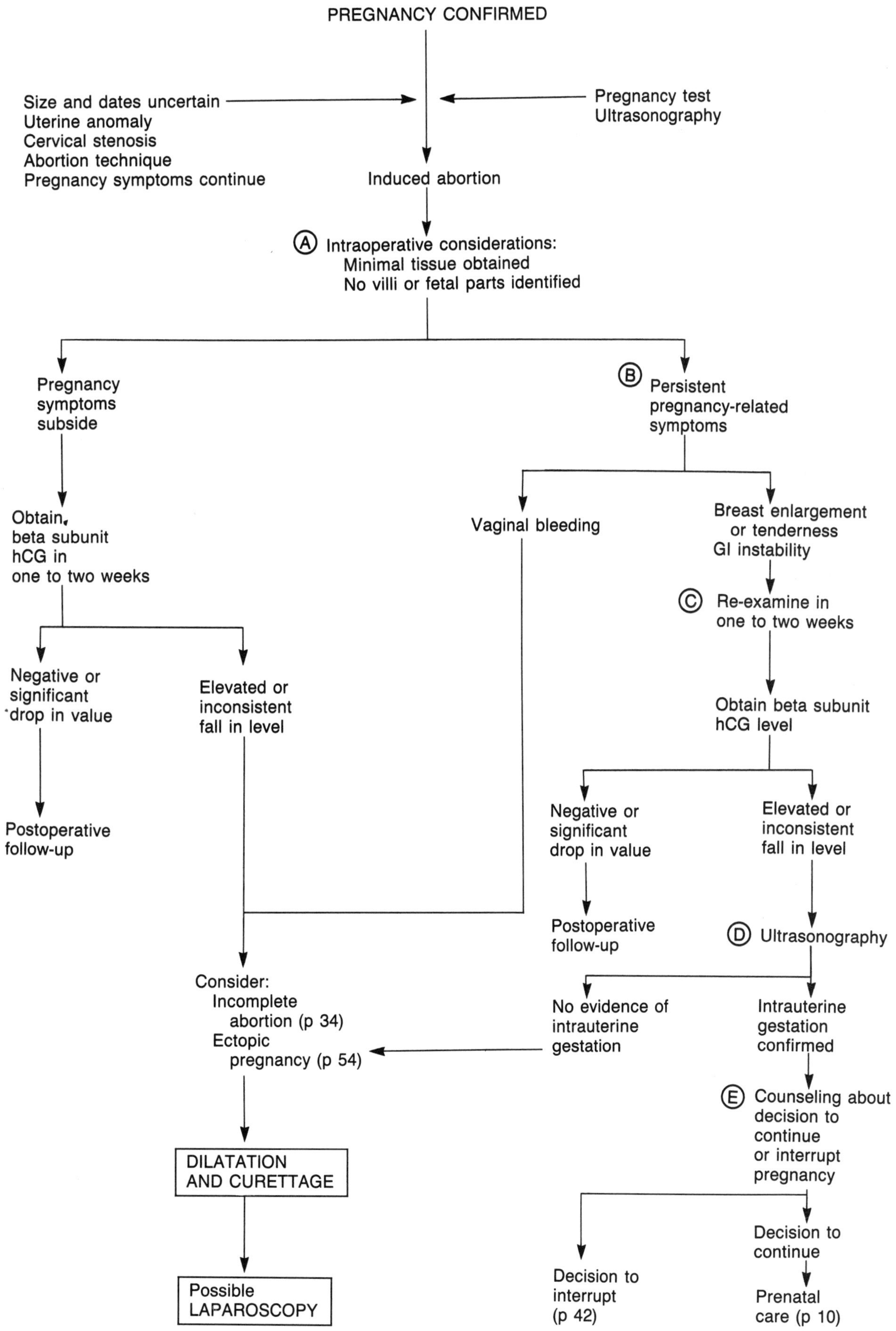

PREGNANCY CONFIRMED

Size and dates uncertain
Uterine anomaly
Cervical stenosis
Abortion technique
Pregnancy symptoms continue

Pregnancy test
Ultrasonography

Induced abortion

Ⓐ Intraoperative considerations:
  Minimal tissue obtained
  No villi or fetal parts identified

Pregnancy
symptoms
subside

Ⓑ Persistent
pregnancy-related
symptoms

Obtain
beta subunit
hCG in
one to two weeks

Vaginal bleeding

Breast enlargement
or tenderness
GI instability

Ⓒ Re-examine in
one to two weeks

Negative or
significant
drop in value

Elevated or
inconsistent
fall in level

Obtain beta subunit
hCG level

Postoperative
follow-up

Negative or
significant
drop in value

Elevated or
inconsistent
fall in level

Postoperative
follow-up

Ⓓ Ultrasonography

Consider:
Incomplete
abortion (p 34)
Ectopic
pregnancy (p 54)

No evidence of
intrauterine
gestation

Intrauterine
gestation
confirmed

Ⓔ Counseling about
decision to
continue
or interrupt
pregnancy

DILATATION
AND CURETTAGE

Possible
LAPAROSCOPY

Decision to
interrupt
(p 42)

Decision to
continue

Prenatal
care (p 10)

MISSED ABORTION

Max Borten, M.D.

A. Missed abortion is a term applied to intrauterine retention of a dead conceptus when the diagnosis is verified by ultrasonography or by prolonged retention of a dead abortus without evidence of growth or development. The urinary pregnancy test usually remains positive for long periods, but beta subunit hCG levels tend to remain stable or fall. One has to recognize that hCG levels are generally expected to fall toward the end of the first trimester. Characteristically the uterus stops growing in missed abortion cases. Sometimes the uterine size actually diminishes, but the reliability of uterine growth for diagnosis is marginal at best.

B. Obtain coagulation studies whenever the diagnosis of missed abortion is entertained, because disseminated intravascular coagulation is a potentially serious complication. Although overt manifestations of disseminated intravascular coagulation are seldom seen until four to six weeks after fetal death, difficulty in assessing the exact time of the demise makes it important to begin coagulation studies early and to repeat them at least every week.

C. Ultrasonography makes it possible to diagnose fetal death with a high degree of reliability (p 6). Intervention was often delayed in the past because one could not always be certain that the fetus was dead. The techniques for interrupting such pregnancies were also more hazardous and less reliable than those available today.

D. If ultrasonography is not readily available, it is best to wait at least four to six weeks, re-evaluating periodically, before taking action. If a complication arises, such as vaginal bleeding, infection, or disseminated intravascular coagulation, requiring intervention in the interim, action may become necessary. The delay is needed because lack of uterine growth is not a reliable indicator of fetal death. Even in a normal pregnancy, the uterus need not appear to be growing at a constant rate. During this observation period, serial bimanual abdominopelvic examinations for uterine size, fetal heart auscultations, and hCG determinations are done.

E. The techniques outlined for induced abortion (p 44) are generally applicable here as well. Prostaglandin E_2 vaginal suppositories are effective in advanced second trimester missed abortion, but they produce frequent gastrointestinal side effects. If instrumentation proves to be necessary, suction evacuation is preferable to sharp curettage. It is relatively easy to denude the endometrium by a sharp curette as a consequence of the decidual necrosis that occurs with missed abortion. Intrauterine synechiae characteristic of Asherman's syndrome may thus be avoided by the more gentle practice of suction aspiration.

References

Gustavii B. Missed abortion and uterine contractility. Am J Obstet Gynecol 130:18, 1978.

Lauersen NH, Wilson KH. Induction of labor in patients with missed abortion and fetal death in utero with prostaglandin E_2 suppositories. Am J Obstet Gynecol 127:609, 1977.

McFadyen IR. Missed abortion, and later spontaneous abortion, in pregnancies clinically normal at 7–12 weeks. Eur J Obstet Gynecol Reprod Biol 20:381,1985.

Romero R, Jeanty P, Hobbins JC. Diagnostic ultrasound in the first trimester of pregnancy. Clin Obstet Gynecol 27:286, 1984.

Tan KC, Karim SM, Ratnam SS, Kottegoda SR. Epidemiologic analysis of fetal death in utero in Singapore. Int J Gynaecol Obstet 22:181, 1984.

FAILURE OF UTERINE GROWTH

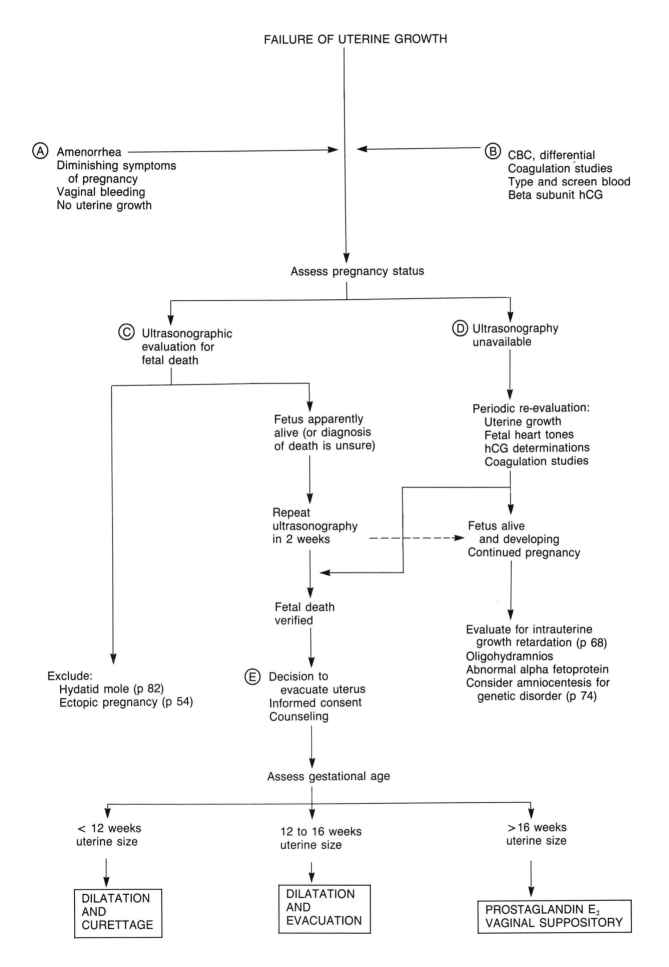

Ⓐ Amenorrhea
Diminishing symptoms
of pregnancy
Vaginal bleeding
No uterine growth

Ⓑ CBC, differential
Coagulation studies
Type and screen blood
Beta subunit hCG

Assess pregnancy status

Ⓒ Ultrasonographic
evaluation for
fetal death

Ⓓ Ultrasonography
unavailable

Fetus apparently
alive (or diagnosis
of death is unsure)

Periodic re-evaluation:
Uterine growth
Fetal heart tones
hCG determinations
Coagulation studies

Repeat
ultrasonography
in 2 weeks

Fetus alive
and developing
Continued pregnancy

Fetal death
verified

Exclude:
Hydatid mole (p 82)
Ectopic pregnancy (p 54)

Ⓔ Decision to
evacuate uterus
Informed consent
Counseling

Evaluate for intrauterine
growth retardation (p 68)
Oligohydramnios
Abnormal alpha fetoprotein
Consider amniocentesis for
genetic disorder (p 74)

Assess gestational age

< 12 weeks
uterine size

12 to 16 weeks
uterine size

>16 weeks
uterine size

DILATATION
AND
CURETTAGE

DILATATION
AND
EVACUATION

PROSTAGLANDIN E₂
VAGINAL SUPPOSITORY

HABITUAL ABORTION

Louis Burke, M.D.

A. Spontaneous abortion is generally stated to occur in 15 to 20 percent of all pregnancies, but recent data based on early detection of pregnancy by beta subunit hCG blood levels suggest that the rate is closer to 30 to 50 percent or even higher. This sheds doubt on the risk rates cited for pregnancy loss after one or more spontaneous abortions. Nonetheless the risk of recurrent abortion is probably increased after one or two spontaneous abortions, and even more so after three consecutive abortions, although the true frequency (in excess of expected loss rates) is unclear. Habitual abortion is usually defined as three or more pregnancy losses prior to the 20th week of gestation.

B. Fetal wastage in the first trimester is often associated with problems of conception and embryogenesis. Such losses may also be related to sexually transmitted and debilitating systemic diseases, such as hypothyroidism, lupus erythematosus, and renal disease. Second trimester abortion can also result from infection, especially with Toxoplasma, Listeria, Chlamydia, and Ureaplasma. More commonly, however, it is due to uterine anomalies, cervical incompetence (p 52) and structural and functional effects of exposure in utero to diethylstilbestrol. Be alert to a history of possible cervical trauma, especially by conization, vigorous dilatation (prior to curettage), or complicated delivery. Intrauterine exposure to diethylstilbestrol may not be known, but telltale signs of vaginal adenosis with a typical cervical hood and ectopy confirm it. Smoking may lower the luteinizing hormone level and affect steroid production in early pregnancy, which in turn can lead to fetal wastage.

C. At least half of first trimester abortuses have chromosomal abnormalities: 4 percent are trisomic, 2 percent have a 45X karyotype, and 1.5 percent are polyploid; a 45X pattern results in abortion 99 percent of the time. Couples experiencing habitual abortion have a 4.4 percent incidence of chromosomal abnormality (6.6 percent for the female and 2.6 percent for the male partner). Advanced maternal and paternal age increases the risk of blighted ova. Chromosomal studies should be done on both fetus and placenta, and the parents should be checked for balanced translocation. Genetic screening and counseling are useful. Some habitual abortions may be due to immunologic rejection resulting from the absence of serum lymphocytic blocking factors in the gravida specific for paternal antigen, analogous to the tissue rejection phenomenon in a host-graft reaction.

D. Try to discover and provide treatment for multiple factors that may exist. Consider possible psychogenic influences; supportive psychotherapy and counseling may help (80 percent success rates have been reported). The tests with the highest yield in detecting etiologic factors, many of which may be correctable, are hysterosalpingography (applicable in the nonpregnant state only), peripheral lymphocyte karyotyping, and cervical cultures for sexually transmitted infectious agents. A woman whose evaluations yield entirely normal results can be counseled that she has a good chance (estimated to be 77 percent) that the next pregnancy will result in a live birth. Even women with some abnormality can be encouraged by the great likelihood of a gratifying outcome in the next pregnancy.

E. Cervical incompetence is generally an acquired condition due to various types of trauma, such as occurs at delivery, abortion, or forceful instrumental dilatation. It may also be associated with congenital conditions involving both histologic and anatomic defects. This is especially true for the women exposed to diethylstilbestrol in utero. The presence of a major uterine anomaly increases the risk of cervical incompetence. One can recognize cervical incompetence clinically by the pattern of progressive midtrimester cervical effacement and dilatation unaccompanied by uterine contractions (until just prior to evacuation). A cerclage procedure should be done if the membranes are still intact and there are no contractions. Tocolytic drugs may be helpful afterward to keep the uterus quiescent. The McDonald procedure is preferable to the Shirodkar procedure. Both are equally effective, but no tissue dissection is involved with the McDonald procedure, producing less morbidity.

References

Caudle MR, Rote NS, Scott JR, et al. Histocompatibility in couples with recurrent spontaneous abortion and normal fertility. Fertil Steril 39:793, 1983.

Cowchock S, Dehoratius RD, Wapner RJ, et al. Subclinical autoimmune disease and unexplained abortion. Am J Obstet Gynecol 150:367, 1984.

Harger JH, Archer DF, Marchese SG, et al. Etiology of recurrent pregnancy losses and outcome of subsequent pregnancies. Obstet Gynecol 62:574, 1983.

Rock JA, Zacus HA. The clinical management of repeated early pregnancy wastage. Fertil Steril 39:123, 1983.

Stray-Pedersen B, Stray-Pedersen S. Etiologic factors and subsequent reproductive performance in 195 couples with a prior history of habitual abortion. Am J Obstet Gynecol 148:140, 1984.

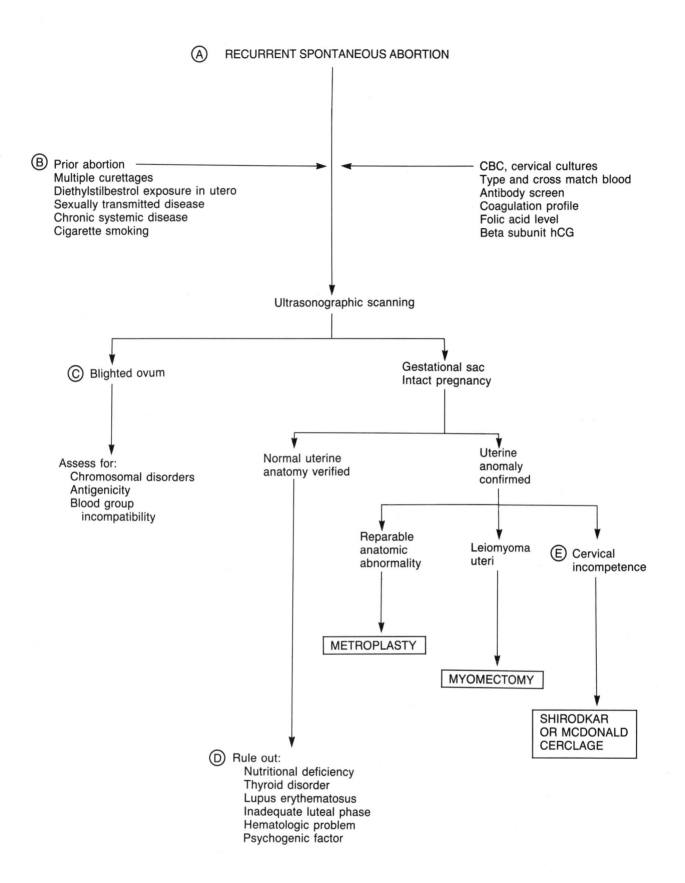

Ⓐ RECURRENT SPONTANEOUS ABORTION

Ⓑ Prior abortion
Multiple curettages
Diethylstilbestrol exposure in utero
Sexually transmitted disease
Chronic systemic disease
Cigarette smoking

CBC, cervical cultures
Type and cross match blood
Antibody screen
Coagulation profile
Folic acid level
Beta subunit hCG

Ultrasonographic scanning

Ⓒ Blighted ovum

Assess for:
  Chromosomal disorders
  Antigenicity
  Blood group
    incompatibility

Gestational sac
Intact pregnancy

Normal uterine
anatomy verified

Uterine
anomaly
confirmed

Reparable
anatomic
abnormality

Leiomyoma
uteri

Ⓔ Cervical
incompetence

METROPLASTY

MYOMECTOMY

SHIRODKAR
OR MCDONALD
CERCLAGE

Ⓓ Rule out:
  Nutritional deficiency
  Thyroid disorder
  Lupus erythematosus
  Inadequate luteal phase
  Hematologic problem
  Psychogenic factor

CERVICAL INCOMPETENCE

Susan B. Wilson, M.D.

A. An obstetrical history suggestive of cervical incompetence includes a history of recurrent midtrimester losses, painless cervical dilatation, second trimester rupture of membranes prior to contractions, and a history of short labors without significant uterine activity. Women with a double uterus or other uterine anomaly are at increased risk as are those who were exposed to diethylstilbestrol during their intrauterine life or whose cervix may have been traumatized by vigorous dilatation or surgical conization.

B. Prepregnancy evaluation of cervical competence can be done by determining whether there is characteristic cervical funneling on hysterosalpingography or easy passage of a number 8 Hegar dilator through the internal os. Antenatal evaluation involves serial manual or ultrasonographic examinations of the cervix for progressive dilatation. Ultrasound may increase the specificity of the diagnosis and help avoid an unnecessary cerclage; however, its predictive and diagnostic reliability has been questioned.

C. It is important to avoid cerclage placement during the first trimester when up to 20 percent of pregnancies may result in miscarriage. Cerclage is most successful between 14 and 20 weeks in the woman with a minimally dilated and effaced cervix. Cerclage should be avoided once viability has been reached because it is unlikely to succeed and is not innocuous. Risks include pregnancy loss, ruptured membranes, cervical laceration, bleeding, cervical stenosis, ruptured uterus, and infection, which may even be fatal.

D. Among the currently available techniques, the McDonald and Shirodkar procedures are equally effective. In McDonald cerclage (Fig. 1) a nonabsorbable purse-string suture is placed around the cervix as close to the internal os as possible without reflecting the bladder, whereas the Shirodkar cerclage advances the bladder first (thereby adding some risk of bleeding and perhaps infection) and ensures that the suture is entirely submucosal. An abdominal approach may be considered if the cervix is destroyed.

E. Conservative measures are sometimes effective when the surgical approach is not appropriate or feasible. Prolonged bed rest may work by neutralizing gravity and perhaps reversing the dynamics of the condition, especially in the head-down Trendelenburg position (which is poorly tolerated). Use of a pessary (Hodge-Smith) may also divert pressure away from the internal os and allow the cervix to re-form.

F. In most instances, vaginal delivery is feasible after removal of the suture at 38 weeks or at the onset of labor. Cervical stenosis is estimated to occur in just under 5 percent and may require cesarean delivery.

References

Barford DAG, Rosen MG. Cervical incompetence: Diagnosis and outcome. Obstet Gynecol 64:159, 1984.

Feingold M, Brook I, Zakut H. Detection of cervical incompetence by ultrasound. Acta Obstet Gynecol Scand 63:407, 1984.

Harger JH. Comparison of success and morbidity in cervical cerclage procedures. Obstet Gynecol 56:543, 1980.

Jackson G, Pendleton HJ, Nichol B, Whittman BK. Diagnostic ultrasound in the assessment of patients with incompetent cervix. Br J Obstet Gynaecol 91:232, 1984.

Michaels WH, Montgomery C, Karo J, Temple J, Ager J, Olson J. Ultrasound differentiation of the competent from the incompetent cervix: Prevention of preterm delivery. Am J Obstet Gynecol 154:537, 1986.

Witter FR. Negative sonographic findings followed by rapid cervical dilatation due to cervical incompetence. Obstet Gynecol 64:136, 1984.

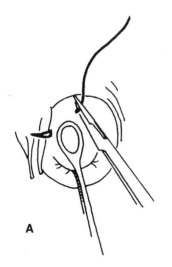
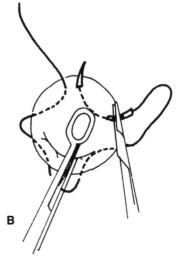

Figure 1 McDonald cerclage technique. The anterior lip of cervix is held by ring forceps. *A*, Mucosal suture is placed into right upper quadrant. *B*, Circumferential purse-string suture is being completed before tying anteriorly.

A

B

PAINLESS CERVICAL DILATATION

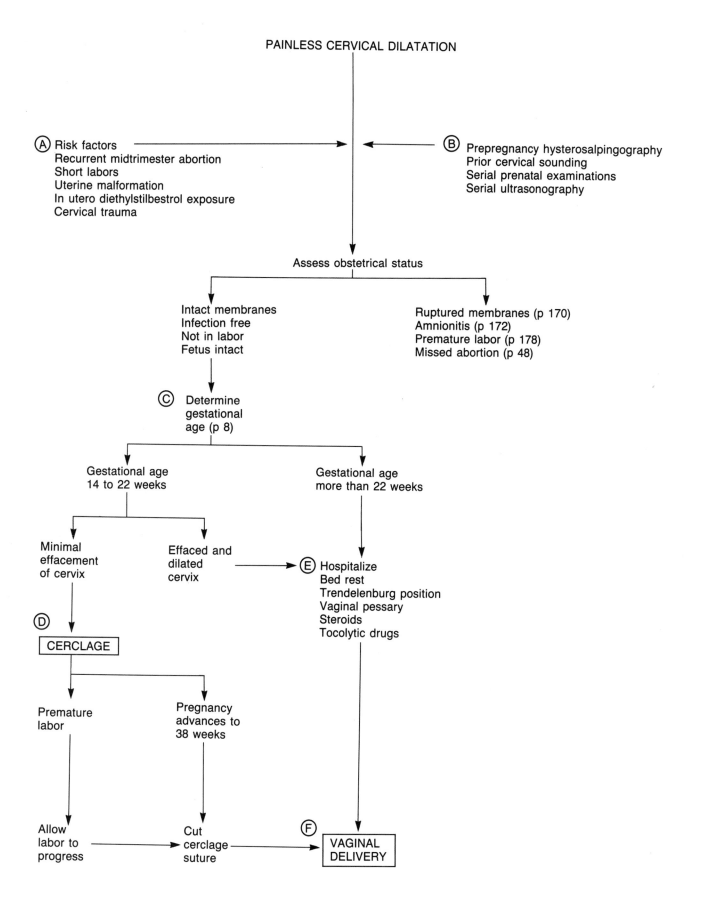

Ⓐ Risk factors
  Recurrent midtrimester abortion
  Short labors
  Uterine malformation
  In utero diethylstilbestrol exposure
  Cervical trauma

Ⓑ Prepregnancy hysterosalpingography
  Prior cervical sounding
  Serial prenatal examinations
  Serial ultrasonography

Assess obstetrical status

Intact membranes
Infection free
Not in labor
Fetus intact

Ruptured membranes (p 170)
Amnionitis (p 172)
Premature labor (p 178)
Missed abortion (p 48)

Ⓒ Determine
  gestational
  age (p 8)

Gestational age
14 to 22 weeks

Gestational age
more than 22 weeks

Minimal
effacement
of cervix

Effaced and
dilated
cervix

Ⓔ Hospitalize
  Bed rest
  Trendelenburg position
  Vaginal pessary
  Steroids
  Tocolytic drugs

Ⓓ
CERCLAGE

Premature
labor

Pregnancy
advances to
38 weeks

Allow
labor to
progress

Cut
cerclage
suture

Ⓕ
VAGINAL
DELIVERY

ECTOPIC PREGNANCY

David S. Chapin, M.D.

A. Any patient with menstrual irregularity should be suspected of having an ectopic pregnancy. The relative incidence among pregnancies has been rising over the past few decades apparently as a consequence of more effective and widespread use of effective contraception (to prevent intrauterine implantation) coupled with an increased prevalence of pelvic inflammatory disease. Be alert to a range of risk factors, including pelvic infection, prior abdominal surgery, use of an intrauterine contraceptive device, and a history of ectopic pregnancy. The characteristic presenting clinical pattern consists of a period of amenorrhea followed by irregular bleeding, abdominal pain (often unilateral) and, if ruptured, syncope related to hypotension from intra-abdominal bleeding. The picture is inconsistent, however, and usually requires a high index of suspicion. If in doubt, assume that an ectopic pregnancy is present to avoid the serious hazard of missing the diagnosis and permitting life-threatening hemorrhage to develop when the patient is away from hospital resources.

B. In the presence of a positive beta subunit hCG test with pelvic pain or vaginal bleeding, hospitalization for observation, including ultrasonography, is mandatory, unless spontaneous abortion is obvious. Urinary pregnancy tests are generally unreliable in these cases. A falling hematocrit level strongly suggests occult bleeding, particularly if unassociated with hemodilution by intravenous fluids or active vaginal bleeding. Especially valuable for diagnosis is the ultrasonographic finding of no intrauterine gestational sac after the sixth week (dating from last normal menstrual period).

C. In stable patients, the quantitative beta subunit hCG serum level should be expected to double every three days (or increase by 66 percent in two days) in the normal intrauterine pregnancy. While tubal pregnancy is not ordinarily associated with this sequence, it may occasionally be; moreover, intrauterine pregnancy need not

always follow the expected pattern, especially if it is in the process of aborting or contains a blighted ovum. By five to six weeks after the last menstrual period, a well defined gestational sac should be seen in the uterus. Its presence effectively rules out an ectopic pregnancy except for the very rare situation of simultaneous intrauterine and extrauterine pregnancy. Less often, ultrasonographic screening can identify the sac in the region of the adnexa. Even more rarely, interstitial pregnancy may have to be ruled out (Fig. 1).

D. Culdocentesis, although helpful in diagnosing hemoperitoneum, is less helpful than quantitative serum pregnancy tests and ultrasonography combined. A negative tap may just mean that the tubal pregnancy has not yet begun to bleed intra-abdominally or that the needle did not enter the peritoneal cavity; a positive tap for nonclotted (lysed) blood does not establish the site of bleeding.

E. Unless the patient's condition is unstable or the diagnosis is clear-cut, laparoscopy should be done before open exploratory surgery (except when contraindicated) for the purpose of documenting the need for major surgery. Patients in whom incomplete abortion has not been ruled out definitively should undergo endometrial curettage first. Finding tissue within the uterus, confirmed if necessary by frozen section pathologic examination, will avert an unnecessary surgical procedure.

F. Salpingostomy may be performed in the patient desiring future pregnancy if the tube is not already ruptured and irreparable. Some centers have the skills and resources to perform salpingostomy through the laparoscope. Segmental resection of the tube is occasionally indicated, preserving as much as possible for future tuboplasty repair. It is generally inappropriate to undertake delicate plasty techniques during this emergency operation, especially if the patient's condition is unstable and microsurgical resources are unavailable. "Milking" the pregnancy tissue out through the fimbriated end of the tube is contraindicated because it has been shown to be associated with poor prognostic results in regard to future successful pregnancy. Even if both tubes are no longer fuctional, bear in mind that in vitro fertilization techniques (p 28) are now available to by-pass the tube and permit intrauterine implantation. It is therefore important to preserve ovarian and uterine integrity.

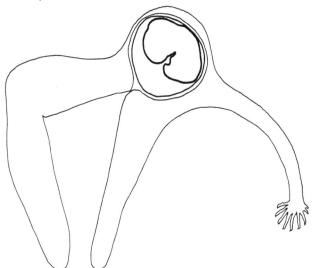

Figure 1 Uterus with interstitial pregnancy, showing intact endometrial cavity and fallopian tube.

References

Borten M. Ectopic pregnancy. In Borten M. Laparoscopic Complications: Prevention and Management. Toronto: BC Decker, 1986.

DeCherney AH, Jones EE. Ectopic pregnancy. Clin Obstet Gynecol 28:365, 1985.

Weckstein LN. Current perspective on ectopic pregnancy. Obstet Gynecol Surv 40:259, 1985.

Weckstein LN, Boucher AR, Tucker H, et al. Accurate diagnosis of early ectopic pregnancy. Obstet Gynecol 65:393, 1985.

SUSPICION OF ECTOPIC PREGNANCY

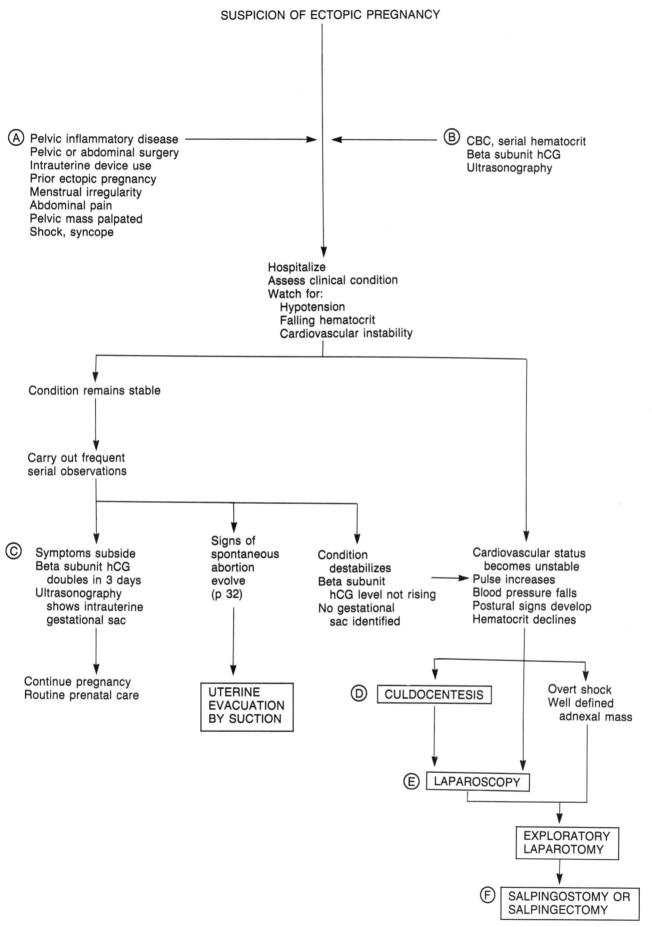

(A) Pelvic inflammatory disease
Pelvic or abdominal surgery
Intrauterine device use
Prior ectopic pregnancy
Menstrual irregularity
Abdominal pain
Pelvic mass palpated
Shock, syncope

(B) CBC, serial hematocrit
Beta subunit hCG
Ultrasonography

Hospitalize
Assess clinical condition
Watch for:
  Hypotension
  Falling hematocrit
  Cardiovascular instability

Condition remains stable

Carry out frequent
serial observations

(C) Symptoms subside
Beta subunit hCG
  doubles in 3 days
Ultrasonography
  shows intrauterine
  gestational sac

Signs of
spontaneous
abortion
evolve
(p 32)

Condition
destabilizes
Beta subunit
  hCG level not rising
No gestational
  sac identified

Cardiovascular status
  becomes unstable
Pulse increases
Blood pressure falls
Postural signs develop
Hematocrit declines

Continue pregnancy
Routine prenatal care

UTERINE
EVACUATION
BY SUCTION

(D) CULDOCENTESIS

Overt shock
Well defined
adnexal mass

(E) LAPAROSCOPY

EXPLORATORY
LAPAROTOMY

(F) SALPINGOSTOMY OR
SALPINGECTOMY

HORMONAL EXPOSURE

Johanna F. Perlmutter, M.D.

A. In the past, progesterone was used for pregnancy maintenance and progestins were given as a pregnancy test by invoking withdrawal. These drugs were thus sometimes given early in the first trimester during the critical period of fetal organogenesis. Available limited data do not appear to implicate progesterone as the cause of any fetal anomalies.

B. Progestins are the synthetic progesterone congeners included in birth control pills; they are sometimes taken inadvertently in early pregnancy. Pregnancy may occur as a result of failure of contraception and the patient, unaware of the gestation, continues to take the pills. Abnormalities have been reported, but the relationship of these abnormalities to the steroids taken in pregnancy has not been established.

C. The fetal risks of progestins are unclear. Retrospective analyses show a wide variety of defects, but only genital changes can be confirmed, specifically, minor degrees of androgenization of female genitalia (such as clitoral enlargement and labial adhesions). On the basis of our current knowledge, one can support with equal vigor and rationale the patient's decision to continue the pregnancy or not to continue it.

D. Estrogens were once widely used for pregnancy maintenance, especially in women who had had a spontaneous abortion or who were threatening to abort in the current pregnancy; when used for these purposes, they were given throughout pregnancy. Diethylstilbestrol was the drug most commonly used in this way. Because of their potentially serious fetal sequelae (see F) and documented ineffectiveness, estrogen compounds must not be used in pregnancy.

E. Although no longer formally recommended for clinical practice, high doses of estrogen (such as diethylstilbestrol) given within 72 hours after unprotected coitus are effective in preventing conception. The risks to the fetus from such a single exposure are not known, but it is important to counsel the patient about known diethylstilbestrol risks beforehand and to ascertain whether the patient will accept abortion in the event that pregnancy occurs. Induced abortion is indicated because of the risk of fetal anomalies from the drug under these circumstances.

F. Only reproductive tract anomalies have been reported thus far to result from exposure to estrogens in utero for both male and female offspring. In males, benign nodulation of the epididymis and a reduced sperm count may cause infertility. In females, clear cell carcinoma of the vagina is a rare but very serious occurrence; more common is the development of vaginal adenosis and a deformed lower uterine segment with reduced ability to carry a pregnancy to term. Women exposed in utero to exogenous estrogenic hormones have been noted to have a fourfold increase in preterm labor and delivery. Bed rest and tocolytic drugs may be required if premature labor occurs (p 178); cervical cerclage may be needed for cervical incompetence (p 52).

References

Driscoll SG, Taylor SH. Effects of prenatal maternal estrogens on the male urogenital system. Obstet Gynecol 56:537, 1980.

Herbst AL. Diethylstilbestrol and other sex hormones during pregnancy. Obstet Gynecol 58:35s, 1981.

Sandberg EC, Riffle NL, Higdon JV. Pregnancy outcome in women exposed to diethylstilbestrol in utero. Am J Obstet Gynecol 140:194, 1981.

Schardein JL. Congenital abnormalities and hormones during pregnancy: A clinical review. Teratology 22:251, 1980.

FETAL EXPOSURE TO HORMONE

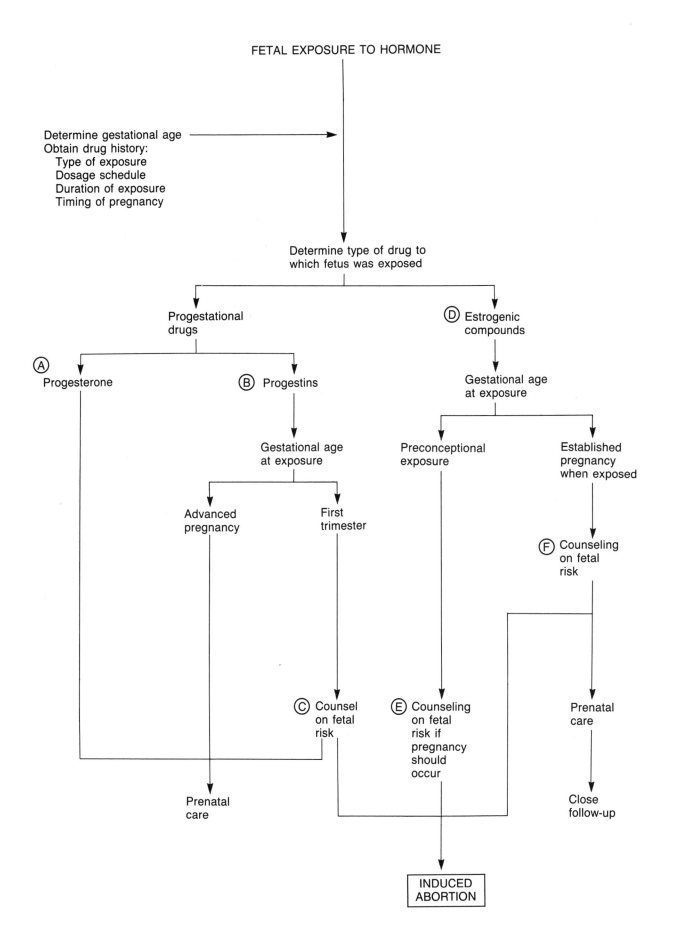

Determine gestational age
Obtain drug history:
    Type of exposure
    Dosage schedule
    Duration of exposure
    Timing of pregnancy

Determine type of drug to which fetus was exposed

Progestational drugs

Ⓓ Estrogenic compounds

Ⓐ Progesterone

Ⓑ Progestins

Gestational age at exposure

Gestational age at exposure

Advanced pregnancy

First trimester

Preconceptional exposure

Established pregnancy when exposed

Ⓕ Counseling on fetal risk

Ⓒ Counsel on fetal risk

Ⓔ Counseling on fetal risk if pregnancy should occur

Prenatal care

Prenatal care

Close follow-up

INDUCED ABORTION

TERATOGENIC DRUGS

Janet L. Mitchell, M.D.

A. The list of teratogens includes any agent, energy source, or condition that produces a harmful structural effect on the developing fetus. This includes irradiation, chemotherapy (p 62), drugs, environmental pollutants, infectious organisms, and a variety of maternal illnesses (especially diabetes mellitus). While congenital malformation is their primary effect, they can produce a range of clinically recognizable disorders, such as spontaneous abortion, stillbirth or neonatal mortality, intrauterine growth retardation, malignant disease, altered sex ratio, and chromosomal abnormality. Because the effects of many potential teratogens are incompletely known (many thousands of exposed cases are required to identify a small risk), a good general guide is to urge pregnant women to avoid any drug intake during gestation unless it is clearly indicated for therapeutic purposes (when the risk of not taking a medication may be greater than that of taking it).

B. The effect produced depends upon the specificity of the agent, the dosage administered and that capable of crossing the placenta to the fetus, the stage of embryologic development at the time of exposure (Fig. 1), the duration of the exposure, the susceptibility of the mother and especially of the fetus, and interactions with other agents. The period of organogenesis during the first eight weeks of gestation (dating from conception) is the time of greatest sensitivity; this can be specified in somewhat more practical terms in relation to the interval dating from last menstrual period of 31 to 71 days. Prior to this time, from conception up to about 17 days (31 days from the last menstrual period), a teratogen will either have a fa-

tal effect or no apparent effect at all. Beyond the period of organ formation, adverse effects can still occur, but they tend to be limited to less apparent (but not necessarily less important) structural damage to tissues that are actively differentiating, such as the brain. Most agents have a dose-response effect such that the greater the exposure, the more adverse the effect; moreover, below a certain threshold dose, no effect should be seen. The defect produced often depends on the specific organs developing at the time the fetus is exposed.

C. Although there may be animal evidence of teratogenicity for many agents, and therefore a theoretical risk to humans, the actual number of proved teratogens in humans is small, including thalidomide, aminopterin, warfarin, alcohol, and both androgenic and estrogenic (diethylstilbestrol) steroids. The risk with others, such as anticonvulsants and lithium, is less clear. Data based on laboratory animal studies are not necessarily applicable to the human fetus because effects are often species specific. Consultation should be sought if any uncertainty exists about the risk of a drug to humans before prescribing it or advising a gravida who has taken it about the risks to her fetus.

D. First trimester investigation is limited to ultrasonographic examination for blighted ovum and chorionic villus sampling, if available, for genetic assessment. Many structural anomalies can be identified as early as the middle of the second trimester with improved ultrasonographic technology. Amniocentesis can be helpful for alpha fetoprotein (p 76), karyotyping, and cell culture for a wide

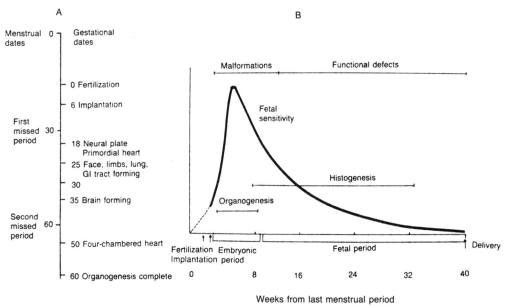

Figure 1 Timetable of embryogenesis. *A*, Events associated with period of organogenesis; *B*, Embryonic and fetal functional stages and relative sensitivity to adverse environment.

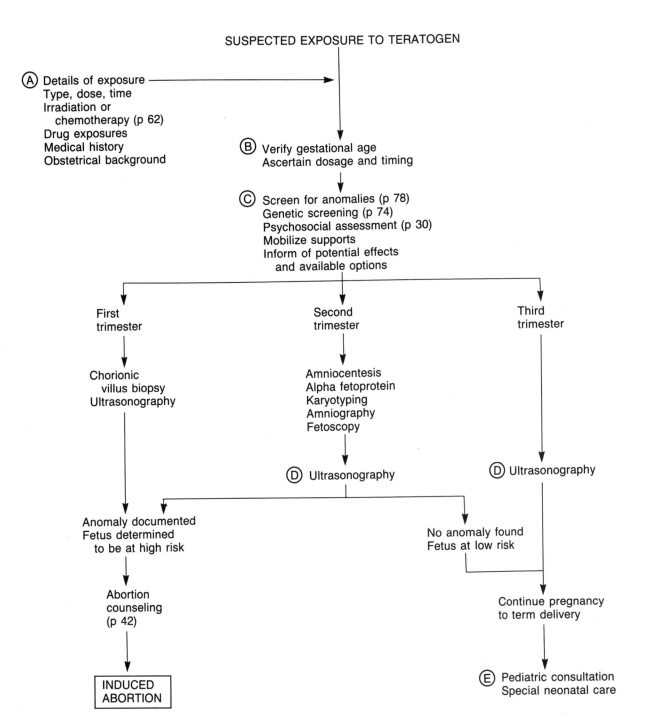

SUSPECTED EXPOSURE TO TERATOGEN

(A) Details of exposure
Type, dose, time
Irradiation or
    chemotherapy (p 62)
Drug exposures
Medical history
Obstetrical background

(B) Verify gestational age
Ascertain dosage and timing

(C) Screen for anomalies (p 78)
Genetic screening (p 74)
Psychosocial assessment (p 30)
Mobilize supports
Inform of potential effects
    and available options

First
trimester

Second
trimester

Third
trimester

Chorionic
    villus biopsy
Ultrasonography

Amniocentesis
Alpha fetoprotein
Karyotyping
Amniography
Fetoscopy

(D) Ultrasonography

(D) Ultrasonography

Anomaly documented
Fetus determined
    to be at high risk

No anomaly found
Fetus at low risk

Abortion
counseling
(p 42)

Continue pregnancy
to term delivery

INDUCED
ABORTION

(E) Pediatric consultation
Special neonatal care

variety of metabolic disorders characterized by abnormal biochemical mechanisms (p 74). Direct fetoscopic observation of the fetus is also possible in some centers.

E. Pediatric consultation is appropriate at any time during pregnancy but especially if the pregnancy is continued in order to determine the long-term prognosis and explore therapeutic interventions just after delivery.

References

Harrison MR, Golbus MS, Filly RA. The Unborn Patient. New York: Grune & Stratton, 1984.

Hemminki K, Lindbohm ML, Taskinen H. Transplacental toxicity of environmental chemicals. In: Milunsky A, Friedman EA, Gluck L. Advances in Perinatal Medicine. New York: Plenum Medical Book Co., 1986, Vol 5.

Hill LM, Kleinberg F. Effects of drugs and chemicals on the fetus and newborn. Mayo Clinic Proc 59:707, 755, 1984.

Niebyl JR. Drug use in pregnancy. In: Pitkin RM, Zlatnik FJ (Editors). Year Book of Obstetrics and Gynecology. Chicago: Year Book Medical Publishers, 1984.

Shepard TH. Catalog of Teratogenic Drugs. 5th ed. Baltimore: Johns Hopkins University Press, 1986.

Simpson JL, Golbus MS, Martin AO, Sarto GE. Genetics in Obstetrics and Gynecology. New York: Grune & Stratton, 1982.

NEUROBEHAVIORAL EFFECTS OF DRUGS

Janet L. Mitchell, M.D.

A. There exist legitimate concerns on the part of both health care providers and patients about the long term impact on the mother and the infant of many of the medications and treatment modalities commonly used in obstetrical practice. There are particular concerns about the effects on the fetus of the analgesic and anesthetic drugs used for the relief of pain during labor and at delivery. These drugs have been widely studied in regard to their neurobehavioral effects. The action a drug may have, if any, is dependent on the route of administration, the dosage, the time elapsing from its administration to delivery, the pharmacology of the drug, and the gestational age of the fetus. There is minimal documentary evidence that any of the alterations reported to occur actually lasts beyond a few days. Drugs and anesthetics can affect the fetus directly by transplacental transmission or indirectly by adversely influencing uteroplacental blood flow and oxygenation. Essentially every drug administered to the gravida reaches the fetus, although it might be in altered form or in diminished amount. Drugs that cross readily include low molecular weight, lipid soluble, nonionized, and unbound compounds. Preterm infants are more susceptible to the depressive effects of narcotic analgesics (p 180), which are best avoided or minimized, if possible, in the labor management of these cases.

B. Among the range of systemically administered medications used for pain relief in labor (p 186), barbiturates, diazepam, and narcotic analgesics appear to decrease neurobehavioral scores but only in the first few hours of life, with some isolated effects persisting somewhat longer, such as a depressed sucking reflex and habituation to bell ringing. Narcotic antagonists administered to the mother just prior to delivery, such as naloxone, have been found to be of no real benefit in averting or correcting these effects.

C. The anesthetic drugs used in regional anesthesia or for local blocks vary in their effects depending more on the route of administration than on the type of drug. No long-term effect has been noted beyond 24 to 48 hours. Narcotic drugs used for peridural or intrathecal anesthesia do not appear to have any residual long-term effects either.

D. With the use of general anesthesia, neonatal neurobehavioral scores are found to be deleteriously influenced by both induction and anesthetic maintenance drugs, varying with the dosage, duration of use, and the time elapsing from administration to delivery. Although associated with more frequent and intense short-term effects than those seen with regional block anesthesia and analgesia, no differences have been shown to exist at 10 days of life or subsequently in the newborn infant exposed to general inhalation anesthetic drugs at delivery.

E. The neurobehavioral status of the newborn is evaluated by examining for muscle tone and the ability of the infant to alter the arousal state, to suppress intrusive stimuli, and to respond to external events. There are a number of formal testing procedures available to assess neurobehavioral performance. Some of the better known and more widely used are the Brazelton Neonatal Behavioral Assessment Scale (NBAS), the Scanlon Early Neonatal Neurobehavioral Scale (ENNS), and the Amiel-Tison, Barrier, and Shnider Neonatal Neurologic and Adaptive Capacity Score (NACS). The Apgar Score (p 260) is a superficial but standardized assessment based on rapid examination of only the most primitive of responses in the first minutes of life; its value for determining neurobehavioral effects is therefore very limited, being confined to detection of only the most severe narcotic depression.

References

Chantigian RC, Ostheimer GW. Effect of maternally administered drugs on the fetus and newborn. In: Milunsky A, Friedman EA, Gluck L (Editors). Advances in Perinatal Medicine. New York: Plenum Medical Book Co., 1986, Vol. 5.

Dailey PA, Baysinger CL, Levinson G, Shnider SM. Neurobehavioral testing of the newborn infant: Effects of obstetric anesthesia. Clin Perinatal 9:191, 1982.

Kileff ME, James FM, Dewan DM, Floyd HM. Neonatal neurobehavioral response after epidural anesthesia for cesarean section using lidocaine and bupivacaine. Anesth Analg 63:413, 1984.

Stefani S, Hughes S, Shnider S, et al. Neonatal neurobehavioral effects of inhalation analgesia for vaginal delivery. Anesthesiology 56:351, 1982.

CONCERN ABOUT NEUROBEHAVIORAL EFFECTS OF DRUGS

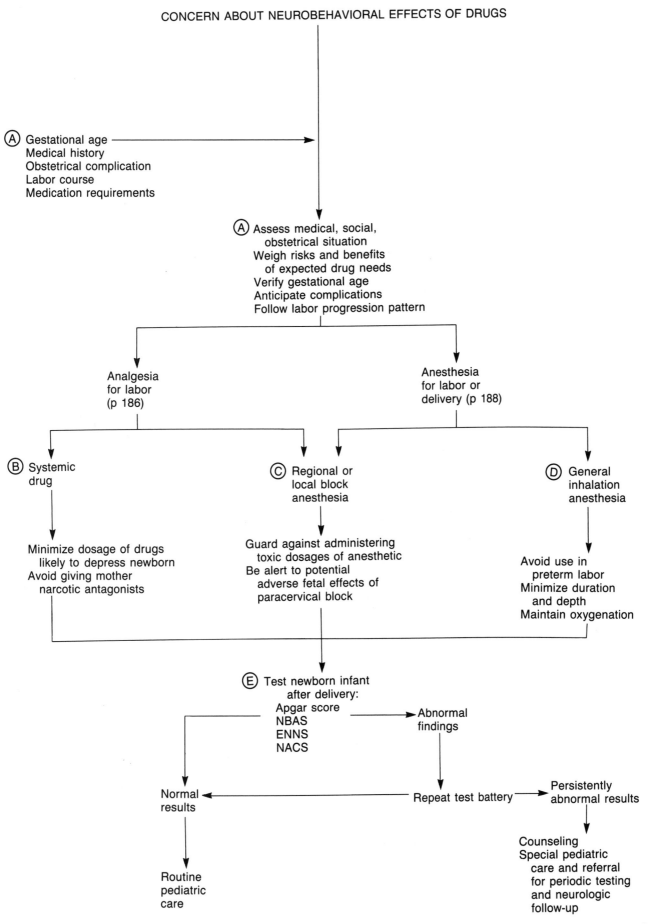

Ⓐ Gestational age
Medical history
Obstetrical complication
Labor course
Medication requirements

Ⓐ Assess medical, social,
obstetrical situation
Weigh risks and benefits
of expected drug needs
Verify gestational age
Anticipate complications
Follow labor progression pattern

Analgesia
for labor
(p 186)

Anesthesia
for labor or
delivery (p 188)

Ⓑ Systemic
drug

Ⓒ Regional or
local block
anesthesia

Ⓓ General
inhalation
anesthesia

Minimize dosage of drugs
likely to depress newborn
Avoid giving mother
narcotic antagonists

Guard against administering
toxic dosages of anesthetic
Be alert to potential
adverse fetal effects of
paracervical block

Avoid use in
preterm labor
Minimize duration
and depth
Maintain oxygenation

Ⓔ Test newborn infant
after delivery:
Apgar score
NBAS
ENNS
NACS

Abnormal
findings

Normal
results

Repeat test battery

Persistently
abnormal results

Routine
pediatric
care

Counseling
Special pediatric
care and referral
for periodic testing
and neurologic
follow-up

RADIATION OR CHEMOTHERAPEUTIC EXPOSURE

Lenard R. Simon, M.D.

A. The adverse fetal impact of diagnostic levels of radiation is as yet unproved. While no threshold dose of radiation below which it can be considered harm-free has been established, current objective data strongly suggest that exposure to less than 10 rads causes no apparent harm (the "critical level" at which any discernible fetal damage actually occurs may be as much as 10 times higher). Few diagnostic x-ray studies today exceed one-tenth this level even when there are multiple exposures. This should not be interpreted to mean that unnecessary x-ray examinations are acceptable in pregnancy. The risk, however remote, must be weighed against the possible benefits of the test being done. Radioisotopic iodine (^{131}I) for thyroid function study is contraindicated in pregnancy, especially after the 14th week when the fetal thyroid gland is functioning sufficiently to concentrate this material so that it is thereby likely to cause irreparable damage.

B. In the first trimester, the rapidly developing fetus is particularly sensitive to the teratogenic effects of both radiation and chemotherapy. To avoid even the theoretical risk to the zygote in the immediate postconception period, it has been recommended that elective radiographic studies of the pelvis or abdomen in women of reproductive age be limited to the first half of the menstrual cycle (since unrecognized pregnancy is possible in the second half). The basis for this practice is dubious in the absence of documented harm. Gravidas subjected to therapeutic radiation (not diagnostic levels) in the first trimester have a high frequency of fetal wastage, approaching 80 percent. Such women include patients being treated for malignant disease involving the breast, lymphoreticular system, gynecologic structures, and bone, as well as those with skin melanoma.

C. Intense therapeutic exposure is likely to affect the pregnancy adversely. Comparable to their action against tumor cells, radiation and chemotherapy can damage or destroy the rapidly dividing cells of the fetus and placenta, especially during early organogenesis in the first trimester. In this regard, all chemotherapeutic drugs and irradiation modalities, when given in the large doses required for the aggressive treatment of patients with cancer, are potentially mutagenic or teratogenic. The incidence of recessive mutation under these circumstances is unknown; if mutations occur, they may not be manifest for several generations, if ever, although it is likely that significantly adverse mutations will be lethal and therefore unrecognized.

D. Continued pregnancy may affect the disease process for which the radiation or chemotherapy was given. For example, malignant tumors arising in tissues that are under endocrine control may be deleteriously affected by the hormones produced in such large amounts during pregnancy. The anatomic or physiologic changes that occur during pregnancy may mask or totally obscure subtle changes in cases of malignant disease, making clinical detection and periodic assessment difficult. A typical example is breast cancer, which can be especially difficult to detect and follow in pregnancy because of the mammary enlargement and engorgement that so commonly take place. Moreover, the increased vascularity accompanying gestation may facilitate metastasis. In addition, the natural immunosuppression associated with pregnancy, especially when combined with the possibly immunosuppressive effects of chemotherapeutic drugs or radiation therapy, may enhance tumor dissemination.

References

Baker DC. Medical radiation exposure and genetic risks. South Med J 73:1247, 1980.

Brent RL. Radiation teratogenesis. Teratology 21:281, 1980.

Harris JW. Prepregnancy counselling of premalignant and malignant disease. Clin Obstet Gynaecol 9:171, 1982.

Rittenour ER. Health effects of low level radiation: Carcinogenesis, teratogenesis, and mutagenesis. Semin Nucl Med 16:106, 1986.

Williams SF, Bitran JD. Cancer and pregnancy. Clin Perinatol 12:609, 1985.

EXPOSURE TO RADIATION OR A CHEMOTHERAPEUTIC DRUG

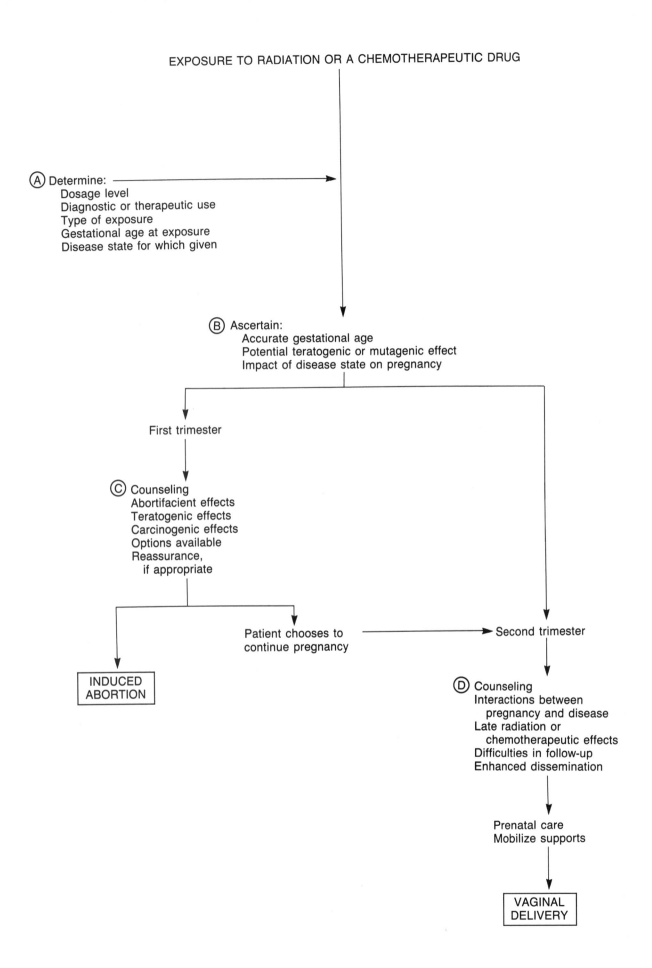

Ⓐ Determine:
Dosage level
Diagnostic or therapeutic use
Type of exposure
Gestational age at exposure
Disease state for which given

Ⓑ Ascertain:
Accurate gestational age
Potential teratogenic or mutagenic effect
Impact of disease state on pregnancy

First trimester

Ⓒ Counseling
Abortifacient effects
Teratogenic effects
Carcinogenic effects
Options available
Reassurance,
if appropriate

Patient chooses to
continue pregnancy

Second trimester

INDUCED
ABORTION

Ⓓ Counseling
Interactions between
pregnancy and disease
Late radiation or
chemotherapeutic effects
Difficulties in follow-up
Enhanced dissemination

Prenatal care
Mobilize supports

VAGINAL
DELIVERY

ASSESSMENT OF FETAL WELL-BEING

Henry Klapholz, M.D.

A. All fetuses at risk by virtue of a maternal disorder risk attribute warrant early and frequent antepartum testing. If the risk status reverts to normal (that is, if the mother's condition is corrected), further testing may no longer be indicated, but it is often prudent to continue nevertheless, particularly if the risk condition may persist or recur.

B. Fetal activity assessment is principally subjective, but it is sometimes helpful in flagging a fetal problem. The gravida should count and record the movements she feels in a 30 minute period two to three times daily. The fetus tends to be most active during the first half hour after a meal. Decreased fetal movement or its absence, even though not a completely reliable sign, warrants assessment of fetal status.

C. Ultrasonographic scanning can reliably measure the fetal biparietal diameter (within 1 to 2 mm). Expected growth up to about 34 weeks is 2 to 3 mm per week; later in pregnancy, growth slows. Abnormally slow growth should alert one to a potential problem, such as intrauterine growth retardation or a fetal anomaly (p 68).

D. A biophysical profile score (p 70) in excess of 6 suggests a state of normal fetal oxygenation. Among the factors that make up the score, pay particular attention to the presence of marked oligohydramnios, which can be an ominous sign.

E. The nonstress test consists of monitoring the external fetal heart rate to detect accelerations with fetal movements. A reactive test is one with two movement-associated accelerations in a 20 minute interval. Accelerations are recognized as being at least 15 beats per minute above the baseline fetal heart rate and lasting at least 15 seconds.

F. The frequency of reassessment depends on the nature of the risk factor. In general, ultrasonography is done at two week intervals. Fetal activity can be assessed every six hours, if necessary. Nonstress tests are usually repeated weekly, but intervals of two to three days may be more appropriate in some sick patients, such as diabetics or hypertensives.

G. An oxytocin challenge test (or contraction stress test) monitors the response of the fetal heart rate to oxytocin in-

duced uterine contractions. Give oxytocin by controlled intravenous drip or preferably pump. Late fetal heart rate decelerations are ominous, although false positive results are common. If a contraction frequency of 3 per 10 minutes (or more) fails to develop late decelerations, a good fetal status is reasonably assured because false negative results are rare.

H. Fetal lung maturity is tested in amniotic fluid samples by lecithin/sphingomyelin ratio and disaturated phosphatidylcholine level. A lecithin/sphingomyelin below 2.0 and a disaturated phosphatidylcholine level below 800 indicate the likelihood of severe respiratory distress. The limits of normal are higher for amniotic fluid from diabetic gravidas.

I. Use of corticosteroids to accelerate lung maturity seems helpful between 26 and 34 weeks. We use betamethasone, 24 mg parenterally divided into two doses over a 48 hour period.

J. Delivery is indicated for the fetus in jeopardy. Induction is often successful (p 182) although careful monitoring is essential. Cesarean section may not be required if induction can be carried out expeditiously with intensive, continuous electronic surveillance of the fetal status (p 192).

References

Lavery JP. Nonstress fetal heart rate testing. Clin Obstet Gynecol 25:689, 1982.

Manning FA. Assessment of fetal condition and risk: Analysis of single and combined biophysical variable monitoring. Semin Perinatol 9:168, 1985.

Platt LD, Eglinton GS, Sipos L, Broussard PM, Paul RH. Further experience with the fetal biophysical profile. Obstet Gynecol 61:480, 1983.

Rayburn WF. Clinical implications from monitoring fetal activity. Am J Obstet Gynecol 144:967, 1982.

Thacker SB, Berkelman RL. Assessing the diagnostic accuracy and efficacy of selected antepartum fetal surveillance techniques. Obstet Gynecol Surv 41:121, 1986.

ASSESSING FETAL WELL-BEING

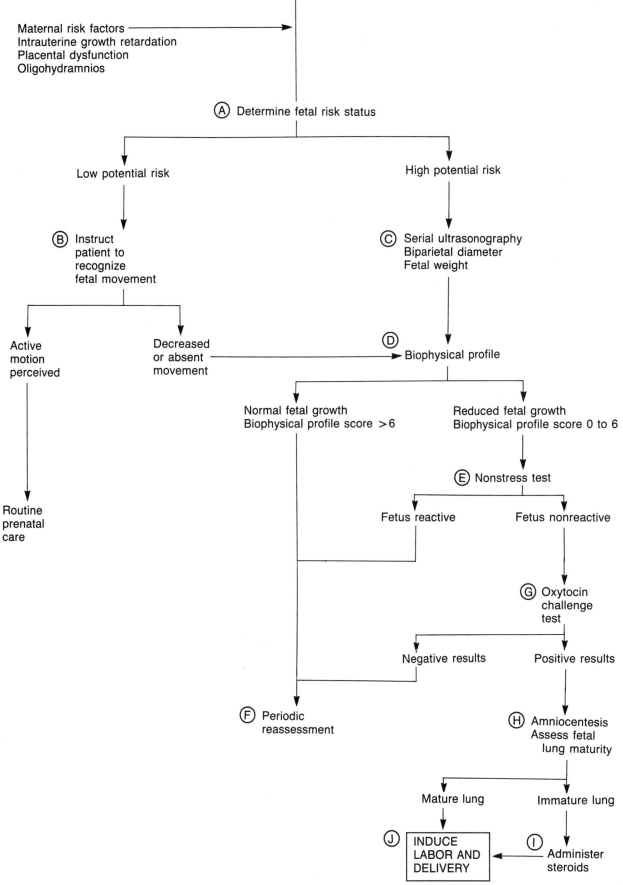

Maternal risk factors
Intrauterine growth retardation
Placental dysfunction
Oligohydramnios

(A) Determine fetal risk status

Low potential risk

High potential risk

(B) Instruct patient to recognize fetal movement

(C) Serial ultrasonography
Biparietal diameter
Fetal weight

Active motion perceived

Decreased or absent movement

(D) Biophysical profile

Routine prenatal care

Normal fetal growth
Biophysical profile score >6

Reduced fetal growth
Biophysical profile score 0 to 6

(E) Nonstress test

Fetus reactive

Fetus nonreactive

(G) Oxytocin challenge test

Negative results

Positive results

(F) Periodic reassessment

(H) Amniocentesis
Assess fetal lung maturity

Mature lung

Immature lung

(J) INDUCE LABOR AND DELIVERY

(I) Administer steroids

ASSESSMENT OF FETAL GROWTH

Henry Klapholz, M.D.

A. Every obstetrical patient should be evaluated to disclose the presence of high risk background factors that will make close surveillance of fetal growth and development essential. Among obstetrical events in the past that carry a relatively poor prognosis are delivery of a premature or growth retarded infant, perinatal loss, and recurrent late abortion. Assess nutritional factors even though only extreme malnutrition affects fetal growth significantly. Calorie supplementation may increase the birth weight, but starvation causes little (if any) measurable intellectual impairment. Adequate weight gain in pregnancy is also important in this regard (p 14). The social status may be an index of nutritional deprivation. Watch for signs of maternal illnesses that adversely affect the fetus, such as hypertension, vascular disease, Rh isoimmunization, and diabetes mellitus. More than one-third of all cases of fetal growth retardation occur in association with placental vascular insufficiency attributable to hypertension or related disorders of placental perfusion.

B. Chromosomal variants account for fewer than 10 percent of the cases of growth retardation. Maternal smoking reduces the average fetal weight, as do high altitude and chronic exposure to carbon monoxide. Toxoplasmosis and cytomegalovirus and rubella infections may reduce fetal growth and retard brain development. Even without direct fetal infection, placental infection may retard growth. Potentially teratogenic substances such as alcohol, Coumadin, hydantoin, heroin, methadone, nicotine, and antimetabolites can also impede fetal development.

C. Measurement of uterine size is of only limited value, but sequential observations at each prenatal visit neverthe-less help one to assess growth objectively. Measure from the upper margin of the symphysis pubis to the top of the fundus. Most clinicians prefer to use the tape measure (McDonald's measurements) for this purpose. Each centimeter of fundal height measured in this way corresponds to one week of gestational age between 20 and 36 weeks. For example, 28 cm is equivalent to 28 weeks, 30 cm to 30 weeks, and so on. Additionally, the circumference measured by tape is a better guide to intrauterine volume than the measurement obtained by means of the calipers. Relating the fundal height to an anatomic landmark, such as the xyphoid or umbilicus, is a poor practice. From 20 to 36 weeks, the uterine size increases 3.5 cm per month, reaching about 35 cm. This varies somewhat with race, parity, and maternal weight. Obesity, a distended bowel, full bladder, hydramnios, a multiple gestation, transverse lie, and a pendulous abdomen obscure the significance of fundal height measurements and make them difficult to interpret meaningfully. Fundal height generally recedes near term as the fetal head engages, but reduced uterine size may also reflect oligohydramnios or leakage of amniotic fluid.

D. Serial ultrasonographic measurements of fetal anatomic structures, such as the biparietal diameter (Fig. 1), abdominal circumference, and femoral length, may be made with great accuracy using real-time techniques. An accuracy of ± 2 mm is possible, permitting one to estimate the fetal weight accurately to within 15 percent. Because the fetal head is larger than the abdomen until 36 weeks, the head-to-abdomen ratio may help distinguish symmetric from asymmetric (head sparing) growth retardation. If the fetus fails to show weight gain ultrasonographically over a two week interval, intrauterine growth retardation is likely. Furthermore, the finding of oligohydramnios (no pocket of amniotic fluid larger than 2 cm) should alert the clinician to the probability of placental dysfunction as well. Oligohydramnios often accompanies true intrauterine growth retardation.

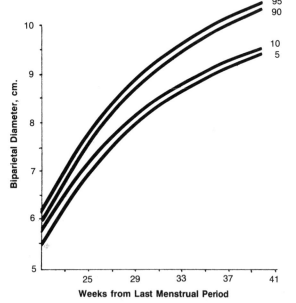

Figure 1 Relation between fetal biparietal diameter as measured by ultrasonography and gestational age, showing 5, 10, 90, and 95 percentiles of distribution.

References

Brown JE, Jacobson HN, Askue LH, Peieck MG. Influence of pregnancy weight gain on the size of infants born to underweight women. Obstet Gynecol 57:13, 1981.

Chervenak FA, Jeanty P, Hobbins JC. Current status of fetal age and growth assessment. Clin Obstet Gynecol 10:423, 1983.

Jones OW. Genetic factors in the determination of fetal size. J Reprod Med 21:305, 1978.

Knox GE. Influence of infection on fetal growth and development. J Reprod Med 21:352, 1978.

Seeds JW. Impaired fetal growth: Definition and clinical diagnosis. Obstet Gynecol 64:303, 1984.

ASSESSING FETAL GROWTH

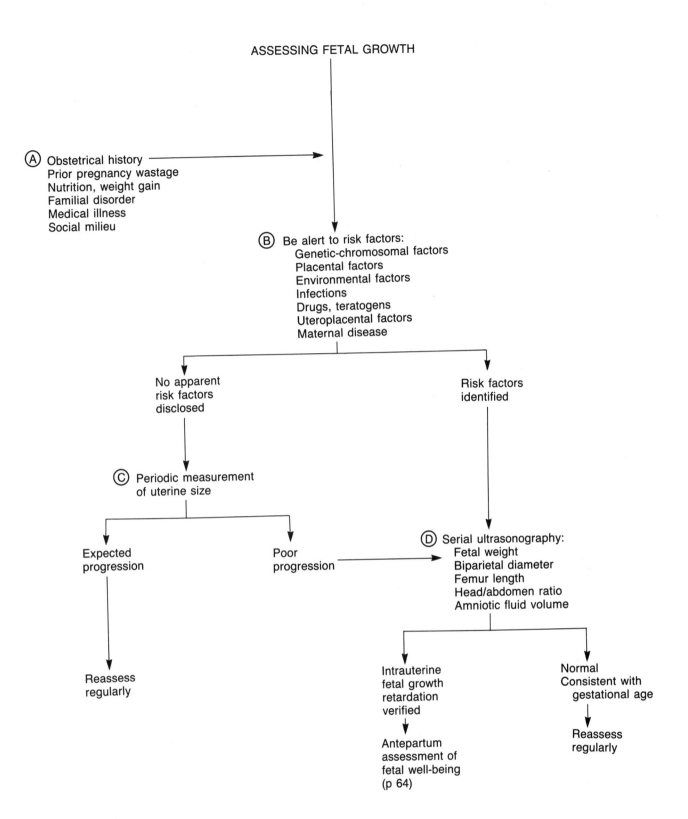

Ⓐ Obstetrical history
  Prior pregnancy wastage
  Nutrition, weight gain
  Familial disorder
  Medical illness
  Social milieu

Ⓑ Be alert to risk factors:
    Genetic-chromosomal factors
    Placental factors
    Environmental factors
    Infections
    Drugs, teratogens
    Uteroplacental factors
    Maternal disease

No apparent
risk factors
disclosed

Risk factors
identified

Ⓒ Periodic measurement
  of uterine size

Expected
progression

Poor
progression

Ⓓ Serial ultrasonography:
    Fetal weight
    Biparietal diameter
    Femur length
    Head/abdomen ratio
    Amniotic fluid volume

Reassess
regularly

Intrauterine
fetal growth
retardation
verified

Normal
Consistent with
gestational age

Antepartum
assessment of
fetal well-being
(p 64)

Reassess
regularly

INTRAUTERINE GROWTH RETARDATION

Henry Klapholz, M.D.

A. Among the risk factors for intrauterine growth retardation are an obstetrical history of growth retardation, twins in the current pregnancy, maternal disease, malnutrition, smoking, and inadequate weight gain.

B. Fetal growth can be evaluated quantitatively by sequential ultrasonography every two to three weeks during the last trimester. Failure of the uterine fundus to grow normally as pregnancy advances (p 8) requires such ultrasonographic assessments. Fetal biparietal diameter measurements are easily made. Growth of the biparietal diameter slows from 3 to 3.5 mm per week at 28 weeks to 2.5 mm per week at 28 to 32 weeks, and reaches 1.7 mm per week from then to term. Since the ultrasound error is about 2 mm, three week intervals are needed to differentiate true growth retardation. Brain sparing in early pregnancy (asymmetric growth retardation) results in normal head growth in a fetus that is smaller than expected. Serial measurements of the thorax or abdomen diameter provide head-to-abdomen or head-to-thorax ratios. In most cases of intrauterine growth retardation head-to-thorax ratios are above the 95th percentile for the gestational age. Symmetric growth retardation is often seen earlier in pregnancy as a result of chronic infection, chromosomal anomalies, and cigarette smoking. These infants tend to have a poor long-term prognosis. The total intrauterine volume as measured by ultrasound may help to assess the overall uterine growth and detect oligohydramnios or polyhydramnios associated with poor fetal development. Total fetal weight assessment requires complex calculations based on multiple ultrasound images of the fetal thorax and abdomen. Correlations within 10 percent of actual fetal weight can be achieved by measuring the abdominal circumference and the biparietal diameter.

C. Complete cessation of growth over an interval of two to three weeks is serious. Consider delivery at once if the fetus is physiologically mature as determined by the amniotic fluid lecithin:sphingomyelin ratio, the disaturated phosphatidylcholine level, or the ratio of phosphatidylinositol to phosphatidyglycerol.

D. The effects of reduced fetal growth are often detectable by periodic antepartum testing of the fetal status by a biophysical profile or nonstress test (and contraction stress test, if indicated). Evidence of placental insufficiency should prompt the undertaking of measures to effect delivery. In the face of a reactive nonstress test and a good biophysical profile or negative contraction stress test, allow the pregnancy to continue until spontaneous labor begins.

E. Since intrauterine growth retardation may be associated with chromosomal anomalies, an amniocentesis is helpful in providing information for counseling the couple before delivery. Fetal blood for IgM titers can also be obtained from cord blood by means of ultrasonographically controlled fetal vein puncture. Viral or parasitic infection may thus be detected before delivery to alert the pediatrician who will be caring for the infant.

F. Induction of labor and subsequent vaginal delivery are preferable to cesarean section. However, associated placental insufficiency may make it impossible to effect strong uterine contractions without producing fetal hypoxia. This necessitates abdominal delivery for fetal salvage. Continous electronic fetal heart rate monitoring is critical in these cases throughout the course of labor.

References

Bowes WA. Delivery of the low birth weight infant. Clin Perinatol 8:183, 1980.

Hadlock FP, Deter RL, Harrist RB. Sonographic detection of abnormal fetal growth patterns. Clin Obstet Gynecol 27:342, 1984.

Seeds JW. Impaired fetal growth: Ultrasonic evaluation and clinical management. Obstet Gynecol 64:577, 1984.

Tambyraja RL, Ratnam SS. The small fetus: Growth-retarded and preterm. Clin Obstet Gynecol 9:517, 1982.

SUSPICION OF INTRAUTERINE GROWTH RETARDATION

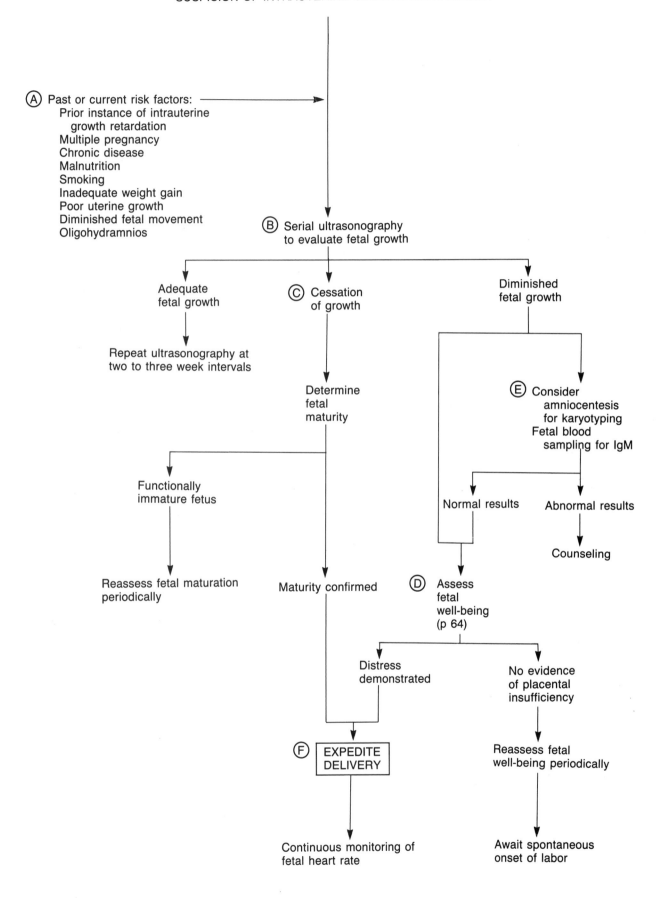

(A) Past or current risk factors:
  Prior instance of intrauterine
    growth retardation
  Multiple pregnancy
  Chronic disease
  Malnutrition
  Smoking
  Inadequate weight gain
  Poor uterine growth
  Diminished fetal movement
  Oligohydramnios

(B) Serial ultrasonography
    to evaluate fetal growth

Adequate
fetal growth

(C) Cessation
    of growth

Diminished
fetal growth

Repeat ultrasonography at
two to three week intervals

Determine
fetal
maturity

(E) Consider
    amniocentesis
    for karyotyping
    Fetal blood
    sampling for IgM

Functionally
immature fetus

Normal results

Abnormal results

Reassess fetal maturation
periodically

Maturity confirmed

(D) Assess
    fetal
    well-being
    (p 64)

Counseling

Distress
demonstrated

No evidence
of placental
insufficiency

(F) EXPEDITE
    DELIVERY

Reassess fetal
well-being periodically

Continuous monitoring of
fetal heart rate

Await spontaneous
onset of labor

BIOPHYSICAL PROFILE

Benjamin P. Sachs, M.B., B.S., D.P.H.

A. The biophysical profile is a screening test for uteroplacental insufficiency that utilizes ultrasonographic techniques. Typically it is combined with a nonstress test. A score of 0 to 2 is given for each of several observations. The sum of these subscores gives an overall index of fetal well-being. There are a number of different systems in current use, variously measuring such factors as fetal breathing movement, gross body motion, muscle tone, amniotic fluid volume, reactive fetal heart rate, and placental grade. The objective of the biophysical profile is to assess a number of fetal factors simultaneously, thereby to acquire a more meaningful evaluation of the fetal status than any single measure might provide. As is true for any screening test, the capacity of the biophysical profile test to predict fetal distress is dependent on the level of risk; the higher the risk, the better the predictive value. Thus, if it is used to screen a low risk population, it will prove even less valuable as a predictor. It is most useful, therefore, as a means for detecting developing fetal compromise in situations in which the fetus is at greatest risk, such as pregnancy induced hypertension, diabetes mellitus, and postdate pregnancy. It is useful not only to report an overall score for the biophysical profile but to break it down into individual components. This gives the obstetrician an opportunity to give differential weight to some factors. Oligohydramnios, for example, is generally considered an especially ominous indicator, particularly when coupled with intrauterine growth retardation.

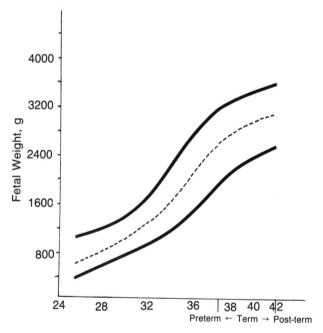

Figure 1   Distribution of birthweight by gestational age, illustrating 10, 50 (median), and 90 percentiles.

B. Amniotic fluid volume is a useful signal of placental insufficiency in postdate pregnancy. If no pocket of fluid exceeds 2 cm, oligohydramnios is likely to exist; if none is greater than 1 cm, the situation may be critical. However, at 36 weeks' gestation these criteria may be too liberal because more fluid is generally present at this gestational age. This means that criteria have to be different at different gestational ages. The skilled ultrasonographer should therefore interpret the volume accordingly and provide serial observations as to whether the amniotic fluid volume is decreasing.

C. The usefulness of fetal breathing movements is questionable at best. If there are no episodes of respiration-like chest movements lasting at least 30 seconds within a 30 minute span, this factor is generally considered abnormal. However, periods of fetal apnea may occur in a normal fetus for up to 120 minutes without signifying any problem.

D. Placental morphologic characteristics discernible by ultrasonography appear to be related to fetal maturity. More mature fetuses are associated with calcium deposition, echo-sparing central areas, chorionic plate indentations with larger densities (capable of casting acoustical shadows), and basal layer echogenic densities. A grade III (mature) placenta is very common and of no particular prognostic value in a postdate pregnancy. However, if such a pattern is seen in conjunction with a fetus suspected of being growth retarded at less than 36 weeks' gestation, it is highly significant.

E. One should expect to see at least three gross movements of the fetal body or limbs in a 30 minute interval of observation. A sequence of movements occurring with no interruption is considered one episode. Similarly, active extension and flexion of a limb or hand show good muscle tone, whereas slow extension with a return to partial extension or limb movement only in full extension indicates poor tone. These signs are always important indicators because they seem to be the last to develop in cases of progressive fetal hypoxia.

References

Jones TB, Frigoletto FD. Fetal condition and the biophysical profile. Postgrad Radiol 5:47, 1985.

Kazzi G, Gross T, Sokol R, Kazzi S. Noninvasive prediction of hyaline membrane disease: An optimized classification of sonographic placental maturation. Am J Obstet Gynecol 152:213, 1985.

Manning FA, Morrison I, Lange IR, et al. Fetal assessment based on fetal biophysical profile scoring: Experience in 12,620 referred high-risk pregnancies: I. Perinatal mortality by frequency and etiology. Am J Obstet Gynecol 151:343, 1985.

Phelan JP, Platt LD, Yeh SY, et al. The role of ultrasound assessment of amniotic fluid volume in the management of the postdate pregnancy. Am J Obstet Gynecol 151:304, 1985.

PATIENT WITH SUSPECTED UTEROPLACENTAL INSUFFICIENCY

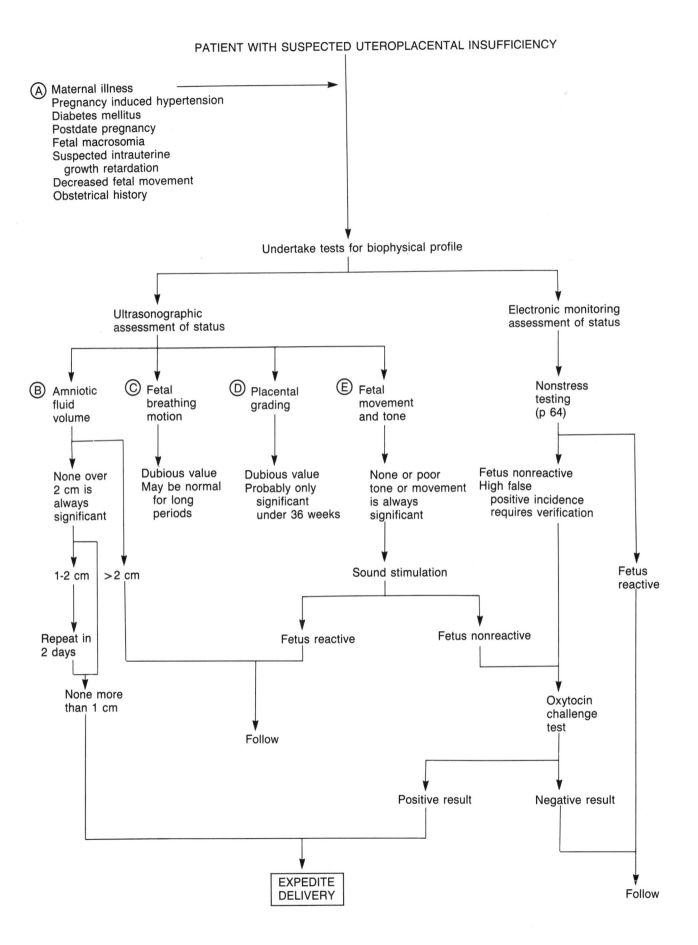

(A) Maternal illness
Pregnancy induced hypertension
Diabetes mellitus
Postdate pregnancy
Fetal macrosomia
Suspected intrauterine
   growth retardation
Decreased fetal movement
Obstetrical history

Undertake tests for biophysical profile

Ultrasonographic
assessment of status

Electronic monitoring
assessment of status

(B) Amniotic
fluid
volume

(C) Fetal
breathing
motion

(D) Placental
grading

(E) Fetal
movement
and tone

Nonstress
testing
(p 64)

None over
2 cm is
always
significant

Dubious value
May be normal
for long
periods

Dubious value
Probably only
significant
under 36 weeks

None or poor
tone or movement
is always
significant

Fetus nonreactive
High false
   positive incidence
   requires verification

1-2 cm   >2 cm

Sound stimulation

Fetus
reactive

Repeat in
2 days

Fetus reactive

Fetus nonreactive

None more
than 1 cm

Follow

Oxytocin
challenge
test

Positive result

Negative result

EXPEDITE
DELIVERY

Follow

FETAL CARDIAC ARRHYTHMIA

Henry Klapholz, M.D.

A. Fetal heart rates that are consistently above 170 or below 80 per minute should alert one to the possibility that a fetal cardiac rhythm disturbance exists. Heart block and supraventricular tachycardias are not uncommon. Extreme swings in variability should be viewed with suspicion as well. Arrhythmias, such as atrial fibrillation, may present a picture of extreme variability. Premature beats (Fig. 1) also may appear as wide fluctuations in rate on the continuous electronic fetal heart rate monitor tracing.

B. Arrhythmia must be distinguished from artifacts due to poor electrode connection, maternal electrocardiographic conduction to the fetal electrode (combining maternal and fetal signals into an uninterpretable pattern), or even a dead fetus, with the maternal signal being recorded alone. The external monitoring mode (using ultrasound) always introduces some machine logic (suppressing rapid swings in rate) that may obscure the actual rhythm disturbance. Internal monitors allow one to turn off this logic; the switch provided to accomplish this is often hidden at the rear of the monitor or behind the paper tray.

C. Arrhythmias appear to be regularly irregular so that a definable pattern develops. Artifacts produce no recognizable pattern that can be identified.

D. Whenever the rate pattern on the monitor is irregular, one should first auscultate the fetal heart with a stethoscope (DeLee fetoscope) or Doppler ultrasound device (Doptone). If auscultation also reveals an irregular rate, an arrhythmia exists. This step should be followed by direct fetal internal monitoring, if possible. If the arrhythmia is detected before labor has begun, it is likely to have been present for a long time. Under these circumstances,

there is no reason to intervene or deliver. The fetal status should be checked frequently, however, and the pediatrician alerted to the condition (see G).

E. A fetal electrocardiogram may be obtained by connecting an electrocardiography machine to the electrocardiographic output connector on the rear of most electronic fetal heart rate monitors. The machine will require an attenuator or an appropriate interface cable.

F. In cases of persistent bradycardia or tachycardia, fetal congestive heart failure is possible. Its presence can be determined by the use of real-time ultrasonography, looking for pericardial effusion, ascites, and anasarca. A fetal blood sample, if obtainable, may give useful information about the fetal status. Additionally, fetal cardiac anatomy should be evaluated ultrasonographically to rule out major congenital heart disease, which may prove to be the cause of the arrhythmia and require expeditious evaluation and management soon after the baby is born. If congenital heart disease is found, one might consider transferring the mother to a regionalized center where the infant's condition can be managed promptly at birth.

G. A pediatrician should be available at delivery. The type of arrhythmia should be determined in advance of the delivery, if at all feasible, and this information should be conveyed directly to the physician who will be caring for the infant. Cardiologic consultation is prudent. Fetal heart block serves as an indicator that the mother may have systemic lupus erythematosus. It is advisable to search for the lupus antigen in these cases.

H. If the auscultated rate is regular and is clearly not maternal in origin, another modality of monitoring must be used. A maternal-to-fetal conduction artifact can be corrected by changing to an external monitor. Repositioning the scalp electrode so that the metal grounding tabs touch the mother may also be of help in correcting this problem.

References

Beall MH, Paul RH. Artifacts, blocks, and arrhythmias: Confusing nonclassical heart rate tracings. Clin Obstet Gynecol 29:83, 1986.

Crawford D, Chapman M, Allan L. The assessment of persistent bradycardia in prenatal life. Br J Obstet Gynaecol 92:941, 1985.

DeVore GR, Siassi B, Platt LD. Fetal echocardiography. III. The diagnosis of cardiac arrhythmias using real-time-directed M-mode ultrasound. Am J Obstet Gynecol 146:792, 1983.

Kleinman CS, Donnerstein RL, Jaffe CC, et al. Fetal echocardiography: A tool for evaluation of in utero cardiac arrhythmias and monitoring of in utero therapy: Analysis of 71 patients. Am J Cardiol 51:237, 1983.

Stewart PA, Tonge HM, Wladimiroff JW. Arrhythmia and structural abnormalities of the fetal heart. Br Heart J 50:550, 1983.

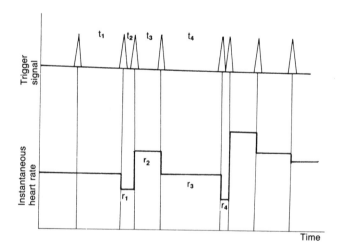

Figure 1 Cardiotachometry concept showing trigger signal developed from QRS or ultrasound complex for each cardiac cycle. A heart rate (r_1) is computed for each trigger-to-trigger interval (t_1) and recorded on the monitor tracing.

ABNORMAL FETAL HEART RATE PATTERN

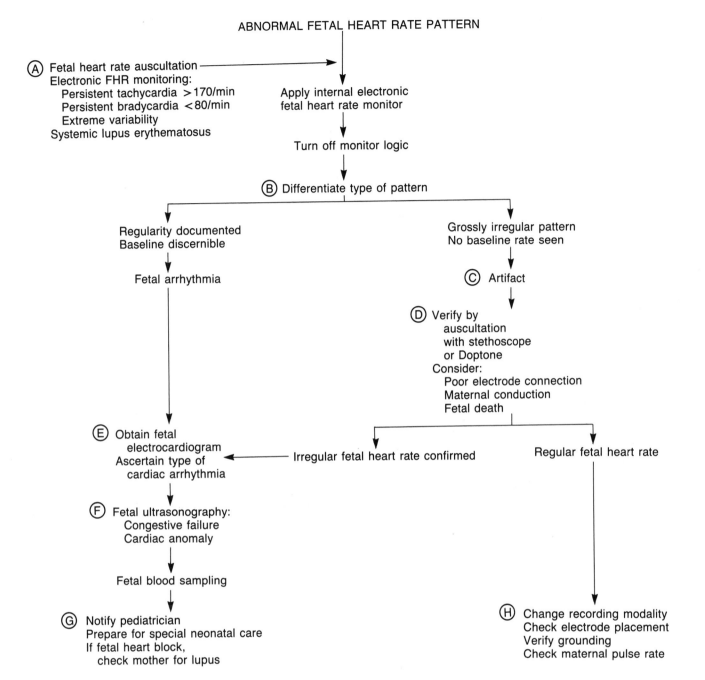

Ⓐ Fetal heart rate auscultation
Electronic FHR monitoring:
    Persistent tachycardia >170/min
    Persistent bradycardia <80/min
    Extreme variability
  Systemic lupus erythematosus

Apply internal electronic
fetal heart rate monitor

Turn off monitor logic

Ⓑ Differentiate type of pattern

Regularity documented
Baseline discernible

Fetal arrhythmia

Grossly irregular pattern
No baseline rate seen

Ⓒ Artifact

Ⓓ Verify by
  auscultation
  with stethoscope
  or Doptone
Consider:
  Poor electrode connection
  Maternal conduction
  Fetal death

Ⓔ Obtain fetal
  electrocardiogram
Ascertain type of
  cardiac arrhythmia

Irregular fetal heart rate confirmed

Regular fetal heart rate

Ⓕ Fetal ultrasonography:
  Congestive failure
  Cardiac anomaly

Fetal blood sampling

Ⓖ Notify pediatrician
Prepare for special neonatal care
If fetal heart block,
  check mother for lupus

Ⓗ Change recording modality
Check electrode placement
Verify grounding
Check maternal pulse rate

PRENATAL GENETIC SCREENING

Benjamin P. Sachs, M.B., B.S., D.P.H.

A. A careful genetic history is essential in the management of every pregnant woman, in a search for mental retardation or birth defects. The ethnic background may guide the evaluation: Screen for Tay-Sachs disease among Ashkenazi Jews or French Canadians, and check Southeast Asians for alpha thalassemia. Drug or radiation exposure is important (p 58, 62). Inquire about antecedent infant deaths, stillbirths, and abortions. Habitual abortion (p 50) warrants blood chromosome karyotyping to detect balanced translocation carriers. Ask about consanguinity as a clue to autosomal recessive inheritance. Since the father of the fetus may not be identifiable, it may be difficult to establish paternity; this may interfere with the construction of a meaningful family tree.

B. Prenatal genetic testing is indicated if the gravida is age 35 years or more, if either parent is a carrier of a chromosome rearrangement or a recessive gene, if the mother is a carrier of an X linked gene, or if a previous child had an extra chromosome or a neural tube defect.

C. Amniocentesis is performed at 15 to 17 weeks to obtain fetal cells from the amniotic fluid for study. The procedure carries a 0.5 percent risk of spontaneous abortion; this risk may be greatly reduced if the procedure is carried out under ultrasonographic guidance. Tissue culture techniques take two to three weeks for chromosome analysis. Counsel patients about this delay in advance because it is a period of great anxiety. Moreover, they must be advised that it is possible that the fetal cells will not grow in culture, necessitating a second amniocentesis and still more delay. Alpha fetoprotein testing for a neural tube defect (p 76) is generally done with the amniotic fluid specimen obtained at this time.

D. An alternative to amniocentesis is the recently introduced technique of chorionic villus biopsy (Fig. 1). It has several distinct advantages: It can be done much earlier in pregnancy and results are often available sooner. It may reduce the period of time the patient must wait for an answer (direct cell preparation of the specimen requires only 48 hours, but tissue culture takes longer) and permits decisions concerning pregnancy termination to be made at a much more acceptable time in pregnancy. It is carried out under ultrasonographic guidance at nine to 11 weeks. The risk of spontaneous abortion is as yet unknown, but it is undoubtedly somewhat higher than for amniocentesis; serious maternal infections have also occurred.

E. Chorionic villus biopsy cannot be used to screen for neural tube defects. The serum alpha fetoprotein level (p 76) should therefore be determined at 15 weeks. Moreover, a gravida whose fetus is at increased risk for spina bifida is strongly advised to undergo amniocentesis at the appropriate time (see C) for an alpha fetoprotein assay.

F. Prenatal diagnosis through DNA analysis has become very sophisticated. New probe methods are becoming increasingly available for prenatal diagnosis. Examples of diseases now amenable to diagnosis are cystic fibrosis and muscular dystrophy. Because the discipline is changing so rapidly, it is strongly advised that a geneticist be consulted to help investigate and counsel a couple with a history of an inherited disease.

G. Fetoscopy is mostly used for fetal skin biopsy in cases of hereditary dermatologic disorders. Fetal blood analysis is occasionally required for prenatal genetic screening. An example is beta thalassemia, which does not lend itself to DNA analysis and in which abnormal chromosomes have been found even though fetal disease cannot be documented. Fetal blood can be obtained by either fetoscopy or percutaneous umbilical venous blood sampling (p 80). The latter carries a somewhat lower incidence of complications and may be done successfully at 16 to 20 weeks.

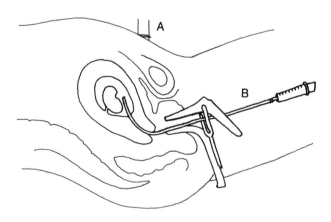

Figure 1 Chorionic villi sampling technique. *A*, ultrasonographic transducer for monitoring catheter placement and *B*, metal sampling catheter entering chorion frondosum site for suction biopsy.

References

Barela AI, Kleinman GE, Golditch IM, et al. Septic shock with renal failure after chorionic villus sampling. Am J Obstet Gynecol 154:1100, 1986.

Simoni G, Brambati B, Danesino C, et al. Efficient direct chromosome analyses and enzyme determinations from chorionic villi samples in the first trimester of pregnancy. Hum Genet 63:349, 1983.

DESIRE FOR GENETIC SCREENING

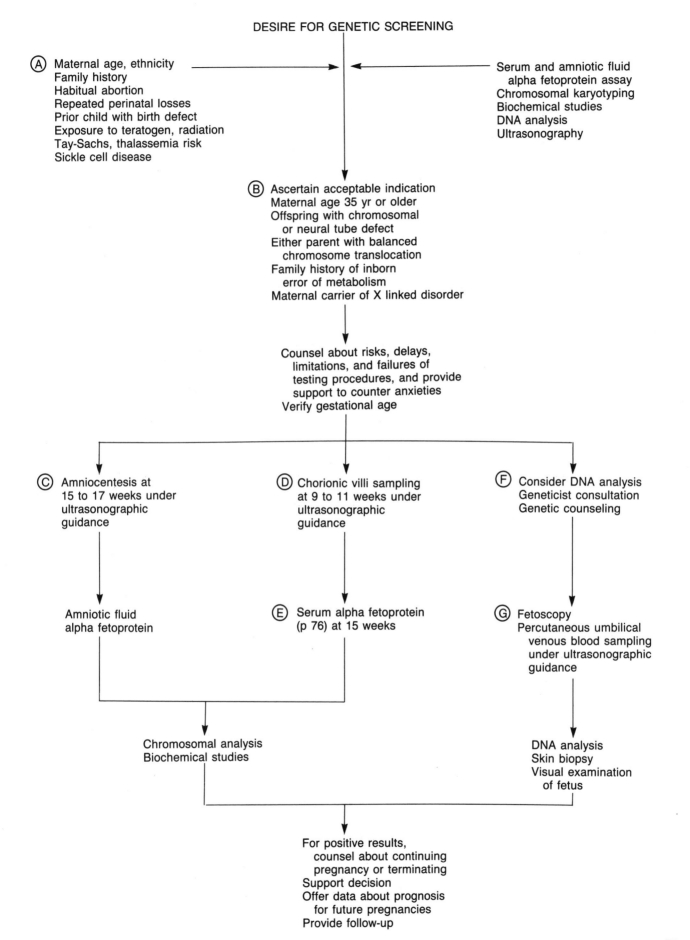

Ⓐ Maternal age, ethnicity
Family history
Habitual abortion
Repeated perinatal losses
Prior child with birth defect
Exposure to teratogen, radiation
Tay-Sachs, thalassemia risk
Sickle cell disease

Serum and amniotic fluid
alpha fetoprotein assay
Chromosomal karyotyping
Biochemical studies
DNA analysis
Ultrasonography

Ⓑ Ascertain acceptable indication
Maternal age 35 yr or older
Offspring with chromosomal
or neural tube defect
Either parent with balanced
chromosome translocation
Family history of inborn
error of metabolism
Maternal carrier of X linked disorder

Counsel about risks, delays,
limitations, and failures of
testing procedures, and provide
support to counter anxieties
Verify gestational age

Ⓒ Amniocentesis at
15 to 17 weeks under
ultrasonographic
guidance

Ⓓ Chorionic villi sampling
at 9 to 11 weeks under
ultrasonographic
guidance

Ⓕ Consider DNA analysis
Geneticist consultation
Genetic counseling

Amniotic fluid
alpha fetoprotein

Ⓔ Serum alpha fetoprotein
(p 76) at 15 weeks

Ⓖ Fetoscopy
Percutaneous umbilical
venous blood sampling
under ultrasonographic
guidance

Chromosomal analysis
Biochemical studies

DNA analysis
Skin biopsy
Visual examination
of fetus

For positive results,
counsel about continuing
pregnancy or terminating
Support decision
Offer data about prognosis
for future pregnancies
Provide follow-up

75

ALPHA FETOPROTEIN ASSESSMENT

Benjamin P. Sachs, M.B., B.S., D.P.H.

A. Use of the maternal serum alpha fetoprotein (AFP) level for routine prenatal screening for neural tube defects, specifically anencephaly and open spina bifida, is now widespread. However, the effectiveness is not well established because its value is dependent on the incidence of neural tube defects and the sophistication of ultrasonography facilities. It is especially indicated in gravidas who have a family history or have themselves delivered a child with a neural tube defect; there is a 5 percent risk of recurrence if one sibling is affected, a 12 percent risk if two siblings are affected, a 4 percent risk if one parent, a 2 percent risk if a second degree relative, and a 1 percent risk if a third degree relative. Combining serum screening with amniotic fluid study and ultrasonography improves the accuracy considerably.

B. The serum AFP level rises progressively over the course of pregnancy. The concentrations in fetal serum and amniotic fluid peak at about 13 weeks and fall rapidly thereafter. Critical levels are thus very much dependent on accurate dating of the gestational age. Interpretation requires reliable information about the duration of the pregnancy. Specifically, underestimating gestational age gives a false impression that the serum AFP level is elevated. Similarly maternal age and weight may affect the interpretation. Because the serum AFP level is so imperfect for screening, many recommend repeating the test before taking action because of an elevated level.

C. The AFP can be elevated for reasons other than a neural tube defect. These include omphalocele, gastroschisis, congenital nephrosis, multiple gestation, threatened abortion, Turner's syndrome (45,XO), sacrococcygeal teratoma, bladder exstrophy, focal dermal hypoplasia, Meckel's syndrome, Rh isoimmunization, and intrauterine fetal death. False negative results can occur with a fetus with a closed neural tube defect and even in rare cases of open spina bifida. An elevated serum AFP level may be verified by repeating the test in one week; alternatively one may proceed to ultrasonographic surveillance. Ultrasonography helps confirm the gestational age and rule out fetal death or multiple gestation. High resolution ultrasonography performed by a skilled and experienced professional should also disclose many gross malformations. Obstetrical attendants who have only limited acquaintance with these disorders should be circumspect about reassuring patients in regard to findings (or more relevantly, absence of findings).

D. If ultrasonography has verified the gestational age and the absence of grossly identifiable anomalies, amniocentesis should be performed (Fig. 1). The optimal time is 15 to 17 weeks, which provides enough opportunity for chromosome studies and a decision about continuing the pregnancy. The amniotic fluid AFP level should be determined. If it is elevated, measure the acetylcholinesterase level; if the level is not elevated in parallel with AFP level, it is likely that the latter is a spurious finding. Even if ultrasonography reveals that there are no major birth defects, chromosome analysis is nonetheless generally done with fetal cells obtained from the amniotic fluid specimen.

E. An elevated serum AFP level with a normal amniotic fluid AFP level appear to place the gravida in a high risk category, with reports of up to a 30 percent risk of perinatal complications, such as prematurity, intrauterine growth retardation, and fetal demise. It is advisable to follow these patients in the third trimester with serial ultrasonography, careful assessments of fetal size and growth, periodic antenatal fetal testing, and electronic fetal heart rate monitoring.

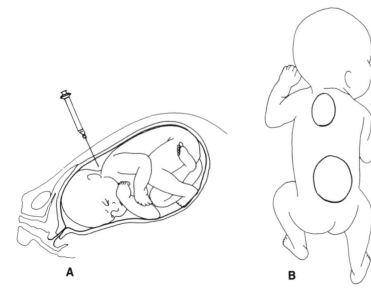

A   B

Figure 1 *A*, site for amniocentesis by inserting needle suprapubically to gain access to amniotic fluid located behind the fetal neck. *B*, characteristic locations of spina bifida with thoracic or lumbar meningomyelocele

SERUM ALPHA FETOPROTEIN SCREENING

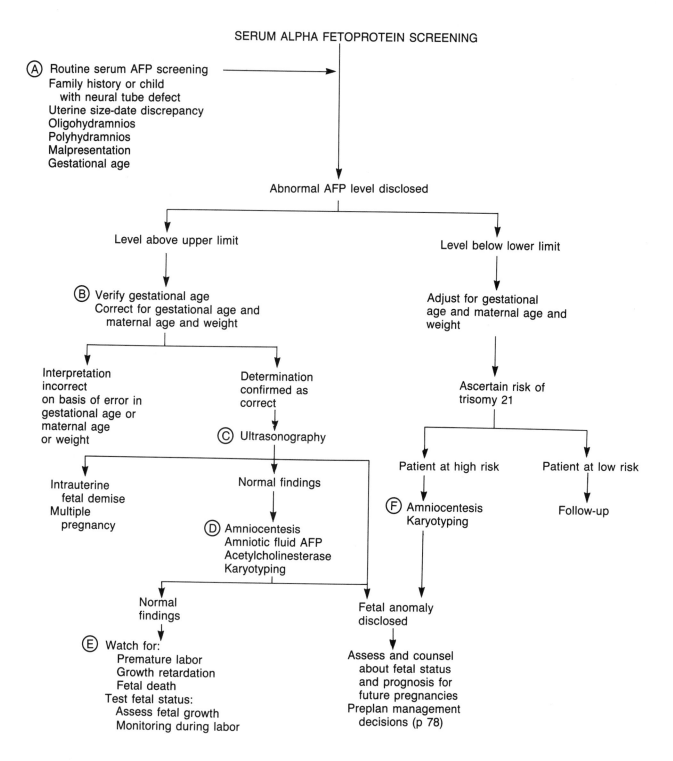

Ⓐ Routine serum AFP screening
Family history or child
  with neural tube defect
Uterine size-date discrepancy
Oligohydramnios
Polyhydramnios
Malpresentation
Gestational age

Abnormal AFP level disclosed

Level above upper limit

Level below lower limit

Ⓑ Verify gestational age
Correct for gestational age and
  maternal age and weight

Adjust for gestational
age and maternal age and
weight

Interpretation
incorrect
on basis of error in
gestational age or
maternal age
or weight

Determination
confirmed as
correct

Ⓒ Ultrasonography

Ascertain risk of
trisomy 21

Patient at high risk

Patient at low risk

Intrauterine
fetal demise
Multiple
pregnancy

Normal findings

Ⓕ Amniocentesis
Karyotyping

Follow-up

Ⓓ Amniocentesis
Amniotic fluid AFP
Acetylcholinesterase
Karyotyping

Normal
findings

Fetal anomaly
disclosed

Ⓔ Watch for:
  Premature labor
  Growth retardation
  Fetal death
Test fetal status:
  Assess fetal growth
  Monitoring during labor

Assess and counsel
about fetal status
and prognosis for
future pregnancies
Preplan management
decisions (p 78)

F. A low serum AFP level adjusted for maternal age, gestational age, and maternal weight is an indication for amniocentesis for chromosome analysis because of a
statistical relationship with fetal trisomy 21. The level at
which a low serum AFP level is considered significant
has to be determined by each laboratory performing the
assay. It helps identify gravidas under the age of 35 years
who should undergo amniocentesis. It cannot apply to
those over 35 (who are at increased risk for this anomaly) by virtue of its relatively limited sensitivity.

References

Davenport DM, Macri JN. The clinical significance of low maternal serum alpha-fetoprotein. Am J Obstet Gynecol 146:657,
  1983.
Haddow JE, Kloza EM, Smith DE, Knight GJ. Data from an alpha-
  fetoprotein pilot screening program in Maine. Obstet Gynecol 62:556, 1983.
Hamilton MP, Abdalla HI, Whitfield CR. Significance of raised
  maternal serum alpha-fetoprotein in singleton pregnancies
  with normally formed fetuses. Obstet Gynecol 65:465, 1985.

ASSESSMENT FOR FETAL ANOMALIES

Benjamin P. Sachs, M.B., B.S., D.P.H.
Beryl R. Benacerraf, M.D.

A. About 2 to 4 percent of all pregnancies result in the birth of a child with a major congenital anomaly. Many can be detected by currently available high resolution ultrasonography. This examination is essential for all gravidas at risk. Whether routine use can be justified is a matter of conjecture, but there is a wide range of acceptable indications, from poor gestational dating to evaluation of fetal growth and well-being. Many gravidas request a fetal scan for detection of birth defects; these requests should be honored.

B. A persistently abnormal presentation may be associated with central nervous system or musculoskeletal abnormalities with hypotonia. A discrepancy in uterine size relative to dates may indicate a fetal malformation associated with oligohydramnios or polyhydramnios. An abnormally low maternal serum alpha fetoprotein level (p 76) may provide a clue to chromosome abnormalities; a high level suggests an open spinal defect. Premature labor and a personal or family history of a child with a congenital defect are other reasons to evaluate the current fetus.

C. Except for the most obvious defects, such as anencephaly or gross hydrocephalus, errors of commission and omission are common. To avoid unnecessary parental anxiety (or inappropriate reassurances) engendered by incorrect ultrasonographic interpretation, it is prudent to refer the gravida to an ultrasonographer who is especially skilled and experienced in the detection of fetal malformations. Subtle defects can be easily missed, such as those involving the chambers of the heart and the major exiting arterial trunks, which constitute about one-fourth of all major fetal anomalies. Serial studies are recommended, regardless of whether abnormality is found, to reduce the chance of an error and to observe whether the defect is changing as pregnancy advances.

D. The detection of anencephaly during the first half of pregnancy permits consideration of pregnancy termination (p 44). While ethical and legal constraints may interdict such intervention late in pregnancy, some have recently suggested that this practice be extended into the third trimester if the gravida desires.

E. Appropriate consultation should be sought with experts knowledgeable about the immediate and long-term management of fetuses and infants with specific con genital lesions. This aids the primary clinician in formulating a plan that takes into account fetal considerations, the options open to the family, and societal ethics. Resources, such as published birth defect compendiums or experienced consultants, aid the clinician in linking the detected defect to possible chromosomal aberrations. Cardiac and central nervous system lesions (hydrocephaly and microcephaly) are examples of such linked conditions. Fetal and parental karyotyping is then indicated. Similarly, consider serologic studies or blood cultures to identify a possible infectious etiology, such as the TORCH organisms (p 150, 158).

F. Some gravidas and their in situ fetuses may benefit from transfer to a perinatal center. If the appropriate choice is to remain with the primary clinican, the team of involved health care providers should discuss the issues together with the gravida and her partner so that they can agree in advance on a mutually acceptable plan for labor, delivery, and neonatal care. Clarify medicolegal ramifications with a representative of the hospital's administrative or risk management personnel. The minimum basic objectives should be to determine the preferred route of delivery and to decide whether specific antepartum treatment should be given, whether electronic fetal monitoring should be used during labor, and whether resuscitation or heroic measures should be invoked at delivery.

References

Campbell S, Pearce JM. The prenatal diagnosis of fetal structural anomalies by ultrasound. Clin Obstet Gynecol 10:475, 1983.

Nelson LH, Clark CE, Fishburne JI, et al. Value of serial sonography in the in utero detection of duodenal atresia. Obstet Gynecol 59:657, 1982.

Romero R, Cullen M, Grannum P, et al. Antenatal diagnosis of renal anomalies with ultrasound: III. Bilateral renal agenesis. Am J Obstet Gynecol 151:38, 1985.

Sabbagha RE, Sheikh Z, Tamura RK, et al. Predictive value, sensitivity, and specificity of ultrasonic targeted imaging for fetal anomalies in gravid women at high risk for birth defects. Am J Obstet Gynecol 152:822, 1985.

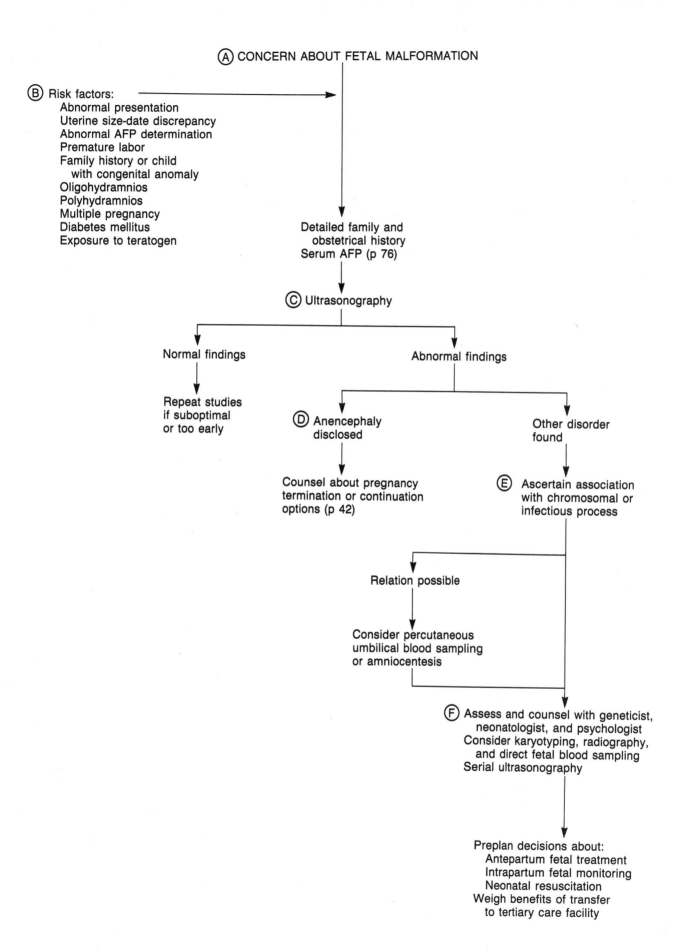

A CONCERN ABOUT FETAL MALFORMATION

B Risk factors:
   Abnormal presentation
   Uterine size-date discrepancy
   Abnormal AFP determination
   Premature labor
   Family history or child
     with congenital anomaly
   Oligohydramnios
   Polyhydramnios
   Multiple pregnancy
   Diabetes mellitus
   Exposure to teratogen

Detailed family and
obstetrical history
Serum AFP (p 76)

C Ultrasonography

Normal findings

Repeat studies
if suboptimal
or too early

Abnormal findings

D Anencephaly
disclosed

Counsel about pregnancy
termination or continuation
options (p 42)

Other disorder
found

E Ascertain association
with chromosomal or
infectious process

Relation possible

Consider percutaneous
umbilical blood sampling
or amniocentesis

F Assess and counsel with geneticist,
   neonatologist, and psychologist
Consider karyotyping, radiography,
   and direct fetal blood sampling
Serial ultrasonography

Preplan decisions about:
   Antepartum fetal treatment
   Intrapartum fetal monitoring
   Neonatal resuscitation
   Weigh benefits of transfer
     to tertiary care facility

NEW PRENATAL APPROACHES

Benjamin P. Sachs, M.B., B.S., D.P.H.

A. At the first prenatal visit, determine whether there has been exposure to medication, radiation, or drugs since conception (p 58) and whether there is a family or personal history of recurrent spontaneous abortions, stillbirths, birth defects, or mental retardation. Also at risk are older gravidas (age 35 years or more) and known carriers of a chromosome rearrangement or a recessive or X linked gene. Referral for expert genetic consultation is generally prudent in these cases.

B. Although amniocentesis is still the most frequently used prenatal diagnostic procedure to detect these abnormalities, the procedure cannot be performed until 15 to 17 weeks and tissue culture usually requires two to three weeks for completion. Chorionic villus biopsy (p 74) provides an earlier (nine to 11 weeks) and more rapid (three days to three weeks) diagnosis. Experience is limited and it is not yet widely available. Most newly developing techniques such as this are being done only at large perinatal centers.

C. Gravidas at serious risk should undergo intensive ultrasonography by a clinician especially skilled in detecting abnormalities. Office ultrasonography by the obstetrician may be suggestive, but findings must be verified before any definitive clinical decision is made on this basis.

D. Percutaneous umbilical vein puncture (Fig. 1) is a means for direct access to the fetus for blood sampling, transfusion, or injection. It is accomplished by transplacental puncture to the base of the cord or by direct venipuncture under fetoscopic observation. The severely affected premature fetus suffering from intrauterine hemolytic anemia due to Rh isoimmunization (p 138) will benefit from referral to a perinatal center where intraperitoneal or direct umbilical vein transfusion can be done. The initial good experience with direct intrauterine umbilical vein transfusion has encouraged some investigators to expand the indications for this procedure to include sampling fetal blood for rapid chromosome analysis, fetal platelet count and hematocrit, fetal acid-base determination, as well as confirmation of fetal infection or beta thalassemia and perhaps sophisticated DNA analyses.

E. A number of prenatal surgical procedures have been developed to deal with certain diagnosed fetal problems. These are being done only at centers equipped to work out the complex details where teams of perinatologists, pediatric surgeons, neonatologists, geneticists, psychologists, and social workers can integrate their activities and pool their expertise. Informed consent is a critical consideration. The treatment of hydrocephalus by implanting a shunt, although still an experimental procedure, will probably benefit only a small number of fetuses because major chromosomal or anatomic abnormalities are so often associated. Results to date are not encouraging. Other equally serious central nervous system lesions (such as porencephaly and hydranencephaly) must be differentiated. For urinary obstruction, a vesicouterine shunt may be indicated to salvage renal function in a very premature fetus with bilateral hydronephrosis. Unilateral hydronephrosis requires only routine obstetrical care with sequential ultrasonography and neonatal evaluation. The renal agenesis and oligohydramnios of Potter's syndrome are not treatable. Similarly, no intrauterine surgery is available to treat bowel and abdominal wall defects identified by ultrasonography. Nonetheless, it is important to make the diagnosis, because atraumatic delivery in a center equipped to treat the neonate at birth offers the opportunity for salvage and recovery. Fetal pleural and pericardial effusions can be drained under ultrasonographic control. The extent of the underlying pulmonary or cardiac defect determines the optimal management. Referral to a perinatal center is recommended in these cases.

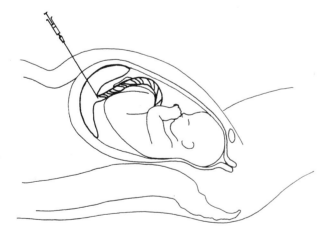

Figure 1   Means for obtaining sample of fetal blood. Needle is inserted percutaneously through the placenta under ultrasonographic guidance into the umbilical vein at the site of the cord insertion into the placenta.

References

Berkowitz RL, Chitkara U, Goldberg JD, et al. Intravascular transfusion in utero: The percutaneous approach. Am J Obstet Gynecol 154:622, 1986.

Daffos F, Capella-Pavlovsky M, Forestier F. A new procedure for fetal blood sampling in utero: Preliminary result of fifty-three cases. Am J Obstet Gynecol 146:985, 1983.

Elias S, Annas GJ. Perspectives on fetal surgery. Am J Obstet Gynecol 145:807, 1983.

McFayden IR, Wigglesworth JS, Dillon MJ. Fetal urinary tract obstruction: Is active intervention before delivery indicated? Br J Obstet Gynaecol 90:342, 1983.

SUSPICION OF FETAL ANOMALY

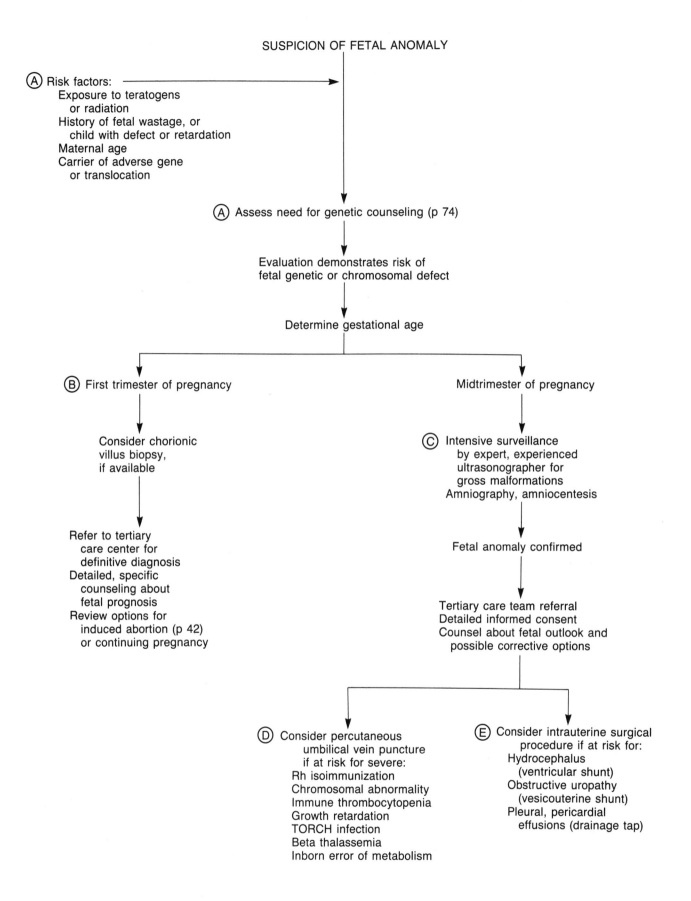

Ⓐ Risk factors:
   Exposure to teratogens
      or radiation
   History of fetal wastage, or
      child with defect or retardation
   Maternal age
   Carrier of adverse gene
      or translocation

Ⓐ Assess need for genetic counseling (p 74)

Evaluation demonstrates risk of
fetal genetic or chromosomal defect

Determine gestational age

Ⓑ First trimester of pregnancy

Consider chorionic
villus biopsy,
if available

Refer to tertiary
   care center for
   definitive diagnosis
Detailed, specific
   counseling about
   fetal prognosis
Review options for
   induced abortion (p 42)
   or continuing pregnancy

Midtrimester of pregnancy

Ⓒ Intensive surveillance
      by expert, experienced
      ultrasonographer for
      gross malformations
   Amniography, amniocentesis

Fetal anomaly confirmed

Tertiary care team referral
Detailed informed consent
Counsel about fetal outlook and
   possible corrective options

Ⓓ Consider percutaneous
      umbilical vein puncture
      if at risk for severe:
   Rh isoimmunization
   Chromosomal abnormality
   Immune thrombocytopenia
   Growth retardation
   TORCH infection
   Beta thalassemia
   Inborn error of metabolism

Ⓔ Consider intrauterine surgical
      procedure if at risk for:
   Hydrocephalus
      (ventricular shunt)
   Obstructive uropathy
      (vesicouterine shunt)
   Pleural, pericardial
      effusions (drainage tap)

HYDATIDIFORM MOLE

Lenard R. Simon, M.D.

A. One should be alert to the possibility of a hydatidiform mole if uterine growth is excessively rapid, although this is not a completely reliable sign, when present, and is often absent in patients with a mole. It should be more strongly suspected, however, if no fetal heart can be heard by ultrasonographic auscultation (Doptone) after eight to 10 weeks. Other manifestations encountered with a molar pregnancy include prolonged and heavy vaginal bleeding, anemia, hyperemesis gravidarum, hypertension in the first or second trimester (indistinguishable at times from the clinical picture of pregnancy induced hypertension of the third trimester), hyperthyroidism, hemoptysis, cough, dyspnea, or chest pain. Pulmonary symptoms reflect lung metastasis.

B. A history of a gestational trophoblastic neoplasm is an important signal for the physician. All subsequent pregnancies must be followed carefully because of the danger of repetition of this event. Ultrasonographic scanning helps diagnose the condition by showing the absence of a gestational sac and characteristically scattered intrauterine echoes. Quantitative beta subunit hCG determinations may be helpful if levels are markedly elevated. However, they need not be elevated with a mole (even if aggressively malignant), especially with rapidly proliferating neoplastic tissue undergoing necrosis.

C. The patient's risk status needs to be carefully assessed by pretreatment evaluation of the hCG level, liver function, thyroid status, coagulation profile, chest x-ray views, and stool guaiac test. When they are indicated on the basis of suggestive symptoms or physical findings, one should undertake studies of lung, brain, and liver for tumor metastases by tomography, arteriography, or computed tomography. Comorbid conditions that may affect clinical management and prognosis include hyperthyroidism, pregnancy induced hypertension, trophoblastic embolization, and disseminated intravascular coagulation.

D. In the interest of an optimal outcome for the patient with advanced disease, the treatment of metastatic gestational trophoblastic neoplastic disease is preferably done at regionalized centers where there are skilled personnel available with experience in carrying out the sometimes complicated therapeutic protocols, in detecting and managing complications as they arise, and in following these women carefully during the prolonged recuperative phase. A combination of methotrexate with citrovorum factor rescue is the regimen of choice. For women with liver dysfunction, actinomycin D is used in place of methotrexate, which is potentially hepatotoxic. Actinomycin D may also be used prophylactically in cases classified as being high risk by virtue of associated comorbid factors or special presenting manifestations in order to avert metastatic sequelae; the benefits of this mode of treatment seem to outweigh its risks in these cases. Such prophylactic use, if undertaken, should begin three days before evacuation, if delay is feasible.

E. Quantitative beta subunit hCG determinations are obtained weekly until the level falls to zero (undetectable) for three consecutive weeks and then monthly for six months. Chest x-ray examination is done before treatment and again after four weeks. The patient should avoid subsequent pregnancy during the follow-up interval; the placental hCG of pregnancy will make it impossible to interpret follow-up hCG levels meaningfully. Effective contraception should therefore be used until the hCG levels have been normal for at least six months to ensure against superimposing a new pregnancy.

F. A subsequent course of chemotherapy will be needed if the hCG levels remain stable (that is, if they do not continue to fall) for more than two weeks, if the levels begin to rise, or if evidence of metastasis appears. The recommended regimen for repeat treatment is actinomycin D. Patients failing to respond promptly should be considered for a more intensive multiple agent chemotherapy program.

References

Elston CW. The pathology of trophoblastic disease: Current status. Clin Obstet Gynaecol 11:135, 1984.

Goldstein DP, Berkowitz RS. Gestational Trophoblastic Neoplasms: Clinical Principles of Diagnosis and Management. Philadelphia: WB Saunders, 1982.

McDonald TW, Ruffolo EH. Modern management of gestational trophoblastic disease. Obstet Gynecol Surv 38:67, 1983.

Runowicz CD. Clinical aspects of gestational trophoblastic disease. Mt Sinai J Med 52:35, 1985.

SUSPICION OF HYDATIDIFORM MOLE

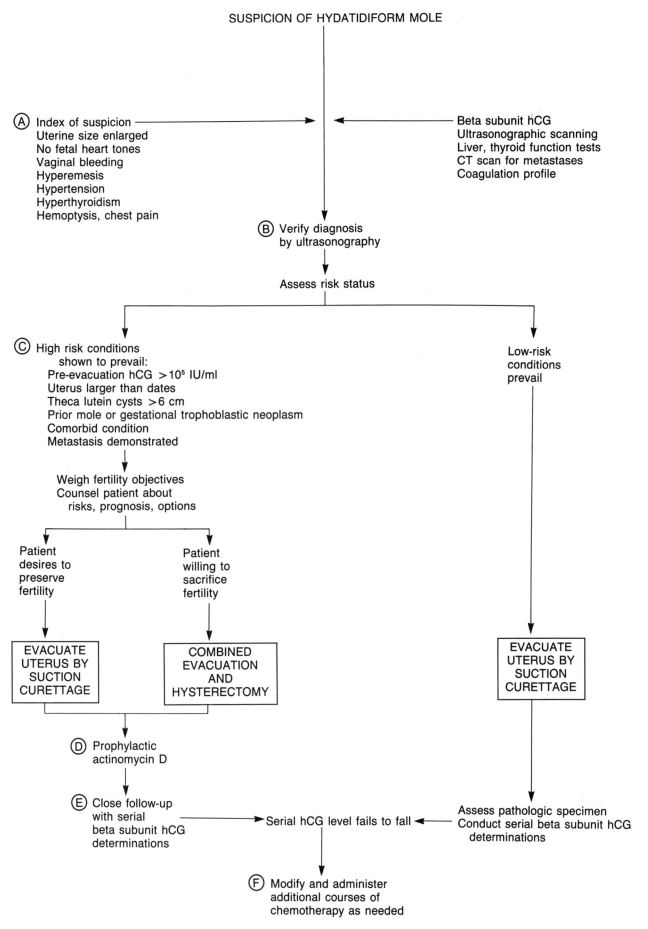

(A) Index of suspicion
    Uterine size enlarged
    No fetal heart tones
    Vaginal bleeding
    Hyperemesis
    Hypertension
    Hyperthyroidism
    Hemoptysis, chest pain

Beta subunit hCG
Ultrasonographic scanning
Liver, thyroid function tests
CT scan for metastases
Coagulation profile

(B) Verify diagnosis
    by ultrasonography

Assess risk status

(C) High risk conditions
        shown to prevail:
    Pre-evacuation hCG >10^5 IU/ml
    Uterus larger than dates
    Theca lutein cysts >6 cm
    Prior mole or gestational trophoblastic neoplasm
    Comorbid condition
    Metastasis demonstrated

    Weigh fertility objectives
    Counsel patient about
        risks, prognosis, options

Patient
desires to
preserve
fertility

Patient
willing to
sacrifice
fertility

Low-risk
conditions
prevail

EVACUATE
UTERUS BY
SUCTION
CURETTAGE

COMBINED
EVACUATION
AND
HYSTERECTOMY

EVACUATE
UTERUS BY
SUCTION
CURETTAGE

(D) Prophylactic
    actinomycin D

(E) Close follow-up
    with serial
    beta subunit hCG
    determinations

Serial hCG level fails to fall

Assess pathologic specimen
Conduct serial beta subunit hCG
determinations

(F) Modify and administer
    additional courses of
    chemotherapy as needed

HYPEREMESIS GRAVIDARUM

Susan B. Wilson, M.D.

A. More than half of pregnant women experience nausea and some vomiting during the first 12 to 18 weeks of pregnancy. Nearly three-quarters of primigravidas are affected. In most cases, hydration and nutrition can be maintained by symptomatic relief and minor dietary adjustment until this unpleasant manifestation of early pregnancy subsides. Fewer than 2 percent experience true hyperemesis gravidarum unresponsive to supportive measures and characterized by progressive dehydration, ketonuria, tachycardia, and weight loss. It is generally regarded as more likely to occur in adolescents, primigravidas, obese women, and nonsmokers. Rarely do serious complications develop, provided the condition is recognized and treated aggressively. If persistent vomiting is neglected or treatment is ineffectual, it can cause erosion of the esophageal mucosa even to the point of rupture, as well as disruption of esophageal varices, mediastinal abscess formation, or aspiration pneumonitis.

B. Hyperemesis gravidarum occurs more commonly with multiple gestation and hydatidiform mole than in otherwise uncomplicated pregnancies. Intercurrent problems, such as hyperthyroidism, hepatitis, gastric or duodenal ulcer, cholelithiasis, hiatus hernia, inflammatory bowel disease, gastric carcinoma, pyelonephritis, gastroenteritis, intestinal obstruction, pancreatitis, diabetic ketoacidosis, and central nervous system tumor, must be ruled out along with alcoholism and emotional disturbance.

C. Determine the frequency of vomiting and inquire about the details of diet, stresses, and supports. A history of oliguria is an index of dehydration. Physical examination should seek evidence of pathologic conditions that may be causative or contributory. Assess for dehydration (in skin turgor and dry mucous membranes), ketoacidosis, uterine growth, and fetal status. Ultrasonography may reveal gallbladder disease, hydronephrosis, a mole, or twins.

D. Most patients do well with minor dietary modifications, such as frequent feedings. They usually tolerate bland, dry, nonfatty foods best. Explanation and sympathetically reassuring support are essential. Hypnosis has been reported to result in a decrease in symptoms after one to three sessions in most receptive patients. Avoid antiemetics, unless symptoms clearly warrant, because of their theoretical fetal risks (thus far unproved).

E. For gravidas with mild degrees of dehydration and ketonuria, outpatient therapy with intravenous hydration and antiemetics may be tried first. The risks of any drug used in pregnancy must be weighed carefully against its benefits. Doxylamine succinate, meclizine, promethazine, or prochlorperazine may be considered because only rare reports of adverse fetal outcomes exist despite widespread use over many years. Nonetheless, use of these drugs should be restricted to cases in which they are clearly indicated.

F. Severe hyperemesis gravidarum needs close sequential surveillance of electrolyte levels, renal and liver function tests, and acid-base balance. Thyroid function tests are indicated as well. Deaths have occurred as a result of renal and hepatic damage. Wernicke's encephalopathy may develop secondary to thiamine deficiency.

G. Hospital care includes aggressive management with intravenous replacement of fluids, glucose, electrolytes, and vitamins for the correction of ketoacidosis, dehydration, and nutritional deficiency. Oral intake is initially restricted. Nasogastric suction and antiemetic drugs may be necessary. Gradual increments in oral intake follow. Counseling or psychiatric care may be required. Visitor restriction may have to be imposed when interpersonal relations appear to be causative or aggravating.

H. Hyperalimentation has been used successfully to treat hyperemesis gravidarum. It should be tried before considering termination of the pregnancy. Induced abortion may prove necessary, however, as a lifesaving measure in a gravida whose unremitting hyperemesis fails to respond to the most aggressive in-hospital regimen.

References

Dozeman R, Kaiser FE, Cass O, Pries J. Hyperthyroidism appearing as hyperemesis gravidarum. Arch Intern Med 143:2202, 1983.

Klebanoff MA, Koslowe PA, Kaslow R, et al. Epidemiology of vomiting in early pregnancy. Obstet Gynecol 66:612, 1985.

Rayburn W, Wolk R, Mercer N, Roberts J. Parenteral nutrition in obstetrics and gynecology. Obstet Gynecol Surv 41:200, 1986.

Schulman PK. Hyperemesis gravidarum: An approach to the nutritional aspects of care. J Am Diet Assoc 80:577, 1982.

UNREMITTING NAUSEA AND VOMITING

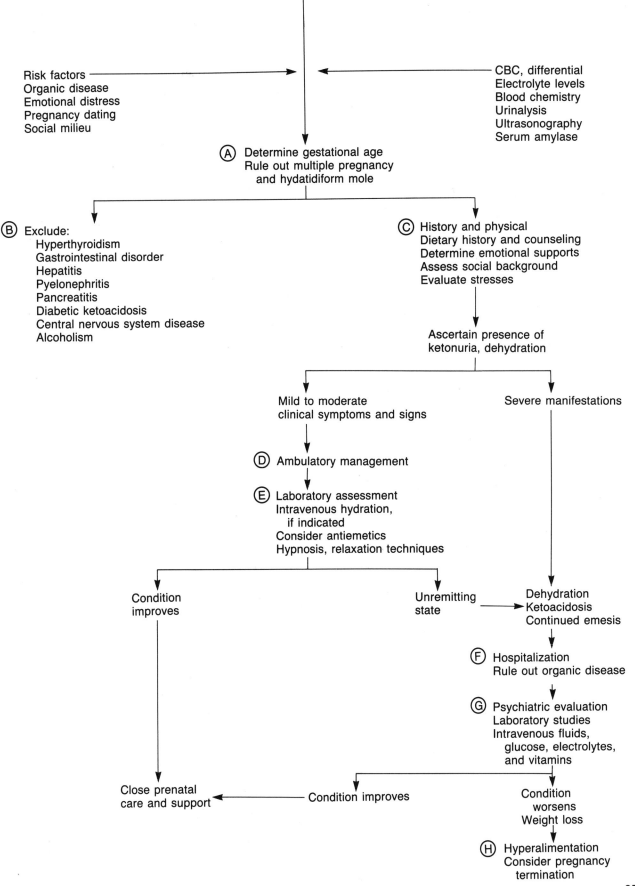

Risk factors
Organic disease
Emotional distress
Pregnancy dating
Social milieu

CBC, differential
Electrolyte levels
Blood chemistry
Urinalysis
Ultrasonography
Serum amylase

Ⓐ Determine gestational age
Rule out multiple pregnancy
and hydatidiform mole

Ⓑ Exclude:
Hyperthyroidism
Gastrointestinal disorder
Hepatitis
Pyelonephritis
Pancreatitis
Diabetic ketoacidosis
Central nervous system disease
Alcoholism

Ⓒ History and physical
Dietary history and counseling
Determine emotional supports
Assess social background
Evaluate stresses

Ascertain presence of
ketonuria, dehydration

Mild to moderate
clinical symptoms and signs

Severe manifestations

Ⓓ Ambulatory management

Ⓔ Laboratory assessment
Intravenous hydration,
if indicated
Consider antiemetics
Hypnosis, relaxation techniques

Condition
improves

Unremitting
state

Dehydration
Ketoacidosis
Continued emesis

Ⓕ Hospitalization
Rule out organic disease

Ⓖ Psychiatric evaluation
Laboratory studies
Intravenous fluids,
glucose, electrolytes,
and vitamins

Close prenatal
care and support

Condition improves

Condition
worsens
Weight loss

Ⓗ Hyperalimentation
Consider pregnancy
termination

85

PREGNANCY INDUCED HYPERTENSION

Eric D. Lichter, M.D.

A. The factors that place a gravida at special risk for developing pregnancy induced hypertension include diabetes mellitus, renal disease, pyelonephritis, as well as a family background and personal history of hypertension.

B. Be alert to the cardinal manifestations of hypertension and proteinuria. Edema is an unreliable sign. A mid-trimester mean arterial blood presssure (diastolic pressure + one-third the difference between diastolic and systolic pressures) of 90 mm Hg or more signals pregnancy induced hypertension well in advance. In the third trimester, blood pressure levels exceeding 135/85 (rather than 140/90) should be considered abnormal along with a 15 mm Hg diastolic or 30 mm Hg systolic rise above prepregnancy or first trimester levels and proteinuria (more than a trace). No preventive effects have been shown by use of salt restriction, antihypertensive or diuretic medication, or weight control measures.

C. The course can be fulminating with rapid progression over a period of hours to convulsion, coma, and death. Therefore, hospitalization is essential at the earliest manifestations. Carry out frequent observations of the blood pressure, urinary output, reflexes, retinal vasospasm (Fig. 1), and condition of the sensorium. Watch for progression of the disease.

D. Patients with severe pregnancy induced hypertension show blood pressures of 160 mm Hg systolic or 110 mm Hg diastolic or more and proteinuria of at least 5 g per 24 hours. Oliguria less than 400 ml per 24 hours is ominous as is cerebral or visual disturbance, pulmonary edema or cyanosis, and evidence of the constellation of hemolysis, elevated liver function test results, and low platelet count (HELLP syndrome). The earlier in pregnancy the onset of disease, the worse the prognosis. Aggressive management of severe disease yields the best results.

E. Seizure (eclampsia) is generally preceded by progressive hyperreflexia with clonus. Expeditious intervention is mandatory, aimed at stopping the convulsions, maintaining adequate oxygenation, avoiding pulmonary aspiration, preventing or treating heart failure, and emptying the uterus as soon as it is safe to do so (after stabilization) by cesarean section, unless vaginal delivery is imminent.

F. Magnesium sulfate is the primary treatment of pregnancy induced hypertension. An initial loading dose of 20 ml of a 20 percent solution is given very slowly by intravenous push over at least a three minute period, testing the knee jerk and watching the respirations. Stop the administration when the deep tendon reflexes diminish. Have calcium gluconate available to counteract the magnesium effect if respirations should stop (a sign of overdose). Supplemental magnesium can be given by intravenous drip or by periodic intramuscular injections, titrated according to the return of hyperreflexia or serum magnesium levels, if rapidly available. The urinary output should be monitored by an indwelling bladder catheter to ensure proper drug clearance and excretion. Hydralazine (5 to 10 mg intravenously every 15 to 20 minutes as needed) should be used if the diastolic pressure increases above 100 to 105 mm Hg to prevent a cerebrovascular accident.

G. Although the pathophysiologic mechanism underlying pregnancy induced hypertension is as yet unknown, the process continues until the pregnancy ends even though its overt manifestations may subside. The patient remains at high risk. Frequent follow-up is essential, with rehospitalization and aggressive management for recurrence.

H. Once the patient's condition is stabilized, maintain control with magnesium sulfate and proceed in six to 12 hours to deliver. Even with an unfavorable cervix, labor induction with a carefully titrated oxytocin infusion (p 182) may prove unexpectedly successful. Continuous electronic monitoring of the fetal heart rate is essential. If induction fails, cesarean section is appropriate for patients with severe pregnancy induced hypertension after they have been brought under control. Delay risks exacerbation or complications such as abruptio placentae or fetal hypoxia from placental insufficiency. Continue postpartum observations to detect and manage exacerbations expediently.

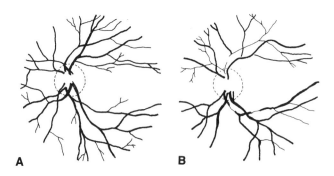

A　　　　　　**B**

Figure 1 Retinal vasospasm in severe pregnancy induced hypertension. *A,* Normal vascular pattern seen by ophthalmoscopy. *B,* Typical pre-eclamptic pattern with arteriolar narrowing and spasm shown as localized constrictions of terminal retinal vessels, especially in medially located arterioles.

References

Chesley LC. Hypertensive Disorders in Pregnancy. New York: Appleton-Century-Crofts, 1978.

Pritchard JA. The use of magnesium sulfate in preeclampsia-eclampsia. J Reprod Med 23:107, 1979.

Sibai BM, Taslimi M, Abdella, TN, et al. Maternal and perinatal outcome of conservative management of severe preeclampsia in midtrimester. Am J Obstet Gynecol 152:32, 1985.

Weinstein L. Syndrome of hemolyses, elevated liver enzymes, and low platelet count: A severe consequence of hypertension in pregnancy. Am J Obstet Gynecol 142:159, 1982.

Zuspan FP. Hypertension and reneal disease in pregnancy. Clin Obstet Gynecol 27:797, 1984.

SUSPICION OF PREGNANCY INDUCED HYPERTENSION

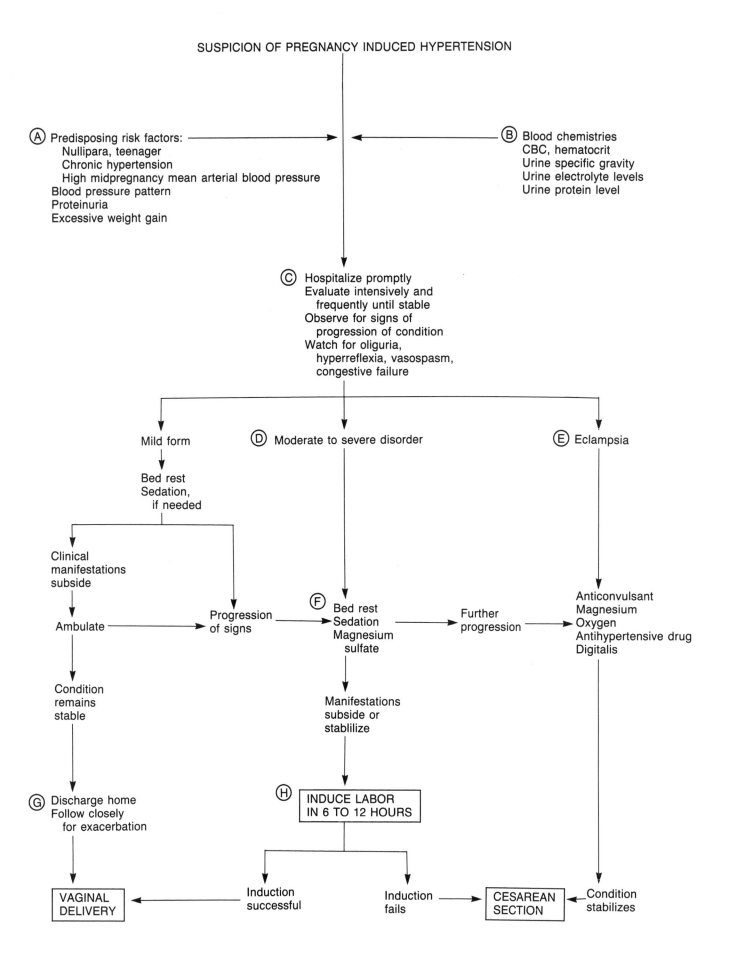

Ⓐ Predisposing risk factors:
    Nullipara, teenager
    Chronic hypertension
    High midpregnancy mean arterial blood pressure
  Blood pressure pattern
  Proteinuria
  Excessive weight gain

Ⓑ Blood chemistries
  CBC, hematocrit
  Urine specific gravity
  Urine electrolyte levels
  Urine protein level

Ⓒ Hospitalize promptly
Evaluate intensively and
  frequently until stable
Observe for signs of
  progression of condition
Watch for oliguria,
  hyperreflexia, vasospasm,
  congestive failure

Mild form

Bed rest
Sedation,
  if needed

Ⓓ Moderate to severe disorder

Ⓔ Eclampsia

Clinical
manifestations
subside

Ambulate

Progression
of signs

Ⓕ Bed rest
Sedation
Magnesium
sulfate

Further
progression

Anticonvulsant
Magnesium
Oxygen
Antihypertensive drug
Digitalis

Condition
remains
stable

Manifestations
subside or
stablilize

Ⓖ Discharge home
Follow closely
  for exacerbation

Ⓗ INDUCE LABOR
IN 6 TO 12 HOURS

VAGINAL
DELIVERY

Induction
successful

Induction
fails

CESAREAN
SECTION

Condition
stabilizes

PLACENTA PREVIA

Henry Klapholz, M.D.

A. Although it is rare for the first episode of bleeding from placenta previa to be profuse and life-threatening, the problem nonetheless can be potentially catastrophic. This is true especially if an internal examination is done that unwittingly disrupts the placental site to cause exsanguinating hemorrhage.

B. It is acceptable to undertake a speculum examination to rule out local sources of bleeding, such as a cervical polyp, cancer, vaginal laceration, or a ruptured varix. It should be done gently and with great care to avoid undue pressure or trauma to the cervix or lower uterine segment, thereby potentially impinging on the placental site. No other form of intravaginal examination or manipulation should be done until placenta previa has been clearly ruled out because digital vaginal or rectal examinations can invoke uncontrollable bleeding in these cases if the cervical canal is entered (Fig. 1).

C. Ultrasonography is an especially valuable examination for confirming the presence of placenta previa. It is also helpful for assessing the fetal size and status, providing important information pertaining to maturity and well-being for guiding the management. Conservative expectancy, if feasible, is in order for the preterm fetus; more aggressive intervention is called for if the fetus is at term or in jeopardy.

D. Profuse bleeding is life-threatening to the mother. It may jeopardize the fetus as well, since up to 10 percent of the blood lost is fetal in origin. If bleeding is not profuse, amniocentesis is in order to ascertain the stage of fetal pulmonary maturity. If the fetal lungs are not mature, consideration may be given to the administration of corticosteroids to the mother in order to accelerate fetal lung maturation. This is done in anticipation of a significant bleeding episode that might occur as the pregnancy advances; because such hemorrhage would necessitate intervention, it is prudent to try to prevent respiratory distress in the preterm infant by this means.

E. If it is possible, expectant management is desirable and should be pursued until the fetus reaches 37 weeks' gestation. At this point, an amniocentesis is done to ensure maturity of fetal pulmonary function.

F. As the lower uterine segment develops, the placental site may appear on ultrasonographic scanning to "migrate" away from the internal os. Therefore, ultrasonography should be repeated periodically if bleeding begins early. Such serial examinations may serve to rule out placenta previa and permit ambulation and subsequent routine prenatal care until the spontaneous onset of labor.

G. Any intravaginal manipulation, examination, or procedure, except gentle speculum examination, must be done in the operating room with the patient fully informed and everything in readiness for immediate surgery. Preparations needed before proceeding include the following: adequate large bore intravenous lines open; blood already typed and cross matched and immediately available; operating room equipment, instruments, and assistant medical and nursing personnel scrubbed and gowned; and an anesthetist informed and prepared for immediate action.

H. If placenta previa is encountered in a patient who has had a prior cesarean section, consider the possibility of placenta accreta (p 90). Obtain consent in advance for a possible hysterectomy in case placenta accreta is actually found.

I. If the cervix is favorable and bleeding is minimal or absent, undertake induction of labor. Constant surveillance of the fetal and maternal status is essential, with the operating room in readiness and blood on hand for immediate use if indicated. The membranes are generally ruptured in these cases to effect tamponade of the fetal head against the edge of the placenta, thereby preventing bleeding as labor progresses and as the cervix dilates to separate the low-lying placenta from its attachment near the internal os and at the lower uterine segment.

References

Artis AA, Bowie JD, Rosenberg ER, Rauch RF. The fallacy of placental migration: Effect of sonographic techniques. Am J Radio 144:79, 1985.
Clark SL, Koonings PP, Phelan JP. Placenta previa/accreta and prior cesarean section. Obstet Gynecol 66:89, 1985.
McShane PM, Heyl PS, Epstein MF. Maternal and perinatal morbidity resulting from placenta previa. Obstet Gynecol 65:176, 1985.
Newton ER, Barss V, Cetrulo CL. The epidemiology and clinical history of asymptomatic midtrimester placenta previa. Am J Obstet Gynecol 148:743, 1984.
Silver R, Depp R, Sabbagha RE, et al. Placenta previa: Aggressive expectant management. Am J Obstet Gynecol 150:15, 1984.

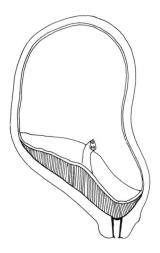

Figure 1 Central or total placenta previa overlying the internal cervical os. Hemorrhage can be invoked by digital examination or by intrinsic cervical dilatation.

PAINLESS VAGINAL BLEEDING

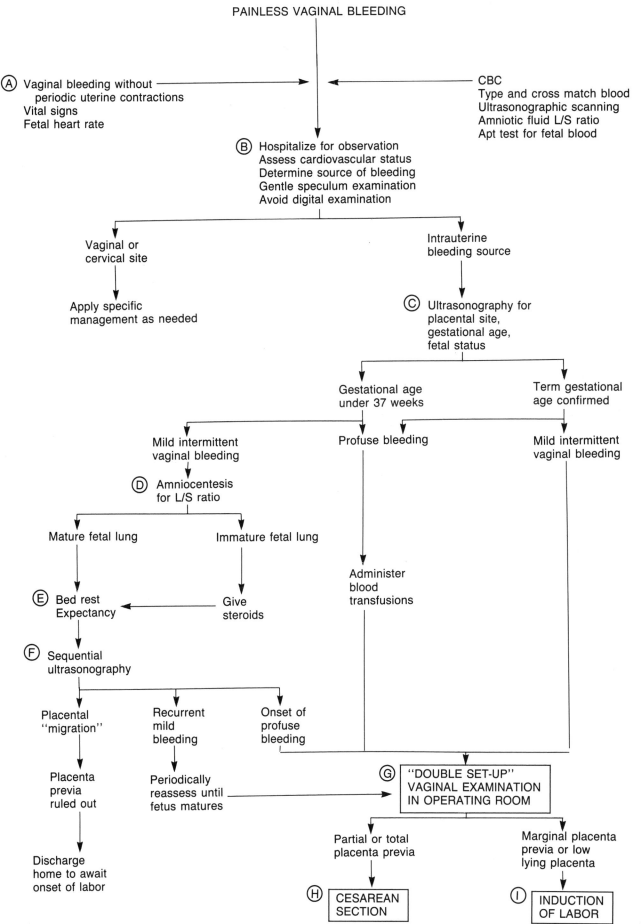

Ⓐ Vaginal bleeding without
    periodic uterine contractions
Vital signs
Fetal heart rate

CBC
Type and cross match blood
Ultrasonographic scanning
Amniotic fluid L/S ratio
Apt test for fetal blood

Ⓑ Hospitalize for observation
Assess cardiovascular status
Determine source of bleeding
Gentle speculum examination
Avoid digital examination

Vaginal or
cervical site

Apply specific
management as needed

Intrauterine
bleeding source

Ⓒ Ultrasonography for
placental site,
gestational age,
fetal status

Gestational age
under 37 weeks

Term gestational
age confirmed

Mild intermittent
vaginal bleeding

Profuse bleeding

Mild intermittent
vaginal bleeding

Ⓓ Amniocentesis
for L/S ratio

Mature fetal lung

Immature fetal lung

Ⓔ Bed rest
Expectancy

Give
steroids

Administer
blood
transfusions

Ⓕ Sequential
ultrasonography

Placental
"migration"

Recurrent
mild
bleeding

Onset of
profuse
bleeding

Placenta
previa
ruled out

Periodically
reassess until
fetus matures

Ⓖ "DOUBLE SET-UP"
VAGINAL EXAMINATION
IN OPERATING ROOM

Discharge
home to await
onset of labor

Partial or total
placenta previa

Marginal placenta
previa or low
lying placenta

Ⓗ CESAREAN
SECTION

Ⓘ INDUCTION
OF LABOR

PLACENTA ACCRETA

Harold W. Rubin, M.D.

A. In this condition there is abnormal adherence of all or part of the placenta to the uterine wall with no intervening decidua basalis. There are three recognized types: placenta accreta, in which the placenta is adherent to the myometrium; placenta increta, in which the myometrium is invaded; and placenta percreta, in which the myometrium is invaded to or beyond the serosa. They are generally distinguishable only retrospectively by pathologic examination of the uterus at the placental site. The only clinically relevant distinction is between total and partial accreta (see D and E). Past history of placenta previa, cesarean section, uterine malformation, myomectomy, manual removal of the placenta, uterine infection, retained placenta, hemorrhage, and postpartum or postabortal curettage are predisposing factors and should alert one to the possibility of placenta accreta.

B. Whenever placenta accreta is considered or encountered, preparations must be made for anticipated acute blood loss and surgical intervention. Blood should be made rapidly available for transfusion as needed, coagulation studies undertaken (and repeated serially), and the operating room facilities and personnel mobilized immediately to permit emergency intervention and support.

C. The only way to establish the diagnosis of placenta accreta clinically is to initiate an attempt to remove the placenta manually. No cleavage plane will be found in the case of total accreta; in partial accreta, the cleavage plane is found but complete separation cannot be accomplished. The manual exploration is performed under anesthesia in the operating room, with blood ready or actually infusing, the surgical assistants and nurses scrubbed and gowned, and all the necessary instruments for abdominal surgery in readiness.

D. Complete (total) accreta is generally asymptomatic. Since there is no separation, there is generally no bleeding unless a false plane is artificially created.

E. Partial placenta accreta usually presents with acute hemorrhage because the placenta is partially detached from its uterine implantation site and the uterus is unable to contract adequately to control the bleeding effectively. Placenta accreta associated with placenta previa (p 88) is also accompanied by considerable bleeding because the lower uterine segment cannot contract well even under optimal circumstances.

F. Emergency measures are frequently necessary to maintain cardiovascular integrity. These include rapid administration of volume expanders and blood replacement. Bilateral internal iliac artery ligation may also prove necessary as a life-saving approach in these cases.

G. It has been well established that once the clinical diagnosis of placenta accreta is made, the best results are obtained when a hysterectomy is performed (about 6 percent mortality); by contrast, the mortality rate in patients treated conservatively is four times as great (nearly 26 percent). Expeditious intervention usually makes the difference between a good outcome and an adverse one. Despite the need for rapid action, care should nonetheless be taken to avoid injury to the ureters during the surgery.

References

Breen JL, Neubacker R, Gregori CA, Franklin JE. Placenta accreta, increta and percreta: Survey of 40 cases. Obstet Gynecol 49:43, 1977.

Clark SL, Koonings PP, Phelan JP. Placenta previa/accreta and prior cesarean section. Obstet Gynecol 66:89, 1985.

Innes G, Rosen P. An unusual cause of abdominal pain and shock in pregnancy: Case report and review of the literature. J Emerg Med 2:361, 1985.

Read JA, Cotton DB, Miller FC. Placenta accreta: Changing clinical aspects and outcome. Obstet Gynecol 56:31, 1980.

RETAINED PLACENTA

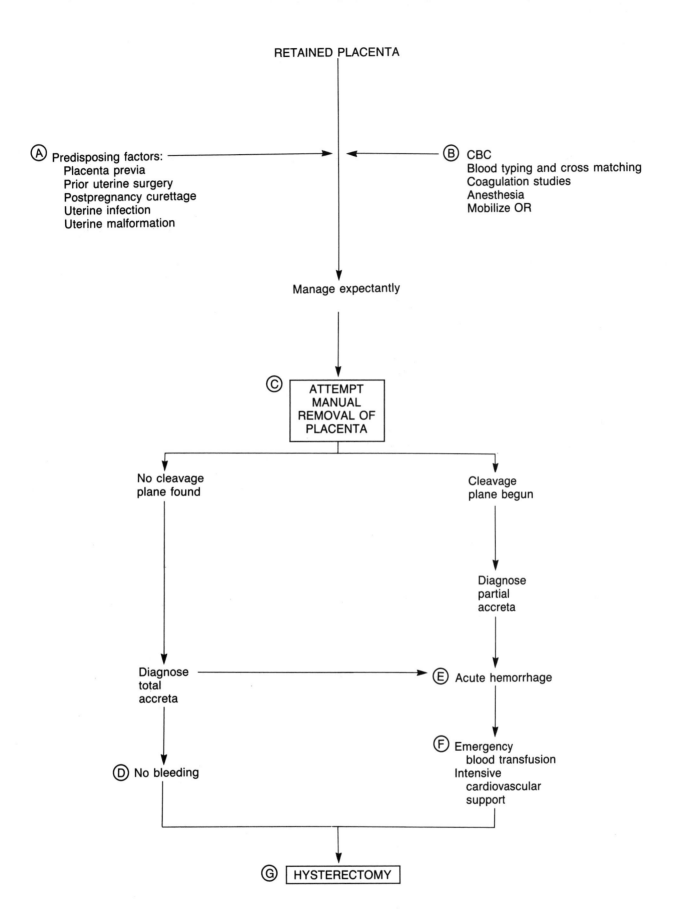

A Predisposing factors:
  Placenta previa
  Prior uterine surgery
  Postpregnancy curettage
  Uterine infection
  Uterine malformation

B CBC
  Blood typing and cross matching
  Coagulation studies
  Anesthesia
  Mobilize OR

Manage expectantly

C ATTEMPT MANUAL REMOVAL OF PLACENTA

No cleavage plane found

Cleavage plane begun

Diagnose partial accreta

Diagnose total accreta

E Acute hemorrhage

D No bleeding

F Emergency blood transfusion Intensive cardiovascular support

G HYSTERECTOMY

ABRUPTIO PLACENTAE

Louis Burke, M.D.

A. Although the pathophysiologic mechanisms and etiology of premature separation of the placenta are unclear, the condition is reported to be associated with high parity, chronic and pregnancy induced hypertension, direct uterine or abdominal trauma (as in a motor vehicle accident), a short umbilical cord (especially late in labor as the fetus descends), sudden uterine decompression (as with the sudden release of amniotic fluid in hydramnios or delivery of the first twin), uterine anomaly, and (perhaps) folic acid deficiency. It has also been reported to occur after cocaine use. Women suffering previous episodes of abruptio placentae may be at increased risk for recurrence. The condition should be considered in a gravida who develops sudden, intense, usually focalized uterine pain with or without vaginal bleeding. Characteristically the uterus is quite tender, with increased tone, often of a boardlike nature. Occult retroplacental bleeding may produce a shock state out of proportion to the vaginal bleeding. Disseminated intravascular coagulation may develop, especially in the more severe cases. Although the clinical picture is usually clear-cut, ultrasonographic study may be used to demonstrate the site of retroplacental hematoma formation. If a bleeding site can be identified, serial ultrasonography may prove useful in following the course of the condition, although the clinical picture is generally a more sensitive indicator.

B. It is useful to classify cases according to clinical severity. In the mild form, placental separation is minimal, involving less than one-sixth of the surface. The blood loss is generally less than 500 ml. The maternal condition remains good, and no evidence of an adverse effect is demonstrated on continuous electronic monitoring of the fetal heart rate. In general, no intervention is necessary in mild cases, although hospitalization can be foreshortened if definitive care is rendered to those at term (by inducing labor if conditions are favorable). Severe abruptio placentae involves separation of more than two-thirds of the placenta, accompanied by severe pain, tetanic uterine contractions, and fetal distress or intrauterine death. The maternal condition may be unstable, with hypotension, tachycardia, coagulopathy, and even renal failure. In such cases, intervention is mandatory in the interests of the mother; if the fetus is alive and sufficiently mature, one must try to salvage the fetus as well. In moderately severe cases there is blood loss of 500 to 1,000 ml, uterine irritability, and incipient cardiovascular instability, although fetal distress is not usually present.

C. After placenta previa has been ruled out by a "double set-up" examination (p 88), amniotomy should be done and oxytocin infusion begun. Titrated oxytocin stimulation of labor (p 182), even under suboptimal cervical conditions, is often effective in promoting rapid cervical dilatation followed by fetal descent and vaginal delivery. Intensive surveillance of maternal status (and fetal well-being if fetal salvage is feasible and intended) is mandatory throughout. If one encounters evidence that the condition of the mother (or the fetus) is deteriorating, the process should be interrupted at once in favor of cesarean section. In some severe cases, cesarean section may be indicated on an emergency basis as the primary approach because maternal jeopardy is already apparent; this applies for purposes of preserving the gravida regardless of the fetal status. Unsensitized Rh negative women are candidates for anti-D (RhoGam) prophylaxis with the added precaution of ensuring adequate dosage by postdelivery quantitative assessment of the peripheral blood to determine the amount of fetomaternal transfusion. If the number of fetal red blood cells in the maternal circulation is large, supplementary anti-D should be given.

References

Acker D, Sachs BP, Tracey KJ, et al. Abruptio placentae associated with cocaine use. Am J Obstet Gynecol 146:220, 1983.

Grimes DA, Stelle AO, Hatcher RA. Rh immunoglobulin use with placenta previa and abruptio placentae. South Med J 76:743, 1983.

Hurd WW, Miadovnik M, Hertzberg V, et al. Selective management of abruptio placentae: A prospective study. Obstet Gynecol 61:467, 1983.

Ness PM, Budzymski AZ, Olexa SA, et al. Congenital hypofibrinogenemia and recent placental abruption. Obstet Gynecol 61:519, 1983.

Rivera-Alsina MB, Saldana LR, Maklad N, et al. The use of ultrasound in the expectant management of abruptio placentae. Am J Obstet Gynecol 146:924, 1983.

PAIN AND BLEEDING

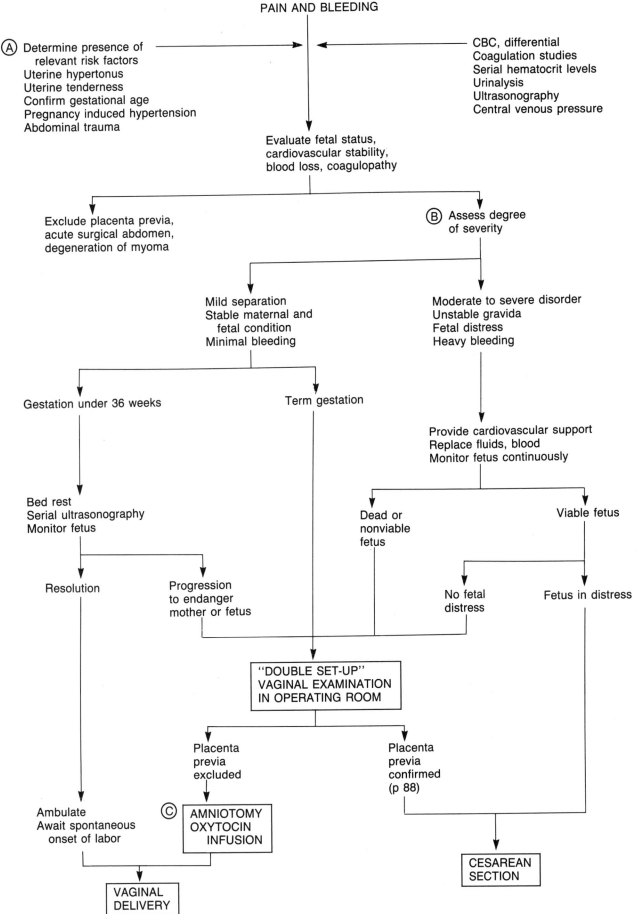

Ⓐ Determine presence of
   relevant risk factors
Uterine hypertonus
Uterine tenderness
Confirm gestational age
Pregnancy induced hypertension
Abdominal trauma

CBC, differential
Coagulation studies
Serial hematocrit levels
Urinalysis
Ultrasonography
Central venous pressure

Evaluate fetal status,
cardiovascular stability,
blood loss, coagulopathy

Exclude placenta previa,
acute surgical abdomen,
degeneration of myoma

Ⓑ Assess degree
   of severity

Mild separation
Stable maternal and
   fetal condition
Minimal bleeding

Moderate to severe disorder
Unstable gravida
Fetal distress
Heavy bleeding

Gestation under 36 weeks

Term gestation

Provide cardiovascular support
Replace fluids, blood
Monitor fetus continuously

Bed rest
Serial ultrasonography
Monitor fetus

Dead or
nonviable
fetus

Viable fetus

Resolution

Progression
to endanger
mother or fetus

No fetal
distress

Fetus in distress

"DOUBLE SET-UP"
VAGINAL EXAMINATION
IN OPERATING ROOM

Placenta
previa
excluded

Placenta
previa
confirmed
(p 88)

Ambulate
Await spontaneous
onset of labor

Ⓒ AMNIOTOMY
   OXYTOCIN
   INFUSION

CESAREAN
SECTION

VAGINAL
DELIVERY

VASA PREVIA

Eric D. Lichter, M.D.

A. In cases of velamentous insertion of the fetal umbilical vessels distant from the edge of the placenta, those vessels sometimes may course over the fetal membranes on the lower uterine segment and cross directly over the internal os of the cervix. Occasionally they can be palpated by an astute observer during vaginal examination, but more often they are unrecognized until after the delivery when the placenta is examined. Since these vessels are unsupported and unprotected by either the umbilical cord or placental tissue, they may rupture. This happens concurrently with rupture of the chorioamniotic membranes, although it rarely occurs spontaneously. Aside from its association with a velamentous cord, vasa previa also can be seen with a bilobate placenta, a succenturiate lobe, and twins. Despite increasing awareness of this condition and rapid recognition and intervention by cesarean section, fetal mortality remains very high, at more than 50 percent.

B. Suspect vasa previa in all cases of vaginal bleeding accompanied by fetal heart irregularity, deceleration, or bradycardia, especially if the bleeding begins at or just after rupture of the membranes. The clinical signs and symptoms of abruptio placentae (p 92) are absent in these cases, but the asymptomatic bleeding of placenta previa (p 88) is indistinguishable. Therefore, one has to maintain a high index of suspicion for vasa previa at all times. If not, diagnosis and management will be delayed to the detriment of a fetus that is at significant risk from blood loss.

C. Since the blood lost is all fetal in origin, rapid assessment to determine its source (fetus versus mother) will quickly establish the diagnosis. Speed is important here because even a relatively small amount of vaginal bleeding, by maternal standards, can reflect the loss of a sizable proportion of the fetal blood volume. The Apt test is based on the resistance of fetal hemoglobin to alkali. A Wright stained smear of the blood can also be used to identify nucleated fetal red blood cells. A Kleihauer-Betke (acid elution) analysis is still another means for identifying and quantitating fetal blood. Bear in mind that up to 10 percent of the blood lost in placenta previa may be fetal in origin. Thus, the diagnosis of vasa previa cannot be made with certainty unless the proportion of fetal erythrocytes or hemoglobin is correspondingly high.

D. In the absence of fetal red blood cells, other causes of vaginal bleeding must be sought. An appropriate workup to diagnose placenta previa or abruptio placentae should be undertaken.

E. Velamentous vessels may rupture before or during labor. Early diagnosis is essential to prevent fetal exsanguination. The diagnosis can be made prior to rupture if the forelying fetal vessels are palpated through the dilated cervix. Confirmation may be attempted by visualizing the vessels in the membranes over the internal os (Fig. 1). For this purpose, one can undertake a speculum examination or amnioscopy with good light and assistance to provide needed exposure. Care must be taken to avoid damaging or occluding the vessels during this examination. Once the diagnosis has been confirmed, proceed to cesarean section unless vaginal delivery is imminent.

F. If the blood is shown to be derived exclusively from the fetus, prompt action is mandatory for fetal salvage. If there is a question of fetal viability and time permits, determine the gestation age, fetal size, physiologic maturity, and functional well-being by ultrasonographic examination, fetal monitoring, and other appropriate tests (p 70) as indicated. If the fetus is alive and likely to survive and immediate vaginal delivery cannot be accomplished atraumatically, emergency cesarean section should be performed. All too often the fetus is already dead; under these circumstances, labor should be allowed to evolve spontaneously without operative intervention.

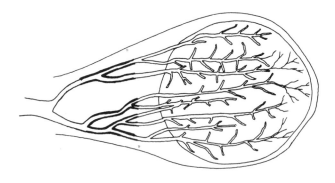

Figure 1 Velamentous insertion of the cord with umbilical vessels splaying between amnion and chorion (drawn heavily) before reaching margin of the placenta. Vasa previa occurs when such vessels traverse the internal os.

References

Kouyoumdjian A. Velamentous insertion of the umbilical cord. Obstet Gynecol 56:737, 1980.

Robinson LK, Jones KL, Benirshke K. The nature of structural defects associated with velamentous and marginal insertion of the umbilical cord. Am J Obstet Gynecol 146:191, 1982.

SUSPICION OF VASA PREVIA

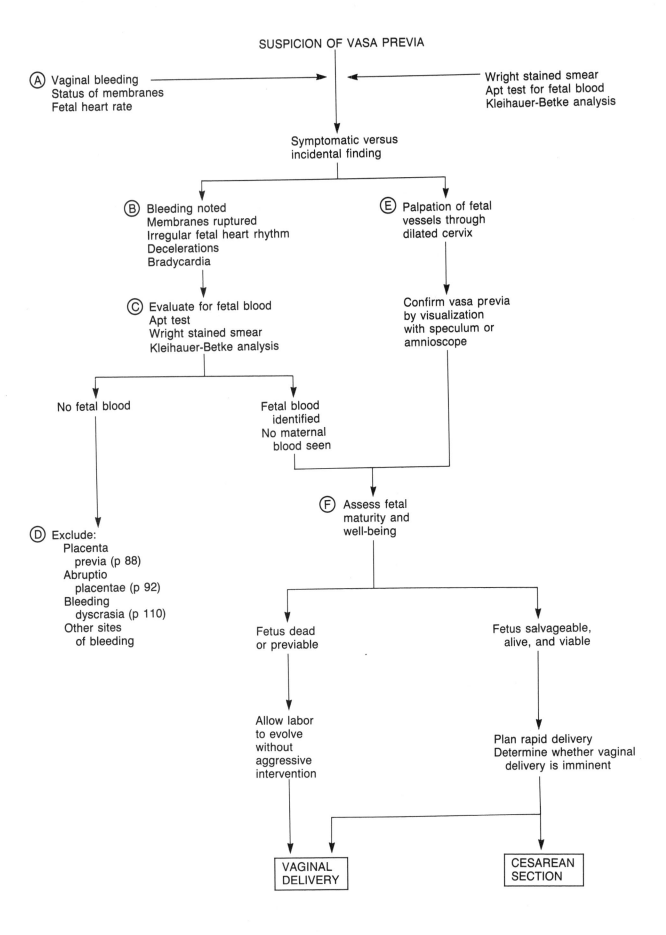

Ⓐ Vaginal bleeding
Status of membranes
Fetal heart rate

Wright stained smear
Apt test for fetal blood
Kleihauer-Betke analysis

Symptomatic versus
incidental finding

Ⓑ Bleeding noted
Membranes ruptured
Irregular fetal heart rhythm
Decelerations
Bradycardia

Ⓔ Palpation of fetal
vessels through
dilated cervix

Ⓒ Evaluate for fetal blood
Apt test
Wright stained smear
Kleihauer-Betke analysis

Confirm vasa previa
by visualization
with speculum or
amnioscope

No fetal blood

Fetal blood
identified
No maternal
blood seen

Ⓓ Exclude:
Placenta
previa (p 88)
Abruptio
placentae (p 92)
Bleeding
dyscrasia (p 110)
Other sites
of bleeding

Ⓕ Assess fetal
maturity and
well-being

Fetus dead
or previable

Fetus salvageable,
alive, and viable

Allow labor
to evolve
without
aggressive
intervention

Plan rapid delivery
Determine whether vaginal
delivery is imminent

VAGINAL
DELIVERY

CESAREAN
SECTION

DIABETES MELLITUS

Henry Klapholz, M.D.

A. One must be alert to the importance of a prior stillbirth, a history of traumatic delivery, or delivery of an infant with a congenital anomaly or one weighing over 9 pounds, as well as an elevated blood sugar level, glycosuria, or recurrent moniliasis. It has recently been recommended that all pregnant women over age 30 years be routinely screened for glucose intolerance, even though no risk factor exists, because half the cases ultimately determined to be diabetic come from the otherwise normal population of gravidas.

B. At each visit, evaluate for glycosuria, fetal growth, and hydramnios. Ultrasonography may be indicated to verify a clinical suspicion of macrosomia or excess amniotic fluid.

C. A blood sugar level determined one hour after the oral administration of 50 g of glucose is a useful screen. Levels greater than 135 mg per deciliter require a full three hour glucose tolerance test.

D. The maximum normal glucose levels after a 100 g oral glucose intake are shown in Table 1. If any two values are abnormal, the glucose tolerance test result must be considered abnormal. Diagnose class A diabetes if the fasting blood sugar level is normal and at least class B if the fasting blood sugar level is abnormal.

E. The patient with class A diabetes needs close observation and dietary control (2,000 to 2,200 calorie ADA diet). The patient should be seen every two weeks. The outcome is usually good. Delivery is undertaken at 40 weeks to avoid post-term pregnancy and macrosomia and the labor and delivery complications that can ensue as a consequence. Premature induction should be avoided in these cases because of fetal functional immaturity (despite the large size). Rigid control of the blood sugar level within a narrow range of normal is essential.

F. At special risk are patients with elevated fasting blood sugar levels (class B or worse) and those who develop pregnancy induced hypertension or hydramnios.

G. Brief hospitalization is needed to evaluate the daily blood sugar patterns and to carry out baseline renal function studies, retinal examination, urinalysis, and urine cultures.

H. Frequent antepartum testing must be done because the fetus may deteriorate very rapidly. Carry out nonstress or oxytocin challenge tests twice weekly, biophysical profiles weekly, ultrasonography for fetal growth every two weeks, and renal function studies monthly.

I. Hospitalize the diabetic patient at 34 weeks if the diabetes is class C or worse. Provide insulin as needed in divided doses to regulate the blood sugar to normal levels (fasting blood sugar level 100 mg per deciliter or less), aiming at day-long stability. A careful home monitoring program may be a safe alternative to hospitalization. Periodic glycosylated hemoglobin levels are useful for ensuring that control has been maintained adequately.

J. Amniocentesis at 36 weeks is done to check fetal lung maturity. For diabetes, lecithin-sphingomyelin ratios of 4.0 or greater should be achieved; better yet, a disaturated phosphatidycholine value of at least 800 (and preferably 1,200) mg per deciliter ensures against neonatal respiratory distress.

K. Deliver as soon as the fetus is fully mature. If the fetus is deteriorating, interrupt earlier. Induction is preferred, but cesarean section may be needed if macrosomia is suspected or fetal distress develops.

L. Regulate the blood sugar level at about 100 mg per deciliter with intravenous doses of insulin (given at four hour intervals or by continuous infusion at 2 to 8 U per hour), while giving 5 percent glucose (150 ml per hour). Monitor the blood sugar level every four hours and titrate the insulin dose accordingly.

References

Felig P, Bergman M. Intensive ambulatory treatment of insulin dependent diabetes. Ann Intern Med 97:225, 1982.

Gabbe SG. Management of diabetes mellitus in pregnancy. Am J Obstet Gynecol 153:824, 1985.

Health and Public Policy Committee, American College of Physicians. Glycosylated hemoglobin assays in the management and diagnosis of diabetes mellitus. Ann Intern Med 101:710, 1984.

Kaplan SA, Lippe BM, Brinkman CR, et al. Diabetes mellitus. Ann Intern Med 96:635, 1982.

Peacock I, Tattersall R. Methods of self monitoring of diabetic control. Clin Endocrinol Metab 11:485, 1982.

Willman SP, Leveno KJ, Guzick DS, et al. Glucose threshold for macrosomia in pregnancy complicated by diabetes. Am J Obstet Gynecol 154:470, 1986.

TABLE 1

	Fasting	1 hour	2 hours	3 hours
Whole blood	90	165	145	125
Plasma	110	200	150	130

SUSPICION OF DIABETES

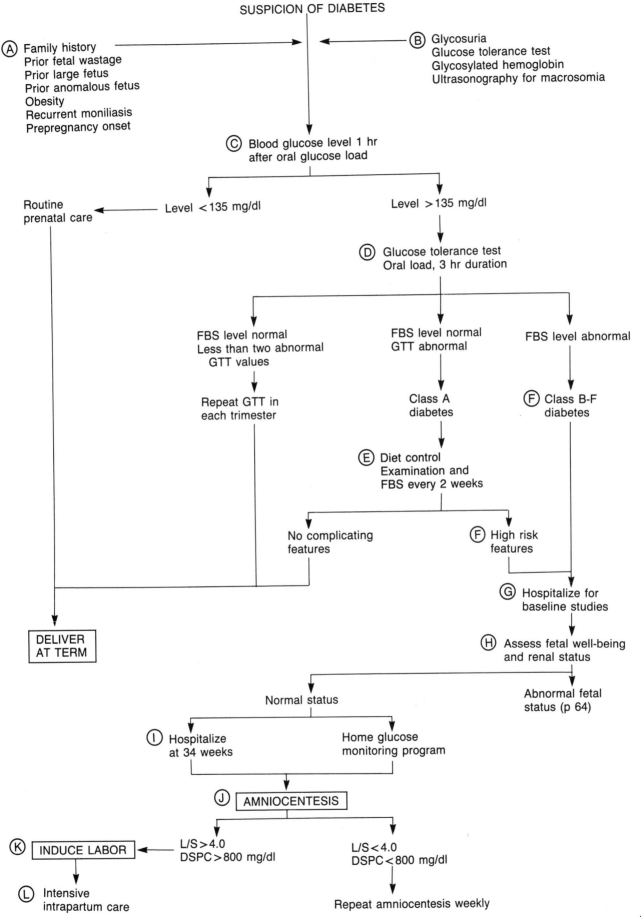

(A) Family history
Prior fetal wastage
Prior large fetus
Prior anomalous fetus
Obesity
Recurrent moniliasis
Prepregnancy onset

(B) Glycosuria
Glucose tolerance test
Glycosylated hemoglobin
Ultrasonography for macrosomia

(C) Blood glucose level 1 hr
after oral glucose load

Level <135 mg/dl → Routine prenatal care

Level >135 mg/dl

(D) Glucose tolerance test
Oral load, 3 hr duration

FBS level normal
Less than two abnormal
GTT values

FBS level normal
GTT abnormal

FBS level abnormal

Repeat GTT in
each trimester

Class A
diabetes

(F) Class B-F
diabetes

(E) Diet control
Examination and
FBS every 2 weeks

No complicating
features

(F) High risk
features

(G) Hospitalize for
baseline studies

(H) Assess fetal well-being
and renal status

Normal status

Abnormal fetal
status (p 64)

DELIVER
AT TERM

(I) Hospitalize
at 34 weeks

Home glucose
monitoring program

(J) AMNIOCENTESIS

(K) INDUCE LABOR ← L/S>4.0
DSPC>800 mg/dl

L/S<4.0
DSPC<800 mg/dl

(L) Intensive
intrapartum care

Repeat amniocentesis weekly

CHRONIC HYPERTENSIVE DISEASE

Henry Klapholz, M.D.

A. Special attention should be paid to gravidas who have a family history of hypertension, labile hypertension early in childhood, renal disease, hematuria, frequent urinary tract infections, and childhood nephritis. Characteristic symptoms that serve to alert one to the possibility of chronic hypertension include recurrent headaches and nosebleeds. It is essential that women at risk be identified as early in pregnancy as possible.

B. Thorough baseline evaluation should be done when the patient is first seen. Blood pressure levels of 140/90 or greater are abnormal, but lower levels should be encountered in midtrimester. Failure of the blood pressure to fall in midpregnancy suggests hypertension. Complete renal function evaluation includes microscopic urinalysis and examination of a 24 hour urine collection for protein, catecholamines, and VMA, as well as blood urea nitrogen, uric acid, and electrolyte levels and creatinine clearance. Bear in mind that the normal laboratory values in pregnancy are influenced by an increased glomerular filtration rate. X-ray studies are best avoided in pregnancy, unless there is an overriding reason to counterbalance the fetal risk of radiation exposure. Renal ultrasonography may help. Auscultation of the abdomen can detect the renal artery bruit associated with renal arterial stenosis. Examine the retina to assess for hemorrhages, exudates, and vascular changes.

C. Treatment of a patient with a blood pressure less than 170/110 does not improve the fetal outcome. Higher blood pressures, however, not only yield poor fetal results but may threaten the mother's well-being by causing a cerebrovascular accident. This is particularly the case if there is an area of intracranial vascular compromise, such as an arteriovenous malformation or aneurysm. The risk of sudden abruptio placentae also mandates the treatment of such patients.

D. Avoid the use of thiazides in pregancy, because severe fetal and maternal electrolyte imbalance may result. Hemorrhagic pancreatitis is a further risk. Beta blockers have been shown to be effective hypotensive drugs with little apparent fetal risk. Alpha methyldopa and hydralazine are acceptable alternatives. None of these drugs appears to be capable of preventing superimposed pregnancy induced hypertension, however.

E. Since these patients are at a fivefold increased risk of developing superimposed pregnancy induced hypertension, they have to be followed closely. They should be seen at least at two week intervals until 36 weeks and then weekly or more often until term or delivery. Be watchful for failing cardiac and renal reserve. Repeat renal function studies no less often than every two months, including creatinine clearance, blood urea nitrogen level, and a full urinalysis. Serial coagulation studies should be undertaken to detect impending pregnancy induced hypertension.

F. Begin testing the fetal status at 28 weeks. Deterioration (as shown by two or more clearly abnormal test results) calls for delivery. A single suspicious test of the fetal status warrants amniocentesis and evaluation of fetal maturity. Deliver a fetus that is objectively determined to be mature. If the dates are well documented, hypertensive women should not be permitted to go beyond term. If in doubt, amniocentesis is done to evaluate fetal pulmonary maturity.

References

Ferris TF. How should hypertension during pregnancy be managed? An internist's approach. Med Clin North Am 68:491, 1984.

Lindheimer MD, Katz Al. Hypertension in pregnancy. New Engl J Med 313:675, 1985.

Murnaghan GA. Cardiovascular disorders and hypertension. Clin Obstet Gynaecol 9:59, 1982.

Zuspan FP. Chronic hypertension in pregnancy. Clin Obstet Gynaecol 27:854, 1984.

BLOOD PRESSURE ELEVATION

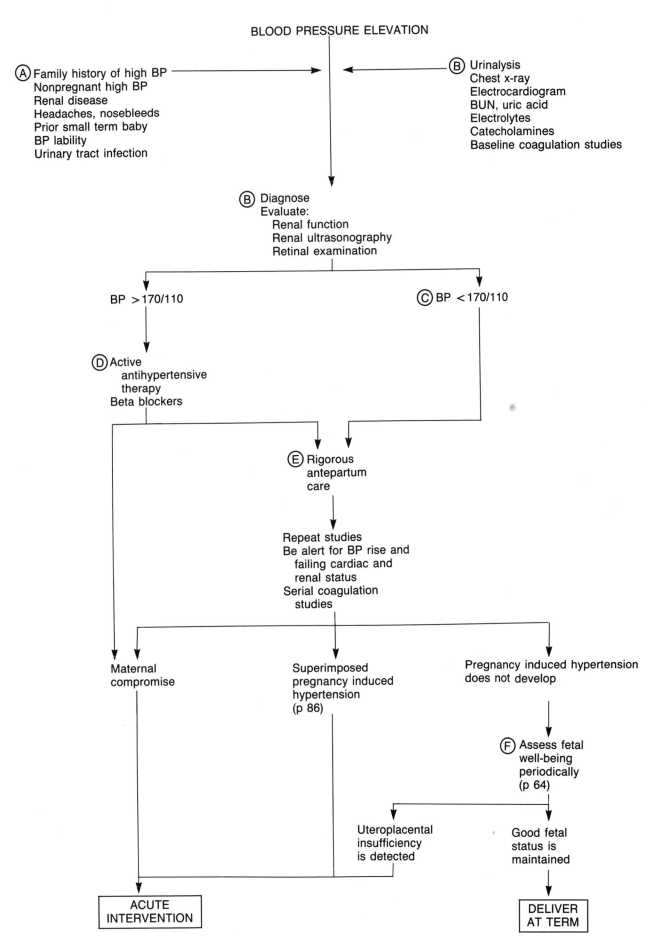

Ⓐ Family history of high BP
Nonpregnant high BP
Renal disease
Headaches, nosebleeds
Prior small term baby
BP lability
Urinary tract infection

Ⓑ Urinalysis
Chest x-ray
Electrocardiogram
BUN, uric acid
Electrolytes
Catecholamines
Baseline coagulation studies

Ⓑ Diagnose
Evaluate:
    Renal function
    Renal ultrasonography
    Retinal examination

BP >170/110

Ⓒ BP <170/110

Ⓓ Active
    antihypertensive
    therapy
Beta blockers

Ⓔ Rigorous
    antepartum
    care

Repeat studies
Be alert for BP rise and
    failing cardiac and
    renal status
Serial coagulation
    studies

Maternal
compromise

Superimposed
pregnancy induced
hypertension
(p 86)

Pregnancy induced hypertension
does not develop

Ⓕ Assess fetal
    well-being
    periodically
    (p 64)

Uteroplacental
insufficiency
is detected

Good fetal
status is
maintained

ACUTE
INTERVENTION

DELIVER
AT TERM

99

RENAL DISEASE

Balmookoot Balgobin, M.D.

A. Kidney disease should be suspected if symptoms are referable to the urinary tract or if there is a history of urinary tract disorders, diabetes, gout, hyperparathyroidism, heart failure, or collagen disease. Persistent bacteriuria (p 164) is also important in this regard.

B. One should survey renal function bearing in mind that pregnancy normally increases renal blood flow and glomerular filtration. Blood urea nitrogen levels are lower than in nonpregnant adults; concentrations considered normal in the nonpregnant state may reflect azotemia in pregnancy. The creatinine clearance is especially valuable. Urinary concentration or dye excretion is often unreliable. The uric acid level may be falsely elevated after diuretic drugs are given. Baseline studies should include serum electrolyte, blood urea nitrogen, and serum creatinine and uric acid levels, as well as creatinine clearance. With heavy proteinuria, carry out 24 hour urinary protein, serum protein, and cholesterol tests. Additional laboratory studies may be needed to rule out orthostatic proteinuria, autoimmune disease, and diabetes.

C. If possible, the specific underlying condition should be diagnosed, provided the diagnostic tests do not jeopardize the fetus or the mother. Unless strongly indicated, x-ray studies and renal biopsy are best avoided. Intravenous pyelography is not done without a clear indication (although a single-film exposure may be appropriate). Ultrasonography is acceptable, however, and often can aid in the diagnosis of renal tumors, renal calculi, hydronephrosis, and hydroureter. The history, previous investigations, and course of the disease state may help make the diagnosis. General guidelines for care pertain to specific conditions. Acute glomerulonephritis can be expected to resolve if managed medically; consider interruption of the pregnancy only if there is no improvement after two weeks of treatment. Diabetic nephropathy demands strict control of the diabetes,

recognizing the added risk to both mother and fetus. Renal calculi are treated expectantly with analgesics. Intervention is reserved for unremitting ureteral obstruction. Such patients should be screened for hyperparathyroidism, gout and cystinuria.

D. Evidence of impaired or failing renal function is alarming. It signifies that the pregnancy is having an adverse effect on the mother. Interrupting the pregnancy may be in the best interest of the gravida, especially if renal decompensation is progressive.

E. Although there are reported cases of liveborn infants with and without growth retardation born to gravidas subjected to hemodialysis during pregnancy for renal failure, the prognosis generally remains poor in such cases.

F. The optimal timing of the delivery depends on maternal or fetal risk. If the mother is in peril, one can justify interrupting the pregnancy at any gestational age. If the fetus shows evidence of compromise, however, interruption can be rationalized only if the infant is mature enough to survive.

References

Drago JR. Management of renal calculi in pregnancy. Urology 20:578, 1982.

Hou SH, Grossman SD, Madias NE. Pregnancy in women with renal disease and moderate renal insufficiency. Am J Med 78:185, 1985.

Katz AI, Davison JM, Hayslett JP, et al. Pregnancy in women with kidney disease. Kidney Int 18:192, 1980.

Kitzmiller JL, Brown ER, Phillippe M, et al. Diabetic nephropathy and perinatal outcome. Am J Obstet Gynecol 141:741, 1981.

Registration Committee of European Dialysis and Transplant Association. Successful pregnancies in women treated with dialysis and kidney transplants. Br J Obstet Gynaecol 87:839, 1980.

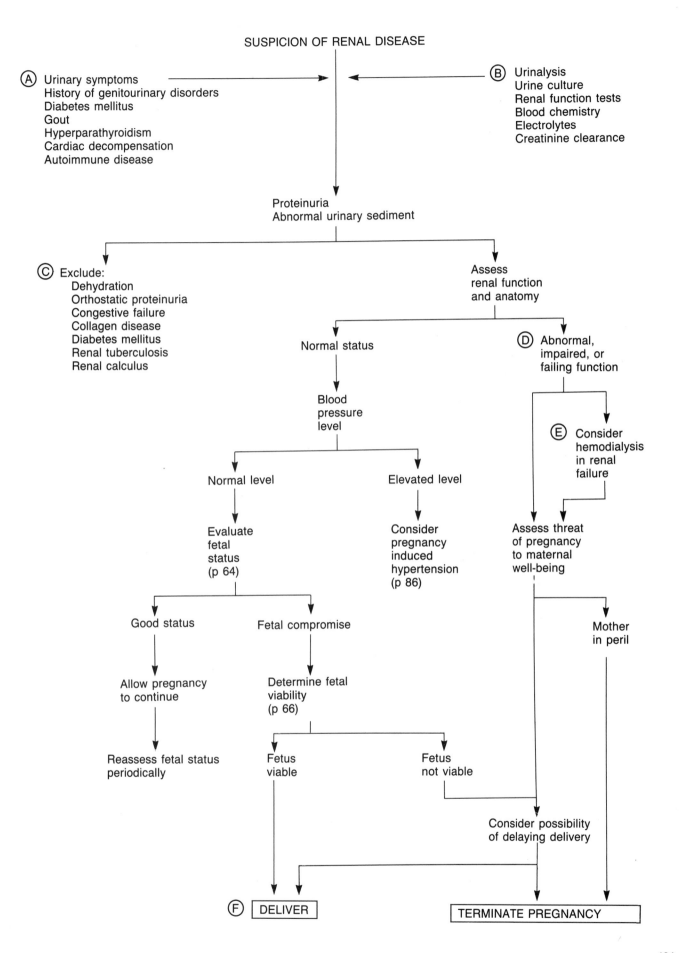

SUSPICION OF RENAL DISEASE

Ⓐ Urinary symptoms
History of genitourinary disorders
Diabetes mellitus
Gout
Hyperparathyroidism
Cardiac decompensation
Autoimmune disease

Ⓑ Urinalysis
Urine culture
Renal function tests
Blood chemistry
Electrolytes
Creatinine clearance

Proteinuria
Abnormal urinary sediment

Ⓒ Exclude:
Dehydration
Orthostatic proteinuria
Congestive failure
Collagen disease
Diabetes mellitus
Renal tuberculosis
Renal calculus

Assess
renal function
and anatomy

Normal status

Ⓓ Abnormal,
impaired, or
failing function

Blood
pressure
level

Ⓔ Consider
hemodialysis
in renal
failure

Normal level

Elevated level

Evaluate
fetal
status
(p 64)

Consider
pregnancy
induced
hypertension
(p 86)

Assess threat
of pregnancy
to maternal
well-being

Good status

Fetal compromise

Mother
in peril

Allow pregnancy
to continue

Determine fetal
viability
(p 66)

Reassess fetal status
periodically

Fetus
viable

Fetus
not viable

Consider possibility
of delaying delivery

Ⓕ DELIVER

TERMINATE PREGNANCY

101

RENAL TRANSPLANT RECIPIENT

Eric D. Lichter, M.D.

A. Because renal failure is a cause of infertility, conception was rarely seen in the past among such women. However, the advent of dialysis and renal transplantation has changed the outlook greatly. Although pregnancy in patients who have undergone renal transplant is still fairly uncommon, the numbers increase every year. As a general rule, these women are much like gravidas with diminished renal function, in that they are at high potential risk for pregnancy induced hypertension, premature delivery, and urinary tract infection (the last more frequently related to immunosuppressive therapy). These patients require counseling about the risks of conception and carefully integrated care between the obstetrician and an internist with expertise in renal disease. A successful outcome of pregnancy can be achieved only with early and frequent antepartum assessments (preferably beginning before pregnancy is undertaken), planning, and an intensive management program. Chronic hemodialysis in a woman in renal failure is also compatible with a successful pregnancy, although the outlook is much less favorable than for the gravida with a transplanted kidney.

B. The best results in pregnancy can be expected in patients who fulfill certain criteria—good health for at least two years following transplantation, a health status otherwise compatible with a good obstetrical outcome, no proteinuria or significant hypertension, no evidence of graft rejection, no evidence of renal pelvicalyceal distention on a recent excretory urogram, a plasma creatinine level of 2 mg per deciliter or less, a prednisone requirement of 15 mg per day or less, and an azathioprine dose of 2 mg per kilogram day or less. Even with these criteria fulfilled, however, close observation and care are essential because the effect of pregnancy is unpredictable so that progressive reduction in renal function or even graft rejection may occur.

C. Pregnant patients who have undergone renal transplantation have to be considered at high risk. Special attention must be paid to renal function and the blood pressure status, with periodic evaluations to detect developing anemia, urinary tract infection, and bone disease. Advise a schedule of prenatal visits every two weeks (or more often, if indicated) until 32 weeks and then weekly thereafter until delivery. At each visit obtain a complete blood count, serum electrolyte and blood urea nitrogen levels, a 24 hour creatinine clearance, a urine protein level, and a midstream urine culture. Every six weeks determine the plasma protein, calcium, and phosphate levels, as well as cytomegalovirus and herpesvirus titers. Since the incidence of preterm delivery and intrauterine growth retardation is high, monitor fetal growth by serial ultrasonography (p 66). Immunosuppressive therapy should be maintained at prepregnancy levels. Watch for hepatic toxicity from azathioprine by checking liver function tests periodically and observing for jaundice; a reduction in dosage may prove necessary. Hospitalize as indicated.

D. Patients who have undergone renal transplantation and who are taking immunosuppressive therapy are particularly vulnerable to infection. Therefore, meticulous aseptic technique is even more critical than ordinarily in all surgical and obstetrical procedures undertaken. Antibiotics should be administered prophylactically before and immediately following these operations. Soft tissue dystocia (p 246) due to obstruction from the renal graft is uncommon, because the transplanted kidney is generally placed in the false pelvis adjacent to the iliac fossa (Fig. 1). Unless induction is undertaken because of failing renal function, the spontaneous onset of labor can be anticipated. Cesarean section may be indicated for maternal problems (renal compromise, pregnancy induced hypertension, or pelvic osteodystrophy, for example) or for fetal problems (such as fetoplacental insufficiency), but vaginal delivery ordinarily should be expected.

E. Most newborn infants have no problems. The offspring of transplant patients may develop thymic atrophy, leukopenia, bone marrow hypoplasia, septicemia, hypoglycemia, hypocalcemia, and adrenocortical insufficiency. In general, however, except perhaps for prematurity related complications, they tend to do well. Reports of long term follow-up thus far fail to show any lasting adverse effects from fetal intrauterine exposure to immunosuppressive therapy.

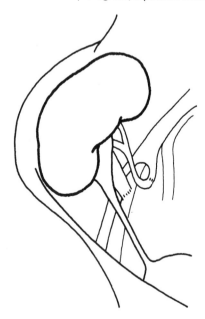

Figure 1 Grafted kidney in the iliac fossa on the psoas major muscle. Ureter is implanted in bladder, and the renal artery and vein are anastomosed to the internal iliac artery and external iliac vein, respectively.

PATIENT WHO HAS UNDERGONE KIDNEY GRAFTING OR IS ON DIALYSIS

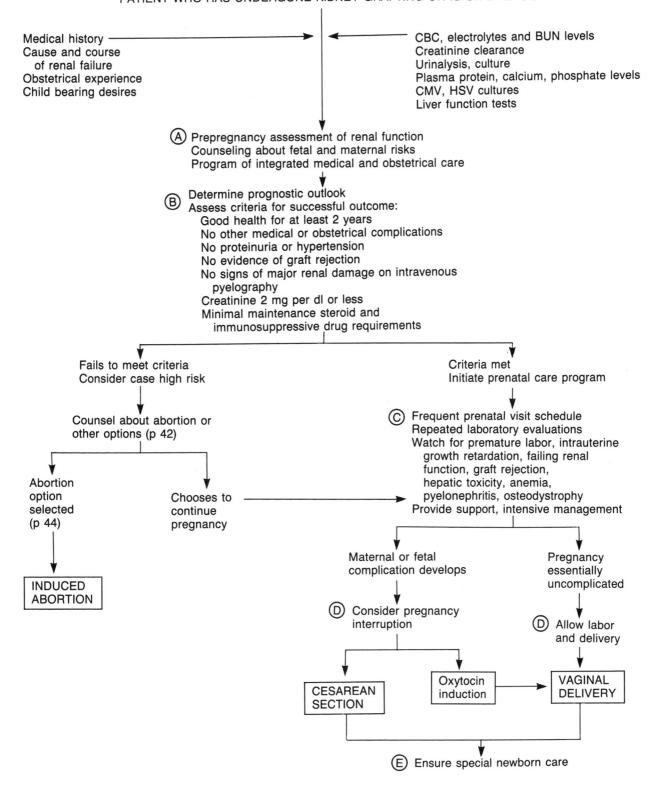

Medical history
Cause and course
  of renal failure
Obstetrical experience
Child bearing desires

CBC, electrolytes and BUN levels
Creatinine clearance
Urinalysis, culture
Plasma protein, calcium, phosphate levels
CMV, HSV cultures
Liver function tests

Ⓐ Prepregnancy assessment of renal function
  Counseling about fetal and maternal risks
  Program of integrated medical and obstetrical care

Ⓑ Determine prognostic outlook
  Assess criteria for successful outcome:
    Good health for at least 2 years
    No other medical or obstetrical complications
    No proteinuria or hypertension
    No evidence of graft rejection
    No signs of major renal damage on intravenous
      pyelography
    Creatinine 2 mg per dl or less
    Minimal maintenance steroid and
      immunosuppressive drug requirements

Fails to meet criteria
Consider case high risk

Criteria met
Initiate prenatal care program

Counsel about abortion or
other options (p 42)

Ⓒ Frequent prenatal visit schedule
  Repeated laboratory evaluations
  Watch for premature labor, intrauterine
    growth retardation, failing renal
    function, graft rejection,
    hepatic toxicity, anemia,
    pyelonephritis, osteodystrophy
  Provide support, intensive management

Abortion
option
selected
(p 44)

Chooses to
continue
pregnancy

Maternal or fetal
complication develops

Pregnancy
essentially
uncomplicated

INDUCED
ABORTION

Ⓓ Consider pregnancy
  interruption

Ⓓ Allow labor
  and delivery

CESAREAN
SECTION

Oxytocin
induction

VAGINAL
DELIVERY

Ⓔ Ensure special newborn care

References

Davison JM, Lindheimer MD. Pregnancy in renal transplant recipients. J Reprod Med 27:613, 1982.

Kobayashi H, Matsumoto Y, Otsubo O, et al. Successful pregnancy in a patient undergoing chronic hemodialysis. Obstet Gynecol 57:382, 1981.

Registration Committee of the European Dialysis and Transplant Association: Successful pregnancies in women treated by dialysis and kidney transplantation. Br J Obstet Gynaecol 87:839, 1980.

Whetham JCG, Cardella C, Harding M. Effect of pregnancy on graft function and graft survival in renal cadaver transplant patients. Am J Obstet Gynecol 145:193, 1983.

CARDIAC DISEASE

Henry Klapholz, M.D.

A. One should suspect heart disease in a gravida who develops exertion induced dyspnea, cyanosis, chest pain, palpitations, or arrhythmias; check carefully any patient with a history of rheumatic fever or limitations of activities or one in whom a heart murmur is heard. Many otherwise normal pregnant women have a widely split S_1 heart sound, a third sound, and a systolic murmur at the left sternal border. It is important to diagnose the condition early and to classify it on a functional basis in regard to limitation of activity. Any patient with marked limitation of activity because of respiratory or chest symptoms requires special intense cardiologic consultation, evaluation, and continued integrated care, beginning as early in pregnancy as possible and preferably before conception.

B. One should undertake periodic arterial blood gas determinations, especially if cyanosis or dyspnea is present. Chest x-ray examinations are done periodically to check for changing heart size and the development of pulmonary edema. Serial chest auscultation detects progressive left sided failure; right sided failure is reflected in pitting pretibial edema. Weigh the patient frequently to detect fluid retention. Electrocardiograms show rhythm disturbances; the axis changes associated with normal cardiac displacement result from the enlarging uterus. Cardiac catheterization studies are not generally required except in the cyanotic patient; echocardiography is safe in pregnancy and may prove diagnostically useful.

C. Fetal growth and development need to be evaluated, especially in patients with cyanotic heart disease. Increasing cardiac failure diminishes placental perfusion. If there is significant evidence of fetal jeopardy, consider delivery unless the fetus is too immature.

D. Reduce the gravida's physical activity as pregnancy advances; ensure periods of rest daily. The sodium intake should be restricted to 2 to 4 g per day. Give digitalis for congestive failure; diuretics may be required for congestive failure unresponsive to rest alone. Administer oxygen by controlled Venturi mask for cyanotic patients; oxygen is especially needed in patients with pulmonary hypertension. One might consider cardiac surgery for unresponsive critically ill patients, but this is rarely required. Limit weight gain to 15 pounds to minimize the cardiac workload.

E. If fetal or maternal deteriorization is evident, elective oxytocin induction may be an option. It has the advantage of orderly mobilization of staff, specialists, and facilities. Candidates should be easily inducible on the basis of a high Bishop score (p 182).

F. Vaginal delivery under regional block anesthesia is better than cesarean section because it ensures circulatory stability. The objectives of care in labor and delivery are to relieve pain, avoid the Valsalva maneuver (expulsive bearing down), maintain a stable blood volume by careful fluid administration and hemostasis, and accomplish delivery by elective low forceps technique. Balanced general anesthesia is preferred for delivery in gravidas with pulmonary congestion to control alveolar ventilation. A pulmonary arterial (Swan-Ganz) catheter is invaluable for management (Fig. 1). The prophylactic use of antibiotics is appropriate for these patients to prevent bacterial endocarditis if organic heart disease exists. Give ampicillin (1 g) and gentamycin (80 mg) intravenously at the time the patient enters the active phase and for three additional doses over the course of labor and in the immediate postpartum period.

G. The immediate postdelivery period is critical. The blood pressure must be maintained. Special attention is given to avoid blood loss from uterine atony and to prevent acute congestive failure from fluid overload. A Swan-Ganz or central venous pressure line is especially useful to guide fluid management. Appropriate counseling is essential post partum for contraception and future medical care. Children born to women with heart disease are themselves at increased risk of having cardiac problems.

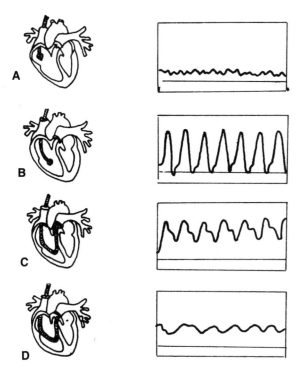

Figure 1 Swan-Ganz catheter pressure patterns as the tip is advanced. *A*, right atrium; *B*, right ventricle, with zero or negative baseline; *C*, pulmonary artery, with high diastolic baseline; *D*, pulmonary capillary wedge pressure shown when balloon occludes arterial flow.

References

Elkayam U, Gleicher N. Cardiac problems in pregnancy. I. Maternal aspects: The approach to the pregnant patient with heart disease. JAMA 251:2838, 1984.

Lang RM, Borow KM. Pregnancy and heart disease. Clin Perinatol 12:551, 1985.

Northcote RJ, Knight PV, Ballantyne D. Systolic murmurs in pregnancy: Value of echocardiographic assessment. Clin Cardiol 8:327, 1985.

SUSPICION OF HEART DISEASE

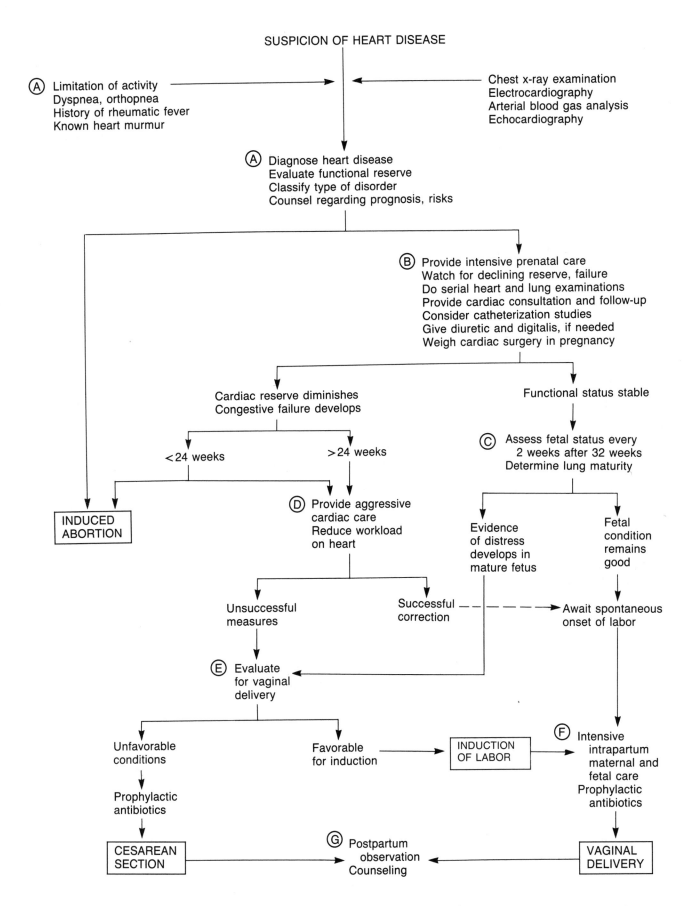

(A) Limitation of activity
Dyspnea, orthopnea
History of rheumatic fever
Known heart murmur

Chest x-ray examination
Electrocardiography
Arterial blood gas analysis
Echocardiography

(A) Diagnose heart disease
Evaluate functional reserve
Classify type of disorder
Counsel regarding prognosis, risks

(B) Provide intensive prenatal care
Watch for declining reserve, failure
Do serial heart and lung examinations
Provide cardiac consultation and follow-up
Consider catheterization studies
Give diuretic and digitalis, if needed
Weigh cardiac surgery in pregnancy

Cardiac reserve diminishes
Congestive failure develops

Functional status stable

<24 weeks   >24 weeks

(C) Assess fetal status every
2 weeks after 32 weeks
Determine lung maturity

INDUCED
ABORTION

(D) Provide aggressive
cardiac care
Reduce workload
on heart

Evidence
of distress
develops in
mature fetus

Fetal
condition
remains
good

Unsuccessful
measures

Successful
correction

Await spontaneous
onset of labor

(E) Evaluate
for vaginal
delivery

Unfavorable
conditions

Favorable
for induction

INDUCTION
OF LABOR

(F) Intensive
intrapartum
maternal and
fetal care
Prophylactic
antibiotics

Prophylactic
antibiotics

CESAREAN
SECTION

(G) Postpartum
observation
Counseling

VAGINAL
DELIVERY

Sugrue D, Blake S, Troy P, MacDonald D. Antibiotic prophylaxis against infective endocarditis after normal delivery: Is it necessary? Br Heart J 44:499, 1980.

Whittemore R, Hobbins JC, Engle MA. Pregnancy and its outcome in women with and without surgical treatment of congenital heart disease. Am J Cardiol 50:641, 1982.

SICKLE CELL DISEASE

Balmookoot Balgobin, M.D.

A. Episodic crises, recurrent infection, and refractory or hemolytic anemia suggest the diagnosis of sickle cell disease. Both mother and fetus may be at serious risk.

B. A positive sickle cell preparation test is useful for screening, but definitive diagnosis rests with hemoglobin electrophoresis. If the father also has sickle cell disease or the trait, the infant may be affected. Prenatal diagnosis is possible in some centers by studying fetal erythrocytes obtained by fetoscopy. With more recent advances, the diagnosis now can be made by restriction endonuclease analysis of fetal DNA applied to amniocytes obtained in midpregnancy by amniocentesis or to placental tissue obtained in the first trimester by chorionic villus biopsy (p 74).

C. Infection, severe anemia, and a sickle cell crisis pose a constant threat to the mother and fetus. All are aggravated by the stress of pregnancy. Spontaneous abortion and stillbirth account for a 30 to 40 percent incidence of fetal loss. Intrauterine growth retardation and placental insufficiency are common. The patient can be offered the options of abortion or of continuing the pregnancy under rigorous prenatal care and close fetal surveillance.

D. Evaluate at least every two weeks. Give folic acid supplements with iron, if indicated. Screen periodically for infection, including the urine for bacteriuria; if infection is found, treat aggressively. If the hematocrit level falls below 25 percent or the proportion of red blood cells that sickle exceeds 60 percent, give an exchange transfusion with packed red blood cells to reduce the likelihood of crisis and improve fetal salvage. Transfusion is not without risks, especially hepatitis and late alloimmunization. Hospitalize the patient for severe anemia or an acute crisis, and prophylactically late in pregnancy.

E. A sickle cell crisis is a serious complication. Manage aggressively with exchange transfusion, intravenous fluid administration, oxygen, and sedation; treat acidosis, infections, and congestive heart failure; anticoagulation is given for pulmonary emboli. Acute crises in the first or second trimester warrant consideration of induced abortion; in the third trimester, induction or cesarean section may be indicated.

F. Close fetal surveillance is essential, including serial ultrasonography, a biophysical profile, and nonstress tests, as well as oxytocin challenge tests, if indicated.

G. Vaginal delivery is preferred, if feasible. The patient should be kept warm, well oxygenated, and not oversedated. Anesthesia consultation is useful to ensure appropriate pain relief while minimizing risk.

H. Because most of the infant's hemoglobin is fetal, hemolytic anemia is generally not present at birth. Hypoxia will cause sickling in an affected infant only after the fetal hemoglobin has been replaced by hemoglobin S. Such infants should be kept well oxygenated.

References

Carache S, Scott J, Niebyl J, Bonds D. Management of sickle cell disease in pregnant patients. Obstet Gynecol 55:407, 1980.

Chang JC, Kan YW. A sensitive new prenatal test for sickle cell anemia. New Engl J Med 307:30, 1982.

Cunningham FG, Pritchard JA, Mason R. Pregnancy and sickle hemoglobinopathy: Results with and without prophylactic transfusions. Obstet Gynecol 62:419, 1983.

Miller JM, Horger EO, Key TC, Walker EM. Management of sickle hemoglobinopathies in pregnant patients. Am J Obstet Gynecol 141:237, 1981.

Old JM, Ward RHT, Karagozlu F, Petrou M, Modell B, Weatherall DJ. First trimester fetal diagnosis for haemoglobinopathies. Lancet 2:1414, 1982.

Sergeant GR. Sickle hemoglobin and pregnancy. Br Med J 287:628, 1983.

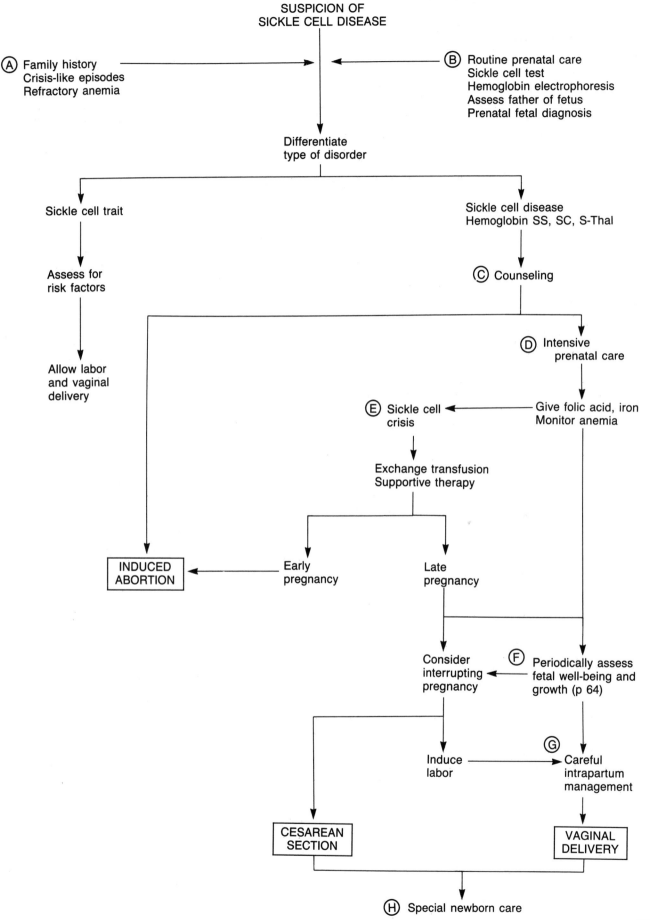

SUSPICION OF
SICKLE CELL DISEASE

(A) Family history
Crisis-like episodes
Refractory anemia

(B) Routine prenatal care
Sickle cell test
Hemoglobin electrophoresis
Assess father of fetus
Prenatal fetal diagnosis

Differentiate
type of disorder

Sickle cell trait

Sickle cell disease
Hemoglobin SS, SC, S-Thal

Assess for
risk factors

(C) Counseling

Allow labor
and vaginal
delivery

(D) Intensive
prenatal care

(E) Sickle cell
crisis

Give folic acid, iron
Monitor anemia

Exchange transfusion
Supportive therapy

INDUCED
ABORTION

Early
pregnancy

Late
pregnancy

Consider
interrupting
pregnancy

(F) Periodically assess
fetal well-being and
growth (p 64)

(G)
Induce
labor

Careful
intrapartum
management

CESAREAN
SECTION

VAGINAL
DELIVERY

(H) Special newborn care

107

THROMBOCYTOPENIC PURPURA

Balmookoot Balgobin, M.D.

A. Autoimmune or idiopathic thrombocytopenic purpura results from the destruction of platelets by circulating IgG antibodies that attach themselves to platelet antigens. IgG antibodies can cross the placenta to cause fetal thrombocytopenia. The patient with idiopathic thrombocytopenic purpura may be asymptomatic or suffer from easy bruising, petechiae, or mucosal bleeding.

B. The evaluation includes relevant laboratory studies to detect thrombocytopenia (<100,000 per ml), increased capillary fragility, poor clot retraction, and an increased (or normal) bleeding time.

C. Give prednisone (60 to 100 mg daily in divided doses) for bleeding or severe thrombocytopenia (platelet level <50,000 per ml) to correct abnormal capillary fragility and increase the platelet count. Reduce to the lowest dose needed to maintain hemostasis and the platelet count. Maternal prednisone may also protect the fetus somewhat. To minimize the risk of fetal bleeding during labor and delivery, give 10 to 20 mg of prednisone daily for 10 to 14 days before delivery.

D. Splenectomy is indicated if bleeding continues, but it should be avoided in pregnancy, if possible, because of the high associated maternal (9 to 10 percent) and fetal (25 to 30 percent) mortality rates.

E. If all else fails, platelet transfusion is given. If the mother's life is threatened, immunosuppressant therapy may be tried (e.g., cyclophosphamide, vincristine, or azathioprine), but they carry great fetal risk. Danazol has recently been reported to be of some value in unresponsive cases, but it may virilize the female fetus. The efficacy of high dose gammaglobulin therapy is as yet unknown in pregnancy.

F. Fetal thrombocytopenia subjects the fetus to hemorrhagic complications during the course of labor, especially intracerebral bleeding. If the fetus is at risk, therefore, cesarean section is in order. This applies for the splenectomy patient with persistent IgG antibodies that may adversely affect the fetus. Assess the fetal platelet count by means of scalp blood sampling during labor. If the fetal platelet count is above 50,000 per ml, labor and vaginal delivery can be permitted. Supplementary intravenous doses of steroids are indicated during labor and at delivery for patients who have been receiving them. Platelet transfusion may be necessary for hemostasis. The concentration of circulating antiplatelet antibody in the maternal serum frequently reflects the severity of fetal thrombocytopenia; its value is limited in the management of labor because it is not entirely consistent in this regard.

G. Thrombocytopenia in the newborn infant is self-limiting, the platelet level returning to normal in three to four weeks. The lowest counts occur at about the sixth day. Daily counts should be obtained during the first week of life. If petechiae or purpura develops, steroid therapy is given. Reduce the dosage to the lowest amount to maintain the desired effect and continue for three weeks. Active bleeding requires platelet transfusion and exchange transfusion. Splenectomy is contraindicated.

References

Cines DB, Dusak, B, Tomaski A, Menutti M, Schreiber AD. Immune thrombocytopenic purpura and pregnancy. New Engl J Med 306:826, 1982.

Karpatkin M, Porges RF, Karpatkin S. Platelet counts in infants of women with autoimmune thrombocytopenia. New Engl J Med 305:936, 1981.

Kelton JG, Innwood MJ, Barr RM, Effer SB, Hunter D, Wilson WE, Gainsburg DA, Power PF. The prenatal prediction of thrombocytopenia in infants of mothers with clinically diagnosed immune thrombocytopenia. Am J Obstet Gynecol 144: 449, 1982.

Scott JR, Cruikshank DP, Kochenour NK, Pitkin RM, Warenski JC. Fetal platelet counts in the obstetric management of immunologic thrombocytopenic purpura. Am J Obstet Gynecol 136:495, 1980.

Scott JR, Rote NS, Cruikshank DP. Antiplatelet antibodies and platelet counts in pregnancies complicated by autoimmune thrombocytopenic purpura. Am J Obstet Gynecol 145:932, 1983.

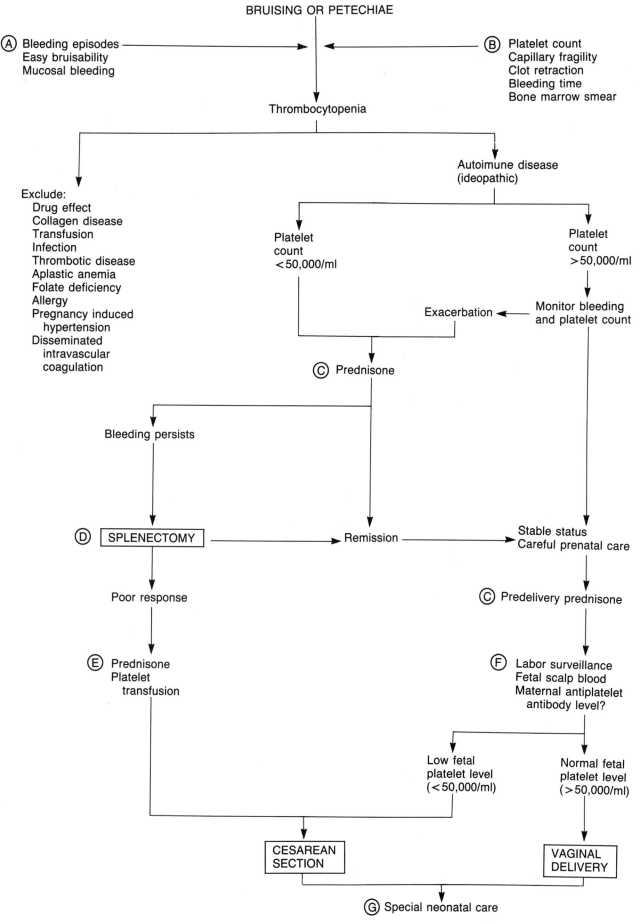

BRUISING OR PETECHIAE

(A) Bleeding episodes
Easy bruisability
Mucosal bleeding

(B) Platelet count
Capillary fragility
Clot retraction
Bleeding time
Bone marrow smear

Thrombocytopenia

Exclude:
    Drug effect
    Collagen disease
    Transfusion
    Infection
    Thrombotic disease
    Aplastic anemia
    Folate deficiency
    Allergy
    Pregnancy induced
        hypertension
    Disseminated
        intravascular
        coagulation

Autoimmune disease
(ideopathic)

Platelet
count
<50,000/ml

Platelet
count
>50,000/ml

Exacerbation ← Monitor bleeding
and platelet count

(C) Prednisone

Bleeding persists

(D) SPLENECTOMY → Remission → Stable status
Careful prenatal care

Poor response

(C) Predelivery prednisone

(E) Prednisone
Platelet
transfusion

(F) Labor surveillance
Fetal scalp blood
Maternal antiplatelet
antibody level?

Low fetal
platelet level
(<50,000/ml)

Normal fetal
platelet level
(>50,000/ml)

CESAREAN
SECTION

VAGINAL
DELIVERY

(G) Special neonatal care

HEREDITARY HEMORRHAGIC DISORDER

Balmookoot Balgobin, M.D.

A. Any unusual bleeding or a family history of a bleeding disorder should serve to alert one to the possibility of a hereditary hemorrhagic problem. It requires careful investigation. Clotting and prothrombin times may be normal. The partial thromboplastin time is a more sensitive indicator. However, even if the results of these tests are normal, specific assays of coagulation factors should be done.

B. Von Willebrand's disease is manifested by easy bruising and bleeding, epistaxis, gastrointestinal bleeding, and menorrhagia. Reductions in factor VIII activity (VIIIC), factor VIII related antigen (VIIIR:Ag), and factor VIII related ristocene cofactor (VIIIRCo) activity occur with a prolonged bleeding time, a positive tourniquet test, and decreased platelet adhesiveness. Most cases are characterized by mild manifestations. Offspring are variably affected but seldom seriously unless the parents are homozygous.

C. Both hemophilia A (factor VIIIC deficiency) and hemophilia B (Christmas disease, factor IX deficiency) are sex linked disorders. Unless homozygous, females are usually asymptomatic. Male fetuses are more likely to manifest the disease. The carrier state for hemophilia A shows a reduced ratio of factor VIIIC to factor VIIIR:Ag (ratio 1:2). No comparable indicator exists for carriers of hemophilia B; they can be detected with reasonable confidence only on the basis of factor IX assays in about 25 percent of the cases. With the rapidly advancing field of DNA technology, carriers of hemophilia A and hemophilia B can now be identified by DNA analysis.

D. Males affected by hemophilia suffer life threatening bleeding with resulting soft tissue and joint damage. Amniocentesis or chorionic villus biopsy for chromosome analysis will identify the fetal gender. A male fetus has a 50 percent chance of being affected. Carrier gravidas may elect to terminate pregnancies in which a male fetus is identified as being affected.

E. Fetoscopy for direct fetal blood sampling can identify the unaffected male fetus and avert abortion. More exciting are recent advances in DNA analysis that enable some centers to determine the fetal gender as well as the hemophiliac status directly from tissue obtained by chorionic villus biopsy or cells obtained by means of amniocentesis.

F. Serial assays of the relevant factors should be done monthly throughout pregnancy. The levels of these coagulation factors normally tend to rise as gestation advances. If the level is below 50 percent activity, consider transfusion of fresh frozen plasma or cryoprecipitate prior to surgery or induction of labor as well as during labor and post partum. Transfusion may also be indicated at any time bleeding occurs. Note that cryoprecipitate lacks factor IX; if it is specifically needed, give fresh frozen plasma or factor IX concentrate instead. Avoid aspirin use because it interferes with platelet function.

G. There are no reports of fetal hemorrhage during labor in these cases. This makes the vaginal route preferable for delivery. Intervention by cesarean section is strictly reserved for obstetrical indications.

H. Daily monitoring of coagulation factors is necessary for at least seven days after delivery. Maintain the coagulation factor assay levels above 50 percent by appropriate transfusion, if necessary. Bleeding from an incision or episiotomy wound also requires transfusion. The infant should be screened for evidence of disease, deferring circumcision until it has been ruled out reliably.

References

Caldwell DC, Williamson RA, Goldsmith JC. Hereditary coagulopathies in pregnancy. Clin Obstet Gynecol 28:53, 1985.

Gianelli F, Choo KH, Winship PR, et al. Characterization and use of an intragenic polymorphic marker for detection of carriers of haemophilia B (factor IX deficiency). Lancet 1:239, 1984.

Hoyer LW, Carta CA, Mahoney MJ. Detection of hemophilia carriers during pregnancy. Blood 60:1407, 1982.

Lipton RA, Ayromlooi J, Coller BS. Severe von Willebrand's disease during labor and delivery. JAMA 248:1355, 1982.

Oberle I, Camerino G, Heilig R, et al. Genetic screening for hemophilia A (classic hemophilia) with a polymorphic DNA probe. New Engl J Med 312:682, 1985.

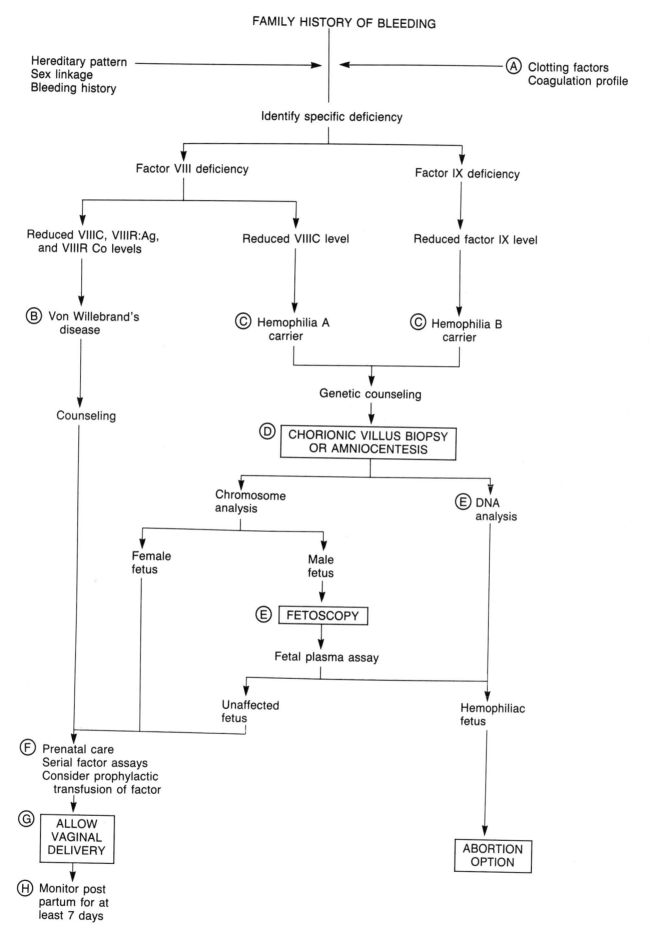

FAMILY HISTORY OF BLEEDING

Hereditary pattern
Sex linkage
Bleeding history

Ⓐ Clotting factors
Coagulation profile

Identify specific deficiency

Factor VIII deficiency

Factor IX deficiency

Reduced VIIIC, VIIIR:Ag,
and VIIIR Co levels

Reduced VIIIC level

Reduced factor IX level

Ⓑ Von Willebrand's
disease

Ⓒ Hemophilia A
carrier

Ⓒ Hemophilia B
carrier

Counseling

Genetic counseling

Ⓓ CHORIONIC VILLUS BIOPSY
OR AMNIOCENTESIS

Chromosome
analysis

Ⓔ DNA
analysis

Female
fetus

Male
fetus

Ⓔ FETOSCOPY

Fetal plasma assay

Unaffected
fetus

Hemophiliac
fetus

Ⓕ Prenatal care
Serial factor assays
Consider prophylactic
transfusion of factor

Ⓖ ALLOW
VAGINAL
DELIVERY

ABORTION
OPTION

Ⓗ Monitor post
partum for at
least 7 days

ANEMIA

Balmookoot Balgobin, M.D.

A. Screening for anemia should be done at the first prenatal visit, at 28 to 32 weeks, and again at 36 to 38 weeks. On each occasion, determine the hemoglobin and hematocrit levels, red cell count, blood cell indices, and differential white count. A routine sickle cell preparation is useful in black women once during the course of pregnancy. Urinalysis helps reveal infection (p 164). If the serum is icteric, evaluate for liver disease and hemolytic anemia.

B. Iron and folic acid prophylaxis is warranted in all obstetrical patients because of gestational hemodilution and increased nutritional demands. Gravidas with hematocrit levels below 30 percent (or a hemoglobin level below 10 g per deciliter) should be evaluated. This also applies to those who are refractory to prophylactic treatment. Be alert to patients who are noncompliant in regard to the treatment prescribed for them. Also inquire into and evaluate for poor diet, vomiting, malabsorption, bleeding, chronic disease, drug dependency, liver disease, hemoglobinopathy, and multiple pregnancy.

C. Study the peripheral blood smear, serum iron level, total iron binding capacity, percentage of iron saturation, serum and erythrocyte folate levels, and serum vitamin B_{12} level. Red cell indices may be helpful guides to the type of anemia and its management. Use the serum ferritin level to assess iron stores and hemoglobin electrophoresis to identify hemoglobinopathy.

D. Iron deficiency anemia is common in pregnancy. Microcytosis precedes hypochromia. Clinical manifestations are rare. Typically the mean corpuscular volume (MCV) is less than 80, mean corpuscular hemoglobin concentration (MCHC) less than 30 percent, serum iron less than 50, iron saturation less than 15 percent, and serum ferritin less than 10 ng per milliliter.

E. Folic acid deficiency is much less common. Pancytopenia may be intense. The red cells are macrocytic; megaloblasts are seen in buffy coat smears or the peripheral blood. The MCV is greater than 100, serum folate less than 3 ng per deciliter, and red cell folate less than 150 mg per deciliter. Smears of the peripheral blood show more than 3 percent hypersegmented neutrophils.

F. Infection is a common cause of hypochromic microcytic anemia with low serum iron levels and total iron binding capacity. Unless infection is identified and treated, the anemia generally fails to respond to hematinic therapy.

G. Iron deficiency anemia is best treated with a good diet and oral doses of iron (ferrous sulfate, 300 mg three times daily) combined with prophylactic oral doses of folic acid, 1 mg daily. Follow the response with sequential reticulocyte counts and peripheral blood smears. The intravenous or intramuscular administration of iron has no real advantage except in patients with vomiting, intolerance to oral iron therapy, or a malabsorption syndrome. Folic acid deficiency is treated with oral doses of folic acid, 1 to 5 mg daily. Iron is given concurrently. Vitamin B_{12} deficiency should be ruled out first by assessing the serum vitamin B_{12} level even though such deficiency is rare; specific treatment consists of vitamin B_{12} injections. If blood transfusion is indicated, packed red blood cells are used; avoid cardiac failure by careful surveillance or exchange transfusion.

References

Harrison KA. Anemia, malaria and sickle cell disease. Clin Obstet Gynaecol 9:445, 1982.

Kaneshige E. Serum ferritin as an assessment of iron stores and other parameters during pregnancy. Obstet Gynecol 57:238, 1981.

Shojania AM. Folic acid and B_{12} deficiency in pregnancy and in the neonatal period. Clin Perinatol 11:433, 1984.

Taylor DJ. Prophylaxis and treatment of anaemia during pregnancy. Clin Obstet Gynaecol 8:297, 1981.

Taylor DJ, Mallen C, McDougall N, Lind T. Effect of iron supplementation on serum ferritin levels during and after pregnancy. Br J Obstet Gynaecol 89:1011, 1982.

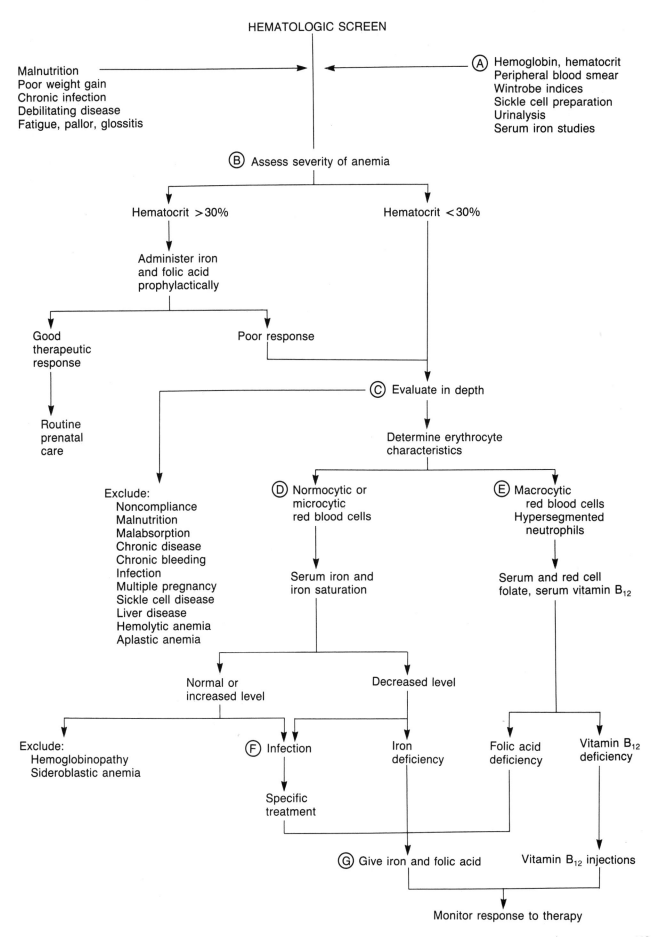

HEMATOLOGIC SCREEN

Malnutrition
Poor weight gain
Chronic infection
Debilitating disease
Fatigue, pallor, glossitis

(A) Hemoglobin, hematocrit
Peripheral blood smear
Wintrobe indices
Sickle cell preparation
Urinalysis
Serum iron studies

(B) Assess severity of anemia

Hematocrit >30%

Hematocrit <30%

Administer iron
and folic acid
prophylactically

Good
therapeutic
response

Poor response

Routine
prenatal
care

(C) Evaluate in depth

Determine erythrocyte
characteristics

Exclude:
 Noncompliance
 Malnutrition
 Malabsorption
 Chronic disease
 Chronic bleeding
 Infection
 Multiple pregnancy
 Sickle cell disease
 Liver disease
 Hemolytic anemia
 Aplastic anemia

(D) Normocytic or
microcytic
red blood cells

(E) Macrocytic
red blood cells
Hypersegmented
neutrophils

Serum iron and
iron saturation

Serum and red cell
folate, serum vitamin B$_{12}$

Normal or
increased level

Decreased level

Exclude:
 Hemoglobinopathy
 Sideroblastic anemia

(F) Infection

Iron
deficiency

Folic acid
deficiency

Vitamin B$_{12}$
deficiency

Specific
treatment

(G) Give iron and folic acid

Vitamin B$_{12}$ injections

Monitor response to therapy

113

COAGULOPATHY

Balmookoot Balgobin, M.D.

A. Consumption coagulopathy (disseminated intravascular coagulation) rarely develops spontaneously in pregnancy. It is usually associated with some apparent predisposing condition, such as prolonged retention of a dead fetus (p 226), abruptio placentae (p 92), septic abortion (p 36), or pregnancy induced hypertension (p 86). Survivors of catastrophic amniotic fluid embolism (p 132) may also develop intense, life threatening coagulopathy.

B. Observation of clot formation, retraction, and dissolution offers a simple means for obtaining useful information concerning fibrinogen, platelets, and fibrin degradation products; the last reflect the process of fibrinolysis. The fibrinogen level, prothrombin time, and partial thromboplastin time are valuable tests along with a peripheral blood smear and platelet count. Deficiencies of specific coagulation factors can be determined by laboratory analysis as well.

C. With a retained dead fetus (p 226), consumption coagulopathy may develop slowly and silently. It can be detected only by serial laboratory studies. The development of the process is reflected well in advance of clinical symptoms by falling fibrinogen levels.

D. Although heparin therapy is controversial, it may block the coagulation process in the patient who has prolonged retention of a dead fetus, especially in the absence of overt bleeding. Coagulation factors and platelet counts improve spontaneously once the process has been arrested. After correction, steps can be taken to empty the uterus. One must avoid trauma and pay meticulous attention to hemostasis. Currently heparin is not recommended as treatment for any other coagulopathy in obstetrics.

E. The patient with acute bleeding resulting from disseminated intravascular coagulation must be monitored carefully. Blood volume and tissue perfusion are maintained by replacing large volumes of blood and fluids rapidly to prevent cardiovascular collapse while observing for and guarding against congestive heart failure by central venous pressure or Swan-Ganz catheter monitoring.

F. The main goal of therapy is to correct the underlying condition. If this cannot be done expeditiously, one may try to correct the hypofibrinogenemia temporarily by giving cryoprecipitate or fresh frozen plasma that also contains factor V and factor VIII. If there is significant thrombocytopenia, the patient can be treated with platelet transfusion. The risk of serum hepatitis has to be weighed in the treatment plan. It may also be necessary to consider giving fresh frozen plasma and platelet transfusion to provide hemostasis in patients with coagulopathy who require surgery (e.g., cesarean section) and who are actively bleeding (or can be expected to bleed).

G. The specific therapy for most patients with pregnancy related coagulopathy consists of uterine evacuation. Once the source of the underlying problem is corrected (by uterine evacuation or control of sepsis), the accelerated coagulation mechanism and spiral of consumption of coagulation factors cease. With intact liver function, coagulation factors are synthesized rapidly, normal function resumes, and bleeding stops. In fulminant cases, when all other measures fail, continued fresh blood replacement in large volumes and surgical hemostasis (such as internal iliac ligation) may be in order.

References

Killam A. Amniotic fluid embolism. Clin Obstet Gynecol 28:32, 1985.

Price TM, Baker VV, Cefalo RC. Amniotic fluid embolism: Three case reports with a review of the literature. Obstet Gynecol Surv 40:462, 1985.

Romero R, Copel JA, Hobbins JC. Intrauterine fetal demise and hemostatic failure: The fetal death syndrome. Clin Obstet Gynecol 28:24, 1985.

Sher G, Statland BE. Abruptio placentae with coagulopathy: A rational basis of management. Clin Obstet Gynecol 28:15, 1985.

Talbert LM, Blatt PM. Disseminated intravascular coagulation in obstetrics. Clin Obstet Gynecol 22:889, 1979.

White PF, Coe V, Dworsky WA, Margolis A. Disseminated intravascular coagulation following midtrimester abortions. Anesthesiology 58:99, 1983.

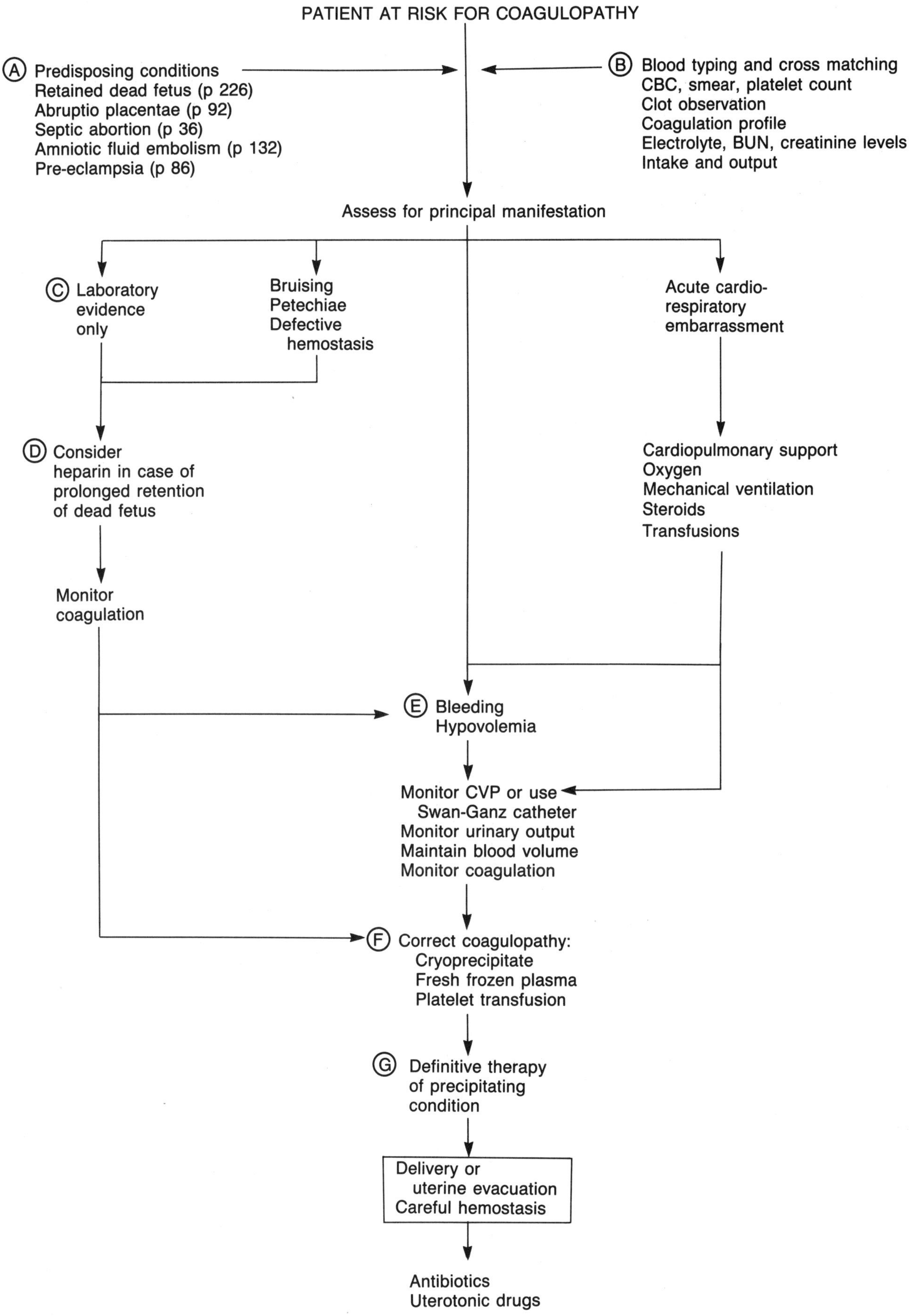

PATIENT AT RISK FOR COAGULOPATHY

Ⓐ Predisposing conditions
Retained dead fetus (p 226)
Abruptio placentae (p 92)
Septic abortion (p 36)
Amniotic fluid embolism (p 132)
Pre-eclampsia (p 86)

Ⓑ Blood typing and cross matching
CBC, smear, platelet count
Clot observation
Coagulation profile
Electrolyte, BUN, creatinine levels
Intake and output

Assess for principal manifestation

Ⓒ Laboratory
evidence
only

Bruising
Petechiae
Defective
hemostasis

Acute cardio-
respiratory
embarrassment

Ⓓ Consider
heparin in case of
prolonged retention
of dead fetus

Cardiopulmonary support
Oxygen
Mechanical ventilation
Steroids
Transfusions

Monitor
coagulation

Ⓔ Bleeding
Hypovolemia

Monitor CVP or use
Swan-Ganz catheter
Monitor urinary output
Maintain blood volume
Monitor coagulation

Ⓕ Correct coagulopathy:
Cryoprecipitate
Fresh frozen plasma
Platelet transfusion

Ⓖ Definitive therapy
of precipitating
condition

Delivery or
uterine evacuation
Careful hemostasis

Antibiotics
Uterotonic drugs

THYROID DISORDER

Machelle M. Seibel, M.D.
Jeffrey R. Garber, M.D.

A. Pregnancy may obscure or mimic characteristic symptoms and physical findings of hypo- or hyperthyroidism, and the laboratory test parameters for diagnosing these conditions in the nonpregnant state are not necessarily applicable in gestation. Be alert for an obstetrical history of fetal wastage from abortion, preterm delivery, and perinatal mortality.

B. The common physical manifestations of thyroid disease may be masked by pregnancy, just as the physical signs of pregnancy may resemble those of thyroid dysfunction, including thyroid enlargement and bruit, widened pulse pressure, increased heart rate, palmar erythema, and warm moist palms. Not otherwise found in an uncomplicated pregnancy are the characteristic ocular signs of stare, lid lag, pretibial myxedema, exophthalmos, onycholysis, and hip and shoulder myopathy.

C. Interpret the results of laboratory tests with caution in pregnancy. The basal metabolic rate normally rises well into the abnormal range. Radioiodine cannot be used for diagnosis or treatment because it is readily taken up by the fetal thyroid from about 12 to 14 weeks' gestational age. The diagnosis is made by estimating the blood levels of free thyroxine (T_4), free triiodothyronine (T_3) and the free T_4 or T_3 index. The last are determined by multiplying the total T_4 or total T_3 by the T_3 resin uptake. Thyroid stimulating hormone (TSH) and antithyroid antibodies are used to evaluate for hypothyroidism. Normal pregnancy affects the results of some of these tests. Since the thyroxin binding globulin (TBG) level rises, T_3 and T_4 levels increase, mostly bound to TBG; T_3 uptake falls owing to an excess of unsaturated TBG binding sites. Active T_3 and T_4 levels, however, remain normal.

D. Gravidas who develop hypothyroidism may or may not show reduced levels of T_4. A low T_3 uptake with a normal or low normal T_4 level is suggestive. Primary hypothyroidism shows an elevated TSH level and often a positive antithyroid antibody test.

E. As in the nonpregnant adult, primary hypothyroidism in pregnancy is treated with thyroid replacement. Thyroxine is the treatment of choice. The dosage is adjusted by following the clinical response and changing TSH, T_3 uptake, and T_4 levels.

F. In the hyperthyroid gravida the free T_4, total T_3 and T_4, and TBG blood levels increase. As a result, T_3 uptake is usually normal or increased. The diagnosis rests on a combination of clinical signs, symptoms, and laboratory analyses. The tests also provide a means for assessing the severity and the response to therapy. In the case of Graves' disease, measuring stimulator immunoglobulin (LATS, TSI, TBII) levels may help gauge disease activity.

G. Propylthiouracil (PTU) is used to treat the gravida with hyperthyroidism. Use the lowest possible dosage to reduce the risk of fetal goiter and hypothyroidism. Patients with pre-existing thyrotoxicosis may improve in late pregnancy. It is necessary, therefore, to reduce therapy accordingly. Avoid iodides, especially for long term usage. Use caution if it is necessary to give propranolol for thyrotoxic symptoms because of uterine tetany and neonatal effects. Determine the T_3, T_4, and T_3 uptake periodically to help adjust treatment. Subtotal thyroidectomy is reserved for patients who are resistant or significantly allergic to suppressive drugs. Life threatening thyroid storm may be precipitated by labor or cesarean section. Integrate acute management with PTU, cortisol, fluids, and hypothermia, as well as propranolol and iodides, if indicated. Test the newborn infant for signs of thyroid dysfunction.

H. After delivery, patients with thyroid nodules of indeterminate nature should undergo radioactive iodine scan to identify a "hot" or autonomous nodule indicating no risk of malignant disease.

References

Burrow GN. The management of thyrotoxicosis in pregnancy. New Engl J Med 313:562, 1985.

Geelhoed GW. Surgery of the endocrine glands in pregnancy. Clin Obstet Gynecol 26:865, 1983.

Ingbar SH. The thyroid gland. In: Wilson JD, Foster DW (Editors). Williams Textbook of Endocrinology. 7th ed. Philadelphia: W.B. Saunders, 1985.

Mestman JH. Thyroid disease in pregnancy. Clin Perinatol 12:651, 1985.

Wall JR, Kuroki T. Immunologic factors in thyroid disease. Med Clin North Am 69:1913, 1985.

SUSPICION OF THYROID DISEASE

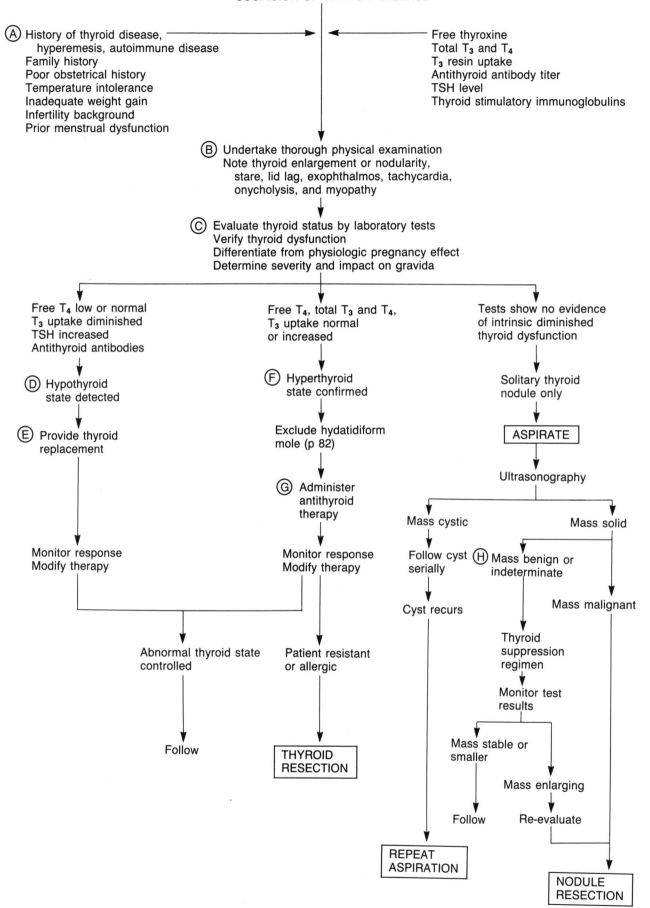

Ⓐ History of thyroid disease,
   hyperemesis, autoimmune disease
Family history
Poor obstetrical history
Temperature intolerance
Inadequate weight gain
Infertility background
Prior menstrual dysfunction

Free thyroxine
Total T₃ and T₄
T₃ resin uptake
Antithyroid antibody titer
TSH level
Thyroid stimulatory immunoglobulins

Ⓑ Undertake thorough physical examination
Note thyroid enlargement or nodularity,
stare, lid lag, exophthalmos, tachycardia,
onycholysis, and myopathy

Ⓒ Evaluate thyroid status by laboratory tests
Verify thyroid dysfunction
Differentiate from physiologic pregnancy effect
Determine severity and impact on gravida

Free T₄ low or normal
T₃ uptake diminished
TSH increased
Antithyroid antibodies

Free T₄, total T₃ and T₄,
T₃ uptake normal
or increased

Tests show no evidence
of intrinsic diminished
thyroid dysfunction

Ⓓ Hypothyroid
   state detected

Ⓕ Hyperthyroid
   state confirmed

Solitary thyroid
nodule only

Ⓔ Provide thyroid
   replacement

Exclude hydatidiform
mole (p 82)

ASPIRATE

Ultrasonography

Ⓖ Administer
   antithyroid
   therapy

Mass cystic

Mass solid

Monitor response
Modify therapy

Monitor response
Modify therapy

Follow cyst
serially

Ⓗ Mass benign or
   indeterminate

Cyst recurs

Mass malignant

Abnormal thyroid state
controlled

Patient resistant
or allergic

Thyroid
suppression
regimen

Monitor test
results

Follow

THYROID
RESECTION

Mass stable or
smaller

Mass enlarging

Follow

Re-evaluate

REPEAT
ASPIRATION

NODULE
RESECTION

SEIZURE DISORDER

Jerold M. Carlson, M.D., M.P.H.

A. Seizure disorders should be classified initially as obstetrically related or intercurrent on the basis of a pre-existing disease related to the central nervous system (p 120), endocrinopathy, electrolyte imbalance, neoplasm, drug or drug withdrawal, trauma, infection, or vascular accident. Differentiate pseudoseizures due to syncope, hysteria, or hyperventilation. Consider any gravida who has a generalized convulsion in the last trimester to have eclampsia until proved otherwise; this applies especially if there is no history of seizures or hypertension and proteinuria exist. The diagnosis may be complicated if the severe hypertension produces a secondary intracranial hemorrhage. The absence of characteristic signs of pregnancy induced hypertension (p 86), such as hypertension, proteinuria, hyperreflexia, and retinal vasospasm, makes another cause likely.

B. If the seizure was observed, a description is sometimes very useful for diagnosis, concentrating on where it started, how it progressed, whether it was focalized, the associated mental status, antecedent vomiting, headache, fever, visual changes, and postictal confusion or paralysis. Obtain a detailed probing history to detect underlying neurologic, liver, renal, and pulmonary diseases and drug exposure. This may not be possible, given the patient's postictal state and the need to expedite acute care, but information is often available from the family or friends. Physical examination should be thorough with special attention to neurologic and ocular findings. Laboratory studies should include a baseline complete blood count, platelet count, blood sugar, urea nitrogen, and serum electrolyte levels, and a urinalysis. Unless there is evidence of elevated intracranial pressure, undertake lumbar puncture to diagnose meningitis or gross subarachnoid hemorrhage. The cerebrospinal fluid protein level may be somewhat elevated with eclampsia, but not with milder forms of pregnancy induced hypertension. Electroencephalography may be needed to diagnose epilepsy. Skull x-ray views, a brain scan, a computed tomographic scan, and a cerebral angiogram may also be required to make a definitive diagnosis of an intrinsic central nervous system disorder (p 120), such as aneurysm, anomaly, neoplasm, thromboembolism, or bleeding.

C. Medical management should be instituted to correct the underlying etiology, if it is known. Eclamptic seizure therapy involves anticonvulsant control, maintaining oxygenation and the cardiovascular status, and proceeding as soon as feasible to deliver the fetus (if still in utero). Status epilepticus demands intensive effort to prevent permanent damage. Establish a good airway for ventilation and prevention of aspiration. Correct fluid and electrolyte imbalance quickly. Give appropriate medications, such as Valium, Dilantin, and phenobarbital, as needed. If these are ineffectual, consider general anesthesia. Once the patient is controlled, begin a long term maintenance regimen, taking advantage of neurologic consultation for guidance. Medication needs may change as pregnancy advances. Monitor drug levels at least monthly during gestation and post partum to ensure adequate coverage. Dilantin teratogenicity yields facial dysmorphism, microcephaly, and developmental delay. Thus, if the patient has been free of idiopathic seizures for years, consider stopping the drug before conception, but continue it if there is still a risk of convulsions, giving vitamin K supplements to counter the effect. Metabolic disorder, infection, drug withdrawal, and tumor are managed by measures aimed at the specific causative problem.

D. Cesarean section is generally indicated only for obstetrical reasons. Vaginal delivery is preferable except in cases of increased intracranial pressure in which labor may be interdicted. Concern about the effects of the Valsalva maneuver during second stage expulsive efforts can be assuaged by use of effective regional block anesthesia to inhibit reflex bearing down. The second stage can be allowed to proceed long enough for the fetal presenting part to reach the perineum, where the use of atraumatic low forceps technique can effect delivery with relative safety.

References

Barrett JM, Van Hooydonk JE, Boehm FH. Pregnancy-related rupture of arterial aneurysms. Obstet Gynecol Surv 37:557, 1982.

Dalessio DJ. Seizure disorders and pregnancy. N Engl J Med 312:559, 1985.

Graham JG. Neurological complications of pregnancy and anaesthesia. Clin Obstet Gynaecol 9:333, 1982.

Greenspoon JS, Paul RH. Paraplegia and quadriplegia: Special considerations during pregnancy and labor and delivery. Am J Obstet Gynecol 155:738, 1986.

PATIENT WITH SEIZURE OR HISTORY OF SEIZURE

Ⓐ Personal history of convulsion ———————
Prior central nervous system disease
Electrolyte imbalance
Drug use or abuse
Head trauma
Infection
Vascular accident

————— CBC, differential
Sedimentation rate
Drug screen
Serum electrolyte levels, chemistries
Arterial blood gas levels
Catecholamine level, VMA level
Spinal fluid analysis

Ⓑ Obtain description of convulsion,
    site of onset, progression pattern,
    antecedent events, status, symptoms
  Probe history in detail
  Thorough physical examination
  Neurologic and ocular examination

  Intensive laboratory survey
  Lumbar puncture for spinal fluid study

  Consider electroencephalography,
    skull x-ray examination, brain scan, computed
    tomography, angiography as needed
    for definitive diagnosis

  Establish differential diagnosis

Ⓒ Diagnose
  eclampsia
  (p 86)

Manage
  aggressively
Establish airway
Stop seizure
Control blood pressure
Stabilize
Consider timely
  delivery
  by cesarean
  section

Ⓒ Diagnose epilepsy

Ensure airway patency
Stop seizure
Undertake
  anticonvulsive
  regimen
Monitor drug
  levels
Consider potential
  teratogenicity

Rule out
pseudoseizure

Consider:
  Syncope
  Hysteria
  Hyperventilation

Reassure
Support

Diagnose central nervous system
  disease or central nervous
  system manifestation of systemic
  disorder
Provide specific therapy

Consider:
  Pheochromocytoma
  Metabolic disorder
  Berry aneurysm
  Meningitis
  Skull trauma
  Intracranial hemorrhage
  Cerebral vein thrombosis
  Hypertensive encephalopathy
  Water intoxication
  Thrombotic
    thrombocytopenic purpura
  Anesthetic drug toxicity

Ⓓ Conduct labor and delivery management
    according to obstetrical indications
  Maintain astute surveillance in labor
  Weigh need to avoid bearing down
  Use regional block as indicated
  Shorten second stage with low forceps

NEUROLOGIC DISORDER

Jerold M. Carlson, M.D., M.P.H.

A. Neurologic symptoms that may arise in pregnancy range from headaches and neurologic deficits to convulsions and coma. Probe for current medications, exposure to toxic agents, prior neurologic and vascular disorders, endocrinopathy, electrolyte imbalance, trauma, infection, and drug abuse.

B. A neurologic examination, in addition to laboratory studies, such as a complete blood count, electrolyte levels, urinalysis, sickle cell preparation, serology for syphilis, and chemistries, should be done to rule out an organic disorder.

C. Peripheral neuropathies are seen in pregnancy or post partum. Bell's (facial nerve) palsy, the carpal tunnel syndrome (median nerve), meralgia paresthetica (lateral cutaneous nerve), brachial plexus neuropathy, foot drop (nerve trunk compression during difficult labor or from stirrup positioning), and femoral neuropathy (retractor pressure during cesarean section) are usually self-limited.

D. Headaches may be vascular, muscular, infectious, or neoplastic or may be due to pregnancy induced hypertension (p 86). The cause is often elucidated in the history, physical, and neurologic examination. If headaches are persistent, unresponsive to mild analgesia, or concurrent with neurologic manifestations, they warrant expeditious evaluation and expert care.

E. Cerebrovascular disease from ischemia, hemorrhage, or thrombosis with infarction may be preceded by headache, nausea and vomiting, hypertension, visual disturbances, mental confusion, and paresthesias. Suspect subarachnoid hemorrhage in a patient with fever, leukocytosis, proteinuria, hypertension, and erythrocytes in the cerebrospinal fluid. Rule out abruptio placentae (p 92), disseminated intravascular coagulation (p 114), eclampsia, and subacute bacterial endocarditis. Computed tomographic scanning and cerebral angiography are diagnostic. Venous thrombosis is generally treated with anticoagulants and anticonvulsants, whereas corrective neurosurgery is reserved for bleeding from a ruptured aneurysm.

F. If an intracranial neoplasm is suspected, electroencephalography, computed tomographic scanning, and angiography may be helpful in making the diagnosis. Emergency neurosurgical extirpation may be indicated if the tumor is deemed malignant and still potentially operable or is causing serious symptoms. Weigh a decision to treat against the benefits of delay in order to deliver (or induce abortion).

G. Multiple sclerosis is characterized by exacerbations and remissions, but it is not believed to influence pregnancy or to be affected by pregnancy, although puerperal relapse is common. The diagnosis is based on the neurologic history and the physical examination. Weakness, diplopia, and sensory changes occur in an unpredictable chronic course extending over decades. Since there is no known diagnostic test, the diagnosis is made by exclusion. Patients need support and encouragement. Bed rest and steroids may be helpful.

H. Myasthenia gravis is manifested by fatigability, especially of muscles supplied by the cranial nerves, with diplopia, ptosis, dysphagia, dysarthria, and hypoventilation. Pregnancy is generally unaffected, but transient symptoms can appear in the newborn infant. Anticholinesterases are effective; give neostigmine, 15 mg orally four times a day, or pyridostigmine, 60 mg daily. Follow frequently to adjust the dosage as needed. During the first three days after delivery, observe the infant carefully. Breast feeding is contraindicated because of antibody transfer.

I. In general the management of labor and delivery is based only on obstetrical considerations. These patients should be considered at risk and managed in a facility capable of providing specialized care. Vaginal delivery is often feasible if pain relief can be provided and Valsalva maneuvers can be minimized or avoided in the second stage. Consider elective cesarean section only for an untreated arteriovenous anomaly.

References

Chaudhuri P, Wallenburg HC. Brain tumors and pregnancy: Presentation of a case and a review of the literature. Eur J Obstet Gynecol Reprod Biol 11:109, 1980.

Ghezzi A, Caputo D. Pregnancy: A factor influencing the course of multiple sclerosis? Eur Neurol 20:115, 1981.

Minielly R, Yuzpe AA, Drake CG. Subarachnoid hemorrhage secondary to ruptured cerebral aneurysm in pregnancy. Obstet Gynecol 53:64, 1979.

Plauché WC. Myasthenia gravis in pregnancy: An update. Am J Obstet Gynecol 135:691, 1979.

Weinberger J, Lauersen NH. Vascular headache in pregnancy. Am J Obstet Gynecol 143:842, 1982.

PATIENT WITH SUSPICION OF NEUROLOGIC DISORDER

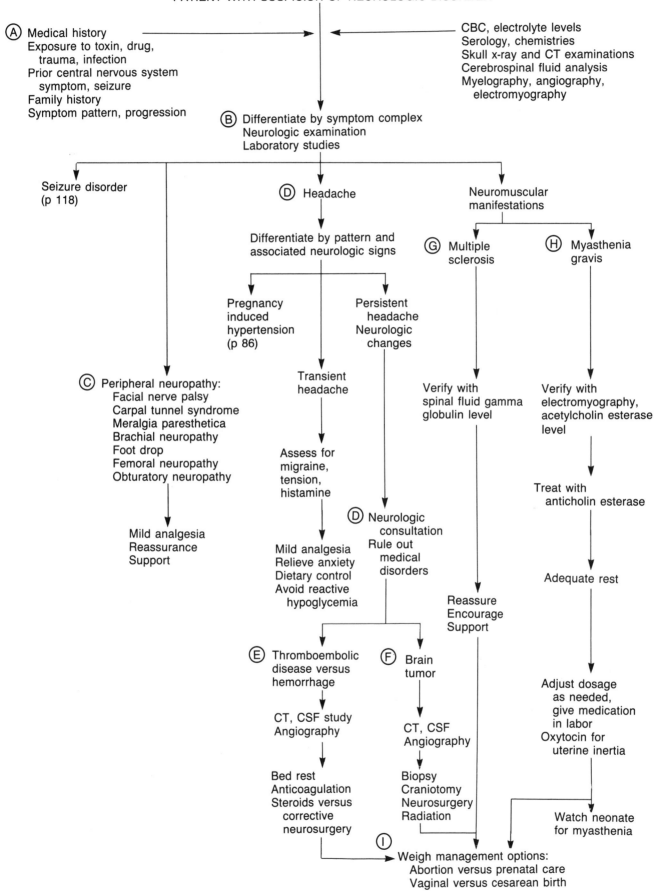

Ⓐ Medical history
Exposure to toxin, drug,
    trauma, infection
Prior central nervous system
    symptom, seizure
Family history
Symptom pattern, progression

CBC, electrolyte levels
Serology, chemistries
Skull x-ray and CT examinations
Cerebrospinal fluid analysis
Myelography, angiography,
    electromyography

Ⓑ Differentiate by symptom complex
Neurologic examination
Laboratory studies

Seizure disorder
(p 118)

Ⓓ Headache

Differentiate by pattern and
associated neurologic signs

Neuromuscular
manifestations

Ⓖ Multiple
sclerosis

Ⓗ Myasthenia
gravis

Pregnancy
induced
hypertension
(p 86)

Persistent
headache
Neurologic
changes

Ⓒ Peripheral neuropathy:
    Facial nerve palsy
    Carpal tunnel syndrome
    Meralgia paresthetica
    Brachial neuropathy
    Foot drop
    Femoral neuropathy
    Obturatory neuropathy

Transient
headache

Verify with
spinal fluid gamma
globulin level

Verify with
electromyography,
acetylcholin esterase
level

Assess for
migraine,
tension,
histamine

Treat with
anticholin esterase

Mild analgesia
Reassurance
Support

Ⓓ Neurologic
consultation
Rule out
medical
disorders

Adequate rest

Mild analgesia
Relieve anxiety
Dietary control
Avoid reactive
    hypoglycemia

Adjust dosage
as needed,
give medication
in labor
Oxytocin for
uterine inertia

Ⓔ Thromboembolic
disease versus
hemorrhage

Ⓕ Brain
tumor

Reassure
Encourage
Support

CT, CSF study
Angiography

CT, CSF
Angiography

Bed rest
Anticoagulation
Steroids versus
    corrective
    neurosurgery

Biopsy
Craniotomy
Neurosurgery
Radiation

Watch neonate
for myasthenia

Ⓘ Weigh management options:
    Abortion versus prenatal care
    Vaginal versus cesarean birth

PREGNANT ADDICT

Janet L. Mitchell, M.D.
Patricia S. Stewart, M.S., M.S.W.

A. Although pregnancy can be a strong motivation for a change in life style, addiction in itself is a serious counterbalancing force as well as a debilitating disease. The most successful programs for improving the obstetrical outcome in addicted pregnant women combine intensive medical surveillance with a strong psychosocial support program. The addicted person responds best in a structured environment where limits are set and clearly outlined. Medical assessment should include objectively establishing the gestational age (sometimes difficult because menstrual irregularity is common in women taking drugs), screening for sexually transmitted diseases, and a search for all intercurrent diseases, especially those related to the use of illicit drugs, such as hepatitis and acquired immunodeficiency syndrome (AIDS). In addition, it is important to evaluate the nutritional status of the gravida. Prognostically the gravida who acknowledges and shows concern about the risk to her fetus, is compliant with a structured counseling and obstetrical program, complies with toxic screening requirements periodically, and exhibits no overt antisocial behavior (see p 30) can be expected to do much better than one who denies her problem, is unconcerned about the effect on the fetus, has a chaotic life style, and refuses to participate in a drug counseling program.

B. Most addicts are polydrug abusers. Alcohol consumption and cigarette smoking are common in these women as well. Random urine toxicologic screening increases self-reporting and provides valuable information for both the obstetrical and pediatric staffs. Screening for AIDS should be considered, since many of these women are either intravenous drug users or prostitutes (the latter to provide income for their expensive habit); both are characteristics that place the person at high risk for AIDS.

C. Women taking street narcotics should be stabilized on a methadone dosage and encouraged to enter a formal therapeutic treatment program. This approach is helpful insofar as its impact on the gravida's nutrition is concerned. The outcome for both the patient and her fetus is decidedly improved. The use of cocaine and its derivatives is a growing problem. Presently there is no drug substitute available. Its use in pregnancy has been associated with abruptio placentae and premature delivery.

D. Maintain the patient on the lowest dosage of methadone possible. Total detoxification in pregnancy is difficult and hazardous because it increases the risk of antepartum and perinatal mortality.

E. The life style associated with addiction increases the risk of premature delivery, intrauterine growth retardation, and pregnancy induced hypertension. These patients require intensive prenatal care and continuing counseling with attention to emotional and social supports and encouragement.

F. The management of labor can be difficult because most addicted women have a high tolerance for the analgesics commonly used. Pain relief for them is best accomplished by regional block anesthesia.

G. The pediatric staff should be advised (preferably in advance) of the birth of an infant of an addicted mother and provided with the results of her urine toxicologic screen. Neonatal drug withdrawal, especially from methadone, can be delayed for up to one month. Manifestations of withdrawal from other drugs can appear as early as 72 hours after delivery; they may constitute a life threatening constellation, especially when compounded by prematurity and low birth weight, requiring concerted pediatric care.

References

Acker DB, Sachs BP, Tracey KJ, Wise WE. Abruptio placentae associated with cocaine use. Am J Obstet Gynecol 146:220, 1983.

Center for Disease Control. Recommendation for assisting in the prevention of perinatal transmission of human T-lymphotropic virus type III/lymphadenopathy associated virus and acquired immunodeficiency syndrome. Morbid Mortal Weekly Rep 34:721, 1985.

Hingson R, Zuckerman B, Amaro H, et al. Maternal marijuana and neonatal outcome: Uncertainty posed by self-reports. Am J Publ Health 76:667, 1986.

Suffet F, Brotman R. A comprehensive care program for pregnant addicts: Obstetrical, neonatal and child development outcomes. Internat J Addict 19:199, 1984.

Zuckerman BS, Parker SJ, Hingson R, Alpert JJ, Mitchell JL. Substance abuse during pregnancy and neonatal outcome: An update. In: Milunsky A, Friedman EA, Gluck L. (Editors). Advances in Perinatal Medicine. New York: Plenum Medical Book Co., 1986, Vol. 5.

PATIENT WITH SUSPICION OR HISTORY OF DRUG ABUSE

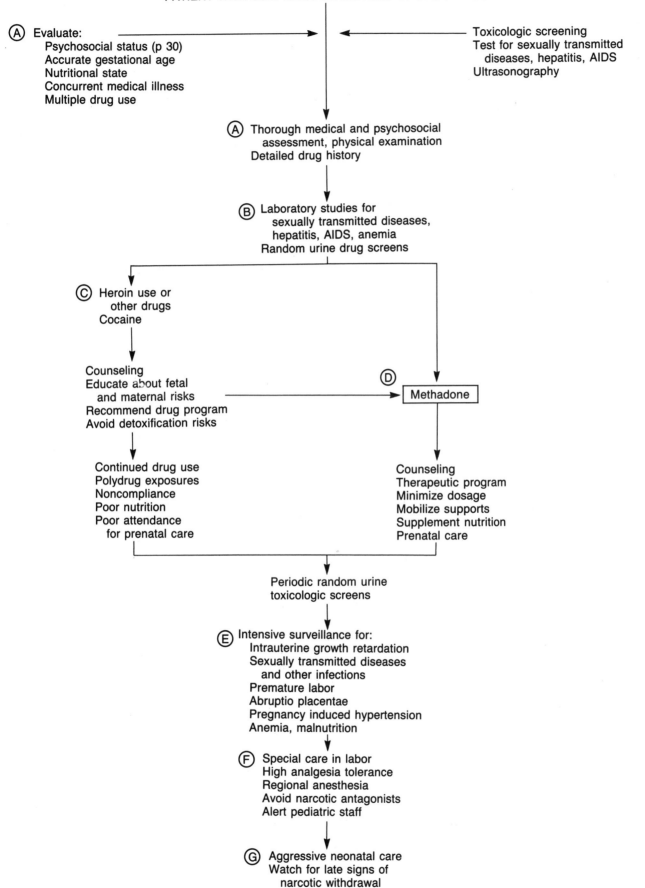

Ⓐ Evaluate:
    Psychosocial status (p 30)
    Accurate gestational age
    Nutritional state
    Concurrent medical illness
    Multiple drug use

Toxicologic screening
Test for sexually transmitted
    diseases, hepatitis, AIDS
Ultrasonography

Ⓐ Thorough medical and psychosocial
    assessment, physical examination
    Detailed drug history

Ⓑ Laboratory studies for
    sexually transmitted diseases,
    hepatitis, AIDS, anemia
    Random urine drug screens

Ⓒ Heroin use or
    other drugs
    Cocaine

Counseling
Educate about fetal
    and maternal risks
Recommend drug program
Avoid detoxification risks

Ⓓ Methadone

Continued drug use
Polydrug exposures
Noncompliance
Poor nutrition
Poor attendance
    for prenatal care

Counseling
Therapeutic program
Minimize dosage
Mobilize supports
Supplement nutrition
Prenatal care

Periodic random urine
toxicologic screens

Ⓔ Intensive surveillance for:
    Intrauterine growth retardation
    Sexually transmitted diseases
        and other infections
    Premature labor
    Abruptio placentae
    Pregnancy induced hypertension
    Anemia, malnutrition

Ⓕ Special care in labor
    High analgesia tolerance
    Regional anesthesia
    Avoid narcotic antagonists
    Alert pediatric staff

Ⓖ Aggressive neonatal care
    Watch for late signs of
        narcotic withdrawal

TRAUMA IN PREGNANCY

Lynn H. Galen, M.D.

A. Falls are the most frequent cause of minor blunt trauma, generally without serious injury to the fetus or mother. The uterus is well protected by the bony pelvis, especially in the first trimester, and amniotic fluid cushions the fetus against injury. Minor injuries are managed just as they are in the nongravid patient. If x-ray views are needed, shield the abdomen. If indicated, give tetanus prophylaxis as well.

B. The normal physiologic changes of pregnancy may alter the effects of trauma. The gravida can sustain a large amount of blood loss before vital signs change, even though nonvital organs, including the uterus, may not be well perfused. Fetal hypoxia may thus occur; this can be compounded by the reduced cardiac output associated with supine hypotension. Increased oxygen consumption and decreased functional residual capacity cause hypoxemia more readily, with low oxygenation and greater sensitivity to gas anesthesia. The risk of aspiration is increased (p 266). The typical peritoneal signs are masked.

C. Focus the initial management on aggressive maternal resuscitation. Evaluate the ventilatory status and establish an airway, if necessary. Assess the cardiovascular status and provide venous access with large bore catheters. Carry out appropriate laboratory studies; cross match blood for transfusion. Arterial blood gas levels may also be needed. A central venous pressure or Swan-Ganz catheter is essential for cardiovascular monitoring and managing fluid and blood replacement. Follow the urinary output with an indwelling catheter. Displace the uterus off the vena cava. Support the blood pressure with appropriate fluids; if it fails to respond to adequate volume replacement, give vasopressors, such as ephedrine or metaphedrin, which can raise arterial pressure without compromising the uterine blood flow.

D. After the patient has been initially stabilized, evaluate the fetus by auscultation. Check the uterus for contractions, rupture, or abruptio placentae. Evaluate the cervix, looking for amniotic fluid and blood. Ultrasonography helps confirm the gestational age and fetal maturity and well-being and can be used to scan for evidence of overt injury. If alive and mature enough to survive, the fetus should be continuously monitored. Abruptio placentae causes fetal death most often in cases of blunt trauma; late decelerations may be the earliest sign. Penetrating uterine trauma frequently produces fetal injury or death. Individualize the fetal management according to the maternal and fetal status. Intervene if fetal distress develops or give tocolytic drugs if the maternal condition permits. Do not discharge the patient before assessing fetal well-being.

E. Assess the extent of maternal injury and treat. Carry out appropriate studies and obtain consultations. For blunt abdominal injury, perform peritoneal lavage to detect blood and to identify a perforated viscus. Injury to the urinary tract requires urologic study. With a pelvic fracture, look for urinary tract injury and retroperitoneal hemorrhage. Open reduction and fixation of fractures are preferable to traction in order to avoid prolonged immobilization. Laparotomy is done in cases of penetrating abdominal trauma or suspicion of intra-abdominal bleeding, bowel or bladder damage, and uterine rupture. Do not empty the uterus for exposure unless this is technically not avoidable. This applies especially if the fetus is immature or not in distress.

F. An agonal or postmortem cesarean section is indicated if the undelivered gravida expires and the fetus is considered salvageable. The fetal prognosis depends on the cause of maternal death, adequacy of interim resuscitation, foregoing fetal status, and gestational age. The prognosis is poor if the elapsed time from death to delivery is over 15 minutes. A classic uterine incision is most expeditious. Despite cerebral death from trauma, maternal cardiac and respiratory function sometimes can be adequately supported for a long time to allow the fetus to mature before cesarean section is done.

References

Higgins SD, Garite TJ. Late abruptio placentae in trauma patients: Implications for monitoring. Obstet Gynecol 63:10S, 1984.

Mossman KL, Hill LT. Radiation risks in pregnancy. Obstet Gynecol 60:237, 1982.

Patterson RM. Trauma in pregnancy. Clin Obstet Gynecol 27:32, 1984.

Rayburn W, Smith B, Feller I, et al. Major burns during pregnancy: Effect on fetal well-being. Obstet Gynecol 63:392, 1984.

Rose PG, Strohm PL, Zuspan FP. Fetomaternal hemorrhage following trauma. Am J Obstet Gynecol 153:844, 1985.

PATIENT WITH TRAUMATIC INJURY INCURRED DURING PREGNANCY

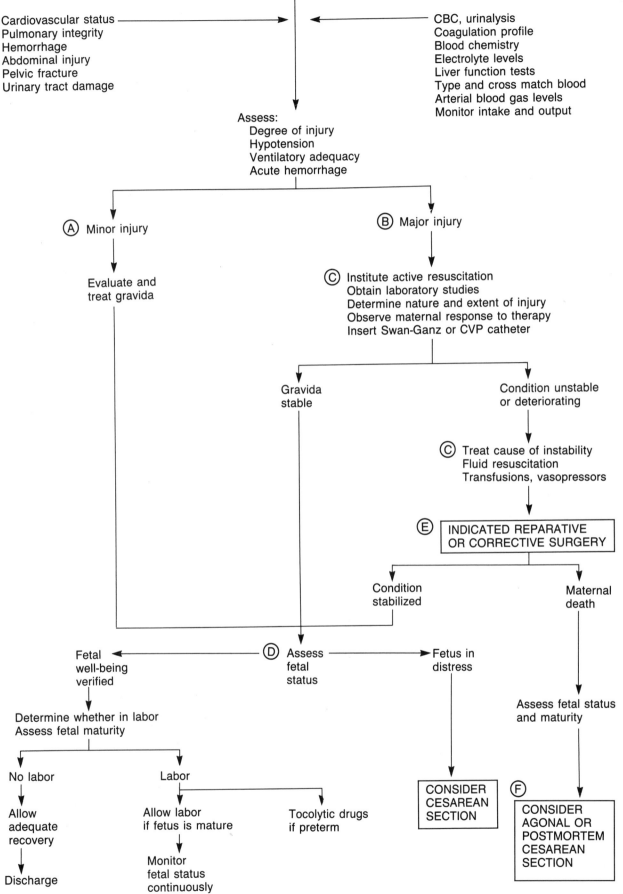

Cardiovascular status
Pulmonary integrity
Hemorrhage
Abdominal injury
Pelvic fracture
Urinary tract damage

CBC, urinalysis
Coagulation profile
Blood chemistry
Electrolyte levels
Liver function tests
Type and cross match blood
Arterial blood gas levels
Monitor intake and output

Assess:
    Degree of injury
    Hypotension
    Ventilatory adequacy
    Acute hemorrhage

Ⓐ Minor injury

Ⓑ Major injury

Evaluate and
treat gravida

Ⓒ Institute active resuscitation
   Obtain laboratory studies
   Determine nature and extent of injury
   Observe maternal response to therapy
   Insert Swan-Ganz or CVP catheter

Gravida
stable

Condition unstable
or deteriorating

Ⓒ Treat cause of instability
   Fluid resuscitation
   Transfusions, vasopressors

Ⓔ INDICATED REPARATIVE
   OR CORRECTIVE SURGERY

Condition
stabilized

Maternal
death

Fetal
well-being
verified

Ⓓ Assess
   fetal
   status

Fetus in
distress

Assess fetal status
and maturity

Determine whether in labor
Assess fetal maturity

No labor

Labor

CONSIDER
CESAREAN
SECTION

Ⓕ CONSIDER
   AGONAL OR
   POSTMORTEM
   CESAREAN
   SECTION

Allow
adequate
recovery

Allow labor
if fetus is mature

Tocolytic drugs
if preterm

Discharge

Monitor
fetal status
continuously

ORTHOPEDIC DISORDER

Eric D. Lichter, M.D.

A. Pelvic bony abnormalities affecting pregnancy, labor, and delivery are rare in the reproductive age group. A routine history and physical examination at the time of the initial antepartum visit alert the physician to possible problems. A history of developmental disease, rickets, kyphoscoliosis, pelvis fracture, or poliomyelitis may indicate the possibility of a pelvic malformation, especially if these conditions preceded puberty. The same applies for the presence of neuromuscular disease elsewhere in the body. A long-standing limp suggests musculoskeletal abnormalities, which may have hindered or altered normal pelvic development. Pelvic examination aids in diagnosing benign osteochondroma, malunion of pelvic fractures with resulting deformity, and spondylolisthesis (Fig. 1). The anterior vertebral projection associated with spondylolisthesis or kyphoscoliosis can potentially reduce pelvic capacity greatly.

B. A history and physical findings consistent with pelvic malformation warrant formal x-ray pelvimetry (p 24) in the third trimester. With this information available, one can begin to discuss the method of delivery at this time. Gross malformation severely restricting pelvic capacity may require cesarean section for delivery.

C. Osteogenesis imperfecta is a connective tissue disorder characterized by severe osteoporosis, blue sclerae, middle ear deafness, and multiple deformities secondary to repeated fractures. Two forms of the disease, congenita and tarda, can be distinguished. The congenita form is associated with fetal death in utero or in the immediate neonatal period and is inherited as an autosomal recessive trait. The tarda form is inherited as an autosomal dominant trait; it is milder in expression and appears later in infancy. X-ray views for fetal fractures and deformities and for pelvimetry should be obtained if labor is contemplated. Fetal fractures indicate intrauterine osteogenesis imperfecta, contraindicating vaginal delivery. Maternal pelvic deformation may also limit vaginal delivery.

D. Kyphoscoliosis may yield a markedly distorted, asymmetric pelvic deformation. The lower the spinal curvature deformity, the greater the effect on the pelvis. The gravida's problems are further compounded by a severe reduction in the available space for uterine growth in the abdomen as well as reduced ventilatory excursion in the thoracic cavity; this combination of adverse effects can be especially hazardous for the afflicted gravida. A reduced vital capacity and altered hemodynamics can result in congestive heart failure, which must be anticipated and managed aggressively to avoid a potentially fatal outcome (p 104).

E. Softening and laxity of the pelvic ligaments occur in pregnancy, perhaps in response to endogenous relaxin. These phenomena are coupled with the pressure exerted by the fetal head as it engages and descends in the birth canal before or during labor to produce diastasis of the pubic symphysis in some gravidas. Symphyseal separation can occur spontaneously at delivery or, more likely, as a consequence of forceful forceps traction or hyperabduction of the lower extremities in the lithotomy position for delivery. This condition, which destabilizes the weight bearing function of the pelvis, is characterized by persistent pubic pain on motion and associated difficulty in walking. Sacroiliac pain is also noted frequently. Examination reveals tenderness over the symphysis and sacroiliac regions. X-ray study shows the separation of the anterior rami of the pubic bones. Mild symptoms respond to firm pelvic support and a bedboard. Severe symptoms require a prolonged period of bed rest with a tight pelvic compression by strapping to encourage healing.

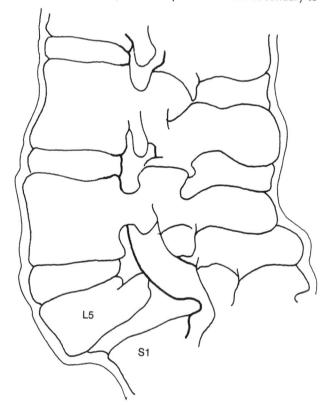

Figure 1 Spondylolisthesis showing subluxating forward projection of fifth lumbar (L5) vertebral body with potential impingement on nerve roots and reduction of pelvic inlet capacity at sacral promontory (S1).

References

Cherry SH, Berkowitz RL, Kuse NG. Medical, Surgical and Gynecologic Complications of Pregnancy. 3rd ed. Baltimore: Williams & Wilkins, 1985.

Rothman R, Simeone S, Beruine P. Lumbar disk disease. In: The Spine. 2nd ed. Philadelphia: W.B. Saunders, 1982.

White AA. Back School and Other Conservative Approaches to Low Back Pain. St. Louis: C.V. Mosby, 1983.

ORTHOPEDIC DISORDER IDENTIFIED

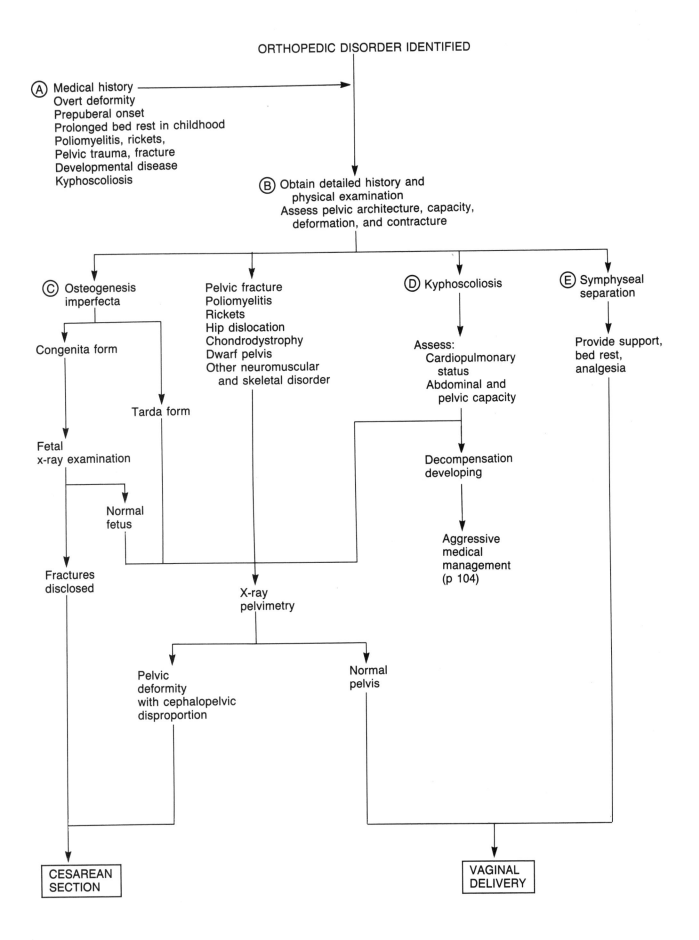

(A) Medical history
Overt deformity
Prepuberal onset
Prolonged bed rest in childhood
Poliomyelitis, rickets,
Pelvic trauma, fracture
Developmental disease
Kyphoscoliosis

(B) Obtain detailed history and
physical examination
Assess pelvic architecture, capacity,
deformation, and contracture

(C) Osteogenesis
imperfecta

Pelvic fracture
Poliomyelitis
Rickets
Hip dislocation
Chondrodystrophy
Dwarf pelvis
Other neuromuscular
and skeletal disorder

(D) Kyphoscoliosis

(E) Symphyseal
separation

Congenita form

Tarda form

Assess:
Cardiopulmonary
status
Abdominal and
pelvic capacity

Provide support,
bed rest,
analgesia

Fetal
x-ray examination

Normal
fetus

Decompensation
developing

Fractures
disclosed

X-ray
pelvimetry

Aggressive
medical
management
(p 104)

Pelvic
deformity
with cephalopelvic
disproportion

Normal
pelvis

CESAREAN
SECTION

VAGINAL
DELIVERY

HANDICAPPED GRAVIDA

Lynn H. Galen, M.D.

A. Optimally prepregnancy counseling should enable the couple to make an informed decision about childbearing. Detail the patient's medical history and do a complete physical examination. Counsel about the effects of pregnancy on her illness and of her disability on the fetus. Review medications and modify them, if possible, to avoid potential teratogenic action. If a medication is essential, yet potentially harmful to the fetus, outline those risks. Patients with disabilities of genetic origin should be referred for genetic counseling. Encourage the patient to discuss her concerns about her disability and childbearing. Review her support systems.

B. A team approach is generally called for during pregnancy. Mobilize community resources as needed. Childbirth education classes should be adapted to her needs; for example, a translator might interpret for the deaf gravida. Make contact with other mothers who have successfully dealt with similar disabilities for support and practical advice. Attend to nutritional and exercise needs. Refer those with spinal cord injuries to a physical therapist. Inform the hospital staff in advance of possible admission so that appropriate planning and preparation can be made for any special needs.

C. Patients with spinal cord injury have special problems of recurrent urinary tract infection, renal and bladder calculi, anemia, decibitus ulcer, leg and perineal muscle spasm, premature labor, and autonomic hyperreflexia. Chronic urinary tract infection does not contraindicate pregnancy if renal function is normal; give long term suppressive therapy with methylmandelic acid or nitrofurantoin. Bowel dysfunction aggravated by iron therapy is aided by stool softeners. Ensure meticulous care of decubitus ulcers to avoid sepsis. These gravidas risk premature labor. Spinal transection above the tenth thoracic level yields painless labor. Since the patient is unaware of contractions, weekly examinations are necessary, beginning at 28 weeks, to monitor cervical changes.

D. Uterine contractions are not affected by cord transection and labor may proceed rapidly. Sensation remains intact in patients with paraplegia related to anterior horn cell disease, such as poliomyelitis. Lesions above T7 may cause an autonomic mass discharge with contractions; it is associated with an abrupt rise in blood pressure (risking seizure or hemorrhage), headache, diaphoresis, extreme anxiety, pilomotor erection, flushing, and bradycardia. Avoid bladder distention by use of an indwelling catheter; minimize skin stimulation by internal monitoring. Epidural anesthesia is effective in blocking this response. Titrated doses of a short acting ganglionic blocking drug may also be needed. The fetus generally tolerates the labor well. Cesarean section is done for obstetrical indications only. Gravidas with paraplegia or quadriplegia are at increased risk of deep vein thrombosis. Early mobilization and physical therapy are indicated; consider heparin, 5,000 units twice daily. Patients with orthopedic (p 126) or neuromuscular disorders (p 120) and those who were subjected to unequal weight bearing in childhood may have a deformed pelvis, requiring careful assessment of architecture and capacity. Women with severe kyphoscoliosis may have limited cardiorespiratory reserve and should be managed as one would a gravida with cardiac disease (p 104).

E. Give contraceptive counseling post partum. Community resources, such as public health nursing and new mother and infant support groups, should be called upon to help her cope with her disability and devise adaptive mechanisms to best care for her infant.

References

Asrael W. An approach to motherhood for disabled women. Rehab Lit 43:214, 1982.

Tabsh KMA, Brinkman CR, Reff RA. Autonomic dysreflexia in pregnancy. Obstet Gynecol 60:119, 1982.

Taylor P. Ganglion stimulating and blocking agents. In: Gilman LS, Goodman AG, Rall TW, Murad F (Editors). Goodman and Gilman's The Pharmacological Basis of Therapeutics. 7th ed. New York: Macmillan, 1985.

Young BK, Katz M, Klein SA. Pregnancy after spinal cord injury: Altered maternal and fetal response to labor. Obstet Gynecol 62:59, 1983.

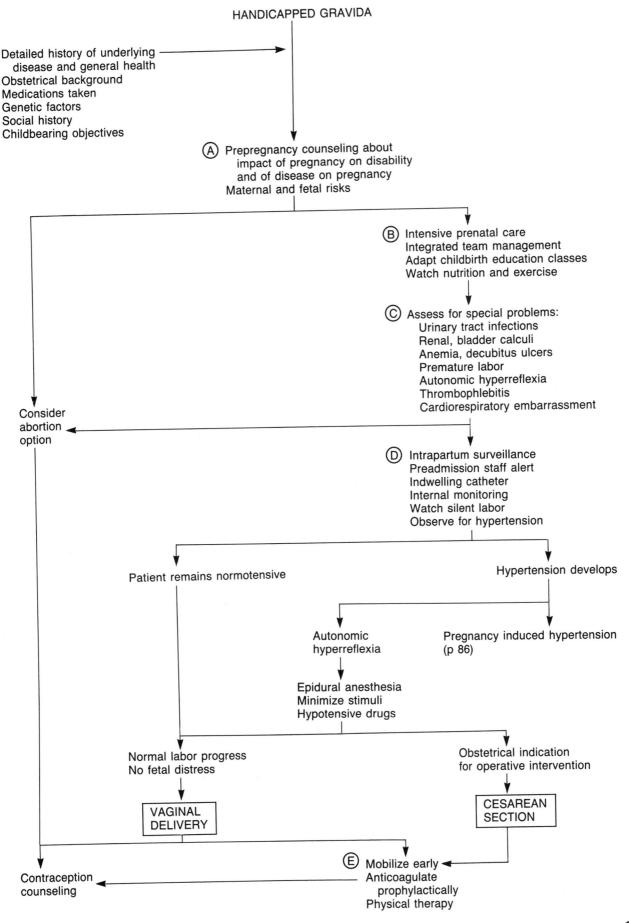

HANDICAPPED GRAVIDA

Detailed history of underlying
  disease and general health
Obstetrical background
Medications taken
Genetic factors
Social history
Childbearing objectives

Ⓐ Prepregnancy counseling about
  impact of pregnancy on disability
  and of disease on pregnancy
  Maternal and fetal risks

Ⓑ Intensive prenatal care
  Integrated team management
  Adapt childbirth education classes
  Watch nutrition and exercise

Ⓒ Assess for special problems:
  Urinary tract infections
  Renal, bladder calculi
  Anemia, decubitus ulcers
  Premature labor
  Autonomic hyperreflexia
  Thrombophlebitis
  Cardiorespiratory embarrassment

Consider
abortion
option

Ⓓ Intrapartum surveillance
  Preadmission staff alert
  Indwelling catheter
  Internal monitoring
  Watch silent labor
  Observe for hypertension

Patient remains normotensive

Hypertension develops

Autonomic
hyperreflexia

Pregnancy induced hypertension
(p 86)

Epidural anesthesia
Minimize stimuli
Hypotensive drugs

Normal labor progress
No fetal distress

Obstetrical indication
for operative intervention

VAGINAL
DELIVERY

CESAREAN
SECTION

Ⓔ Mobilize early
  Anticoagulate
    prophylactically
  Physical therapy

Contraception
counseling

PULMONARY EMBOLISM

Henry Klapholz, M.D.

A. Patients at risk are those with prior peripheral venous disease, thrombophlebitis, or pulmonary embolism, those with pelvic infection, and those undergoing prolonged surgery, trauma, or protracted periods of immobilization or bed rest. Patients with antithrombin III deficiency are at special risk. Sudden precordial or substernal chest pain is seen with radiation to the neck or shoulder, as well as pleuritic pain, shortness of breath, anxiety, agitation, and restlessness.

B. Physical findings include hypotension, tachycardia, and tachypnea. Peripheral and circumoral cyanosis also occur.

C. Transient electrocardiographic changes may be seen, reflecting acute cor pulmonale (typically an $S_1Q_3T_3$ pattern, right axis deviation, or right bundle branch block). Serial electrocardiograms are sometimes helpful. Chest x-ray examination may show pulmonary infiltrates, increased radiolucency, an elevated diaphragm, or pleural effusion. Lung scan techniques are useful and safe for screening, especially for detecting lung perfusion defects in the patient with normal chest x-ray findings. Pulmonary function studies show increased ventilatory dead space and reduced alveolar Pco_2 and normal arterial Pco_2 values. A low arterial Po_2 value (below 90 mm Hg) on room air together with a positive lung scan helps establish the diagnosis (with a consistent history and physical examination). Although more hazardous than scanning, pulmonary angiography permits direct visualization of the pulmonary vessels and is therefore definitive for the diagnosis of this condition. It should be done in doubtful cases before committing a patient to a prolonged course of treatment.

D. Immediate anticoagulant therapy is essential to prevent fatal complications. Heparin is the preferred treatment because it does not cross the placenta to affect the fetus adversely. Continuous intravenous infusion of about 1000 units of heparin per hour is effective. The partial thromboplastin time is used to titrate the dosage; which should be adjusted until the partial thromboplastin time is twice the control value. Bed rest, oxygen, analgesics, and antibiotics are needed. Digitalis may be indicated for cardiac failure. Give isoproterenol and dopamine, if indicated, for hypotension and diuretics for pulmonary edema. After a few days one can switch to intermittent subcutaneous heparin therapy, continuing to term.

E. At term, vaginal delivery is preferable to cesarean section. It is important to avoid a traumatic vaginal delivery. Delivery, even by cesarean section (if obstetrically indicated), can be carried out safely under full heparinization. If bleeding occurs, protamine counteracts the heparin effect quickly and effectively; it should be held in reserve until needed.

F. Coumadin may be substituted for heparin post partum in an overlapping regimen. Warfarin is given daily in 10 to 15 mg doses for two to three days until the prothrombin time is two to three times the control level. Then the heparin dosage may be reduced and finally discontinued. The patient should avoid breast feeding while she is taking Coumadin because it passes readily into the milk. The larger heparin molecule offers no such direct risk to either fetus or infant.

References

Bell WR, Bartholomew JR. Pulmonary thromboembolic disease. Curr Probl Cardiol 10:1, 1985.

Bell WR, Simon TL. Current status of pulmonary thromboembolic disease: Pathophysiology, diagnosis, prevention, and treatment. Am Heart J 103:239, 1982.

de Swiet M. Thromboembolism. Clin Haematol 14:643, 1985.

Schafer AI. The hypercoagulable states. Ann Intern Med 102:814, 1985.

Weiner CP. Diagnosis and management of thromboembolic disease during pregnancy. Clin Obstet Gynecol 28:107, 1985.

SUSPICION OF PULMONARY EMBOLISM

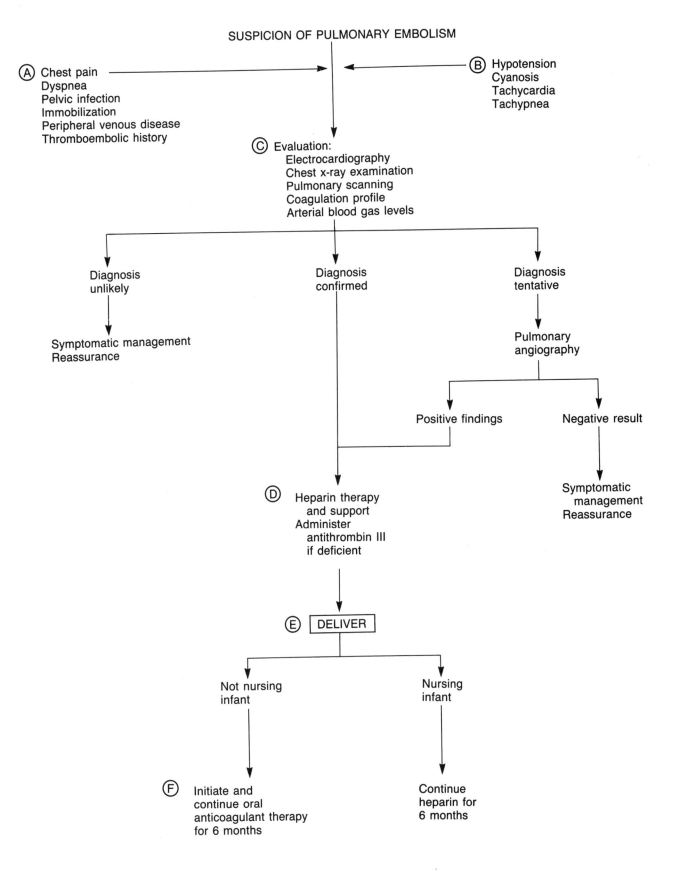

(A) Chest pain
Dyspnea
Pelvic infection
Immobilization
Peripheral venous disease
Thromboembolic history

(B) Hypotension
Cyanosis
Tachycardia
Tachypnea

(C) Evaluation:
Electrocardiography
Chest x-ray examination
Pulmonary scanning
Coagulation profile
Arterial blood gas levels

Diagnosis
unlikely

Diagnosis
confirmed

Diagnosis
tentative

Symptomatic management
Reassurance

Pulmonary
angiography

Positive findings

Negative result

(D) Heparin therapy
and support
Administer
antithrombin III
if deficient

Symptomatic
management
Reassurance

(E) DELIVER

Not nursing
infant

Nursing
infant

(F) Initiate and
continue oral
anticoagulant therapy
for 6 months

Continue
heparin for
6 months

AMNIOTIC FLUID EMBOLISM

Henry Klapholz, M.D.

A. If amniotic fluid gains access to the maternal circulation in the course of labor or in the immediate postpartum period by way of open maternal venous sinuses, the resulting clinical picture can be devastating with acute respiratory embarrassment leading rapidly in most cases to death. Although it is rare and still associated with a high mortality rate, patients with amniotic fluid embolism can be salvaged if personnel are astute and act expeditiously and aggressively. Since the condition nearly always arises in a delivery unit setting, often with anesthesia personnel already in attendance, facilities and personnel are generally available to deal with this crisis. The pathogenetic mechanism appears to be obstruction of the pulmonary vascular tree by a combination of amniotic fluid debris (squames, vernix, mucin, lanugo, and meconium), reflex vasospasm, and particulate microclots resulting from the thromboplastin-like material contained in amniotic fluid. The sequence of cor pulmonale and disseminated intravascular coagulation follows rapidly if the patient survives the initial hypoxic event. Patients at particular risk for amniotic fluid embolism include multiparas, women with very rapid tumultuous labors, especially those in whom labor is being augmented with oxytocin, as well as gravidas with uterine overdistention from polyhydramnios or multiple pregnancy and women in whom the uterus is being subjected to operative manipulation. It can also be seen with induced abortion, most commonly those done after 20 weeks.

B. This is a catastrophic event that presents with respiratory distress, hypotension, profuse bleeding with uterine atony, cyanosis, peripheral vasoconstriction, and tonic-clonic seizures. Typically the patient is in the final stages of the delivery or has just delivered. She may sit bolt upright and complain of chest pain; she becomes deeply cyanotic, gasping for air, and promptly collapses in shock. Only if she survives this initial episode do hemorrhagic manifestations become apparent. A less fulminating form of this condition may also occur with slowly developing signs over a period of hours, usually beginning post partum.

C. Amniotic fluid embolism is to be differentiated from a pulmonary embolism secondary to a peripheral or pelvic venous clot (p 130), acute myocardial infarction, congestive heart failure, and coagulopathy due to sepsis. Pulmonary arterial blood may now be sampled by means of a pulmonary arterial (Swan-Ganz) catheter and examined cytologically for evidence of fetal cells to make a definitive antemortem diagnosis (Fig. 1). Regrettably, however, most cases are still confirmed by finding pulmonary vascular plugging with amniotic fluid debris at autopsy.

D. The immediate concern is to establish ventilation in a patient who is in cardiopulmonary collapse and provide adequate oxygenation for tissue perfusion. Mechanical ventilation is essential with positive end expiratory pressure to combat pulmonary edema. Since uterine bleeding is usually very brisk, many units of blood have to be cross matched to accommodate replacement needs. Fresh frozen plasma and platelet concentrate are also required to treat the intense coagulopathy that results. Give platelet transfusions if the count falls below 25,000 per mm³. Examine blood or urine for evidence of fibrin degradation products to confirm the presence of disseminated intravascular coagulation. Two large bore intravenous catheters should be placed. One of these should be a central venous line or preferably a Swan-Ganz pulmonary wedge catheter. An intra-arterial line is also useful for monitoring blood gas levels.

E. If the blood pressure continues to fall despite the administration of oxygen, blood, and fluid, vasopressors such as dopamine and levophed should be used. Steroids have been variably successful in treating this event. Heparin and aspirin as well as proteases have offered some hope, but their use is still controversial. The mortality from amniotic fluid embolism remains high.

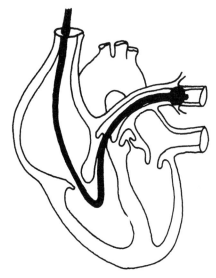

Figure 1 Technique for obtaining sample of pulmonary arterial blood by way of a Swan-Ganz catheter traversing the right heart to gain access to the pulmonary circulation. Finding fetal squames and vernix makes the diagnosis of amniotic fluid embolism.

References

Clark SL, Pavlova Z, Greenspoon J, et al. Squamous cells in the maternal pulmonary circulation. Am J Obstet Gynecol 154:104, 1986.

Killam A. Amniotic fluid embolism. Clin Obstet Gynecol 28:32, 1985.

Masson RG, Ruggieri J. Pulmonary microvascular cytology: A new diagnostic application of the pulmonary artery catheter. Chest 88:908, 1985.

Turner R, Gusack M. Massive amniotic fluid embolism. Ann Emerg Med 13:359, 1984.

PATIENT WITH SUSPICION OF AMNIOTIC FLUID EMBOLISM

Ⓐ Risk factors:
    Multiparous pregnancy
    Tumultuous labor
    Oxytocin stimulation
    Uterine overstimulation
    Uterine manipulation

Type and cross match blood
Coagulation studies
Fibrin split products
Arterial blood gas levels
Central venous pressure or Swan-Ganz catheter

Ⓑ Recognize characteristic clinical pattern:
    Acute respiratory embarrassment
    Chest pain, cyanosis, hypotension,
      collapse, seizures, and hemorrhage

Ⓒ Differentiate from other acute conditions

Ⓒ Pulmonary thromboembolism
  Myocardial infarction
  Congestive heart failure
  Septic shock

Ⓓ Provide mechanical ventilation
  Positive end expiratory pressure
  Rapid laboratory assessment
  Large bore intravenous lines
  Transfuse whole blood, fresh frozen
    plasma, and platelets, as indicated
  Monitor by central venous pressure or
    Swan-Ganz pulmonary wedge catheter
  Intra-arterial line for serial
    arterial blood gas levels
  Cytology of pulmonary blood

Ⓔ Progressive or
  unremitting
  hypotension
  or shock state

Coagulopathy

Patient recovers
Maintains oxygenation
Normotensive
Adequate tissue perfusion

Consider:
  Vasopressors
  Corticosteroids
  Heparin
  Protease

Treat bleeding
problem aggressively;
replacing factors
and transfusing

Provide symptomatic
relief as required

Expect high
mortality

Expect recovery
without residua

TUBERCULOSIS

Jerold M. Carlson, M.D., M.P.H.

A. For many years the incidence of tuberculosis was believed to be falling to the vanishing point, aided in no small measure by effective treatment regimens. Recently, however, there has been an upsurge in cases found because of the rapid influx of émigrés from Southeast Asia. Whereas the problem had almost become an academic curiosity, it is now once again of considerable practical importance for physicians. Although other routes of infection occur (as from milk), the pulmonary route is primary. Tuberculosis is caused mainly by the airborne acid fast bacillus *Mycobacterium tuberculosis*. Be especially alert to the possibility of infection, even in asymptomatic patients, among gravidas whose socioeconomic background reflects indigency, crowded housing, and poor medical care. Characteristic symptoms of pulmonary tuberculosis include hemoptysis, chest pain, fatigue, night sweats, weight loss, pneumonia, and chronic debilitation. A thorough evaluation into each person's family, medical, surgical, and obstetrical history should therefore be carried out. It is reassuring to know that there is no adverse fetal effect of this disease when it is treated early and effectively, nor does pregnancy have an impact on the disease or the effectiveness of treatment.

B. The physical examination should focus on the cardiopulmonary status. A tuberculin skin test (PPD) is used for surveillance. In cases suspicious for tuberculosis, a chest x-ray examination with the abdomen shielded is mandatory. This is especially indicated in any patient with a previously negative skin test who develops a positive reaction, and even more so if she also has respiratory or systemic symptoms. Although the radiation dose to the fetus is negligible, some recommend waiting until after the first trimester, but delay cannot be condoned in view of the serious risk of the disease. Obtain three consecutive first-morning expectoration specimens for sputum culture and acid fast stained smears. These provide a definitive diagnosis if positive. Use aerosolized hypertonic saline to stimulate sputum production if necessary. Sputum cultures are positive in the majority of patients with active disease. Bronchoscopy is reserved for patients whose diagnosis is in question. Because cultures take so long, however, treatment is generally begun well before the results are known.

C. The medical management of a patient with tuberculosis is modified to ensure against potentially harmful fetal effects of the drugs. In the first trimester, daily doses of isoniazid, 300 mg, with supplemental pyridoxine and ethambutol, 15 mg per kilogram, are the drugs of choice. Monitor the SGOT levels to detect a reaction to isoniazide and, by stopping the drug, avoid toxic hepatitis. Beginning in the second trimester, rifampin, 600 mg daily, may be substituted for ethambutol, although the regimen may be continued if it is well tolerated. Because of the potential for ototoxicity, streptomycin should be avoided in pregnancy if possible; its use is reserved for the most unresponsive cases. Up to two years of therapy is generally recommended; shorter periods of treatment are less efficacious. Hospitalization with isolation, good nutrition, and general medical care are also essential. Defer prophylactic isoniazid treatment for high risk patients, whose skin test has converted but who have no detectable tubercular lesion or positive culture, until after delivery.

D. Optimal obstetrical management is based on maternal or fetal considerations. Institute appropriate isolation during labor, delivery, and the postpartum period. The placenta should be cultured and the infant tested for evidence of tuberculosis. Whereas transplacental infection is rather rare, the baby risks infection from respiratory exposure to a mother who has active disease. For protection of the newborn infant who shows no evidence of active disease, give either isoniazid or BCG vaccination.

References

American Thoracic Society. Guidelines for short course tuberculosis chemotherapy. Am Rev Resp Dis 121:611, 1980.

Charles D. Infections in Obstetrics and Gynecology. Philadelphia: W.B. Saunders, 1980.

Niles RA. Puerperal tuberculosis with death of an infant. Am J Obstet Gynecol 144:131, 1982.

Snider DE, Layde PM, Johnson MW, Lyle MA. Treatment of tuberculosis during pregnancy. Am Rev Resp Dis 122:65, 1980.

PATIENT WITH SUSPICION OF TUBERCULOSIS

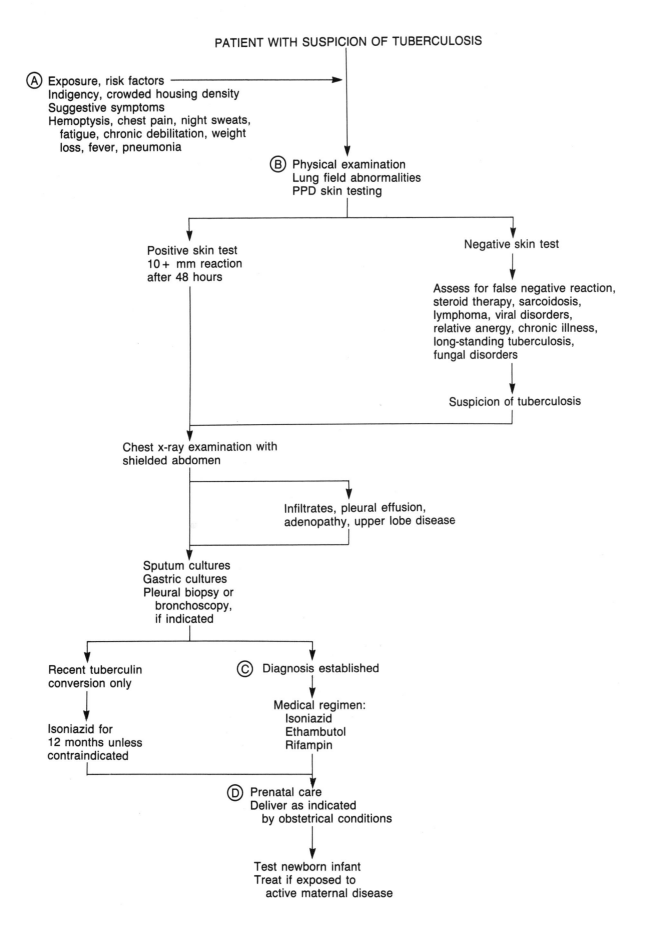

Ⓐ Exposure, risk factors
Indigency, crowded housing density
Suggestive symptoms
Hemoptysis, chest pain, night sweats,
 fatigue, chronic debilitation, weight
 loss, fever, pneumonia

Ⓑ Physical examination
Lung field abnormalities
PPD skin testing

Positive skin test
10 + mm reaction
after 48 hours

Negative skin test

Assess for false negative reaction,
steroid therapy, sarcoidosis,
lymphoma, viral disorders,
relative anergy, chronic illness,
long-standing tuberculosis,
fungal disorders

Suspicion of tuberculosis

Chest x-ray examination with
shielded abdomen

Infiltrates, pleural effusion,
adenopathy, upper lobe disease

Sputum cultures
Gastric cultures
Pleural biopsy or
 bronchoscopy,
 if indicated

Recent tuberculin
conversion only

Ⓒ Diagnosis established

Isoniazid for
12 months unless
contraindicated

Medical regimen:
 Isoniazid
 Ethambutol
 Rifampin

Ⓓ Prenatal care
Deliver as indicated
 by obstetrical conditions

Test newborn infant
Treat if exposed to
 active maternal disease

OBSTRUCTIVE PULMONARY DISEASE

Henry Klapholz, M.D.

A. Many more patients with cystic fibrosis are now surviving to adulthood in sufficiently good health to consider reproduction. Although many of them can survive pregnancy, labor, and delivery without serious compromise, both medical evaluation for functional reserve (Fig. 1) and appropriate genetic counseling about the hereditary risks are clearly in order. Newer prenatal diagnostic tests can detect cystic fibrosis in the fetus. A history of allergies or wheezing (especially in response to stress, dust, cold, exercise, or infection) with the characteristic physical findings of expiratory obstructive disease helps diagnose bronchial asthma. Asthmatics deserve close care to prevent adverse outcomes.

B. Patients with obstructive pulmonary disease can be differentiated for purposes of management into those who have mild and readily treated episodic attacks, those with chronic disorders with some degree of deficient pulmonary function that may or may not produce hypoxia, and those with the serious life threatening disorder of acute status asthmaticus. Compromising situations can arise without warning in these patients, requiring astute and expeditious care.

C. Episodic attacks lend themselves to periodic treatment with bronchodilators (such as ephedrine, 10 mg orally four times daily, or terbutaline, 2.5 to 5 mg four times a day). Orally administered theophylline, 100 mg or more three times per day, is also generally satisfactory. Epinephrine (up to 0.5 mg subcutaneously in a dilute solution) may be given for the acute manifestations, but because adverse reactions have been reported, it is best held in reserve, if possible. These drugs do not seem to harm the fetus.

D. Gravidas with uncomplicated episodic disease can be cared for in a routine manner during pregnancy except at times of acute attacks. Cromolyn inhalation may help avoid allergic or exercise induced attacks when used in a prophylactic regimen; it is ineffective for the acute episode.

E. Patients with arterial PO_2 levels below 80 mm Hg should be hospitalized for aggressive care. This applies especially in the presence of hypercarbia (PCO_2 greater than 38 mm Hg), dyspnea, or cyanosis. Supplemental oxygen may be needed. Check the fetal status periodically from 28 weeks on for evidence of hypoxia. Verify fetal growth by ultrasonography.

F. Vigorous pulmonary toilet, including chest physical therapy, steam inhalation, and increased fluid intake, may prevent bronchopulmonary infection. Give aerosol bronchodilators and steroids, such as prednisone, 30 to 40 mg per day for three to five days, slowly tapering by 5 mg per day to a maintenance dosage of 10 to 15 mg per day. Antibiotics, such as ampicillin, penicillin, or cefaclor (a cephalosporin effective against Gram negative organisms, especially *H. influenzae*), may be helpful. Avoid tetracycline because of its fetal effect.

G. Uncontrolled acute status asthmaticus is a medical emergency requiring immediate hospitalization. Watch for hypoxemia and hypercarbia by periodic use of arterial blood gas determinations. The patient who fails to respond to a standard regimen (e.g., 0.2 to 0.5 ml of 1:1,000 epinephrine subcutaneously) is treated with intermittent positive pressure breathing, supplemental oxygen to maintain arterial PO_2 levels, and high dose steroid therapy (such as Solu-Cortef, 250 mg intravenously every four to six hours). Maintain hydration and provide reassurance. Consider endotracheal intubation and mechanical ventilation if the arterial PCO_2 level rises above 40 mm Hg. Maintain such patients on long term therapy with bronchodilators and steroids. Chest x-ray examination, if indicated by physical findings, may confirm complicating pneumonitis, mediastinal emphysema, or atelectasis.

H. Deliver under controlled conditions by induction of labor when conditions are optimal. During labor, pain relief and hydration are essential. Have bronchodilators, including epinephrine, terbutaline, or aminophylline, readily available. Avoid inhalation anesthesia unless status asthmaticus occurs; then an anesthetic such as halothane may be beneficial for relieving bronchospasm. Even with conduction anesthesia, attentive care is necessary because inspiratory effort may be impeded.

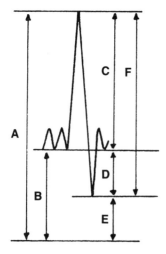

Figure 1 Lung volume compartments as demonstated by spirometry. *A*, total capacity; *B*, functional residual capacity (falls in pregnancy); *C*, inspiratory capacity; *D*, expiratory reserve (falls); *E*, residual volume (falls); *F*, vital capacity.

References

Bukowskyj M, Nakatsu K, Munt PW. Theophylline reassessed. Ann Intern Med 101:63, 1984.

Lalli CM, Raju L. Pregnancy and chronic obstructive pulmonary disease. Chest 80:759, 1981.

Lenfant C, Schweizer M. Pulmonary research: Advances and clinical implications. Am J Med 70:1155, 1981.

Palmer J, Dillon-Baker C, Tecklin JS, et al. Pregnancy in patients with cystic fibrosis. Ann Intern Med 99:596, 1983.

Spector SL. Reciprocal relationship between pregnancy and pulmonary disease: State of the art. Chest 86:1S, 1984.

SUSPICION OF PULMONARY DISEASE

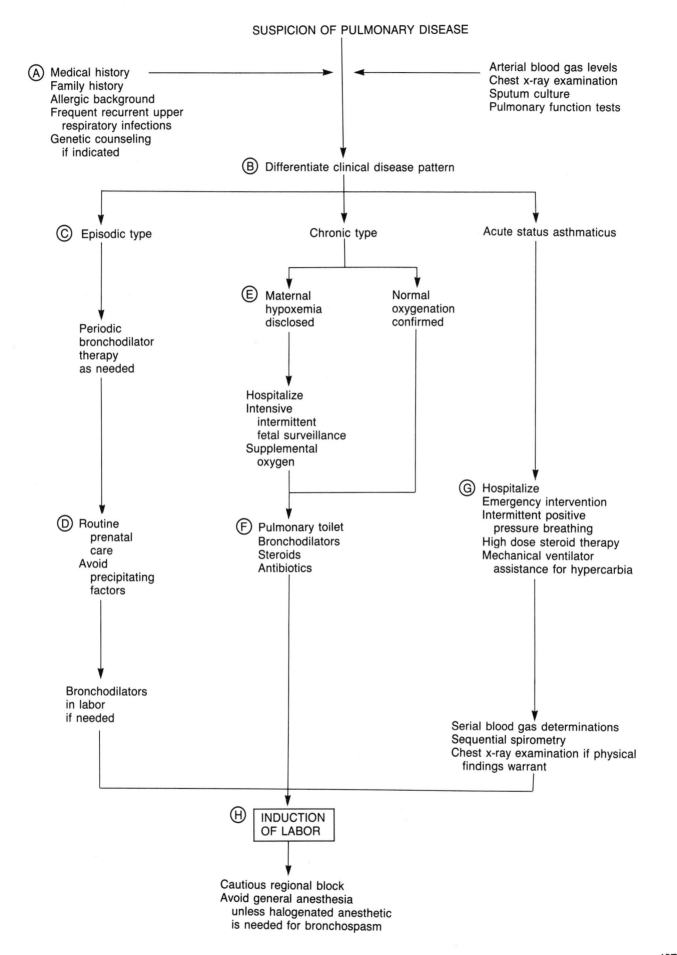

Ⓐ Medical history
Family history
Allergic background
Frequent recurrent upper
    respiratory infections
Genetic counseling
    if indicated

Arterial blood gas levels
Chest x-ray examination
Sputum culture
Pulmonary function tests

Ⓑ Differentiate clinical disease pattern

Ⓒ Episodic type

Chronic type

Acute status asthmaticus

Periodic
bronchodilator
therapy
as needed

Ⓔ Maternal
hypoxemia
disclosed

Normal
oxygenation
confirmed

Hospitalize
Intensive
    intermittent
    fetal surveillance
Supplemental
    oxygen

Ⓖ Hospitalize
Emergency intervention
Intermittent positive
    pressure breathing
High dose steroid therapy
Mechanical ventilator
    assistance for hypercarbia

Ⓓ Routine
    prenatal
    care
Avoid
    precipitating
    factors

Ⓕ Pulmonary toilet
Bronchodilators
Steroids
Antibiotics

Bronchodilators
in labor
if needed

Serial blood gas determinations
Sequential spirometry
Chest x-ray examination if physical
    findings warrant

Ⓗ INDUCTION
OF LABOR

Cautious regional block
Avoid general anesthesia
    unless halogenated anesthetic
    is needed for bronchospasm

Rh ISOIMMUNIZATION

David B. Acker, M.D.

A. Confirm the gravida's complete history, especially noting any blood transfusions, and details of her obstetrical background in regard to abortion, ectopic pregnancy, stillbirth, and the neonatal course of prior infants (jaundice, anemia, transfusion). Obtain written reports from all treating physicians. Every prenatal patient should have blood typed and an antibody screen performed at the first prenatal visit. Ultrasonography for gestational dating is also done, if needed.

B. To avoid errors in quantitation of antibody titers that make interpretation difficult, send specimens only to laboratories that have a substantive background and continuing experience with this problem.

C. An Rh negative gravida who is anti-D antibody negative and who experiences vaginal bleeding or an abortion during the first trimester should receive 50 μg of immune globulin (anti-D, RhoGam) intramuscularly to protect against sensitization from fetomaternal transfusion. Amniocentesis undertaken for genetic testing, and second trimester termination require 300 μg of immune globulin. The same applies to intrauterine fetal demise from any cause, especially if one chooses conservative expectancy, awaiting spontaneous labor.

D. If the result of initial anti-D antibody screening is negative and the course of the pregnancy is uncomplicated, no further testing is necessary until the 28th gestational week. At that time carry out a repeat study. If the result is still negative, 300 μg of immune globulin should be administered intramuscularly as prophylaxis against a silent fetomaternal bleeding episode.

E. If amniocentesis is needed to determine fetal lung maturity and the delivery is not expected to take place within 48 hours, a postamniocentesis dose of 300 μg of immune globulin should be given; if delivery is not expected to be delayed, a single postpartum dose will suffice. A large fetomaternal transfusion may occur with abruptio placentae, manual removal of the placenta, or incision through the placenta. Quantitate the amount of fetal blood in the maternal circulation so that an appropriate dose of immune globulin can be given.

F. A gravida given immune globulin prophylactically at 28 weeks may have sufficient exogenous antibody to cause the neonatal direct Coombs test to be positive. This represents passive antibody administration, not active immunization. The mother is still a candidate for postpartum immune globulin therapy.

G. Each laboratory should determine its own critical anti-D antibody titer as the level below which no severely erythroblastotic neonate or stillbirth has been noted. The critical titer of 1:16 reflects our experience.

H. If the anti-D titer exceeds the critical titer, further management is based on amniocentesis and spectrophotometric analysis of bilirubin breakdown products (Fig. 1). The severity and timing of complications in prior pregnancies determine when to do the first amniocentesis, usually between the 24th and 28th weeks. Use an opaque envelope to shield amniotic fluid specimens from light because it alters the bilirubin metabolites and falsely lowers the reading.

I. The severity of fetal compromise and the timing of sequential amniocenteses are based on the pigment level and gestational age (Liley curves). The higher the level and the more rapid the rise over time, the greater the urgency to effect either delivery (if near term) or intrauterine transfusion (if immature). Ultrasonography, biophysical testing, and pulmonary maturity studies guide the care. Consultation and transfer to a tertiary care center are in the patient's best interests. Highly sophisticated skills can be brought to bear for early detection of fetal hydrops, administration of intrauterine transfusion, and provision of other developing techniques applicable to these cases.

References

Bowman JM, Manning FA. Intrauterine transfusions: Winnipeg 1982. Obstet Gynecol 61:203, 1983.

Bowman JM, Pollack J. Rh isoimmunization in Manitoba: Progress in prevention and management. Can Med Assoc J 129:343, 1983.

Management of Isoimmunization in Pregnancy. Technical Bulletin number 90. Washington, DC: American College of Obstetricians and Gynecologists, 1986.

Prevention of Rho(D) Isoimmunization. Technical Bulletin number 79. Washington, DC: American College of Obstetricians and Gynecologists, 1984.

Seeds JW, Bowes WA. Ultrasound-guided fetal intravascular transfusion in severe rhesus immunization. Am J Obstet Gynecol 154:1105, 1986.

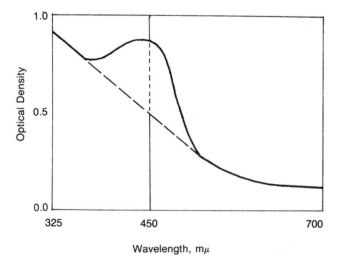

Figure 1 Amniotic fluid spectrophotometric absorption curve. Peak representing blood breakdown pigments at 450 mμ is demonstrated above interpolated baseline (broken line) in Rh-sensitized pregnancy.

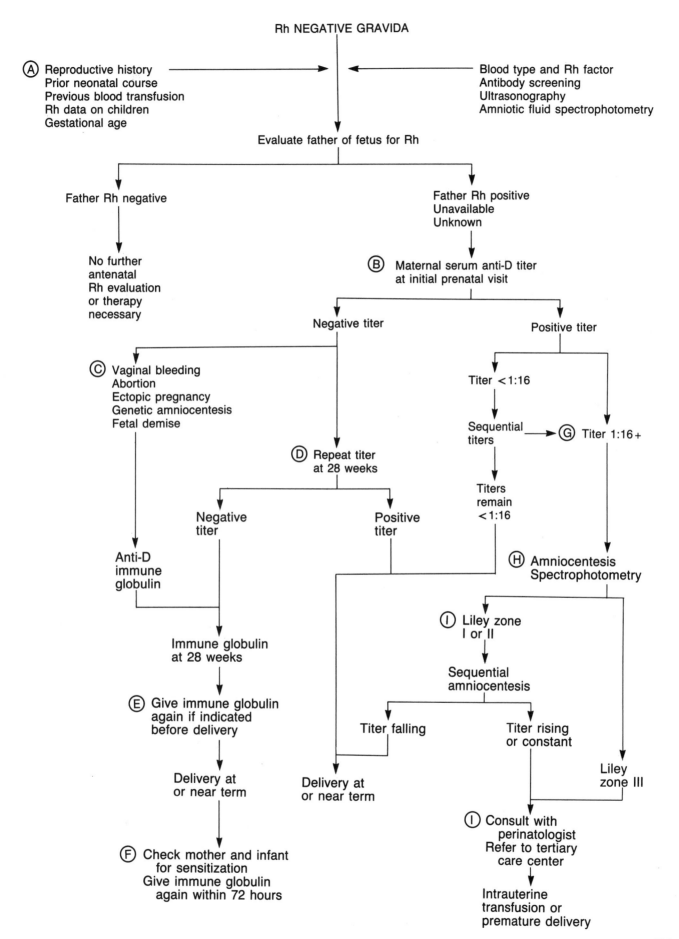

Rh NEGATIVE GRAVIDA

Ⓐ Reproductive history
Prior neonatal course
Previous blood transfusion
Rh data on children
Gestational age

Blood type and Rh factor
Antibody screening
Ultrasonography
Amniotic fluid spectrophotometry

Evaluate father of fetus for Rh

Father Rh negative

No further
antenatal
Rh evaluation
or therapy
necessary

Father Rh positive
Unavailable
Unknown

Ⓑ Maternal serum anti-D titer
at initial prenatal visit

Negative titer

Positive titer

Ⓒ Vaginal bleeding
Abortion
Ectopic pregnancy
Genetic amniocentesis
Fetal demise

Titer <1:16

Sequential
titers

Ⓖ Titer 1:16+

Ⓓ Repeat titer
at 28 weeks

Titers
remain
<1:16

Negative
titer

Positive
titer

Anti-D
immune
globulin

Ⓗ Amniocentesis
Spectrophotometry

Immune globulin
at 28 weeks

Ⓘ Liley zone
I or II

Ⓔ Give immune globulin
again if indicated
before delivery

Sequential
amniocentesis

Delivery at
or near term

Titer falling

Titer rising
or constant

Liley
zone III

Delivery at
or near term

Ⓙ Consult with
perinatologist
Refer to tertiary
care center

Ⓕ Check mother and infant
for sensitization
Give immune globulin
again within 72 hours

Intrauterine
transfusion or
premature delivery

NONIMMUNE HYDROPS FETALIS

Benjamin P. Sachs, M.B., B.S., D.P.H.

A. Exposure to foreign blood antigens as a result of pregnancy or blood transfusion may result in the production of antibodies that have the potential for causing hemolytic disease in the fetus by crossing transplacentally to the fetus where they can destroy fetal erythrocytes. The most common immunologic form, until recently, was related to the anti-D antibody in the Rh system (p 138). As the incidence of immune hydrops has fallen with the effective use of anti-D preparations (RhoGam), nonimmune hydrops has taken on greater significance. Regardless of the Rh status, all gravidas should undergo an antibody screening test at the first prenatal visit.

B. If an antibody is detected, ascertain the risk of hemolytic disease. Two commonly detected antibody systems, Lewis and cold agglutinin, pose no fetal threat. By contrast, the Kell antibody often behaves in a more aggressive fashion than the Rh (anti-D) antibody. Consultation with experienced clinicians is recommended in these cases.

C. Maternal risk factors for nonimmune hydrops include twin pregnancy, infection—specifically cytomegalovirus disease (p 150) and syphilis (p 154)—diabetes mellitus (p 96), thalassemia (p 110), and pregnancy induced hypertension (p 86).

D. Because the onset of nonimmune hydrops cannot be predicted with any degree of accuracy, it is suggested that ultrasonographic fetal evaluation in the asymptomatic gravida be done at 26 to 30 weeks and again at about 34 weeks. For the symptomatic gravida, clinical events dictate the timing of the ultrasonography.

E. The most common reason for undertaking ultrasonography for this condition is a uterus that is larger than anticipated for the dates. Decreased fetal movements coupled with a nonreactive nonstress test should warrant investigation. Occasionally hydrops fetalis is disclosed as an incidental finding in an ultrasonographic study done for an unrelated reason.

F. Hydrops fetalis is a nonspecific descriptive designation for the manifestation of generalized fetal edema with ascites, pleural or pericardial effusion, and anasarca. A wide variety of illnesses, some fatal but many amenable to medical or surgical treatment, are associated with this condition.

G. Evaluate for specific fetal problems, paying special attention to the cardiac anatomy, rate, and rhythm and searching for pulmonary malformations, mediastinal and other chest masses, bowel volvulus, retroperitoneal neuroblastoma, hydronephrotic kidney, and sacrococcygeal teratoma.

H. The twin-to-twin transfusion syndrome associated with monochorionic-diamniotic multiple fetuses is often heralded by acute polyhydramnios (p 216). Watch for discordant fetal weights. If the technique is available, consider fetal umbilical vein blood sampling (p 80).

I. Approximately one-seventh of the cases are idiopathic. In this group, recovery sometimes can be expected if appropriate antenatal treatment is given. This may require sequential drainage of collected effusions to relieve intracavity pressure and thereby help maintain the fetal cardiovascular status to permit the fetus to continue to grow and develop in utero until it is mature enough to be delivered without risk of compromise in the neonatal period.

References

Anderson HM, Drew JH, Bencher NA, et al. Non-immune hydrops fetalis: Changing contribution to perinatal mortality. Br J Obstet Gynaecol 90:636, 1983.

Fleisher AC, Killam AP, Boehm FH, et al. Hydrops fetalis: Sonographic evaluation and clinical implications. Radiology 141:163, 1981.

Hutcheson AA, Drew JH, Yu VY, et al. Non-immunological hydrops fetalis: A review of 61 cases. Obstet Gynecol 59:347, 1982.

Watson J, Cambell S. Antenatal evaluation and management in non-immune hydrops fetalis. Obstet Gynecol 67:589, 1986.

PATIENT WITH SUSPICION OF NONIMMUNE HYDROPS

Risk factors:
  Multiple pregnancy
  Intrauterine infection
  Diabetes mellitus
  Hereditary coagulation disorder
  Pregnancy induced hypertension
  Discrepant uterine size
  Hydramnios
  Decreased fetal movement

CBC
Blood type and Rh
Antibody screen
Hemoglobin electrophoresis
G6PD-pyruvate kinase level
Alpha fetoprotein level
Glucose tolerance test
Serology for syphilis
TORCH titers

(A) Assess risk for immune hydrops fetalis
Screen for maternal antibodies

(B) Antibody detected:
Lewis, cold agglutinin,
Kell antibody

No antibody found

Consultation or referral

(C) Evaluate for risk of
nonimmune hydrops fetalis:
  Multiple pregnancy
  Cytomegalovirus, syphilis
  Diabetes, thalassemia, pregnancy induced hypertension

Identify and undertake
program of testing and
pregnancy management
for isoimmunization
(p 138)

Risk factor disclosed

No risk factor

(E) Clinical suspicion only

(D) Ultrasonography to diagnose
hydrops and detect malformations

(F) Hydrops fetalis diagnosed
Ascites, pleural and pericardial
effusions, and anasarca

(G) Structural fetal
abnormality

No anatomic fetal
malformation seen

Counsel
Provide
specific
therapy if
feasible

(H) Multiple
fetuses
(p 220)

(I) Single
fetus

Note discordant size
Acute polyhydramnios
Consider twin-twin
transfusion syndrome

Identify and
treat maternal
disorder

(I) Consider:
  Fetomaternal
   transfusion
  Genetic disease
  Viral infection
  Idiopathic cause

COLLAGEN DISEASE

Jerold M. Carlson, M.D., M.P.H.

A. The three principal autoimmune connective tissue disorders, systemic lupus erythematosus, scleroderma, and rheumatoid arthritis, share many but not all histologic and clinicopathologic characteristics. Other collagen diseases, such as dermatomyositis and periarteritis nodosa, are especially rare among gravidas. The diagnoses are based on clinical manifestations and are confirmed by demonstration of various autoantibodies. Extensive evaluation of the multisystem disease process is recommended before pregnancy is undertaken.

B. Skin lesions, fever, arthralgia, nephritis, and hypertension as well as cardiac, pulmonary, and central nervous system manifestations should raise a suspicion of the diagnosis. Certain medications, such as orally administered contraceptives, anticonvulsants, and antihypertensive drugs, may cause a lupus reaction.

C. Laboratory studies can document autoimmune phenomena. Normochromic normocytic anemia, leukopenia, increased platelets, a high sedimentation rate, and hypergammaglobulinemia are commonly seen. Rheumatoid arthiritis is further characterized by joint swelling and stiffness and rheumatoid nodules with a positive rheumatoid factor, synovial fluid inflammatory exudate, and soft tissue swelling and osteoporosis on x-ray examination. Scleroderma is associated with Raynaud's phenomenon, skin and visceral involvement, and a positive antinuclear antibody test. Systemic lupus erythematosus appears with a characteristic butterfly malar rash and arthralgia, photosensitivity, pleuritic symptoms, seizures, a false positive serologic test for syphilis, and a positive antinuclear antibody test and LE preparation.

D. Systemic lupus erythematosus is generally unaffected by pregnancy, although infertility, spontaneous abortion, prematurity, and perinatal mortality are increased. Corticosteroids are often effective for management. Give prednisone, 40 to 100 mg daily in divided doses, for exacerbations, tapering gradually. If the patient is already being treated, continue therapy in pregnancy, including both glucocorticoids and azathioprine. Most worrisome is lupus nephritis, often masked as pregnancy induced hypertension. Watch for falling serum complement (C3 and C4) levels, failing renal function, and hemolytic anemia.

E. Scleroderma does not appear to be accelerated by pregnancy, but severe cardiac, renal, or gastrointestinal involvement may adversely affect pregnancy and threaten the gravida's life and well-being. Watch for reduced renal function, unremitting hypertension, and dysphagic manifestations. Treatment consists of supportive measures and, if needed, antacids and corticosteroids.

F. Generally there is a decrease in the symptoms of rheumatoid arthritis during pregnancy, perhaps in response to enhanced blood cortisol levels. The treatment consists of physical therapy and medical management as needed. Anti-inflammatory drugs, mainly aspirin in dosages up to 3 to 4 g daily, are the treatment of choice. If this is not effective, consider corticosteroids first and then immunosuppressives. The fetal effects of aspirin have to be accepted, including bleeding and delayed labor.

G. If significant fetal or maternal complications occur, delivery is indicated. The mode of delivery may be mandated by compromise of the maternal renal or cardiac status. Contracture of extremities (by rheumatoid arthritis) or soft tissue (by scleroderma) may interdict vaginal delivery.

H. Postpartum exacerbation is common, possibly due to steroid withdrawal. Treatment by corticosteroids is generally effective. The newborn must be followed for transient or permanent disease. Watch for perinatal heart block in cases of lupus erythematosus. Growth retardation may also occur.

References

Bear R. Pregnancy and lupus nephritis: A detailed report of six cases with a review of the literature. Obstet Gynecol 47:715, 1976.

Fine LG, Barnett EV, Danovitch GM, et al. Systemic lupus erythematosus in pregnancy. Ann Int Med 94:667, 1981.

Gimovsky ML, Montoro M, Paul RH. Pregnancy outcome in women with systemic lupus erythematosus. Obstet Gynecol 63:686, 1984.

Kohler PF, Vaughan J. The autoimmune diseases. JAMA 248:2646, 1982.

Zurier RB, Argyros TG, Urman JD, et al. Systemic lupus erythematosus: Management during pregnancy. Obstet Gynecol 51:178, 1978.

PATIENT WITH SUSPICION OF COLLAGEN DISEASE

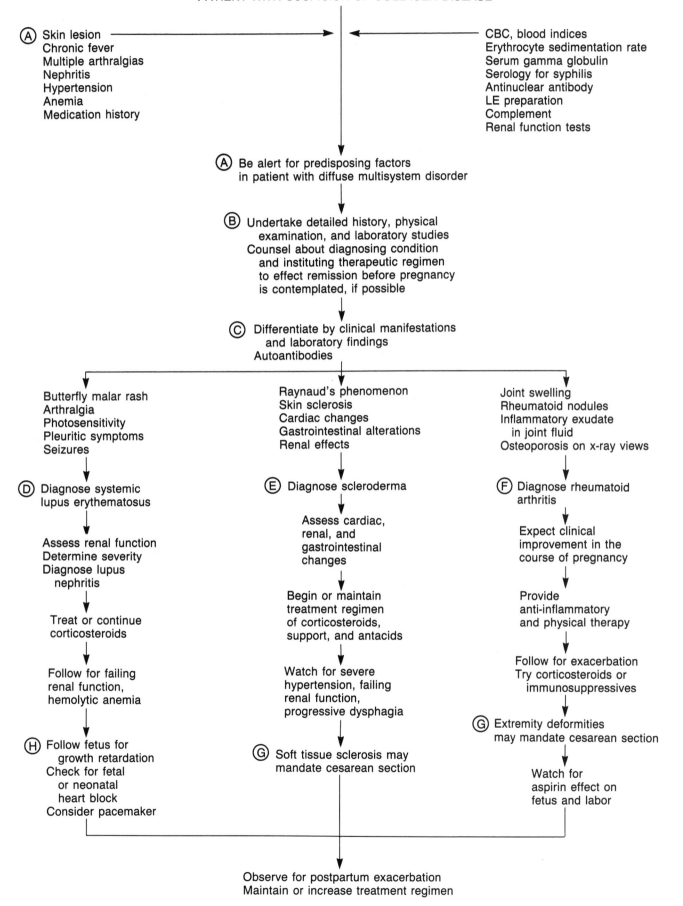

(A) Skin lesion
Chronic fever
Multiple arthralgias
Nephritis
Hypertension
Anemia
Medication history

CBC, blood indices
Erythrocyte sedimentation rate
Serum gamma globulin
Serology for syphilis
Antinuclear antibody
LE preparation
Complement
Renal function tests

(A) Be alert for predisposing factors
in patient with diffuse multisystem disorder

(B) Undertake detailed history, physical
examination, and laboratory studies
Counsel about diagnosing condition
and instituting therapeutic regimen
to effect remission before pregnancy
is contemplated, if possible

(C) Differentiate by clinical manifestations
and laboratory findings
Autoantibodies

Butterfly malar rash
Arthralgia
Photosensitivity
Pleuritic symptoms
Seizures

Raynaud's phenomenon
Skin sclerosis
Cardiac changes
Gastrointestinal alterations
Renal effects

Joint swelling
Rheumatoid nodules
Inflammatory exudate
in joint fluid
Osteoporosis on x-ray views

(D) Diagnose systemic
lupus erythematosus

(E) Diagnose scleroderma

(F) Diagnose rheumatoid
arthritis

Assess renal function
Determine severity
Diagnose lupus
nephritis

Assess cardiac,
renal, and
gastrointestinal
changes

Expect clinical
improvement in the
course of pregnancy

Treat or continue
corticosteroids

Begin or maintain
treatment regimen
of corticosteroids,
support, and antacids

Provide
anti-inflammatory
and physical therapy

Follow for failing
renal function,
hemolytic anemia

Watch for severe
hypertension, failing
renal function,
progressive dysphagia

Follow for exacerbation
Try corticosteroids or
immunosuppressives

(H) Follow fetus for
growth retardation
Check for fetal
or neonatal
heart block
Consider pacemaker

(G) Soft tissue sclerosis may
mandate cesarean section

(G) Extremity deformities
may mandate cesarean section

Watch for
aspirin effect on
fetus and labor

Observe for postpartum exacerbation
Maintain or increase treatment regimen

ACUTE SURGICAL ABDOMEN

Henry Klapholz, M.D.

A. The presenting clinical pictures associated with acute abdominal surgical disorders are often markedly altered by pregnancy. This makes it very difficult to differentiate them from obstetrical conditions or intercurrent medical illnesses. There are a number of physiologic conditions in pregnancy that cause pain. Indeed some discomfort is commonly experienced by gravidas. A frequent form of pain, one that may be distressing but resolves spontaneously, is caused by round ligament tension. Nonetheless intense persistent pain must be evaluated expeditiously. In addition to pain, pregnancy may normally present other symptoms that serve to flag surgical problems in the nonpregnant state, such as nausea and vomiting. However, if vomiting is protracted, profuse, or projectile and is accompanied by pain or abdominal distention, a surgical problem must be considered likely. The common symptoms of transient syncope seen so often in pregnancy are readily distinguished from those of shock with progressive cardiovascular instability, which occurs in some intra-abdominal surgical emergencies. Hypoglycemia should also be investigated.

B. There are many different nonsurgical conditions that can present in pregnancy with signs and symptoms almost indistinguishable from those of acute surgical disorders. Although acute salpingitis, for example, is unusual in pregnancy, it can occur and should be considered in a gravida who has a history of pelvic inflammatory disease or sexually transmitted disease and whose clinical picture includes episodic pain and fever. Take into account the constellation of the history, physical findings, and laboratory evidence to help diagnose urinary, cardiac, or inflammatory bowel disease or other medical disorders. In relative terms, complications related to pregnancy are even more common. Those that constitute true surgical crises, such as ectopic pregnancy (p 54), must be evaluated with all due haste and managed aggressively as emergencies. Maintain a high index of suspicion and follow the patient's changing clinical and laboratory picture closely in order to make the proper diagnosis as soon as feasible.

C. Gratifyingly, it is rare to encounter a true surgical emergency in pregnancy. If diagnosis and appropriate intervention are delayed, however, morbidity and mortality increase considerably. Pregnancy may modify presenting manifestations somewhat. The focus of pain and tenderness in association with acute appendicitis, for example, is commonly moved progressively cephalad as the antececal appendix is advanced by the growing uterus (p 146). Because manifestations are so often atypical, one must be especially alert for this condition.

D. Critical decision making in managing gravidas with acute surgical conditions has to weigh the hazards associated with delaying surgical intervention against the risks of surgery in pregnancy. Although nonsurgical approaches are preferable, surgery is clearly indicated for patients who show evidence of progression of an acute surgical process, who develop cardiovascular instability from intraperitoneal bleeding, who show spreading peritonitis, or who are deemed to have a life threatening problem, such as acute appendicitis, twisted ovarian cyst, intestinal obstruction, ruptured viscus, or volvulus. A careful examination should be performed to rule out an incarcerated inguinal or umbilical hernia. Peritonitis offers the greatest risk because it can quickly become generalized in pregnancy. Well conducted surgery and anesthesia uncomplicated by hypoxia and hypotension carry little fetal risk, especially if one can avoid manipulating or operating on the gravid uterus. Postoperative tocolytic therapy may help preserve the pregnancy (p 178) during the early phase of recovery.

E. If the gravida is in stable condition and her disease is not progressive, it may be justified to consider an expectant approach. Gallbladder disease, for example, can be treated in this way in the absence of jaundice or obstruction by a common duct stone. Similarly acute pancreatitis may also be managed conservatively in most cases. Continue close observation and periodic testing. Surgery can be undertaken at any time it becomes apparent that the problem is not under control.

References

Barron WM. Medical evaluation of the pregnant patient requiring nonobstetric surgery. Clin Perinatol 12:481, 1985.

Cooperman M. Complications of appendectomy. Surg Clin North Am 63:1233, 1983.

DeVore GR. Acute abdominal pain in the pregnant patient due to pancreatitis, acute appendicitis, cholecystitis or peptic ulcer disease. Clin Perinatol 7:349, 1980.

Klein EA. Urologic problems of pregnancy. Obstet Gynecol Surv 39:605, 1984.

Stevenson RJ. Abdominal pain unrelated to trauma. Surg Clin North Am 65:1181, 1985.

GRAVIDA WITH ABDOMINAL PAIN

Persistent abdominal pain
Protracted vomiting
Cardiovascular instability
Abdominal distention
Vascular collapse
Stool changes
Hematemesis, melena
Jaundice

Serial WBC, differential
Erythrocyte sedimentation rate
Urinalysis and culture
Serum electrolyte and amylase levels
Ultrasonography
Genitourinary and gastrointestinal x-ray studies
Liver function tests

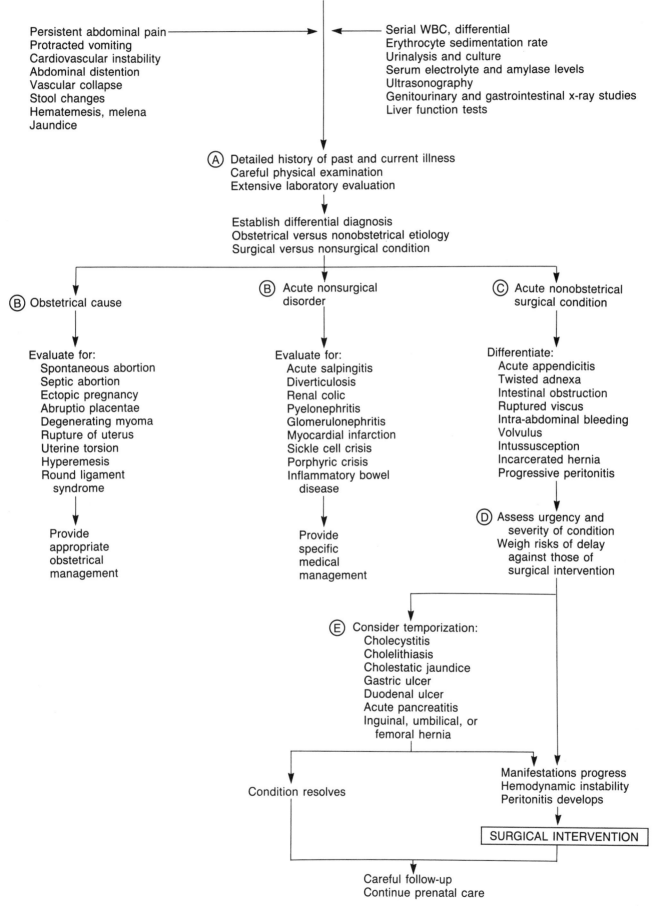

Ⓐ Detailed history of past and current illness
Careful physical examination
Extensive laboratory evaluation

Establish differential diagnosis
Obstetrical versus nonobstetrical etiology
Surgical versus nonsurgical condition

Ⓑ Obstetrical cause

Ⓑ Acute nonsurgical disorder

Ⓒ Acute nonobstetrical surgical condition

Evaluate for:
    Spontaneous abortion
    Septic abortion
    Ectopic pregnancy
    Abruptio placentae
    Degenerating myoma
    Rupture of uterus
    Uterine torsion
    Hyperemesis
    Round ligament
        syndrome

Evaluate for:
    Acute salpingitis
    Diverticulosis
    Renal colic
    Pyelonephritis
    Glomerulonephritis
    Myocardial infarction
    Sickle cell crisis
    Porphyric crisis
    Inflammatory bowel
        disease

Differentiate:
    Acute appendicitis
    Twisted adnexa
    Intestinal obstruction
    Ruptured viscus
    Intra-abdominal bleeding
    Volvulus
    Intussusception
    Incarcerated hernia
    Progressive peritonitis

Provide
appropriate
obstetrical
management

Provide
specific
medical
management

Ⓓ Assess urgency and
severity of condition
Weigh risks of delay
against those of
surgical intervention

Ⓔ Consider temporization:
    Cholecystitis
    Cholelithiasis
    Cholestatic jaundice
    Gastric ulcer
    Duodenal ulcer
    Acute pancreatitis
    Inguinal, umbilical, or
        femoral hernia

Condition resolves

Manifestations progress
Hemodynamic instability
Peritonitis develops

SURGICAL INTERVENTION

Careful follow-up
Continue prenatal care

GASTROINTESTINAL DISORDER

Jerold M. Carlson, M.D., M.P.H.

A. The diagnosis and management of intercurrent medical and or surgical problems arising in the obstetrical patient are often difficult and confusing. This is especially pertinent when timely diagnosis and intervention are critical, as in cases of acute surgical abdomen (p 144). The developing clinical picture helps to clarify the condition and guide management. A history of pre-existing gastrointestinal, renal, or cardiac disorders or of trauma, tumor, diabetes mellitus, or drug use alerts one to the proper diagnosis and course of action.

B. Persistent pain or vomiting demands immediate attention. The differential diagnosis includes hyperemesis gravidarum (p 84), ulcer disease, bilary tract disease, appendicitis, pancreatitis, and a number of other surgical and medical disorders, such as sickle cell crisis, porphyria, salpingitis, intestinal obstruction, hernia, enteritis, inflammatory bowel disease, renal colic, and adnexal accident. Evaluation includes appropriate laboratory studies to rule out an acute process and serial observations to assess changing conditions with the passage of time.

C. The diagnosis of ulcer disease and reflux esophagitis is most often made by endoscopy; x-ray confirmation is rarely needed and is best avoided in pregnancy, if possible, to reduce fetal exposure to radiation. This admonition should not be misinterpreted to mean that x-ray studies are never indicated in pregnancy. They should be done when it is clear that their benefit outweighs the risk (p 62). Management includes the use of hydration, small meals, antacids, and dietary restrictions.

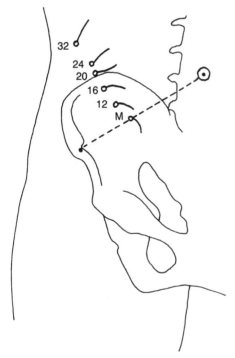

Figure 1 Expected location of a freely mobile antececal appendix as it rises during the course of pregnancy from McBurney's point (M) to a subcostal site, being displaced by the enlarging gravid uterus. Weeks of gestational age shown.

D. If maternal progression of symptoms is evident by the appearance of fever, increasing pain, and jaundice, serial blood tests are needed to detect a rising white blood count and shifting differential (suggestive of inflammation), falling hematocrit level (reflecting hemorrhage), altered serum enzyme and electrolyte levels, and changes in chemistry results. The stool should be examined for blood and, if indicated, for ova and parasites.

E. If biliary tract disease is suspected, abdominal ultrasonography is useful for diagnosing acute cholecystitis and sometimes cholelithiasis as well. One should also find leukocytosis and increased levels of serum alkaline phosphatase, SGOT, and sometimes amylase and lipase, but usually a normal bilirubin level. For acute cholecystitis, admit the patient to the hospital for supportive and symptomatic management until her condition has stabilized. Provide bed rest, intravenous hydration, and analgesia, as needed. Surgery is called for only if the patient is unstable or her condition is progressive. Surgical management usually can be deferred until after delivery.

F. Pancreatitis is associated with many different etiologic conditions, including drug or alcohol abuse, infectious biliary tract disease, trauma to the pancreas, and metabolic disorders. Laboratory study shows a rising serum amylase level, an increased serum lipase level, an increased or normal serum bilirubin level, increases in LDH, SGOT, and alkaline phosphatase levels, an increased white blood count, and increases in hematocrit and blood sugar levels. Conservative medical therapy is often effective in pregnancy. Inflammatory bowel disease may be aggravated by pregnancy, although this is not invariably the case. A chronic course is characteristic. Steroid therapy in addition to antibiotics, antispasmodics, and sedatives helps control the acute flare-up. Positional x-ray evaluation is needed to confirm an intestinal obstruction by demonstrating dilated loops of bowel containing fluid-gas interface levels. Ultrasonography is useful for identifying an abscess cavity or visualizing an enlarged pancreas. In general, the therapy of gastrointestinal disorders is the same in pregnancy as in nonpregnant adults, except that use of x-ray examination should be minimized. Obstetrical management of labor and delivery should be carried out as indicated, modifying the approach only if the maternal or fetal status deteriorates.

References

DeVore GR. Acute abdominal pain in the pregnant patient due to acute pancreatitis, acute appendicitis, cholecystitis or peptic ulcer disease. Clin Perinatol 7:349, 1980.

McKay AJ, O'Neill J, Imrie CW. Pancreatitis, pregnancy and gallstones. Br J Obstet Gynaecol 87:47, 1980.

Young KR. Acute pancreatitis in pregnancy: Two case reports. Obstet Gynecol 60:653, 1982.

SUSPICION OF GASTROINTESTINAL DISORDER

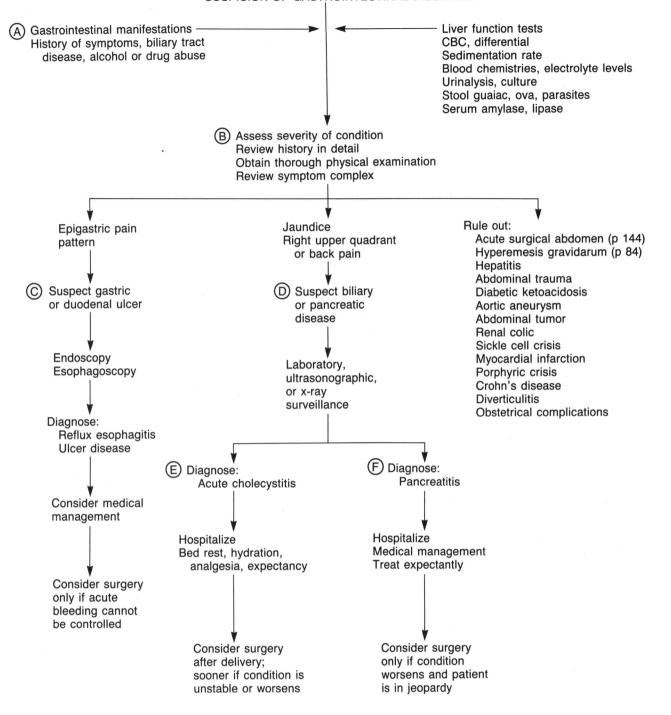

(A) Gastrointestinal manifestations
History of symptoms, biliary tract
disease, alcohol or drug abuse

Liver function tests
CBC, differential
Sedimentation rate
Blood chemistries, electrolyte levels
Urinalysis, culture
Stool guaiac, ova, parasites
Serum amylase, lipase

(B) Assess severity of condition
Review history in detail
Obtain thorough physical examination
Review symptom complex

Epigastric pain
pattern

Jaundice
Right upper quadrant
or back pain

Rule out:
Acute surgical abdomen (p 144)
Hyperemesis gravidarum (p 84)
Hepatitis
Abdominal trauma
Diabetic ketoacidosis
Aortic aneurysm
Abdominal tumor
Renal colic
Sickle cell crisis
Myocardial infarction
Porphyric crisis
Crohn's disease
Diverticulitis
Obstetrical complications

(C) Suspect gastric
or duodenal ulcer

(D) Suspect biliary
or pancreatic
disease

Endoscopy
Esophagoscopy

Laboratory,
ultrasonographic,
or x-ray
surveillance

Diagnose:
Reflux esophagitis
Ulcer disease

(E) Diagnose:
Acute cholecystitis

(F) Diagnose:
Pancreatitis

Consider medical
management

Hospitalize
Bed rest, hydration,
analgesia, expectancy

Hospitalize
Medical management
Treat expectantly

Consider surgery
only if acute
bleeding cannot
be controlled

Consider surgery
after delivery;
sooner if condition is
unstable or worsens

Consider surgery
only if condition
worsens and patient
is in jeopardy

ABDOMINAL MASS

Susan B. Wilson, M.D.

A. An abdominal mass in pregnancy signals the need for astute evaluation, whether symptomatic or incidental. The differential diagnosis requires careful physical examination and a detailed history to reveal the pain pattern and associated symptoms.

B. If the tumor is growing at a rate consistent with gestation, consider it to be related to the pregnancy. First verify that the patient is actually pregnant. Ultrasonography helps differentiate a blighted ovum, ectopic pregnancy, and hydatidiform mole and also determines the presence, size, consistency (solid versus cystic), and site of the mass.

C. It is important to learn whether the mass is intrinsic to the gravid uterus (intraluminal or intramural) or distinct from it. This information differentiates adnexal, intra-abdominal, or retroperitoneal lesions. An asymptomatic leiomyoma uteri needs no special care in pregnancy, although it may obstruct labor. However, acute degeneration with pain, fever, and leukocytosis necessitates symptomatic treatment, often requiring much analgesia until the acute phase subsides. An acute surgical problem must be ruled out first. Myomectomy is rarely indicated in these cases because it is seldom necessary and risks hemorrhage, infection, abortion, fetal hypoxia, and premature birth.

D. If the gestational size is consistent with the duration of pregnancy on the basis of the last menstrual period, the mass is probably extrauterine, most often adnexal. If the uterus is larger than expected, assess for complications of pregnancy, including hydatidiform mole, multiple pregnancy or hydramnios, or a uterine myoma or malformation.

E. Pregnancy related extrauterine masses most often arise in the ovary, usually a corpus luteum of pregnancy or theca lutein cysts. However, they also may represent concurrent inflammatory bowel disease.

F. Be alert to the possibility of an ovarian neoplasm even though it is rare in young women of reproductive age. This applies especially if the mass is hard, nodular, and bilateral. Look for a fluid wave, admittedly difficult to detect in pregnancy. Ascites may be the first overt sign. The common benign ovarian mass is cystic, smooth, mobile, nontender, and unilateral.

G. Staging laparotomy for ovarian cancer requires a midline suprapubic incision for adequate exploration and observation. Collect ascitic fluid for a cell block; if there is no ascites, take peritoneal saline washings. Carefully document the extent of the lesion, especially implants on the undersurface of the diaphragm, omentum, mesentery, bowel, and paracolic gutters. Obtain biopsy specimens of representative implants and palpable aortic nodes. Oncologic consultation is important for determining the optimal surgical therapy and subsequent adjunctive therapy.

H. Delay surgery, if possible, until the second trimester to avoid the fetal risks of anesthesia and intraoperative hypoxia during embryonic organogenesis (p 58). Functional or luteal cysts often subside spontaneously. Symptomatic adnexal accidents usually require prompt surgical intervention for definitive care. Early in the third trimester, each week of delay improves the fetal chances of survival. Consider administering steroids to accelerate lung maturity (p 178).

References

Lavery JP, Koontz WL, Layman L, et al. Sonographic evaluation of the adnexa during early pregnancy. Surg Gynecol Obstet 163:319, 1986.

Roberts JA. Management of gynecologic tumors during pregnancy. Clin Perinatol 10:369, 1983.

Winer-Muran HT, Muram D, Gillieson MS, et al. Uterine myomas in pregnancy. Can Med Assoc J 128:949, 1983.

PATIENT WITH ABDOMINAL MASS DISCLOSED IN PREGNANCY

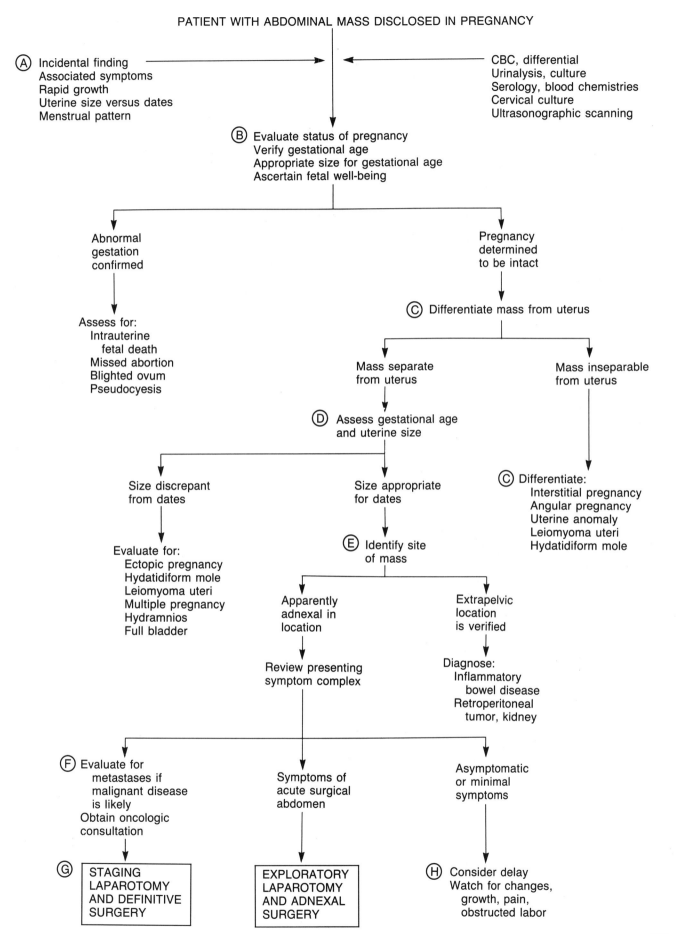

Ⓐ Incidental finding
Associated symptoms
Rapid growth
Uterine size versus dates
Menstrual pattern

CBC, differential
Urinalysis, culture
Serology, blood chemistries
Cervical culture
Ultrasonographic scanning

Ⓑ Evaluate status of pregnancy
Verify gestational age
Appropriate size for gestational age
Ascertain fetal well-being

Abnormal
gestation
confirmed

Pregnancy
determined
to be intact

Assess for:
Intrauterine
fetal death
Missed abortion
Blighted ovum
Pseudocyesis

Ⓒ Differentiate mass from uterus

Mass separate
from uterus

Mass inseparable
from uterus

Ⓓ Assess gestational age
and uterine size

Ⓒ Differentiate:
Interstitial pregnancy
Angular pregnancy
Uterine anomaly
Leiomyoma uteri
Hydatidiform mole

Size discrepant
from dates

Size appropriate
for dates

Evaluate for:
Ectopic pregnancy
Hydatidiform mole
Leiomyoma uteri
Multiple pregnancy
Hydramnios
Full bladder

Ⓔ Identify site
of mass

Apparently
adnexal in
location

Extrapelvic
location
is verified

Review presenting
symptom complex

Diagnose:
Inflammatory
bowel disease
Retroperitoneal
tumor, kidney

Ⓕ Evaluate for
metastases if
malignant disease
is likely
Obtain oncologic
consultation

Symptoms of
acute surgical
abdomen

Asymptomatic
or minimal
symptoms

Ⓖ STAGING
LAPAROTOMY
AND DEFINITIVE
SURGERY

EXPLORATORY
LAPAROTOMY
AND ADNEXAL
SURGERY

Ⓗ Consider delay
Watch for changes,
growth, pain,
obstructed labor

149

ACUTE VIRAL INFECTION

Henry Klapholz, M.D.

A. Maternal cytomegalovirus infection is usually asymptomatic, but may appear with mononucleosis-like manifestations. Fetal infection occurs in about 10 percent of the cases, but in most there are no adverse effects. In some there may be devastating consequences, including microcephaly, retardation, hearing loss, chorioretinitis, and cerebral calcifications. The diagnosis is made by viral culture from the cervix, urine, or liver biopsy. Complement fixation, fluorescent antibody, and indirect hemagglutination inhibition assays are confirmatory. There is no known treatment or prevention.

B. Varicella is more severe in adults than in children, but the clinical course is not altered by pregnancy. Diagnose by the characteristic chickenpox rash appearing in crops, mostly on the trunk, often with fever and malaise. The virus incubates for 10 to 21 days and is communicable from one to two days before the eruption until two to five days later. The treatment is symptomatic. Fluorescent antibody membrane antigen or viral recovery from vesicular fluid aids in diagnosis. Late pregnancy infection can cause severe fetal problems, including skin scarring, muscle atrophy, hypoplastic extremities, atrophic digits, microphthalmia, cataracts, and optic atrophy. Fatal disseminated infection or congenital varicella pneumonia may result from maternal infection within four days after delivery (or in the newborn period). Neonatal varicella may develop from maternal illness acquired within three weeks of delivery. Isolation is essential. Treat exposed nonimmune gravidas (and infants) with zoster immune globulin.

C. The fetus is generally unaffected by respiratory illnesses, but the infected newborn may appear septic, especially if premature. Nursery influenza and parainfluenza virus outbreaks are seen. Late pregnancy influenza, which can be seriously complicated by pneumonia, may resemble a common cold or produce high fever, myalgia, sore throat, and cough. Give influenza vaccine to gravidas at high risk.

D. Both rubella and rubeola are infrequent today as a result of effective immunization programs. Measles develops after an incubation period of 10 to 12 days, with catarrhal symptoms, fever, and Koplik spots. The virus can be isolated from the throat, and serologic diagnosis is possible. Pneumonia is the main problem in the mother. Congenital measles occurs in 30 percent of the cases arising within one week after delivery; infected infants may develop severe otitis media or even fatal pneumonia. Congenital defects have been reported, especially in first trimester infections. Provide passive immunization with immune serum globulin to exposed nonimmune mothers. About half of first trimester rubella infections may produce congenital malformations involving cardiac anomalies, deafness, and cataract. Immunization is therefore imperative for all females before embarking on childbearing.

E. Jaundice, loss of appetite, and malaise suggest hepatitis. Hepatitis A is spread by the oral or fecal route. Immunoglobulin M (IgM) antibody may be detected. Fetal infection is rare; give exposed infants immune serum globulin. Hepatitis B is potentially more serious as a major cause of cirrhosis and hepatocellular carcinoma. It has little effect on the pregnancy if acquired early, but in the third trimester, premature delivery may occur. Fetal transmission is common transplacentally or by direct contact during delivery. Most infants remain asymptomatic, but some develop severe chronic disease. Antibody to hepatitis surface antigen HBsAg develops and can be detected at about eight weeks (Fig. 1). Some patients become chronic carriers. Treat infants promptly with hepatitis B immune globulin and hepatitis B vaccine.

References

Cherry JD. Viral exanthems. Curr Prob Pediatr 13:1, 1983.

Hethcote HW. Measles and rubella in the United States. Am J Epidemiol 117:2, 1983.

Minkoff H. Hepatitis. Clin Obstet Gynecol 26:178, 1983.

Snydman DR. Hepatitis in pregnancy. N Engl J Med 313:1398, 1985.

Stagno S, Whitley RJ. Herpesvirus infections of pregnancy. Part I: Cytomegalovirus and Epstein-Barr virus infections. N Engl J Med 313:1270, 1985.

Stagno S, Whitley RJ. Herpesvirus infections of pregnancy. Part II: Herpes simplex virus and varicella-zoster virus infections. N Engl J Med 313:1327, 1985.

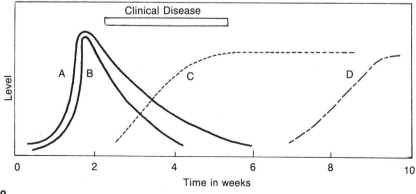

Figure 1 Immunological indices of hepatitis B infection based on changing laboratory titers over time relative to the overt manifestations of clinical disease. *A*, HBsAg; *B*, HBeAg; *C*, HBcAb; *D*, HBsAb.

PATIENT WITH SUSPICION OF VIRAL ILLNESS

Upper respiratory disease ──────────►
Exanthem
Malaise
Jaundice
Adenopathy
Hydramnios

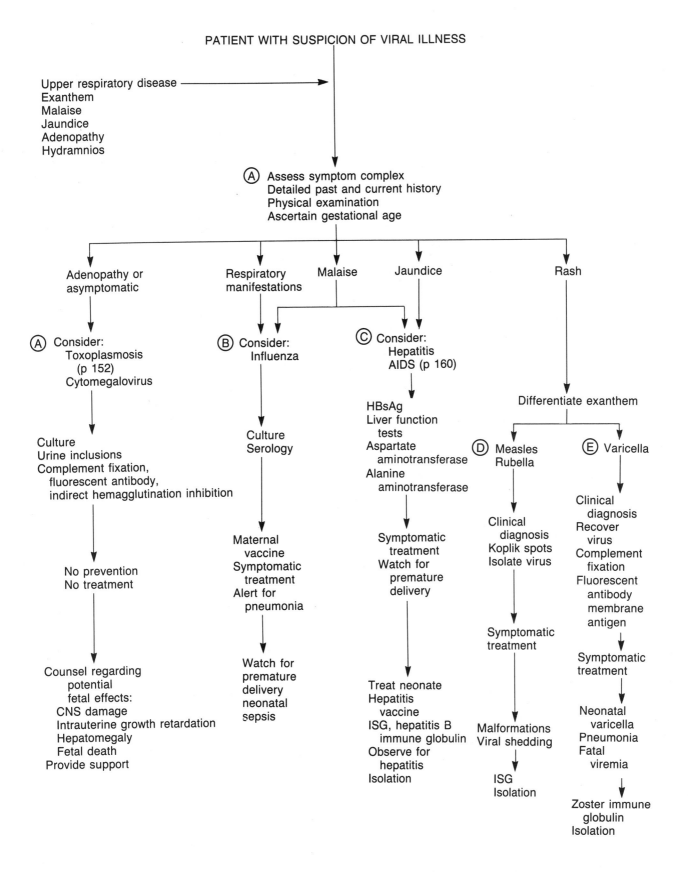

(A) Assess symptom complex
    Detailed past and current history
    Physical examination
    Ascertain gestational age

Adenopathy or   Respiratory   Malaise   Jaundice   Rash
asymptomatic   manifestations

(A) Consider: (B) Consider: (C) Consider:
    Toxoplasmosis   Influenza   Hepatitis
    (p 152)   AIDS (p 160)
    Cytomegalovirus

                                            HBsAg
                                            Liver function   Differentiate exanthem
                                                tests
Culture   Culture   Aspartate   (D) Measles   (E) Varicella
Urine inclusions   Serology   aminotransferase   Rubella
Complement fixation,   Alanine
    fluorescent antibody,   aminotransferase   Clinical
    indirect hemagglutination inhibition   diagnosis
                                                                                   Recover
                                            Symptomatic   Clinical   virus
                                                treatment   diagnosis   Complement
No prevention   Maternal   Watch for   Koplik spots   fixation
No treatment   vaccine   premature   Isolate virus   Fluorescent
                       Symptomatic   delivery   antibody
                           treatment   membrane
                       Alert for   antigen
                           pneumonia   Symptomatic
                                                                    treatment   Symptomatic
Counsel regarding   treatment
    potential   Watch for   Treat neonate
    fetal effects: premature   Hepatitis
CNS damage   delivery   vaccine   Neonatal
Intrauterine growth retardation neonatal ISG, hepatitis B   Malformations   varicella
Hepatomegaly   sepsis   immune globulin   Viral shedding   Pneumonia
Fetal death   Observe for   Fatal
Provide support   hepatitis   viremia
                                           Isolation   ISG
                                                                Isolation   Zoster immune
                                                                                       globulin
                                                                                   Isolation

TOXOPLASMOSIS

Henry Klapholz, M.D.

A. The primary source of toxoplasmosis infection in the United States is raw meat that is ingested. The parasite is very sensitive to heat, and even a small amount of cooking prevents the disease. Adequate hand washing after handling raw meat must be emphasized to pregnant patients. The common house cat, if infected, can excrete millions of infectious oocysts (Fig. 1) in a single stool; these may survive for days. No other animal appears to excrete the parasite in feces. Patients who own cats, especially if they have access to the outdoors where they can acquire the organism, have to be counseled accordingly.

B. Common screening tests use the hemagglutination-inhibition (HI) test. They may yield false positive results but are inexpensive. Routine prenatal screening can detect prior infection on the basis of elevated HI titers; a low level indicates susceptibility. If a woman has had an infected baby, she stands a negligible risk of ever having another such child, although repeated infestations are possible.

C. The usual presentation of the clinical disease in adults is a flulike illness, usually only a few days in duration with little or no fever. Lymphadenopathy is common. Severe intrauterine infestation produces marked acute polyhydramnios. This may serve to alert the astute clinician.

D. A fourfold increase in HI titer (or more) over a period of two weeks is suggestive of an acute infection. This should be verified by the Sabin-Feldman (SF) dye test. There are no known false positives with this test. This is in sharp contrast to the HI screening tests, which yield elevated titers with many other diseases, including most collagen diseases. Between 20 and 24 weeks of gestation, consider fetal blood sampling for immunoglobulin M (IgM) levels. This can now be achieved in many centers by fetoscopic or ultrasonographically guided techniques.

E. If the Sabin-Feldman dye test is positive, infection is likely. An elevated toxoplasmosis specific IgM titer in the mother and especially in the fetus indicates recent infection. One should consider pregnancy termination under these circumstances, if still possible and desired by the patient. The likelihood is very high that the infant, if infected, will be damaged. Early infection often results in spontaneous abortion; later infection, however, may produce congenital toxoplasmosis in the fetus. Major neurologic and developmental sequelae are associated with intracranial calcification, hydrocephalus, microcephaly, and chorioretinitis.

F. If pregnancy termination is not a viable alternative, treatment may be undertaken. The treatment of choice is Spiramycin, which regrettably has not yet been formally approved for clinical use in this country. Currently available drugs include pyrimethamine and sulfapyrimidine, both of which are relatively toxic to the developing embryo. Treatment of the infected newborn is more acceptable.

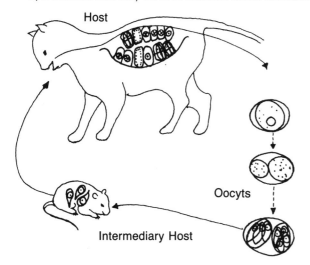

Figure 1 Probable life cycle of Toxoplasma. Oocysts in host (cat) feces, when ingested directly by man, mouse or other intermediary host, produce acute infection. Trophozoites are excreted in turn by the intermediary host. Infection is spread by fecal excretion of trophozoites or by ingestion of animal tissues containing cysts.

References

Desmonts G, Daffos F, Forestier F, et al. Prenatal diagnosis of congenital toxoplasmosis. Lancet 2:500, 1985.

Foulon W, Naessens A, Volckaert M, et al. Congenital toxoplasmosis: A prospective study in Brussels. Br J Obstet Gynaecol 91:419, 1984.

Hunter K, Stagno S, Capps E, Smith RJ. Prenatal screening of pregnant women for infections caused by cytomegalovirus, Epstein-Barr virus, herpesvirus, rubella, and Toxoplasma gondii. Am J Obstet Gynecol 145:269, 1983.

Ritter SE, Vermund SH. Congenital toxoplasmosis. J Obstet Gynecol Neonatal Nurs 14:435, 1985.

PATIENT WITH POTENTIAL EXPOSURE TO TOXOPLASMOSIS

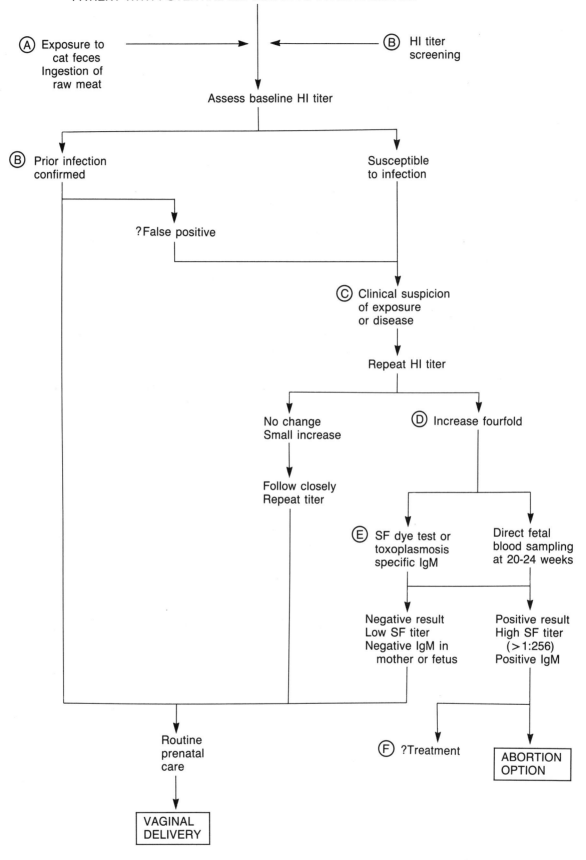

Ⓐ Exposure to cat feces Ingestion of raw meat

Ⓑ HI titer screening

Assess baseline HI titer

Ⓑ Prior infection confirmed

Susceptible to infection

?False positive

Ⓒ Clinical suspicion of exposure or disease

Repeat HI titer

No change Small increase

Ⓓ Increase fourfold

Follow closely Repeat titer

Ⓔ SF dye test or toxoplasmosis specific IgM

Direct fetal blood sampling at 20-24 weeks

Negative result Low SF titer Negative IgM in mother or fetus

Positive result High SF titer (>1:256) Positive IgM

Routine prenatal care

Ⓕ ?Treatment

ABORTION OPTION

VAGINAL DELIVERY

SEXUALLY TRANSMITTED DISEASE

David S. Chapin, M.D.

A. In the symptomatic gravida with a frothy vaginal discharge and an itch, a wet mount examination should be done. Examine a drop of the discharge diluted with normal saline under high power microscopy. The typical trichomonad is a motile, flagellated, one celled organism seen within a field of white blood cells. Limit first trimester treatment to vinegar douches or the topical application of clotrimazole because the safety of metronidazole is unclear. Give metronidazole thereafter in a single dose regimen (eight 250 mg tables taken orally) if needed. Treat the sexual partner as well. Side effects include nausea, headache, a metallic taste, and diarrhea. Warn against the intake of alcohol during treatment.

B. If gonorrhea is suspected on the basis of exposure, obtain both a culture and a Gram stained smear for Gram negative intracellular diplococci. Treat as for nonpregnant women, but avoid tetracycline. Even if the Gram stained smear and culture are negative, proceed to treat if the gravida has been exposed to a confirmed gonococcal contact. Specific single dose regimens combine oral doses of probenecid, 1 g, with amoxicillin, 3.5 g, or aqueous procaine penicillin, 4.8 million units. *Chlamydia trachomatis* infection is so common among women with gonorrhea (more than one third) that it should be looked for and treated simultaneously. It may cause endometritis, premature rupture of membranes, low birth weight in the neonate, neonatal conjunctivitis, and pneumonia. Obtain a culture or antibody test (direct immunofluorescent or enzyme linked) if disease is suspected. Therapeutic regimens consist of probenecid combined with amoxicillin, 3.0 g, or ampicillin, 3.5 g, followed by oral doses of erythromycin (not the estolate form), 500 mg four times daily for seven days. Sulfonamides are also effective but may not be innocuous in pregnancy. Treat the partner with oral doses of tetracycline or doxycycline.

C. A positive culture after treatment indicates reinfection, noncompliance, or the emergence of resistant organisms. Retreatment regimens include intramuscular doses of spectinomycin, 2 g, cefoxitin, 2.0 g (both with probenecid), or ceftriaxone, 250 mg.

D. All pregnant women should undergo serologic testing for syphilis (either Venereal Disease Research Laboratory [VDRL] test or rapid plasma reagin [RPR] test) at the first prenatal visit. False positive reactions may result from viral infection, immunization, autoimmune disease, narcotic use, and pregnancy itself. If the patient is at high risk for syphilis, repeat the nontreponemal test in the third trimester and again on a cord blood sample obtained at delivery.

E. A patient with a seroreactive pattern should be evaluated promptly. Undertake another thorough history and physical examination, and have a darkfield examination of any lesion (chancre or rash) done by an experienced consultant. The fluorescent treponemal antibody absorption (FTA-ABS) test is a more specific test to confirm the diagnosis. Institute therapy while awaiting the results; discontinue it if the test result proves negative. Treat for early syphilis with single dose benzathine penicillin G, 2.4 million units intramuscularly, or erythromycin (not estolate), 500 mg orally four times daily for 15 days. Long-term disease or neurosyphilis requires special consultation and management. Repeat quantitative nontreponemal tests monthly; treat again if there is a fourfold rise in titer. Evaluate all partners as well.

F. If prior treatment was adequate, retreatment is not necessary unless there is clinical (a darkfield positive lesion) or serologic (a fourfold rise in titer) evidence of reinfection.

G. One may withhold or discontinue treatment if the FTA-ABS test result is negative, but consider continuing it if there is doubt. Evaluate for biologic false positive reactions. Repeat tests for syphilis in four weeks.

References

Center for Disease Control. Sexually Transmitted Disease Treatment Guidelines. Atlanta: 1985.

FitzSimmons J, Callahan C, Shanahan B, Jungkind D. Chlamydial infections in pregnancy. J Reprod Med 31:19, 1986.

Hart G. Syphilis tests in diagnostic and therapeutic decision making. Ann Int Med 104:368, 1986.

Roe FJC. Toxicologic evaluation of metronidazole with particular reference to carcinogenic, mutagenic, and teratogenic potential. Surgery 93:158, 1983.

Sweet RL, Gibbs RS. Infectious Diseases of the Female Genital Tract. Baltimore: Williams & Wilkins, 1985.

PATIENT WITH SUSPICION OF SEXUALLY TRANSMITTED DISEASE

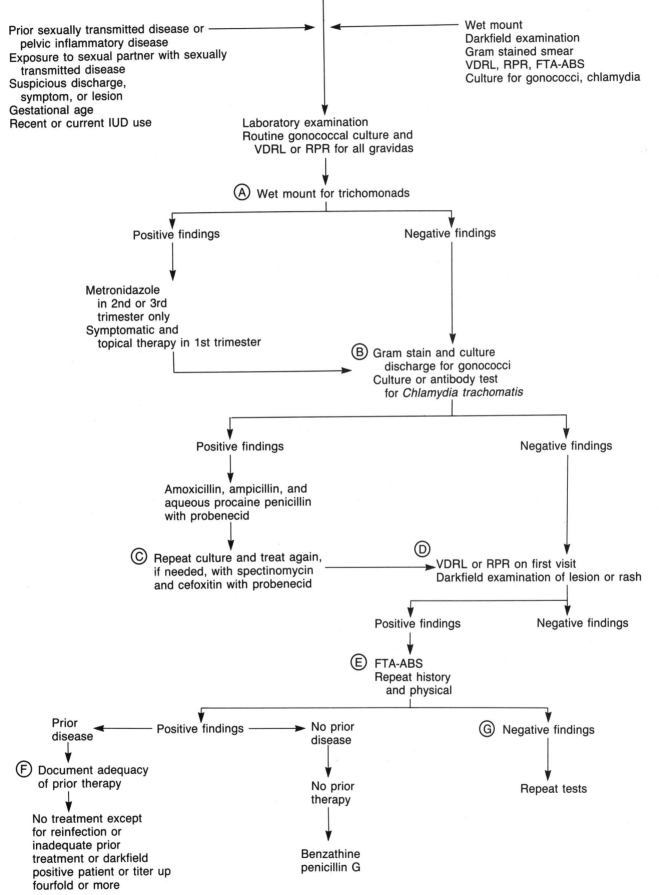

Prior sexually transmitted disease or
  pelvic inflammatory disease
Exposure to sexual partner with sexually
  transmitted disease
Suspicious discharge,
  symptom, or lesion
Gestational age
Recent or current IUD use

Wet mount
Darkfield examination
Gram stained smear
VDRL, RPR, FTA-ABS
Culture for gonococci, chlamydia

Laboratory examination
Routine gonococcal culture and
VDRL or RPR for all gravidas

(A) Wet mount for trichomonads

Positive findings   Negative findings

Metronidazole
  in 2nd or 3rd
  trimester only
Symptomatic and
  topical therapy in 1st trimester

(B) Gram stain and culture
    discharge for gonococci
    Culture or antibody test
    for *Chlamydia trachomatis*

Positive findings   Negative findings

Amoxicillin, ampicillin, and
aqueous procaine penicillin
with probenecid

(C) Repeat culture and treat again,
    if needed, with spectinomycin
    and cefoxitin with probenecid

(D) VDRL or RPR on first visit
    Darkfield examination of lesion or rash

Positive findings   Negative findings

(E) FTA-ABS
    Repeat history
    and physical

Prior   Positive findings   No prior   (G) Negative findings
disease   disease

(F) Document adequacy   No prior   Repeat tests
    of prior therapy   therapy

No treatment except   Benzathine
for reinfection or   penicillin G
inadequate prior
treatment or darkfield
positive patient or titer up
fourfold or more

155

CONDYLOMA ACUMINATUM

Louis Burke, M.D.
David S. Chapin, M.D.

A. Condyloma acuminatum is a sexually transmitted lesion of the cervix, vagina, vulva, perineum, anus, and urethra caused by a DNA-containing human papovavirus. Certain forms (serotypes) of the virus are implicated as being carcinogenic. This magnifies the clinical significance of the condition, making it important to diagnose and treat in both sexual partners. Immunity seems to play an important role. Immunosuppressed patients are likely to develop condylomas. These include those who have had an organ transplant or are being treated with chemotherapy or radiation for lymphoma or other malignant disease or with corticosteroids for various medical disorders. The virus seems to flourish in a warm moist environment.

B. Since the disease is sexually transmitted, other venereal diseases such as gonorrhea, syphilis, and herpes should be ruled out (pp 154, 158) in all cases in which condylomas are encountered.

C. During the past 20 years the number of patients seen for condyloma acuminatum has increased more than fivefold, reflecting the greater sexual activity of the young adult population. Among asymptomatic women screened by routine cervical cytology, 2 percent are found to have condylomas. Most of them have only subclinical genital tract disease recognizable by its histologic characteristics. Colposcopic examination may show a typical warty pattern, but the lesions are more often flat acetowhite patches with multiple small projections. One-third of the patients have identifiable exophytic condylomas. Condylomas often involve both the vagina and the cervix. In women with extensive lesions the condylomas may also be seen extending onto the vulva and over the perineum.

D. Obtain biopsy specimens of all lesions, including flat, pigmented, and giant bleeding ulcerated lesions as well as those that have not responded to treatment. Because flat condylomas are associated with a high frequency of dysplastic change, all should be subjected to biopsy for careful histologic examination. Typically one sees perinuclear cytoplasmic halos; dysplastic changes are common, especially in the basal layers of the epidermis.

E. Between 65 and 85 percent of the women who have condylomas have been in contact with men who have similar disease. All sexual partners of infected individuals should therefore be examined. A meticulous search may be necessary because penile lesions are usually sparse and difficult to find.

F. Condylomas tend to enlarge and grow more rapidly during pregnancy. They may even become so large as to obstruct the pelvic outlet. If these large lesions are traumatized during delivery, they may cause major bleeding. Treatment can generally be carried out safely up until 28 weeks of gestation. In more advanced pregnancy, bleeding is a frequent complication and there is an associated risk of premature labor. Various modes of therapy are available, including topical applications of 50 to 85 percent trichloroacetic acid, cryocautery, electrocautery, or laser ablation. Podophyllin should never be used during pregnancy because it is readily absorbed and can have a toxic effect on the fetus. Absorption from the vagina and cervix has been associated with neuropathy, bone marrow depression, respiratory failure, and even death. The antimetabolite 5-fluorouracil blocks nucleic acid synthesis and must therefore be avoided in pregnancy.

G. There may be a causative relationship between genital warts in the mother and the development of laryngeal papillomas in the infant. It has been reported that most affected infants are delivered vaginally. Although the number of cases is small, laryngeal tumors in infants are particularly difficult to treat and cause great morbidity. Extensive involvement of the birth canal and condylomas at the time of delivery may thus be an indication for cesarean section.

References

Ferenczy A, Mitao M, Nagai N, et al. Latent papillomavirus and recurring genital warts. N Engl J Med 313:784, 1985.

Levine RU, Crum CP, Herman E, et al. Cervical papillomavirus infection and intraepithelial neoplasia: A study of male sexual partners. Obstet Gynecol 64:16, 1984.

Meisels A, Morin C. Human papillomavirus and cancer of the uterine cervix. Gynecol Oncol 12:111S, 1981.

Purola EE, Halila H, Vesterinen E. Condyloma and cervical epithelial atypias in young women. Gynecol Oncol 16:34, 1983.

Singer A, Wilters J, Walker P, et al. Comparison of prevalence of human papillomavirus antigen in biopsies from women with cervical intraepithelial neoplasia. J Clin Pathol 38:855, 1985.

PATIENT WITH SUSPICION OF CONDYLOMA ACUMINATUM

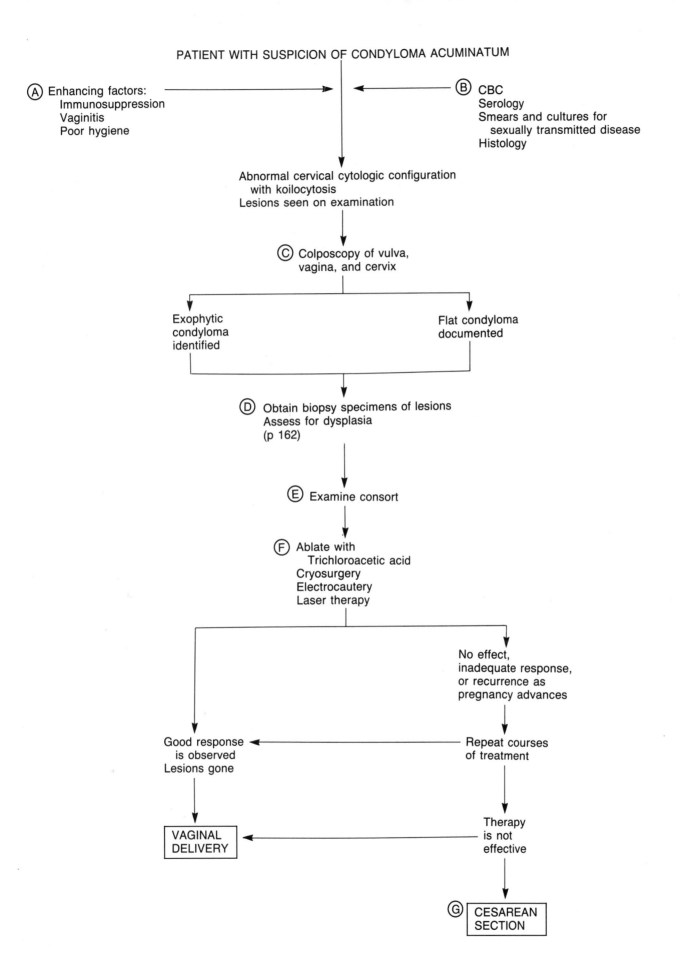

Ⓐ Enhancing factors:
Immunosuppression
Vaginitis
Poor hygiene

Ⓑ CBC
Serology
Smears and cultures for
sexually transmitted disease
Histology

Abnormal cervical cytologic configuration
with koilocytosis
Lesions seen on examination

Ⓒ Colposcopy of vulva,
vagina, and cervix

Exophytic
condyloma
identified

Flat condyloma
documented

Ⓓ Obtain biopsy specimens of lesions
Assess for dysplasia
(p 162)

Ⓔ Examine consort

Ⓕ Ablate with
Trichloroacetic acid
Cryosurgery
Electrocautery
Laser therapy

No effect,
inadequate response,
or recurrence as
pregnancy advances

Good response
is observed
Lesions gone

Repeat courses
of treatment

VAGINAL
DELIVERY

Therapy
is not
effective

Ⓖ CESAREAN
SECTION

HERPES INFECTION

Benjamin P. Sachs, M.B., B.S., D.P.H.

A. The risk factors for herpex simplex virus (HSV) infection include exposure to multiple sexual partners, poor hygiene, other sexually transmitted diseases (p 154), and a history of herpes simplex virus lesions. Primary infections are usually associated with viremia, fever, myalgia, malaise, and regional adenopathy. Secondary or recurrent infections are usually limited to the site. Infections tend to recur. A host immunologic response does not rule out the presence of the virus. Of the two types of herpes simplex virus, HSV-I tends to be associated with infections of the face and upper body and HSV-II with genital lesions, but both are potential genital and perinatal pathogens.

B. Although fetal malformation does not result from first trimester infection, spontaneous abortion may occur. Offer reassurance about the immediate effect, but emphasize the importance of late pregnancy surveillance to detect recurrence and virus shedding near term.

C. The virus can be isolated and identified by tissue culture methods; rub the base of the lesion to obtain a swab specimen from a vesicle or ulcer. If culture is unavailable, a Papanicolaou or Tzanck smear can show multinucleated giant cells. The high incidence of false negative results reduces the reliability of smears.

D. Obtain herpes simplex virus cultures weekly near term. Begin at 32 to 36 weeks' gestation. If risk factors for premature delivery exist (p 176), it is important to start early.

E. Active herpes infection in labor exposes the newborn infant to a 40 to 60 percent risk of infection. Of these cases, devastating effects (death or severe neurologic damage) may occur in half. Since herpes simplex virus infections are common and serious neonatal disease is rare, these data may be questioned. Neonatal herpes simplex virus infection is usually acquired by direct contact during parturition. Infrequent cases of transplacental spread have been reported to result from primary maternal infection with viremia.

F. In the past, fetal infection was thought to be unavoidable if the membranes were ruptured for more than four hours. This made cesarean section inappropriate. Because the original evidence was based on only a few cases, many now recommend cesarean section even if the membranes have been ruptured for as long as 24 hours.

G. Active extragenital herpes lesions do not interdict vaginal delivery, provided the vaginal cultures are negative. Cover the affected areas during delivery.

H. Despite all preventive measures, not every neonatal infection can be prevented. Up to half may derive from apparently asymptomatic gravidas. Even with two recent negative herpes simplex virus cultures, there may be viral shedding in labor. Nonetheless vaginal delivery is recommended if cultures remain negative and there are no discernible lesions.

I. Neonatal infection is usually manifest in two to 10 days. Some infants show only the characteristic lesions, usually confined to the skin, eyes, and mouth. Others have central nervous system involvement, with lethargy, poor feeding, fever, and irritability. Generalized infection may present with jaundice, purpura, shock, and respiratory signs; neurologic and ophthalmic sequelae occur in surviving infants. The recently introduced drug acyclovir may improve the long term prognosis, but this has not yet been confirmed. Breast feeding is acceptable even if the mother has an active lesion (except for one on the breast). Careful handwashing is necessary. Keep the baby with the mother (rooming in) or impose special nursery precautions.

References

Binkin NJ, Koplan JP, Cates W. Preventing neonatal herpes: The value of weekly viral cultures in pregnant women with recurrent genital herpes. JAMA 251:2816, 1984.

Brown ZA, Vontver LA, Benedetti J, et al. Genital herpes in pregnancy: Risk factors associated with recurrences and asymptomatic viral shedding. Am J Obstet Gynecol 153:24, 1985.

Daling JR, Wolf ME. The role of decision and cost analysis in the treatment of a pregnant woman with recurrent genital herpes. JAMA 251:2828, 1985.

Monif GRG, Kellner KR, Donnelly WH. Congenital herpes simplex type II infection. Am J Obstet Gynecol 152:1000, 1985.

PATIENT WITH SUSPICION OF HERPESVIRUS INFECTION

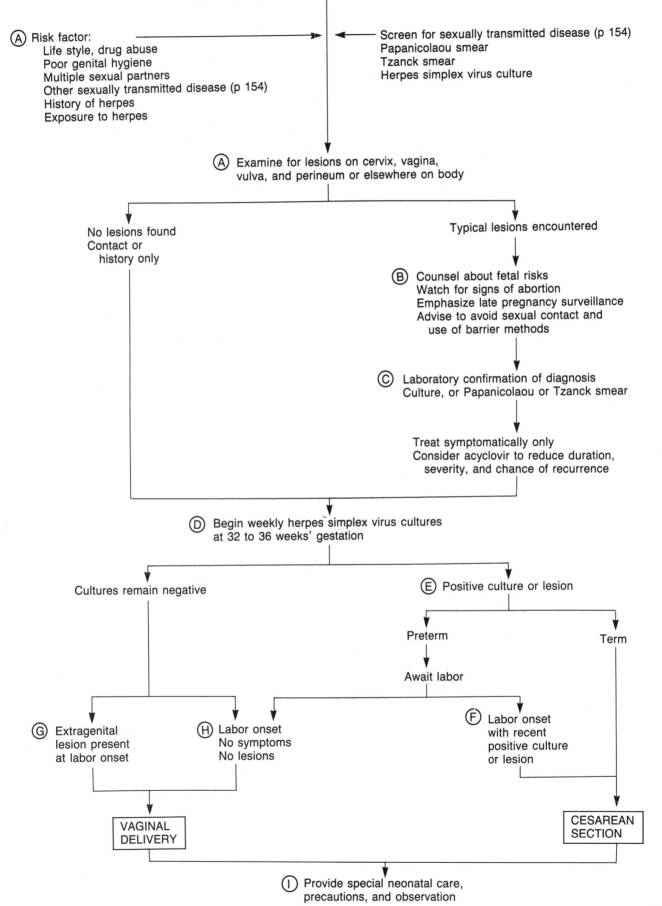

Ⓐ Risk factor:
  Life style, drug abuse
  Poor genital hygiene
  Multiple sexual partners
  Other sexually transmitted disease (p 154)
  History of herpes
  Exposure to herpes

Screen for sexually transmitted disease (p 154)
Papanicolaou smear
Tzanck smear
Herpes simplex virus culture

Ⓐ Examine for lesions on cervix, vagina,
  vulva, and perineum or elsewhere on body

No lesions found
Contact or
history only

Typical lesions encountered

Ⓑ Counsel about fetal risks
  Watch for signs of abortion
  Emphasize late pregnancy surveillance
  Advise to avoid sexual contact and
    use of barrier methods

Ⓒ Laboratory confirmation of diagnosis
  Culture, or Papanicolaou or Tzanck smear

Treat symptomatically only
Consider acyclovir to reduce duration,
  severity, and chance of recurrence

Ⓓ Begin weekly herpes simplex virus cultures
  at 32 to 36 weeks' gestation

Cultures remain negative

Ⓔ Positive culture or lesion

Preterm

Term

Await labor

Ⓖ Extragenital
  lesion present
  at labor onset

Ⓗ Labor onset
  No symptoms
  No lesions

Ⓕ Labor onset
  with recent
  positive culture
  or lesion

VAGINAL
DELIVERY

CESAREAN
SECTION

Ⓘ Provide special neonatal care,
  precautions, and observation

159

ACQUIRED IMMUNODEFICIENCY SYNDROME

Benjamin P. Sachs, M.B., B.S., D.P.H.

A. The prevalence of the acquired immunodeficiency syndrome (AIDS) is growing rapidly among heterosexual men and women, and more recently the disease has begun to appear in pregnant women and their offspring. The infants are thought to have been infected principally through perinatal transmission of the causative human immunodeficiency virus (HIV). The affected gravidas are principally intravenous drug users or women whose sexual partners are either intravenous drug users or bisexual men. Women who are HIV antibody positive are at increased risk of becoming symptomatic during pregnancy. The irreversible immunosuppression characteristic of this disease is manifested by lymphadenopathy, chronic infection by opportunistic organisms (for example, Pneumocystis), and the appearance of certain neoplasms (such as Kaposi's sarcoma). Many are asymptomatic for long periods of time before the overt indolent course begins.

B. Because of the potentially high risk of perinatal transmission, routine screening should be urged for all women identified as being at high risk. A woman who is HIV antibody positive should have the information so that she can choose between the options of induced abortion or follow-up medical care for her child. She should also be counseled about safe sex practices (specifically use of condoms) to prevent spread to partners. The disadvantages of the test are the anxiety that it provokes and some medicolegal ramifications. Although legislation exists (or is pending) to ensure confidentiality of AIDS test results, the HIV antibody status of an individual may affect her employability, interpersonal relationships, and insurability.

C. The best time for screening is before pregnancy. If this is not possible, undertake screening before 23 weeks' gestational age. The HIV serologic test detects antibodies to the virus, but it does not necessarily identify individuals with the disease. More sophisticated testing is needed for this purpose. If the patient is shown to be positive for HIV as well as on the ELISA and Western blot tests, she must be considered to be infected with HIV and to risk transmitting the virus to her fetus. She should be provided with detailed counseling about the disease, its prognosis for her, and the option of an induced abortion (p 42). If the patient has a negative result on the HIV antibody blood test, the test should be repeated in the third trimester.

D. AIDS is an infectious disease that health care providers should protect themselves against. Others include cytomegalovirus, hepatitis, and herpes. Adequate protection needed in the labor and delivery unit includes protective eyeglasses, gowns, and gloves. Although it is obvious that such protective measures must be used in identified cases, it is less evident that they should also be used in all others. Unless they are invoked routinely, potential exposure of personnel is inevitable, because some patients refuse to be tested for AIDS or fail to realize that they are at risk, perhaps having become infected without recognizing their exposure. Despite the trend away from strict aseptic techniques for delivery, it is imperative that appropriate routine measures be reinstituted to protect against this serious disorder. The same precautions apply here in regard to contamination by body fluids as for hepatitis.

E. Perinatal transmission of HIV is estimated to occur in 15 to 65 percent of the cases. Because the route is hematogenous, it cannot be prevented by cesarean delivery. Most infants who have acquired the infection in utero become symptomatic.

References

CDC recommendations for assisting in the prevention of perinatal transmission of HTLV-III/LAV and AIDS. Morb Mortal Wkly Report 34:245, 1985.

Selik R, Haverkos H, Curran J. Acquired immune deficiency syndrome (AIDS) trends in the United States, 1978–1982. Am J Med 76:493, 1984.

Ziegler JB, Cooper DA, Johnson RO, et al. Postnatal transmission of AIDS-associated retrovirus from mother to infant. Lancet 1:896, 1985.

PATIENT AT RISK FOR AIDS

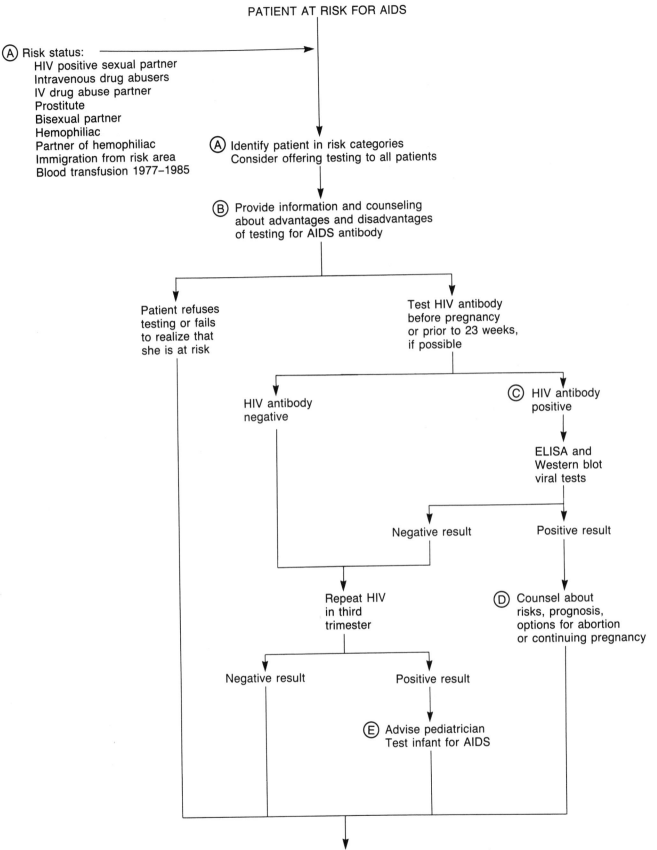

(A) Risk status:
   HIV positive sexual partner
   Intravenous drug abusers
   IV drug abuse partner
   Prostitute
   Bisexual partner
   Hemophiliac
   Partner of hemophiliac
   Immigration from risk area
   Blood transfusion 1977–1985

(A) Identify patient in risk categories
    Consider offering testing to all patients

(B) Provide information and counseling
    about advantages and disadvantages
    of testing for AIDS antibody

Patient refuses testing or fails to realize that she is at risk

Test HIV antibody before pregnancy or prior to 23 weeks, if possible

HIV antibody negative

(C) HIV antibody positive

ELISA and Western blot viral tests

Negative result

Positive result

Repeat HIV in third trimester

(D) Counsel about risks, prognosis, options for abortion or continuing pregnancy

Negative result

Positive result

(E) Advise pediatrician
    Test infant for AIDS

Enforce precautionary practices for all personnel to avoid exposure to contaminated body fluids

ABNORMAL CERVICAL CYTOLOGY

Louis Burke, M.D.

A. In every prenatal patient Papanicolaou smear should be obtained routinely at the first prenatal visit. Be especially alert for gravidas presenting with factors placing them at special risk for cervical dysplasia, including an early age at first coitus, multiple partners, and sexually transmitted disease. Postcoital staining may signal a problem, but most patients are asymptomatic. Abnormal smears showing cervical intraepithelial neoplasia (CIN) can be expected in 40 to 50 of every 1,000 asymptomatic women screened; of these two to three have overt cancer. Considerably more cases of cervical intraepithelial neoplasia are now observed among the younger population, probably reflecting the current wide exposure to the papovavirus of condyloma (p 156). There is a 3 to 4 percent incidence of abnormal cytologic findings among pregnant women. Cervical dysplasia is often a forerunner of carcinoma in situ and must therefore be considered precancerous. Although management tends to be conservative in pregnancy to avoid disturbing the gestation, it is important to investigate thoroughly to rule out invasive disease, which has to be treated expeditiously.

B. Investigation should be undertaken as soon as the first smear is obtained showing dysplastic cells. Do not merely repeat the smear in the hope that the lesion will correct itself. Delays in actual ablative management until after vaginal delivery are permissible in the presence of cervical intraepithelial neoplasia, but invasive cancer must be aggressively attacked without delay. While ruling out the remote possibility of invasion, however, one must avoid injury to the fetus, premature labor, and harm to the mother, such as hemorrhage from deep biopsy or conization. Colposcopy is the primary mode of evaluation to assess the presence and pattern of the lesion, its extent, and the best sites for biopsy. Watch for punctation, a mosaic pattern, and especially abnormal subsurface vascular architecture. Dilute acetic acid identifies the areas to be examined. Colposcopically directed biopsy has made it possible to evaluate these patients effectively and at the same time avoid cervical conization in more than 90 percent (see F). Cervical intraepithelial neoplasia can be documented in 10 to 25 percent of the patients with mildly atypical cytologic smears; in half these patients the disease is at an advanced stage, although invasion is gratifyingly rare.

C. A satisfactory examination is one in which the entire lesion, squamocolumnar junction, and transformation zone can be clearly visualized, examined, and subject-ed to biopsy. Normal endocervical columnar epithelium must be seen cephalad to these areas.

D. An unsatisfactory examination is one that does not meet the aforementioned criteria (see C). Typically the upper edge of the lesion extends up into the endocervical canal and is not readily accessible for colposcopic visualization or biopsy. Under such circumstances one cannot assume that the pattern of the lesion seen on the exocervix necessarily continues unchanged into the canal. Despite the real risk of bleeding in pregnancy, conization or wedge biopsy is generally indicated here; it is done in an operating room with adequate facilities.

E. Lesions may be graded according to the method of Coppleson, based on color, surface texture, vascular atypia, and intercapillary distance. Invasive carcinoma is never associated with a grade 1 lesion (that is, one showing minimal colposcopic changes). Therefore, if the cytologic study suggests CIN 1 (mild dysplasia) only, it may not be necessary to obtain a biopsy specimen of the lesion during pregnancy. Biopsy specimens of all other lesions should be obtained for careful histologic study to rule out invasion below the basement membrane.

F. An important guiding principle is to avoid cervical conization in pregnancy if at all possible, because hemorrhage, infection, rupture of membranes, cervical incompetence, and premature labor (or abortion) may result. If a diagnosis cannot be made by any other means, however, conization may have to be done. It is essential to weigh the risks and fully inform the patient so that she can be directly involved in the decision to proceed.

References

Hacker NF, Berek JS, Lagasse LD, et al. Carcinoma of the cervix associated with pregnancy. Obstet Gynecol 59:735, 1982.

Kohan S, Beckman E, Bigelow B, et al. The role of colposcopy in the management of cervical intraepithelial neoplasia during pregnancy and postpartum. J Reprod Med 25:279, 1980.

McDonnell JM, Mylotte MJ, Gustafson RC, et al. Colposcopy in pregnancy: A twelve year review. Br J Obstet Gynaecol 88:414, 1981.

Soutter WP, Wisdom S, Brough AK, et al. Should patients with mild atypia in a cervical smear be referred for colposcopy? Br J Obstet Gynaecol 93:70, 1986.

Townsend DB, Richard RM. Can colposcopy replace conization? Cancer 32:85, 1982.

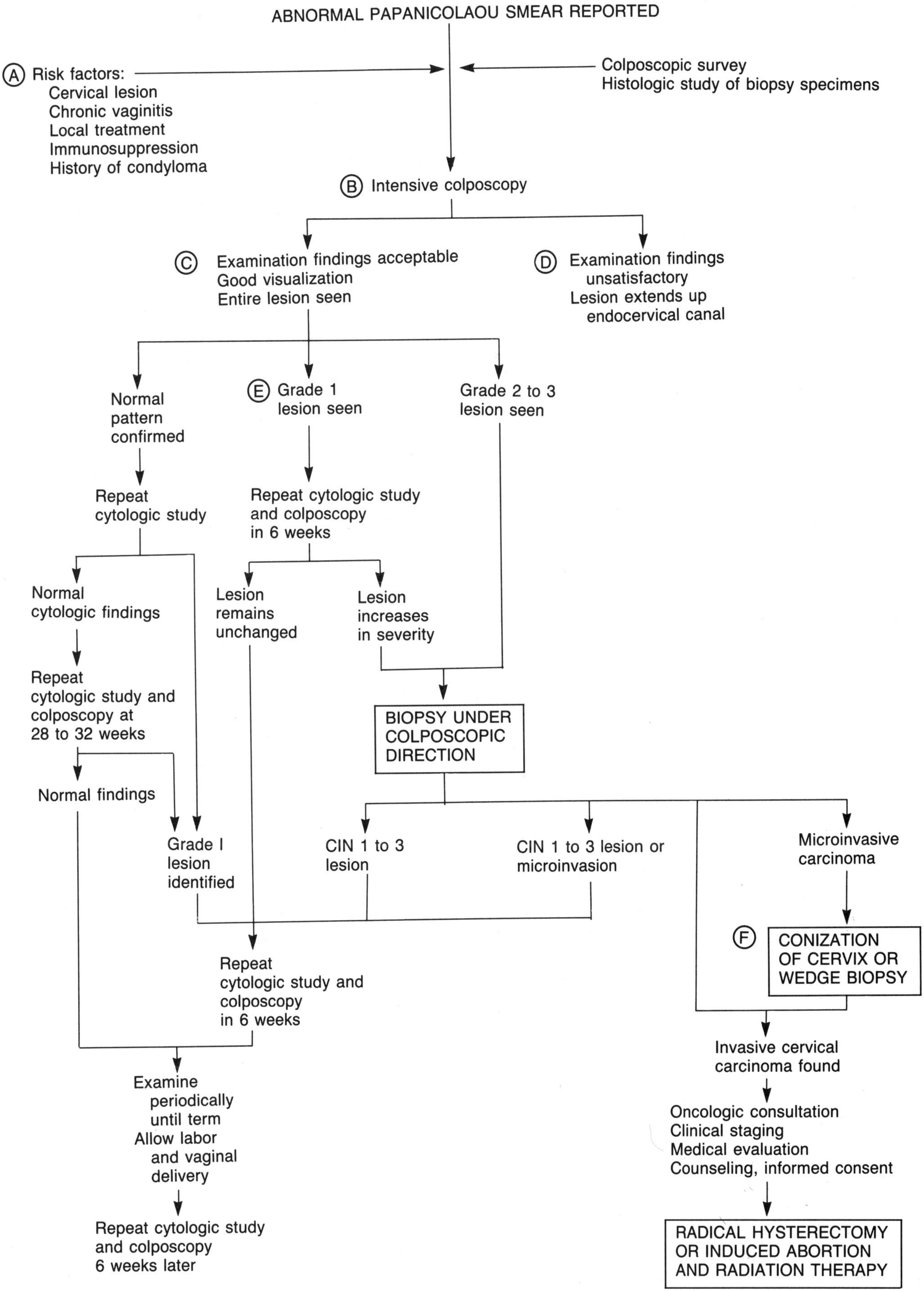

ABNORMAL PAPANICOLAOU SMEAR REPORTED

(A) Risk factors:
    Cervical lesion
    Chronic vaginitis
    Local treatment
    Immunosuppression
    History of condyloma

Colposcopic survey
Histologic study of biopsy specimens

(B) Intensive colposcopy

(C) Examination findings acceptable
Good visualization
Entire lesion seen

(D) Examination findings
unsatisfactory
Lesion extends up
endocervical canal

Normal
pattern
confirmed

(E) Grade 1
lesion seen

Grade 2 to 3
lesion seen

Repeat
cytologic study

Repeat cytologic study
and colposcopy
in 6 weeks

Normal
cytologic findings

Lesion
remains
unchanged

Lesion
increases
in severity

Repeat
cytologic study and
colposcopy at
28 to 32 weeks

BIOPSY UNDER
COLPOSCOPIC
DIRECTION

Normal findings

Grade I
lesion
identified

CIN 1 to 3
lesion

CIN 1 to 3 lesion or
microinvasion

Microinvasive
carcinoma

Repeat
cytologic study and
colposcopy
in 6 weeks

(F) CONIZATION
OF CERVIX OR
WEDGE BIOPSY

Examine
periodically
until term
Allow labor
and vaginal
delivery

Invasive cervical
carcinoma found

Oncologic consultation
Clinical staging
Medical evaluation
Counseling, informed consent

Repeat cytologic study
and colposcopy
6 weeks later

RADICAL HYSTERECTOMY
OR INDUCED ABORTION
AND RADIATION THERAPY

BACTERIURIA

Balmookoot Balgobin, M.D.

A. Quantitative urine culture, using an aerobic agar pour plate dilution technique to give the number of colonies per milliliter, is accurate but time consuming and expensive. Fortunately recent introduction of the semiautomated urine screen (Bac-T-Screen) has facilitated the detection of asymptomatic bacteriuria in obstetrical patients. For reliable culture data, uncontaminated urine specimens are needed. The clean catch method is widely used. It avoids catheterization with its risk of introducing infection. The patient washes her hands and cleanses the vulva. Then, separating the labia, she begins to void, collecting only the middle portion of the stream in a sterile container. Specimens are cultured immediately or refrigerated. Specimens can be evaluated first by the Bac-T-Screen, if available, and those found positive are then subjected to culture and sensitivity tests. Alternative techniques that may be considered in exceptional circumstances for collecting uncontaminated urine include catheterization of suprapubic aspiration. Colony counts exceeding 100,000 per ml of clean catch urine indicate significant bacteriuria (especially if found in two consecutive specimens). A Gram stained smear is sometimes helpful for guiding treatment if significant bacteriuria is present.

B. Antibiotic choice is guided by urinary Gram staining, culture, and sensitivity tests. Take care to avoid undesirable maternal and fetal effects. Suitable outpatient programs for asymptomatic bacteriuria or simple cystitis include ampicillin (500 mg four times daily for 10 days), sulfisoxazole (Gantrisin, 1 g four times daily for 10 days), or nitrofurantoin (Macrodantin, 100 mg four times daily for 10 days). Single dose therapy is an alternative regimen that should especially be considered in noncompliant patients, it consists of ampicillin (2 g) with probenecid (1 g), amoxicillin (3 g), sulfisoxazole (2 g), or nitrofurantoin (200 mg). Significant bacteriuria should be treated even if it is asymptomatic because 20 to 40 percent of untreated women develop acute pyelonephritis with the attendant risks of renal damage and prematurity. Asymptomatic bacteriuria alone, however, is not a significant risk factor for prematurity.

C. Acute pyelonephritis may reduce the glomerular filtration rate, making the choice of antibiotic difficult. Renal function should be evaluated, therefore, with attention to intake and output, serum urea nitrogen and creatinine levels, and creatinine clearance.

D. Patients with acute pyelonephritis require hospitalization for hydration with intravenous fluid administration and vigorous antibiotic therapy, such as ampicillin intravenously (1 g every six hours until afebrile for 48 hours, then 500 mg orally four times daily for 14 days). Gentamicin may also be used, but its ototoxicity must be borne in mind; it may be avoided by maintaining serum levels below 10 μg per ml. In life threatening situations, kanamycin or gentamicin may be considered despite their known toxicity; they may also be indicated in patients who are allergic to penicillin or who have infections with organisms that are resistant to penicillin and cephalosporin.

E. In unremitting cases, suspect obstructive disease or a urinary tract abnormality. Ultrasonography may detect hydronephrosis, hydroureter, and occasionally even renal or ureteral calculi. Ureteral calculi pass spontaneously with conservative therapy in about half the cases. Reserve the use of intravenous pyelography for resistant cases. In severe symptomatic obstruction, manipulation via cystoscopy or retrograde ureteral catheterization may help provide drainage or dislodge the stone. Rarely persistent obstruction requires surgical intervention. All patients with recurrent or persistent urinary tract infections should be given prophylactic therapy (e.g., nitrofurantoin, 100 mg daily) throughout the rest of the pregnancy. They deserve a complete urologic evaluation about three months post partum.

References

Davis JR, Stager CE. Detection of asymptomatic bacteriuria in obstetric patients with a semiautomated urine screen. Am J Obstet Gynecol 151:1069, 1985.

Gilstrap LC, Cunningham FG, Whalley PJ. Acute pyelonephritis in pregnancy: An anterospective study. Obstet Gynecol 57:409, 1981.

Harris RE, Gilstrap LC, Pretty A. Single-dose antimicrobial therapy for asymptomatic bacteriuria during pregnancy. Obstet Gynecol 59:546, 1982.

Masterton RG, Evans DC, Strike PW. Single dose amoxicillin in the treatment of bacteriuria in pregnancy and the puerperium: A controlled clinical trial. Br J Obstet Gynaecol 92:498, 1985.

McGrady GA, Daling JR, Peterson DR. Maternal urinary tract infection and adverse fetal outcome. Am J Epidemiol 121:377, 1985.

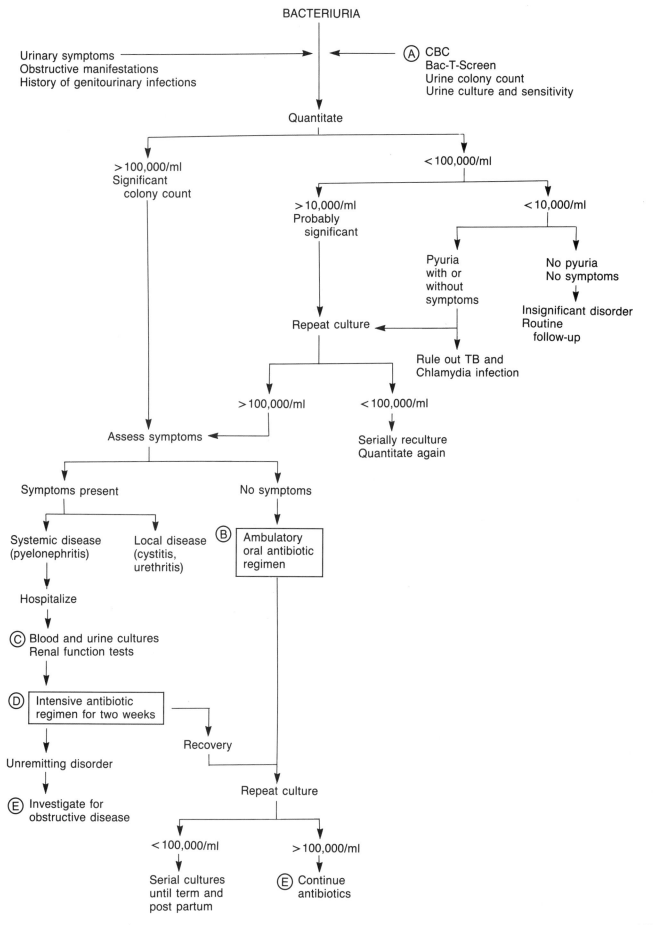

BACTERIURIA

Urinary symptoms
Obstructive manifestations
History of genitourinary infections

(A) CBC
Bac-T-Screen
Urine colony count
Urine culture and sensitivity

Quantitate

>100,000/ml
Significant
colony count

<100,000/ml

>10,000/ml
Probably
significant

<10,000/ml

Pyuria
with or
without
symptoms

No pyuria
No symptoms

Repeat culture

Insignificant disorder
Routine
follow-up

Rule out TB and
Chlamydia infection

>100,000/ml

<100,000/ml

Assess symptoms

Serially reculture
Quantitate again

Symptoms present

No symptoms

Systemic disease
(pyelonephritis)

Local disease
(cystitis,
urethritis)

(B) Ambulatory
oral antibiotic
regimen

Hospitalize

(C) Blood and urine cultures
Renal function tests

(D) Intensive antibiotic
regimen for two weeks

Recovery

Unremitting disorder

Repeat culture

(E) Investigate for
obstructive disease

<100,000/ml

>100,000/ml

Serial cultures
until term and
post partum

(E) Continue
antibiotics

BREAST MASS

Max Borten, M.D.

A. The physician must always be alert to risk factors for breast cancer in the patient's family and personal history. Women should be taught periodic breast self-examination and encouraged to practice it regularly. In this way many lesions can be detected early. Delayed recognition is common in pregnancy because of the congestion that accompanies gestation. This makes astute surveillance by the obstetrical attendant all the more important.

B. Enlargement of the breast during pregnancy and lactation tends to mask parenchymal masses. Nevertheless a thorough breast examination ought to be performed at some point during prenatal care, preferably at the first visit, and again post partum. Any concern expressed by the patient about a possible lump or change in consistency or lobularity warrants re-examination. One of the most significant factors adversely affecting the prognosis for patients with breast cancer during pregnancy and the puerperium is physician delay in making the diagnosis and instituting therapy.

C. Ultrasonographic evaluation of a breast lump identifies the cystic nature of fluid filled masses. Identification of a solid tumor requires further study and exploration. A preoperative low dose (soft tissue technique) mammogram can help disclose smaller secondary lesions in the affected breast as well as any unsuspected abnormalities in the contralateral mammary gland.

D. Fine needle aspiration of a cystic breast mass during pregnancy ought to be performed promptly. This decompresses the cyst and simultaneously provides material for cytologic evaluation. Clear or straw colored fluid is considered a benign finding, and the specimen can therefore be discarded. Bloody fluid, by contrast, raises the question of malignancy and must be studied microscopically. If the cystic mass forms again, reaspiration is required. It is important to re-examine the breast after aspiration to determine whether the mass can still be palpated. If so, it must not be ignored. Failure to decompress any breast mass by aspiration requires a biopsy of the lesion irrespective of the apparently benign characteristics of the fluid obtained.

E. A biopsy specimen of all clinically malignant or suspicious breast masses must be obtained even if the cytologic evaluation reveals benign findings. The histologic features of mammary cancers associated with pregnancy or lactation are the same as in those occurring in nonpregnant women. Survival incidence is also comparable, although some hold that they are worse in pregnancy because the disease tends to be more advanced as a consequence of delay in detection and diagnosis sometimes seen in these cases. It has not been shown that pregnancy accelerates the course of the breast cancer. If a malignant tumor of the breast is identified, surgical exploration of the axillary lymph nodes is generally required. The prognosis is considerably worsened when the axillary nodes are involved.

F. The management of breast cancer during pregnancy does not differ from that provided to nonpregnant women. Survival is not improved by pregnancy termination; nevertheless it can be considered in patients in whom the prognosis for long term survival is poor. Surgical treatment presents little danger to the fetus provided maternal hypotension and hypoxia are prevented. Avoid radiation and chemotherapy if the pregnancy is to be continued. Subsequent pregnancy is not medically contraindicated for women who are still apparently free of disease after a suitable period of time (at least two years and preferably five years) has elapsed.

References

Canter JW, Oliver GC, Zaloudek CJ. Surgical diseases of the breast during pregnancy. Clin Obstet Gynecol 26:853, 1983.

Clark RM, Reid J. Carcinoma of the breast in pregnancy and lactation. Int J Radiat Oncol Biol Phys 4:693, 1978.

Donegan WL. Mammary carcinoma and pregnancy. Major Prob Clin Surg 5:448, 1979.

Russ JE, Winchester DP, Scanlon EF, Christ MA. Cytologic findings of aspiration of tumors of the breast. Surg Gynecol Obstet 146:407, 1978.

Sahni K, Sanyal B, Agrawal MS, et al. Carcinoma of breast associated with pregnancy and lactation. J Surg Oncol 16:167, 1981.

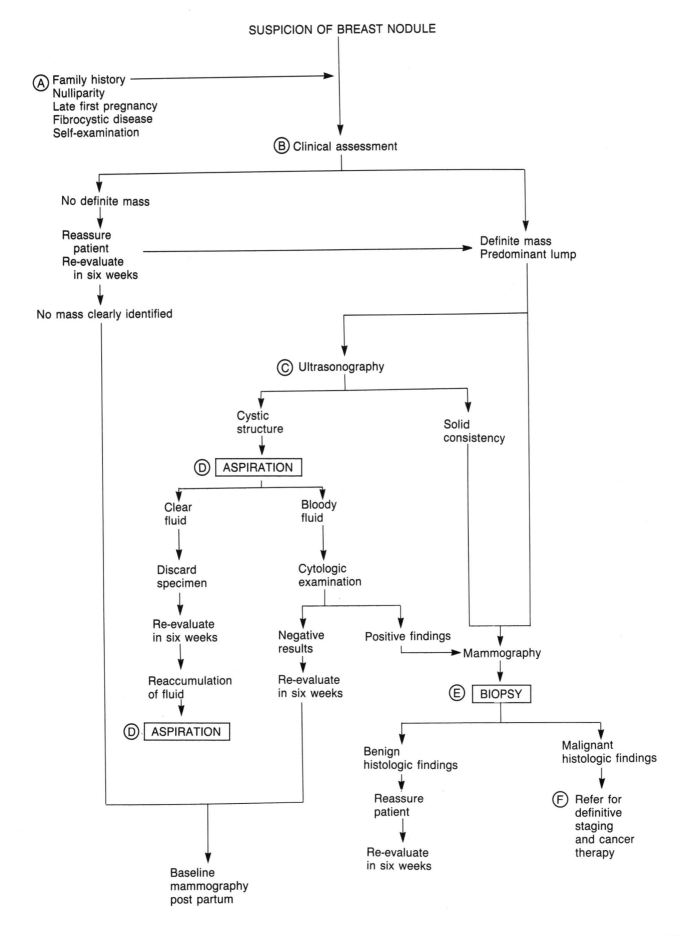

SUSPICION OF BREAST NODULE

(A) Family history
Nulliparity
Late first pregnancy
Fibrocystic disease
Self-examination

(B) Clinical assessment

No definite mass

Reassure
patient
Re-evaluate
in six weeks

No mass clearly identified

Definite mass
Predominant lump

(C) Ultrasonography

Cystic
structure

Solid
consistency

(D) ASPIRATION

Clear
fluid

Bloody
fluid

Discard
specimen

Cytologic
examination

Re-evaluate
in six weeks

Negative
results

Positive findings

Reaccumulation
of fluid

Re-evaluate
in six weeks

Mammography

(D) ASPIRATION

(E) BIOPSY

Benign
histologic findings

Malignant
histologic findings

Reassure
patient

(F) Refer for
definitive
staging
and cancer
therapy

Re-evaluate
in six weeks

Baseline
mammography
post partum

NURSING ASSESSMENT IN LABOR

Maureen J. McRae, R.N., M.S.

A. The nurse responsible for the gravida must initially and regularly assess the stage of labor and its progression (p 234), attend to the gravida's comfort and needs, and monitor fetal well-being. Note the physical and emotional condition and the patient's desires about the birthing process. Previous health care experiences may affect her attitude. Be alerted by the history or evidence of undue anxiety, fear, anger, or hostility. Discuss relevant findings with the physician of record, and exchange information about special needs, plans, complications, consultations, and orders.

B. Ascertain the extent of childbirth preparation at formal classes or exercise programs and exposure to current literature. Coach and aid in relaxation and breathing techniques already learned. Assess the role of the partner or support person in regard to attendance at childbirth classes and the anticipated active or passive role. Learn whether analgesia and anesthesia are desired. Inquire about the desire for breastfeeding before delivery.

C. Assess the labor status by noting the time of onset, uterine contractile pattern, status of membranes, cervical dilatation and effacement, and fetal station. Evaluate the contractile pattern by palpation to assess the frequency, duration, and intensity. External tocodynamometry does not measure contractile strength. Frequent periodic re-examinations provide essential information about normal labor progress and the fetal status (see E).

D. Determine the status of the membranes. Note the time of rupture and the color and odor of the fluid. Auscultate the fetal heart rate immediately after the membranes rupture and several times over the ensuing half hour. Check vaginally for the fetal station and possible cord prolapse. If the fetal head is not engaged, place the patient at bed rest. Report and record the appearance of meconium with a vertex presentation. Request and institute internal electronic monitoring of the fetal heart rate by scalp electrode for optimal fetal surveillance.

E. Continuous electronic monitoring is preferable, especially if the fetal risk is high. If such monitoring is not used, auscultate the fetal heart rate in all cases and record it every 30 minutes during early first stage labor and at least every 15 minutes during the active phase and second stage. Listen for 30 seconds at a minimum, beginning at the end of each contraction to detect late decelerations (p 198). Listen more often if the risk status or meconium in the amniotic fluid dictates.

F. Report any questionable or abnormal pattern of the fetal heart rate at once and document. Change the maternal position, give oxygen, increase (or initiate) hydration, and discontinue oxytocin (p 194).

G. Nursing support and coaching are required throughout labor. Encouragement, comfort measures, assistance with breathing and relaxation, and analgesia and anesthesia (on the physician's order) are all integral aspects of care, modified by the labor progress and coping pattern. Do not withhold requested analgesia to achieve the goal of natural childbirth. Initial goals and plans may have to be changed if labor complications arise.

H. A position change may prove useful for comfort. Delivery need not take place on a bed or delivery table. Squatting, a lateral Sims position, and even the knee-chest position may be more suitable for some patients. Avoid the supine position for both labor and delivery to prevent hypotension as a result of aortocaval compression by the large gravid uterus.

I. Support family integration after delivery by encouraging bonding between the infant and parent(s). Delay giving prophylactic ophthalmic treatment in order to foster eye contact. Initiate breast feeding at this time if desired. Unless it is medically indicated, do not separate the mother and infant during this sensitive period. Hospital policies should be supportive in this regard.

References

The Nurse's Role in Electronic Fetal Monitoring. Technical Bulletin number 7. Washington, DC:NAACOG, 1980.

Rising S. Fourth stage of labor: Family integration. Am J Nursing 74:870, 1974.

ADMISSION TO LABOR UNIT

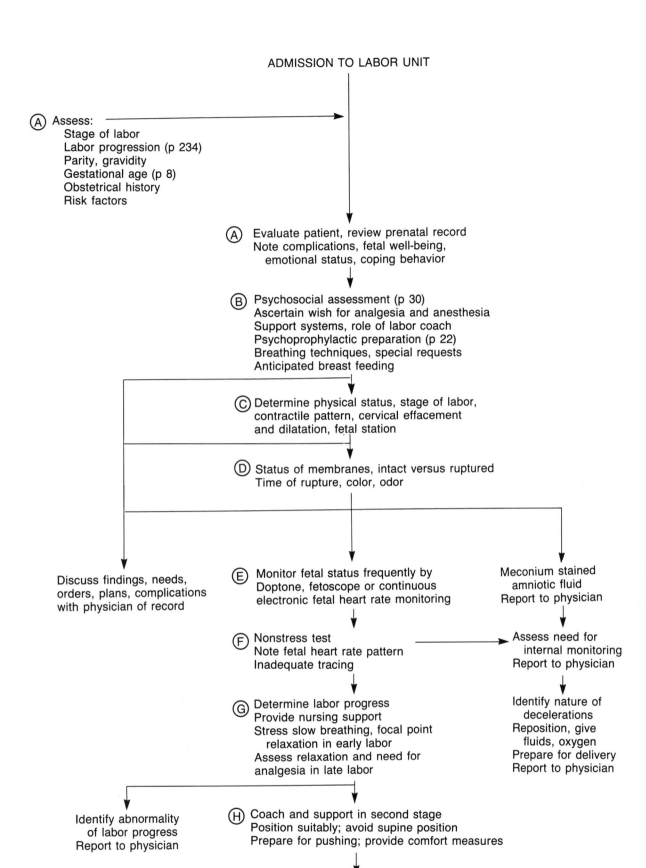

Ⓐ Assess:
　　Stage of labor
　　Labor progression (p 234)
　　Parity, gravidity
　　Gestational age (p 8)
　　Obstetrical history
　　Risk factors

Ⓐ Evaluate patient, review prenatal record
　　Note complications, fetal well-being,
　　　emotional status, coping behavior

Ⓑ Psychosocial assessment (p 30)
　　Ascertain wish for analgesia and anesthesia
　　Support systems, role of labor coach
　　Psychoprophylactic preparation (p 22)
　　Breathing techniques, special requests
　　Anticipated breast feeding

Ⓒ Determine physical status, stage of labor,
　　contractile pattern, cervical effacement
　　and dilatation, fetal station

Ⓓ Status of membranes, intact versus ruptured
　　Time of rupture, color, odor

Discuss findings, needs,
orders, plans, complications
with physician of record

Ⓔ Monitor fetal status frequently by
　　Doptone, fetoscope or continuous
　　electronic fetal heart rate monitoring

Meconium stained
amniotic fluid
Report to physician

Ⓕ Nonstress test
　　Note fetal heart rate pattern
　　Inadequate tracing

Assess need for
internal monitoring
Report to physician

Ⓖ Determine labor progress
　　Provide nursing support
　　Stress slow breathing, focal point
　　　relaxation in early labor
　　Assess relaxation and need for
　　　analgesia in late labor

Identify nature of
decelerations
Reposition, give
　fluids, oxygen
Prepare for delivery
Report to physician

Identify abnormality
of labor progress
Report to physician

Ⓗ Coach and support in second stage
　　Position suitably; avoid supine position
　　Prepare for pushing; provide comfort measures

Ⓘ Support postdelivery family integration
　　Encourage infant bonding
　　Withhold prophylactic eye medications
　　Foster eye contact, infant to breast
　　Medicate for postpartum discomfort
　　Initiate teaching program

PREMATURE RUPTURE OF MEMBRANES

Max Borten, M.D.

A. Although the chorioamniotic membranes commonly rupture spontaneously before labor, the longer the membranes are ruptured before delivery, the greater the risk of infection for both the mother and the fetus. When rupture occurs well before term, it is further complicated by premature delivery, which is likely to take place in a few days. There are currently two acceptable approaches to management. One favors aggressive intervention; the other, conservative expectancy. Either can be justified, provided the risk-benefit relationship is understood and taken into account for the individual gravida and her fetus. Conservative management, coupled with careful periodic evaluation for the earliest manifestations of amnionitis, usually yields good results. By contrast, it is essential to intervene early and aggressively once signs of infection appear. Lacking evidence of infection, one need not intervene in most cases.

B. It is essential to confirm rupture of the membranes whenever it is clinically suspected. Characteristically the gravida relates that she experienced a sudden gush of fluid from the vagina, but it may appear only as a slow trickle indistinguishable from vaginal discharge or involuntary loss of urine. To verify membrane rupture, a sterile speculum examination is done, testing the vaginal pool fluid for pH with Nitrazine paper; if alkaline, it is probably amniotic fluid. A drop of the specimen is placed on a glass slide and flame-dried to evaluate for ferning. The arborization so typical of dried amniotic fluid is readily recognized at all gestational ages, reflecting crystallization of dissolved protein and electrolytes. Under the microscope one may also see fetal squamous cells and lanugo. If there is any remaining doubt about the diagnosis, inject dye (not methylene blue, which may produce fetal methemoglobinemia) into the uterine cavity by amniocentesis; the appearance of dye in the vagina clearly confirms rupture of the membranes. Ultrasonographic evaluation of the intrauterine amniotic fluid volume provides valuable information about oligohydramnios (see E).

C. Watch carefully for the earliest signs of infection. Obtain a sample of the amniotic fluid (e.g., by means of a sheathed sterile transcervical catheter) for Wright and Gram stained smears and culture. Although bacteria and polymorphonuclear leukocytes do not prove infection, their absence is reassuring. Examination of a fluid sample obtained by amniocentesis clarifies doubtful results. A serum C-reactive protein determination may signal chorioamnionitis. The maternal temperature, white blood cell count, and differential are useful but late indices of the systemic response to infection.

D. Evaluate the fetal maturity (p 66) by the menstrual history, antenatal records, and ultrasonography. Vaginal pool phospholipid analysis helps measure fetal lung maturity. In a preterm gestation it is critical to weigh the risk of interference to effect delivery against the potential risk of infection if the pregnancy is allowed to continue. Administration of corticosteroids may avert the respiratory distress syndrome if delivery becomes necessary. The uncomplicated preterm pregnancy can justifiably be permitted to continue provided surveillance can be assured; this policy may avoid prematurity, failed or complicated induction, and even cesarean section. If conditions for induction are optimal at or near term, the hazard of infection from delay probably outweighs that of induction.

E. Premature rupture of the membranes before the fetus is viable is often complicated by oligohydramnios. Although this is not the oligohydramnios seen with placental insufficiency (p 70) but rather a consequence of outflow exceeding production, it is associated with a poor neonatal prognosis. The perils of pulmonary hypoplasia and deformation from amniotic bands must be discussed with the patient; serious consideration has to be given to interrupting the pregnancy, especially if the fetus is mature.

References

Borten M. Premature rupture of membranes. In: Nelson NM (Editor). Current Therapy in Neonatal-Perinatal Medicine 1985-1986. Toronto: B.C. Decker, 1985.

Borten M, Friedman EA. Amniotic fluid ferning in early gestation. Am J Obstet Gynecol 154:628, 1986.

Morales WJ, Diebel ND, Lazar AJ, Zadrozny D. The effect of antenatal dexamethasone administration on the prevention of respiratory distress syndrome in preterm gestations with premature rupture of membranes. Am J Obstet Gynecol 154:591, 1986.

Romem Y, Artal R. C-reactive protein as a predictor for chorioamnionitis in cases of premature rupture of the membranes. Am J Obstet Gynecol 150:546, 1984.

Thibeault DW, Beatty EC, Hall RT, et al. Neonatal pulmonary hypoplasia with premature rupture of fetal membranes and oligohydramnios. J Pediatr 107:273, 1985.

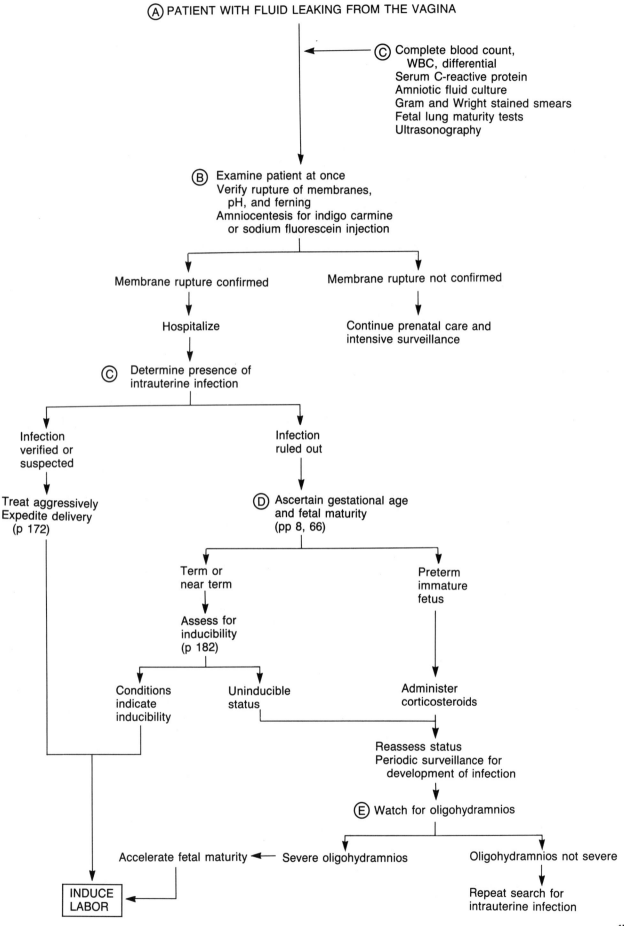

Ⓐ PATIENT WITH FLUID LEAKING FROM THE VAGINA

Ⓒ Complete blood count,
   WBC, differential
   Serum C-reactive protein
   Amniotic fluid culture
   Gram and Wright stained smears
   Fetal lung maturity tests
   Ultrasonography

Ⓑ Examine patient at once
   Verify rupture of membranes,
     pH, and ferning
   Amniocentesis for indigo carmine
     or sodium fluorescein injection

Membrane rupture confirmed

Membrane rupture not confirmed

Hospitalize

Continue prenatal care and
intensive surveillance

Ⓒ Determine presence of
   intrauterine infection

Infection
verified or
suspected

Infection
ruled out

Treat aggressively
Expedite delivery
(p 172)

Ⓓ Ascertain gestational age
   and fetal maturity
   (pp 8, 66)

Term or
near term

Preterm
immature
fetus

Assess for
inducibility
(p 182)

Conditions
indicate
inducibility

Uninducible
status

Administer
corticosteroids

Reassess status
Periodic surveillance for
development of infection

Ⓔ Watch for oligohydramnios

Accelerate fetal maturity ← Severe oligohydramnios

Oligohydramnios not severe

Repeat search for
intrauterine infection

INDUCE
LABOR

171

AMNIONITIS

Max Borten, M.D.

A. Because chorioamnionitis is associated with high fetal morbidity and mortality rates, it is a serious complication of the third trimester of gestation. It is usually preceded by premature rupture of the membranes of some duration (p 170) or a prolonged and difficult labor, but it may also occur de novo by ascending infection even through intact membranes. Serious maternal sepsis may occur with septicemia. Early diagnosis, thorough evaluation, and treatment are critical. The premonitory signs are those of systemic infection with fever, chills, leukocytosis, and a differential shift to the left, usually accompanied by uterine tenderness; a foul vaginal discharge is only occasionally encountered.

B. Infection can be a complication of transcervical or transabdominal puncture in the course of amniocentesis, chorionic villus biopsy, intrauterine transfusion, fetoscopy, or percutaneous umbilical vein sampling. A difficult procedure with multiple punctures or breaks in aseptic technique increases the likelihood of infection.

C. Since amnionitis is often associated with premature labor, suspect infection in gravidas who fail to respond to tocolytic therapy (p 178). Obtain a sample of amniotic fluid by amniocentesis for the identification of white blood cells and bacteria by smear and culture. Serum C reactive protein may be an early marker. Tocolytic drugs to arrest labor and corticosteroids to enhance pulmonary maturity are contraindicated with amnionitis.

D. Take normal pregnancy changes into account when interpreting the results of laboratory tests done to confirm the diagnosis. Both the erythrocyte sedimentation rate and the white blood count rise in pregnancy. Polymorphonuclear leukocytes and bacteria on a smear of amniotic fluid (especially if obtained by amniocentesis) make the diagnosis of chorioamnionitis likely. Their absence, by contrast, points to an extrauterine infection.

E. As soon as the diagnosis is made, obtain appropriate cultures and give wide spectrum antibiotics. If vaginal delivery is expected soon and fetal salvage is deemed reasonable on the basis of gestational age, consider transferring the gravida to a tertiary center to ensure availability of intensive neonatal care. Under these circumstances one might delay administration of antibiotics to enable the pediatrician to obtain meaningful cultures from the newborn infant. No adverse puerperal effects appear to result from such brief delays unless the maternal condition is critical. Involve the neonatologist in the management planning; his presence at delivery is important as well for purposes of resuscitation, rapid assessment, and expeditious treatment.

F. The labor course with chorioamnionitis is sometimes dysfunctional owing to decreased uterine contractility. Induction or augmentation of labor may require higher than ordinary doses of oxytocin to effect progress. Electronic fetal heart rate monitoring may show an absence of beat-to-beat variability and fetal tachycardia, usually reflecting maternal fever rather than hypoxia but deserving astute evaluation (p 200) nevertheless. Patients must be carefully followed after delivery for postpartum uterine atony (p 254), hemorrhage, and endometritis.

G. It is important for maternal well-being that the infected uterus be emptied as quickly as is compatible with circumstances. Vaginal delivery is clearly preferable if it can be accomplished in a reasonable period of time. Eight hours is a goal, but not rigidly adhered to if it is evident that labor is progressing well and the gravida's general condition is good. Cesarean section should be limited to those requiring abdominal delivery for obstetrical complications unless the infection is under poor control or the prospects of delivery are remote. The extraperitoneal approach offers no special advantages.

References

Duff P, Sanders R, Gibbs RS. The course of labor in term patients with chorioamnionitis. Am J Obstet Gynecol 147:391, 1983.

Ferguson MG, Rhodes PG, Morrison JC, Puckett CM. Clinical amniotic fluid infection and its effect on the neonate. Am J Obstet Gynecol 151:1058, 1985.

Hameed C, Tejani N, Verma UL, Archbald F. Silent chorioamnionitis as a cause of preterm labor refractory to tocolytic therapy. Am J Obstet Gynecol 149:726, 1984.

Romem Y, Artal R. C-reactive protein as a predictor for chorioamnionitis in cases of premature rupture of the membranes. Am J Obstet Gynecol 150:546, 1984.

FEVER IN PREGNANCY

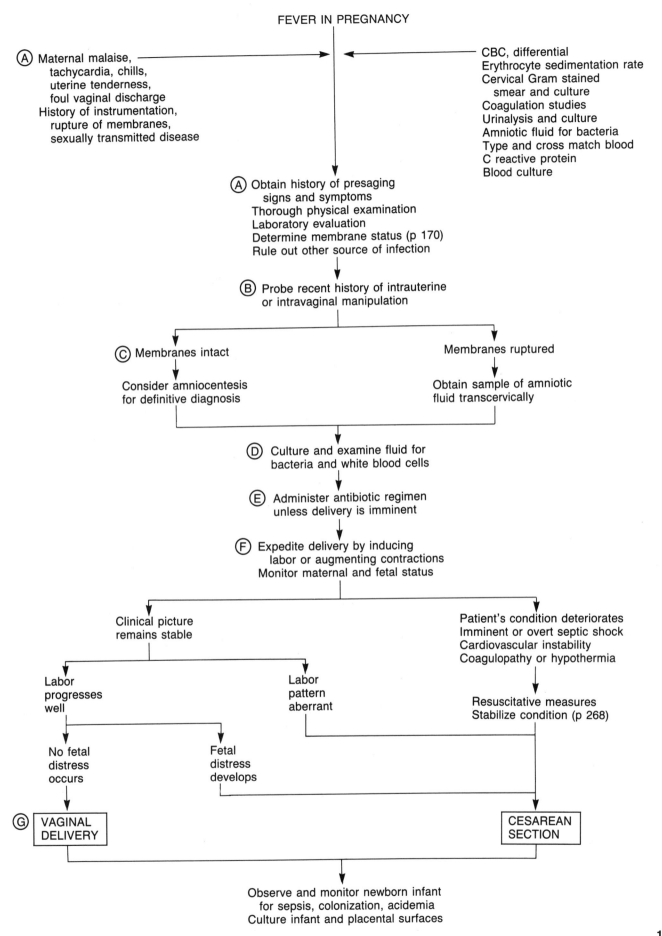

A Maternal malaise,
   tachycardia, chills,
   uterine tenderness,
   foul vaginal discharge
History of instrumentation,
   rupture of membranes,
   sexually transmitted disease

CBC, differential
Erythrocyte sedimentation rate
Cervical Gram stained
   smear and culture
Coagulation studies
Urinalysis and culture
Amniotic fluid for bacteria
Type and cross match blood
C reactive protein
Blood culture

A Obtain history of presaging
   signs and symptoms
Thorough physical examination
Laboratory evaluation
Determine membrane status (p 170)
Rule out other source of infection

B Probe recent history of intrauterine
   or intravaginal manipulation

C Membranes intact

Consider amniocentesis
for definitive diagnosis

Membranes ruptured

Obtain sample of amniotic
fluid transcervically

D Culture and examine fluid for
   bacteria and white blood cells

E Administer antibiotic regimen
   unless delivery is imminent

F Expedite delivery by inducing
   labor or augmenting contractions
Monitor maternal and fetal status

Clinical picture
remains stable

Patient's condition deteriorates
Imminent or overt septic shock
Cardiovascular instability
Coagulopathy or hypothermia

Labor
progresses
well

Labor
pattern
aberrant

Resuscitative measures
Stabilize condition (p 268)

No fetal
distress
occurs

Fetal
distress
develops

G VAGINAL
DELIVERY

CESAREAN
SECTION

Observe and monitor newborn infant
for sepsis, colonization, acidemia
Culture infant and placental surfaces

COUNSELING FOR PREMATURE BIRTH

Susan B. Wilson, M.D.
Franci Sheehan-Weber, R.N.C., M.S.

A. A high risk obstetrical team, composed of an obstetrician-perinatologist, geneticist, internist, nurse practitioner, social worker, and nutritionist, can optimally assess and provide care for the high risk obstetrical patient. Such ideal evaluation and management can be anticipated to improve the maternal and fetal prognosis for most conditions if diagnosed early and treated aggressively, by reducing the incidence of complications, fetal malformations, and stress and averting the need for preterm intervention for delivery.

B. Prepregnancy counseling is essential for patients with medical problems, especially those with diabetes mellitus (p 96), hypertension (p 98), and cardiovascular disorders (p 104), to minimize patient risk, the incidence of fetal anomalies, and the chances of preterm birth. Prepregnancy weight loss is recommended for obese patients, who can be expected to have a high incidence of pregnancy complications. Detailed informative genetic counseling (p 74) is essential to help identify patients who may need artificial insemination with sex-selected sperm, chorionic villus biopsy, genetic amniocentesis, or even newer techniques of percutaneous umbilical vein blood sampling for genetic testing (p 80).

C. Outreach programs to high risk populations, such as pregnant adolescents and diabetics, may be successful in fostering early enrollment for prenatal care. Educational programs for physicians, including both general obstetricians and family practitioners, regarding new concepts and technologies for managing high risk patients increase awareness of their needs and the means for early and definitive identification. Facilitated referral and consultative mechanisms are important to ensure beneficial intervention in pregnancies at risk.

D. A continuing educational program should be available for all obstetrical patients. Every pregnant woman should know the normal symptoms and changes of pregnancy in addition to warning signs of contractions, leakage of amniotic fluid, bleeding, cervical dilatation, bleeding, and pre-eclampsia. Prompt attention to the patient's questions and problems is important. Patients need to be counseled about the importance of prenatal visits, good nutrition, and the harmful effects of drugs, alcohol, and cigarette smoking. Women at high risk for a preterm birth should visit the special care nursery to familiarize themselves in advance with the facilities, personnel, and operations. All their questions about preterm delivery risks and survival rates should be addressed realistically. A reasonable balance should be struck between reassurance and reality in regard to prognostication to avoid generating undue anxiety while at the same time providing meaningful information about the serious potential risks for immediate and long term outcome results.

E. Continuation of team care for both inpatient and outpatient management is important. Specific problems, such as drug addiction, malnutrition, urinary tract infection, hypertension, and diabetes mellitus, need coordinated care and counseling from several different members of the high risk team. Preventive measures (p 176) should be discussed at length to ensure that the patient understands their rationale, thereby enlisting her cooperation to ensure compliance and help reduce the likelihood of preterm labor and delivery.

F. If the pregnancy ends in a preterm birth, it is important that the physicians carefully review the events leading to the delivery to relieve feelings of guilt and responsibility. Facilitate and coordinate communication between the parents and the neonatologist. Parents of preterm infants deserve the education, reassurance, and support that can be provided for them by both the nursing and social service team members.

References

Gilstrap LC, Hauth JC, Bell RE, et al. Survival and short-term morbidity of the premature neonate. Obstet Gynecol 65:37, 1985.

Goldenberg RL, Nelson KG, Hale CD, et al. Survival of infants with low birth weight and early gestational age, 1979 to 1981. Am J Obstet Gynecol 149:508, 1984.

Harley JMG. Pre-pregnancy counselling in obstetrics. Clin Obstet Gynaecol 9:1, 1982.

Hollingsworth DR, Jones OW, Resnik R. Expanded care in obstetrics for the 1980s: Preconception and early postconception counseling. Am J Obstet Gynecol 149:811, 1984.

Merkatz IR. Preterm birth. Clin Obstet Gynecol 27:537, 1984.

PATIENT AT RISK FOR PREMATURE DELIVERY

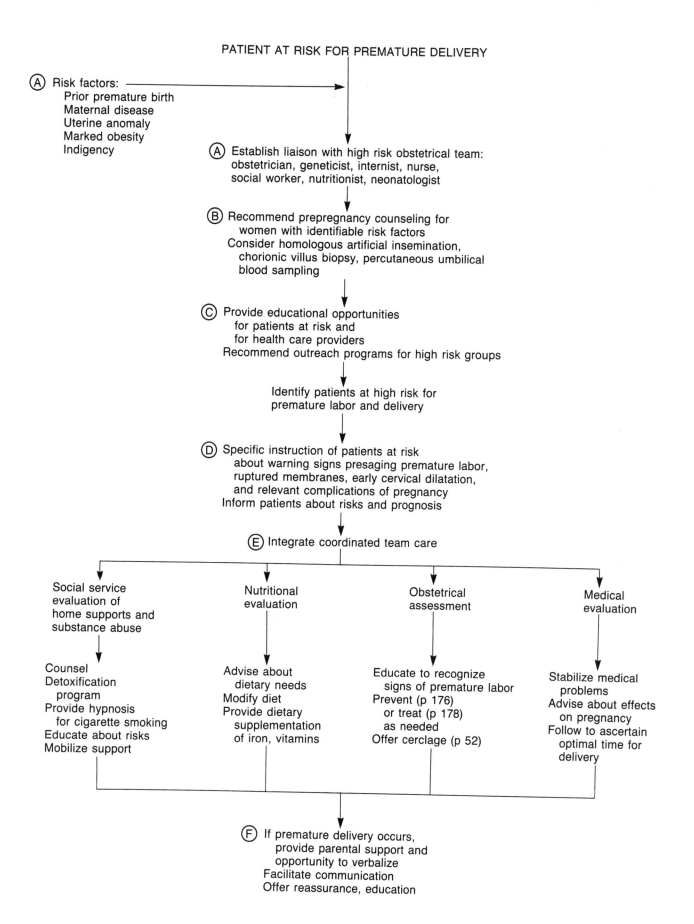

(A) Risk factors:
    Prior premature birth
    Maternal disease
    Uterine anomaly
    Marked obesity
    Indigency

(A) Establish liaison with high risk obstetrical team:
    obstetrician, geneticist, internist, nurse,
    social worker, nutritionist, neonatologist

(B) Recommend prepregnancy counseling for
    women with identifiable risk factors
    Consider homologous artificial insemination,
    chorionic villus biopsy, percutaneous umbilical
    blood sampling

(C) Provide educational opportunities
    for patients at risk and
    for health care providers
    Recommend outreach programs for high risk groups

Identify patients at high risk for
premature labor and delivery

(D) Specific instruction of patients at risk
    about warning signs presaging premature labor,
    ruptured membranes, early cervical dilatation,
    and relevant complications of pregnancy
    Inform patients about risks and prognosis

(E) Integrate coordinated team care

Social service
evaluation of
home supports and
substance abuse

Nutritional
evaluation

Obstetrical
assessment

Medical
evaluation

Counsel
Detoxification
    program
Provide hypnosis
    for cigarette smoking
Educate about risks
Mobilize support

Advise about
    dietary needs
Modify diet
Provide dietary
    supplementation
    of iron, vitamins

Educate to recognize
    signs of premature labor
Prevent (p 176)
    or treat (p 178)
    as needed
Offer cerclage (p 52)

Stabilize medical
    problems
Advise about effects
    on pregnancy
Follow to ascertain
    optimal time for
    delivery

(F) If premature delivery occurs,
    provide parental support and
    opportunity to verbalize
    Facilitate communication
    Offer reassurance, education

PREVENTION OF PREMATURE LABOR

Susan B. Wilson, M.D.

A. A variety of factors may be associated with preterm labor. These should be searched for in every gravid patient to identify those at special risk and needing active preventive care. However, it should be emphasized that although a number of prenatal scoring systems are in vogue (and recommended for use) for determining the probability of preterm delivery, none has been shown to predict pregnancy outcome accurately. Known risk factors include a history of premature labor, uterine malformation, leiomyoma uteri, multiple gestation, abruptio placentae, chronic hypertension, drug abuse, alcohol and cigarette use, young maternal age, low socioeconomic class, and low maternal weight. Pregnancies at high risk of premature delivery should be managed by a team composed of a physician, nurse, and social worker with consultation with an internist, a nutritionist, and a perinatologist, as indicated.

B. Laboratory evaluation should be undertaken in a search for hemoglobinopathy, anemia, pelvic and urinary tract infection, and diabetes mellitus. Abnormal alpha fetoprotein levels have been associated with a poor pregnancy outcome (p 76). Ultrasonographic evaluation is important to establish the gestational age and fetal size accurately and to demonstrate uterine anomalies or leiomyomas. Psychosocial assessment (p 30) is appropriate in a gravida who falls into the group at high risk for premature delivery, especially if the presenting risks are behavioral factors (drug or alcohol use, smoking, poor nutrition) and potentially capable of correction. Education and counseling are important components of prenatal care in these patients.

C. Aggressive prenatal care can significantly reduce the risks of premature rupture of membranes, low birth weight in the infant, premature delivery, and perinatal death, minimizing the need for neonatal intensive care and diminishing the hospital cost. A program of optimal care includes early and frequent prenatal visits, patient education, periodic re-examinations to detect problems, and attention to the patient's concerns and questions, noting especially canceled appointments or failure to comply with recommendations. Enrollment in outreach programs should be considered for such high risk gravidas as adolescent mothers (p 18). Obstetrical visits should involve screening for signs of hypertension, diabetes, urinary tract infection, premature contractions, and evidence of cervical effacement and dilatation. Serial vaginal examinations may aid in predicting the onset of premature labor; these should be carried out with great gentleness, avoiding any digital pressure or probing of the cervical os, to ensure against the obviously counterproductive possibility of stimulating labor to begin. The use of prophylactic measures, such as tocolytics, although not fully documented to be of real value, is advocated by some as being helpful in prolonging pregnancy in gravidas who are at risk of premature labor, especially when coupled with careful outpatient monitoring.

D. Cervical effacement and dilatation occurring without accompanying perceived uterine contractions are evidence of cervical incompetence. If they are documented in the midtrimester, consider cervical cerclage (p 52); if they occur later in pregnancy, prescribe bed rest and tocolytic drugs as indicated by the appearance of contractions.

E. Premature labor should be aggressively treated with tocolytic drugs (p 178) unless contraindications, such as chorioamnionitis or abruptio placentae, exist. Consider giving steroid therapy to enhance fetal pulmonary maturity and transferring the gravida to a tertiary care center if delivery is likely.

References

Bouyer J, Papiernik E, Dreyfus J, et al. Maturation signs of the cervix and prediction of preterm birth. Obstet Gynecol 68:209, 1986.

Gonik B, Creasy RK. Preterm labor: Its diagnosis and management. Am J Obstet Gynecol 154:3, 1986.

Herron MA, Katz M, Creasy RK. Evaluation of a preterm birth prevention program: A preliminary report. Obstet Gynecol 59:452, 1982.

Katz M, Gill PJ, Newman RB. Detection of preterm labor by ambulatory monitoring of uterine activity for the management of oral tocolysis. Am J Obstet Gynecol 154:1253, 1986.

GRAVIDA AT RISK OF PREMATURE LABOR

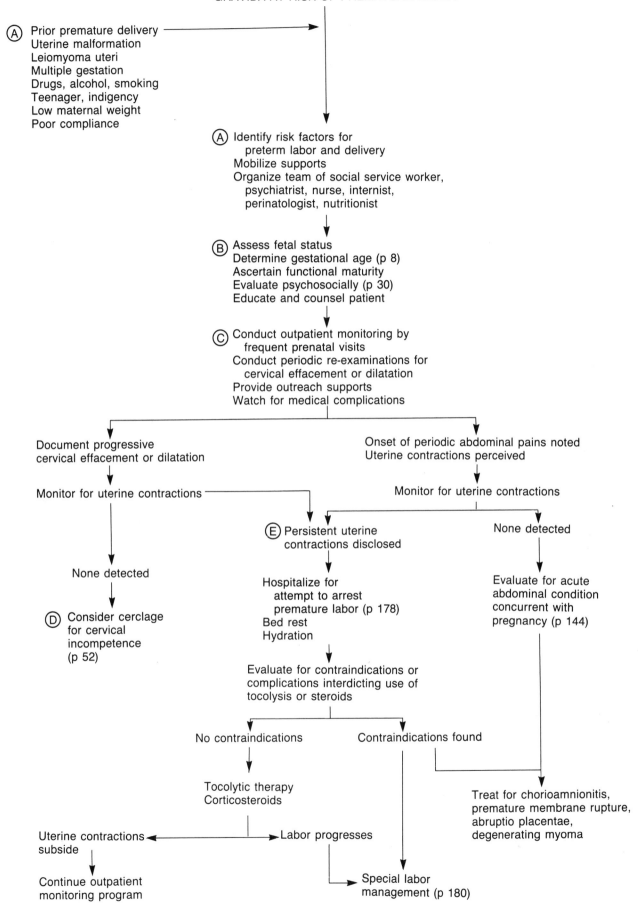

(A) Prior premature delivery
Uterine malformation
Leiomyoma uteri
Multiple gestation
Drugs, alcohol, smoking
Teenager, indigency
Low maternal weight
Poor compliance

(A) Identify risk factors for
preterm labor and delivery
Mobilize supports
Organize team of social service worker,
psychiatrist, nurse, internist,
perinatologist, nutritionist

(B) Assess fetal status
Determine gestational age (p 8)
Ascertain functional maturity
Evaluate psychosocially (p 30)
Educate and counsel patient

(C) Conduct outpatient monitoring by
frequent prenatal visits
Conduct periodic re-examinations for
cervical effacement or dilatation
Provide outreach supports
Watch for medical complications

Document progressive
cervical effacement or dilatation

Onset of periodic abdominal pains noted
Uterine contractions perceived

Monitor for uterine contractions

Monitor for uterine contractions

(E) Persistent uterine
contractions disclosed

None detected

None detected

(D) Consider cerclage
for cervical
incompetence
(p 52)

Hospitalize for
attempt to arrest
premature labor (p 178)
Bed rest
Hydration

Evaluate for acute
abdominal condition
concurrent with
pregnancy (p 144)

Evaluate for contraindications or
complications interdicting use of
tocolysis or steroids

No contraindications

Contraindications found

Tocolytic therapy
Corticosteroids

Treat for chorioamnionitis,
premature membrane rupture,
abruptio placentae,
degenerating myoma

Uterine contractions
subside

Labor progresses

Continue outpatient
monitoring program

Special labor
management (p 180)

ARRESTING PREMATURE LABOR

Benjamin P. Sachs, M.B., B.S., D.P.H.

A. Premature labor is easy to diagnose if associated with regular contractions and a changing cervix. Unfortunately if one waits for obvious progress to occur, treatment becomes less and less effective in stopping labor. Although the diagnosis of premature labor without any change in the cervix can lead to inappropriate management, it may be prudent to undertake some measures nonetheless with the patient's full knowledge and consent. If the initial examination shows the cervix already 2 to 3 cm dilated and effaced, it would clearly be inappropriate to wait for a further change in the cervix to make a definitive diagnosis of premature labor, because the labor would likely be so far advanced by the time another examination is done that no measures could be expected to be effective in arresting progress.

B. The initial assessment should include fetal monitoring and ultrasonography for the purposes of estimating fetal weight, verifying gestational age, and ascertaining information about the fetal presentation, malformation, placental site, amniotic fluid volume, and fetal sex. Administer intravenous hydration rapidly and confine the patient to bed rest in the left lateral position as a first step in management, because these simple measures sometimes can cause the contractions to subside, thereby obviating the need for tocolytic therapy.

C. Determine whether there are any conditions that would make it preferable to proceed with delivery rather than attempting to arrest the labor. Foremost among them is amnionitis. If there are signs of intrauterine infection (p 172), tocolytic therapy is contraindicated and the fetus should be delivered. In addition, premature rupture of the membranes makes it unlikely that such treatment will work (aside from the potential risk of infection from prolonged delays). Obviously if the mother or the fetus exhibits a problem necessitating expeditious delivery, tocolysis should not be considered either.

D. Carefully ascertain the gestational age, using all available information and objective tests (p 8). If the fetus is obviously too immature by dates (less than 34 weeks) to ensure an uneventful neonatal course, one should attempt to forestall delivery if it is feasible to do so. However, the fetal lungs may be immature even if the gestational duration exceeds 34 weeks. Before making a decision to allow labor to progress, therefore, obtain amniotic fluid for fetal pulmonary indices whenever possible, unless it is well established that the fetus is at or near term. In case of immature indices, consider giving corticosteroid therapy to accelerate maturation, if time permits.

E. Before undertaking tocolytic therapy with beta sympathomimetic drugs, it is essential to evaluate the gravida's metabolic and cardiologic status carefully, including serum electrolyte and blood sugar levels, electrocardiography, and a thorough examination of the heart and lungs. These should be repeated periodically during treatment and again afterward. Avoid these measures if there is evidence of cardiopulmonary disease, hyperthyroidism, acute or chronic hypertension, or diabetes mellitus.

F. The beta sympathomimetic regimen should begin parenterally (e.g., ritodrine, 50 to 100 μg per minute, increasing by 50 μg per minute every 10 to 15 minutes until contractions stop or side effects prevent continuation, to a maximum of 350 μg per minute) and, if successful, changing after 12 hours to oral doses (10 to 20 mg at two to six hour intervals; daily maximum 120 mg). Watch closely for signs suggestive of congestive failure. Symptoms of chest tightness, shortness of breath, orthopnea, and irritability should alert the clinician to the possibility of developing pulmonary edema. Discontinue ritodrine therapy at once if edema occurs. At special risk are gravidas with multiple pregnancy or heart disease, those with fluid overload, and those using steroids concomitantly.

References

Souney PF, Kaul AF, Osathanondh R. Pharmacotherapy of preterm labor. Clin Pharm 2:29, 1983.

Tejani NA, Verma UL. Effect of tocolysis on incidence of low birth weight. Obstet Gynecol 61:566, 1983.

Williams RL, Chen PM. Identifying the sources of the recent decline in prenatal mortality rates in California. New Engl J Med 306:207, 1982.

ONSET OF LABOR IN PRETERM PREGNANCY

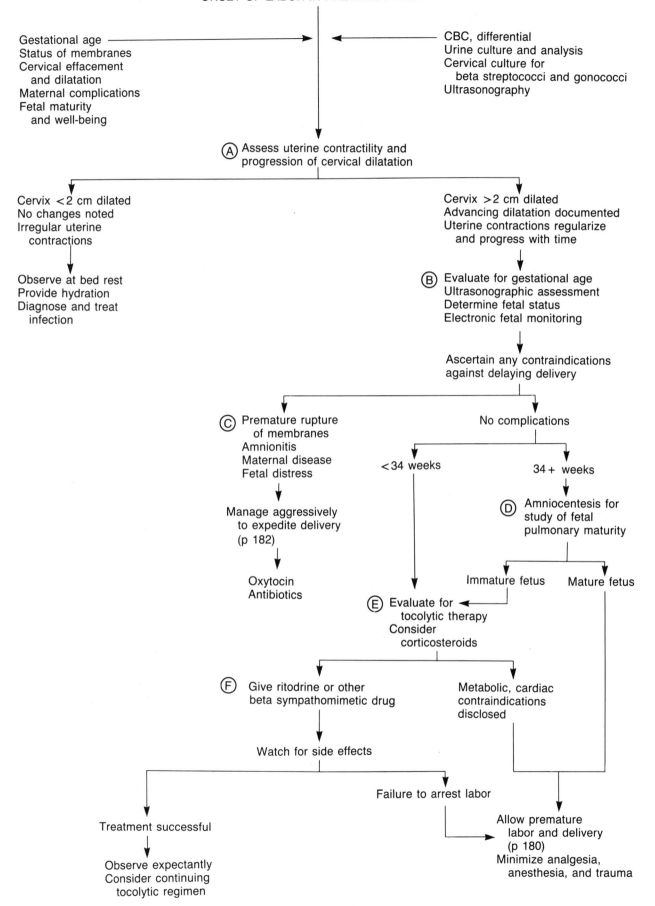

Gestational age
Status of membranes
Cervical effacement
  and dilatation
Maternal complications
Fetal maturity
  and well-being

CBC, differential
Urine culture and analysis
Cervical culture for
  beta streptococci and gonococci
Ultrasonography

Ⓐ Assess uterine contractility and
   progression of cervical dilatation

Cervix <2 cm dilated
No changes noted
Irregular uterine
  contractions

Cervix >2 cm dilated
Advancing dilatation documented
Uterine contractions regularize
  and progress with time

Observe at bed rest
Provide hydration
Diagnose and treat
  infection

Ⓑ Evaluate for gestational age
   Ultrasonographic assessment
   Determine fetal status
   Electronic fetal monitoring

Ascertain any contraindications
against delaying delivery

Ⓒ Premature rupture
   of membranes
   Amnionitis
   Maternal disease
   Fetal distress

No complications

<34 weeks

34 + weeks

Manage aggressively
to expedite delivery
(p 182)

Ⓓ Amniocentesis for
   study of fetal
   pulmonary maturity

Oxytocin
Antibiotics

Immature fetus   Mature fetus

Ⓔ Evaluate for
   tocolytic therapy
   Consider
   corticosteroids

Ⓕ Give ritodrine or other
   beta sympathomimetic drug

Metabolic, cardiac
contraindications
disclosed

Watch for side effects

Failure to arrest labor

Treatment successful

Allow premature
labor and delivery
(p 180)
Minimize analgesia,
  anesthesia, and trauma

Observe expectantly
Consider continuing
  tocolytic regimen

PREMATURE LABOR AND DELIVERY

Benjamin P. Sachs, M.B., B.S., D.P.H.

A. The management of premature labor and delivery of a very immature fetus has to take into account the facts that the very low birth weight fetus has little reserve in regard to its potential for developing hypoxia, it is easily traumatized, it is frequently in a malpresentation, and the labor is often complicated by maternal disease (diabetes, pregnancy induced hypertension, chorioamnionitis) or an obstetrical disorder (abruptio placentae, placenta previa, premature rupture of membranes, cord prolapse). If preventive measures have failed or cannot be applied because they are inappropriate or actually contraindicated (p 178), the inevitability of delivery must be accepted. Prepare the parents (p 174) as well as time permits, and alert the neonatologist of the impending delivery. Consider transferring the mother to a tertiary care center in anticipation of the delivery so that the full panoply of neonatal intensive care can be made available without exposing the newborn infant to the substantive risks of neonatal transport.

B. Aside from laboratory assessments for infection and general maternal health status, it is important to perform ultrasonography as part of the initial evaluation. This should include a thorough evaluation for fetal anomalies malpresentation, weight, and sex, as well as placental localization. Look for uterine malformation. Information about fetal well-being can be obtained by this approach at the same time, examining for body movement, breathing excursions, muscle tone, and amniotic fluid volume (p 70).

C. Because the diameters of the head of a premature fetus are relatively so much larger than those of the body, there is a growing trend toward delivering any with malpresentation by cesarean section. This practice, although it has found wide approval, is based on intuitive logic; there are as yet no objective data to support it, because many of those delivered by section may still succumb to problems related to immature physiologic development.

D. For premature fetuses presenting by the vertex, vaginal delivery should be attempted if labor progress is normal and there is no evidence of fetal distress. The labor should be monitored carefully by continuous internal electronic fetal heart rate monitoring. Use scalp blood pH determinations if they are indicated to clarify any suspicious decelerations. Since beat-to-beat variabiity may not yet be developed in the very premature fetus, this feature cannot always be evaluated.

E. The fetus of very low birth weight (below 1,500 g) is at special risk in regard to potential trauma during its passage through the birth canal; therefore one should weigh the option of cesarean section, particularly if there is any complicating feature, such as infection or bleeding. Here again the benefit of aggressive intervention has not yet been proved. Nevertheless the practice is being advocated widely. The good results with cesarean section for maternal or fetal complications in these cases indicate that early recourse to operative delivery can be justified if such complications arise during labor.

F. Premature labor should be conducted with minimal analgesia. Peridural anesthesia is useful, but hypotension should be avoided. Uterotonic stimulation should not be used, if possible, to prevent the forces of labor from becoming excessive. Gentleness is critical. A large episiotomy is made for delivery to minimize the perineal pressures on the fetal head. The use of forceps, widely recommended in the past ostensibly to protect the fetal head, is now recognized to effect compression instead and is therefore less preferable to permitting a gentle, controlled, spontaneous delivery.

References

Jovanovic R. Incision of the pregnant uterus and delivery of low-birth-weight infants. Am J Obstet Gynecol 152:971, 1985.

Rayburn WF, Dunn SM, Kolin MG, et al. Obstetric care and intraventricular hemorrhage in the low birth weight infant. Obstet Gynecol 62:408, 1983.

Rosen MG, Chik L. The association between cesarean birth outcome in vertex presentation: Relative importance of birth weight, Dubowitz scores, and delivery route. Am J Obstet Gynecol 150:775, 1984.

Sachs BP, McCarthy BJ, Rubin G, et al. Cesarean section: Risks and benefits for mother and fetus. JAMA 250:2157, 1983.

GRAVIDA IN PREMATURE LABOR

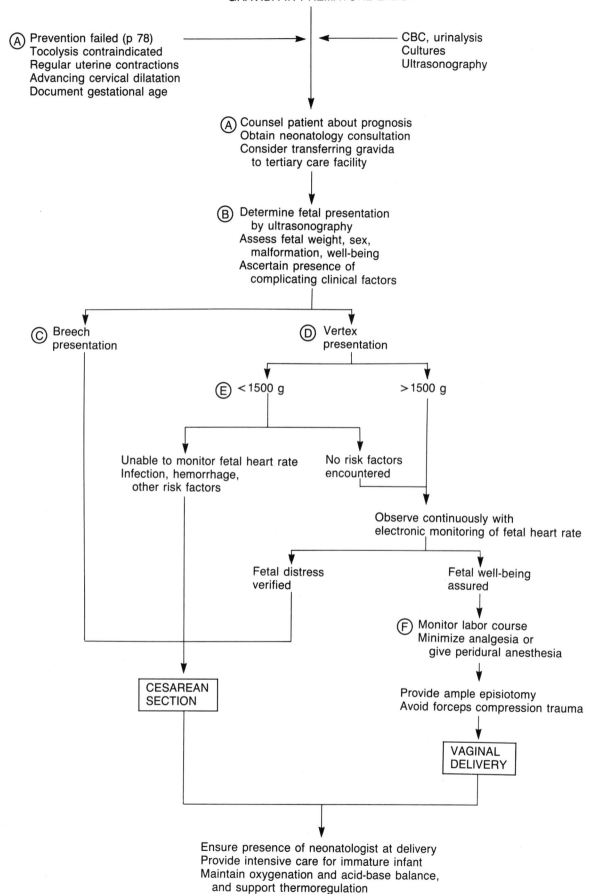

Ⓐ Prevention failed (p 78)
Tocolysis contraindicated
Regular uterine contractions
Advancing cervical dilatation
Document gestational age

CBC, urinalysis
Cultures
Ultrasonography

Ⓐ Counsel patient about prognosis
Obtain neonatology consultation
Consider transferring gravida
to tertiary care facility

Ⓑ Determine fetal presentation
by ultrasonography
Assess fetal weight, sex,
malformation, well-being
Ascertain presence of
complicating clinical factors

Ⓒ Breech
presentation

Ⓓ Vertex
presentation

Ⓔ <1500 g

>1500 g

Unable to monitor fetal heart rate
Infection, hemorrhage,
other risk factors

No risk factors
encountered

Observe continuously with
electronic monitoring of fetal heart rate

Fetal distress
verified

Fetal well-being
assured

Ⓕ Monitor labor course
Minimize analgesia or
give peridural anesthesia

CESAREAN
SECTION

Provide ample episiotomy
Avoid forceps compression trauma

VAGINAL
DELIVERY

Ensure presence of neonatologist at delivery
Provide intensive care for immature infant
Maintain oxygenation and acid-base balance,
and support thermoregulation

LABOR INDUCTION

Lynn H. Galen, M.D.

A. Because of the increased risks to both the fetus and the mother, elective induction of labor is no longer considered to be acceptable medical practice. Strong indications that outweigh the known risks need be present before proceeding. Indications for the induction of labor include pregnancy induced hypertension, prolonged gestation, intrauterine growth retardation, chronic hypertension, fetal demise, Rh sensitization, amnionitis, abruptio placentae, and diabetes mellitus, among others.

B. An examination should be done prior to beginning an induction of labor to assess the fetal presentation, adequacy of pelvic dimensions, and cervical condition. Amniocentesis is undertaken if fetal lung maturity is in question (p 64). Contraindications to induction include fetal malpresentation, prematurity, cephalopelvic disproportion, uterine overdistention, and fetal distress. One should ensure there are trained personnel present to recognize and deal with complications that may arise. The patient should be fully informed and the physician must be present.

C. The degree of cervical ripeness and fetal station correlates with the ease of induction. This can be assessed by use of the Bishop score (Table 1). A score of 4 or less is associated with a 20 percent failure rate; if it is 9 or more, inducibility usually can be expected. In the face of a poor Bishop score, one must carefully weigh the risk-benefit relationship.

D. If the indication for induction is strong, an amniotomy is done and an infusion of a dilute solution of oxytocin begun: 10 IU of oxytocin is added to 1 liter of a balanced salt solution, giving a concentration of 1 mU of oxytocin per 0.1 ml of solution. An infusion pump is recommended with the oxytocin line "piggybacked" to the main intravenous line. The infusion is begun at a rate of 2 mU per minute and increased by 2 mU at 20 minute intervals until good quality labor is established. One generally should not have to exceed a dose of 20 mU per minute of oxytocin. The lowest dose of oxytocin necessary to achieve cervical dilatation is used. After optimal uterine activity is achieved, close mintoring should be maintained. It may prove necessary to reduce the oxytocin dosage as labor advances.

E. If the patient presents with a poor Bishop score and indications for induction are weak, one should consider postponing the induction. Sometimes a trial of oxytocin may be undertaken as a "staged" induction—that is, repeated daily until the cervix is sufficiently ripened that a successful induction can be expected. Amniotomy can then be done when labor ensues.

F. Cervical priming with such techniques as the use of Laminaria, cervical balloons, or prostaglandins is not as yet routinely used in clinical practice. It has not been shown to decrease the induction-to-delivery time, but it does increase uterine sensitivity to oxytocin. The total amount of oxytocin needed to achieve dilatation is thereby diminished and the chance of failure of induction is decreased.

G. Active stimulation of uterine contractions with oxytocin increases the risk of hypertonic contractions and fetal distress. The fetal status and uterine contractions should be constantly monitored; electronic surveillance is strongly recommended. Vital signs are assessed every 15 minutes. In the presence of ruptured membranes, vaginal examinations are kept to a minimum. In the event of excessive duration of contractions (over 90 seconds), a rise in uterine tone with poor relaxation between contractions, or evidence of fetal distress (p 200), the infusion should be stopped and the patient re-evaluated. Because of its potent antidiuretic action, oxytocin is not given in conjunction with free water solutions. Postpartum hemorrhage may result from uterine atony and should be anticipated following delivery.

H. Failure to establish strong regular contractions or to achieve progressive cervical dilatation is a known complication of attempted induction of labor. Cesarean section is done for failed induction only if immediate delivery is clearly warranted on the basis of the maternal or fetal condition.

TABLE 1 Components of the Bishop Score

Bishop Score	0	1	2	3
Cervical dilatation	Closed	1–2 cm	3–4 cm	5 cm +
Effacement	0–30%	40–50%	60–70%	80% +
Consistency	Firm	Medium	Soft	
Fetal station	−3	−2	−1,0	+1,+2
Cervical position	Posterior	Midposition	Anterior	

References

Anderson KE, Forman A, Olmsten U. Pharmacology of labor. Clin Obstet Gynecol 26:56, 1983.

Arulkumaran S, Gibb DM, Ratnam SS, Lun KC, Heng SH. Total uterine activity in induced labor: An index of cervical and pelvic tissue resistance. Br J Obstet Gynaecol 92:693, 1985.

Graves GR, Baskett TF, Gray JH, Luther ER. The effect of vaginal administration of various doses of PGE$_2$ gel on cervical ripening and induction of labor. Am J Obstet Gynecol 151:178, 1985.

Jagani N, Schulman H, Fleischer A, Mitchell J, Blattner P. Role of prostaglandin induced cervical changes in labor induction. Obstet Gynecol 63:225, 1984.

PATIENT UNDER CONSIDERATION FOR LABOR INDUCTION

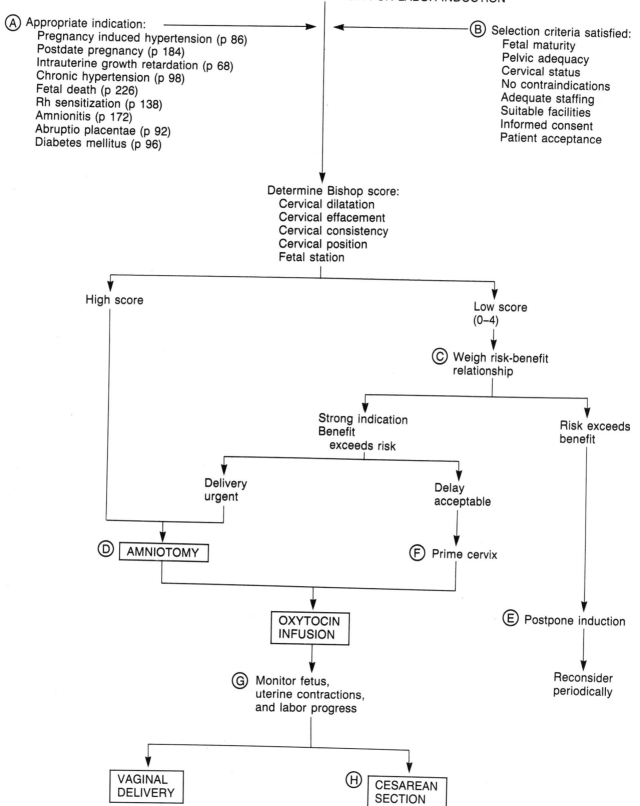

(A) Appropriate indication:
    Pregnancy induced hypertension (p 86)
    Postdate pregnancy (p 184)
    Intrauterine growth retardation (p 68)
    Chronic hypertension (p 98)
    Fetal death (p 226)
    Rh sensitization (p 138)
    Amnionitis (p 172)
    Abruptio placentae (p 92)
    Diabetes mellitus (p 96)

(B) Selection criteria satisfied:
    Fetal maturity
    Pelvic adequacy
    Cervical status
    No contraindications
    Adequate staffing
    Suitable facilities
    Informed consent
    Patient acceptance

Determine Bishop score:
    Cervical dilatation
    Cervical effacement
    Cervical consistency
    Cervical position
    Fetal station

High score

Low score
(0–4)

(C) Weigh risk-benefit
    relationship

Strong indication
Benefit
exceeds risk

Risk exceeds
benefit

Delivery
urgent

Delay
acceptable

(D) AMNIOTOMY

(F) Prime cervix

(E) Postpone induction

OXYTOCIN
INFUSION

Reconsider
periodically

(G) Monitor fetus,
    uterine contractions,
    and labor progress

VAGINAL
DELIVERY

(H) CESAREAN
    SECTION

POST - TERM PREGNANCY

David B. Acker, M.D.

A. Management of the post-term pregnancy should begin at the very first antenatal visit. For all gravidas, accurate evaluation of gestational age and calculation of the estimated date of confinement should be done at the earliest opportunity. Although routine ultrasonographic confirmation of gestational length is not required in all pregnancies, if any difficulty is encountered in the physical assessment of uterine size (due to body habitus or abdominal scars) or if the uterus is larger than expected, ultrasonography should be performed promptly. After all available information has been gathered and the estimated date of confinement calculated (and written in the chart), only the most convincing and definitive new information should tempt the obstetrician to change it. Clinical decisions are generally best based on the earliest available calculation.

B. Gravidas with coexisting medical conditions, especially those associated with uteroplacental insufficiency (hypertension, overt diabetes, hemoglobinopathies) or women carrying fetuses already compromised by an adverse uterine environment (growth retardation, Rh isoimmunization, hydrops), should ordinarily be delivered prior to completion of the 42nd week.

C. Obstetrical management of the postdate (or almost postdate uncomplicated pregnancy has become polarized. Some favor frequent (twice weekly) fetal status testing and await the onset of labor. Others favor induction, if the cervix is favorable, at 42 weeks (some even at the end of 41 weeks). Care for specific patients can be individualized. If pregnancy is permitted to continue, antenatal testing must be done, including a nonstress test, contraction stress test, or biophysical profile. Although some wait until 42 weeks to begin, it is preferable to start earlier in order to get baseline data. Testing should be done twice weekly. All pregnancies that progress beyond 42 weeks deserve this type of antenatal surveillance. Insufficient evidence is available to recommend sole reliance on a patient documented fetal "kick" count. Nipple stimulation contraction stress testing may be associated with prolonged fetal bradycardia and is currently not recommended.

D. The biophysical profile gives valuable information about amniotic fluid volume, fetal tone, movement, and breathing. It is especially useful for detecting oligohydramnios and fetal anomalies. Oligohydramnios (no pocket of amniotic fluid larger than 1 to 2 cm on ultrasonography) is ominous; when it is noted, induction should be initiated promptly. The presence of fetal anomalies may alter antepartum and intrapartum management, including the choice of the hospital at which delivery should take place.

E. The patient should be instructed to come to the delivery unit at the onset of contractions, regardless of how irregular they are. Early labor may irreversibly stress the fetus. The policy of awaiting regular, frequent, and strong contractions prior to coming to the hospital is inappropriate for the management of postdate pregnancy. The fetus should be electronically monitored throughout. Intermittent monitoring is unacceptable. Delivery units without fetal monitoring capabilities should not be delivering postdate gravidas. Meconium is common (25 to 50 percent) and serves as a marker, but not necessarily as an accurate indicator, of possible fetal distress.

F. After the 43rd postmenstrual week, continued management of the high risk pregnancy must be carefully weighed. The gravida must understand the risks and benefits of all alternatives. Whereas individualization of care is still important, delivery is generally most prudent at this time, if it can be accomplished safely. Further delay is justifiable only if the maternal and fetal status warrants it. The plan should be documented in the patient's chart.

G. A prolonged contraction stress test has two distinct advantages: Repetitive contractions over a period of hours may unmask previously undetected uteroplacental insufficiency, and the test itself may initiate labor.

References

Eden RD, Gregely RZ, Schifrin BS, et al. Comparison of antepartum testing schemes for the management of postdate pregnancy. Am J Obstet Gynecol 144:683, 1982.

Johnson JM, Harman CR, Lange IR, et al. Biophysical profile scoring in the management of the postterm pregnancy: An analysis of 307 patients. Am J Obstet Gynecol 154:269, 1986.

Phalen JP, Platt LD, Yeh SY, et al. The role of ultrasound measurement of amniotic fluid volumes in the management of postdate pregnancy. Am J Obstet Gynecol 151:304, 1985.

Yeh SY, Read JA. Management of postterm pregnancy in a large obstetric population. Obstet Gynecol 60:282, 1982.

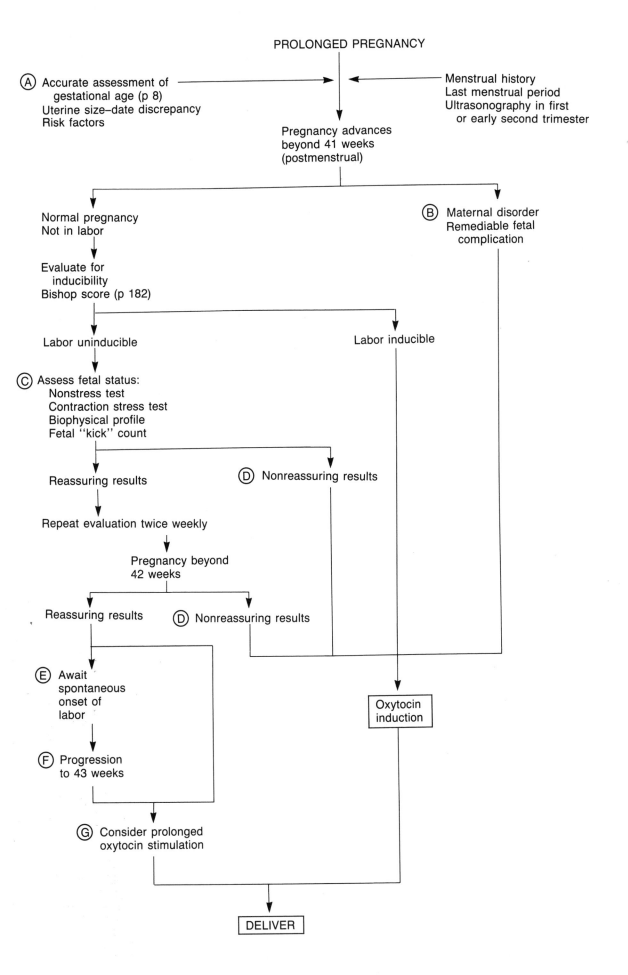

PROLONGED PREGNANCY

(A) Accurate assessment of
gestational age (p 8)
Uterine size–date discrepancy
Risk factors

Menstrual history
Last menstrual period
Ultrasonography in first
or early second trimester

Pregnancy advances
beyond 41 weeks
(postmenstrual)

Normal pregnancy
Not in labor

(B) Maternal disorder
Remediable fetal
complication

Evaluate for
inducibility
Bishop score (p 182)

Labor uninducible

Labor inducible

(C) Assess fetal status:
Nonstress test
Contraction stress test
Biophysical profile
Fetal ''kick'' count

Reassuring results

(D) Nonreassuring results

Repeat evaluation twice weekly

Pregnancy beyond
42 weeks

Reassuring results

(D) Nonreassuring results

(E) Await
spontaneous
onset of
labor

Oxytocin
induction

(F) Progression
to 43 weeks

(G) Consider prolonged
oxytocin stimulation

DELIVER

LABOR ANALGESIA

Nancy E. Oriol, M.D.

A. One should try to tailor the analgesic regimen to the individual gravida while simultaneously minimizing risk and ensuring safety. The medications used should not adversely affect the labor process or unfavorably affect the fetus. One's choice of the analgesic drug and dosage schedule varies according to the patient's emotional stability, level of anxiety, and her desire regarding pain relief and degree of wakefulness over the course of labor and during the delivery. The choice also must take into account her medical condition and any labor or fetal complications. Epidural analgesia decreases catecholamine levels; this effect can be particularly beneficial to the gravida with pregnancy induced hypertension. Similarly, peridural anesthesia increases intervillous blood flow, which can help ameliorate the fetal condition. Nonetheless, use of peridural analgesia in patients with pregnancy induced hypertension requires meticulous attention to the cardiovascular status, because the constricted intravascular volume can be destabilized by the associated vasodilatation. Most cardiac patients are helped in labor by the effective relief of pain and stress resulting from epidural analgesia. However, this does not apply for all heart diseases. Gravidas afflicted with certain types, especially if associated with cyanosis or a potential left to right shunt, may be put into serious jeopardy by the sympathetic block caused by the anesthesia; the peridural administration of opiates may be considered as a potentially useful alternative.

B. Progress in the latent phase is adversely affected by narcotic analgesic drugs, and more so by large doses. The same effect is seen with regional block anesthesia. If peridural anesthesia must be used at this phase of labor, its inhibitory effects can be overcome by use of oxytocin infusion, but because the combination may diminish uterine blood flow, prehydration and continuous electronic fetal heart monitoring are necessary. Early labor is less inhibited by barbiturates such as secobarbital. Nevertheless they are not recommended because prolonged neonatal depression may occur, including somnolence, hypoventilation, and hypotonia in addition to diminished attention span for up to two to four days. Sedative hypnotic drugs, such as scopolamine, may be amnesic, but they are not analgesic in labor and may actually induce such unpleasant side effects as paradoxical excitement and disorientation in the presence of pain. Patients who become hyperkinetic and uncontrollable may injure themselves or attendant personnel; they become difficult nursing management problems as a consequence.

C. Narcotic analgesia is being used less frequently these days as more women insist on reduced use of these drugs in the interest of remaining alert to participate actively in the birthing process and also to avoid potentially adverse neonatal affects. Despite this trend, narcotic drugs are given more often for analgesia than any other measures. They are best used in combination with ataractic tranquilizers; the synergism effectively reduces the analgesic dosage needed. Narcotic analgesics are administered during the active phase of labor, titrated to reduce rather than to eliminate pain. Dosages should be minimized to avert respiratory depression, peripheral vasodilatation (which will cause postural hypotension), and diminished gastric motility (enhancing the risk of aspiration). They may result in neonatal respiratory depression if given within two to three hours before the delivery. Therefore, avoid these drugs if labor is progressing quickly and delivery is likely to take place in the next several hours. The type and route are chosen according to the onset and duration of action desired for the specific patient.

References

Fishburne JI. Systemic analgesia during labor. Clin Perinatol 9:29, 1982.

Jouppila P, Jouppila R, Hollmén A, Koivula A. Lumbar epidural analgesia to improve intervillous blood flow during labor in severe preeclampsia. Obstet Gynecol 59:158, 1982.

Scanlon JW. Effects of obstetric anesthesia and analgesia on the newborn: A select annotated bibliography for the clinician. Clin Obstet Gynecol 24:649, 1981.

Shnider SM. Choice of anesthesia for labor and delivery. Obstet Gynecol 58:245S, 1981.

Shnider SM, Abboud TK, Artal R, et al. Maternal catecholamines decrease during labor after lumbar epidural anesthesia. Am J Obstet Gynecol 147:13, 1983.

GRAVIDA IN LABOR

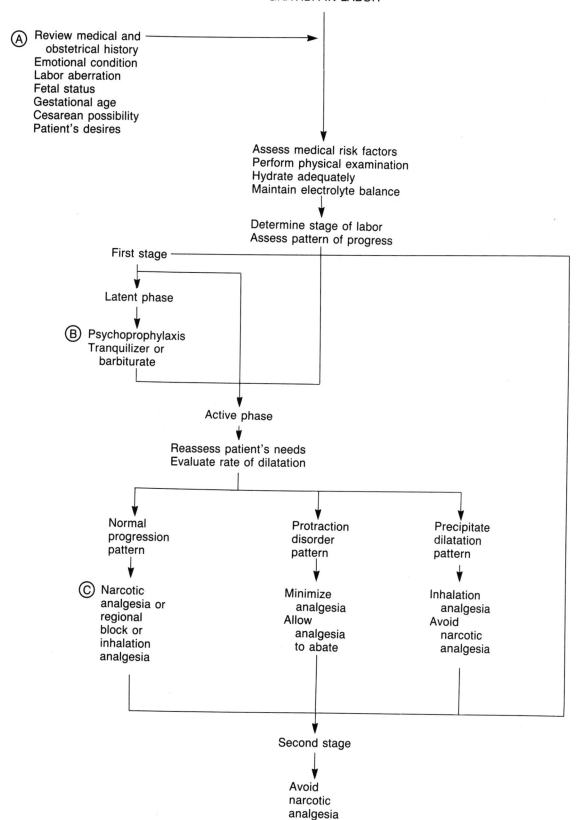

Ⓐ Review medical and
    obstetrical history
Emotional condition
Labor aberration
Fetal status
Gestational age
Cesarean possibility
Patient's desires

Assess medical risk factors
Perform physical examination
Hydrate adequately
Maintain electrolyte balance

Determine stage of labor
Assess pattern of progress

First stage

Latent phase

Ⓑ Psychoprophylaxis
Tranquilizer or
   barbiturate

Active phase

Reassess patient's needs
Evaluate rate of dilatation

Normal
progression
pattern

Protraction
disorder
pattern

Precipitate
dilatation
pattern

Ⓒ Narcotic
analgesia or
regional
block or
inhalation
analgesia

Minimize
analgesia
Allow
  analgesia
  to abate

Inhalation
analgesia
Avoid
  narcotic
  analgesia

Second stage

Avoid
narcotic
analgesia

DELIVERY ANESTHESIA

Nancy E. Oriol, M.D.

A. The skills, experience, and capabilities of the available anesthesia personnel, the mother's general state of health, any complications that may arise in the course of labor and delivery, and her desire to be awake or asleep for the delivery are the principal factors upon which the choice of anesthesia is based. A preanesthetic history and physical examination are essential. Determine when the patient ate last.

B. Anesthesia requirements are different for vaginal and cesarean delivery in regard to type, depth or level, and duration. Consideration has to be given to any time constraints that may exist or develop without forewarning. Emergency situations demand rapid induction. A full stomach may interdict inhalation anesthesia without special measures to avoid aspiration (see F).

C. For the patient who desires to remain awake at delivery, it is important to provide counseling. Prior psychoprophylactic preparation (p 22) is helpful in this regard. Care must be taken to avoid toxic dosages of the drugs used for local or pudendal block anesthesia. Paracervical block anesthesia has been reported to be associated with fetal complications (sometimes serious), especially if the fetal condition is marginal beforehand; if used at all, electronic fetal heart rate monitoring should be instituted first to ensure fetal well-being and then continued throughout.

D. Analgesic drugs used in labor can be supplemented, if needed, by such drugs as ketamine, nitrous oxide, or methoxyflurane (Penthrane), all in small amounts. Knowledge about the physiologic pulmonary function changes occurring in pregnancy is critical for the use of inhalation analgesia. It must be given very cautiously, because functional residual lung capacity is decreased and alveolar ventilation is increased in pregnancy, while the minimum alveolar concentrations of the drugs given are diminished. Anesthesia (rather than the desired analgesia) may be induced, risking aspiration (p 266).

E. Forceps procedures usually require more than local infiltration or pudendal block for adequate pain relief. Uterine relaxation, if needed for manipulation, cannot be accomplished with regional block anesthesia alone; it requires third plane general anesthesia. The deeper the anesthesia, the greater the maternal risks. Halogenated drugs in high concentrations readily relax the uterus, but the resulting uterine atony is resistant to uterotonic drugs post partum, sometimes causing hemorrhage that is difficult to control.

F. Since emergencies requiring cesarean section may arise at any time, every obstetrical unit must have the capability to carry out the procedure in no more than 30 minutes from the time the decision is made to proceed. Suitably trained and competent personnel, equipment, an operating theater, laboratory, and blood bank are critical. General anesthesia is preferable for emergencies unless a regional block has already been started and is functional. One should assume that the patient's stomach is full. Premedicate with a nonparticulate antacid solution and metoclopramide (p 266). Prevent gastric acid aspiration by endotracheal intubation using a tube with an occlusive tracheal cuff. Apply cricoid pressure first to occlude the esophagus and then induce anesthesia rapidly by the intravenous administration of thiopental, maintaining anesthesia with nitrous oxide (50 percent mixture with oxygen) and a muscle relaxant.

G. Use of peridural anesthesia requires both technical skill and experience as well as close continuing attention to the patient to detect hypotension and drug reactions promptly. It offers the advantage of decreased morbidity and faster recovery. Pudendal block, local infiltration, or saddle block is effective for most vaginal deliveries, but a fuller block (such as spinal or peridural anesthesia to T4) is required for cesarean section. Prehydrating with 1000 to 1500 ml of lactated Ringer's solution and giving a vasopressor prophylactically are effective means for averting hypotension from vasodilatation. Hypotension from regional block may compound hypovolemia from blood loss and make treatment more difficult. If acute hemorrhage may occur, it is preferable to choose general anesthesia.

References

Crawford JS. Anaesthesia for obstetric emergencies. Br J Anaesth 45:844, 1973.

Morgan BM, Barker JP, Goroszeniuk T, et al. Anaesthetic morbidity following caesarean section under epidural or general anaesthesia. Lancet 1:328, 1984.

Scott DB, Sinclair CJ. Advances in regional anaesthesia and analgesia. Clin Obstet Gynaecol 9:273, 1982.

ANESTHESIA FOR DELIVERY*

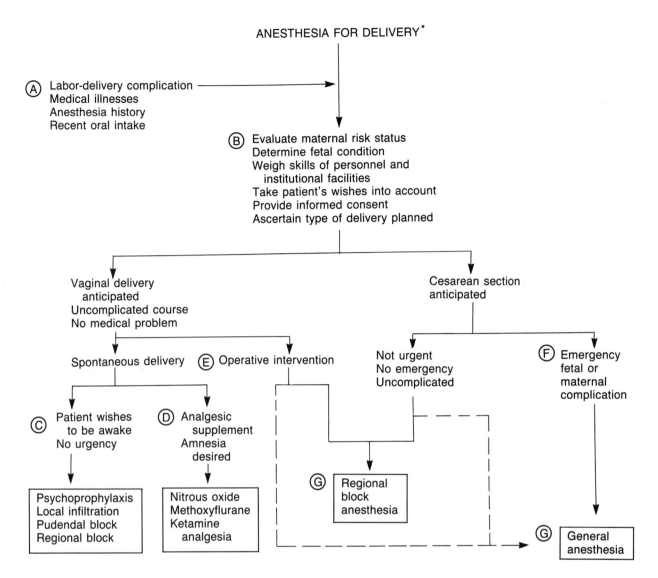

A Labor-delivery complication
   Medical illnesses
   Anesthesia history
   Recent oral intake

B Evaluate maternal risk status
   Determine fetal condition
   Weigh skills of personnel and
     institutional facilities
   Take patient's wishes into account
   Provide informed consent
   Ascertain type of delivery planned

Vaginal delivery
anticipated
Uncomplicated course
No medical problem

Cesarean section
anticipated

Spontaneous delivery   E Operative intervention

Not urgent
No emergency
Uncomplicated

F Emergency
   fetal or
   maternal
   complication

C Patient wishes
   to be awake
   No urgency

D Analgesic
   supplement
   Amnesia
   desired

Psychoprophylaxis
Local infiltration
Pudendal block
Regional block

Nitrous oxide
Methoxyflurane
Ketamine
analgesia

G Regional
   block
   anesthesia

G General
   anesthesia

* Broken line indicates a less preferable option

MATERNAL POSITION IN LABOR

Jerold M. Carlson, M.D., M.P.H.

A. Controversy exists as to the relationship between maternal position in labor and labor duration, subjective discomfort, and fetal outcome. Custom and practice habits often dictate that a limited number of positions (or even a single one) should be recommended by attendant personnel for all parturients throughout labor and delivery. It is clear that labor is a complex and dynamic process, and it is probably inappropriate for the maternal position to be arbitrarily fixed in labor. There is no substantive basis for any such recommendation in most cases if all is going well. Certain specific conditions, however, do appear to warrant special positioning (see C).

B. Gravidas in labor tend to change position frequently if left on their own; the left lateral recumbent position is assumed most often, but far from exclusively. In the absence of any contraindications, ambulation is generally encouraged in early labor. In active labor, parturients generally prefer to be in bed, moving from position to position, seeking comfort. They should be allowed to assume any posture in which they feel most comfortable. The same applies in the second stage (p 244), although an upright position, such as sitting or squatting, might be considered because of its capacity to enhance bearing-down expulsive efforts and fetal descent. Only the supine position should be avoided, because the pressure of the large gravid uterus on the inferior vena cava reduces venous return and cardiac output, causing the blood pressure to fall (supine hypotension syndrome) and uterine blood flow to diminish proportionally, with resulting fetal hypoxia. This admonition is even more important in the presence of multiple pregnancy, hydramnios, and fetal macrosomia, which tend to enhance caval (and aortic) compression. Moreover, if epidural anesthesia is in effect, reduced intraluminal resistance increases the gravida's susceptibility to supine hypotension.

C. A number of clinical situations call for modification or limitation of the position in which the gravida may labor. High risk patients may have to be confined to bed to provide the necessary continuous electronic fetal heart rate monitoring. Telemetric techniques are also available, permitting ambulation if suitable. Bed rest nevertheless may be required for these affected women by virtue of the prevailing risk status. The left lateral recumbent position, for example, is essential for gravidas with pregnancy induced hypertension (p 86) to help improve both uterine and renal blood flow. The same is true in cases of fetal distress (p 200) resulting from placental insufficiency. Cord compression fetal heart rate patterns (p 196) necessitate turning the patient from side to side in an effort to correct the problem by dislodging the loop of cord. Cord prolapse, whether occult or overt, may benefit from placing the patient in the knee-chest (kneeling with the pelvis elevated and the chest down) or deep Trendelenburg position because it may relieve pressure on the cord by the presenting part. Remember to move the uterus off the inferior vena cava by laterally applied pressure whenever the Trendelenburg position is being used. Maternal shock from any cause (p 268) can also be helped transiently by a head-down position, although counterbalancing elevation of the diaphragm by the liver and large uterus may interfere with ventilation. The head-up Fowler position, by contrast, is recommended for patients with acute pyelonephritis. When technical considerations mandate the supine position, as for cesarean section, for example, inserting a wedge bolster under one flank ensures sufficient left lateral tilt to move the uterus off the inferior vena cava (p 188). Prophylaxis against aspiration (p 266) requires the lateral position during recovery from general anesthesia.

References

Carlson JM, Diehl JA, Sachleben-Murray M, et al. Maternal position during parturition in normal labor. Obstet Gynecol 68:443, 1986.

Friedman EA. Labor: Clinical Evaluation and Management. 2nd ed. New York: Appleton-Century-Crofts, 1978.

Hemminki E, Saarikoski S. Ambulation and delayed amniotomy in the first stage of labour. Eur J Obstet Gynaecol 15:129, 1983.

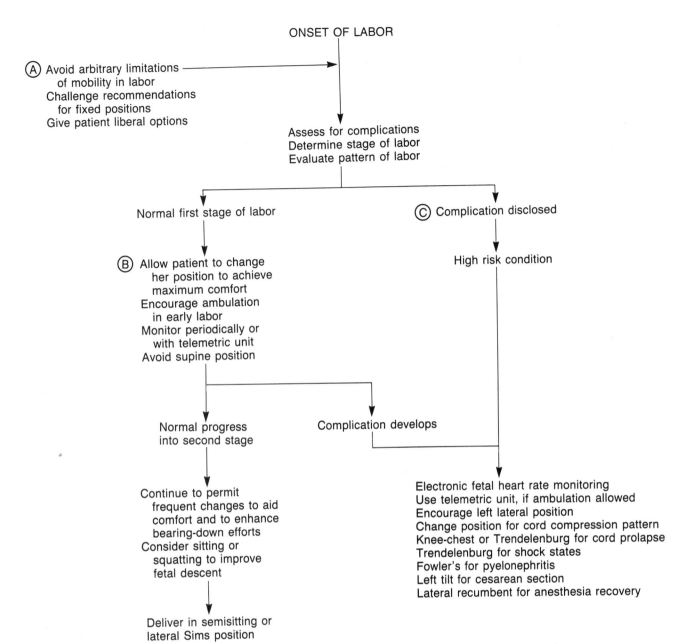

ONSET OF LABOR

Ⓐ Avoid arbitrary limitations
    of mobility in labor
  Challenge recommendations
    for fixed positions
  Give patient liberal options

Assess for complications
Determine stage of labor
Evaluate pattern of labor

Normal first stage of labor

Ⓒ Complication disclosed

High risk condition

Ⓑ Allow patient to change
    her position to achieve
    maximum comfort
  Encourage ambulation
    in early labor
  Monitor periodically or
    with telemetric unit
  Avoid supine position

Normal progress
into second stage

Complication develops

Continue to permit
  frequent changes to aid
  comfort and to enhance
  bearing-down efforts
Consider sitting or
  squatting to improve
  fetal descent

Electronic fetal heart rate monitoring
Use telemetric unit, if ambulation allowed
Encourage left lateral position
Change position for cord compression pattern
Knee-chest or Trendelenburg for cord prolapse
Trendelenburg for shock states
Fowler's for pyelonephritis
Left tilt for cesarean section
Lateral recumbent for anesthesia recovery

Deliver in semisitting or
lateral Sims position

FETAL MONITORING IN LABOR

Henry Klapholz, M.D.

A. Auscultation by stethoscope, fetoscope, or Doptone monitor is generally inadequate for detecting any but the most obvious decelerations of the fetal heart rate. These tend to be the innocuous variety of variable decelerations (p 196). The more ominous late decelerations (p 198) are less often detected and subtle, but important loss of beat-to-beat variability cannot be identified at all by auscultation. Such detection requires continuous electronic fetal heart rate monitoring, which should be available in all well conducted obstetrical units today and used regularly in all high risk cases. The absence of periodic fetal heart rate changes (that is, decelerations from the baseline) and the presence of good reactivity (fetal heart rate accelerations in association with fetal movement) are sufficient to assure fetal well-being. External electronic monitors that utilize ultrasound transducers display artifactually increased variability owing to the frequent changes that occur in the timing of the reflected fetal signals from the heart valves. Nonetheless the absence of variability on an external electronic fetal heart rate tracing does indicate the likelihood that there is really no variability of the fetal heart rate. Abdominal wall electrocardiography displays variability more accurately, but it is useful (that is, it gives a usable signal) in only about half the cases. Maternal obesity and gestational prematurity tend to reduce the effectiveness of this technique still further.

B. Grossly irregular rates and persistent bradycardia or tachycardia may be secondary to fetal arrhythmia (p 72). Such cases warrant examination of the fetal electrocardiogram obtained directly from the fetal scalp eletrode.

C. Beat-to-beat variability is an accurate indicator of cerebral function since it reflects the fetal arousal state. It is reduced by the maternal administration of narcotics and sedatives as well as by vagal blocking drugs and magnesium sulfate. It is often diminished (that is, not yet functionally developed) in premature fetuses. Major morphologic alterations in brain structure result in altered variability patterns. Although one must be alert to its possible significance, it is important not to assume that all cases of reduced variability are secondary to hypoxia and intervene without verification by clinical investigation. A careful ultrasonographic examination of every fetus exhibiting chronically diminished or no short term variability is in order.

D. Internal monitoring of the fetal heart rate by means of a fetal scalp electrode usually provides the most reliable electrocardiographic signal for electronic processing into useful meaningful information about fetal well-being. Continuous beat-to-beat rates are recorded and displayed, thus depicting short term fetal heart rate variability accurately. The internal monitoring technique is relatively free of complications, except for rare scalp infections (sometimes leading to systemic infection in the newborn, however). To apply the electrode, the cervix must be at least 1 to 2 cm dilated, the fetal head no higher than − 1 station, and the membranes ruptured. Variability is difficult to quantitate, but a variation of four to 10 beats per minute from the baseline is acceptable. Change from external to internal monitoring mode, if possible, whenever the external electronic fetal heart rate tracing shows evidence of an abnormal fetal heart rate pattern or when conditions strongly indicate the need (e.g., meconium staining of amniotic fluid).

E. If periodic decelerations from the baseline are encountered, they should be examined to determine their temporal relation to uterine contractions (monitored simultaneously by either an external tokodynamometer or an internal catheter attached to a strain gauge). Late decelerations (p 198) are characteristically symmetrical, beginning at least 20 seconds after the onset of a contraction, reaching their nadir after the peak of the uterine contraction, and continuing somewhat beyond the time the contraction has subsided; the intensity of the deceleration is proportional to the amplitude of the contraction. Late decelerations, which are diagnostic of placental insufficiency, are characteristically repetitive. Variable decelerations (p 196), by contrast, rise and fall rapidly; they have a variable shape, variable onset, and variable ending in relation to uterine contractions; they may even occur between contractions. Variable decelerations signify compression of the umbilical cord.

References

Brioschi PA, Extermann P, Terracina D, et al. Antepartum non-stress fetal heart rate monitoring: Systematic analysis of baseline patterns and decelerations as an adjunct to reactivity in the prediction of fetal risks. Am J Obstet Gynecol 153:633, 1985.

Clark SL, Paul RH. Intrapartum fetal surveillance: The role of fetal scalp blood sampling. Am J Obstet Gynecol 153:717, 1985.

Helfand M, Marton K, Ueland K. Factors involved in the interpretation of fetal monitor tracings. Am J Obstet Gynecol 151:737, 1985.

Krebs HB, Petres RE, Dunn LJ, Smith PJ. Intrapartum fetal heart rate monitoring. VI. Prognostic significance of accelerations. Am J Obstet Gynecol 142:297, 1982.

CONSIDERATION OF FETAL HEART RATE MONITORING

Weigh indications:
  High risk status
  Abnormality auscultated
  Meconium stained fluid
  Medical complication
  Post-term pregnancy
Educate, inform, reassure

(A) External electronic
monitoring of fetal heart rate

(A) Normal rate
  and rhythm
Fetus reactive

Continue external
monitoring of fetal
heart rate as long as pattern
remains normal

Nonreactive pattern
Decelerations seen
Tachycardia found
Technically inadequate
tracing produced

(C) Chronically poor
variability
encountered

(B) Irregular
pattern
encountered

Evaluate for
arrhythmia (p 72)

Assess fetal well-being
by ultrasonography (p 70)

(D) Internal electronic
monitoring of fetal heart rate

Normal
pattern

Periodic fetal heart rate
decelerations

(E) Determine temporal
relation of decelerations
to uterine contractions

Early decelerations
Good variability
Normal fetal heart rate

Late decelerations
Variable decelerations
Loss of variability
Tachycardia
Bradycardia

Continue internal fetal heart rate
monitoring as long as pattern
remains normal

Evaluate for fetal
distress (pp 194–200)
Intervene as indicated

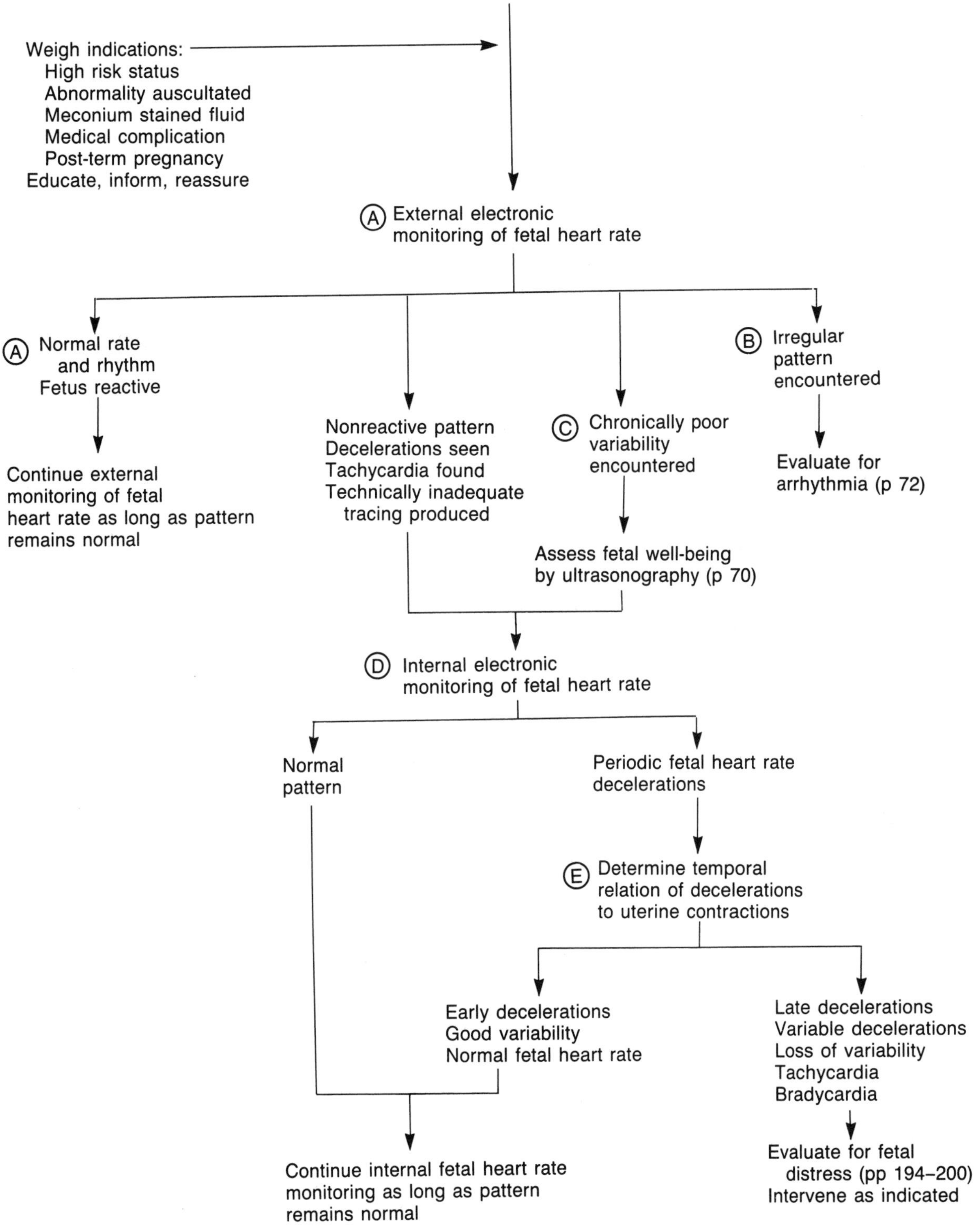

THE NURSE'S ROLE IN MONITORING LABOR

Jeanette Blank, R.N.

A. Important in the care rendered by the intrapartum nurse is continuous electronic monitoring of the fetal heart rate as a tool for fetal assessment during labor. As the professional who assumes responsibility for making meaningful observations, collecting clinical data, and compiling that information into a utilitarian plan for individual care, the nurse must gain expertise in using monitoring equipment, producing interpretable tracings, recognizing suspicious, threatening, or ominous fetal heart rate patterns, and taking appropriate action when indicated. Formal training programs are necessary to ensure adequate knowledge and technical competence for all nurses responsible for this important activity. Periodic testing of the level of skill achieved during and after training is equally important to verify that each nurse can function independently, even when supervision may be close at hand.

B. Each institution should have a written nursing protocol for electronic fetal heart rate monitoring outlining practices, interpretations, and interventions consistent with the obstetrical policies of that institution. The nurse also should be skilled in inserting an intravenous line unless physician availability can always be assured. Frequent auscultation of the fetal heart tones is carried out over the course of labor (p 168) as an integral part of routine intrapartum care. High risk patients deserve the benefits of continuous electronic fetal heart rate monitoring; this applies to gravidas with medical or obstetrical problems placing the fetus at risk of an adverse outcome. Use all information from prenatal records and intrapartum observations to determine the presence of such risk factors. If they are present, apply the external monitor. Similarly, if slowing of the rate is heard by fetoscope or Doptone, switch to the external monitor. If the pattern looks suspicious or worse, seek internal monitoring by means of a scalp electrode. A change in the fetal heart rate baseline, a decrease in variability, or the presence of decelerations must be reported to the physician. The nurse must be able to recognize when a tracing is unreadable and know what measures must be taken to correct it.

C. When an abnormal fetal heart rate pattern is identified, the nurse must initiate treatment and notify the physician at once. Placing the gravida in the left lateral position, giving oxygen by mask, increasing blood volume and uterine blood flow by means of rapid intravenous infusion, and decreasing uterine contractility by discontinuing oxytocin may be beneficial. Changing the maternal position from side to side or placing her in a knee-chest position may alleviate cord entrapment. Educating the gravida and her partner to the needs and benefits of such intrauterine resuscitative measures helps ensure her cooperation. At this time also review with them other interventions that may become necessary, such as direct electrocardiographic monitoring for arrhythmia or fetal scalp sampling for pH, to help minimize anxiety and concern.

D. Continuous reassessment of the fetal heart rate pattern indicates whether resuscitative measures have been successful in correcting the problem. If the pattern is corrected, no further interventions other than continuous electronic monitoring are necessary. If the abnormal pattern persists or returns with increased uterine contractility, further intervention is necessary. Anticipating and preparing for fetal scalp blood sampling are important aspects of the role of the intrapartum nurse. If the fetal heart rate pattern deteriorates or fetal acidosis is documented by fetal scalp blood sampling (serially performed, if necessary), the nurse must prepare for prompt delivery. She must continually be aware of her responsibility to function as a health care professional, interpreting clinical information, anticipating events and needs, and implementing appropriate action as indicated.

References

Blank J. Electronic fetal monitoring: Nursing management defined. J Obstet Gynecol Neonatal Nurs 14:463, 1985.

The Nurse's Role in Electronic Fetal Monitoring. Technical Bulletin No. 7. Washington: Nurses Association of the American College of Obstetricians and Gynecologists, 1980.

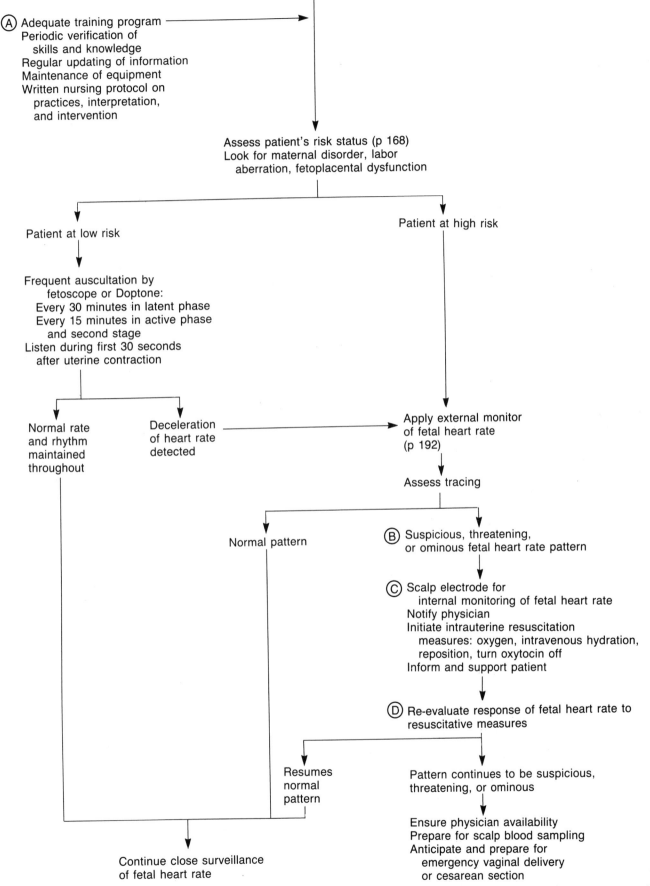

GRAVIDA ADMITTED IN LABOR

Ⓐ Adequate training program
Periodic verification of
  skills and knowledge
Regular updating of information
Maintenance of equipment
Written nursing protocol on
  practices, interpretation,
  and intervention

Assess patient's risk status (p 168)
Look for maternal disorder, labor
  aberration, fetoplacental dysfunction

Patient at low risk

Patient at high risk

Frequent auscultation by
  fetoscope or Doptone:
  Every 30 minutes in latent phase
  Every 15 minutes in active phase
    and second stage
  Listen during first 30 seconds
    after uterine contraction

Normal rate
and rhythm
maintained
throughout

Deceleration
of heart rate
detected

Apply external monitor
of fetal heart rate
(p 192)

Assess tracing

Normal pattern

Ⓑ Suspicious, threatening,
  or ominous fetal heart rate pattern

Ⓒ Scalp electrode for
  internal monitoring of fetal heart rate
Notify physician
Initiate intrauterine resuscitation
  measures: oxygen, intravenous hydration,
  reposition, turn oxytocin off
Inform and support patient

Ⓓ Re-evaluate response of fetal heart rate to
  resuscitative measures

Resumes
normal
pattern

Pattern continues to be suspicious,
threatening, or ominous

Ensure physician availability
Prepare for scalp blood sampling
Anticipate and prepare for
  emergency vaginal delivery
  or cesarean section

Continue close surveillance
of fetal heart rate

VARIABLE DECELERATIONS

Henry Klapholz, M.D.

A. The fetal heart rate pattern of variable deceleration (Fig. 1) is seen quite commonly in the course of electronically monitored labors. The decelerations are usually innocuous and require no intervention. This does not mean that they should be entirely ignored. Certain characteristics help identify cases demanding investigation possibly leading to intervention (see B). The wave form of variable decelerations characteristically falls rapidly and also rises rapidly back to the original baseline rate. Such decelerations are due to an electromechanical insult, namely, occlusion of the umbilical cord with resultant fetal hypertension and bradycardia. They are variable in onset insofar as their temporal relation to uterine contractions is concerned, although they often appear concurrently with contractions. This would not be unexpected, especially after the membranes have ruptured or in second stage labor, when a contraction is most likely to cause compression of a segment of the cord between the fetus and an adjacent part of the uterine wall. The depth of a variable deceleration may be proportional to the amplitude of a contraction, but this is not always the case. Although atropine abolishes variable decelerations, it merely obscures the warning signal and has no beneficial effect on the problem of the cord occlusion. Persistent deep variable decelerations suggest umbilical cord prolapse.

B. Variable decelerations that do not recover promptly to the fetal heart rate baseline, but rather exhibit a slow return, signify that the fetus was asphyxiated during the antecedent bradycardia. A progressive rise in the baseline rate with developing tachycardia over a series of variable decelerations also reflects fetal hypoxia. Absence of variability during the recovery between decelerations is particularly ominous. Internal electronic fetal heart rate monitoring by use of a scalp electrode is essential for adequate evaluation.

C. The most important treatment modality is left lateral positioning of the mother. Mechanical factors may be alleviated in this way by dislodging the cord from the site at which it is compressed. It is a common practice (often proving effective) to turn the patient first to one lateral position and then to the other and perhaps back again, monitoring all the while to determine whether the series of maneuvers has corrected the problem. The patient is examined vaginally to rule out a cord prolapse. Oxygen given by face mask may be of some benefit as well. Fluids should be administered rapidly by intravenous infusion to enhance blood volume and uterine blood flow, thereby increasing fetal oxygenation between contractions. Elevation of the fetal vertex by applying firm cephalad pressure digitally to the fetal head during the vaginal examination and placing the gravida into the knee-chest position may be of value if other measures fail. Amnioinfusion of saline to expand the intra-amniotic space and, as a consequence, relieve the cord compression has been reported to alleviate these decelerations when delivery was not yet possible.

D. If the variable decelerations disappear in response to the measures taken to effect correction, expectancy and observation are in order. Close surveillance is essential over the remaining course of the labor to detect recurrence and reinstitute corrective programs in the event that the problem recurs. Partial recovery or a continuing adverse pattern requires one to proceed with fetal scalp blood pH analysis to confirm hypoxia by the objective demonstration of secondary fetal acidosis.

E. A pH less than 7.25 verifies fetal hypoxia and therefore calls for delivery. If the pH is greater than 7.25, the determination should be repeated in 15 minutes unless the pattern improves. Proceed with delivery by whatever means is appropriate and expedient in the presence of confirmatory acidosis or a persistent pattern of adverse variable decelerations. This means vaginal delivery, if possible in an expeditious and atraumatic manner, or cesarean section, if not.

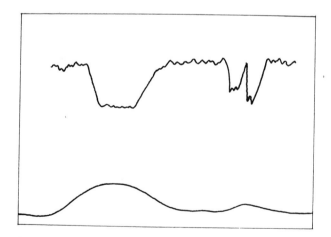

Figure 1 Variable decelerations, Rapid decline in fetal heart rate (upper tracing) to a relatively flat trough, and rapid return to baseline without consistent temporal relation to contractions (lower tracing).

References

Dashow EE, Read JA. Significant fetal bradycardia during antepartum heart rate testing. Am J Obstet Gynecol 148:187, 1984.

Gilstrap LC, Hauth JC, Toussaint S. Second stage fetal heart rate abnormalities and neonatal acidosis. Obstet Gynecol 63:209, 1984.

Hutson JM, Mueller-Heubach E. Diagnosis and management of intrapartum reflex fetal heart rate changes. Clin Perinatol 9:325, 1982.

Martin CB. Physiology and clinical use of fetal heart rate variability. Clin Perinatol 9:339, 1982.

Welt SI. The fetal heart rate W-sign. Obstet Gynecol 63:405, 1984.

APPEARANCE OF VARIABLE DECELERATIONS

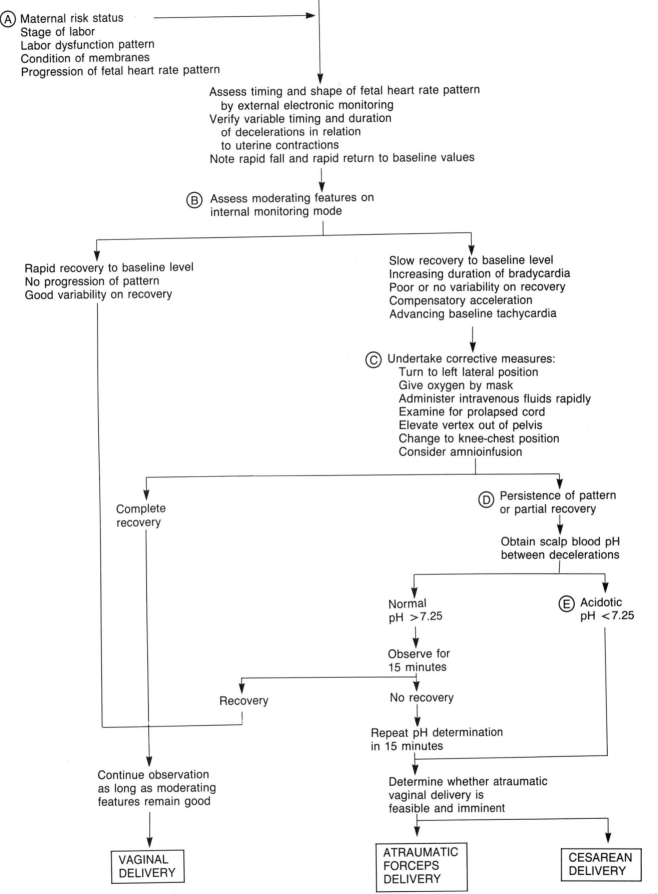

(A) Maternal risk status
Stage of labor
Labor dysfunction pattern
Condition of membranes
Progression of fetal heart rate pattern

Assess timing and shape of fetal heart rate pattern
by external electronic monitoring
Verify variable timing and duration
of decelerations in relation
to uterine contractions
Note rapid fall and rapid return to baseline values

(B) Assess moderating features on
internal monitoring mode

Rapid recovery to baseline level
No progression of pattern
Good variability on recovery

Slow recovery to baseline level
Increasing duration of bradycardia
Poor or no variability on recovery
Compensatory acceleration
Advancing baseline tachycardia

(C) Undertake corrective measures:
Turn to left lateral position
Give oxygen by mask
Administer intravenous fluids rapidly
Examine for prolapsed cord
Elevate vertex out of pelvis
Change to knee-chest position
Consider amnioinfusion

Complete
recovery

(D) Persistence of pattern
or partial recovery

Obtain scalp blood pH
between decelerations

Normal
pH >7.25

(E) Acidotic
pH <7.25

Observe for
15 minutes

Recovery

No recovery

Repeat pH determination
in 15 minutes

Continue observation
as long as moderating
features remain good

Determine whether atraumatic
vaginal delivery is
feasible and imminent

VAGINAL
DELIVERY

ATRAUMATIC
FORCEPS
DELIVERY

CESAREAN
DELIVERY

197

LATE DECELERATIONS

Henry Klapholz, M.D.

A. Routine auscultation of the fetal heart rate in the course of labor may detect late decelerations (Fig. 1) if attention is given to the rate at the end of the uterine contraction and for the ensuing 20 to 30 seconds. When alerted in this way or by external electronic fetal heart rate monitoring, apply a scalp electrode. Measures should be taken for rapid evaluation and attempts at correction as well as intervention if necessary. Late decelerations are considered diagnostic of placental insufficiency. Associated fetal hypoxia may result from decreased uterine blood flow, increased resistance to perfusion, diminished placental exchange surface (by separation or infarction), maternal hypoxia, and uterine hypercontractility or hypertonus. The last named factors cause fetal hypoxia by mechanically constricting the uterine vessels. To help interpretation of the electronic fetal heart rate tracing, it is important to recognize that true late decelerations do not occur as isolated entities. A single deceleration is probably innocuous. To be clinically meaningful, late decelerations are usually repetitive, recurring with each contraction. Their depth below the fetal heart rate baseline and their duration are generally proportional to the strength of the contraction, reflecting the aforementioned effect of the contraction on the uterine blood flow.

B. Late decelerations should always be considered clinically important. They cannot be ignored. However, if the baseline beat-to-beat variability is good, it is less likely that any associated fetal hypoxia is significant. Watch for progressive changes in the pattern. Increasing depth or duration signifies progressive hypoxia or acidosis, usually accompanied by progressively diminished variability. If this sequence is seen, aggressive measures are mandated.

C. Late decelerations can develop after the administration of peridural anesthesia. They arise especially if the gravida has not been prehydrated. The disorder results from the reduced uterine blood flow associated with splanch-

nic vasodilation and decreased cardiac output caused by the anesthesia. Injudicious administration of oxytocin (or another uterotonic drug) often results in late decelerations by producing hypercontractility. However, even normal contractions may be capable of invoking late decelerations if fetal oxygen reserves are marginal because of a pre-existing or concurrent problem. Uterine hypertonus secondary to abruptio placentae also can cause late decelerations.

D. Late decelerations are treated by repositioning the mother to the left lateral position so as to increase venous return and thereby improve cardiac output and uterine blood flow in turn. The intravenous administration of fluids, especially normal saline or lactated Ringer's solution, helps increase cardiac output as well if administration is rapid. Oxygen is of minimal value but should nonetheless be given by mask. Conduction anesthesia should not be renewed; it can be allowed to abate if its adverse fetal effects persist. Oxytocin is contraindicated and must be discontinued at once if it is being given. Uterine relaxants (tocolytic drugs, p 180) have been employed to reduce uterine tone and stop contractions if the late decelerations cannot be corrected and prompt delivery is not feasible.

E. If the late decelerations subside in the course of corrective therapy, no further action is required other than continued intensive observation of the fetal status for the remainder of the labor. Partial, negligible, or no improvement calls for fetal scalp blood sampling to verify that the fetus is truly hypoxic by demonstrating acidosis. This is done because there is a high frequency of false positive cases.

F. A pH greater than 7.25 indicates that the fetus is probably not hypoxic. A pH less than 7.25 mandates delivery. Quickly assess whether it is feasible to undertake vaginal delivery without subjecting the mother and fetus to serious risks. Delivery under these circumstances is usually accomplished by cesarean section. If delay is elected and late decelerations persist, repeat scalp blood samplings for pH determination at 15 minute intervals, intervening if the pH shows developing acidosis.

References

Baxi LV. Current status of fetal oxygen monitoring. Clin Perinatol 9:423, 1982.

Gimovsky ML, Caritis SN. Diagnosis and management of hypoxic fetal heart rate patterns. Clin Perinatol 9:313, 1982.

Martin CB. Physiology and clinical use of fetal heart rate variability. Clin Perinatol 9:339, 1982.

Schellpfeffer MA, Hoyle D, Johnson JW. Antepartal uterine hypercontractility secondary to nipple stimulation. Obstet Gynecol 65:588, 1985.

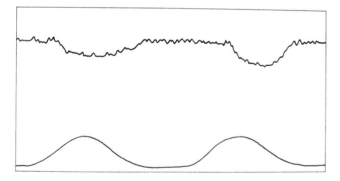

Figure 1 Late decelerations. Repetitive pattern of slowly falling and slowly recovering fetal heart rate (upper tracing) consistently following the onset of the contraction (lower tracing); nadir and duration of deceleration are generally proportional to intensity of contraction.

OCCURRENCE OF LATE DECELERATIONS

High risk maternal condition
Meconium stained fluid
Post-term pregnancy
Labor dysfunction
Progression of fetal heart rate pattern

(A) Verify timing and shape of fetal heart rate pattern
by external electronic monitoring:
Late onset, nadir, and end relative
to uterine contractile pattern
Slow fall and slow return to baseline level
Recurrently repetitive with contractions
Depth proportional to contraction strength

(B) Assess moderating features by
internal monitoring mode

Good baseline variability
between decelerations
No progression of pattern

Progressively deeper decelerations
Progressively longer duration
Progressive loss of variability

(C) Attempt to determine etiology:
Fetal hypoxia
Peridural anesthesia
Oxytocin hyperstimulation
Abruptio placentae
Placental insufficiency

(D) Undertake corrective measures:
Turn to left lateral position
Give oxygen by mask
Administer intravenous fluids rapidly
Turn off oxytocin infusion
Withhold anesthesia or allow to abate
Consider tocolytic drugs

Complete recovery

(E) Persistence of pattern
or partial recovery

Obtain scalp blood pH
between decelerations

Normal
pH >7.25

(F) Acidotic
pH <7.25

pH remains in
normal range

Repeat determination every
15 minutes

Determine whether atraumatic
vaginal delivery is
feasible and imminent

Continue observation
as long as moderating
features remain favorable

VAGINAL
DELIVERY

ATRAUMATIC
FORCEPS
DELIVERY

CESAREAN
SECTION

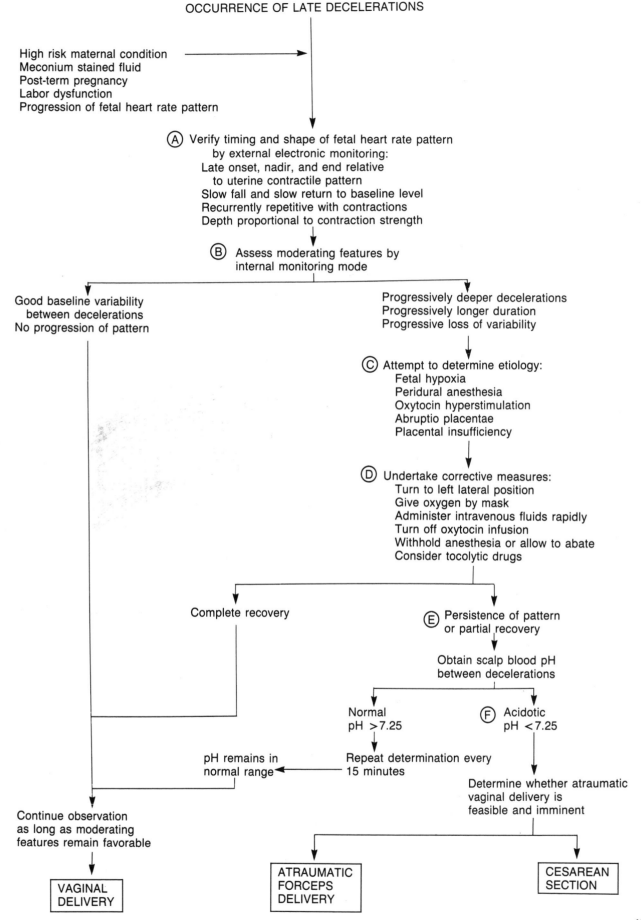

FETAL DISTRESS

Benjamin P. Sachs, M.B., B.S., D.P.H.

A. The basic objective of electronic fetal heart rate monitoring is to detect evidence of fetal compromise. It correlates changes in the fetal heart rate with fetal movement and uterine contractions. Although there has not always been a consensus about nomenclature, certain fetal heart rate patterns are widely recognized. Early decelerations are symmetric in shape and mirror the uterine contractions. They can be largely obliterated by the administration of atropine; this innocuous pattern probably results from increased vagal tone due to pressure on the fetal head. Late decelerations (p 198), which are also symmetric in shape but delayed temporally with regard to uterine contractions and typically repetitive, appear to be due to uteroplacental insufficiency. They are often associated with fetal hypoxia and a poor fetal outcome. The nadir of the late deceleration occurs after the peak of the contraction and returns slowly to the baseline. Variable decelerations (p 196), which result from umbilical cord compression, are variable in their relationship to uterine contractions and in their shape, with a rapid fall in the fetal heart rate and a rapid return to baseline. They are commonly encountered and are ordinarily innocuous. However, if cord occlusion persists for some time, the fetus may become hypoxic and, as a consequence, acidotic. Beat to beat variability in the fetal heart rate (reliably assessed by internal monitoring by way of a scalp electrode only) is a normal finding in the third trimester of pregnancy. In simplistic terms, it can be thought of as resulting from the push and pull of vagal and sympathetic cardiovascular reflexes. Loss of beat to beat variability can result from drugs, such as morphine and magnesium sulfate, or reflect the transient physiologic fetal sleep cycle. However, the absence of beat to beat variability may indicate fetal compromise in some circumstances. Fetal heart rate decelerations unaccompanied by beat to beat variability are likely to be associated with fetal hypoxia and acidosis.

B. In general, a normal fetal heart rate pattern constitutes sufficient reassurance that the baby is not hypoxic. However, an abnormal fetal heart rate tracing often requires further evaluation by fetal scalp blood pH measurement because of the high frequency of false positive deceleration patterns seen with electronic fetal heart rate monitoring.

C. In the event that an abnormal fetal heart rate pattern is encountered, intrauterine resuscitation should first be attempted by administering oxygen, placing the mother in the left lateral position, and giving rapid intravenous hydration. If oxytocin infusion is in place, it must be discontinued at once as well. All these actions are undertaken expeditiously while notifying responsible attendant personnel and mobilizing resources in anticipation of intervention for delivery; the need to proceed will become evident if the resuscitative measures do not satisfactorily correct the problem. Persistently ominous patterns indicate significant distress and warrant prompt delivery. The fluid used for hydration should not include dextrose, because it has been shown that large amounts of dextrose may aggravate the fetal condition by enhancing the accumulation of lactic acid.

D. If the fetal heart rate pattern is suspicious or threatening, clarify with a scalp blood pH determination (Fig. 1). A pH between 7.20 and 7.24 requires repeating within 15 to 20 minutes unless the fetal heart rate tracing deteriorates markedly in the interim; if it does, delivery is essential. If the repeat pH is falling, deliver promptly. If it is stable at these borderline levels, relocate the patient to a delivery room where either a cesarean section or a vaginal delivery can be carried out, as indicated, monitoring her closely for changing fetal status, with an anesthesiologist in attendance to expedite operative delivery if and when it becomes necessary. Measure the umbilical arterial pH after such a delivery because it reflects the fetal status better than that of the umbilical venous blood.

Figure 1 Amnioscope applied transvaginally to presenting fetal head (not at most dependent portion) to expose scalp for purposes of obtaining capillary blood sample for pH determination.

References

Curzen P, Bekir JS, McLintock DG, Patel M. Reliability of cardiotocography in predicting baby's condition at birth. Br Med J 289:1345, 1984.

Edelstone D, Peticca BP, Goldblum LJ. Effects of maternal oxygen administration on fetal oxygenation during reduction of umbilical blood flow in fetal lambs. Am J Obstet Gynecol 152:351, 1985.

MacDonald D, Grant A, Sheridan-Pereira M, et al. The Dublin randomized controlled test of intrapartum fetal heart rate monitoring. Am J Obstet Gynecol 152:524, 1985.

SUSPICION OF FETAL DISTRESS

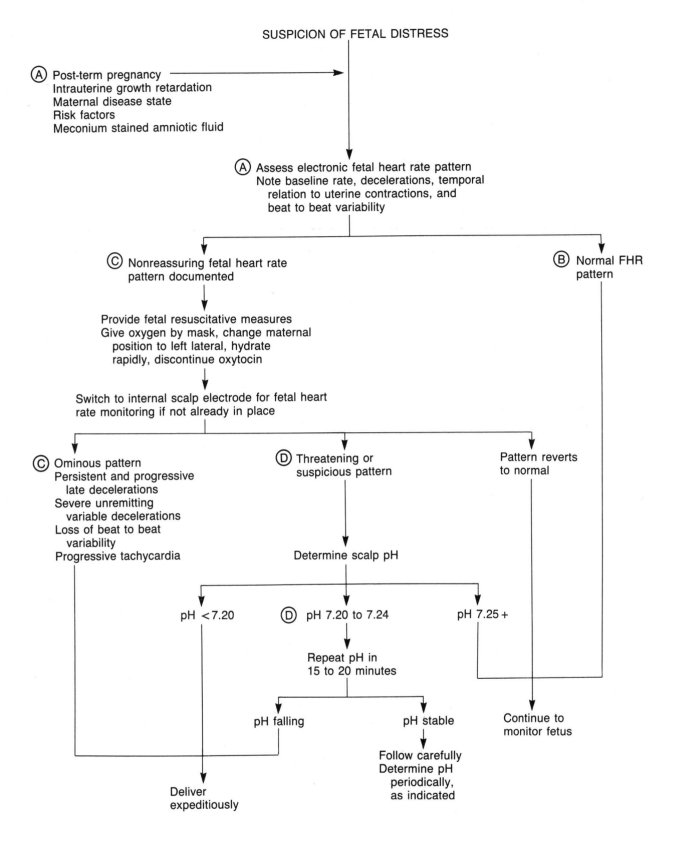

(A) Post-term pregnancy
    Intrauterine growth retardation
    Maternal disease state
    Risk factors
    Meconium stained amniotic fluid

(A) Assess electronic fetal heart rate pattern
    Note baseline rate, decelerations, temporal
        relation to uterine contractions, and
        beat to beat variability

(C) Nonreassuring fetal heart rate
    pattern documented

(B) Normal FHR
    pattern

Provide fetal resuscitative measures
Give oxygen by mask, change maternal
    position to left lateral, hydrate
    rapidly, discontinue oxytocin

Switch to internal scalp electrode for fetal heart
rate monitoring if not already in place

(C) Ominous pattern
    Persistent and progressive
        late decelerations
    Severe unremitting
        variable decelerations
    Loss of beat to beat
        variability
    Progressive tachycardia

(D) Threatening or
    suspicious pattern

Pattern reverts
to normal

Determine scalp pH

pH < 7.20   (D) pH 7.20 to 7.24   pH 7.25 +

Repeat pH in
15 to 20 minutes

pH falling   pH stable

                          Follow carefully
                          Determine pH
                              periodically,
                              as indicated

Continue to
monitor fetus

Deliver
expeditiously

MALPRESENTATION DIAGNOSIS

Louis Burke, M.D.

A. Fetal malpresentation is a common complication with a potentially serious prognosis for the fetus. Early diagnosis reduces the risk because it gives the obstetrician the opportunity to consider measures to correct the problem and, failing that, to intervene to avert harm to the mother and fetus. Examinations of the abdomen at each prenatal visit are essential for early detection. The wider availability of ultrasonography has made it less critical to be definitive in one's palpational skills, but it is still necessary to have sufficient skill to recognize an abnormal lie or deflexion of the fetal head. One should pay special attention to factors that place a gravida at increased risk of having a malpresentation, such as previous pelvic or abdominal surgery, uterine malformation, grand multiparity (especially with a pendulous abdomen), prematurity, multiple pregnancy, hydramnios, fetal death, placenta previa, a small pelvis, and difficult labors in the past.

B. Unless obesity, a tense abdominal wall, or uterine hypertonus interdicts good palpation, abdominal palpation can be used to determine the fetal axis (whether longitudinal, transverse, or oblique) and orientation (cephalic or breech). Location of the fetal heart may provide helpful information. For example, if the heart beat is heard in the upper uterus, breech presentation is likely. Vaginal examination is especially valuable for defining the presenting part in doubtful cases, particularly if obesity obscures abdominal palpation.

C. Palpate the fetal head suprapubically by insinuating the extended examining hands in a caudad direction into the pelvic inlet on either side of the fetal head (this is the so-called fourth maneuver of Leopold). This provides information concerning the cephalic prominence and its relationship to the fetal back. In a well flexed head in a vertex presentation, the cephalic prominence (brow region) is opposite the fetal back. The somewhat deflexed head of a brow presentation is signaled by bilaterally equal cephalic prominences. By contrast, the extended head of a face presentation produces a cephalic prominence (occipital region) on the same side as the fetal back.

D. Digital palpation for vaginal assessment of the cranial fontanelles and sutures of the fetal head is necessary for confirming a brow presentation by finding both fontanelles and the orbital ridge. In contrast to the well flexed head of a vertex presentation when only the triangular posterior fontanelle can be felt, the large diamond shaped anterior fontanelle should be identifiable. If there is much caput formation obscuring the landmarks, try palpating for an ear. In a face presentation one may feel the orbital ridge, eyes (take care to avoid injury), bridge of the nose, nostrils, lips, gums, and the firm alveolar process of the jaws. The irregularity of the presenting part is characteristic of a face presentation, as is the straight line relationship between the projections of the zygomas and nose. This is different from the triangular relationship between ischial tuberosities and coccyx in a breech presentation.

E. If the cervix is dilated, one should be able to palpate the ischial tuberosities, genitals, and anus of the fetus in a breech presentation. If the membranes are ruptured, meconium can be obtained by inserting a finger into the fetal anus, it will not be present on a finger inserted into the fetal mouth. If a limb is encountered, ensure that it is a foot by determining that the toes form a straight line as opposed to the curved line formed by the fingers (Fig. 1). One cannot rely on the presence of a heel configuration, which may not be distinguishable from a sharply angulated wrist.

F. If the pelvis is empty of any palpable presenting head or breech and the uterus forms a transverse ovoid, a transverse lie is almost certain. Palpation of a limb or the characteristic rib cage grid by vaginal examination gives additional confirmation. Ultrasonography is done for confirmation prior to undertaking operative delivery if there is any question of the diagnosis.

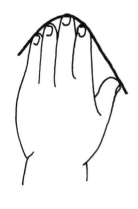

Figure 1 Distinguish fetal foot from hand by palpating straight alignment of toes as distinct from arched alignment of fingers. Heel cannot be readily distinguished from an angulated wrist.

References

Benedetti TJ, Lowensohn RI, Trusscott AM. Face presentation at term. Obstet Gynecol 55:199, 1980.

Luterkort M, Persson P, Weldner B. Maternal and fetal factors in breech presentation. Obstet Gynecol 64:5, 1984.

Phelan JP, Baicher M, Mueller E. The nonlaboring transverse lie: A management dilemma. J Reprod Med 31:184, 1986.

Seeds JW, Cefalo RC. Malpresentations. Clin Obstet Gynecol 25:145, 1982.

ONSET OF LABOR

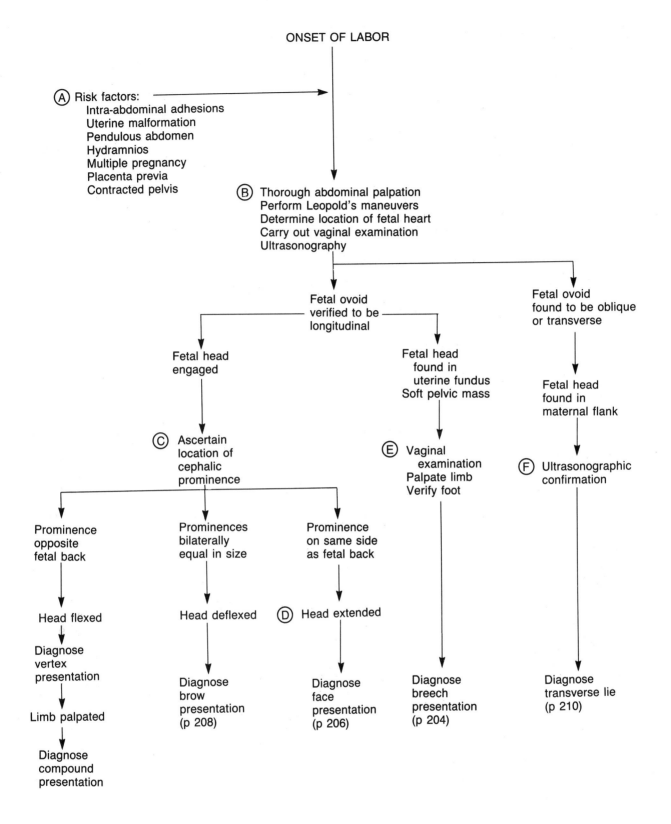

Ⓐ Risk factors:
  Intra-abdominal adhesions
  Uterine malformation
  Pendulous abdomen
  Hydramnios
  Multiple pregnancy
  Placenta previa
  Contracted pelvis

Ⓑ Thorough abdominal palpation
  Perform Leopold's maneuvers
  Determine location of fetal heart
  Carry out vaginal examination
  Ultrasonography

Fetal ovoid verified to be longitudinal

Fetal ovoid found to be oblique or transverse

Fetal head engaged

Fetal head found in uterine fundus
Soft pelvic mass

Fetal head found in maternal flank

Ⓒ Ascertain location of cephalic prominence

Ⓔ Vaginal examination
  Palpate limb
  Verify foot

Ⓕ Ultrasonographic confirmation

Prominence opposite fetal back

Prominences bilaterally equal in size

Prominence on same side as fetal back

Head flexed

Head deflexed

Ⓓ Head extended

Diagnose vertex presentation

Diagnose brow presentation (p 208)

Diagnose face presentation (p 206)

Diagnose breech presentation (p 204)

Diagnose transverse lie (p 210)

Limb palpated

Diagnose compound presentation

BREECH PRESENTATION

Max Borten, M.D.

A. A breech presentation (Fig. 1) frequently turns spontaneously to a vertex presentation, especially those discovered early in the third trimester. However, this occurs less and less often as term approaches, and the probability is very small after 36 to 38 weeks. One should be alert to the possibility of a malpresentation at all times (p 202). Once the breech presentation is diagnosed, whether to attempt external cephalic version is an unresolved matter. Given the growing tendency to subject all or nearly all breech presentations at term to cesarean section, the practice may have renewed appeal. The ability to avoid cesarean section in successfully turned cases (estimated to be about half of all those tried) has to be weighed against the risks of the procedure, including abruptio placentae and fetal distress from cord complications. Such risks are rare, however, if the version is done in a proper setting by skilled personnel and due precautions are taken. It should be performed in a facility with capabilities to permit rapid intervention in the event of a complication. The procedure should not be done without administering a tocolytic drug (p 178) and using continuous external electronic fetal heart rate monitoring. Avoid anesthesia to ensure that the version is done in as gentle a manner as possible. Ultrasonographic control is useful to verify the malpresentation and the progress achieved during the manipulations.

B. Before term, the diameters of the fetal head are larger than those of the body, and the intracranial contents are at greater risk of damage from vaginal delivery than at term. This problem is compounded in breech presentations because there is no opportunity for molding to occur in labor. Therefore, small fetuses weighing less than 2,000 g in breech presentations should preferably be delivered by cesarean section. This need not apply to fetuses with major malformations who can justifiably be delivered vaginally. Ultrasonographic scanning is essential both at term and in premature labor; it provides information about fetal head dimensions, hyperextension of the fetal head (see C), and gross fetal abnormalities.

C. Vaginal breech delivery of a fetus with a hyperextended head may cause catastrophic injury. Transverse sectioning of the infant's cervical spinal cord may result with total paralysis below the neck. Without exception, hyperextension must be ruled out definitively before permitting vaginal delivery of a fetus in breech presentation. Ultrasonography may suffice for this purpose, but x-ray studies are more reliable. Fetal head hyperextension exceeding 90 degrees is an ominous finding and warrants cesarean section. Performing the cesarean section requires special attention to ensure that the hyperextended head is not trapped in the uterine incision, causing the same kind of serious damage that the operation is being done to prevent. This risk is averted by the use of large abdominal and uterine incisions.

D. To justify allowing a trial of labor with a breech presentation, it is important to be reasonably certain that the pelvic capacity is adequate to accommodate the fetus in question. X-ray pelvimetry (p 24) should be available for this purpose; the technique used should be capable of accurately measuring both maternal pelvic and fetal head dimensions, even with the head located in the uterine fundus, and providing a reasonably reliable means for comparing them.

E. A normal labor pattern (p 234) does not guarantee an uneventful breech delivery, but an abnormal labor pattern may presage serious problems. In a vertex presentation, protraction and arrest disorders (p 238, 240) serve

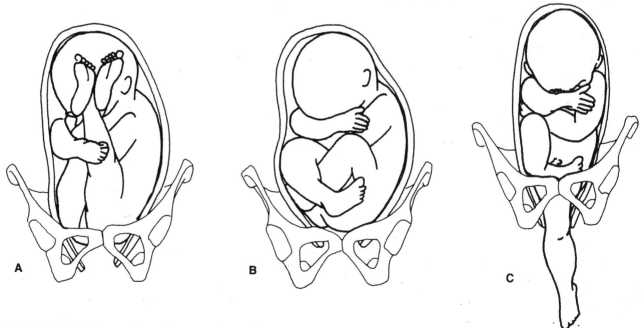

Figure 1 Principal types of breech presentation. *A*, Frank breech; *B*, complete or full breech; *C*, incomplete or single footling breech; double footling breech not shown.

BREECH PRESENTATION IN LABOR

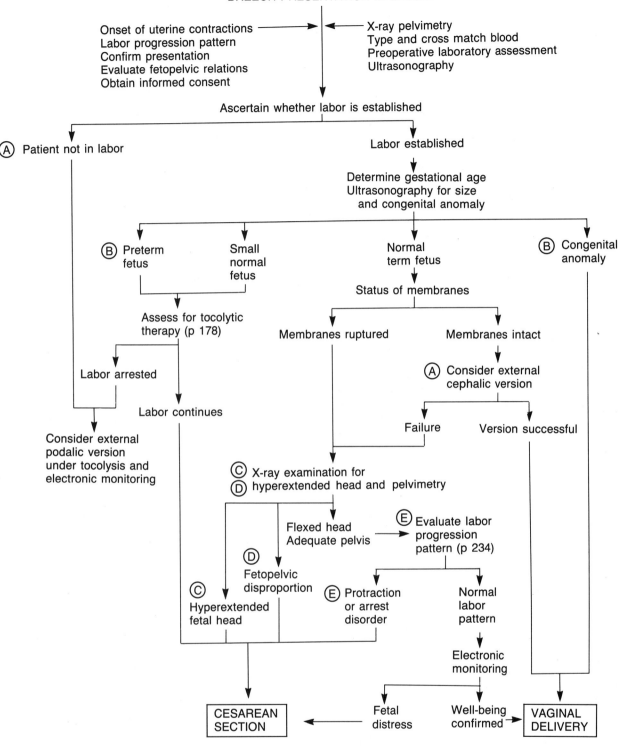

to flag possible fetopelvic disproportion; they may do the same for labors with breech presentations. Frequent periodic assessments of labor progression are therefore critical for detecting abnormal labor patterns as they arise. When encountered, they require prompt evaluation leading to cesarean section.

References

Bodmer B, Benjamin A, McLean FH, Usher RH. Has use of cesarean section reduced the risks of delivery in the pre-

term breech presentation? Am J Obstet Gynecol 154:244, 1986.

Ferguson JE, Dyson DC. Intrapartum external cephalic version. Am J Obstet Gynecol 152:297, 1985.

Morrison JC, Myatt RE, Martin JN, et al. External cephalic version of the breech presentation under tocolysis. Am J Obstet Gynecol 154:900, 1986.

Rosen MG, Debanne S, Thompson K, Bilenker RM. Long-term neurological morbidity in breech and vertex births. Am J Obstet Gynecol 151:718, 1985.

FACE PRESENTATION

Lenard R. Simon, M.D.

A. It is important to recognize a face presentation as early as possible before or during labor to give one the opportunity to evaluate underlying conditions and introduce corrective measures, thereby avoiding a difficult labor and a potentially traumatic delivery. Predisposing factors for face presentation include prematurity and cephalopelvic disproportion. Fetal torticollis or a large neck mass may be an intrinsic cause of hyperextension of the fetal head. Because anomalies are more common among fetuses in face presentation, they should be looked for by ultrasonography. Careful observation should be carried out, searching for anencephaly, encephalocele, goiter, and hygroma.

B. Since prematurity itself is a common etiologic factor in face presentations, one must evaluate both the gestational age (p 8) and the fetal weight (p 66). Discordance also warrants assessment for intrauterine growth retardation (p 68) if the fetus is smaller than expected for the gestational age. Watch for hydramnios, multiple pregnancy, and leiomyoma uteri as well.

C. Because face presentation is so often associated with a contracted pelvis, it follows logically that cephalopelvimetry (p 24) is an essential component of the process of evaluation in these cases. Only if it can be clearly demonstrated that the maternal pelvis is adequate to accommodate the fetal head in a face presentation should the labor be allowed to continue. X-ray examination also helps identify the presence of the aforementioned fetal malformations and growths sometimes encountered in these cases (see A).

D. The graphic recording of cervical dilatation and fetal station against the elapsed time in labor reveals a labor pattern (p 234) in each case. This may prove valuable in detecting abnormal progression of labor. The development of a protraction or arrest disorder (p 238, 240) may be indicative of disproportion. Although oxytocin shortens the labor somewhat, its use is not recommended and its value is unproved in a face presentation. The appearance of a major labor dysfunction in these cases mandates re-evaluation of the cephalopelvic relationships.

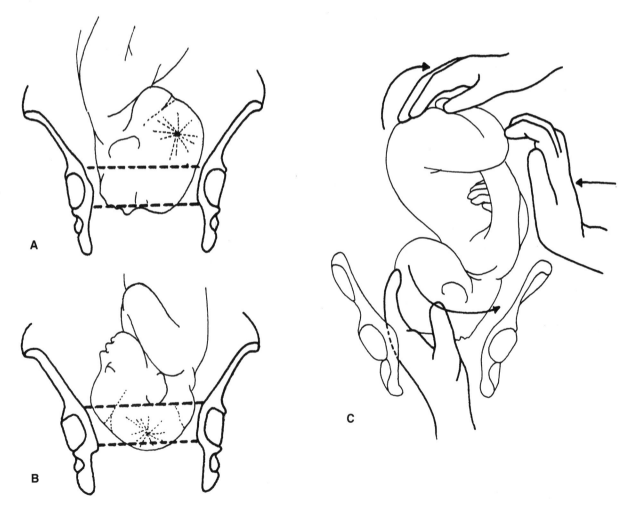

Figure 1 Face presentation (*A*) contrasted with vertex presentation (*B*) to show different level of the widest head dimensions (biparietal diameter) for a given fetal station. Technique for converting face to vertex (*C*) requires combining the forces shown to change S-curve of fetal spine to C-curve.

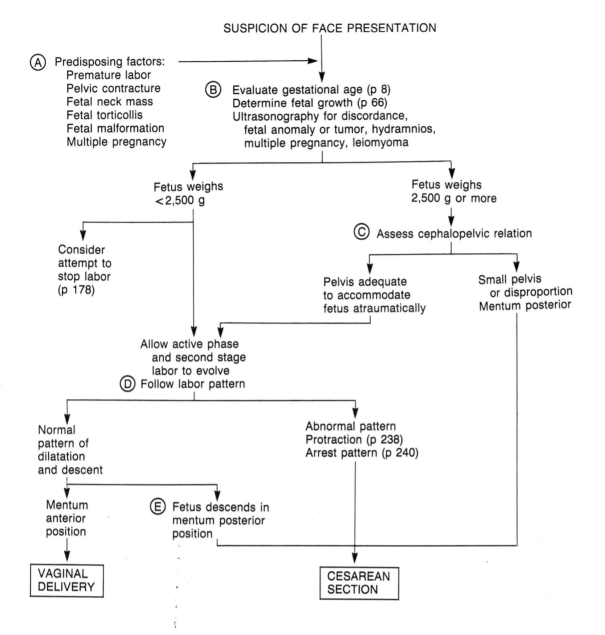

SUSPICION OF FACE PRESENTATION

Ⓐ Predisposing factors:
 Premature labor
 Pelvic contracture
 Fetal neck mass
 Fetal torticollis
 Fetal malformation
 Multiple pregnancy

Ⓑ Evaluate gestational age (p 8)
 Determine fetal growth (p 66)
 Ultrasonography for discordance,
  fetal anomaly or tumor, hydramnios,
  multiple pregnancy, leiomyoma

Fetus weighs <2,500 g

Fetus weighs 2,500 g or more

Ⓒ Assess cephalopelvic relation

Consider attempt to stop labor (p 178)

Pelvis adequate to accommodate fetus atraumatically

Small pelvis or disproportion Mentum posterior

Allow active phase and second stage labor to evolve
Ⓓ Follow labor pattern

Normal pattern of dilatation and descent

Abnormal pattern
Protraction (p 238)
Arrest pattern (p 240)

Mentum anterior position

Ⓔ Fetus descends in mentum posterior position

VAGINAL DELIVERY

CESAREAN SECTION

Unless there is reasonable assurance of ample space for descent and an atraumatic vaginal delivery, the burden of proof rests on the obstetrician who wishes to permit the labor to continue.

E. A fetal head in the mentum posterior position cannot be delivered vaginally without considerable trauma, because the head is already maximally extended (deflexed). In order for delivery to occur over the perineum, it would be necessary for the head to undergo additional extension, an essentially impossible feat without dire consequences. Cesarean section therefore must be done in this circumstance to avoid fetal trauma. Manipulation to rotate a head in the mentum posterior position to mentum anterior is itself often traumatic, especially when the attempt involves a forceps rotation procedure. It is thus of dubious value. One must also recognize that the marked deflexion of the fetal head in these cases means that the widest dimensions of the head are much higher (more cephalad) in the pelvis than they ordinarily are

in a well flexed vertex presentation (Fig. 1). If forceps were to be applied under these circumstances, it would represent an application at a high plane in the pelvis, and the procedure undertaken at that plane could be expected to be considerably more difficult and more hazardous to the mother and fetus.

References

Benedetti TJ, Lowensohn RI, Trusscott AM. Face presentation at term. Obstet Gynecol 55:199, 1980.

Cruikshank DP, Cruikshank JE. Face and brow presentation: A review. Clin Obstet Gynecol 24:333, 1981.

Duff P. Diagnosis and management of face presentation. Obstet Gynecol 57:105, 1981.

Seeds JW, Cefalo RC. Malpresentations. Clin Obstet Gynecol 25:145, 1982.

BROW PRESENTATION

Lenard R. Simon, M.D.

A. The brow presentation, seldom detected before labor, represents the intermediary stage of fetal head deflexion between vertex and face presentations (Fig. 1). Except when it occurs in a small premature fetus, the infant in a brow presentation cannot be delivered vaginally without correction because the deflexion causes the largest head dimension (occipitofrontal) to be presented to the maternal pelvis for accommodation. Predisposing factors include any condition that promotes extension or prevents flexion of the fetal skull. Some degree of pelvic contracture is frequently seen. Low implantation of the placenta may contribute to this condition by occupying and thereby distorting the lower uterine segment. Exceptionally large infants with a resultant degree of relative or absolute cephalopelvic disproportion may develop brow presentation. Deformity or enlargement of the fetal neck or thorax from growths or malformations, such as goiter or hygroma, as well as structural or functional shortening of the cervical muscles, from torticollis, for example, also effectively prevents flexion of the fetal head. Certain congenital anomalies, such as microcephaly, encephalocele, and anencephaly, are also frequently associated with various degrees of deflexion.

B. Gestational age and fetal growth and maturity must be carefully evaluated by both clinical and laboratory means. The latter involves ultrasonography primarily, but other techniques may prove necessary as well (p 66). Special attention should be paid to assessments to detect the aforementioned malformations and growths (see A).

C. Cephalopelvic relationships (p 24) must be carefully evaluated in cases of brow presentation because of its common association with large fetuses or small pelves and obstructed labor. Not only is it imperative to undertake detailed clinical evaluation of the pelvic architecture and the relative fit of the fetal head into the maternal pelvis, but more objective measures, specifically x-ray pelvimetry, are particularly relevant here as well.

D. Follow the course of labor assiduously to detect abnormal progress early (p 234). This means constructing a graph of the course of cervical dilatation and fetal descent to show the labor pattern as it evolves and identify any aberration from the expected pattern as that disorder develops. The appearance of either an arrest or a protraction disorder (p 238, 240) must be considered a strong signal that disproportion probably exists. Under these circumstances cesarean section is clearly warranted unless the brow presentation self-corrects by flexion to a vertex presentation.

E. Spontaneous conversion to a face or vertex presentation frequently occurs as a consequence of the driving forces of a strong labor, provided there is no concurrent disporportion. Such spontaneous conversion obviates any of the dubious maneuvers used in the past to attempt to convert undeliverable brow presentations to vertex. Such maneuvers are of unproven value, are potentially traumatic, and are best avoided. Perhaps the only remaining justifiable situation is the brow (or face) presentation first discovered late in the course of a multiparous labor in which the membranes are still intact (or just ruptured) and the fetal head has not yet descended into the pelvis. Under these unusual circumstances the cervix may

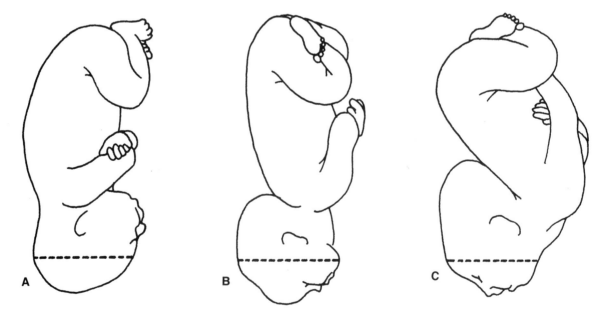

Figure 1 Presenting fetal head dimensions change with extension from sincipital *A*, to brow *B*, and face *C*, presentation. The large occipito-bregmatic (sincipital) and mento-bregmatic (brow) diameters are contrasted with the smaller trachelo-bregmatic (face) and suboccipito-bregmatic (vertex, not shown) diameters.

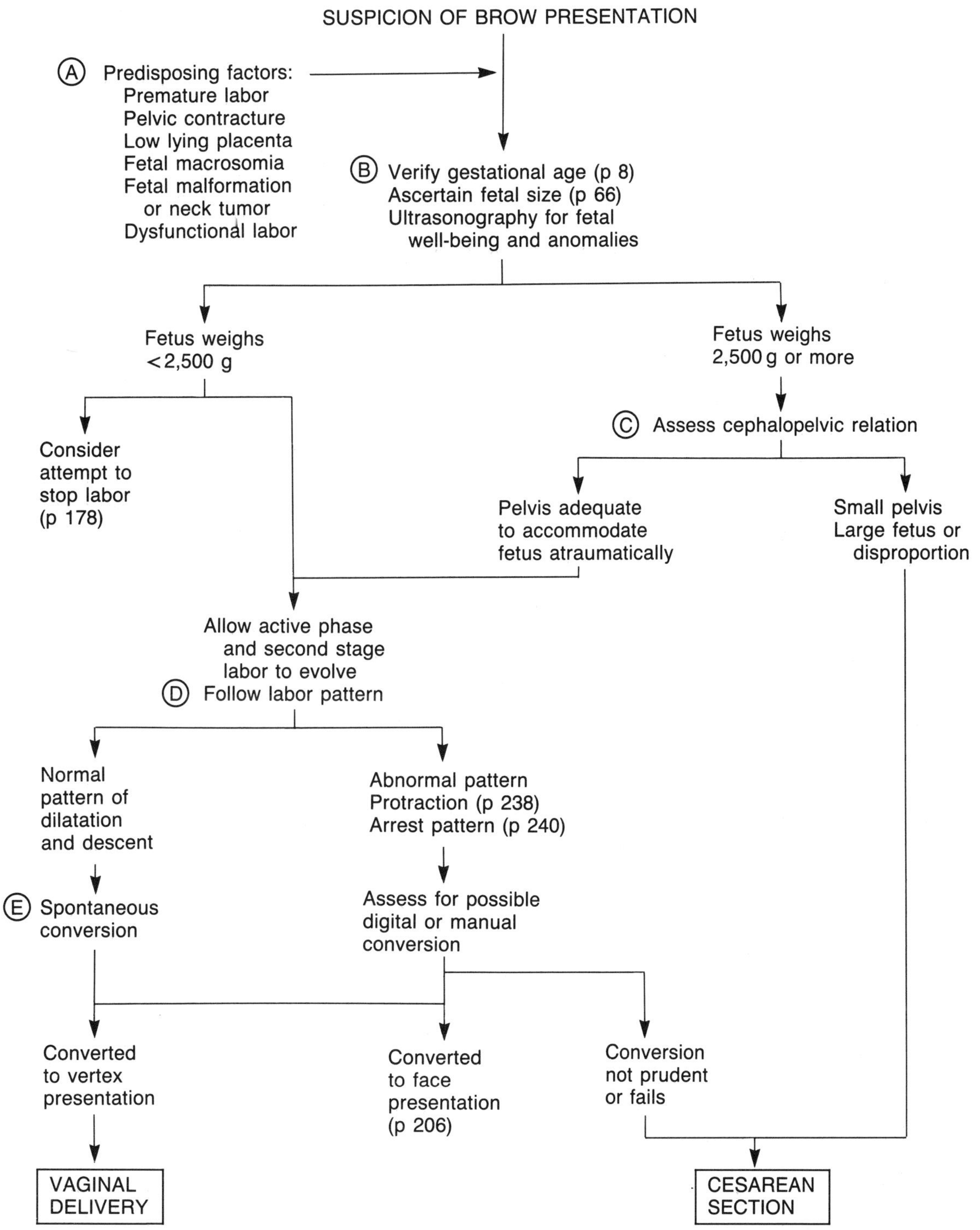

SUSPICION OF BROW PRESENTATION

(A) Predisposing factors:
- Premature labor
- Pelvic contracture
- Low lying placenta
- Fetal macrosomia
- Fetal malformation or neck tumor
- Dysfunctional labor

(B) Verify gestational age (p 8)
Ascertain fetal size (p 66)
Ultrasonography for fetal well-being and anomalies

Fetus weighs <2,500 g

Fetus weighs 2,500 g or more

Consider attempt to stop labor (p 178)

(C) Assess cephalopelvic relation

Pelvis adequate to accommodate fetus atraumatically

Small pelvis Large fetus or disproportion

Allow active phase and second stage labor to evolve
(D) Follow labor pattern

Normal pattern of dilatation and descent

Abnormal pattern Protraction (p 238) Arrest pattern (p 240)

(E) Spontaneous conversion

Assess for possible digital or manual conversion

Converted to vertex presentation

Converted to face presentation (p 206)

Conversion not prudent or fails

VAGINAL DELIVERY

CESAREAN SECTION

be sufficiently dilated and the head mobile enough to permit one to insert a hand through the vagina into the uterus to attempt to flex the head while gentle external pressure is simultaneously applied to the breech (in the same direction) and the thorax (in the opposite direction) to effect conversion. If this fails (avoid persisting) and there is no spontaneous conversion in the second stage, descent cannot be expected to occur. Molding of the fetal head with apparent advancement of the forward leading edge may delude the observer into believing that descent is taking place when it is actually still tightly fixed at or above the inlet. Therefore, always verify des-

cent with concurrent suprapubic palpation under these circumstances (p 240). Failure or arrest of descent in such a case demands cesarean section.

References

Cruikshank DP, Cruikshank JE. Face and brow presentation. A review. Clin Obstet Gynecol 24:333, 1981.

Levy DL. Persistent brow presentation. A new approach to management. South Med J 69:191, 1976.

Seeds JW, Cefalo RC. Malpresentations. Clin Obstet Gynecol 25:145, 1982.

TRANSVERSE LIE

Lenard R. Simon, M.D.

A. Consider the possibility of transverse lie in the gravida whose uterine fundal height is smaller than it should be according to the gestational age and whose flanks are fuller than expected. A short, squat uterus that is broader than it is tall should alert the attendant to this potentially serious condition. A transverse lie (p 202) is generally confirmed by abdominal palpation, using the classic sequence of Leopold's maneuvers. Careful examination reveals a transversely oriented uterus with neither fetal pole (that is, neither head nor breech) in the pelvis. The fetal head should be identifiable by palpation in one iliac fossa and the breech in the other. The pelvis is generally devoid of fetal parts unless the shoulder has become impacted in the inlet or a limb has prolapsed into the lower uterine segment. Vaginal examination may encounter the gridiron configuration of the rib cage. If a limb is palpated, try to distinguish hand from foot by differentiating the straight line of the toes from the curved line of the fingers (p 202). Abnormal relaxation of the abdominal wall, such as is commonly seen in grand multiparas, pelvic contracture, and placenta previa or another soft tissue mass (especially leiomyoma uteri) filling the pelvis may prevent either fetal pole from entering the pelvis.

B. In order to deliver a living, viable infant from the transverse lie it is necessary either to turn it to a longitudinal lie or proceed with operative intervention by cesarean section. If a transverse lie is encountered in the course of labor, attempts at manipulation should be scrupulously avoided because of the inherent risks of serious harm to both mother and fetus, particularly if labor is advanced or the membranes are ruptured. There is renewed interest in external cephalic version (Fig. 1) for correcting a transverse lie if the condition is discovered prior to labor. The risks of this procedure in regard to abruptio placentae and cord accidents have to be weighed against the benefit of averting a cesarean section. It appears possible to minimize these hazards by attempting the version under optimal circumstances, namely, in an appropriate setting where complications can be dealt with expeditiously by skillful personnel, under ultrasonographic and electronic fetal monitoring guidance, with preoperative tocolysis, and in a most gentle manner without anesthesia.

C. Transverse lie in association with a living, previable fetus warrants an attempt to arrest premature labor (p 178). If successful, it may provide an opportunity for spontaneous conversion to a vertex presentation or to effect an external cephalic version (see B). Close follow-up is in order if the labor is successfully arrested. If it fails or is not feasible because labor is far advanced or conditions (such as amnionitis) dictate prompt evacuation, vaginal delivery may be an option, although the chances of intrapartum or neonatal mortality are recognized to be great.

D. If the fetus is known to be dead or is nonviable, the feasibility of vaginal delivery should be weighed. The mechanisms of conduplicato corporis or spontaneous evolution may occur to make vaginal delivery possible. One should always be aware that overdistention of the lower uterine segment is hazardous even if the fetus is relatively small. Under such circumstances the risk of

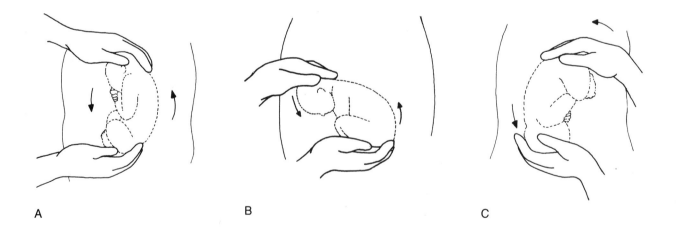

A   B   C

Figure 1 External cephalic version of fetus in breech presentation (A) or transverse lie (B) to vertex (C). The breech is gently dislodged from the pelvis, and the fetus is turned, keeping the head, trunk and limbs flexed, under tocolysis with ultrasonographic guidance and electronic monitoring.

SUSPICION OF TRANSVERSE LIE

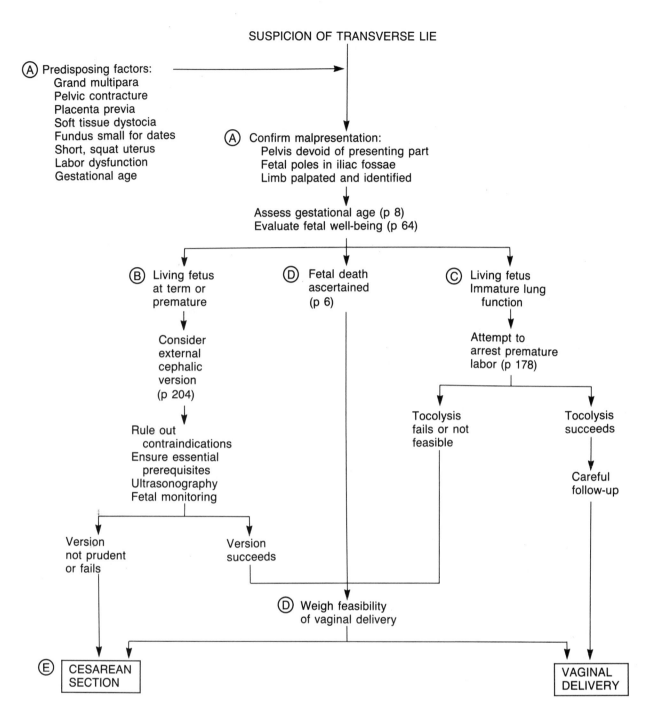

Ⓐ Predisposing factors:
    Grand multipara
    Pelvic contracture
    Placenta previa
    Soft tissue dystocia
    Fundus small for dates
    Short, squat uterus
    Labor dysfunction
    Gestational age

Ⓐ Confirm malpresentation:
    Pelvis devoid of presenting part
    Fetal poles in iliac fossae
    Limb palpated and identified

Assess gestational age (p 8)
Evaluate fetal well-being (p 64)

Ⓑ Living fetus
    at term or
    premature

Ⓓ Fetal death
    ascertained
    (p 6)

Ⓒ Living fetus
    Immature lung
    function

Consider
external
cephalic
version
(p 204)

Attempt to
arrest premature
labor (p 178)

Rule out
  contraindications
Ensure essential
  prerequisites
Ultrasonography
Fetal monitoring

Tocolysis
fails or not
feasible

Tocolysis
succeeds

Version
not prudent
or fails

Version
succeeds

Careful
follow-up

Ⓓ Weigh feasibility
   of vaginal delivery

Ⓔ CESAREAN
   SECTION

VAGINAL
DELIVERY

uterine rupture exists, especially if labor progress becomes arrested. These patients have to be followed carefully, therefore, and cesarean section done whenever it is clear that vaginal delivery cannot occur without serious maternal risk.

E. The choice of a uterine incision for delivering a fetus in transverse lie by cesarean section depends upon the position of the back relative to the pelvic inlet as well as concurrent conditions, such as placenta previa or pelvic tumor. A lower uterine segment incision is acceptable only if the fetal back is up and the lower segment well formed. This allows one to grasp the fetal legs for a breech extraction or to manipulate the fetal head into the incision for delivery. If the back is down or the low-

er segment is not well formed, a classic incision is preferable. It provides enough room to deliver the infant easily and without trauma.

References

Jabbar A, Meshari A. Etiology and management of transverse lie. Int J Gynaecol Obstet 18:448, 1980.

Phelan JP, Boucher M, Mueller E, et al. The nonlaboring transverse lie: A management dilemma. J Reprod Med 31:184, 1986.

Phelan JP, Stine LE, Edwards NB, et al. The role of external version in the intrapartum management of the transverse lie presentation. Am J Obstet Gynecol 151:724, 1985.

PERSISTENT OCCIPUT POSTERIOR

Lenard R. Simon, M.D.

A. The major predisposing factor leading to a persistent occiput posterior position is the type of pelvic architecture, especially anthropoid and android pelves. The position may also be seen in mixed pelvic types when there is an associated contracture of the forepelvis or midplane dimensions. The failure of the fetal head to rotate internally to the occiput anterior position (as it ordinarily should) as it descends in the pelvis appears to be related to the transverse narrowing of the birth canal coupled with the relatively greater amount of compensatory room posteriorly along the sacrum. The latter applies especially to the deep hollow of the sacrum in an anthropoid pelvis.

B. Confirmation of a fetal occiput posterior position is accomplished primarily by vaginal examination, although one may be alerted to its presence by abdominal palpation. Since the fetal back is directed posteriorly, it is generally difficult to palpate the fetus well transabdominally to make out its landmarks. Vaginal examination reveals the fetal head deflexion commonly seen with the occiput posterior position. The sagittal suture is directed anteroposteriorly, and both anterior and posterior fontanelles usually can be felt and identified unless caput formation obscures the demarcating cranial sutures. It is this characteristic deflexion so often associated with an occiput posterior position that makes it a problem because larger fetal head dimensions have to be accommodated by the maternal pelvis than is the case ordinarily. Moreover, the widest diameters of the head are higher (more cephalad) than the forward leading edge assessment (the usual means for determining the fetal station) would suggest. Furthermore, the molding that is almost always seen in these cases compounds the problem.

C. The abnormal labor pattern associated with the occiput posterior position is almost always the result of some degree of cephalopelvic disproportion and not directly related to the fetal position itself. Thus, protraction and arrest disorders are frequently seen (p 238, 240). Conduction anesthesia or excessive sedation may also contribute by reducing the driving force of expulsive efforts in second stage, making it less likely that internal rotation will occur spontaneously as the fetal head reaches the trough of the levator ani muscles.

D. Patients who develop a major labor aberration with the fetus in the occiput posterior position must be considered at high risk because of the probability that cephalopelvic disproportion exists. It is essential, therefore, to evaluate them critically to determine whether the pelvis can accommodate the fetus by clinical means and, if necessary for confirmation, x-ray pelvimetry (p 24). Verification of disproportion warrants cesarean section without a further trial of labor.

E. In most cases in which the pelvis is adequate for the fetus, spontaneous internal rotation occurs to the occiput anterior position. With rare exceptions an uneventful vaginal delivery can be expected. In some the occiput posterior position persists. Here careful reassessment of the pelvic adequacy is essential. The fetus may have descended to a level at which obstruction can now be demonstrated objectively by dynamic assessment (p 24). Even with the head well down in the pelvis, cesarean section may still be indicated because of disproportion. In the absence of evidence of disproportion, one may gently attempt digital rotation to occiput anterior; if this is successful, vaginal delivery should occur in due course. It usually proceeds quickly because the head flexes to present smaller diameters for the remainder of the descent process. In the case of a persistent occiput posterior that cannot be digitally rotated, allowing the fetus to deliver as an occiput posterior is preferable to forceps rotation because the latter risks maternal and fetal damage. Attempts at forceps rotation or forceps delivery of the fetus from the midpelvis are generally unwarranted because of the high frequency of fetal damage associated with these procedures. They are contraindicated unless it can be shown that the risks of alternative actions, including expectancy, are greater (p 284).

References

Holmberg NG, Lilieqvist B, Magnusson S, Segerbraud E. The influence of the bony pelvis in the persistent occiput posterior position. Acta Obstet Gynecol Scand 66:49, 1977.

Seeds JW, Cefalo RC. Malpresentations. Clin Obstet Gynecol 25:143, 1982.

Sunderland R. Fetal position and skull shape. Obstet Gynecol Surv 37:401, 1982.

FETUS IN OCCIPUT POSTERIOR POSITION

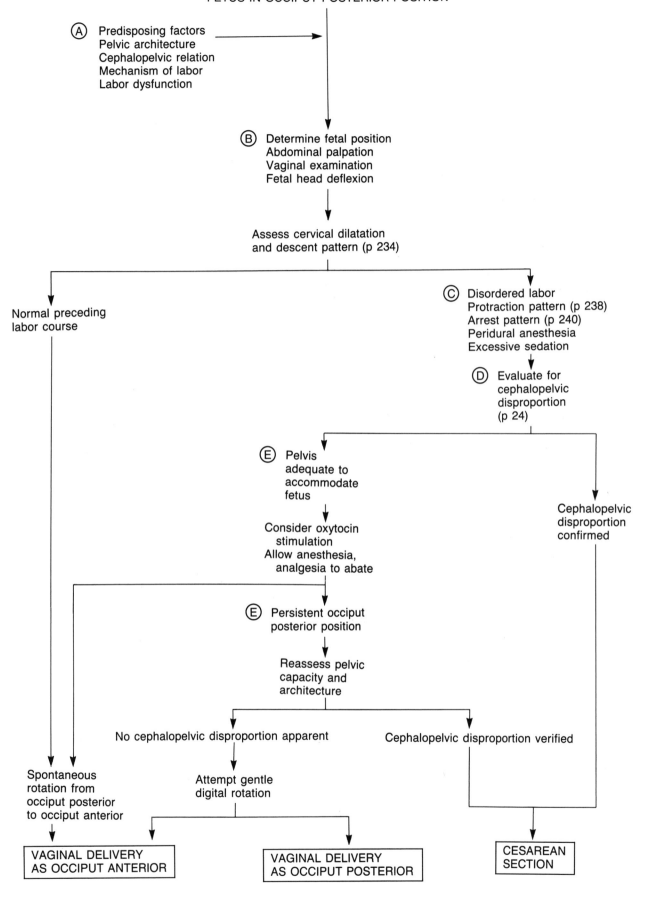

(A) Predisposing factors
Pelvic architecture
Cephalopelvic relation
Mechanism of labor
Labor dysfunction

(B) Determine fetal position
Abdominal palpation
Vaginal examination
Fetal head deflexion

Assess cervical dilatation
and descent pattern (p 234)

Normal preceding
labor course

(C) Disordered labor
Protraction pattern (p 238)
Arrest pattern (p 240)
Peridural anesthesia
Excessive sedation

(D) Evaluate for
cephalopelvic
disproportion
(p 24)

(E) Pelvis
adequate to
accommodate
fetus

Cephalopelvic
disproportion
confirmed

Consider oxytocin
stimulation
Allow anesthesia,
analgesia to abate

(E) Persistent occiput
posterior position

Reassess pelvic
capacity and
architecture

No cephalopelvic disproportion apparent

Cephalopelvic disproportion verified

Spontaneous
rotation from
occiput posterior
to occiput anterior

Attempt gentle
digital rotation

VAGINAL DELIVERY
AS OCCIPUT ANTERIOR

VAGINAL DELIVERY
AS OCCIPUT POSTERIOR

CESAREAN
SECTION

213

PROLAPSED CORD

David B. Acker, M.D.

A. There is a risk of prolapse of the umbilical cord if the presenting part does not effectively block the inlet of the pelvis. Cord prolapse is encountered in association with prematurity, transverse lie, breech presentation (especially single [Fig. 1] or double footling varieties), an unengaged presenting part, compound presentation, multiparity, cephalopelvic disproportion, leiomyoma (particularly intramural or submucosal and occupying the lower uterine segment or cervix), multiple pregnancy, hydramnios, and partial placenta previa or low lying placenta.

B. Overt prolapse seldom occurs prior to labor and is seldom clinically apparent before the membranes rupture. Since overt prolapse carries such a high risk even when managed adroitly, it is preferable to try to detect a forelying cord before it becomes a potential catastrophe, requiring instantaneous mobilization of hospital resources to attempt salvage. To accomplish this, patients with term pregnancies complicated by the aforementioned problems (see A) should be screened by ultrasonography. If the cord is presenting at the internal os, immediate admission is mandated. In the case of a high presenting part (station −2 or higher) in which artificial rupture of the membranes is contemplated, facilities and personnel must be immediately available for intervention in case of cord prolapse.

C. The significance of occult cord prolapse is unclear. It may be asymptomatic or it could cause intrauterine fetal demise. Variable decelerations seen on electronic fetal heart rate monitoring (p 192), especially if unresponsive to corrective treatment, may signal cord occlusion warranting action. Undertake vaginal examination and ultrasonography (if immediately available in the labor unit) to clarify the cause.

D. The obstetrician must decide between expectant management and cesarean section on the basis of the imminence of delivery and the sophistication of the hospital facilities and personnel available. Expectancy requires careful continued surveillance with sequential ultrasonography to evaluate the relationship of the umbilical cord and fetus. One should be able to perform an immediate cesarean section when the need arises.

E. The overtly prolapsed cord can be seen or felt in the vagina or less often protruding from the introitus. Prompt delivery is mandatory to prevent fetal death or damage from compression of the cord by the presenting part and vasoconstriction from exposure to the extrauterine environment. Reposition the patient to a Trendelenburg, elevated lateral Sims', or knee-chest position and elevate the presenting part. Give oxygen by mask, although its value is dubious. Mobilize operating room personnel and pediatricians for immediate surgery.

F. Check the fetal heart rate by auscultation, ultrasonography, or a scalp electrode. Do not palpate the cord to detect pulsations, and do not apply the electrode to the cord. Avoid handling the cord because it will induce vasoconstriction of the umbilical vessels. In situations in which immediate delivery cannot be performed, try filling the bladder with 500 to 700 ml of saline to displace the fetal head away from the cord. A tocolytic drug can be given intravenously to stop contractions.

G. The decision to proceed with cesarean section because of a prolapsed cord when the fetal heart beat cannot be detected depends on the reliability of the detection device, the time elapsing after the heart tones were lost, and the time required to effect the delivery. The wishes of the informed patient have to be taken into account as well. Allow vaginal delivery if the heart tones have been absent for more than 10 minutes. Because a recently dead fetus can transmit electrocardiographic signals from the maternal heart, fetal bradycardia may be mistakenly diagnosed on internal monitoring. Therefore, assess the maternal heart rate simultaneously prior to making any decision.

References

Borten M. Breech presentation. In Cohen WR, Friedman EA (Editors): Management of Labor. Baltimore: University Park Press, 1983.

Katz Z, Lancet M, Borenstein R. Management of labor with umbilical cord prolapse. Am J Obstet Gynecol 142:239, 1982.

Lange IR, Manning FA, Morrison I. Cord prolapse: Is antenatal diagnosis possible? Am J Obstet Gynecol 151:1083, 1985.

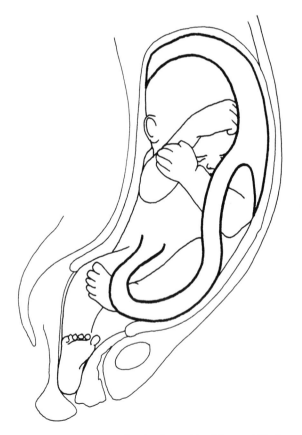

Figure 1 Prolapsed cord showing loop of forelying umbilical cord in a case with single footling breech presentation. The irregular presenting part permits the cord to descend in the birth canal.

PATIENT WITH SUSPICION OF CORD PROLAPSE

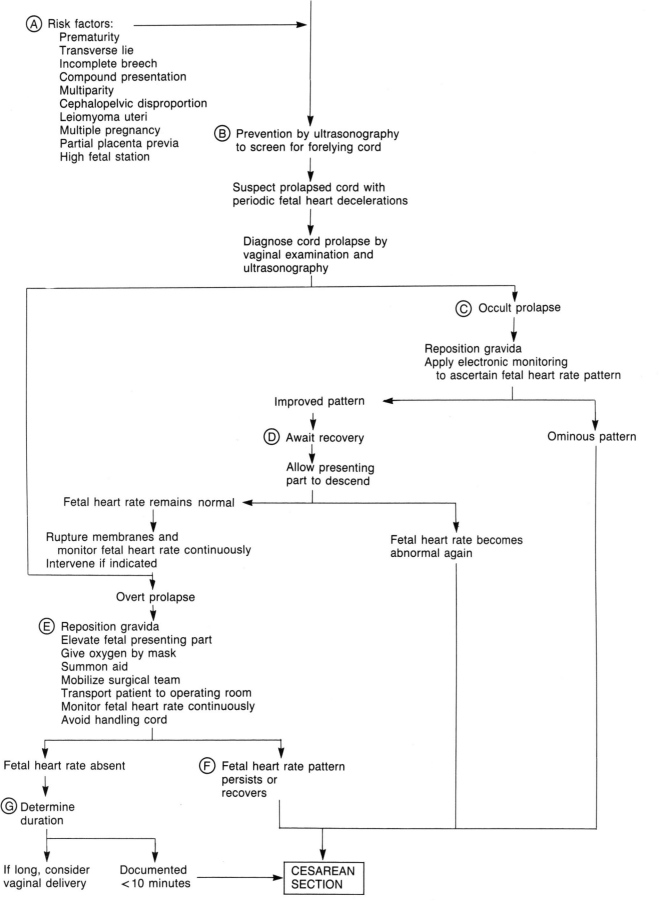

(A) Risk factors:
    Prematurity
    Transverse lie
    Incomplete breech
    Compound presentation
    Multiparity
    Cephalopelvic disproportion
    Leiomyoma uteri
    Multiple pregnancy
    Partial placenta previa
    High fetal station

(B) Prevention by ultrasonography
    to screen for forelying cord

Suspect prolapsed cord with
periodic fetal heart decelerations

Diagnose cord prolapse by
vaginal examination and
ultrasonography

(C) Occult prolapse

Reposition gravida
Apply electronic monitoring
    to ascertain fetal heart rate pattern

Improved pattern

(D) Await recovery

Allow presenting
part to descend

Ominous pattern

Fetal heart rate remains normal

Rupture membranes and
    monitor fetal heart rate continuously
Intervene if indicated

Fetal heart rate becomes
abnormal again

Overt prolapse

(E) Reposition gravida
    Elevate fetal presenting part
    Give oxygen by mask
    Summon aid
    Mobilize surgical team
    Transport patient to operating room
    Monitor fetal heart rate continuously
    Avoid handling cord

Fetal heart rate absent

(F) Fetal heart rate pattern
    persists or
    recovers

(G) Determine
    duration

If long, consider
vaginal delivery

Documented
<10 minutes

CESAREAN
SECTION

HYDRAMNIOS

Henry Klapholz, M.D.

A. Suspect hydramnios, the excessive accumulation of amniotic fluid, whenever uterine growth is more rapid than expected in pregnancy. Serial tape measurements of the fundal height (symphysis pubis to top of uterus) should increase at about 1 cm per week in the second half of gestation. The actual amount of fluid in these cases is usually over 2,000 ml at term; in only about one patient in 1,000 does the volume exceed 3,000 ml. Hydramnios may develop slowly and almost imperceptibly, or suddenly with a rapid weight gain accompanied by a rapid increase in abdominal girth, often with a tense painful abdomen. Considerable stasis edema of the lower extremities develops in these cases. The fetal heart is difficult to hear because of the large volume of intervening fluid. The patient may experience nausea and vomiting. Hydramnios is an important marker of fetal anomalies and infections, multiple pregnancy, maternal diabetes, and Rh isoimmunization.

B. Ultrasonographic scanning is particularly useful for confirming the presence of a large volume of amniotic fluid relative to the fetal size. Volumetric determinations are available to help quantitate the amount. Ultrasonography shows concomitant multiple pregnancy (p 220) and reveals some fetal anomalies, such as anencephalus. If twins are found, suspect monozygous twins, because hydramnios, which is seen in about 10 percent of twins, is more common among them. Sophisticated ultrasonographic equipment may be able to show the absence of intervening membranes between twins, thereby demonstrating the single monoamniotic sac; if membranes are present, their separate layers sometimes can be seen as well.

C. About half the anencephalic fetuses have hydramnios. Fetal esophageal atresia is associated with hydramnios; although the anomaly sometimes can be diagnosed by ultrasonography, x-ray studies are often needed to confirm the diagnosis. The technique involves injecting radiopaque dye into the amniotic fluid; when it is swallowed by the fetus, an upper gastrointestinal study is accomplished. Overall, 29 percent of fetuses with hydramnios have anomalies. Given the large proportion of malformations and the other complicating conditions associated with hydramnios, it is not unexpected that about half the fetuses succumb.

D. It is important to evaluate these cases carefully for fetal infection, maternal diabetes mellitus (p 96), and Rh isoimmunization (p 138). Infection may be detected by obtaining TORCH titers (an acronym for toxoplasmosis, rubella, cytomegalovirus, and herpesvirus). Although toxoplasmosis (p 152) may be treated with spiramycin, the already poor prognosis for fetal survival or well-being is even worse in cases associated with hydramnios.

E. Amniocentesis can be undertaken with the understanding that it is being done only to relieve the intense pressure and respiratory compromise that occur as a result of the greatly overdistended uterus, which not only impinges on the diaphragm but also may cause azotemia by obstructing the ureters where they cross the brim of the pelvis. About 500 ml per hour can be withdrawn safely up to a total of 1,500 ml on each occasion. Removing larger amounts or at more frequent intervals may result in placental separation. Abruptio placentae also may occur in these cases without amniocentesis; it is especially likely to develop at the time the membranes rupture spontaneously, as a consequence of the shearing forces that occur when the uterine volume is suddenly reduced. Unfortunately rapid reaccumulation can be expected. Labor often ensues. A technique for effecting long term drainage, without risking infection, has not yet been developed.

F. There is an increased incidence of amniotic fluid embolism (p 132) complicating this disorder. This is perhaps related to the uterine overdistention and the stretched placental site, exposing maternal venous sinuses to the amniotic fluid. Care therefore should be taken to avoid oxytocin augmentation, if possible, because it could theoretically enhance the risk.

References

Flowers WK. Hydramnios and gastrointestinal atresias: A review. Obstet Gynecol Surv 38:685, 1983.

Montan S, Jorgensen C, Sjoberg NO. Amniocentesis in treatment of acute polyhydramnios in twin pregnancies. Acta Obstet Gynecol Scand 64:537, 1985.

Quinlan RW, Cruz AC, Martin M. Hydramnios: Ultrasound diagnosis and its impact on perinatal management and pregnancy outcome. Am J Obstet Gynecol 145:306, 1983.

Vintzileos AM, Turner GW, Campbell WA, et al. Polydramnios and obstructive renal failure: A case report and review of the literature. Am J Obstet Gynecol 152:883, 1985.

Zamah NM, Gillieson MS, Walters JH, Hall PF. Sonographic detection of polyhydramnios: A five-year experience. Am J Obstet Gynecol 143:523, 1982.

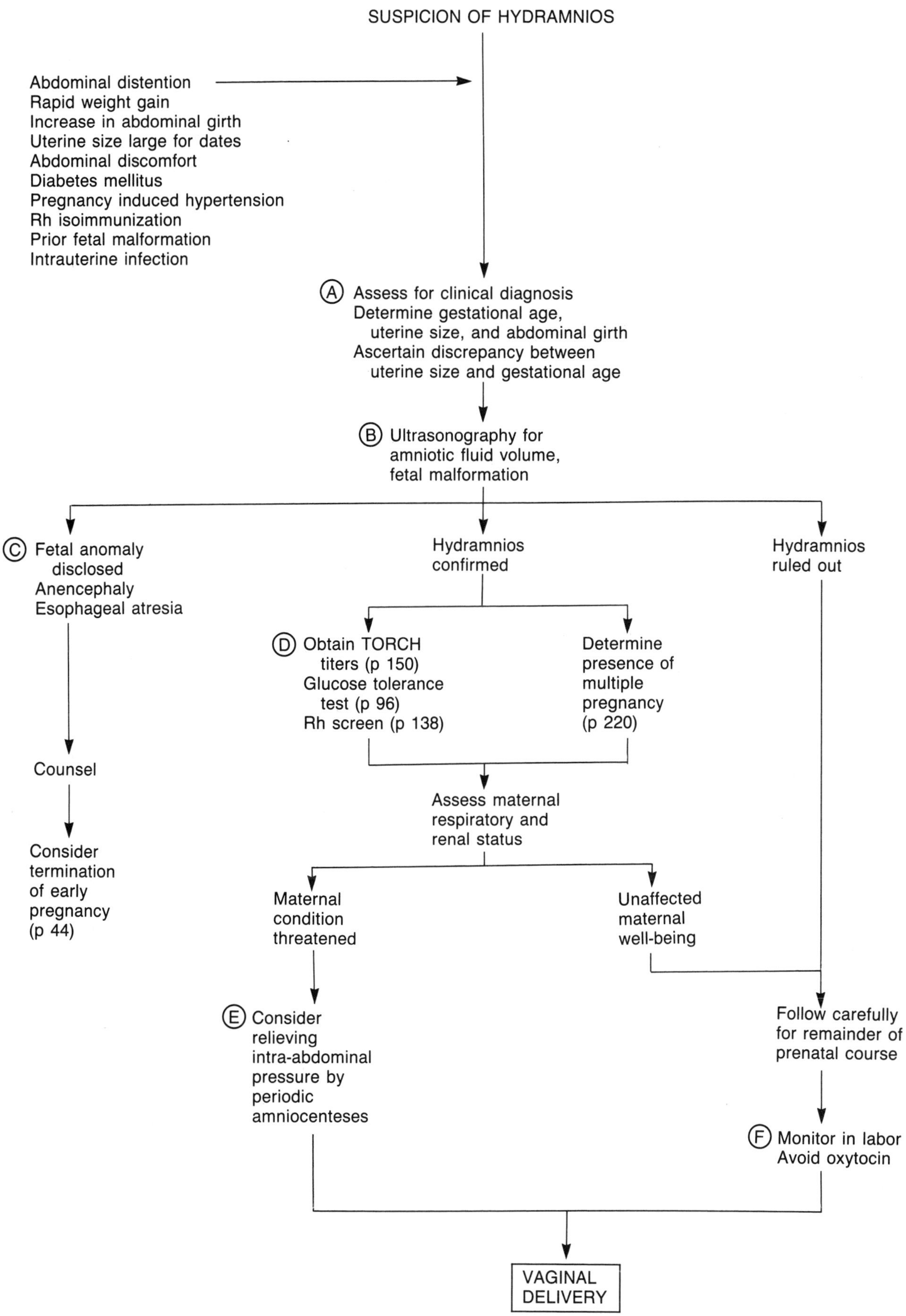

SUSPICION OF HYDRAMNIOS

Abdominal distention
Rapid weight gain
Increase in abdominal girth
Uterine size large for dates
Abdominal discomfort
Diabetes mellitus
Pregnancy induced hypertension
Rh isoimmunization
Prior fetal malformation
Intrauterine infection

(A) Assess for clinical diagnosis
Determine gestational age,
    uterine size, and abdominal girth
Ascertain discrepancy between
    uterine size and gestational age

(B) Ultrasonography for
amniotic fluid volume,
fetal malformation

(C) Fetal anomaly
disclosed
Anencephaly
Esophageal atresia

Hydramnios
confirmed

Hydramnios
ruled out

(D) Obtain TORCH
titers (p 150)
Glucose tolerance
test (p 96)
Rh screen (p 138)

Determine
presence of
multiple
pregnancy
(p 220)

Counsel

Assess maternal
respiratory and
renal status

Consider
termination
of early
pregnancy
(p 44)

Maternal
condition
threatened

Unaffected
maternal
well-being

Follow carefully
for remainder of
prenatal course

(E) Consider
relieving
intra-abdominal
pressure by
periodic
amniocenteses

(F) Monitor in labor
Avoid oxytocin

VAGINAL
DELIVERY

FETAL HYDROCEPHALUS

Benjamin P. Sachs, M.B., B.S., D.P.H.

A. Because hydrocephalus is so frequently accompanied by spina bifida (in one-third of the cases), great care should be taken not to assume it to be an isolated phenomenon. The condition does not follow a mendelian inheritance pattern. Although an X linked type with aqueductal stenosis does exist, it is extremely rare. The recurrence risk in the usual variety of hydrocephalus is approximately 3 percent for a single affected child and 8 percent after two affected children, regardless of the anatomic type. There are several different types of hydrocephalus. Internal hydrocephalus indicates increased cerebrospinal fluid within the ventricles; external hydrocephalus reflects increased fluid in the subdural space. If there is no obstruction to the flow of spinal fluid within the ventricular system or the spinal canal, the condition is termed communicating hydrocephalus. Approximately 80 percent of the infants with obstructed hydrocephalus have associated spina bifida. The hydrocephalus in nearly all cases is due to decreased absorption of spinal fluid, which is produced in normal amounts. The exceptions are choroid plexus papillomas in which there is excessive production of spinal fluid.

B. Early diagnosis is important, but care should be taken in diagnosing ventriculomegaly by ultrasonography in a fetus of less than 24 weeks' gestational age. The ratio of ventricular size to biparietal diameter changes with advancing gestation. The distention of the lateral ventricles is usually obvious in advanced cases in which the cerebral mantle of residual cortex is markedly diminished as a result of compression or failure to develop. The diagnosis is less clear-cut in early cases, and one should try to avoid generating anxiety about the condition until it is demonstrated more reliably by serial ultrasonographic observations.

C. There should be a team approach to the management of a patient carrying an infant diagnosed as hydrocephalic. The team should include a perinatologist, neonatologist, geneticist, psychologist, and pediatric neurosurgeon to help evaluate the condition, the extent of brain damage, any concurrent malformations, the ultimate prognosis, and therapeutic options. The patient should be carefully counseled as to the consequences of the fetal condition and of the different treatment modalities.

D. The evaluation of such a fetus should include chromosomal karyotyping, either by amniotic fluid or fetal blood sampling, as well as viral studies and detailed examination for other anomalies.

E. Transabdominal placement of a ventriculoamniotic shunt in utero (p 80) for decompression of the fetal ventricles has not been shown to be consistently or reliably effective.

F. Delivery of a hydrocephalic infant is indicated on the basis of evidence of rapid enlargement of the biparietal diameter by serial ultrasonography. If the patient chooses, early delivery can be considered once pulmonary maturity has been confirmed. If the decision is to await the onset of labor, consider the likelihood of cephalopelvic disproportion due to the large fetal head size. Breech presentation is also commonly associated. If the biparietal diameter is larger than 100 mm, dystocia will probably occur. Ventriculocentesis can be performed under these circumstances to reduce the head size. Drainage of the excess spinal fluid can be achieved either transabdominally or transcervically under ultrasonographic guidance. Rapid decompression of the spinal fluid may be harmful to the fetus. Vaginal delivery can then be expected to follow uneventfully, although fetal survival cannot be guaranteed. Alternatively, if the patient really desires to have her fetus delivered atraumatically to ensure salvage and she fully understands the adverse prognostic implications in regard to long term neurologic and developmental problems, cesarean section may be offered.

References

Birnholz JC, Frigoletto FD. Antenatal treatment of hydrocephalus. New Engl J Med 304:1021, 1981.

Chervenak FA, Berkowitz RL, Tortora M, et al. The diagnosis of ventriculomegaly prior to fetal viability. Obstet Gynecol 64:652, 1984.

Chervenak FA, Berkowitz RL, Tortora M, Hobbins JC. The management of fetal hydrocephalus. Am J Obstet Gynecol 151:933, 1985.

Chervenak FA, Romero R. Is there a role for fetal cephalocentesis in modern obstetrics? Am J Perinatol 1:170, 1984.

Michejda M, Queenan JT, McCollough D. Present status of intrauterine treatment of hydrocephalus and its future. Am J Obstet Gynecol 155:873, 1986.

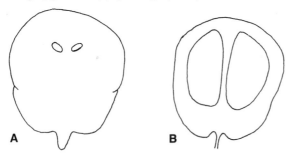

Figure 1 Fetal hydrocephalus can be detected in utero by the ultrasonographic pattern of dilating lateral ventricles. Normal ventricular size at term (*A*) is contrasted with that of a hydrocephalic fetus (*B*) with little residual mantle of cerebral cortex.

SUSPICION OF HYDROCEPHALUS

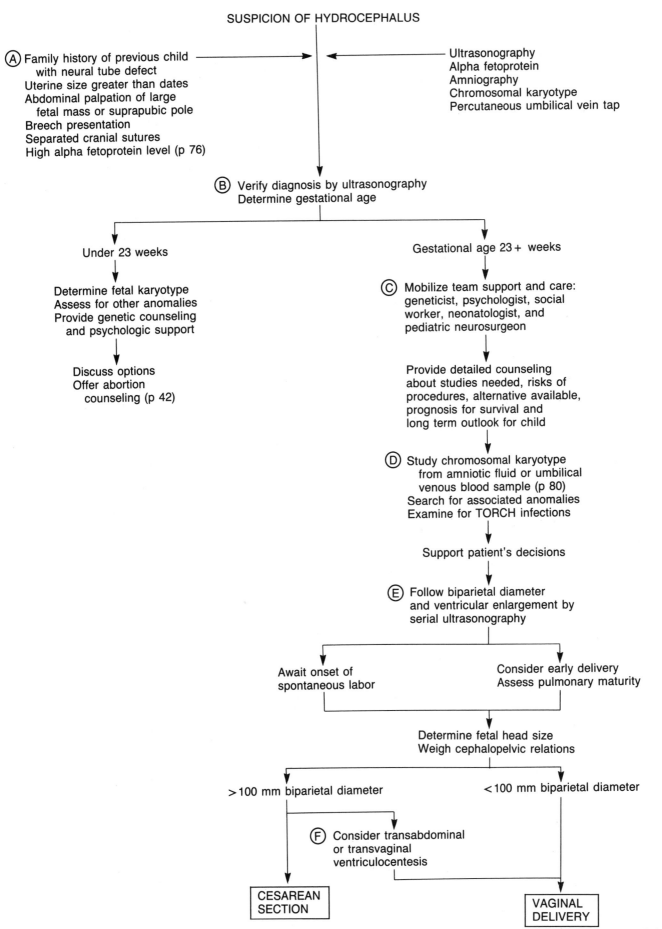

A Family history of previous child
   with neural tube defect
Uterine size greater than dates
Abdominal palpation of large
   fetal mass or suprapubic pole
Breech presentation
Separated cranial sutures
High alpha fetoprotein level (p 76)

Ultrasonography
Alpha fetoprotein
Amniography
Chromosomal karyotype
Percutaneous umbilical vein tap

B Verify diagnosis by ultrasonography
  Determine gestational age

Under 23 weeks

Determine fetal karyotype
Assess for other anomalies
Provide genetic counseling
  and psychologic support

Discuss options
Offer abortion
  counseling (p 42)

Gestational age 23+ weeks

C Mobilize team support and care:
  geneticist, psychologist, social
  worker, neonatologist, and
  pediatric neurosurgeon

Provide detailed counseling
about studies needed, risks of
procedures, alternative available,
prognosis for survival and
long term outlook for child

D Study chromosomal karyotype
  from amniotic fluid or umbilical
  venous blood sample (p 80)
Search for associated anomalies
Examine for TORCH infections

Support patient's decisions

E Follow biparietal diameter
  and ventricular enlargement by
  serial ultrasonography

Await onset of
spontaneous labor

Consider early delivery
Assess pulmonary maturity

Determine fetal head size
Weigh cephalopelvic relations

>100 mm biparietal diameter

<100 mm biparietal diameter

F Consider transabdominal
  or transvaginal
  ventriculocentesis

CESAREAN
SECTION

VAGINAL
DELIVERY

PRENATAL CARE IN MULTIPLE PREGNANCY

Louis Burke, M.D.

A. In the past, no more than half of multiple (or multifetal) pregnancies were correctly diagnosed before labor and delivery. With a high index of suspicion and common use of ultrasonography, the frequency of this error has been markedly reduced. A general impression prevails that there are now more multiple pregnancies. This is based on a small, but real, increase due to use of infertility ovulation-inducing drugs and multiple ovum implantation associated with in vitro fertilization practices. The appearance of more twinning comes from the very early discovery of two or more gestational sacs by ultrasonography in many women who, when followed serially, are found to have absorbed all but the singleton survivor. This phenomenon occurs silently and is likely to have been overlooked in the past. Be alert for factors placing the patient at increased probability of having a multiple pregnancy. Although monozygotic twinning is fairly constant, dizygotic twinning is not. Multiple pregnancies vary among racial groups. Dizygotic twinning is more common among blacks than among whites and least common among orientals. Twinning is correlated with advancing maternal age and with increased parity. Heredity is especially important; a maternal family history is a strong risk factor for twins, especially if the gravida herself is a twin.

B. Suspect multiple pregnancy in patients with presenting risk factors. Watch for it in patients who conceive by in vitro fertilization or while taking infertility drugs. If the uterus is found to be larger than expected by dates, if the serum alpha fetoprotein level is high, if the fetal heart tones are difficult to hear, if the fetal heart is heard in different areas, especially at different rates, if the fetus is difficult to palpate, if one can detect only fetal limbs, or if two disparate fetal poles are felt, proceed with ultrasonography for clarification. Examine the fetuses carefully for malformations. Weight discordance and hydramnios in one fetal sac (often with oligohydramnios in the other) may develop as the pregnancy proceeds, suggesting a twin-twin transfusion syndrome. The hypertransfused recipient fetus is larger, hypervolemic, hyperviscous, and polycythemic with hydramnios and even heart failure, while the underperfused twin becomes growth retarded and anemic. Intervention may be needed to salvage the fetuses before one or the other succumbs, provided they are sufficiently mature to survive. Sophisticated ultrasonographic techniques now permit delineation of the layers of the membranes intervening between fetuses to help determine zygosity. Of special importance is the diagnosis of monoamniotic twinning because of the high frequency of cord and placental complications.

C. The presence of multiple pregnancies leads to an increase in both maternal and fetal complications. Maternal anemia and malnutrition are the result of failure to meet the increased iron, folic acid, and protein requirements; 60 to 100 mg of iron and 300 calories of added dietary intake each day usually suffice. Frequent hemoglobin or hematocrit determinations are essential to detect developing anemia. Urine cultures are also needed in each trimester to reveal urinary tract infections so that they can be treated. Pregnancy induced hypertension occurs more often, is usually more severe, and arises earlier in multiple pregnancies than in singletons. Frequent rest periods with the patient lying on her left side should be encouraged. Both abruptio placentae and placenta previa are possible complications of multiple pregnancy and should be sought.

D. All measures to avoid prematurity should be undertaken (p 176). Screen for urinary tract infections, anemia, and pregnancy induced hypertension to permit initiation of aggressive care as early as possible. Watch for silent cervical dilatation (p 52). In general, hospitalization in the last trimester for bed rest has not been especially beneficial, and complications have occurred more often than in patients whose activities were merely limited at home. The prophylactic use of tocolysis, cerclage, or oral progesterone regimens, although advocated by some, has not been shown to be consistently helpful, although these approaches may be considered for their therapeutic value if clearly indicated.

References

O'Connor MC, Arias E, Royston JP, Dalrymple IJ. The merits of special antenatal care for twin pregnancy. Br J Obstet Gynaecol 88:222, 1981.

O'Leary JA. Prophylactic tocolysis of twins. Am J Obstet Gynecol 154:904, 1986.

Patkos P, Boucher M, Broussard PM, et al. Factors influencing nonstress test results in multiple gestations. Am J Obstet Gynecol 154:1107, 1986.

Saunders MC, Dick JS, Brown IM, et al. The effects of hospital admission for bed rest on the duration of twin pregnancy: A randomised trial. Lancet 2:793, 1985.

Secher NJ, Kaern J, Hansen PK. Intrauterine growth in twin pregnancies: Prediction of fetal growth retardation. Obstet Gynecol 66:63, 1985.

SUSPICION OF MULTIPLE PREGNANCY

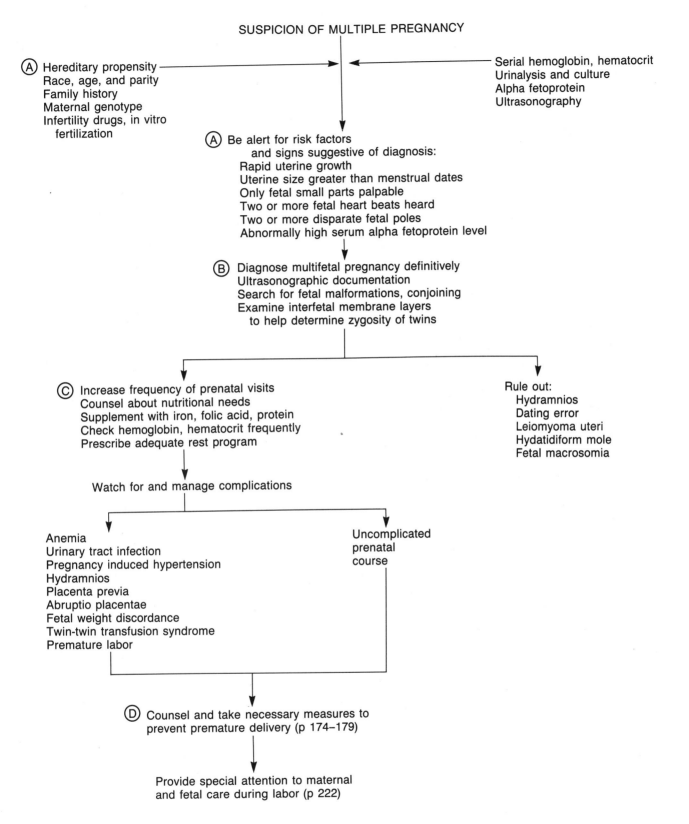

(A) Hereditary propensity
Race, age, and parity
Family history
Maternal genotype
Infertility drugs, in vitro
fertilization

Serial hemoglobin, hematocrit
Urinalysis and culture
Alpha fetoprotein
Ultrasonography

(A) Be alert for risk factors
and signs suggestive of diagnosis:
Rapid uterine growth
Uterine size greater than menstrual dates
Only fetal small parts palpable
Two or more fetal heart beats heard
Two or more disparate fetal poles
Abnormally high serum alpha fetoprotein level

(B) Diagnose multifetal pregnancy definitively
Ultrasonographic documentation
Search for fetal malformations, conjoining
Examine interfetal membrane layers
to help determine zygosity of twins

(C) Increase frequency of prenatal visits
Counsel about nutritional needs
Supplement with iron, folic acid, protein
Check hemoglobin, hematocrit frequently
Prescribe adequate rest program

Rule out:
Hydramnios
Dating error
Leiomyoma uteri
Hydatidiform mole
Fetal macrosomia

Watch for and manage complications

Anemia
Urinary tract infection
Pregnancy induced hypertension
Hydramnios
Placenta previa
Abruptio placentae
Fetal weight discordance
Twin-twin transfusion syndrome
Premature labor

Uncomplicated
prenatal
course

(D) Counsel and take necessary measures to
prevent premature delivery (p 174–179)

Provide special attention to maternal
and fetal care during labor (p 222)

INTRAPARTUM MANAGEMENT OF MULTIPLE PREGNANCY

Louis Burke, M.D.

A. Even optimal prenatal care (p 220) leaves gravidas with multiple pregnancy at increased risk. Consider multiple pregnancy a high risk condition that warrants special care, skill, and facilities. A number of potentially serious prenatal problems may develop, such as pregnancy induced hypertension, acute hydramnios, intrauterine growth retardation, and premature labor, enhanced by a marked increase in blood volume, an elevated diaphragm, respiratory embarrassment, diminished cardiac output (exaggerated supine hypotension syndrome), ureteral obstruction, and postpartum hemorrhage. Pulmonary edema may result from beta adrenergic drugs to control premature labor given with corticosteroids to accelerate fetal pulmonary maturity.

B. Consider transferring the patient to a tertiary care center. Ensure the constant availability of an obstetrician to recognize and deal with problems promptly in labor and at least two for the delivery. An anesthesiologist should be ready if anesthesia becomes necessary for operative intervention or intrauterine manipulation. The team requires two individuals per fetus for resuscitation of the newborn infants. Prepare an adequate intravenous line for rapid access. Monitor both fetuses throughout labor, if possible, by a combination of external and internal electronic methods. It is imperative that the facilities be equipped to permit emergency intervention as conditions dictate.

C. Fetal risks are multiplied for triplets, quadruplets, and quintuplets. Aside from their enhanced risks of premature birth, placental and cord complications, and disordered labor, one or more of the fetuses is almost always found in a malpresentation. Accordingly elective cesarean section is now widely practiced beyond 36 weeks. Awaiting the onset of spontaneous labor in these cases is judged to be less preferable because it does not permit orderly planning and mobilization of personnel and resources. Determine how many fetuses there are by careful ultrasonography. Except for twins, fetal presentations are really not relevant because spatial rearrangement is likely to occur seriatim as each fetus descends and is delivered. Planning the management of twins requires information about the presentations; if the presentation of either is unfavorable, it warrants cesarean section. Although it is possible that the second twin will

correct its malpresentation as the first twin is born, it is preferable to deliver by cesarean section because it avoids the potential hazards of a cesarean section, which may have to be done under suboptimal emergency conditions.

D. The delivery of the first twin is conducted just as if it were a singleton, minimizing analgesia for labor and anesthesia for the delivery. Use local or pudendal block anesthesia, but have general anesthesia available for rapid induction if the delivery of the second twin should require it. Do not clamp and cut a nuchal cord because it may be the cord of the second twin; gently slip it over the infant's head and proceed with the delivery.

E. Promptly after the first twin is born, undertake a vaginal examination to determine the presentation of the second twin. If it is still a longitudinal lie, rupture the membranes and guide the presenting part into the pelvis. Apply a scalp electrode for continuous internal monitoring and permit labor to continue until delivery is accomplished. If it is now a transverse lie and the membranes are still intact, consider external cephalic version. It is likely that the version will not be successful at this late stage, but it is worth trying because cesarean section can be done promptly if a complication arises. Alternatively one may proceed directly to cesarean section.

F. Guide the presenting part into the pelvis, rupture the membranes, and apply a scalp electrode for fetal heart rate monitoring. Allow labor to evolve under close surveillance. Vaginal delivery can be expected provided no cord or placental complications occur.

References

Acker D, Lieberman M, Holbrook, et al. Delivery of second twin. Obstet Gynecol 59:710, 1982.

Chervenak FA, Johnson RE, Berkowitz RL, Hobbins JC. Intrapartum external version of the second twin. Obstet Gynecol 62:160, 1983.

Chervenak FA, Johnson RB, Berkowitz RL, et al. Is routine cesarean section necessary for vertex-breech and vertex-transverse twin gestations? Am J Obstet Gynecol 148:1, 1984.

Chervenak FA, Johnson RE, Youcha S, et al. Intrapartum management of twin gestation. Obstet Gynecol 65:119, 1985.

MULTIPLE PREGNANCY IN LABOR

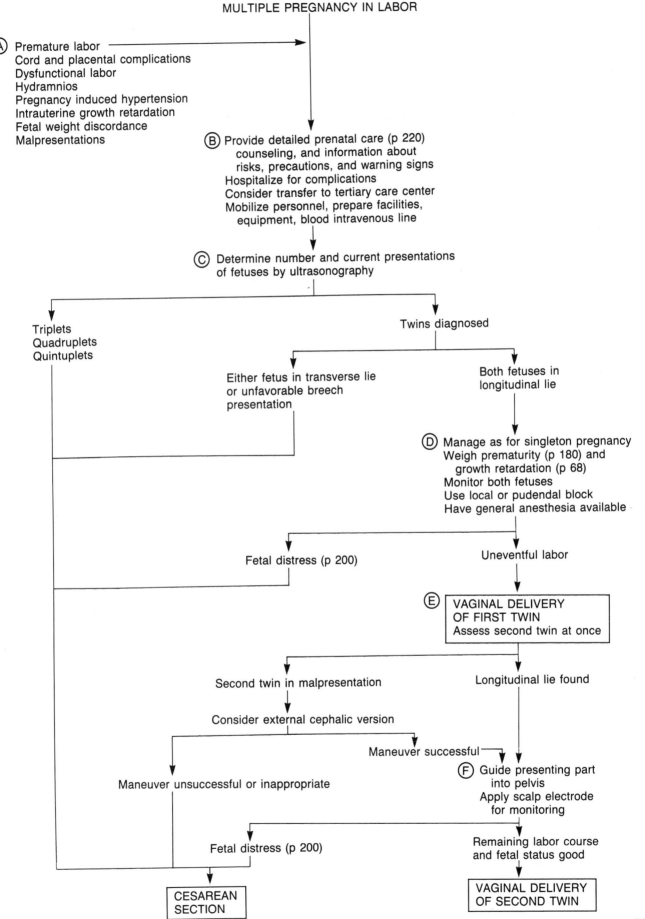

Ⓐ Premature labor
Cord and placental complications
Dysfunctional labor
Hydramnios
Pregnancy induced hypertension
Intrauterine growth retardation
Fetal weight discordance
Malpresentations

Ⓑ Provide detailed prenatal care (p 220)
counseling, and information about
risks, precautions, and warning signs
Hospitalize for complications
Consider transfer to tertiary care center
Mobilize personnel, prepare facilities,
equipment, blood intravenous line

Ⓒ Determine number and current presentations
of fetuses by ultrasonography

Triplets
Quadruplets
Quintuplets

Twins diagnosed

Either fetus in transverse lie
or unfavorable breech
presentation

Both fetuses in
longitudinal lie

Ⓓ Manage as for singleton pregnancy
Weigh prematurity (p 180) and
growth retardation (p 68)
Monitor both fetuses
Use local or pudendal block
Have general anesthesia available

Fetal distress (p 200)

Uneventful labor

Ⓔ VAGINAL DELIVERY
OF FIRST TWIN
Assess second twin at once

Second twin in malpresentation

Consider external cephalic version

Longitudinal lie found

Maneuver successful

Maneuver unsuccessful or inappropriate

Ⓕ Guide presenting part
into pelvis
Apply scalp electrode
for monitoring

Fetal distress (p 200)

Remaining labor course
and fetal status good

CESAREAN
SECTION

VAGINAL DELIVERY
OF SECOND TWIN

LARGE FETUS

David B. Acker, M.D.

A. Fetal macrosomia is defined arbitrarily as 4,000 g or more. It is associated with multiparity, older maternal age, marked obesity, rapid weight gain, diabetes mellitus, and post-term pregnancy, but the predictive value of any single risk factor is low, involving only 6 percent of gestational diabetics, 10 percent of the markedly obese, and 21 percent of post-term gravidas.

B. If unable to evaluate uterine size confidently, carry out ultrasonography, which can rule out multiple pregnancy, hydramnios, leiomyoma uteri, and misdating of gestational duration. Estimating fetal size by ultrasonography, although somewhat more accurate than by physical examination, has a wide range of inherent error (see D).

C. If a glucose screening test is not being routinely performed in all gravidas, the suspicion of a large fetus should now prompt a one hour glucose loading test (obtain a blood glucose level one hour after a 50 g oral glucose intake). If necessary, this is followed by a full three hour glucose tolerance test. Some consider that documenting the presence of a macrosomic fetus in a diabetic gravida is an indication for cesarean section, but the issue is as yet unresolved. It is rationalized on the basis of the high risk of shoulder dystocia and resulting neonatal complications (see F).

D. Physical examination of the maternal abdomen permits the obstetrician to distinguish between small, average, and above average singleton fetuses. Ultrasonography is an improvement upon physical examination; however, regardless of the formulas utilized and the expertise of the evaluating ultrasonographer, the ability to diagnose macrosomia is far from reliable. A 25 percent average error is accepted, and it is probably greater at extremes of fetal weight. Clinicians must avoid the temptation to make management decisions solely on the basis of ultrasonographic data to the exclusion of clinical judgment.

E. Two management plans, which form the focus of much current controversy, attempt to avoid the potential risks of labor and vaginal delivery with a macrosomic fetus. One subjects the gravida with a ripe cervix and a large term fetus to elective induction; the other undertakes cesarean section in the gravida with a fetus estimated to weigh over 4,500 or 5,000 g. Neither plan can yet be recommended as a general policy, although individual patient needs occasionally may be served best by adopting one or the other of these choices. Examples include gravidas who are diabetic or have a contracted pelvis or malpresentation.

F. The most common complication of macrosomia is obstructed labor requiring cesarean section. X-ray pelvimetry should be reserved (if it is necessary to use at all) for laboring gravidas who experience active phase or second stage labor disorders (p 238, 240). Clinical examination of the dynamic relationship between the pelvis and the fetal head is often sufficient to diagnose cephalopelvic disproportion (p 24). An arrest or protraction disorder arising in a gravida with a fetus that is clearly too large to be accommodated by the maternal pelvis warrants cesarean section.

G. Neonatal complications include meconium aspiration, facial or brachial palsy, long bone and skull fractures, and low Apgar scores. These are mainly, but not exclusively, associated with shoulder dystocia (p 250). Vaginal and cervical lacerations and postpartum hemorrhage from uterine atony or rupture are also encountered. The necessary personnel should be summoned in anticipation of these complications to ensure optimal care, especially as regards management of shoulder dystocia. Expert pediatric care is essential as well to deal with the birth injuries, hypoglycemia, respiratory distress, and hyperbilirubinemia to which macrosomal infants appear to be prone.

References

Acker DB, Sachs BP, Friedman EA. Risk factors for shoulder dystocia. Obstet Gynecol 66:762, 1985.

Boyd ME, Usher RH, McLean FH. Fetal macrosomia: Prediction, risks, proposed management. Obstet Gynecol 61:715, 1983.

Shepard MJ, Richards VA, Berkowitz RL, et al. An evaluation of two equations for predicting fetal weight by ultrasound. Am J Obstet Gynecol 142:47, 1982.

Spellacy WN, Miller S, Winegar A, Peterson PQ. Macrosomia: Maternal characteristics and infant complications. Obstet Gynecol 66:158, 1985.

Tamura RK, Sabbagha RE, Depp D, et al. Diabetic macrosomia: Accuracy of third trimester ultrasound. Obstet Gynecol 67:828, 1986.

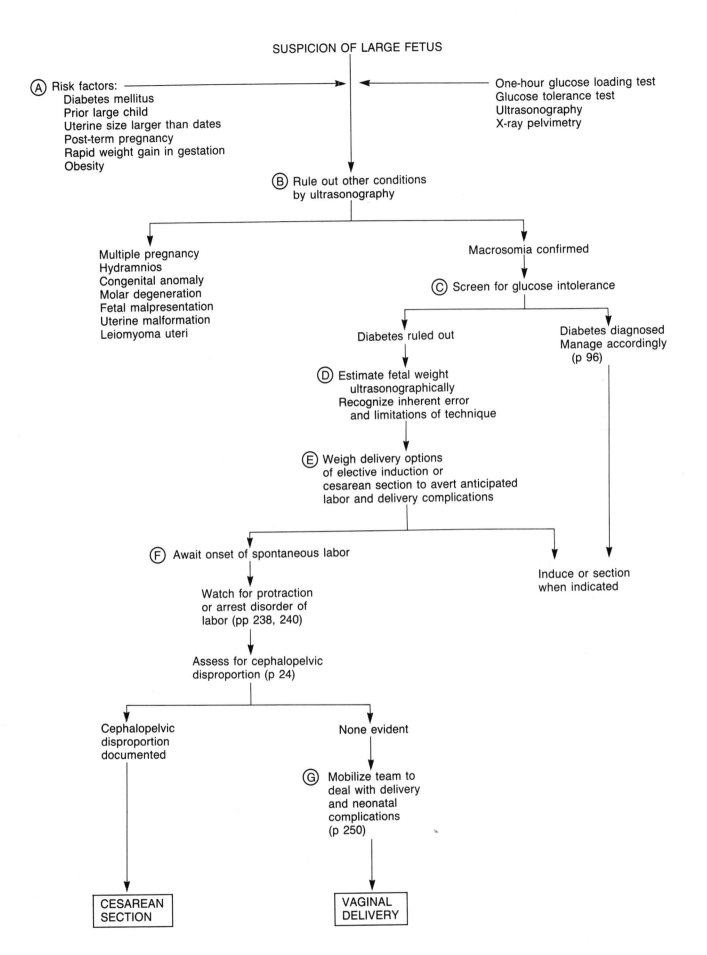

SUSPICION OF LARGE FETUS

Ⓐ Risk factors:
   Diabetes mellitus
   Prior large child
   Uterine size larger than dates
   Post-term pregnancy
   Rapid weight gain in gestation
   Obesity

One-hour glucose loading test
Glucose tolerance test
Ultrasonography
X-ray pelvimetry

Ⓑ Rule out other conditions
   by ultrasonography

Multiple pregnancy
Hydramnios
Congenital anomaly
Molar degeneration
Fetal malpresentation
Uterine malformation
Leiomyoma uteri

Macrosomia confirmed

Ⓒ Screen for glucose intolerance

Diabetes ruled out

Diabetes diagnosed
Manage accordingly
(p 96)

Ⓓ Estimate fetal weight
   ultrasonographically
   Recognize inherent error
   and limitations of technique

Ⓔ Weigh delivery options
   of elective induction or
   cesarean section to avert anticipated
   labor and delivery complications

Ⓕ Await onset of spontaneous labor

Induce or section
when indicated

Watch for protraction
or arrest disorder of
labor (pp 238, 240)

Assess for cephalopelvic
disproportion (p 24)

Cephalopelvic
disproportion
documented

None evident

Ⓖ Mobilize team to
   deal with delivery
   and neonatal
   complications
   (p 250)

CESAREAN
SECTION

VAGINAL
DELIVERY

INTRAUTERINE FETAL DEATH

Benjamin P. Sachs, M.B., B.S., D.P.H.

A. Once intrauterine fetal death has been clearly documented, the patient must be carefully counseled and consoled (p 228). Consider delaying the evacuation procedure to allow the patient to adjust psychologically to the loss (p 42, 228). Delay has the additional advantage of giving the cervix the opportunity to become more favorable. If delivery does not occur promptly after fetal demise, especially in late pregnancy, maternal coagulopathy may result, although it seldom occurs before four to six weeks have elapsed. After three weeks, obtain a clotting profile that includes a platelet count, fibrinogen level, prothrombin time, partial thromboplastin time, and fibrinogen degradation product analysis, and follow serially. Administer Rh immune globulin to all Rh negative gravidas undergoing evacuation unless the father of the fetus is definitely known to be Rh negative. Give a microdose (30 μg) in the first trimester and a full dose in later pregnancy.

B. Application of routine ultrasonography in early pregnancy has demonstrated that fetal death occurs with twin gestations more often than previously appreciated. It is usually asymptomatic, although some vaginal staining may appear. No intervention is needed and uneventful resorption of the affected fetus can be expected. Maternal hypofibrinogenemia is a rare complication and should be watched for in these cases. Consumption coagulopathy can also develop in the living twin. This suggests prompt delivery if the death of one twin occurs in late pregnancy and the maturity of the other twin is assured by amniotic fluid studies of the indices of pulmonary function.

C. Prostaglandin E$_2$ vaginal suppositories (20 mg every three to five hours) are effective for evacuation of a dead fetus in midpregnancy. Although the incidence of success is high, retained placenta may require suction curettage. One can use an intramuscular dose of 15-methylprostaglandin F$_2\alpha$ (250 μg at one and one-half to three and one-half hour intervals) if the membranes rupture. Adjust the dosage schedule to avoid overstimulation. Failure suggests a uterine anomaly. Have aminophylline and terbutaline available to treat bronchospasm if prostaglandins are being given to an asth-

matic. The simultaneous use of oxytocin must be avoided because it risks uterine rupture.

D. If sufficient time has passed since the fetal demise, the uterine size may decrease enough to permit suction evacuation to be performed safely. A coagulation profile, as already described, should be obtained. If it is abnormal, treat the coagulopathy (p 114) and proceed to evacuate. About 85 percent begin labor within two to three weeks. If coagulopathy develops, heparin can be administered to correct it before expediting uterine evacuation, but the use of heparin in these circumstances is not entirely free of hazard. Hysterotomy is almost never indicated unless there has been a previous cesarean birth or myomectomy. The management must be individualized in these cases. Transcervical instrumental evacuation of an advanced second trimester pregnancy requires special skills and experience to avoid perforation and hemorrhage (p 44). Laminaria may be useful beforehand in these cases.

E. All Rh negative gravidas should be given Rh immune globulin (p 138). If an interval of more than 72 hours is anticipated between the fetal demise and delivery, give the appropriate dose immediately. Postdelivery counseling is an important part of the total care of the patient (p 228). Every effort should be made to obtain permission for fetal autopsy, karyotyping, and other indicated studies.

References

Altman AM, Stubblefield PG, Schlam JR. Midtrimester abortion and vacuum evacuation on a teaching service. J Reprod Med 30:601, 1985.

Huisjes HJ. Spontaneous Abortion. New York: Churchill Livingstone, 1984.

Meier PR, Manchester DK, Shikes RH, et al. Perinatal autopsy: Its clinical value. Obstet Gynecol 67:349, 1986.

Romero R, Duffy TP, Berkowitz RL, et al. Prolongation of a preterm pregnancy complicated by death of a single twin in utero and disseminated intravascular coagulation: Effects of treatment with heparin. New Engl J Med 310:772, 1984.

SUSPICION OF FETAL DEATH

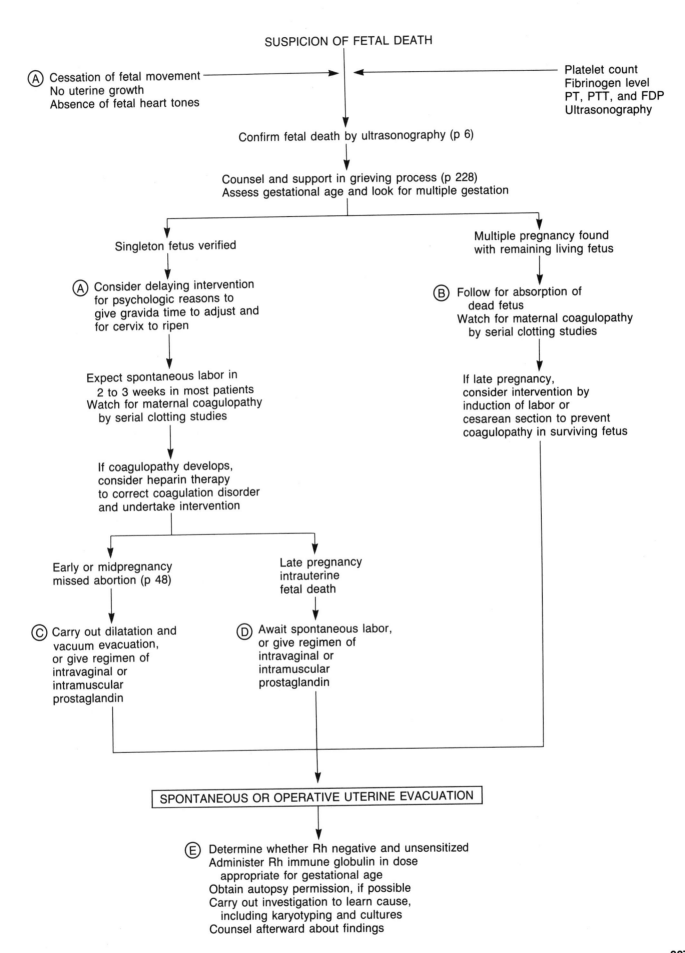

Ⓐ Cessation of fetal movement
No uterine growth
Absence of fetal heart tones

Platelet count
Fibrinogen level
PT, PTT, and FDP
Ultrasonography

Confirm fetal death by ultrasonography (p 6)

Counsel and support in grieving process (p 228)
Assess gestational age and look for multiple gestation

Singleton fetus verified

Multiple pregnancy found
with remaining living fetus

Ⓐ Consider delaying intervention
for psychologic reasons to
give gravida time to adjust and
for cervix to ripen

Ⓑ Follow for absorption of
dead fetus
Watch for maternal coagulopathy
by serial clotting studies

Expect spontaneous labor in
2 to 3 weeks in most patients
Watch for maternal coagulopathy
by serial clotting studies

If late pregnancy,
consider intervention by
induction of labor or
cesarean section to prevent
coagulopathy in surviving fetus

If coagulopathy develops,
consider heparin therapy
to correct coagulation disorder
and undertake intervention

Early or midpregnancy
missed abortion (p 48)

Late pregnancy
intrauterine
fetal death

Ⓒ Carry out dilatation and
vacuum evacuation,
or give regimen of
intravaginal or
intramuscular
prostaglandin

Ⓓ Await spontaneous labor,
or give regimen of
intravaginal or
intramuscular
prostaglandin

SPONTANEOUS OR OPERATIVE UTERINE EVACUATION

Ⓔ Determine whether Rh negative and unsensitized
Administer Rh immune globulin in dose
appropriate for gestational age
Obtain autopsy permission, if possible
Carry out investigation to learn cause,
including karyotyping and cultures
Counsel afterward about findings

ASSESSMENT OF GRIEF

Maureen J. McRae, R.N.

A. Fetal death, regardless of the length of the gestation, is always associated with some degree of grief. All health care providers must be sensitive to the individual needs of the patient and her family. The work of grief resolution begins at the time the fetal death is verified; it continues through the delivery and may extend for months and occasionally for years afterward. The separate stages of the grief response overlap, intertwine, and recur at different times for different individuals. The initial disbelief and denial evolve into physical symptoms, changes in social behavior, and a sense of loneliness, all of which blend into feelings of guilt, hostility, anger, and emptiness. Eventually the patient and her family accept the death and integrate the pain of the loss into their lives as they resume normal relations and activities. Provide support and reassure them that such symptoms are normal.

B. For some, immediate delivery is necessary or desired; for others, a period of delay, if medically acceptable, may aid in the adjustment to the loss. Encourage involvement in labor-delivery planning to help establish the reality of the event.

C. Sedation and analgesia should be kept to the minimum necessary for comfort. Oversedation should be avoided because normal grieving is facilitated by ensuring that the patient is able to experience the technical aspects of the delivery and identify the physical appearance of the fetus. First prepare the gravida and her partner for the appearance of the infant and then encourage them to see, touch, and hold it at a time that seems right for them. The baby should be cleaned and wrapped appropriately so that viewing will emphasize normalcy. An initial reluctance to view and hold the child should be accepted by the staff, but the patient should be assured that she can change her mind. It is useful to photograph the baby, emphasizing its most normal characteristics. The picture should be offered to the parents; if refused, store it in the patient's records for future retrieval if requested. Formally naming the baby may serve to establish its identity for grieving purposes.

D. Private hospital accommodations should be made available if requested by the patient to help with the personal and family grieving process, care being taken to avoid feelings of isolation and abandonment. Nurses skilled in specific postpartum care for grieving parents should be assigned to the couple. The choice of a room in the postpartum or gynecology unit can be made by the patient. Complete all administrative details related to postmortem examination, interment, and genetic tissue studies while the patient is still in the hospital.

E. Normal grief encompasses transient somatic disturbances, guilt, hostility, and anger as well as a period in which there is a breakdown of normal patterns of behavior or conduct. The patient should be advised that these are not abnormal reactions; she should also be encouraged to verbalize her feelings and offered professional counseling or referral to a support group if needed.

F. It is important to be aware of abnormal grief responses. One must recognize when recovery from grief is delayed, anger and hostility are increasing, depression is growing deeper and more agitated, antisocial or destructive behavior is developing, and normal social or work patterns are not being re-established. Once these pathologic manifestations are recognized, prompt professional counseling is essential.

G. The grieving process should be completed before the parents seriously consider another pregnancy. The death must be fully acknowledged and integrated to ensure that the next child will be considered an independent person.

References

Grief Related to Perinatal Death. Technical Bulletin No. 86. Washington, DC: American College of Obstetricians and Gynecologists, 1985.

Friedman R, Gradstein B. Surviving Pregnancy Loss. Boston: Little, Brown, 1982.

Furlong RM, Hobbins JC. Grief in the perinatal period. Obstet Gynecol 61:497, 1983.

McRae M. Condemned to loneliness: A necessary maternity care decree? Am J Mat Child Nurs 2:374, 1977.

FETAL DEATH VERIFIED

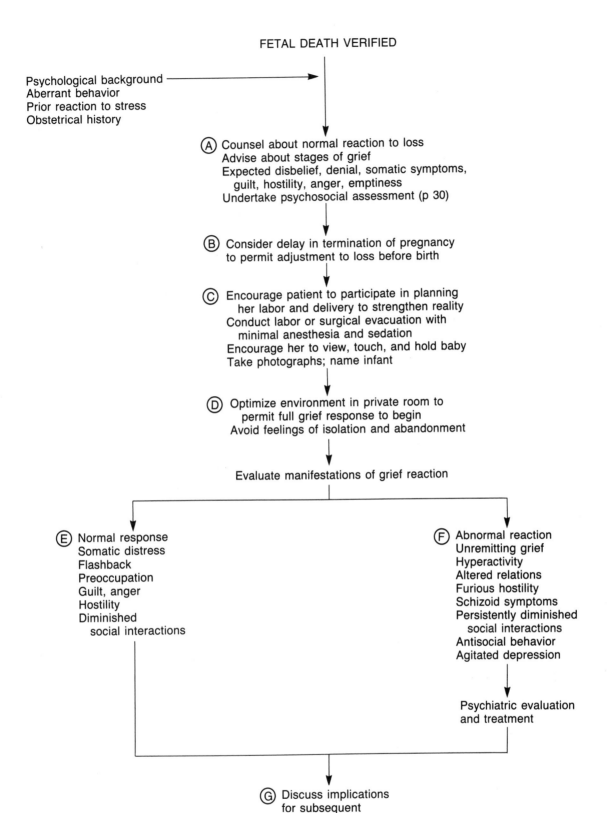

Psychological background
Aberrant behavior
Prior reaction to stress
Obstetrical history

Ⓐ Counsel about normal reaction to loss
    Advise about stages of grief
    Expected disbelief, denial, somatic symptoms,
        guilt, hostility, anger, emptiness
    Undertake psychosocial assessment (p 30)

Ⓑ Consider delay in termination of pregnancy
    to permit adjustment to loss before birth

Ⓒ Encourage patient to participate in planning
    her labor and delivery to strengthen reality
    Conduct labor or surgical evacuation with
        minimal anesthesia and sedation
    Encourage her to view, touch, and hold baby
    Take photographs; name infant

Ⓓ Optimize environment in private room to
    permit full grief response to begin
    Avoid feelings of isolation and abandonment

Evaluate manifestations of grief reaction

Ⓔ Normal response
    Somatic distress
    Flashback
    Preoccupation
    Guilt, anger
    Hostility
    Diminished
        social interactions

Ⓕ Abnormal reaction
    Unremitting grief
    Hyperactivity
    Altered relations
    Furious hostility
    Schizoid symptoms
    Persistently diminished
        social interactions
    Antisocial behavior
    Agitated depression

Psychiatric evaluation
and treatment

Ⓖ Discuss implications
    for subsequent
    pregnancies

RUPTURED UTERUS

Lynn H. Galen, M.D.

A. Uterine rupture can occur in a uterus scarred by surgery or spontaneously (but rarely) in an unscarred uterus. High incidences of morbidity and mortality are seen. Predisposing factors include uterine surgery, intrauterine manipulation, oxytocin hyperstimulation, obstructed labor, and abdominal trauma (p 124).

B. Before delivery, watch for vaginal bleeding, abdominal tenderness, tachycardia, and cessation of uterine contractions and fetal heart tones. Hematuria may result from bladder or ureteral trauma. After delivery, unresponsive bleeding may lead to circulatory collapse, often out of proportion to the amount of blood lost externally. Increasing abdominal girth from intra-abdominal bleeding is a late sign. Clinical patterns vary considerably, but one must recognize the need for operative intervention quickly. Insert at least two large bore intravenous catheters, one of which can serve for monitoring central venous pressure, for the large fluid volumes likely to be necessary.

C. Rupture of a low transverse cesarean section scar is almost always limited to asymptomatic dehiscence seen as an incidental finding at the time of repeat cesarean section. If discovered after a vaginal delivery by uterine exploration, it does not necessarily require any form of treatment. It is perhaps unwise, therefore, to explore manually lest the manipulation produce or extend the dehiscence. Rupture through a low segment vertical scar confined to the noncontractile portion of the uterus probably can be managed in the same way with the same good prognosis. However, some low vertical incisions do extend into the contractile miduterus, and they therefore may behave like classic scars. Rupture of a classic cesarean section scar occurs much more often and with more serious consequences; about one-third rupture prior to the onset of labor. Because of this hazard, a trial of labor to attempt vaginal delivery is contraindicated after classic cesarean section (p 272).

D. The treatment should be individualized according to the type, location, and extent of the uterine laceration. After a successful vaginal delivery, a small asymptomatic lower uterine segment defect (less than 2 cm in size) usually can be treated expectantly. In all other cases evaluate the patient's condition to determine whether immediate surgery is needed. If the patient's condition is stable, there is time to prepare her optimally for the surgery and to discuss the available options. Take the opportunity to mobilize the necessary resources, correct hypovolemia, obtain informed consent, and proceed with surgery in a deliberate fashion without undue haste or risk. If the condition deteriorates, more rapid intervention may become necessary.

E. Although there are no long term studies regarding the outcome of future pregnancies to help determine the best form of management, it is clear that these women are at some increased risk for uterine rupture. Given their frightening experience, it seems prudent to recommend against attempting vaginal delivery again.

F. Life threatening blood loss may be stemmed by direct transabdominal compression of the aorta. This can be done with the hand through an intact abdominal wall. At laparotomy, proceed to clamp the ovarian arteries adjacent to the uterus. Hypogastric or uterine artery ligation can be done as well if bleeding continues (p 272). If conditions warrant and the patient desires to preserve her childbearing capacity, it may be possible to deal with a clean linear laceration by freshening the edges and simply repairing it with well placed sutures. Once hemostasis is achieved, evaluate and proceed as needed. If the laceration extends into the broad ligament and a large hematoma forms, indiscriminate clamping is inadvisable because it risks injury to the ureter and iliac vessels. Under these circumstances hysterectomy is preferable. If the cervix and vagina are uninvolved and the patient's status is marginal, consider suprapubic hysterectomy.

References

Cotton DB. Infant survival with prolonged uterine rupture. Am J Obstet Gynecol 142:1059, 1982.

Lavin JP, Stephens RJ, Miodovnik M, Barden TP. Vaginal delivery in patients with a prior cesarean section. Obstet Gynecol 59:135, 1982.

Plauché WC, Von Almen W, Muller R. Catastrophic uterine rupture. Obstet Gynecol 64:792, 1984.

Zuidema LJ, Goldkrand JW, Work BA. Uterine contractility after rupture of the gravid uterus: A case report. Am J Obstet Gynecol 150:783, 1984.

PATIENT WITH SUSPICION OF RUPTURED UTERUS

(A) Previous uterine surgery
Oxytocin hyperstimulation
Obstructed labor
Abdominal trauma
Acute abdominal pain
Circulatory collapse

Serial hematocrit
Coagulation studies
Type and cross match blood
Central venous pressure
Swan-Ganz catheter

(B) Assess patient's cardiovascular status,
degree of blood loss, ongoing hemorrhage
Establish good intravenous lines for access
Begin intravascular volume replacement
Monitor with central venous pressure
or Swan-Ganz catheter

Rapid hemodynamic evaluation

(C) Incidental finding
at cesarean section
Dehiscence of scar

Hemodynamically stable
Normal or compensated
cardiovascular signs

Hemodynamically unstable
Hypotension, tachycardia,
poor tissue perfusion

(D) Monitor carefully
Assess size and location
of uterine rupture
hematoma formation,
broad ligament extension,
continued bleeding,
any change in status

(F) Stopgap hemostatic measures
Apply aortic compression
Uterine anteflexion,
elevation, compression

Condition remains
stable and process
warrants review
and planning

Condition progresses
Bleeding increases
Status now unstable

Weigh options
Uterine repair versus
extirpation

EXPLORATORY LAPAROTOMY
HYPOGASTRIC AND OVARIAN
ARTERY LIGATIONS

DEBRIDE AND
REPAIR RENT

(E) Advise of risk to
future pregnancies

TOTAL OR SUPRACERVICAL
HYSTERECTOMY

FEVER IN LABOR

Balmookoot Balgobin, M.D.

A. Factors predisposing to infection in labor include poor socioeconomic status and hygiene, severe anemia, poorly controlled diabetes, sickle cell disease, chronic renal or respiratory disease, premature rupture of the membranes, prolonged labor, and multiple vaginal examinations. Internal monitoring, especially with use of an intrauterine pressure catheter, may also place the patient at increased risk. Be alert to localizing symptoms that point to the source. Physical examination may help differentiate appendicitis, pyelonephritis, pneumonia, viremia, or other infection from chorioamnionitis.

B. The most common cause of temperature elevation in labor is dehydration, unless measures are routinely taken to ensure good fluid balance. Rapid intravenous infusion is useful as a therapeutic trial while diagnostic investigations are being simultaneously pursued.

C. A cervical or high vaginal swab for smear and culture may provide helpful information in some cases (e.g., for detection of group B streptococci). Blood cultures are obtained to identify the organisms responsible for bacteremia, especially at the time of a fever spike or when the patient exhibits chills or rigors. In addition, it is most important to rule out amnionitis by examining the amniotic fluid. A sample can be obtained transcervically or, if necessary, by amniocentesis. This is good practice even in the presence of signs suggesting an extrauterine source of infection. Gram staining is useful for demonstrating bacteria and polymorphonuclear leukocytes. The fluid should be cultured as well.

D. The choice of antibiotic therapy is guided by the results of the culture and the sensitivity tests. However, one cannot wait for the results before initiating treatment. Gram staining of smears may help to decide about initial therapy; it can be modified later when the laboratory results are available. One must take into account the undesirable side effects of some antibiotics on the mother and fetus. Because of the risk of kernicterus from hyperbilirubinemia, avoid sulfonamides near term. Tetracycline may cause dysplasia of bone and discoloration of the deciduous teeth; in large doses tetracycline may precipitate jaundice, azotemia, and pancreatitis in the gravida who has impaired renal function. Streptomycin, kanamycin, and gentamicin can be nephrotoxic and ototoxic. Chloramphenicol may produce serious fetal blood dyscrasia, and nitrofurantoin may cause hemolytic anemia in individuals with glucose-6-phosphate dehydrogenase deficiency.

E. In the patient with intrapartum fever due to amnionitis, it is desirable to achieve a short diagnosis-to-delivery interval, preferably under eight to 12 hours. Use oxytocin augmentation, if indicated. After taking cultures, combat the infection by initiating antibiotic therapy. Consider using a combination of antibiotics, such as ampicillin (1 g intravenously every four hours) and gentamicin (80 mg intravenously every eight hours), adding clindamycin after delivery to provide adequate antibiotic coverage for the mixed flora of postpartum endometritis (p 258).

F. One should strive for a spontaneous vaginal delivery whenever possible, because cesarean section is associated with a significant increase in complications, including a five- to tenfold increase in postpartum endometritis relative to vaginal delivery. Intervention is reserved for strict obstetrical indications. In the presence of infection, one should be careful to avoid traumatizing maternal tissues. Thus, instrumentation by forceps, a Credé maneuver or forceful massage, and manual removal of the placenta should be avoided if possible. Check carefully for injuries of the genital tract and repair any lacerations encountered. At the time of delivery, appropriate cultures should be obtained from the mother, infant, and placenta. One should alert the pediatrician beforehand so that appropriate neonatal management can be instituted promptly. Needless to say, good aseptic technique is essential at all times.

References

Bobitt JR, Ledger WJ. Amniotic fluid analysis: Its role in maternal and neonatal infection. Obstet Gynecol 51:56, 1978.

Gibbs RS, Castillo MS. Rodgers PJ. Management of acute chorioamnionitis. Am J Obstet Gynecol 136:709, 1980.

Gibbs RS, Blanco JD, St Clair PJ, Castaneda YS. Quantitative bacteriology of amniotic fluid from patients with clinical intraamniotic infection at term. J Infect Dis 145:1, 1982.

Yoder PR, Gibbs RS, Blanco JD, Castaneda YS, St Clair PJ. A prospective controlled study of maternal and perinatal outcome after intra-amniotic infection at term. Am J Obstet Gynecol 145:695, 1983.

PATIENT WITH FEVER IN LABOR

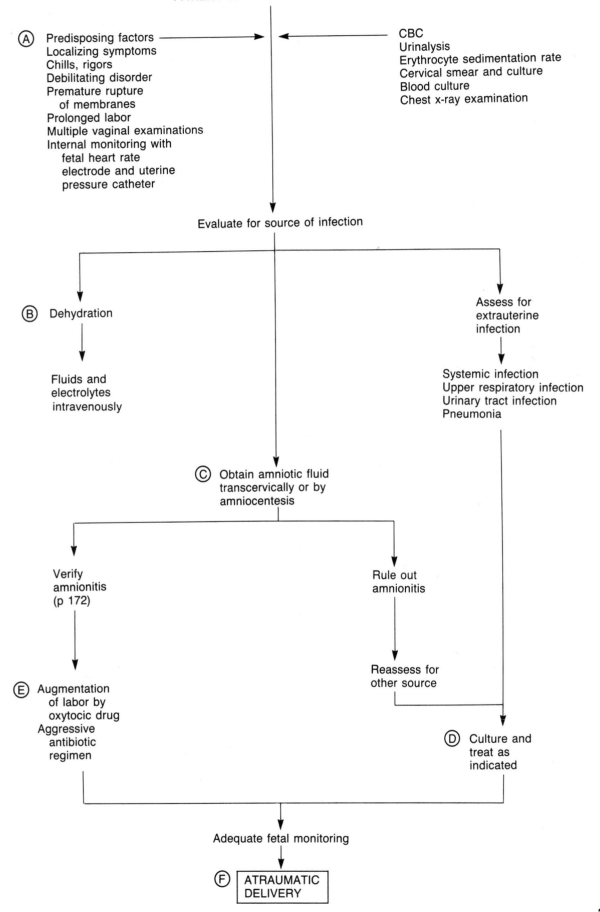

(A) Predisposing factors
Localizing symptoms
Chills, rigors
Debilitating disorder
Premature rupture
    of membranes
Prolonged labor
Multiple vaginal examinations
Internal monitoring with
    fetal heart rate
    electrode and uterine
    pressure catheter

CBC
Urinalysis
Erythrocyte sedimentation rate
Cervical smear and culture
Blood culture
Chest x-ray examination

Evaluate for source of infection

(B) Dehydration

Assess for
extrauterine
infection

Fluids and
electrolytes
intravenously

Systemic infection
Upper respiratory infection
Urinary tract infection
Pneumonia

(C) Obtain amniotic fluid
transcervically or by
amniocentesis

Verify
amnionitis
(p 172)

Rule out
amnionitis

Reassess for
other source

(E) Augmentation
of labor by
oxytocic drug
Aggressive
antibiotic
regimen

(D) Culture and
treat as
indicated

Adequate fetal monitoring

(F) ATRAUMATIC
DELIVERY

ASSESSMENT OF LABOR PROGRESSION

Emanuel A. Friedman, M.D., Sc.D.

A. It is helpful to recognize that the first stage of labor consists of a latent phase, during which little overt clinical change occurs, and an active phase, during which cervical dilatation can be expected to proceed rapidly. Whereas uterine contractions are essential for labor, the contractile pattern (intensity, frequency, duration, and progressive change over time) is not very helpful for judging the progress of labor. In general, the better the contractile pattern, the better the labor, but even this statement cannot be relied upon to guide management or to diagnose abnormal labor. The only clinically reliable means for evaluating labor progress today is to trace the pattern of cervical dilatation and fetal station against the time elapsed in labor from the onset of regular contractions (Fig. 1). This graphic tool shows aberrations of labor as they develop and helps guide evaluation and management.

B. Periodic assessments of the cervix by means of sterile vaginal examinations are important for following the progress of labor. They should be done as often as necessary to create an interpretable labor curve, that is, often (even hourly) if progress is rapid and further apart (at two to four hour intervals) if it is slow. Note cervical dilatation, effacement, consistency, and position relative to the vaginal axis. In addition, at each examination obtain updated information about membrane status, fetal station and position, asynclitism, molding, and caput formation.

C. The gravida who shows no progress in cervical dilatation from the time she is admitted presents a particularly difficult diagnostic problem. If the cervix is closed (or nearly so), she is undoubtedly still in the latent phase or false labor. If dilatation is more advanced, however, she could have begun labor with a dilated cervix; failure to progress could mean either a normal latent phase or secondary arrest. The latter is potentially serious. If the contractions are mild and infrequent, it is likely to be the latent phase. If the situation is unclear, assume that it is a case of arrest to ensure that proper measures are taken to evaluate and treat.

D. The first segment of the dilatation pattern from the onset of labor to the upswing of the curve at the beginning of the active phase, the latent phase, is normally less than 20 hours in nulliparas or 14 hours in multiparas. Durations exceeding these limits warrant a diagnosis of prolonged latent phase.

E. The onset of the active phase is generally unheralded by any identifiable change in contractility pattern. Although uterine contractions continue unaltered, cervical dilatation speeds up. Graphing the observations of dilatation on square-ruled paper (vertical axis) against time (horizontal axis) demonstrates the expected upswing of the curve when the active phase begins. For nulliparas, the normal active phase rate of dilatation is at least 1.2 cm per hour and for multiparas, at least 1.5 cm per hour.

F. The deceleration phase is the last part of the dilatation curve, extending from about 8.5 to 9 cm until full cervical dilatation occurs. It should not ordinarily exceed three hours in nulliparas or one hour in multiparas. Recording the dilatation pattern graphically identifies the deceleration phase and helps make the identification of an abnormally prolonged one easy.

G. Fetal station is determined on vaginal examination by relating the plane of the forward leading edge of the presenting part to the plane of the ischial spines (station zero). For each centimeter the fetus descends below the spines, it has advanced one station (+1) until it reaches and distends the perineum at station +5. Stations cephalad to the spines are designated by negative numbers up to −5 at the true pelvic inlet. Verify that descent is really occurring (rather than just molding of the fetal head) by suprapubic palpation of the fetal head, especially if the rate of descent is slow.

H. The rate of descent generally reaches its maximum when the deceleration phase of dilatation begins. Descent then continues into the second stage until the fetal presenting part reaches the perineum. The normal rate of descent is at least 1 cm per hour in nulliparas or 2 cm per hour in multiparas.

References

Cohen WR. Pelvic division of labor. In: Cohen WR, Friedman EA (Editors). Management of Labor. Baltimore: University Park Press, 1983.

Friedman EA. Labor: Clinical Evaluation and Management. 2nd ed. New York: Appleton-Century-Crofts, 1978.

Friedman EA. Monitoring the labor process. In: Iffy L, Charles D (Editors). Operative Perinatology: Invasive Obstetric Techniques. New York: Macmillan Publishing Co., 1984.

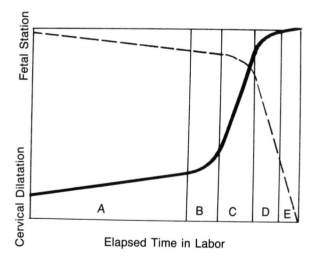

Figure 1 Characteristic graphic patterns of cervical dilatation (heavy line) and fetal descent (broken line) against time in labor. *A*, latent phase; *B*, acceleration phase; *C*, phase of maximum slope; *D*, deceleration phase; *E*, second stage. *B-D* represent the active phase of the first stage.

ASSESSING LABOR PROGRESSION

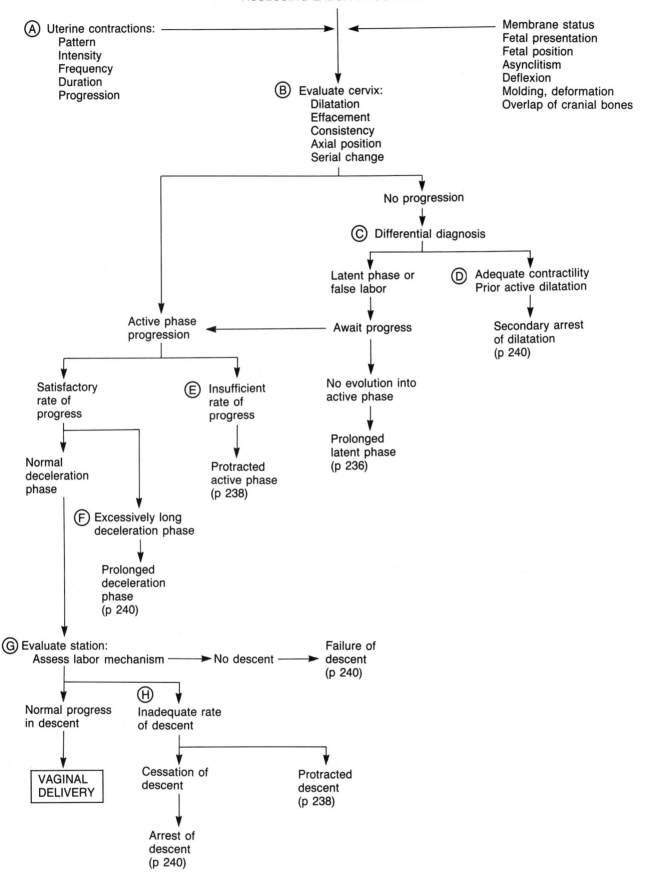

PROLONGED LATENT PHASE

Emanuel A. Friedman, M.D., Sc.D.

A. A considerable period of time may elapse in labor from the onset of regular uterine contractions before any detectable change in cervical dilatation occurs. This is the latent phase of the first stage. Most patients who show no progressive cervical dilatation when they first come under observation are in a perfectly normal latent phase. Those who began labor with some prelabor dilatation may mistakenly be thought to be in the active phase. It is sometimes difficult to differentiate a latent phase from an arrest or protraction pattern. Slow dilatation is sometimes seen in the latent phase, but it is usually less than 0.6 cm per hour. If the rate is more rapid but abnormal (that is, less than 1.2 cm per hour in a nullipara or 1.5 cm per hour in a multipara), consider it to be protracted active phase dilatation for purposes of investigation and care.

B. From the onset of regular contractions to the beginning of the active phase at the upswing of the dilatation curve, the latent phase should not normally exceed 20 hours in nulliparas or 14 hours in multiparas. If it is prolonged beyond these critical limits, one can confidently diagnose the problem as prolonged latent phase (Fig. 1).

C. Excessive narcotic-analgesic-sedative drugs and inhalation or regional block anesthesia are the most frequent causes of abnormal prolongation of the latent phase. Their use should therefore be avoided or minimized in the latent phase; if given and discovered to have had an adverse effect on labor progress, their action can be allowed to abate. False labor, another cause of a prolonged latent phase, can be diagnosed only retrospectively.

D. The recommended approach to the management of a gravida with a prolonged latent phase is a program of therapeutic rest. Morphine sulfate, 15 mg subcutaneously or intramuscularly (20 mg for a large woman), is given in a single dose. After 20 minutes the patient is carefully re-evaluated. Nothing more is given if the contractions have ceased or respirations are depressed. If contractions are continuing, check the cervix for any active phase change; if it is unchanged, administer an additional 10 mg of morphine sulfate. The gravida usually sleeps soundly for six to 10 hours. The time can be used profitably to correct any fluid and electrolyte imbalance.

E. Those gravidas who awaken and are out of labor (10 percent) can be considered to have been in false labor. Once they are sufficiently free of the sedative effects of the morphine they were given earlier, they may be discharged to await the onset of true labor (or to return for another episode of false labor).

F. Most gravidas managed by therapeutic rest (85 percent) awaken with effective uterine contractions and are found to have advanced labor well into the active phase. Their subsequent management is essentially the same as that for other parturients, although they should be observed carefully for the development of other labor aberrations (even though they are not necessarily more prone to have them).

G. The residual few gravidas (5 percent) who are not in the active phase or are out of labor when they awaken constitute those who have failed to respond to the rest regimen. As the morphine effect subsides, they resume ineffectual contractions. They have benefited from the rest and support. Unless contraindicated, oxytocin stimulation may now be invoked to effect active dilatation. A good prognosis can be anticipated.

H. Infrequently (2 percent or less), overriding urgency prevails, requiring expeditious action to conclude the labor as quickly as feasible (short of cesarean section). Careful uterotonic stimulation with oxytocin infusion is then needed instead of the therapeutic rest regimen ordinarily preferred for this condition.

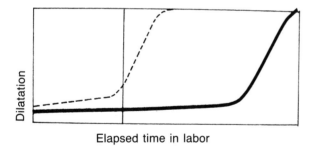

Figure 1 Dilatation pattern of prolonged latent phase (heavy line) contrasted with average curve for normal labor course (broken line).

References

Friedman EA. Labor: Clinical Evaluation and Management. 2nd ed. New York: Appleton-Century-Crofts, 1978.

Peisner DB, Rosen MG. The latent phase of labor in normal patients: A reassessment. Obstet Gynecol 66:644, 1985.

Peisner DB, Rosen MG. Transition from latent to active labor. Obstet Gynecol 68:448, 1986.

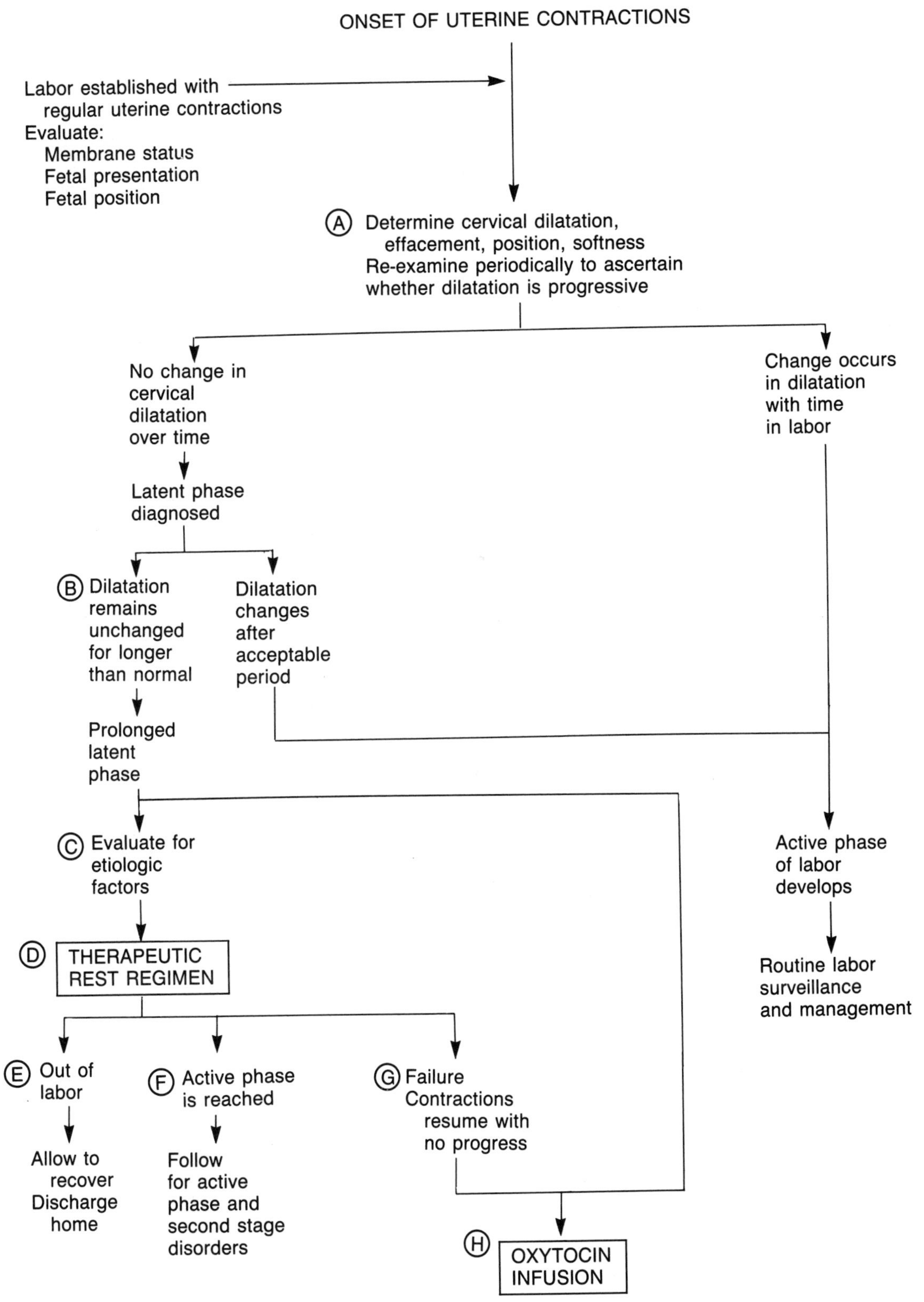

ONSET OF UTERINE CONTRACTIONS

Labor established with
   regular uterine contractions
Evaluate:
   Membrane status
   Fetal presentation
   Fetal position

(A) Determine cervical dilatation,
effacement, position, softness
Re-examine periodically to ascertain
whether dilatation is progressive

No change in
cervical
dilatation
over time

Change occurs
in dilatation
with time
in labor

Latent phase
diagnosed

(B) Dilatation
remains
unchanged
for longer
than normal

Dilatation
changes
after
acceptable
period

Prolonged
latent
phase

(C) Evaluate for
etiologic
factors

Active phase
of labor
develops

Routine labor
surveillance
and management

(D) THERAPEUTIC
REST REGIMEN

(E) Out of
labor

(F) Active phase
is reached

(G) Failure
Contractions
resume with
no progress

Allow to
recover
Discharge
home

Follow
for active
phase and
second stage
disorders

(H) OXYTOCIN
INFUSION

PROTRACTION DISORDER

Emanuel A. Friedman, M.D., Sc. D.

A. The patient whose progress in active labor and second stage is abnormally slow is at increased risk and the fetus is in jeopardy as well. Once the active phase of dilatation has begun, one should expect the cervix to dilate at least at a rate of 1.2 cm per hour in nulliparas or 1.5 cm per hour in multiparas. The rate of dilatation can be obtained by calculation or by graphic representation. If the rate is less than these limits, diagnose protracted active phase dilatation (Fig. 1). Early in the active phase, one may discern the slow progression of the slope of the dilatation curve as the labor undergoes transition from the latent phase to the active phase. Calculating the rate of dilatation before it has reached its maximum slope in the fully developed active phase may thus result in a misdiagnosis of protracted dilatation. The error will correct itself when the true maximum slope is reached.

B. In nulliparas the fetal presenting part usually engages into the pelvis about three weeks before labor begins. Thereafter no further descent generally occurs until late in the active phase of dilatation. Active fetal descent normally reaches its maximum slope about the time cervical dilatation reaches the deceleration phase at 8.5 to 9 cm. It is therefore inappropriate to decide whether descent is occurring normally until after the deceleration phase of dilatation has begun.

C. Fetal descent, once it has reached its maximum rate at or after the deceleration phase of dilatation, should continue without interruption until the perineum is reached. The normal rate of descent is at least 1 cm per hour in nulliparas or 2 cm per hour in multiparas. Periodically reassessing (and recording) the fetal station—the level of the forward leading edge of the presenting part in centimeters above or below the plane of the ischial spines (station zero)—facilitates this calculation (see p 234). These measurements can be entered on a graph to pro-

vide a visual tool for determining progressive change over time in labor. Patients with rates of descent less than these critical limits are diagnosed as having protracted descent. Verify that descent is really occurring, rather than just molding, by simultaneous suprapubic examinations.

D. Since about one-third of gravidas with a protraction disorder also have insurmountable cephalopelvic disproportion, it is essential to evaluate the cephalopelvic relationships in every woman who develops this aberration (see p 24). If disproportion is confirmed, safe vaginal delivery is unlikely and cesarean section is indicated.

E. If disproportion has been ruled out, the patient with a protraction disorder must be followed carefully. Internal electronic fetal heart rate monitoring is essential. Because this form of labor disorder is easily slowed or even stopped by analgesic and anesthetic drugs, their use should be minimized or, if possible, avoided altogether. Arrest disorders (p 240) frequently follow and should be watched for so that they can be re-evaluated and managed properly and expeditiously when encountered.

F. Perinatal morbidity and mortality are increased in offspring delivered after a protraction disorder, especially if delivered by a forceps procedure. The same applies for long term neurologic and developmental problems. Therefore, one should attempt to accomplish spontaneous delivery without instrumentation if it is feasible to do so. This may require permitting the second stage to continue for a long time. This is entirely acceptable provided descent is really occurring (as opposed to deformational molding) and the fetus and mother are documented to remain in good condition throughout. If the fetal head is fixed in the pelvis, an extended second stage may cause intracranial damage and even risk rupture of the uterus from excessive distention and thinning of the lower uterine segment.

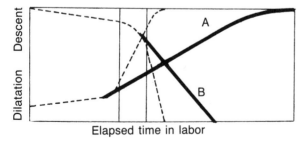

Figure 1 Protraction disorders of labor. *A,* protracted active-phase dilatation pattern; *B,* protracted descent pattern. Mean normal dilatation and descent curves are shown (broken lines) for comparison.

References

Friedman EA. Labor: Clinical Evaluation and Management. 2nd ed. New York: Appleton-Century-Crofts, 1978.

Friedman EA, Neff RK. Labor and Delivery: Impact on Offspring. Littleton, MA: PSG Publishing Co., 1987.

Friedman EA, Sachtleben MR, Dahrouge D, Neff RK. Long-term effects of labor and delivery on offspring: A matched-pair analysis. Am J Obstet Gynecol 150:941, 1984.

ACTIVE PHASE OF LABOR IN PROGRESS

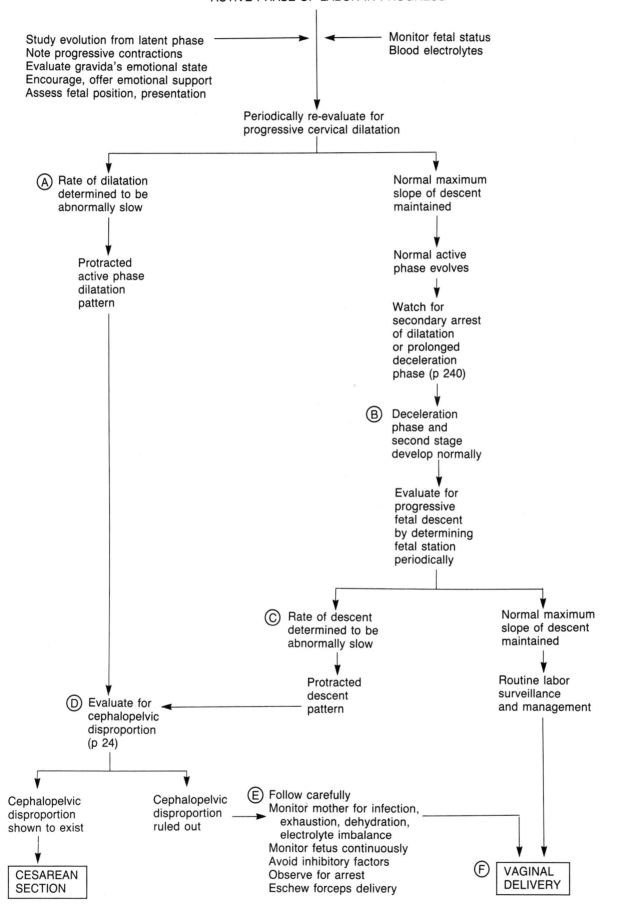

Study evolution from latent phase
Note progressive contractions
Evaluate gravida's emotional state
Encourage, offer emotional support
Assess fetal position, presentation

Monitor fetal status
Blood electrolytes

Periodically re-evaluate for
progressive cervical dilatation

(A) Rate of dilatation
determined to be
abnormally slow

Normal maximum
slope of descent
maintained

Protracted
active phase
dilatation
pattern

Normal active
phase evolves

Watch for
secondary arrest
of dilatation
or prolonged
deceleration
phase (p 240)

(B) Deceleration
phase and
second stage
develop normally

Evaluate for
progressive
fetal descent
by determining
fetal station
periodically

(C) Rate of descent
determined to be
abnormally slow

Normal maximum
slope of descent
maintained

Protracted
descent
pattern

Routine labor
surveillance
and management

(D) Evaluate for
cephalopelvic
disproportion
(p 24)

Cephalopelvic
disproportion
shown to exist

Cephalopelvic
disproportion
ruled out

(E) Follow carefully
Monitor mother for infection,
exhaustion, dehydration,
electrolyte imbalance
Monitor fetus continuously
Avoid inhibitory factors
Observe for arrest
Eschew forceps delivery

CESAREAN
SECTION

(F) VAGINAL
DELIVERY

ARREST DISORDER

Emanuel A. Friedman, M.D., Sc.D.

A. After the latent phase of the first stage ends and active dilatation has begun, cervical dilatation normally can be expected to continue without interruption until the cervix is fully dilated and fully retracted. Dilatation can be documented to have stopped by two vaginal examinations, preferably by the same person, spaced at least two hours apart. If this occurs, secondary arrest of dilatation has developed, a potentially serious labor aberration. Without prior documentation of progression from the latent to the active phase, one has to differentiate the benign condition of a normal latent phase (p 238) from the far more ominous disorder of secondary arrest.

B. In half the gravidas who develop an arrest disorder in labor (Fig. 1), obstructed labor proves to be due to insurmountable cephalopelvic disproportion. To avoid both maternal and fetal risk under these circumstances, evaluate the cephalopelvic relations carefully to rule out disproportion (p 24) before undertaking oxytocin infusion for uterotonic stimulation.

C. Morbidity and mortality risks are increased for both mother and fetus if labor is allowed to proceed and vaginal delivery is attempted in the presence of a combination of disproportion and an arrest pattern. If disproportion cannot be ruled out, one should consider cesarean section to avoid the potential hazards.

D. If disproportion can be effectively ruled out, a carefully titrated oxytocin infusion may be given to augment the effectiveness of the contractile forces. Even in the presence of disproportion, however, additional dilatation and descent are likely to occur. Therefore, it may not be completely safe to use the response to oxytocin as a "trial of the pelvis" in a patient suspected of having dispropor-

tion (see E). Electronic fetal heart rate monitoring must be continued throughout the remainder of the labor.

E. Even though one may believe disproportion to have been ruled out, the degree of response to oxytocin may help signal unsuspected obstructed labor. As oxytocin takes effect, a postarrest pattern of dilatation or descent generally evolves. Compare the measured postarrest slope of progressive dilatation or descent (rate in cm per hour) with the prearrest slope. If the postarrest slope is the same as or greater than the prearrest slope, the prognosis for vaginal delivery is excellent; a lower postarrest slope or nonprogression demands re-evaluation of the pelvic capacity. Cesarean section should be done unless one can be assured that there is ample room to accommodate the fetus and permit its safe delivery vaginally.

F. The deceleration phase is the last part of the active phase, representing a continuation of the dilatation process modified by cephalad retraction of the cervix around the fetal head. Prolongation of this phase may be associated with the same factors seen with other arrest disorders; most important among them is cephalopelvic disproportion. The deceleration phase can be considered abnormal if it continues beyond three hours in nulliparas or one hour in multiparas.

G. Active fetal descent may or may not begin before the deceleration phase. However, if it has not begun by this time in labor, a serious disorder exists, namely, failure of descent. If descent does begin in the late active phase, but the fetal presenting part stops progressing before it reaches the perineum, the related abnormality of arrest of descent is present. It can be diagnosed in the second stage by demonstrating no further descent on two vaginal examinations spaced at least one hour apart. It is important to verify true descent, as opposed to just elongation of the fixed head by molding, with serial suprapubic examinations.

References

Friedman EA. Labor: Clinical Evaluation and Management. 2nd ed. New York: Appleton-Century-Crofts, 1978.

Friedman EA, Neff RK. Labor and Delivery: Impact on Offspring. Littleton MA: PSG Publishing Co., 1987.

Friedman EA, Sachtleben MR, Dahrouge D, Neff RK. Long-term effects of labor and delivery on offspring: A matched-pair analysis. Am J Obstet Gynecol 150:941, 1984.

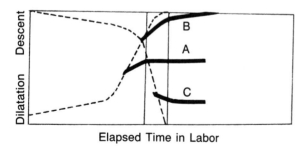

Figure 1 Arrest disorders of labor. *A,* secondary arrest of dilatation; *B,* prolonged deceleration phase; *C,* arrest of descent; failure of descent not shown. Normal dilatation and descent curves (broken lines) also illustrated.

PATIENT IN ACTIVE PHASE OF FIRST STAGE LABOR

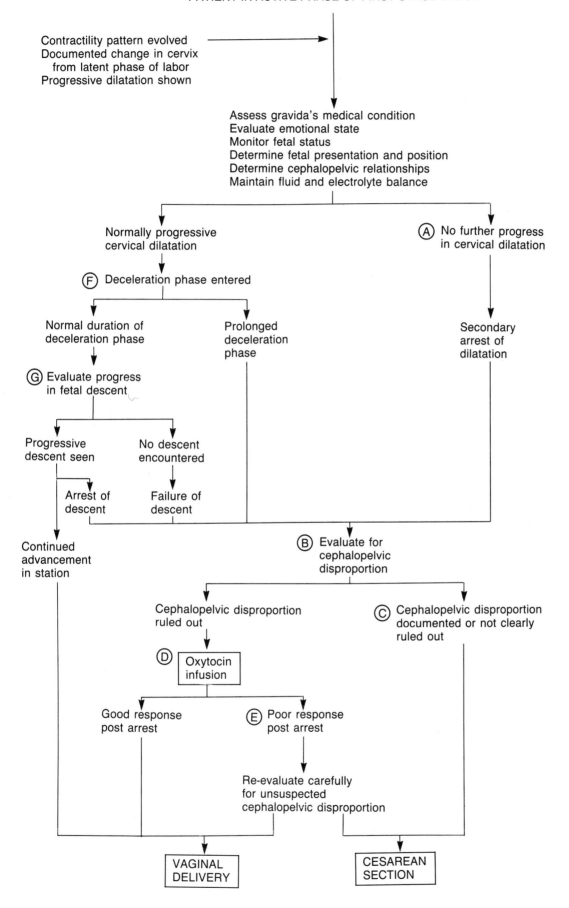

Contractility pattern evolved
Documented change in cervix
  from latent phase of labor
Progressive dilatation shown

Assess gravida's medical condition
Evaluate emotional state
Monitor fetal status
Determine fetal presentation and position
Determine cephalopelvic relationships
Maintain fluid and electrolyte balance

Normally progressive
cervical dilatation

(A) No further progress
in cervical dilatation

(F) Deceleration phase entered

Normal duration of
deceleration phase

Prolonged
deceleration
phase

Secondary
arrest of
dilatation

(G) Evaluate progress
in fetal descent

Progressive
descent seen

No descent
encountered

Arrest of
descent

Failure of
descent

Continued
advancement
in station

(B) Evaluate for
cephalopelvic
disproportion

Cephalopelvic disproportion
ruled out

(C) Cephalopelvic disproportion
documented or not clearly
ruled out

(D) Oxytocin
infusion

Good response
post arrest

(E) Poor response
post arrest

Re-evaluate carefully
for unsuspected
cephalopelvic disproportion

VAGINAL
DELIVERY

CESAREAN
SECTION

FAILURE TO PROGRESS

Emanuel A. Friedman, M.D., Sc.D.

A. The term "failure to progress" is not well defined because it may mean different things under different circumstances. It is used commonly to describe a variety of conditions encompassing a range of situations, some rather serious and others entirely innocuous. A more specific diagnosis of the condition that actually exists is preferable because it can guide evaluation and management to yield optimal results.

B. One should be able to recognize when a patient has entered the active phase of the first stage of labor by the upswing of the cervical dilatation curve characterized by a change in the slope at the end of the latent phase. One can use as a guideline a 0.6 cm per hour maximum rate of dilatation to differentiate between a normal latent phase (no change or a very low slope) and an abnormal active phase (more than 0.6 but less than 1.2 cm per hour. Exceptions do occur, however, making this only a guide and not an absolutely inflexible rule.

C. If labor does not progress with advanced cervical dilatation in a gravida whose prior labor course is undocumented, the differential diagnosis may be difficult. If the degree of dilatation achieved prior to the onset of labor is known (for example, if the patient had recently been examined in the office), this can clarify the situation. Intervening progress, even though it may not have been documented, probably signifies that active phase dilatation has occurred and is now arrested. Otherwise the patient may still be in the latent phase, having begun labor with some dilatation already accomplished. If the differential diagnosis cannot be made with reasonable certainty, it is prudent to assume that arrest of dilatation exists because it is so much more serious.

D. The duration of the normal latent phase is less than 20 hours in nulliparas or 14 hours in multiparas (p 236). "Failure to progress" is normal under these circum-stances. Even a prolonged latent phase, an aberrant labor pattern, is a common and relatively minor problem, which carries a good prognosis if managed conservatively.

E. Secondary arrest of dilatation and failure or arrest of descent (p 240) are readily diagnosed by following the graphic labor pattern traced by plotting cervical dilatation and fetal station against the time in labor. They are far more serious forms of "failure to progress" than a normal or prolonged latent phase. This is so because affected gravidas may require operative intervention for the insurmountable cephalopelvic disproportion that is so often found to be associated.

F. Continuing dilatory progression in dilatation or in descent (p 238) is not actually true arrest, but it is sometimes mistakenly included under the umbrella of "failure to progress." Tracing the graphic curves helps distinguish protraction from arrest patterns. Protraction disorders can be diagnosed only if one is alert to the abnormally slow rate of dilatation or descent, verified by calculation or graphic portrayal; management requires awareness of the refractory nature of these disorders and the poor prognosis based on the likelihood of cesarean section and the potential risk of damage to the fetus.

References

Friedman EA. Labor: Clinical Evaluation and Management. 2nd ed. New York: Appleton-Century-Crofts, 1978.

Friedman EA. Dysfunctional labor. In: Cohen WR, Friedman EA (Editors). Management of Labor. Baltimore: University Park Press, 1983.

Friedman EA. Failure to progress in labor. In: Queenan JT (Editor). Management of High-Risk Pregnancy. 2nd ed. Oradell NJ: Medical Economics Books, 1985.

FAILURE TO PROGRESS

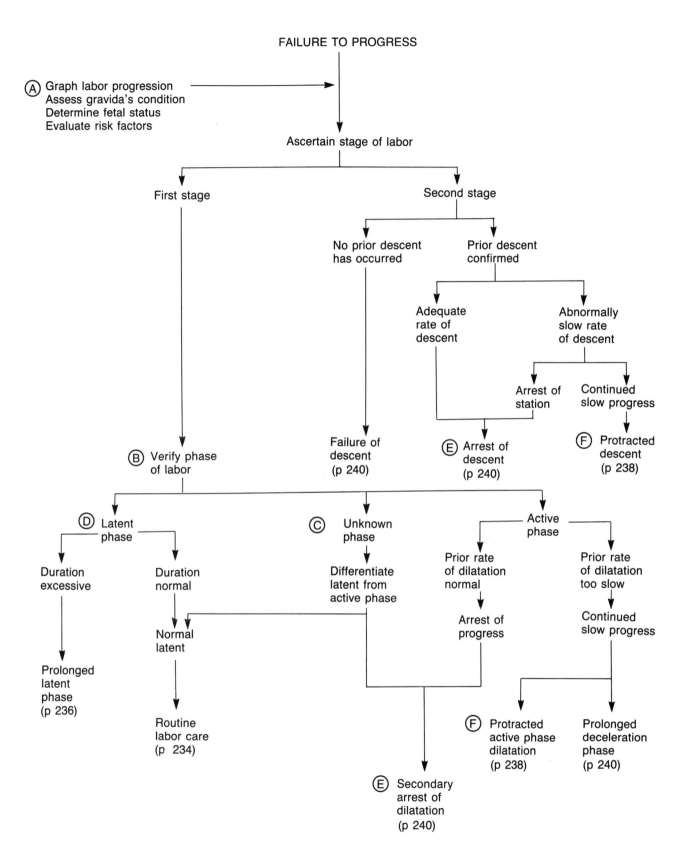

Ⓐ Graph labor progression
Assess gravida's condition
Determine fetal status
Evaluate risk factors

Ascertain stage of labor

First stage

Second stage

No prior descent
has occurred

Prior descent
confirmed

Adequate
rate of
descent

Abnormally
slow rate
of descent

Arrest of
station

Continued
slow progress

Ⓑ Verify phase
of labor

Failure of
descent
(p 240)

Ⓔ Arrest of
descent
(p 240)

Ⓕ Protracted
descent
(p 238)

Ⓓ Latent
phase

Ⓒ Unknown
phase

Active
phase

Duration
excessive

Duration
normal

Differentiate
latent from
active phase

Prior rate
of dilatation
normal

Prior rate
of dilatation
too slow

Normal
latent

Arrest of
progress

Continued
slow progress

Prolonged
latent
phase
(p 236)

Routine
labor care
(p 234)

Ⓕ Protracted
active phase
dilatation
(p 238)

Prolonged
deceleration
phase
(p 240)

Ⓔ Secondary
arrest of
dilatation
(p 240)

SECOND STAGE MANAGEMENT

David B. Acker, M.D.

A. The second stage may be prolonged by fetal macrosomia, malposition, dysfunctional labor, cephalopelvic disproportion, and epidural anesthesia. Not all long second stages are abnormal nor do they necessarily have adverse perinatal effects. Provide necessary support, reassurance, and explanations. Encourage comfortable positions to aid bearing-down efforts and ensure needed rest between contractions. Continuous electronic fetal heart rate monitoring is important.

B. Each labor tests the pelvis anew. Although second stage abnormalities are more common among nulliparas, be alert for abnormalities of descent in all labors because of their relation to birth trauma, febrile morbidity, and postpartum hemorrhage. In the past, a second stage lasting more than two hours was considered abnormal. It is now recognized that the duration is not as important as the absence of progress or an inadequate rate of progress (pp 238, 240). Once active descent begins, the fetal presenting part should progress until it reaches the perineum at a rate of at least 1 cm per hour in nullipara or 2 cm per hour in multipara. To assess progress reliably, observe the fetal station frequently by careful vaginal examinations (Fig. 1), verifying that true descent is occurring by use of suprapubic palpation. If arrest of descent occurs while oxytocin is being administered, it is likely that there is cephalopelvic disproportion.

C. Internal catheter monitoring provides the most accurate information about intrauterine pressure, but it is seldom invoked because it enhances maternal morbidity. Clinical assessment therefore is used to evaluate uterine contractions, which are generally considered adequate if they are strong, last 45 to 60 seconds, and recur every two to three minutes. However, the contractility pattern does not indicate whether a labor is normal. Contractions may become inadequate in response to an insurmountable obstruction or exhaustion. If it is the result of excessive sedation or anesthesia, stimulation or time may be required to allow the inhibiting factor to subside, although one has a positive obligation to rule out bony dystocia. This can be done in late labor by dynamic assessment of the cephalopelvic relations (p 24). Downward pressure on the uterine fundus at the height of a contraction normally produces some descent readily detectable to the examining hand. An advance in station essentially excludes disproportion at that level of the pelvis, whereas fixation of the head strongly suggests obstructed labor. Formal x-ray pelvimetry may help confirm one's suspicions objectively, but it generally is unnecessary if the findings are clear-cut.

D. If labor is permitted to continue, it is essential to follow the ensuing descent course carefully (see B) to ensure that progress is being made. Reassess the cephalopelvic relations periodically as the fetal head descends further in the birth canal. Consider optimizing the efficiency of uterine contractions by allowing analgesia or anesthesia to wear off and perhaps augmenting with oxytocin, if indicated.

E. Given enough time, most patients are able to bring the fetal head to the perineum, provided there is no cephalopelvic disproportion. Uncomplicated atraumatic delivery then can be accomplished. Trauma to the mother and baby may be avoided if a midforceps procedure proves unnecessary. Seldom can the benefits be deemed sufficient to outweigh the risks (p 284).

F. Cesarean section can be exceedingly difficult if performed for disproportion in the second stage of labor, because the fetal head is wedged into the pelvis. It may be necessary for an assistant to dislodge it from below, taking care to distribute pressure on the skull over a broad area. If a low transverse incision is planned, reflect the bladder as far down as possible prior to opening the uterine cavity to ensure that any extension of the incision can be visualized completely. Aerobic and anaerobic cultures should be taken from the uterine cavity. If the patient is not already febrile, the prophylactic administration of antibiotics is strongly recommended.

References

Bergsjo P, Halle C. Duration of second stage of labor. Acta Obstet Gynecol Scand 59:193, 1980.

Cohen WR. The pelvic division of labor. In: Cohen WR, Friedman EA (Editors). Management of Labor. Baltimore: University Park Press, 1983.

Friedman EA. Labor: Clinical Evaluation and Management. 2nd ed. New York: Appleton-Century-Crofts, 1978.

Maresh M, Choong KH, Beard RW. Delayed pushing with lumbar analgesia in labour. Br J Obstet Gynaecol 90:623, 1983.

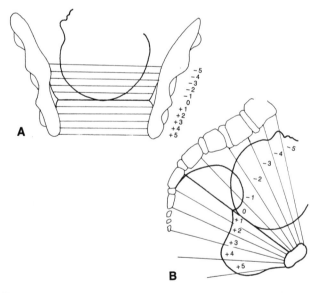

Figure 1 Fetal station designations. *A,* anteroposterior view; *B,* lateral view. Station signifies level of forward leading edge of fetal presenting part in centimeters relative to plane of ischial spines (heavy line); negative numbers designate stations cephalad to the spines; positive, caudad.

PATIENT WITH CERVIX FULLY DILATED

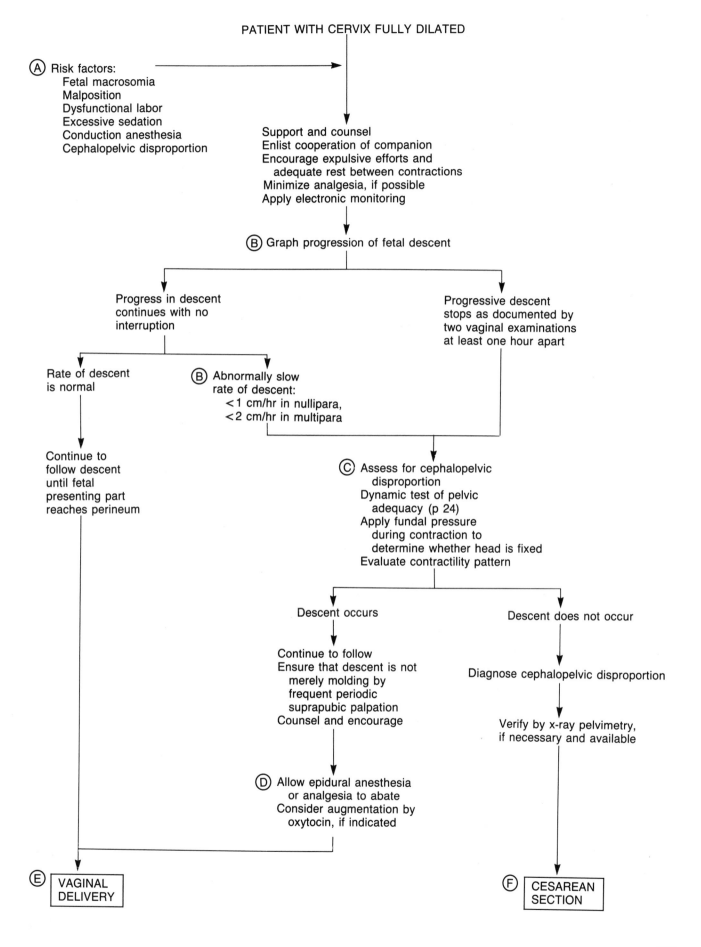

Ⓐ Risk factors:
   Fetal macrosomia
   Malposition
   Dysfunctional labor
   Excessive sedation
   Conduction anesthesia
   Cephalopelvic disproportion

Support and counsel
Enlist cooperation of companion
Encourage expulsive efforts and
   adequate rest between contractions
Minimize analgesia, if possible
Apply electronic monitoring

Ⓑ Graph progression of fetal descent

Progress in descent
continues with no
interruption

Progressive descent
stops as documented by
two vaginal examinations
at least one hour apart

Rate of descent
is normal

Ⓑ Abnormally slow
   rate of descent:
   <1 cm/hr in nullipara,
   <2 cm/hr in multipara

Continue to
follow descent
until fetal
presenting part
reaches perineum

Ⓒ Assess for cephalopelvic
   disproportion
Dynamic test of pelvic
   adequacy (p 24)
Apply fundal pressure
   during contraction to
   determine whether head is fixed
Evaluate contractility pattern

Descent occurs

Descent does not occur

Continue to follow
Ensure that descent is not
   merely molding by
   frequent periodic
   suprapubic palpation
Counsel and encourage

Diagnose cephalopelvic disproportion

Verify by x-ray pelvimetry,
if necessary and available

Ⓓ Allow epidural anesthesia
   or analgesia to abate
Consider augmentation by
   oxytocin, if indicated

Ⓔ | VAGINAL
    | DELIVERY

Ⓕ | CESAREAN
    | SECTION

SOFT TISSUE DYSTOCIA

Eric D. Lichter, M.D.

A. It is unusual for obstructed labor to be due to a soft tissue impediment. Far more often inadequate uterine contractions or cephalopelvic disproportion is found to distort the labor pattern and prevent timely delivery. It is nonetheless important to be aware of the possibility and alert to its occurrence. Sites of obstruction may include the vulva, vagina, cervix, lower uterine segment, bladder, and pelvis. Be alert to features in the history that could be associated with dense fibrous scarring of pelvic tissues, especially operations on or trauma to the cervix.

B. Conglutination of the cervix can result from trauma (resulting from delivery, abortion, or excessively vigorous dilatation) or destructive operative procedures, such as electrocautery, cryosurgery, conization, and amputation. Scarring forms a ring of fibrous tissue preventing dilatation in labor, usually but not exclusively confined to the external os of the cervix. The result is an unusual condition in which the external os remains closed as labor progresses. The lower uterine segment balloons out, and the fetal head descends, pushing the cervix caudad ahead of it. Effacement occurs to form a thin sheet of cervix closely applied to the fetal presenting part or forewaters. The internal os dilates, and all the cervix above the fibrous ring is incorporated into the lower uterine segment. At times it is difficult to find the pinpoint opening that represents the external os. Once it is found, simply insinuating a finger gently into the cervical opening to disrupt the constrictive band should initiate rapid dilatation. Care should be taken to avoid lacerating the cervix during this procedure.

C. The urinary bladder may become overdistended in the course of labor. Although it is a common problem with epidural or spinal anesthesia, it also can occur in the unanesthetized patient. The nursing staff should check for this periodically. It is controversial whether it can cause dystocia, although it is clearly possible. The overdistended bladder is easily treated with catheter drainage, although urethral obstruction by the descending fetal presenting part may make it difficult to insert the catheter without trauma.

D. A uterine leiomyoma or ovarian cyst may obstruct descent of the presenting part if it is impacted in the pelvis.

The decision about the delivery method should not be made prior to the onset of labor, because as labor advances, the mass may rise out of the pelvis. This is likely to be the case in a myoma that is intramural or subserosal in the lower uterine segment. Periodic pelvic examinations in the course of labor may reveal the need for cesarean section.

E. A vaginal septum warrants investigation to disclose associated uterine and urinary tract anomalies. Longitudinal septa may be complete or partial. A complete septum tends to allow satisfactory vaginal dilatation and descent, whereas partial septa are more apt to obstruct labor. Dystocia from a septum in the second stage of labor is treated either by surgical division or, if it is too long or too thick, by cesarean section. A transverse septum may be mistaken for the apex of the vagina and its central opening for the cervix. If it is recognized, the cervix above the ring can be followed until it reaches full dilatation; in second stage, these septa usually open spontaneously to allow descent. Rarely digital stretching or surgical incision is needed. Annular vaginal rings usually soften with advancing pregnancy and produce no problems. Vaginal cysts usually do not impede descent, but they may be aspirated if necessary.

F. Vulvar dystocia may be caused by adhesions or scarring from injury, infection, or surgery. The vulvovaginal outlet also may be inherently small, rigid, or inelastic. The perineal musculature can be developed to excess in professional dancers, acrobats, and equestrians. The resulting dystocia is usually overcome by the forces applied by the fetal head as it descends if enough time is allowed to permit it. Generally a well timed and generous episiotomy or perineotomy is needed in such cases to effect vaginal delivery without extensive perineal lacerations.

References

Heinonen PK. Longitudinal vaginal septum. Eur J Obstet Gynecol Reprod Biol 13:253, 1982.

Kerr-Wilson RHJ, Parham GP, Orr JW. The effect of a full bladder on labor. Obstet Gynecol 62:319, 1983.

NONPROGRESSIVE LABOR

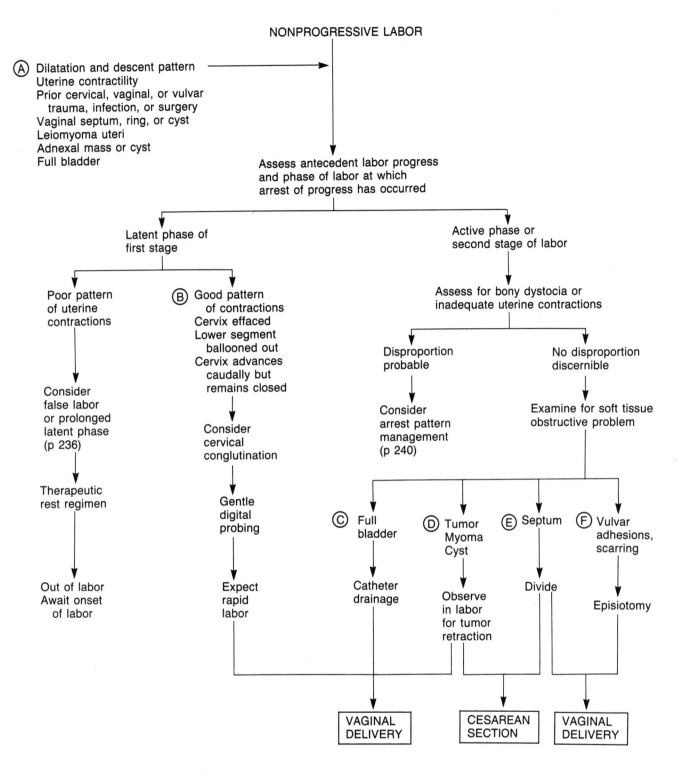

UTERINE TETANY

Lynn H. Galen, M.D.

A. By definition based on common consensus, a uterine contraction that lasts longer than 90 seconds is considered to be a tetanic contraction. It is important clinically because fetal hypoxia can result. Comparable degrees of hypoxia may result from uterine hypertonus (defined by a basal uterine tonus value increased above 12 to 15 mm Hg) or polysystole (frequent contractions with very short intervening resting intervals of less than 30 seconds); these contractile patterns interfere with uterine blood flow and fetal oxygenation in the same way that uterine tetany does. Speed in evaluation and management is critical, because the longer the contraction lasts, the greater its potential for causing fetal death or irreversible brain damage. Thus, while assessing for cause, one should be actively pursuing measures for correcting the problem, determining both fetal and maternal status, and simultaneously preparing for emergency intervention if that should prove necessary.

B. Oxytocin or prostaglandin use and abruptio placentae are the most common identifiable causes of tetanic uterine contractions. They have also been reported to result from nipple stimulation, which some have suggested might be used as a substitute for oxytocin infusion for a contraction stress test of fetal well-being. Uterine tetany can also occur spontaneously or result from the administration of drugs not ordinarily considered to be uterotonic. Aside from ergot preparations (such as those used for treating migraine) and prostaglandins, a wide variety of pharmacologic agents have uterine stimulating effects, including diphenhydramine (especially if given intravenously), vasopressor amines (such as methoxamine and mephentermine), histamine, digoxin (and the related cardiotonic drugs ouabain and strophanthin G), acetylcholine, neostigmine, and pilocarpine. Tetanic contractions caused by these drugs are rare and usually short lived; nonetheless they must be managed carefully and expeditiously to avoid fetal injury. The paradigm for oxytocin induced tetany is applicable here as well.

C. The single most effective means for interrupting a tetanic contraction that occurs in response to oxytocin use is to stop administering the drug. As soon as the intravenous infusion of dilute oxytocin is discontinued, the circulating levels rapidly diminish (half-life about three minutes) and, in consequence, the contraction usually subsides promptly. Giving oxytocin by any other route (that is, intramuscular, intranasal, or buccal) can yield tetanic contractions that are not as readily reversible; thus, these other routes of administration are not recommended.

D. Attempts to stop tetanic uterine contractions by the use of pharmacologic tocolytics, principally beta sympathomimetics (p 178), generally take too long to be very useful. Uterus-relaxing anesthesia is quickly effective, however, especially in the form of halogenated inhalation drugs (e.g., halothane, enflurane); it requires appropriately trained and skilled personnel and suitable facilities to be immediately available. Under most circumstances, by the time everything is in readiness to initiate the anesthesia, tetanic contractions that have been caused by a hypercontractile response to oxytocin infusion will have subsided spontaneously, provided the oxytocin was stopped at once.

References

Caldeyro-Barcia R, Pose SV, Poseiro JJ, Mendez-Bauer C, Escarcena L, Behrman R. Effects of several factors on fetal pO₂ recorded continuously in the fetal monkey. In: Gluck L (Editor). Intrauterine Asphyxia and the Developing Fetal Brain. Chicago: Year Book Medical Publishers, 1977.

Larsen JV, Brits CI, Whittal D. Uterine hyperstimulation and rupture after induction of labor with prostaglandin E2: Case reports. S Afr Med J 65:615, 1984.

Odendaal H. Frequency of uterine contractions in abruptio placentae. S Afr Med J 50:2129, 1976.

Ramsey EM, Donner MW. Placental Vasculature and Circulation. Philadelphia: WB Saunders, 1980.

Viegas OA, Arulkumaran S, Gibb DM, Ratnam SS. Nipple stimulation in late pregnancy causing uterine hyperstimulation and profound fetal bradycardia. Br J Obstet Gynaecol 91:364, 1984.

PATIENT WITH TETANIC CONTRACTION

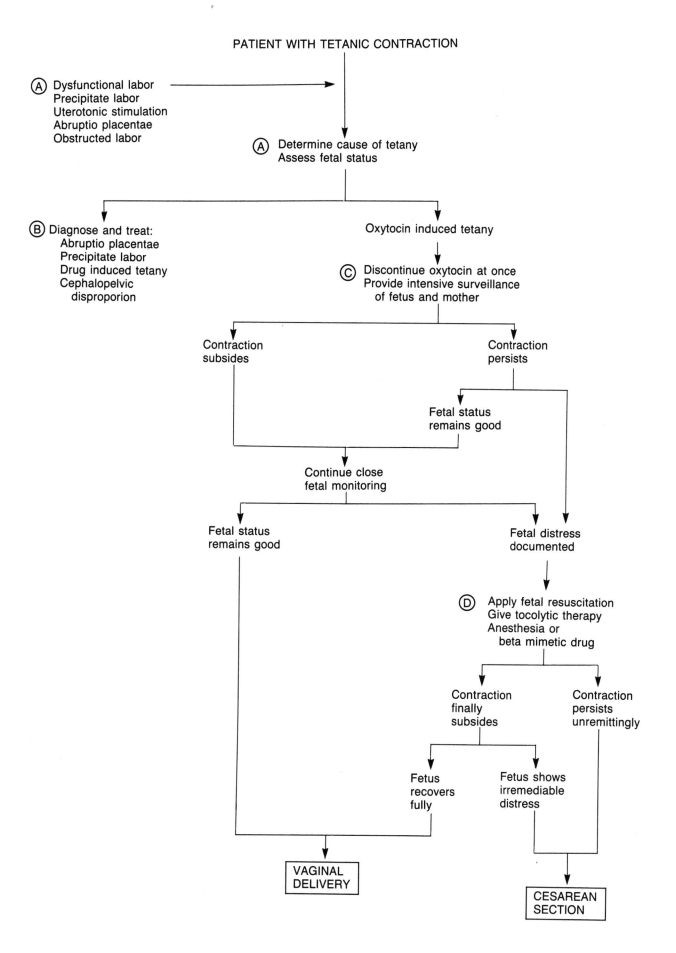

(A) Dysfunctional labor
Precipitate labor
Uterotonic stimulation
Abruptio placentae
Obstructed labor

(A) Determine cause of tetany
Assess fetal status

(B) Diagnose and treat:
Abruptio placentae
Precipitate labor
Drug induced tetany
Cephalopelvic
disproporion

Oxytocin induced tetany

(C) Discontinue oxytocin at once
Provide intensive surveillance
of fetus and mother

Contraction
subsides

Contraction
persists

Fetal status
remains good

Continue close
fetal monitoring

Fetal status
remains good

Fetal distress
documented

(D) Apply fetal resuscitation
Give tocolytic therapy
Anesthesia or
beta mimetic drug

Contraction
finally
subsides

Contraction
persists
unremittingly

Fetus
recovers
fully

Fetus shows
irremediable
distress

VAGINAL
DELIVERY

CESAREAN
SECTION

SHOULDER DYSTOCIA

David B. Acker, M.D.

A. Anticipate shoulder dystocia in the presence of maternal diabetes (even if well controlled), a large fetus, maternal obesity, a large weight gain in pregnancy, a small pelvis, dysfunctional labor (especially an arrest pattern or a prolonged second stage), and midforceps delivery. Recognize, however, that even normal labor and spontaneous delivery may be associated with this complication.

B. For cases at risk for shoulder dystocia, anticipate the complication by delivering the patient in a setting in which corrective and resuscitative measures can be taken promptly. A pediatrician and an anesthesiologist should be alerted in advance to ensure that they will be physically present for the delivery. The obstetrician who has had limited experience should seek support from more expert senior clinicians. Empty the patient's bladder and give perineal anesthesia by pudendal block or local infiltration unless conduction anesthesia is already in place. If shoulder dystocia occurs without forewarning, rapid induction of general anesthesia may be needed instead.

C. Shoulder dystocia is recognizable by the difficulty encountered in effecting delivery of the anterior shoulder; it sometimes is apparent just after the fetal head is delivered when the head is pulled back against the perineum. Make a large mediolateral episiotomy or median

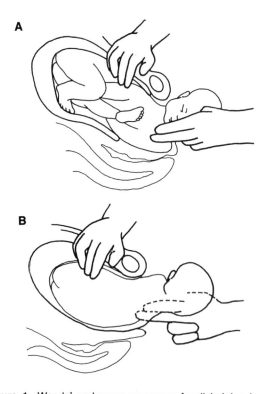

episioproctotomy. Clear the fetal oropharynx rapidly of excessive secretions. Assistants should hyperflex the gravida's thighs against her abdomen (McRoberts' maneuver) to rotate the symphysis pubis cephalad and decrease the pelvic angle of inclination. Although this does not alter the dimensions of the pelvis, it may help free the impacted shoulder so that gentle downward traction on the fetal head will effect delivery.

D. If repositioning fails, insert a hand vaginally behind the anterior shoulder and attempt to rotate it to a more favorable oblique diameter. If this is successful, apply gentle downward traction on the head again but this time in conjunction with suprapubic pressure.

E. A hand is inserted vaginally behind the posterior shoulder to grasp the arm, which is then carefully adducted across the fetal chest. The humerus may fracture in this maneuver, but long term damage is usually negligible or absent. Alternatively the forefinger may be hooked into the posterior axilla for traction to dislodge the posterior shoulder.

F. The Woods or corkscrew technique (Fig. 1) requires the posterior shoulder to have already descended into the hollow of the sacrum. The index and middle fingers are inserted in front of the posterior shoulder. Rotational pressure (with caudad traction) is exerted to turn the posterior shoulder 180 degrees, thereby causing the previously impacted anterior shoulder to rotate posteriorly and inferiorly into the hollow of the sacrum and the previously posterior shoulder to come anteriorly, either stemmed under the symphysis or out of the vagina. The rest of the delivery then may be successfully accomplished in the usual manner with downward head traction. If not, rotate the posterior shoulder (previously anterior) 180 degrees with the opposite hand in the same manner to deliver the remaining shoulder.

G. Seldom is it necessary to fracture the clavicle deliberately to correct shoulder dystocia. Most obstetricians have never had to resort to this technique. It is done with heavy bandage scissors and takes considerable strength. It risks damage to the lung apex. A method recently has been described for replacing the head in the vagina and uterus and then delivering by cesarean section. Without more experience, this potentially hazardous (for the mother) technique cannot yet be recommended.

References

Acker DB, Sachs BP, Friedman EA. Risk factors for shoulder dystocia. Obstet Gynecol 66:762, 1985.

Gonik B, Stringer CA, Held B. An alternate maneuver for management of shoulder dystocia. Am J Obstet Gynecol 145:882, 1983.

Modanlou HD, Komatsu G, Dorchester W, et al. Large-for-gestational-age neonates: Anthropometric reasons for shoulder dystocia. Obstet Gynecol 60:417, 1982.

Sandberg EC. The Zavanelli maneuver: A potentially revolutionary method for the resolution of shoulder dystocia. Am J Obstet Gynecol 152:479, 1985.

Figure 1 Woods' corkscrew maneuver for dislodging impacted shoulders in shoulder dystocia with suprapubic pressure applied to the anterior shoulder, lateral pressure is applied to the posterior shoulder *A*, to rotate it 180° and deliver it under the symphysis pubis *B*; the shoulder now lying posteriorly can be delivered over the perineum with fundal pressure or rotated back to effect its delivery anteriorly.

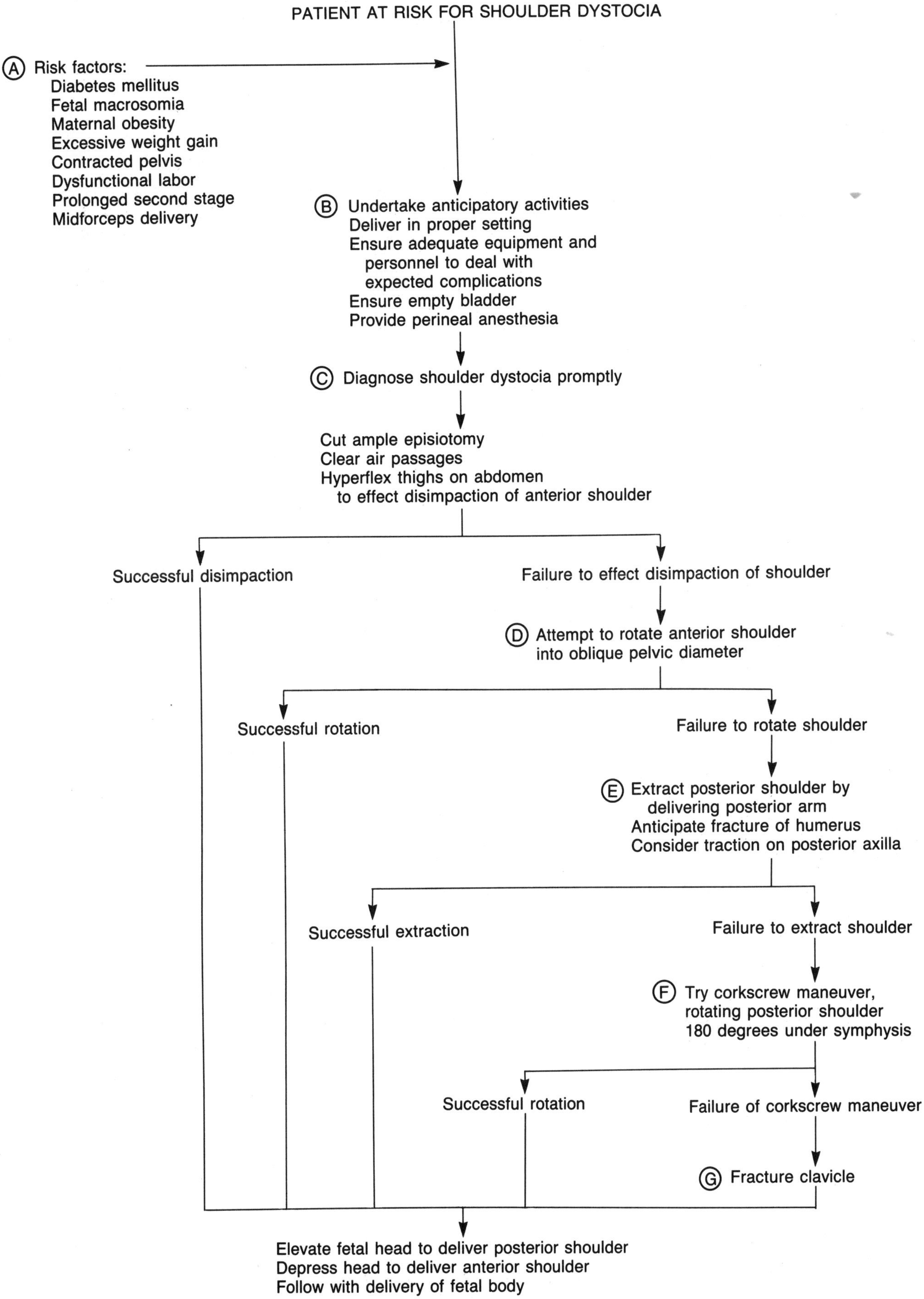

PATIENT AT RISK FOR SHOULDER DYSTOCIA

(A) Risk factors:
   Diabetes mellitus
   Fetal macrosomia
   Maternal obesity
   Excessive weight gain
   Contracted pelvis
   Dysfunctional labor
   Prolonged second stage
   Midforceps delivery

(B) Undertake anticipatory activities
    Deliver in proper setting
    Ensure adequate equipment and
       personnel to deal with
       expected complications
    Ensure empty bladder
    Provide perineal anesthesia

(C) Diagnose shoulder dystocia promptly

Cut ample episiotomy
Clear air passages
Hyperflex thighs on abdomen
   to effect disimpaction of anterior shoulder

Successful disimpaction

Failure to effect disimpaction of shoulder

(D) Attempt to rotate anterior shoulder
    into oblique pelvic diameter

Successful rotation

Failure to rotate shoulder

(E) Extract posterior shoulder by
    delivering posterior arm
    Anticipate fracture of humerus
    Consider traction on posterior axilla

Successful extraction

Failure to extract shoulder

(F) Try corkscrew maneuver,
    rotating posterior shoulder
    180 degrees under symphysis

Successful rotation

Failure of corkscrew maneuver

(G) Fracture clavicle

Elevate fetal head to deliver posterior shoulder
Depress head to deliver anterior shoulder
Follow with delivery of fetal body

251

DELIVERY TRAUMA

Susan B. Wilson, M.D.

A. Risk factors for delivery trauma include precipitate labor, obstructed labor, macrosomia, shoulder dystocia, fetal anomalies, malpresentation, and maternal conditions such as obesity, malnutrition, pelvic varicosities, small pelvic outlet, and grand multiparity. The onset of vaginal bleeding prior to delivery may signify a vaginal or cervical laceration, especially if it occurs in association with a precipitate delivery.

B. When delivery trauma is suspected or anticipated, the patient should be prepared with a large bore intravenous line, and blood and anesthesia should be made available. Adequate visualization of the birth canal requires that the patient be relaxed and that there be adequate lighting, good assistance, and appropriate instruments. The examination is best done in an operating room.

C. Lacerations in the lower vagina and perineum are readily recognized if one has good exposure (Fig. 1). They are repaired after ensuring hemostasis by careful suturing. Special attention should be paid to tears in the vaginal fornices and lateral sulci, because damage to a ureter or the bladder may already exist or be incurred by suturing. Similarly, tears near the ischial spine may damage the pudendal nerve. Lacerations that enter the rectum require meticulous closure in layers, approximating the cut edges of mucosa and anal sphincter. It is essential to follow the hematocrit level and look for signs of infection post partum.

D. If the patient continues to bleed, uterine atony, rupture or inversion, and retained secundines need to be considered. Symptoms may arise secondary to blood loss or to an expanding hematoma.

E. A small, stable hematoma can generally be treated expectantly. If it is progressive with continued bleeding, expanding size, and increasing pain, it must be surgically evacuated with careful attention to hemostasis. Primary closure is sometimes possible, but drainage is usually necessary. Secondary infection mandates evacuation and open drainage.

F. A hematoma in the broad ligament may be difficult to detect. Suspect it if the patient's cardiovascular instability or falling hematocrit level cannot be accounted for by external blood loss. Internal iliac artery ligation is often necessary to stop the bleeding before evacuating and dissecting down to the bleeding source, which is usually a uterine artery or vein. Always bear in mind the risk of ureteral injury.

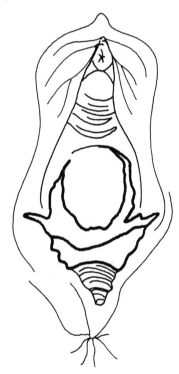

Figure 1 Second-degree perineal laceration through the fascia and muscles of the perineal body, extending upward into both vaginal sulci and exposing the anal sphincter.

References

Herbert WN. Complications of the immediate puerperium. Clin Obstet Gynecol 25:219, 1982.
Lieberman BA. Repair to injuries of the genital tract. Clin Obstet Gynecol 7:621, 1980.

PATIENT WITH HEMORRHAGE

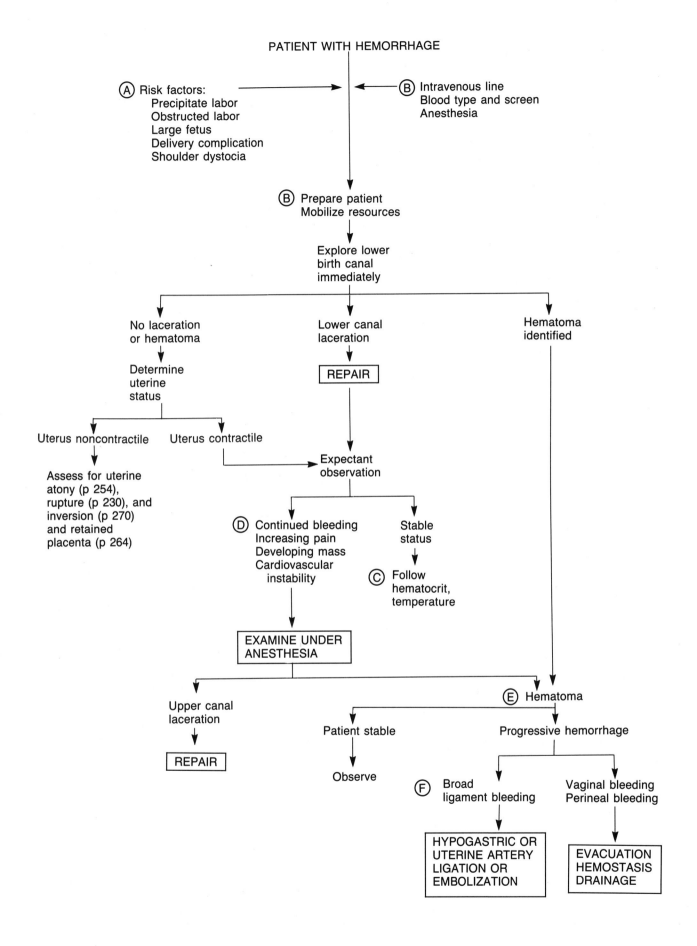

A Risk factors:
  Precipitate labor
  Obstructed labor
  Large fetus
  Delivery complication
  Shoulder dystocia

B Intravenous line
  Blood type and screen
  Anesthesia

B Prepare patient
  Mobilize resources

Explore lower
birth canal
immediately

No laceration
or hematoma

Lower canal
laceration

Hematoma
identified

Determine
uterine
status

REPAIR

Uterus noncontractile   Uterus contractile

Assess for uterine
atony (p 254),
rupture (p 230), and
inversion (p 270)
and retained
placenta (p 264)

Expectant
observation

D Continued bleeding
  Increasing pain
  Developing mass
  Cardiovascular
  instability

Stable
status

C Follow
  hematocrit,
  temperature

EXAMINE UNDER
ANESTHESIA

Upper canal
laceration

E Hematoma

REPAIR

Patient stable

Progressive hemorrhage

Observe

F Broad
  ligament bleeding

Vaginal bleeding
Perineal bleeding

HYPOGASTRIC OR
UTERINE ARTERY
LIGATION OR
EMBOLIZATION

EVACUATION
HEMOSTASIS
DRAINAGE

UTERINE ATONY

Lynn H. Galen, M.D.

A. Uterine atony, in which the uterus fails to contract well after delivery, accounts for most cases of postpartum hemorrhage. Risk factors include grand multiparity, an overdistended uterus from multiple gestation or hydramnios, fetal macrosomia, distention of the uterine cavity by clots, precipitate or prolonged labor, uterotonic stimulation, halogenated or conduction anesthesia, amnionitis, and a history of postpartum hemorrhage.

B. Precautionary intrapartum measures should be taken for patients who are identified as being at high risk for uterine atony. A baseline hematocrit level and blood typing and antibody screening are essential in anticipation of the need for rapid matching of blood for transfusion. Establish a well functioning intravenous line with a large bore catheter. Since large volumes of fluids and blood may be needed, use of a central venous pressure line may be prudent, especially if bleeding is under way and not readily controlled. Carry out baseline coagulation studies as well, if indicated.

C. Effective management needs to be instituted as soon as excessive bleeding is detected to reduce maternal morbidity and mortality. Evaluate the patient immediately for the probable cause, keeping in mind that there may be more than one source of bleeding. Carefully expose the lower birth canal to detect and repair a cervical, vaginal, or perineal laceration. Determine whether the uterus contracts well and stays contracted. Bleeding from a well contracted uterus signifies a cause other than uterine atony. Repeat coagulation studies, and consider the possibility of uterine rupture or an endocervical laceration.

D. Immediate treatment entails bimanual uterine compression, anteflexion, and elevation out of the pelvis. Simultaneously, if not already done, insert two intravenous lines with large bore catheters. Begin uterotonic therapy by administering oxytocin intravenously (30 IU per liter of crystalloid solution) at a rate of 200 ml per hour (do not give a bolus of oxytocin intravenously). Gentle curettage should be carried out to ensure that there is no possibility that placental fragments remain. If atony persists, give 0.2 mg of ergonovine or methylergonovine maleate intramuscularly. A tetanic contraction should occur in a few minutes and last several hours.

E. In the presence of hemorrhagic shock, start rapid volume replacement with cystalloid solutions. Send blood for appropriate laboratory studies at intervals. Monitor the patient's cardiovascular status carefully. Watch the urinary output and fluid balance. Institute central venous pressure monitoring or consider inserting a Swan-Ganz catheter.

F. If the uterus remains atonic, give 250 mg of 15-methylprostaglandin $F_2\alpha$ intramuscularly or directly into the myometrium; this may be repated in five minutes. If this fails, check for amnionitis. For hypertensive or asthmatic patients in whom prostaglandin $F_2\alpha$ is contraindicated, try a 30 mg vaginal or rectal prostaglandin E_2 suppository.

G. If conservative measures fail, one should proceed to surgical management. Rapid blood loss may be stemmed temporarily by the expedient of applying pressure directly on the aorta. Ligating the ovarian arteries at the uterine cornua (not the infundibulopelvic ligaments) is usually beneficial, especially if coupled with bilateral hypogastric artery ligation. Some advocate uterine artery ligation instead. Hysterectomy may prove necessary if bleeding continues and the patient becomes hemodynamically unstable.

H. In patients with uterine atony in whom there is only a moderate rate of blood loss, adjunctive techniques may be a satisfactory alternative to surgical management. Angiographic localization of the specific bleeding vessel can be done with directed selective embolization or a vasopressin infusion to provide effective hemostasis.

References

Clark SL, Phelan JP, Yeh SY, et al. Hypogastric artery ligation for obstetric hemorrhage. Obstet Gynecol 66:353, 1985.

Cruikshank SH. Management of postpartum and pelvic hemorrhage. Clin Obstet Gynecol 29:213, 1986.

Cruikshank SH, Stoelk EM. Surgical control of pelvic hemorrhage: Method of bilateral ovarian artery ligation. Am J Obstet Gynecol 147:724, 1983.

Hayashi RH, Castillo MS, Noah ML. Management of severe postpartum hemorrhage with prostaglandin $F_2\alpha$ analogue. Obstet Gynecol 63:806, 1984.

Sacks BA, Palestrant AM, Cohen WR. Internal iliac artery vasopressin infusion for postpartum hemorrhage. Am J Obstet Gynecol 143:601, 1982.

PATIENT WITH POSTPARTUM VAGINAL BLEEDING

(A) Risk factors:
   Grand multipara
   Dysfunctional or precipitate labor
   Multiple pregnancy or hydramnios
   Fetal macrosomia
   Abruptio placentae or placenta previa
   Prior postpartum hemorrhage
   Amnionitis

(B) CBC, electrolyte levels
   Type blood and screen
      for antibodies
   Serial hematocrit levels
   Coagulation studies
   Central venous pressure
   Pulmonary Swan-Ganz catheter

(C) Evaluate rapidly for bleeding source

Uterine bleeding

Bleeding below uterus

Identify site and repair
laceration or hematoma of
cervix, vagina, or perineum

Noncontractile
uterus

Contractile
uterus

Evaluate and manage:
   Coagulation defect
   Uterine rupture or inversion

(D) Apply uterine massage
   Provide intravascular volume replacement
   Give rapid oxytocin infusion
   Administer ergonovine

Bleeding unremitting

(E) Monitor hemodynamic status
   Maintain blood volume with
      crystalloids and blood
   Insert central venous pressure
      or Swan-Ganz catheter

DILATATION AND EVACUATION
Explore for retained
   placenta or membranes

(F) Give 15-methylprostaglandin $F_2\alpha$

Uterus remains unresponsive

(G) Consider surgical management
   Aggressively stabilize hemodynamically
   Anesthesia consultation

Angiographic localization
of bleeding vessel

EXPLORATORY LAPAROTOMY
Ligate ovarian and hypogastric
   (or uterine) arteries bilaterally
Consider hysterectomy for continued
   bleeding and unstable status

Bleeding controlled

(H) ARTERIAL
EMBOLIZATION

MATERNAL RESUSCITATION

Nancy E. Oriol, M.D.

A. Regional block (even local infiltration and pudendal block) risks adverse reactions to the anesthetic drug. Therefore complete resuscitation equipment must be immediately available and cardiopulmonary resuscitative capability and skills must be provided, optimally by an obstetrical anesthesiologist trained in the resuscitation of pregnant patients and familiar with the treatment of toxic reactions. The minimal resuscitation equipment includes oxygen with bag and mask, suction, an oral airway, cuffed endotracheal tube, and laryngoscope, and drugs for resuscitation (ephedrine, atropine, and epinephrine) and for intubation (succinylcholine). Careful monitoring is critical to detect immediate and delayed reactions and to institute corrective measures instantly. Every gravida receiving regional block should be monitored carefully and never left unattended. Any change in the mental status or hemodynamics warrants action.

B. Adverse reactions may be subtle at first and resemble a physiologic response to anxiety, with dizziness or an altered sensorium. Watch for them, and give oxygen by face mask while simultaneously increasing the intravenous fluid flow and displacing the uterus laterally. Evaluate the anesthesia level. Ask about tinnitus or a metallic taste. Determine whether the hands feel normal and strong. Check the pulse and blood pressure. If symptoms persist or worsen or there is evidence of a problem, call for help; elevate the legs or reposition to a Trendelenburg position. Differentiate a high spinal, toxic, or allergic drug effect from aortocaval compression, vasovagal reaction, thromboembolism, and amniotic fluid embolism.

C. The manifestations of total spinal or high epidural anesthesia reflect hypotension from total sympathetic block, with nausea, vomiting, and syncope. Treat the hypotension and evaluate the anesthesia level by assessing the strength of the patient's hands. Respiratory arrest results primarily from secondary medullary ischemia. Give oxygen (and mechanical ventilation, if needed), fluid resuscitation, vasopressors, and atropine for bradycardia. Reposition to a Trendelenburg position or elevate the legs to increase the venous return. Without hypotension, most patients can breath well even with high spinal anesthesia.

D. Aortocaval compression by the gravid uterus can cause cardiovascular collapse in the supine position. Compensation occurs by upper extremity vasoconstriction to maintain blood flow to the brain and heart, masking the decreased uterine flow. The sympathetic block from regional anesthesia abolishes this compensatory mechanism to produce cardiovascular collapse from decreased venous return. Avoid the supine position, if possible. Treat by left lateral tilting or by turning the patient to the left lateral position. Oxygen and hydration also may help. A history of supine hypotension may interdict regional anesthesia, especially spinal block.

E. Watch for toxic blood levels of the anesthetic drug from inadvertent intravascular injection immediately after a regional block is given or within 10 to 20 minutes as a result of rapid absorption. Early signs of lidocaine toxicity are central nervous system excitation and seizures progressing to depression, respiratory arrest, and coma. Bupivacaine toxicity may produce the same signs or may result in primary cardiovascular toxicity. All local anesthetics are myocardial depressants. Bupivacaine is more cardiotoxic than lidocaine, and its toxicity is greatly enhanced by the hypoxia, hypercarbia, and acidosis that develop with seizures or cardiac arrest. Its avid protein binding may require prolonged resuscitation. In all patients who develop drug reactions, maintain oxygenation and ventilation and treat hypotension aggressively.

References

Adverse reactions with bupivacaine. U.S. Department of Health and Human Services, Publication No. 13, Rockville, Maryland. FDA Drug Bull 3:23, 1983.

Gibbs CP, Krischer J, Peckham BM, et al. Obstetric anesthesia: A national survey. Anesthesiology 65:298, 1986.

Montgomery WH. Standards and guidelines for cardiopulmonary resuscitation (CPR) and emergency care (ECC). JAMA 255:2905, 1986.

Moore DC. Toxicity of local anaesthetics in obstetrics: IV. Management. Clin Anaesthesiol 4:113, 1986.

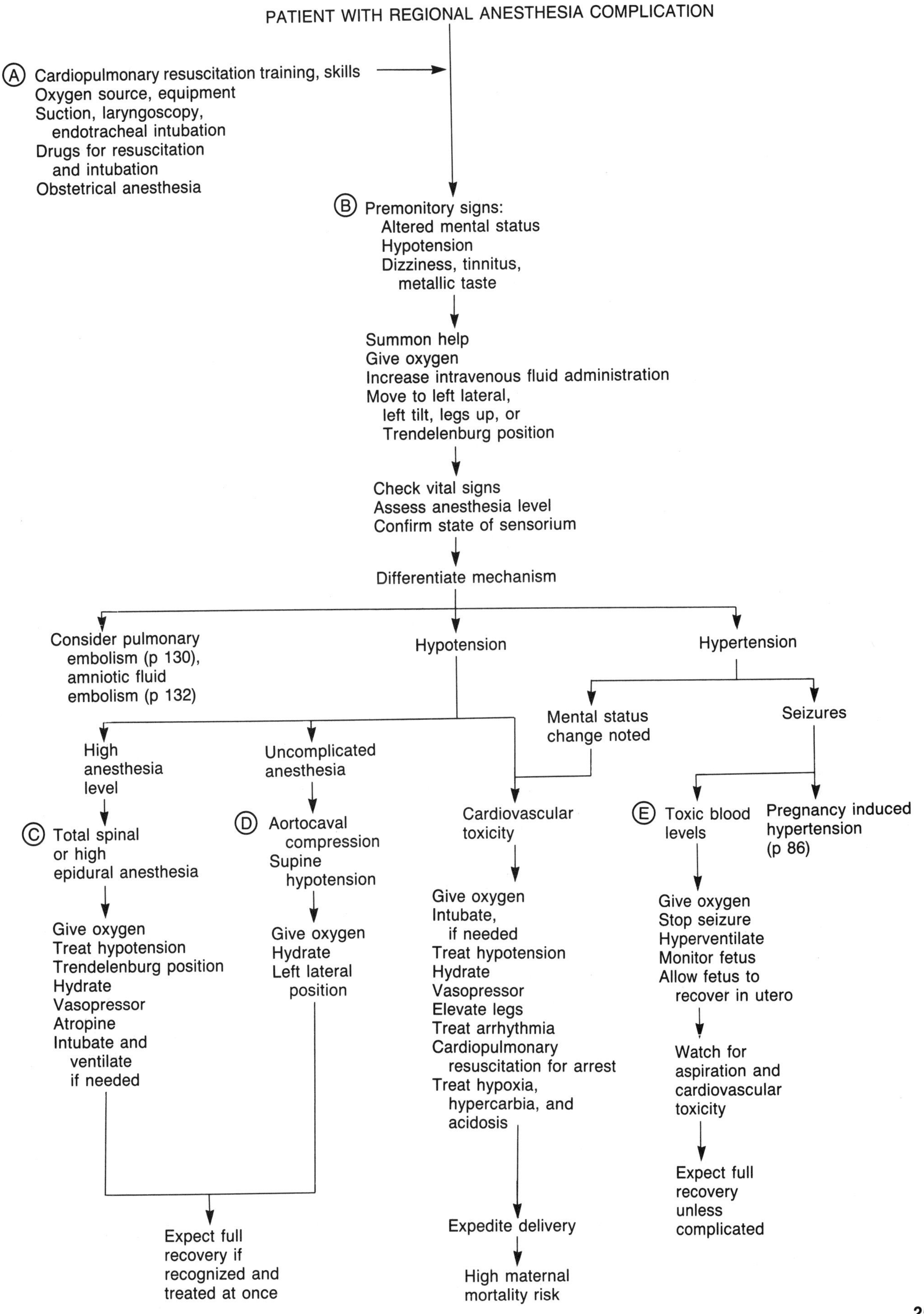

PATIENT WITH REGIONAL ANESTHESIA COMPLICATION

(A) Cardiopulmonary resuscitation training, skills
Oxygen source, equipment
Suction, laryngoscopy,
 endotracheal intubation
Drugs for resuscitation
 and intubation
Obstetrical anesthesia

(B) Premonitory signs:
 Altered mental status
 Hypotension
 Dizziness, tinnitus,
  metallic taste

Summon help
Give oxygen
Increase intravenous fluid administration
Move to left lateral,
 left tilt, legs up, or
 Trendelenburg position

Check vital signs
Assess anesthesia level
Confirm state of sensorium

Differentiate mechanism

Consider pulmonary embolism (p 130), amniotic fluid embolism (p 132)

Hypotension

Hypertension

Mental status change noted

Seizures

High anesthesia level

Uncomplicated anesthesia

(C) Total spinal or high epidural anesthesia

(D) Aortocaval compression Supine hypotension

Cardiovascular toxicity

(E) Toxic blood levels

Pregnancy induced hypertension (p 86)

Give oxygen
Treat hypotension
Trendelenburg position
Hydrate
Vasopressor
Atropine
Intubate and
 ventilate
 if needed

Give oxygen
Hydrate
Left lateral
position

Give oxygen
Intubate,
 if needed
Treat hypotension
Hydrate
Vasopressor
Elevate legs
Treat arrhythmia
Cardiopulmonary
 resuscitation for arrest
Treat hypoxia,
 hypercarbia, and
 acidosis

Give oxygen
Stop seizure
Hyperventilate
Monitor fetus
Allow fetus to
 recover in utero

Watch for
aspiration and
cardiovascular
toxicity

Expect full
recovery if
recognized and
treated at once

Expedite delivery

High maternal
mortality risk

Expect full
recovery
unless
complicated

257

PUERPERAL INFECTION

Harold W. Rubin, M.D.

A. Febrile morbidity is defined as peak temperature elevations to at least 38° C (100.4° F) on any two of the first 10 postpartum days except the first 24 hours. Predisposing factors include prolonged labor, premature rupture of membranes, traumatic delivery, manual removal of the placenta, cesarean section (especially if done after the onset of labor and with internal fetal heart rate monitoring), intrapartum fever, bladder catheterization, and atonic bladder.

B. Both aerobic and anaerobic organisms should be searched for in bacteriologic studies of cultures obtained from the endocervix and uterine cavity as well as blood, throat, and urine. Coagulation parameters should be monitored so that impending disseminated intravascular coagulation can be recognized as early as possible. Ultrasonography is especially useful for identifying an abscess in cases in which it is suspected because an infection is unresponsive to antibiotic management.

C. Antibiotics for use against aerobic and anaerobic bacteria are given at once, as needed, to contain the local infection. The types and doses are adjusted later on the basis of culture reports. Pelvic infections are usually due to mixed flora and therefore require broad spectrum combinations, such as penicillin and streptomycin, clindamycin and kanamycin, or clindamycin, gentamicin, and ampicillin. These drug combinations ensure coverage against both anaerobic and enterococcal pathogens.

D. If there has been no improvement in the patient's general condition within 72 hours, one must consider the possibilities of pelvic thrombophlebitis, abscess formation, and septic embolization.

E. Septic embolization is a rare but potentially life threatening complication of puerperal sepsis. It must be considered if the patient has not responded to appropriate antibiotics in adequate amounts and develops acute chest or pulmonary manifestations.

F. All abscesses must be incised and drained or excised. If the abscess points into the posterior vaginal fornix, it usually can be drained through the vagina; if not, the transabdominal approach is preferable. If the uterus is involved, hysterectomy may be indicated, especially if the condition arose following cesarean section and the uterine incision has dehisced or is the seat of infection.

G. Septic shock is characterized by high fever, unstable cardiovascular status, and a falling white blood count. It demands intensive management with oxygen, volume replacement, blood transfusion, antibiotics, corticosteroids, vasomotor drugs, digitalis, and anticoagulants, as needed.

References

Eshenbach DA, Wager GP, Puerperal infections. Clin Obstet Gynecol 23:1003, 1980.

Gibbs RS. Clinical risk factors for puerperal infection. Obstet Gynecol 55:178S, 1980.

Monif GRG, Hempling RE. Antibiotic therapy for the bacteroidaceae in postcesarean section infections. Obstet Gynecol 57:177, 1981.

Rivlin MF, Hunt JA. Surgical management of diffuse peritonitis complicating obstetric/gynecologic infections. Obstet Gynecol 67:652, 1986.

Sorrell TC, Marshall JR, Yoshimori R, Chow AW. Antimicrobial therapy of postpartum endomyometritis. Am J Obstet Gynecol 141:246, 1981.

FEBRILE MORBIDITY

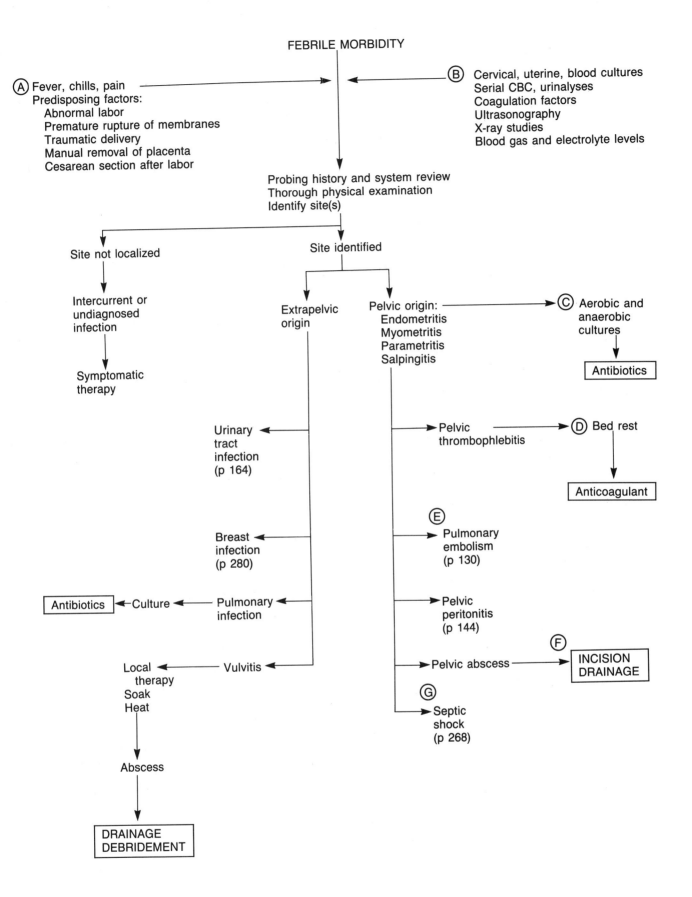

A Fever, chills, pain
Predisposing factors:
  Abnormal labor
  Premature rupture of membranes
  Traumatic delivery
  Manual removal of placenta
  Cesarean section after labor

B Cervical, uterine, blood cultures
  Serial CBC, urinalyses
  Coagulation factors
  Ultrasonography
  X-ray studies
  Blood gas and electrolyte levels

Probing history and system review
Thorough physical examination
Identify site(s)

Site not localized

Site identified

Intercurrent or
undiagnosed
infection

Symptomatic
therapy

Extrapelvic
origin

Pelvic origin:
  Endometritis
  Myometritis
  Parametritis
  Salpingitis

C Aerobic and
  anaerobic
  cultures

Antibiotics

Urinary
tract
infection
(p 164)

Pelvic
thrombophlebitis

D Bed rest

Anticoagulant

Breast
infection
(p 280)

E Pulmonary
  embolism
  (p 130)

Antibiotics ← Culture ← Pulmonary
infection

Pelvic
peritonitis
(p 144)

Local
therapy
Soak
Heat

Vulvitis

Pelvic abscess

F INCISION
  DRAINAGE

G Septic
  shock
  (p 268)

Abscess

DRAINAGE
DEBRIDEMENT

259

EVALUATION OF THE NEWBORN

William D. Cochran, M.D.

A. An important aspect of the perinatal care of the fetus and infant is prenatal and intrapartum involvement of the pediatrician, preferably one with special interest and training in neonatology, in all cases in which a high risk infant is expected to be delivered. Especially relevant in this regard are cases involving serious maternal illnesses, such as diabetes mellitus, pregnancy induced hypertension, Rh isoimmunization, and placental disorders (abruptio placentae and placenta previa), as well as intrauterine growth retardation, premature labor, amnionitis, disordered labor, fetal malposition, prolapsed cord, hydramnios, multiple pregnancy, fetal macrosomia, difficult or potentially traumatic delivery, shoulder dystocia, meconium staining of the amniotic fluid, and fetal distress. By ensuring such active participation by a pediatrician, the obstetrician enhances the probability that decisions pertaining to labor and delivery management practices will take into account the needs of the fetus and that all necessary preparations will be made to provide essential emergency care immediately upon delivery.

B. The Apgar score is a valuable means for quickly evaluating the condition of the newborn infant (Table 1). Of the five factors that make up the score, heart rate and respiratory rate are the best indices of well-being. The simplicity of the Apgar score and the fact that most newborn infants have high scores of 7 or more, especially after 1 minute, should not lull personnel into superficial or inaccurate assessments. Any score below 7 should serve to alert the staff to the need for special expert attention for resuscitation (p 262). A low 1-minute score warrants intensification of resuscitative efforts; it most often reflects transient effects, such as anesthesia. The 5-minute score tends to be a more valuable indicator of prognosis and the need for subsequent special neonatal care; it is correlated with late neurologic and developmental problems, albeit imperfectly.

C. An examination for physical signs of maturity, coupled with information obtained from the history and available laboratory data pertaining to fetal lung maturity, helps determine the gestational age and functional maturity. Look for hypertonic flexion of the extremities, acute popliteal and foot angles, sole creases, breast nodule, cartilaginous earlobe, and descended testes as signs of maturity.

D. Premature infants and those with documented or suspected immature organ system function should be observed and cared for in a special care nursery setting. Similarly, those with recognizable high risk conditions, including hemolytic disease (p 108), congenital anomaly, or intrauterine growth retardation (p 68), or with possible meconium aspiration deserve comparable surveillance and management. If indicated, transfer the infant to a tertiary care facility for more intensive neonatal care to deal with cardiopulmonary support and to provide specialized techniques not otherwise available in less well equipped facilities. If such problems can be anticipated on the basis of prenatal factors, transferring the mother to an appropriate high risk center before delivery has considerable merit.

E. The otherwise normal term infant who develops any manifestation suggesting a serious underlying disorder or deterioration of condition warrants pediatric consultation and special care. If such mature infants improve or stabilize on the basis of evaluation and management, they can be returned to the regular nursery for continued care and observation. One must be especially watchful for respiratory manifestations (grunting, tachypnea, nasal flaring, chest retraction, cyanosis), central nervous system abnormalities (lethargy, seizures, hyperactivity, tremors), abdominal signs (distention, propulsive vomiting, or vomiting of bile colored material), metabolic changes (particularly hypothermia and hypoglycemia), hemolytic effects (positive Coombs test, hepatosplenomegaly, petechiae, and unusual bleeding), infection (manifested by anemia, hepatosplenomegaly, or petechiae), and any anatomic malformations that may compromise the infant's well-being.

TABLE 1 Apgar Score for Evaluating Infant at 1, 5, and 10 Minutes

Sign	Score 0	Score 1	Score 2
Heart rate	Absent	Slow, below 100/min	Over 100/min
Respiratory effort	Absent	Slow, irregular	Good, cry
Muscle tone	Limp	Some flexion of extremities	Active motion, well flexed extremities
Reflex response to stimulus	None	Grimace	Cough, sneeze, cry
Color	Blue or pale	Body pink, extremities blue	Completely pink

DELIVERY OF NEWBORN INFANT

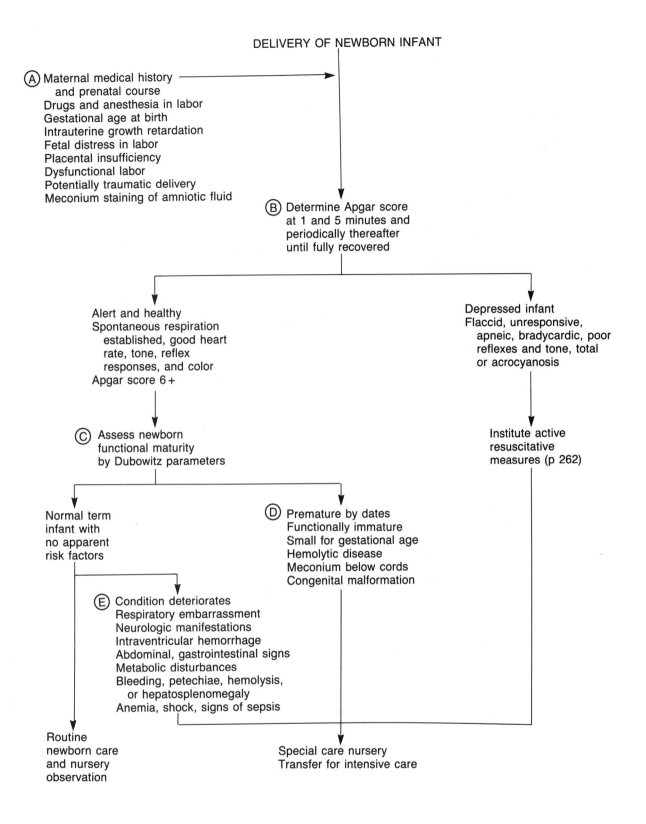

Ⓐ Maternal medical history
    and prenatal course
  Drugs and anesthesia in labor
  Gestational age at birth
  Intrauterine growth retardation
  Fetal distress in labor
  Placental insufficiency
  Dysfunctional labor
  Potentially traumatic delivery
  Meconium staining of amniotic fluid

Ⓑ Determine Apgar score
   at 1 and 5 minutes and
   periodically thereafter
   until fully recovered

Alert and healthy
Spontaneous respiration
  established, good heart
  rate, tone, reflex
  responses, and color
Apgar score 6 +

Depressed infant
Flaccid, unresponsive,
  apneic, bradycardic, poor
  reflexes and tone, total
  or acrocyanosis

Ⓒ Assess newborn
   functional maturity
   by Dubowitz parameters

Institute active
resuscitative
measures (p 262)

Normal term
infant with
no apparent
risk factors

Ⓓ Premature by dates
  Functionally immature
  Small for gestational age
  Hemolytic disease
  Meconium below cords
  Congenital malformation

Ⓔ Condition deteriorates
  Respiratory embarrassment
  Neurologic manifestations
  Intraventricular hemorrhage
  Abdominal, gastrointestinal signs
  Metabolic disturbances
  Bleeding, petechiae, hemolysis,
    or hepatosplenomegaly
  Anemia, shock, signs of sepsis

Routine
newborn care
and nursery
observation

Special care nursery
Transfer for intensive care

References

Avery ME, Taeusch HW (Editors). Shaffer's Diseases of the Newborn. 5th ed. Philadelphia: WB Saunders, 1984.

Phibbs R. Evaluation of the newborn. In: Rudolph A (Editor). Pediatrics. 2nd ed. New York: Appleton-Century-Crofts, 1982.
Scanlon JW, Nelson T, Grylack L, Smith Y. A System of Newborn Physical Examination. Baltimore: University Park Press,
  1979.

NEONATAL RESUSCITATION

William D. Cochran, M.D.

A. Anticipate problems in resuscitating the newborn infant and mobilize full team support. Each member of the team should know his position and review and coordinate specific tasks ahead of time. Remember that a small premature infant with a low Apgar score may still benefit from aggressive resuscitative measures.

B. The obstetrical attendant must take special pains to clear the infant's oropharynx just as the mouth appears over the perineum, preferably before the first breath. This is particularly important if meconium is present. Even if the delivery is being done by cesarean section, such clearing of the oropharynx is still important.

C. In the presence of thick meconium and no crying, the first requisite of resuscitation should be to ascertain whether any meconium has been aspirated below the level of the vocal cords. Endotracheal suctioning is mandatory under such circumstances. Laryngoscopic visualization (Fig. 1A,B) must precede the administration of oxygen under positive pressure to avoid pushing the meconium down into the bronchial tree and the pulmonary alveoli.

D. The moderately depressed infant is resuscitated initially with a flow-through bag fitted with a pop-off valve device and a manometer for proper pressure control. Until one is assured that the chest wall is moving in response to ventilation, pressures up to 60 to 80 cm of water can be used. Thereafter, 40 cm generally suffices. The rate of ventilation should be between 40 and 80 respirations per minute. Listen for air entry by stethoscope.

E. When endotracheal intubation is clearly needed, either orotracheal or nasotracheal intubation is effective as long as it is done correctly—that is, the tube must not be placed in the esophagus. The minimum amount of pressure necessary to move the chest should suffice, but it may require as much as 80 cm of water initially. Listen for air entry. Apply closed chest cardiac massage, with the hands around the chest and the thumbs on the midsternum (Fig. 1C), at a rate of 60 to 80 compressions per minute.

F. By three minutes, the unresponsive infant requires umbilical vein catheterization to correct rapidly developing acidosis. Measure the distance from the umbilicus to the right nipple, subtract 1 cm, and insert the catheter to that distance. If it cannot be inserted that far, inject drugs with extreme caution. Give an equal mixture of 1 M sodium bicarbonate and 10 percent dextrose in water (5 to 8 ml per kilogram). If there is no improvement in one to two minutes, inject epinephrine (1 ml of a 1:10,000 dilution). The epinephrine may be put down the endotracheal tube, if necessary. If there is still no improvement, consider giving Narcan (0.02 mg per milliliter, injecting 1 to 2 ml) as a narcotic antagonist and calcium gluconate (10 percent, injecting 2 ml slowly), rechecking the airway and the chest for air entry. Subsequently one may give whole blood (preferably the infant's own placental blood, 10 to 15 ml per kilogram, since it is immediately available) or 5 percent albumin. One generally terminates efforts after about 30 minutes if there is no response.

References

Cloherty JP, Stark AR. Manual of Neonatal Care. 2nd ed. Boston: Little, Brown, 1985.

Schreiner RL. Care of the Newborn. New York: Raven Press, 1981.

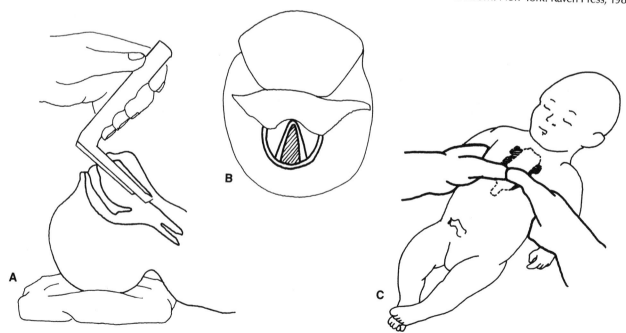

Figure 1 Laryngoscopy of newborn infant. *A*, head elevated and extended while the tip of the laryngoscope is inserted and advanced into the space between tongue and epiglottis. *B*, an endotracheal tube is inserted between the vocal cords, identified as pale white folds. *C*, closed chest cardiac massage is applied by compressing the lower sternum with the thumbs.

DEPRESSED INFANT

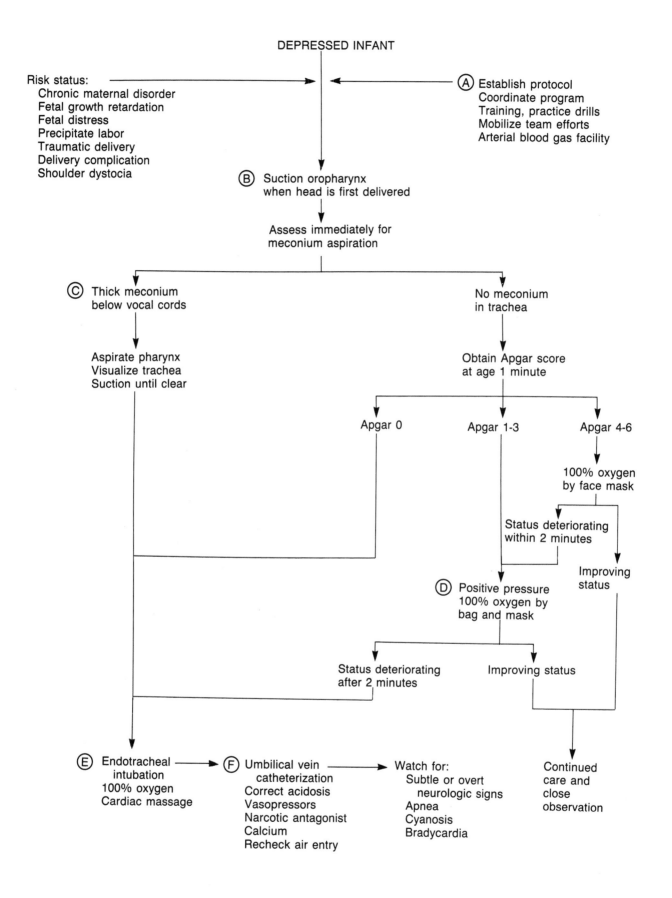

Risk status:
  Chronic maternal disorder
  Fetal growth retardation
  Fetal distress
  Precipitate labor
  Traumatic delivery
  Delivery complication
  Shoulder dystocia

(A) Establish protocol
  Coordinate program
  Training, practice drills
  Mobilize team efforts
  Arterial blood gas facility

(B) Suction oropharynx
  when head is first delivered

Assess immediately for
meconium aspiration

(C) Thick meconium
  below vocal cords

No meconium
in trachea

Aspirate pharynx
Visualize trachea
Suction until clear

Obtain Apgar score
at age 1 minute

Apgar 0   Apgar 1-3   Apgar 4-6

100% oxygen
by face mask

Status deteriorating
within 2 minutes

Improving
status

(D) Positive pressure
  100% oxygen by
  bag and mask

Status deteriorating
after 2 minutes

Improving status

(E) Endotracheal
  intubation
  100% oxygen
  Cardiac massage

(F) Umbilical vein
  catheterization
  Correct acidosis
  Vasopressors
  Narcotic antagonist
  Calcium
  Recheck air entry

Watch for:
  Subtle or overt
    neurologic signs
  Apnea
  Cyanosis
  Bradycardia

Continued
care and
close
observation

RETAINED PLACENTA

Susan B. Wilson, M.D.

A. In most cases (nearly 80 percent), the duration of the third stage is less than 10 minutes; in only 6 percent of women does the third stage last more than 30 minutes, the conventional but arbitrary definition of retained placenta. Predisposing factors for retained placenta are multiple pregnancy, uterine overdistention, uterine atony, desultory labor as well as anatomic defects, such as fibroids, uterine anomalies or scars from prior uterine surgery, and abnormal placentation as occurs with placenta accreta or placental implantation on a uterine septum or scar.

B. When retained placenta is diagnosed, one should prepare for the possibilities of major blood loss and operative intervention by manual removal of the placenta. This requires the placement of a large bore intravenous needle with access for the administration of fluid (and especially blood), blood typing and screening (or actual cross matching if blood bank facilities do not permit rapid availability of blood when needed), and anesthesia. Since placenta accreta, although rare, is a possibility in these cases (see E), emergency surgical facilities may be required as well.

C. The patient should be assessed by a combined abdominopelvic examination under sterile conditions to ascertain whether the placenta has separated and descended into the vagina. Observation shows the cord to be elongating, and vaginal bleeding generally occurs as the placenta separates and begins to descend. Elevating the uterus out of the pelvis while applying slight countertension on the cord demonstrates whether separation has occurred. This is the Brandt-Andrews maneuver (Fig. 1A). It is carried out by placing a hand suprapubically to lift the uterus gently while the umbilical cord is held, but not pulled, at the vulva.

D. If the placenta has not separated or is only incompletely separated from its attachment to the uterine wall, oxytocin should be considered. Intravenous infusion of a dilute solution, analogous to that used for labor induction (p 182), is generally effective. It has recently been shown that 10 IU of oxytocin diluted in 20 ml of saline injected into the umbilical vein helps the placenta separate in a high proportion of cases.

E. Manual removal of the placenta (Fig. 1B) is carried out under sterile conditions in an operating room where facilities can be mobilized rapidly for surgical intervention as needed. An intravenous infusion is essential and the procedure should be done under adequate anesthesia. If a cleavage plane cannot be found and developed completely, one must consider the possibility that placenta accreta exists (p 90). If one persists in the dissection under these circumstances, intense hemorrhage may result.

F. The placenta may be trapped in the endometrial cavity because the uterus is tonically contracted from excessively vigorous uterine massage or the use of uterotonic drugs. Discontinuing the massage, allowing the effect of the uterotonic drug to subside, or administering a general anesthetic, such as halothane, is generally effective in permitting the placenta to be spontaneously evacuated, thereby avoiding the necessity for manual removal.

References

Golan A, Lider AL, Wexler S, David MP. A new method for the management of the retained placenta. Am J Obstet Gynecol 146:708, 1982.

Herbert, WN. Complications of the immediate puerperium. Clin Obstet Gynecol 25:219, 1982.

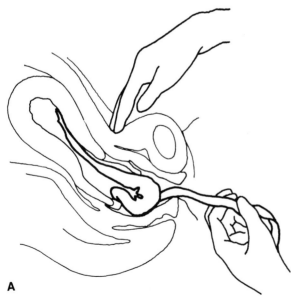

A

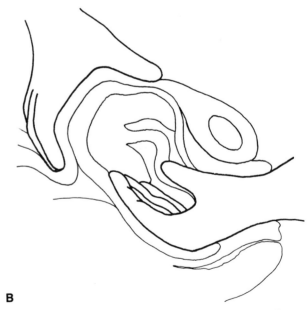

B

Figure 1 Management of retained placenta. *A*, Brandt-Andrews technique for aiding delivery of placenta after it has separated. Lift uterus with suprapubic hand while holding (not pulling) umbilical cord at perineum. *B*, manual removal of placenta by gently advancing dissecting fingers in plane between placenta and uterine wall.

PATIENT WITH RETAINED PLACENTA

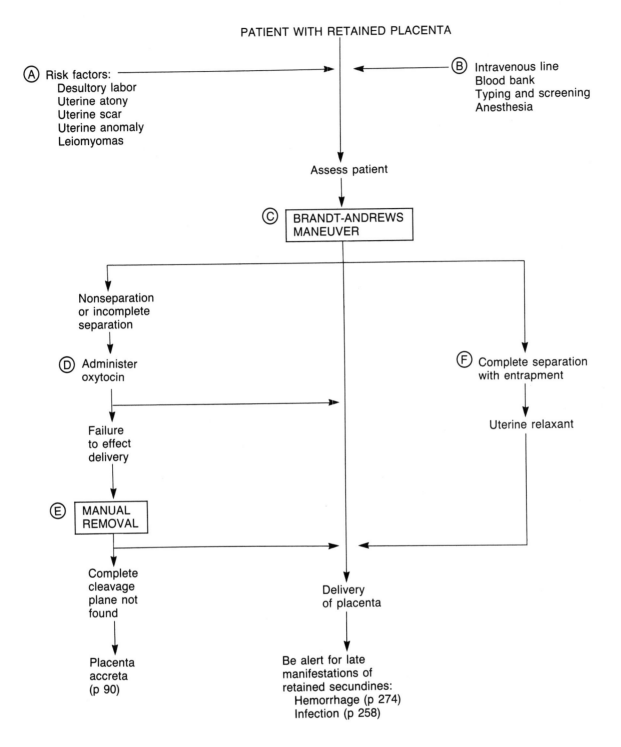

Ⓐ Risk factors:
   Desultory labor
   Uterine atony
   Uterine scar
   Uterine anomaly
   Leiomyomas

Ⓑ Intravenous line
   Blood bank
   Typing and screening
   Anesthesia

Assess patient

Ⓒ BRANDT-ANDREWS
   MANEUVER

Nonseparation
or incomplete
separation

Ⓓ Administer
   oxytocin

Failure
to effect
delivery

Ⓔ MANUAL
   REMOVAL

Ⓕ Complete separation
   with entrapment

Uterine relaxant

Complete
cleavage
plane not
found

Delivery
of placenta

Placenta
accreta
(p 90)

Be alert for late
manifestations of
retained secundines:
   Hemorrhage (p 274)
   Infection (p 258)

ASPIRATION PNEUMONITIS

Nancy E. Oriol, M.D.

A. Aspiration of stomach contents into the lungs is a preventable cause of maternal morbidity and mortality. First described by Mendelson in 1946, it is now the most common cause of anesthesia-related maternal death. A patient is considered at risk for aspiration if her stomach is full from recent eating or drinking or if there is delayed emptying of the normal gastric secretion. In pregnancy, the lower esophageal sphincter allows free reflux of the gastric contents back into the esophagus (explaining heartburn). Once labor begins, gastric emptying is significantly decreased. Even water remains in the stomach until normal gastric function begins after delivery. Digestion also stops in labor; anything eaten persists as large, undigested particles. The practice of allowing laboring patients to drink fluids in labor should be actively discouraged.

B. Prevention is critical. Keep laboring patients from taking anything by mouth, including clear fluids. They should be admonished not to eat at all once labor has begun. Some women, knowing about the restrictions that will be imposed in the hospital, eat before admission. They have to be fully informed about the peril to which they are exposing themselves by this practice. Prior to induction of general anesthesia, use pharmacologic prophylaxis. Give clear antacids periodically in labor to increase the gastric pH, and consider metoclopramide to increase gastric emptying. For elective repeat cesarean section, a histamine-2 blocker, such as cimetidine and ranitidine, may help decrease gastric acid secretion. Whenever possible and appropriate, use regional block instead of general anesthesia. Endotracheal intubation is done if general anesthesia is necessary (or the only option). If difficulty is expected, consider intubating while the patient is still awake, using topical anesthesia.

C. Common reasons for loss of the protective airway reflex are inhalation analgesia, general anesthesia, excessive narcotics, and seizures.

D. If active vomiting or passive regurgitation is observed in a gravida who is not awake with active airway reflexes, quickly place her in the Trendelenburg position and rotate her into an extreme left lateral tilt. Vigorously suction the mouth and airway. Test the pH of the aspirated material and note its amount and particulate content. Early signs of aspiration are wheezing, cyanosis, rales, and rhonchi. Clinical symptoms parallel the volume and nature of the material aspirated; particulate and strongly acid material yields the worst prognosis.

E. Even those who appear to do well at first remain at some risk of late onset respiratory distress. Close surveillance with serial arterial blood gas analyses and chest x-ray examinations is important. Abnormal blood gas values, specifically low PO_2 and high PCO_2 levels, signify respiratory failure. Clinical manifestations include dyspnea and progressive tachypnea. Diffuse, spotty lung infiltrates may advance to pulmonary edema. If the hypoxemia is progressive, ventilatory support will be needed.

F. Intensive care is mandated. Early aggressive management improves the prognosis. Therefore, intubate at once and ventilate mechanically to restore or maintain adequate oxygenation, adding positive end-expiratory pressure (PEEP). Management can be facilitated by a Swan-Ganz catheter, which gives pulmonary capillary wedge and right atrial pressures and cardiac output data. It is essential for correcting fluid imbalance, maintaining hemodynamic support, and monitoring the results of the management program. Steroids do not improve the outcome and may actually interfere with healing. Prophylactic antibiotic administration also does not help and may permit resistant secondary infections to arise. Pulmonary lavage worsens hypoxia. Bronchoscopy is generally unnecessary unless large particles occlude the airway. Prolonged chest physical therapy is usually needed for these cases; the average hospital stay is 21 days. Overall, the prognosis for survival is guarded; mortality after aspiration is approximately 30 percent. Chronic pulmonary problems may occur in survivors.

References

Cohen SE. The aspiration syndrome. Clin Obstet Gynaecol 9:235, 1982.

Eyler SW, Cullen BF, Murphy ME, Welch WD. Antacid aspiration in rabbits: A comparison of Mylanta and Bicitra. Anesth Analg 61:288, 1982.

Howard FA, Sharp DS. Effects of metoclopramide on gastric emptying during labour. Br Med J 1:446, 1973.

Mendelson CL. The aspiration of stomach contents into the lungs during obstetric anesthesia. Am J Obstet Gynecol 52:191, 1946.

Toung T, Cameron JL. Cimetidine as a preoperative medication to reduce the complications of aspiration of gastric contents. Surgery 87:205, 1980.

SUSPICION OF ASPIRATION

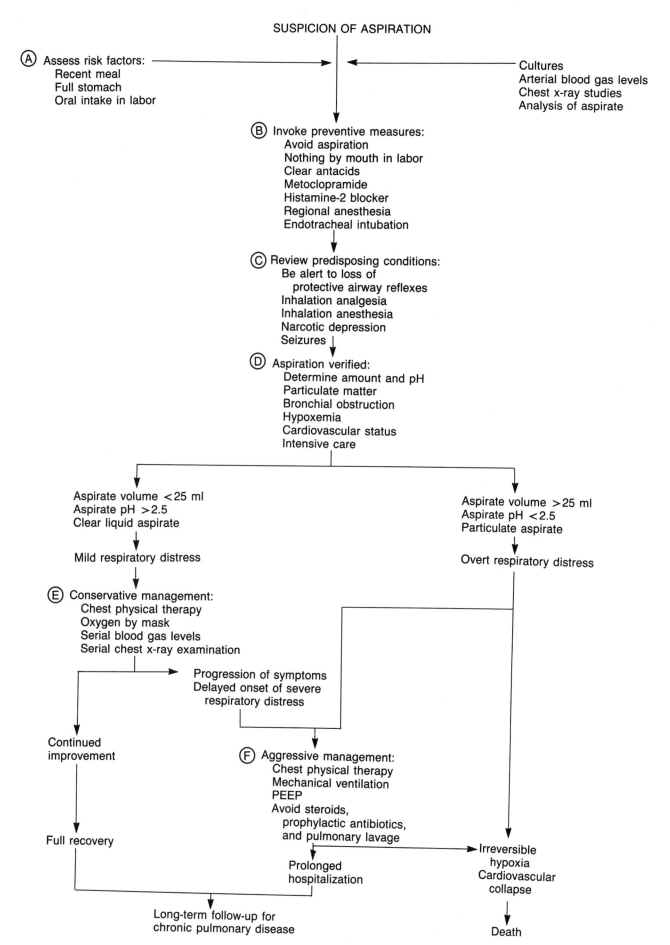

Ⓐ Assess risk factors:
   Recent meal
   Full stomach
   Oral intake in labor

Cultures
Arterial blood gas levels
Chest x-ray studies
Analysis of aspirate

Ⓑ Invoke preventive measures:
   Avoid aspiration
   Nothing by mouth in labor
   Clear antacids
   Metoclopramide
   Histamine-2 blocker
   Regional anesthesia
   Endotracheal intubation

Ⓒ Review predisposing conditions:
   Be alert to loss of
     protective airway reflexes
   Inhalation analgesia
   Inhalation anesthesia
   Narcotic depression
   Seizures

Ⓓ Aspiration verified:
   Determine amount and pH
   Particulate matter
   Bronchial obstruction
   Hypoxemia
   Cardiovascular status
   Intensive care

Aspirate volume <25 ml
Aspirate pH >2.5
Clear liquid aspirate

Aspirate volume >25 ml
Aspirate pH <2.5
Particulate aspirate

Mild respiratory distress

Overt respiratory distress

Ⓔ Conservative management:
   Chest physical therapy
   Oxygen by mask
   Serial blood gas levels
   Serial chest x-ray examination

Progression of symptoms
Delayed onset of severe
respiratory distress

Continued
improvement

Ⓕ Aggressive management:
   Chest physical therapy
   Mechanical ventilation
   PEEP
   Avoid steroids,
     prophylactic antibiotics,
     and pulmonary lavage

Full recovery

Prolonged
hospitalization

Irreversible
hypoxia
Cardiovascular
collapse

Long-term follow-up for
chronic pulmonary disease

Death

SHOCK

Henry Klapholz, M.D.

A. Although one should suspect that shock exists if there is hypotension, the blood pressure may not be a very sensitive indicator of the cardiovascular status. One has to be alert to more meaningful early manifestations, such as peripheral or circumoral cyanosis or pallor (reflecting peripheral vasoconstriction), oliguria, mental confusion, dyspnea, and chest pain. Excessive blood loss and infection place patients at special risk in this regard.

B. The key to management is aggressive, expeditious evaluation. Monitor the pulse and blood pressure constantly. Auscultate the lungs regularly for signs of failure. Check the extremities to assess the peripheral circulation, edema, and reflexes and to determine whether they are warm or cold. Measure the urinary output hourly by means of a continuous indwelling bladder catheter. A central venous pressure catheter is invaluable as well. A large bore intravenous catheter (14 gauge Angiocath, for example) is needed for the rapid administration of drugs and fluids. Obtain blood for cultures, hematocrit and electrolyte levels, coagulation studies—including at least the prothrombin time, partial thromboplastin time, fibrinogen level, and platelet count—and for cross matching whole blood or packed red blood cells (at least four units) for later rapid transfusion, if needed. Chest x-ray examination and electrocardiographic monitoring are useful. When available, a Swan-Ganz pulmonary artery catheter is extremely useful. The information it provides in regard to the pulmonary capillary wedge pressure and cardiac output gives clear insights about the cardiac preload and afterload to facilitate diagnosis and care in the patient in shock. Arterial blood gas analysis is also important; it may have to be repeated sequentially to help determine needed modifications of therapy. The adult respiratory distress syndrome (p 266) often accompanies massive sepsis, blood loss, embolism, and trauma. Endotracheal intubation and mechanically assisted ventilation with positive end-expiratory pressure may be required.

C. Large volumes of electrolyte solutions are generally needed to help bring the central venous pressure of patients in septic shock up to 8 to 10 cm of water. They need triple antibiotic coverage against a broad sprectrum of organisms, such as gentamicin, ampicillin, and clindamycin in large doses. The role of corticosteroids in the treatment of septic shock is in question, because their efficacy is unproved and they may actually increase the risk of death in some patients (especially those who have elevated creatinine levels or who develop secondary infection after treatment begins).

D. Hypovolemic shock demands prompt and adequate replacement of the lost circulatory volume with appropriate volume expanding solutions. Until blood is available, one can give an electrolyte containing solution with crystalloids or colloids, such as Ringer's lactate, normal saline, or 5 percent albumin in saline. Whole blood or packed red blood cells with fresh frozen plasma are optimal for replacing blood loss in kind. It is preferable to give fresh frozen plasma to replace needed coagulation factors.

E. Cardiogenic shock can be managed effectively with a combination of a strong diuretic (such as furosemide, 80 mg intravenously), a pressor drug (such as dopamine), and a digitalis preparation.

F. Potentially fatal amniotic fluid embolism (p 132) may complicate tumultuous labor, especially in grand multiparas, gravidas with polyhydramnios, or those receiving oxytocin infusion. The typical clinical picture involves sudden hypotension, usually at the time of delivery or immediately post partum, accompanied by acute dyspnea, cyanosis, and collapse.

G. Neurogenic shock due to vagal syncope is readily reversed merely by placing the patient in the supine position, taking care to avoid supine hypotension by displacing the large gravid uterus to the left off the inferior vena cava. Atropine can be used in 0.4 to 0.6 mg doses intravenously, along with electrolyte containing fluids, in refractory cases.

References

Herbert WN. Complications of the immediate puerperium. Clin Obstet Gynecol 25:219, 1982.

Hinshaw LB. High-dose corticosteroids in the critically ill patient: Current concept and future developments. Acta Chir Scand 526Suppl:129, 1985.

Houston MC, Thompson WL, Robertson D. Shock: Diagnosis and management. Arch Intern Med 144:1433, 1984.

Karakusis PH. Considerations in the therapy of septic shock. Med Clin North Am 70:933, 1986.

Schwartz RA, Cerra FB. Shock: A practical approach. Urol Clin North Am 10:89, 1983.

Shoemaker WC. Controversies in the pathophysiology and fluid management of postoperative adult respiratory distress syndrome. Surg Clin North Am 65:931, 1985.

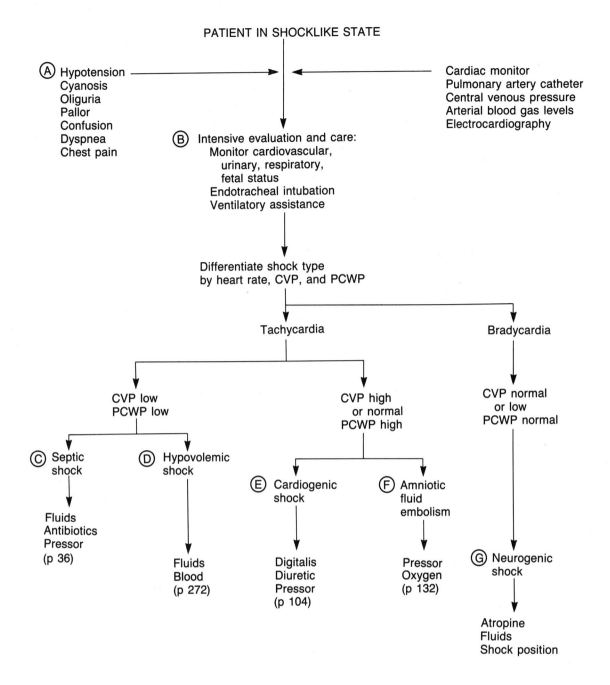

PATIENT IN SHOCKLIKE STATE

Ⓐ Hypotension
Cyanosis
Oliguria
Pallor
Confusion
Dyspnea
Chest pain

Cardiac monitor
Pulmonary artery catheter
Central venous pressure
Arterial blood gas levels
Electrocardiography

Ⓑ Intensive evaluation and care:
Monitor cardiovascular,
urinary, respiratory,
fetal status
Endotracheal intubation
Ventilatory assistance

Differentiate shock type
by heart rate, CVP, and PCWP

Tachycardia

Bradycardia

CVP low
PCWP low

CVP high
or normal
PCWP high

CVP normal
or low
PCWP normal

Ⓒ Septic
shock

Ⓓ Hypovolemic
shock

Ⓔ Cardiogenic
shock

Ⓕ Amniotic
fluid
embolism

Fluids
Antibiotics
Pressor
(p 36)

Fluids
Blood
(p 272)

Digitalis
Diuretic
Pressor
(p 104)

Pressor
Oxygen
(p 132)

Ⓖ Neurogenic
shock

Atropine
Fluids
Shock position

UTERINE INVERSION

Lenard R. Simon, M.D.

A. Although uterine inversion is seldom encountered today, it still occurs with potentially life threatening postpartum hemorrhage and shock. It is caused by excessive pressure applied transabdominally on the uterine fundus, coupled with cord traction, during the third stage of labor in the form of a forceful Credé maneuver. Traction on the umbilical cord alone may cause it if the placenta is attached at the fundus. Inversion is especially likely to occur if the cord is pulled on when the uterus is relaxed. The condition occurs more often in nulliparas than in multiparas and in association with dysfunctional labor, placenta accreta (p 90), and the use of magnesium sulfate (p 86). Third stage management practices that may risk inversion include having the patient bear down and failing to elevate the uterus with the suprapubic hand against the lower uterine segment.

B. The diagnosis is quickly made visually if one recognizes that the adherent placenta is still attached to the fundal implantation site as it is being delivered. The uterine wall may be mistaken for a large myoma in such cases. Abdominal palpation may reveal the deep indentation in the uterine fundus, although in total inversion the uterus usually cannot be palpated abdominally. Partial inversion, although easiest to treat, is most difficult to diagnose. Vaginal examination should disclose the mass representing the fundal wall. Profound shock may occur, accompanied by severe lower abdominal pain or uncontrolled hemorrhage. Rapid diagnosis is important to reduce the difficulty of repositioning the uterus and to minimize morbidity and mortality.

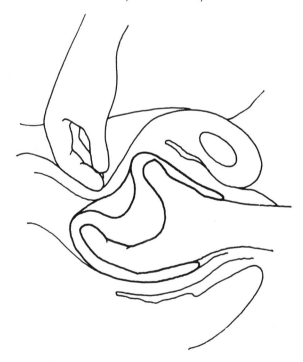

Figure 1   Replacing inverted uterus. Intravaginal hand grasps inverted fundus and applies steady pressure cephalad while spreading cervical ring apart; abdominal hand guides operation by continuous palpation of fundal indentation.

C. Mobilize resources to provide adequate operating facilities, anesthesia, matched blood, an intravenous line, and personnel who have experience in dealing with this problem. Replacement attempts should be done under sterile conditions in an operating room (or a well equipped delivery room) with appropriate resources available for anesthesia and cardiovascular support.

D. Shock resulting from uterine inversion must be treated at once with vasopressors and fluid or blood replacement to correct hypovolemia. Insert large bore intravenous lines for this purpose. It is prudent to monitor by a central venous pressure catheter. Perform a vaginal examination to determine the cervical status (circumferentially around the inverted fundus). If the cervix is still sufficiently open to allow manual replacement, it should be done at once. If not, surgical management is required. This latter is expected if there has been any substantive delay in making the diagnosis; failure to recognize inversion permits the cervix to reform and the lower uterine segment to contract down around the inverted fundus, making manual correction virtually impossible unless tocolytic measures prove effective (see E).

E. If the diagnosis is made before the cervix has had a chance to constrict around the inverted fundus, manual replacement generally can be done easily (Fig. 1). If more than several minutes' time has elapsed, however, it may be difficult. General anesthesia is necessary to permit the procedure to be accomplished. Halogenated drugs in large doses also relax the cervical contraction ring, but skilled anesthesia personnel are required. Tocolytic drugs may be tried for these purposes instead. Magnesium sulfate and betasympathomimetic drugs have been recommended, but they must be used with caution.

F. Surgical intervention to cut the cervical ring and thus permit the inverted uterus corpus to be replaced is rarely, if ever, needed. If the methods for uterine relaxation fail, consider a vaginal (Spinelli) or transabdominal (Huntington or Haultain) approach. The latter is generally safer because it provides good visualization of the bowel and bladder, which may be involved. Prevent recurrence by giving uterotonic drugs, such as oxytocin, ergonovine, or prostaglandin F2α. Uterine packing has also been suggested but is probably unnecessary. Forewarn about recurrence in future pregnancies.

References

Catanzarite VA, Grossman R. How to manage uterine inversion. Contemp Ob Gyn 28:81, 1986.

Harris BA. Acute puerperal inversion of the uterus. Clin Obstet Gynecol 27:134, 1984.

Heyl PS, Stubblefield PG, Phillippe M. Recurrent inversion of the puerperal uterus managed with 15(S)-15-methyl prostaglandin F2α and uterine packing. Obstet Gynecol 63:263, 1984.

Platt LD, Druzin ML. Acute puerperal inversion of the uterus. Am J Obstet Gynecol 141:187, 1981.

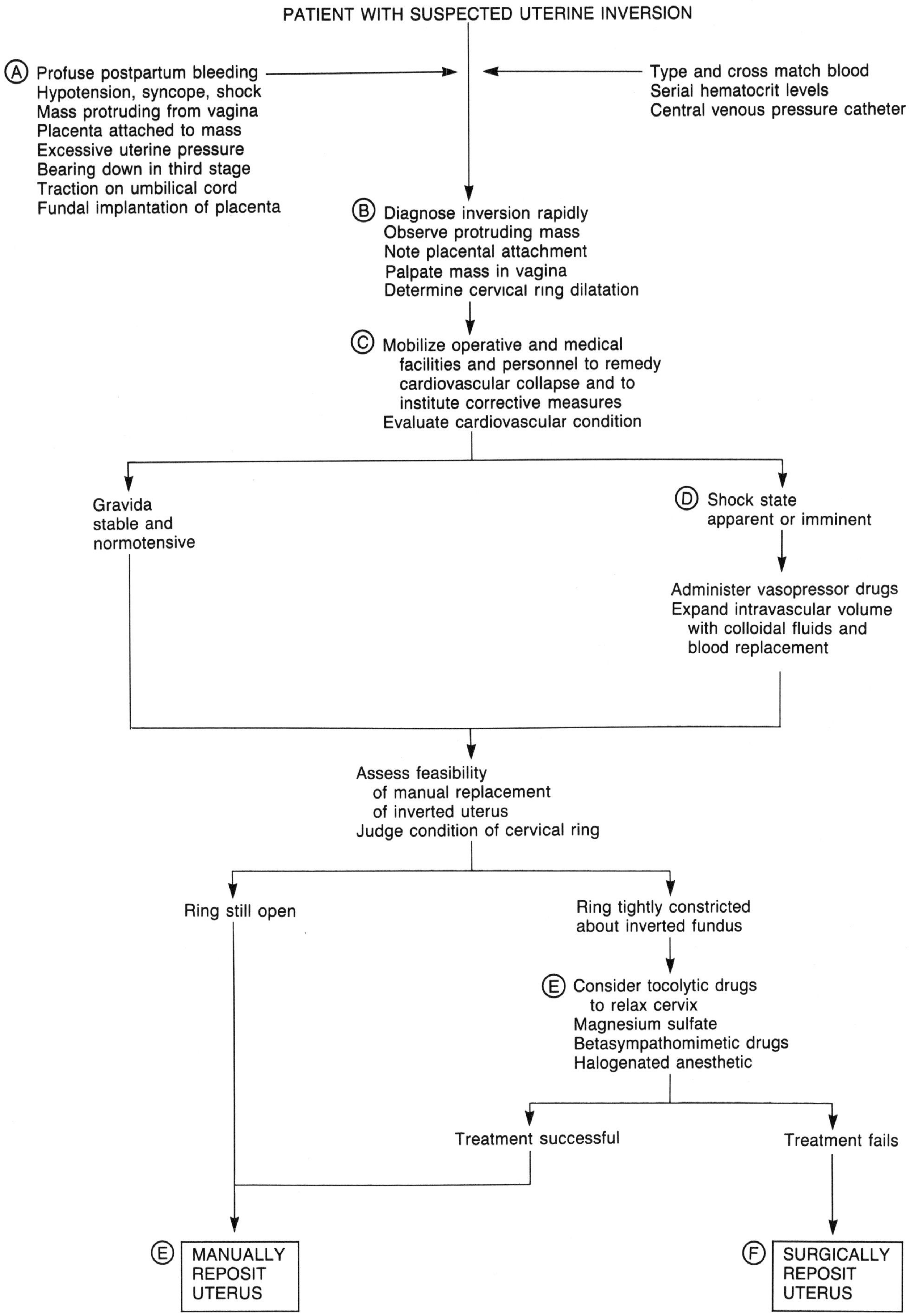

PATIENT WITH SUSPECTED UTERINE INVERSION

(A) Profuse postpartum bleeding
Hypotension, syncope, shock
Mass protruding from vagina
Placenta attached to mass
Excessive uterine pressure
Bearing down in third stage
Traction on umbilical cord
Fundal implantation of placenta

Type and cross match blood
Serial hematocrit levels
Central venous pressure catheter

(B) Diagnose inversion rapidly
Observe protruding mass
Note placental attachment
Palpate mass in vagina
Determine cervical ring dilatation

(C) Mobilize operative and medical
facilities and personnel to remedy
cardiovascular collapse and to
institute corrective measures
Evaluate cardiovascular condition

Gravida
stable and
normotensive

(D) Shock state
apparent or imminent

Administer vasopressor drugs
Expand intravascular volume
with colloidal fluids and
blood replacement

Assess feasibility
of manual replacement
of inverted uterus
Judge condition of cervical ring

Ring still open

Ring tightly constricted
about inverted fundus

(E) Consider tocolytic drugs
to relax cervix
Magnesium sulfate
Betasympathomimetic drugs
Halogenated anesthetic

Treatment successful

Treatment fails

(E) MANUALLY
REPOSIT
UTERUS

(F) SURGICALLY
REPOSIT
UTERUS

POSTPARTUM HEMORRHAGE

Henry Klapholz, M.D.

A. Hemorrhage in excess of 500 ml occurring within the first 24 hours after delivery requires immediate steps to identify the cause and correct it. Evaluate for uterine atony, retained placenta, genital trauma, and unsuspected coagulation defects. Halogenated inhalation anesthetics can cause unresponsive uterine atony with resulting bleeding at delivery.

B. Gravidas at risk are those with high parity, a uterine scar, tumor, or anomaly, prolonged labor (especially a protraction disorder), oxytocin augmented labor, polyhydramnios, multiple pregnancy, traumatic delivery, and a history of a bleeding tendency or prior postpartum hemorrhage.

C. Bleeding associated with a large, boggy uterus or one that is difficult to delineate by palpation is probably due to uterine atony. Atony may occur without apparent cause (as in the patient with dysfunctional labor or an over-distended uterus), but it is frequently associated with retained placental fragments. An atonic uterus should respond to a combination of bimanual massage and oxytocin or ergonovine. Oxytocin can be given intramuscularly or by rapid intravenous infusion (not as a bolus to avoid systemic reaction, particularly hypotension). In the presence of sepsis, these measures may prove ineffectual. If so, prostaglandin $F_2\alpha$ (250 μg) may be given intramuscularly or directly into the myometrium (transabdominally) to give good uterine tone and effective hemostasis. It may be repeated, if needed, within five minutes and every two to three hours thereafter.

D. Retained fragments of placenta or membranes may prevent the uterus from contracting effectively. Bleeding will result. Manual removal of the retained tissue, followed by gentle exploration with a placental forceps, a large blunt curette or a gauze covered hand, in addition to the intramuscular administration of oxytocin or ergonovine, should control the bleeding. If the placental lobe is adherent to the underlying uterine wall, consider the possibility of placenta accreta (p 90).

E. Aggressive, expeditious management is called for if excessive bleeding persists or increases. If the amount of blood loss is great (more than 200 ml per hour), undertake laparotomy promptly for bilateral hypogastric artery ligation. If bleeding is still not adequately controlled, ligate the ovarian arteries at the level of the utero-ovarian ligament (not the infundibulopelvic ligament). Hysterectomy is the last resort, particularly if the woman is of low parity. To temporize, stem acute bleeding by compressing the uterus firmly between a fist in the vagina and an opposing hand on the abdomen (Fig. 1A); one can also encircle the lower uterus with a hand through the abdominal wall to stop uterine bleeding. If bleeding is moderate, consider pelvic angiography for embolizing the internal iliac vessel with Gelfoam or infusing vasopressin into the uterine vessel. Major surgery may thus be averted.

F. Atony and retained placenta can be ruled out with reasonable certainty if the uterus is well contracted; bleeding is then probably due to a traumatic genital laceration. Promptly undertake inspection with good light and exposure; assistance is helpful. Anesthesia may be necessary, especially if manual exploration of the uterus has to be done. Periurethral, vaginal, and cervical lacerations can be repaired without difficulty. Take care to suture above the angle of a cervical laceration to ensure hemostasis (Fig. 1B). Rupture of the uterus demands immediate laparotomy. If the laceration is linear and accessible and the bleeding can be easily controlled, repair may suffice; otherwise hysterectomy is indicated. Preliminary hypogastric artery ligation (see E) may be required for visualizing the damage site.

G. Postpartum hemorrhage may result from von Willebrand's disease or other less common blood dyscrasias (p 110). Fresh frozen plasma or cryoprecipitate in amounts adequate to correct factor VIII levels can be used to control the excessive bleeding. A platelet count is obtained to rule out thrombocytopenia resulting from a viral infection or a bone marrow disorder.

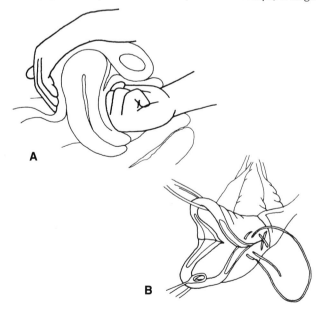

Figure 1 Controlling acute uterine hemorrhage. *A*, compressing, lifting, anteflexing, and massaging the uterus between a fist inserted vaginally and the abdominal hand. *B*, suturing cervical laceration with special care taken to begin it well above the apex to ensure hemostasis.

References

Andrinopoulos GC, Mendenhall HW. Prostaglandin $F_2\alpha$ in the management of delayed postpartum hemorrhage. Am J Obstet Gynecol 146:217, 1983.

Clark SL, Phelan JP, Yeh SY, et al. Hypogastric artery ligation for obstetric hemorrhage. Obstet Gynecol 66:353, 1985.

Evans S, McShane P. The efficacy of internal iliac artery ligation in obstetric hemorrhage. Surg Gynecol Obstet 160:250, 1985.

Hayashi RH, Castillo MS, Noah ML. Management of severe postpartum hemorrhage with a prostaglandin $F_2\alpha$ analogue. Obstet Gynecol 63:806, 1984.

Pais SO, Glickman M, Schwartz P, et al. Embolization of pelvic arteries for control of postpartum hemorrhage. Obstet Gynecol 55:754, 1980.

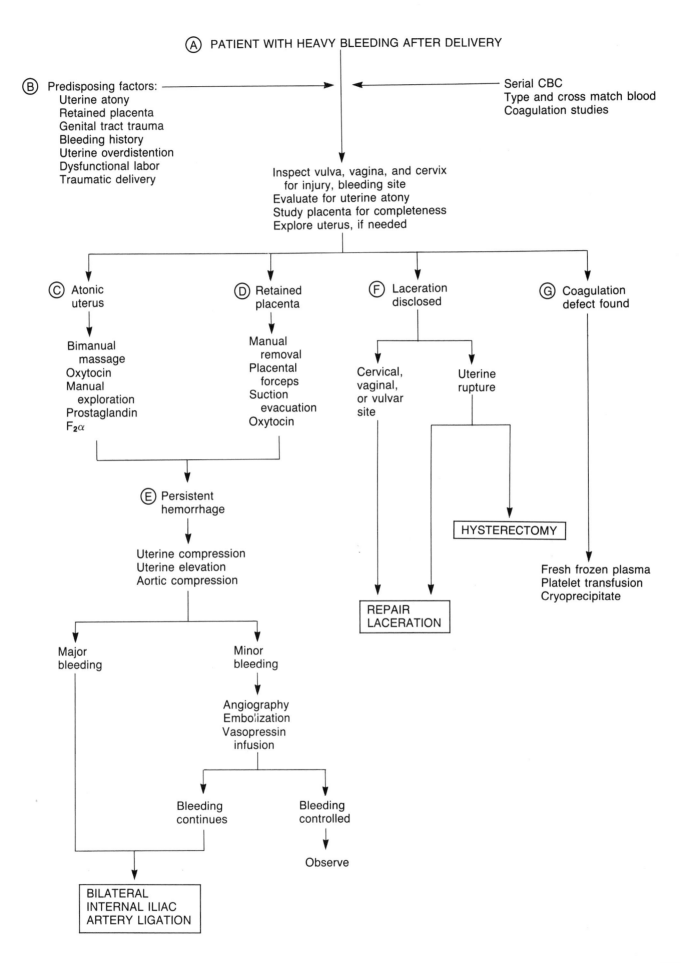

(A) PATIENT WITH HEAVY BLEEDING AFTER DELIVERY

(B) Predisposing factors:
  Uterine atony
  Retained placenta
  Genital tract trauma
  Bleeding history
  Uterine overdistention
  Dysfunctional labor
  Traumatic delivery

Serial CBC
Type and cross match blood
Coagulation studies

Inspect vulva, vagina, and cervix
  for injury, bleeding site
Evaluate for uterine atony
Study placenta for completeness
Explore uterus, if needed

(C) Atonic
uterus

Bimanual
  massage
Oxytocin
Manual
  exploration
Prostaglandin
  $F_2\alpha$

(D) Retained
placenta

Manual
  removal
Placental
  forceps
Suction
  evacuation
Oxytocin

(F) Laceration
disclosed

Cervical,
vaginal,
or vulvar
site

Uterine
rupture

(G) Coagulation
defect found

HYSTERECTOMY

Fresh frozen plasma
Platelet transfusion
Cryoprecipitate

(E) Persistent
hemorrhage

Uterine compression
Uterine elevation
Aortic compression

Major
bleeding

Minor
bleeding

Angiography
Embolization
Vasopressin
  infusion

Bleeding
continues

Bleeding
controlled

Observe

REPAIR
LACERATION

BILATERAL
INTERNAL ILIAC
ARTERY LIGATION

LATE POSTPARTUM HEMORRHAGE

Eric D. Lichter, M.D.

A. Late postpartum hemorrhage (also called delayed or secondary hemorrhage) refers to vaginal bleeding beginning after the first 24 hours following delivery. Although it may develop several months later, it generally occurs in the first seven to nine days. It may start without forewarning, but it is often presaged by fever or uterine cramping. Moreover, it may represent the late overt manifestation of continuing process, such as uterine subinvolution resulting from retained placenta or an occult pelvic hematoma. Chronic or progressive anemia, especially with leukocytosis, should put one on the alert.

B. Late postpartum hemorrhage is most commonly associated with uterine subinvolution, which in turn is usually a consequence of infection, retained products, or abnormal healing of the thrombosed vascular sinuses at the placental implantation site. One should suspect subinvolution on the basis of the physical finding of a softened uterus larger than expected for the time elapsed since delivery. Unless bleeding is active, conservative management with temporization to provide opportunities for antibiotic treatment and ultrasonographic assessment of the uterine contents can replace immediate curettage as the treatment of choice for most of these patients.

C. Ultrasonography has proved very helpful in detecting retained products of conception. The endometrial cavity can be seen with clarity by currently available sophisticated equipment. This approach is appropriate before performing curettage. If the uterus is empty of any echogenic patterns, retained placenta is essentially ruled out; positive findings may represent retained placenta or

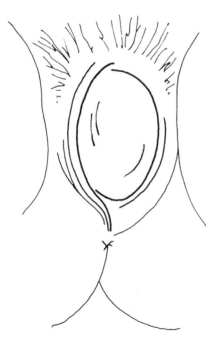

Figure 1 Vulvar hematoma may occur spontaneously from the trauma of delivery of result from inadequate suturing of an episiotomy or laceration; it can extend into the ischiorectal fossa or retroperitoneal space.

merely clots within the uterus. A white blood cell count with a differential may show leukocytosis and a left shift if there is a systemic response to uterine infection. However, local chronic infection may become walled off so that neither the white blood count nor the differential may show the effect, even though subinvolution and bleeding can occur.

D. For patients with normal ultrasonographic findings, conservative medical treatment can be expected to yield a high cure rate. Treatment with antibiotics and a uterotonic drug, such as ergonovine, oxytocin, or prostaglandin $F_2\alpha$, is usually successful. Curettage is reserved for patients who prove to have retained products of conception, who have failed to respond to conservative management, or whose bleeding is so brisk that delay would be imprudent and potentially hazardous.

E. When a hematoma forms as a consequence of bleeding due to spontaneous or traumatic vascular injury, the patient characteristically experiences pain with developing anemia and, if progressive, hypovolemic shock. A mass may be palpable; if superficial in location, it has a typical bluish discoloration. Vulvovaginal hematoma typically presents with unilateral swelling (Fig. 1) with overlying edema and ecchymosis. If uncontrolled, hematomas dissect along the fascial planes. The treatment of a large vulvovaginal hematoma consists of surgical evacuation followed by careful exposure and ligation of the bleeding vessels. Eliminate dead space by suturing in layers or, if not feasible, by packing the vagina firmly.

F. Retroperitoneal hematomas are less obvious and therefore more difficult to diagnose. When they are suspected, undertake ultrasonography, intravenous pyelography, or computed tomographic scanning. Nonsurgical management, using angiography for localization and embolization of the bleeding site, is preferred wherever this technique is practiced because it avoids difficult and hazardous surgical intervention. It is well worth attempting if the patient is hemodynamically stable and time permits. If this approach is not available, transferring the patient to a tertiary care hospital is an option to consider. In an emergency situation with active bleeding and marginal cardiovascular status, surgical exploration must be done to determine the source of the bleeding; ligation of the hypogastric and ovarian arteries is usually necessary.

References

Dehaeck CM. Transcatheter embolization of pelvic vessels to stop intractable hemorrhage. Gynecol Oncol 24:9, 1986.

Herbert WNP, Cefalo RC. Management of postpartum hemorrhage. Clin Obstet Gynecol 27:139, 1984.

Lee CY, Madrazo B, Drukker BH. Ultrasonic evaluation of the postpartum uterus in the management of postpartum bleeding. Obstet Gynecol 58:227, 1981.

Schwartz PE. The surgical approach to severe postpartum hemorrhage. In: Berkowitz RL (Editor). Critical Care of the Obstetric Patient. New York: Churchill Livingstone, 1983.

PATIENT WITH LATE POSTPARTUM VAGINAL BLEEDING

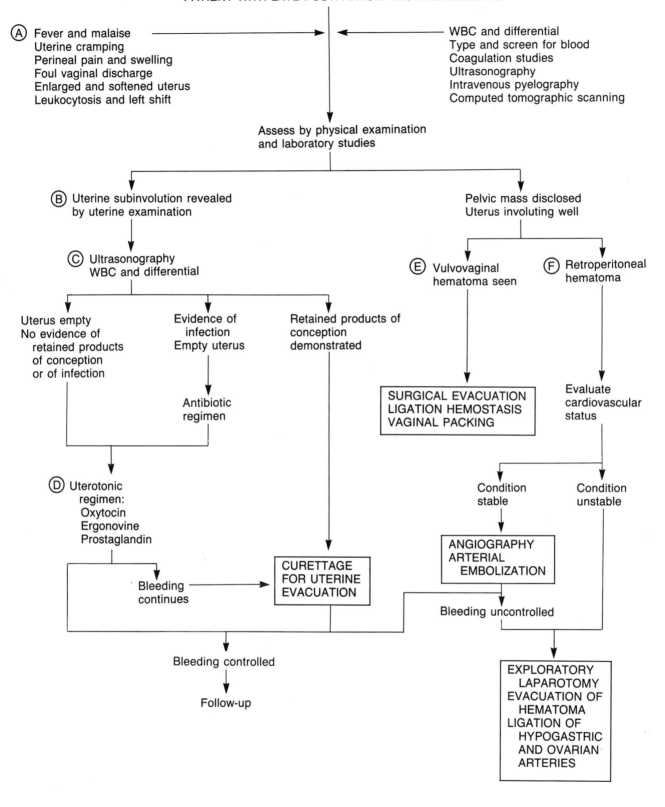

Ⓐ Fever and malaise
Uterine cramping
Perineal pain and swelling
Foul vaginal discharge
Enlarged and softened uterus
Leukocytosis and left shift

WBC and differential
Type and screen for blood
Coagulation studies
Ultrasonography
Intravenous pyelography
Computed tomographic scanning

Assess by physical examination
and laboratory studies

Ⓑ Uterine subinvolution revealed
by uterine examination

Pelvic mass disclosed
Uterus involuting well

Ⓒ Ultrasonography
WBC and differential

Ⓔ Vulvovaginal
hematoma seen

Ⓕ Retroperitoneal
hematoma

Uterus empty
No evidence of
retained products
of conception
or of infection

Evidence of
infection
Empty uterus

Retained products of
conception
demonstrated

Antibiotic
regimen

SURGICAL EVACUATION
LIGATION HEMOSTASIS
VAGINAL PACKING

Evaluate
cardiovascular
status

Ⓓ Uterotonic
regimen:
Oxytocin
Ergonovine
Prostaglandin

Condition
stable

Condition
unstable

Bleeding
continues

CURETTAGE
FOR UTERINE
EVACUATION

ANGIOGRAPHY
ARTERIAL
EMBOLIZATION

Bleeding uncontrolled

Bleeding controlled

Follow-up

EXPLORATORY
LAPAROTOMY
EVACUATION OF
HEMATOMA
LIGATION OF
HYPOGASTRIC
AND OVARIAN
ARTERIES

LACTATION

Max Borten, M.D.

A. Prepare the gravida by discussing the relative benefits of breast and bottle feeding well before delivery. Review psychologic, social, and economic factors affecting her choice. She should not feel pressured to make an unwanted or hurried choice. She should have a realistic view of the constraints it will impose as well as the counterbalancing advantages for the baby as regards nurturing, immunity protection, and psychologic impact. Counsel about the effects of medications or drugs (see E). Pediatric consultation may help in planning.

B. Breast size has no bearing on the ability to produce enough milk for newborn nutrition. Endocrine stimulation causes rapid proliferation of the acini of the lactiferous glands. Thus, small breasts do not interdict breast feeding, which may enhance feelings of self-worth.

C. The only real contraindications involve conditions that make breast feeding a hazard to the mother or baby, such as a local infection (especially herpes) or neoplasm or a maternal disease that is debilitating or requires the use of drugs that are excreted in the milk and toxic to the infant. Maternal breast cancer interdicts lactation and nursing because it could dangerously delay the use of surgery, radiation, or chemotherapy, thereby reducing the potential for cure. Similarly, a cancer located elsewhere should be treated expeditiously; a delay for nursing would be unconscionable if it had an impact on the maternal prognosis.

D. Lactation can be suppressed, if indicated or desired by the recently delivered patient, by physical or pharmaceutical means. Instruct the patient to avoid stimulating her breast by any form of massage or pumping. Provide her with good breast support by the use of a sturdy brassiere or binder. A brief period of congestion and tenderness will follow; it can be readily managed by cold compresses and analgesic drugs. Maintain firm support for several days after the congestion subsides to ensure against recurrence of the lactation sequence. The routine use of lactation suppression drugs is thus not justified, although it is widely practiced. Drugs in current use for lactation suppression include estrogens, but bromocriptine is perhaps the most effective drug for this purpose.

E. Predelivery preparations must include providing information to the gravida about medications that she may or will be taking during lactation. This encompasses prescription as well as over the counter and recreational drugs. Potentially serious undesirable neonatal side effects may result from excretion of drugs in the maternal milk. Blood flow to the breast is increased during lactation, and any drug in the maternal circulation is rapidly diffused into interstitial mammary tissue and alveolar cells. The drug then enters the lumen of the excretory duct by diffusion to appear in the milk. Frequent feedings may increase the transfer of drugs to the milk and thus serve to enhance excretion of diffusible drugs. Close cooperation and exchange of information among the obstetrician, pediatrician, and other treating physicians are important aspects of care to help guide the medicated mother who wishes to nurse her infant.

F. It sometimes may be necessary to delay breast feeding but not suppress it altogether. Examples include premature, anomalous, or sick infants who can be expected to recover sufficiently in time to be nursed. In these cases one should consider mechanical pumping of the breast. This is an excellent method for accumulating breast milk (and keeping it for later use by freezing). It also sustains the gland secretion so that the mother continues to lactate in preparation for later breast feeding when the infant is well enough to participate. A mechanical pump can also be used by women who must work or be otherwise separated from their infant for periods of time (by infection, for example) to yield a milk supply to feed the child in their absence.

References

Lawrence RA. Breastfeeding: A Guide for the Medical Profession. 2nd ed. St. Louis: C.V. Mosby, 1985.

Lemons P, Stuart M, Lemons JA. Breast-feeding the premature infant. Clin Perinatol 13:111, 1986.

Neifert MR, Seacat JM, Jobe WE. Lactation failure due to insufficient glandular development of the breast. Pediatrics 76:823, 1985.

Winikoff B, Laukaran VH, Myers D, Stone R. Dynamics of infant feeding: Mother, professionals, and the institutional context in a large urban hospital. Pediatrics 77:357, 1986.

PATIENT WITH DESIRE TO BREASTFEED INFANT

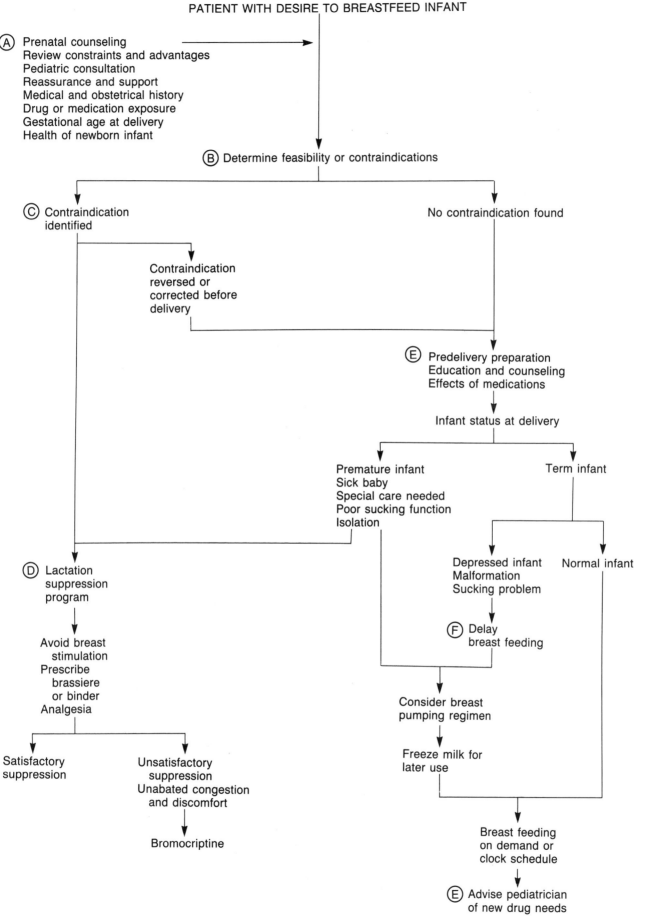

Ⓐ Prenatal counseling
Review constraints and advantages
Pediatric consultation
Reassurance and support
Medical and obstetrical history
Drug or medication exposure
Gestational age at delivery
Health of newborn infant

Ⓑ Determine feasibility or contraindications

Ⓒ Contraindication
identified

No contraindication found

Contraindication
reversed or
corrected before
delivery

Ⓔ Predelivery preparation
Education and counseling
Effects of medications

Infant status at delivery

Premature infant
Sick baby
Special care needed
Poor sucking function
Isolation

Term infant

Ⓓ Lactation
suppression
program

Depressed infant
Malformation
Sucking problem

Normal infant

Avoid breast
stimulation
Prescribe
brassiere
or binder
Analgesia

Ⓕ Delay
breast feeding

Consider breast
pumping regimen

Satisfactory
suppression

Unsatisfactory
suppression
Unabated congestion
and discomfort

Freeze milk for
later use

Bromocriptine

Breast feeding
on demand or
clock schedule

Ⓔ Advise pediatrician
of new drug needs

277

LACTATION DISORDER

Max Borten, M.D.

A. During the initial stages of breast engorgement, manual expression or mechanical pumping is not productive and may even prove to be somewhat traumatic. Generally only a well fitting brassiere is needed while awaiting spontaneous milk flow. At a later stage, gentle manual expression or mechanical pumping (Fig. 1) is helpful. Breast massage, if undertaken, is done in a radial fashion to soften the peripheral lobules. Mild analgesics provide temporary relief of the discomfort so common in these cases. Use of hypnotic drugs may be required to help the patient obtain some rest, although it should be recognized that barbiturates and similar medications are transmitted to the milk.

B. Galactoceles result from occlusion of the lactiferous ducts; they may affect one or more lobules. Compression of the enlarged, affected duct may open the passage and result in milk secretion. This should be done by the physician; the patient should be advised not to massage her breast to avoid aggravating the problem. Spontaneous resolution is not unusual. If the condition fails to subside in 24 to 48 hours, needle aspiration of the accumulated milk is required. This can be done under local anesthesia. Breast feeding does not have to be discontinued unless secondary infection occurs.

C. Painful nipples frequently cause mothers to abandon breast feeding in the early puerperium. Nipple soreness can be prevented or helped by the following measures: (1) Avoid prolonged nursing. Manual expression for the purpose of initiating milk flow hastens the let-down reflex and shortens the feeding time. (2) Expose the nipples to the air for 15 to 20 minutes after each feeding. (3) Apply anhydrous lanolin or vitamin A and D ointment to the irritated areas between feedings to promote healing. (4) Cover the nipples between feedings with a soft cloth. (5) Avoid soaps for washing the breasts before and after feedings. The nipples should be rinsed with plain warm water.

D. Fissures can be circular at the nipple-areolar junction or vertical on the long axis of the nipple. Pain is the principal feature, aggravated by nursing and often compounded by secondary parenchymal mastitis (p 280). Breast feeding should be discontinued from the affected side for 24 to 48 hours. Gentle manual expression or mechanical pumping prevents engorgement. Analgesics, when required, must be short acting (such as codeine) and given immediately after nursing. Anhydrous lanolin or vitamin A and D ointment applied locally is useful for symptomatic relief. The use of a nipple shield is particularly helpful for preventing further irritation of the cracked nipple.

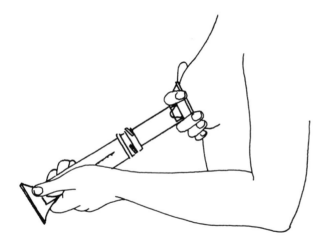

Figure 1 Hand pumping breast by means of a syringe pump to relieve engorgement or to express milk for a preterm or sick child.

References

Almeida OD, Kitay DZ. Lactation suppression for puerperal fever. Am J Obstet Gynecol 154:940, 1986.

Lawrence RA. Breastfeeding: A Guide for the Medical Profession. 2nd ed. St. Louis: C.V. Mosby, 1985.

Thomsen AC, Espersen T, Maigaard S. Course and treatment of milk stasis, noninfectious inflammation of the breast, and infectious mastitis in nursing women. Am J Obstet Gynecol 149:492, 1984.

Thomsen AC, Hansen KB, Møller BR. Leukocyte counts and microbiologic cultivation in the diagnosis of puerperal mastitis. Am J Obstet Gynecol 146:938, 1983.

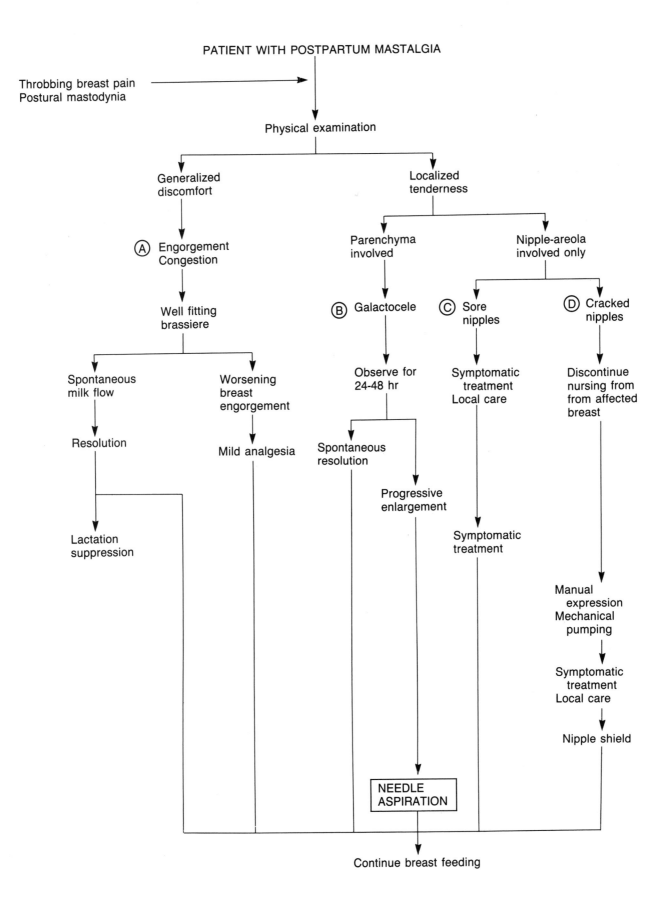

PATIENT WITH POSTPARTUM MASTALGIA

Throbbing breast pain
Postural mastodynia

Physical examination

Generalized discomfort

Localized tenderness

Ⓐ Engorgement Congestion

Parenchyma involved

Nipple-areola involved only

Well fitting brassiere

Ⓑ Galactocele

Ⓒ Sore nipples

Ⓓ Cracked nipples

Spontaneous milk flow

Worsening breast engorgement

Observe for 24-48 hr

Symptomatic treatment Local care

Discontinue nursing from from affected breast

Resolution

Mild analgesia

Spontaneous resolution

Progressive enlargement

Lactation suppression

Symptomatic treatment

Manual expression Mechanical pumping

Symptomatic treatment Local care

Nipple shield

NEEDLE ASPIRATION

Continue breast feeding

PUERPERAL MASTITIS

Harold W. Rubin, M.D.

A. Whereas breast engorgement is almost universal during the first two to three days after delivery, it seldom persists and is usually not accompanied by more than a low grade temperature elevation. Congestion tends to be generalized with enlargement of superficial veins. High fever and a focal distribution of heat, tenderness, and redness should suggest mastitis, especially if accompanied by cracked or macerated nipples. Parenchymatous mastitis generally arises after at least a week or two has elapsed, often preceded by shaking chills, fever, and tachycardia. It is characterized by a painful, indurated, and erythematous breast, but findings may be negligible. *Staphylococcus aureus* is the usual pathogen in cases, derived from the nursing infant's oropharynx and gaining access by way of a nipple fissure to the interlobular breast tissue.

B. Puerperal mastitis at times may become epidemic, especially when antibiotic resistant strains of staphylococci develop and are transmitted from nursery personnel (who are carriers or have infections) to the newborn infant population, who in turn transmit them to their mothers. Prevention involves assiduous efforts to avoid such contamination by excluding any known or suspected carrier or infected individual from nurseries and by regular examinations of all neonates for skin, nose, ear, and cord infections. Meticulous hand washing is essential. Culturing of all personnel is required when an outbreak begins. Although the clinical manifestations of epidemic mastitis may be indistinguishable from those of the sporadic type, it more often involves the lactiferous apparatus (glands and ducts) than the breast parenchyma. Typically pus can be expressed from the nipple.

C. It is often possible to allow nursing to continue in cases of sporadic mastitis when the infection is confined and the discomfort of suckling is not excessive; a nipple shield (p 278) may be helpful for these women. Because the organism in epidemic mastitis is generally present in the milk and is so virulent, nursing should be discontinued. Moreover, nursing tends to be rather painful in these cases. The infant requires observation and, if an organism is colonized, isolation and treatment. Penicillinase resistant antibiotics are given to combat the mastitis along with good breast support and analgesics.

D. Watch for abscess formation (Fig. 1). If it occurs, it necessitates surgical drainage by way of a radial incision over the fluctuant area. Special care should be taken during surgery to ensure adequate drainage of all loculations of pus in the breast. Rapid defervescence can be expected to occur if drainage is instituted properly.

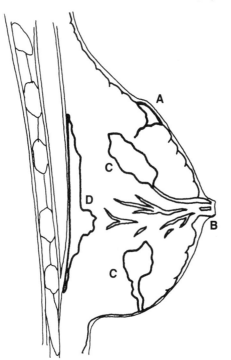

Figure 1 Inflammatory breast disorders of the puerperium, showing possible sites of abscess formation. *A*, subcutaneous; *B*, subareolar; *C*, intramammary; *D*, retromammary.

References

Niebyl JR, Spence MR, Parmley TH. Sporadic (nonepidemic) puerperal mastitis. J Reprod Med 20:97, 1978.

Thomsen AC, Espersen T, Maigaard S. Course and treatment of milk stasis, noninfectious inflammation of breast, and infectious mastitis in nursing women. Am J Obstet Gynecol 149:492, 1984.

Thomsen AC, Hansen KB, Møller BR. Leucocyte counts and microbiologic cultivation in the diagnosis of puerperal mastitis. Am J Obstet Gynecol 146:938, 1983.

PATIENT WITH BREAST TENDERNESS

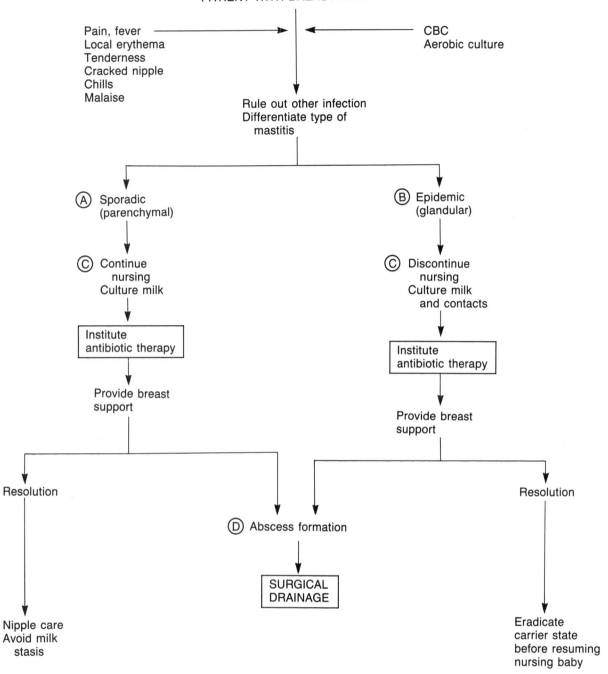

Pain, fever
Local erythema
Tenderness
Cracked nipple
Chills
Malaise

CBC
Aerobic culture

Rule out other infection
Differentiate type of
mastitis

Ⓐ Sporadic
(parenchymal)

Ⓑ Epidemic
(glandular)

Ⓒ Continue
nursing
Culture milk

Ⓒ Discontinue
nursing
Culture milk
and contacts

Institute
antibiotic therapy

Institute
antibiotic therapy

Provide breast
support

Provide breast
support

Resolution

Resolution

Ⓓ Abscess formation

SURGICAL
DRAINAGE

Nipple care
Avoid milk
stasis

Eradicate
carrier state
before resuming
nursing baby

POST-DELIVERY COUNSELING

Max Borten, M.D.

A. It is important to anticipate during the prenatal period which patients are likely to suffer from postpartum depression. Be alert to a history of postpartum depression, behavioral aberration, psychotic episode, serious problems with personal relationships during the gestation, loss of or separation from a supporting person, drug abuse, and extremes of attitude (hostility, anger, anxiety, and fear). Prepregnancy neurotic attitudes are likely to become exacerbated during pregnancy and in the postpartum period. The fastidious woman is likely to encounter difficulty in maintaining her requisite degree of orderliness and cleanliness; her sense of control will be challenged. At the other extreme of life style, the woman whose existence is chaotic and who is essentially incapable of planning ahead may be equally overwhelmed by the burdens of caring for a child. Psychosocial assessment (p 30) is essential as early in pregnancy as feasible in order to prepare for problems that can be expected to arise after delivery.

B. Essentially every pregnancy is associated with emotional conflicts. Adapting and coping mechanisms during the postpartum period depend strongly on the woman's psychological status and prior capacity to deal with major life stresses. Establishment of good rapport between the patient and her obstetrician is essential over the course of the pregnancy. This is particularly difficult if the gravida first appears for care late in pregnancy, because time is limited and such patients are frequently at greater risk than others. They may have put off seeking prenatal care as a consequence of denial, ambivalence, guilt, or shame about the pregnancy. The pregnant woman must be made to feel sufficiently secure to permit her to discuss any subject without fear of embarrassment. Do not rush through the prenatal visit, but try to give each patient enough opportunity to talk about her concerns. Since most fears are entirely unrealistic, the physician's reassurance alone may serve to allay them.

C. During pregnancy, accelerated psychological maturation and regressive states are intermixed. These are most pronounced in the primigravida. The realization of increased responsibilities associated with the forthcoming state of motherhood is in conflict with the gravida's regressive feelings of identification with her fetus. She may thus feel and function in certain aspects like a child, often becoming very dependent. Some degree of regression normal-

ly takes place during pregnancy. The obstetrician's understanding and reassurance help in this regard. Take care to avoid assuming an authoritarian role, however, so as to prevent dependency while providing confidence and support to the patient.

D. Mild postpartum depression ("blues") affects nearly every mother. She may be moody, unresponsive, or irritable and burst into tears without provocation. These manifestations are usually self-limiting and readily respond to reassurance. If they persist beyond the immediate postpartum interval (more than three to five days), the condition becomes a cause for concern. Social service consultation for evaluation provides additional support and establishes contact for further follow-up. Psychiatric referral may be deemed appropriate if the problem becomes serious enough to warrant it, but the mild form rarely does.

E. Early postpartum discharge may aggravate anxiety in the new mother about her capability to care for her infant after leaving the hospital. Awareness of this process enables the obstetrician to understand and deal with these fears. By anticipating this, one can provide discussion and reassurance to help the patient recognize and cope with the problem.

F. Puerperal depression may be premonitory to a more serious underlying depressive psychosis. Confusion, delirium, hallucinations, and delusions are worrisome signs, which demand careful evaluation. Fears about causing injury to the infant or suicidal ideation must also be seriously investigated. Psychiatric consultation must be obtained at once.

References

Hayworth J, Little BC, Carter SB, et al. A predictive study of postpartum depression: Some predisposing characteristics. Br J Med Psychol 53:161, 1980.

Little BC, Hayworth J, Carter SMB, et al. Personal and psychophysiological characteristics associated with puerperal mental state. J Psychiatr Res 25:385, 1981.

Little BC, Hayworth J, Benson P, et al. Psychophysiological antenatal predictors of post-natal depressed mood. J Psychosom Res 26:419, 1982.

Vanderbergh RL. Postpartum depression. Clin Obstet Gynecol 23:1105, 1980.

PATIENT WITH EMOTIONAL RESPONSE TO DELIVERY

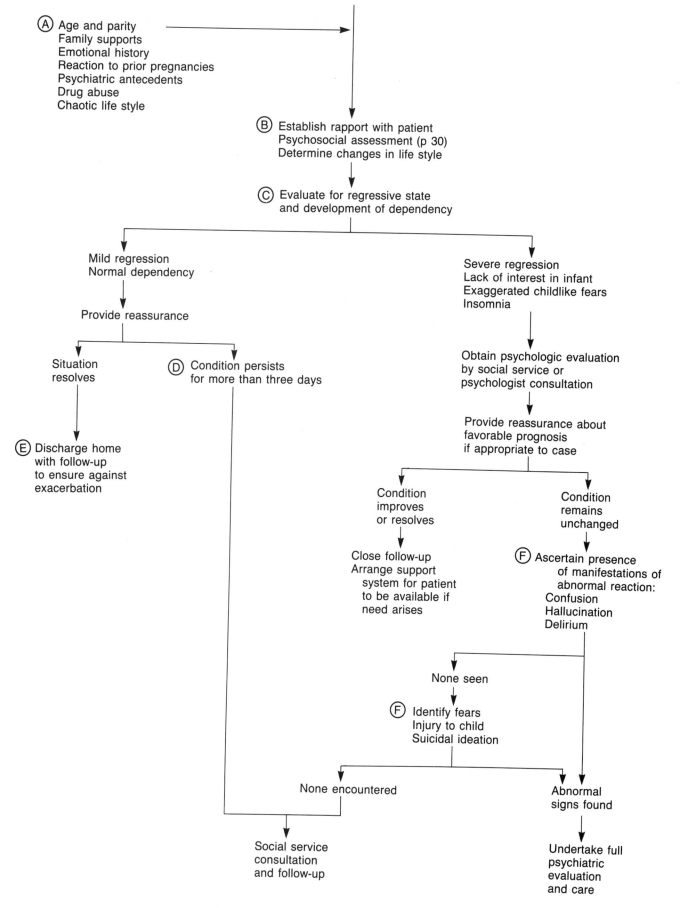

(A) Age and parity
Family supports
Emotional history
Reaction to prior pregnancies
Psychiatric antecedents
Drug abuse
Chaotic life style

(B) Establish rapport with patient
Psychosocial assessment (p 30)
Determine changes in life style

(C) Evaluate for regressive state
and development of dependency

Mild regression
Normal dependency

Provide reassurance

Situation
resolves

(D) Condition persists
for more than three days

(E) Discharge home
with follow-up
to ensure against
exacerbation

Severe regression
Lack of interest in infant
Exaggerated childlike fears
Insomnia

Obtain psychologic evaluation
by social service or
psychologist consultation

Provide reassurance about
favorable prognosis
if appropriate to case

Condition
improves
or resolves

Close follow-up
Arrange support
system for patient
to be available if
need arises

Condition
remains
unchanged

(F) Ascertain presence
of manifestations of
abnormal reaction:
Confusion
Hallucination
Delirium

None seen

(F) Identify fears
Injury to child
Suicidal ideation

None encountered

Abnormal
signs found

Social service
consultation
and follow-up

Undertake full
psychiatric
evaluation
and care

CHOICE OF FORCEPS

Emanuel A. Friedman, M.D., Sc.D.

A. Several important considerations need to be weighed if one is contemplating a forceps operation to effect vaginal delivery. Before using forceps, one must assess the preceding course of labor, cephalopelvic relationship type and capacity of the pelvis, fetal position, station, flexion, synclitism, and molding, as well as the fetal status based on the electronic fetal heart rate pattern.

B. In order to provide justification for a forceps procedure, it is important to weigh its potential risks against its benefits. This means that allowing the labor to continue or delivering by an alternative method can be shown to be more hazardous than proceeding to intervene by forceps in the specific case under consideration. Documenting both the benefits and the relative risks by a detailed note in the patient's chart is good practice for justifying the operation, especially if prevailing conditions for forceps use are not optimal.

C. The clinical conditions in which forceps use may expose the fetus and the gravida to physical damage include a midpelvic fetal station, malposition (occiput transverse or posterior), deflexion, marked molding, cephalopelvic disproportion, and a major labor abnormality, namely, an arrest or protraction disorder.

D. The degree of urgency for delivery depends on the maternal and fetal status. A strong indication for delivery may counterbalance the risk of the delivery procedure. If delay is feasible, however, passage of time to allow labor to progress so that additional descent occurs may make less hazardous options acceptable, such as a spontaneous delivery or a less traumatic forceps delivery. Thus, the indications for intervention have to be carefully assessed to determine whether delivery is required at that time; if so, it becomes essential to decide whether urgency dictates vaginal delivery at once (if it is feasible) or whether one can prepare for and proceed with a timely cesarean section.

E. Delivery with forceps is justified if there is a strong indication for delivery combined with a low potential risk from use of the forceps. By contrast, if conditions are not optimal, it may or may not be justified. One cannot rationalize traumatizing a fetus by undertaking a difficult midforceps operation in a misguided effort to prevent it from being damaged by hypoxia, which may already have taken its toll or which may not yet have had any adverse effect. Cesarean section is a preferable alternative if urgent delivery is called for under conditions that make a forceps operation hazardous. Even when there are strong indications for delivery and urgency dictates rapid intervention, there is usually enough time for cesarean section in institutions prepared for such emergencies.

F. If the indication is equivocal or marginal, such as maternal exhaustion or poor expulsive efforts, the risks of traumatic delivery cannot be justified. Expectancy and support usually prove beneficial. Merely allowing the labor to continue under close surveillance often resolves the problem. Heavy sedation or regional block anesthesia can be permitted to abate so that the contractions can become more effective. If indicated, oxytocin infusion may help improve the contractile pattern and thereby yield progress in fetal descent as well as correction of a malposition.

G. Selecting the proper instrument (p 286) can reduce risks. Use an Elliott type of forceps (with an overlapping shank and a rounded cephalic curve) for an unmolded fetal head and a Simpson type (separated shanks and a tapered curve) for a molded head. Special forceps are applicable for special purposes, including the Kielland (designed for occiput posterior or transverse arrest in a deep anthropoid pelvis) and the Barton forceps (for occiput transverse arrest in a flat pelvis). Because trauma is not uncommon, experience with these special forceps has diminished; thus, fewer and fewer obstetricians have sufficient exposure to justify their continued use in the future. Regardless of the type of forceps chosen, do not persist if any difficulty is encountered with application, rotation, or traction.

References

Chiswick ML, James DK. Kielland's forceps: Association with neonatal morbidity and mortality. Br Med J 1:7, 1979.

Cyr RM, Usher RH, McLean FH. Changing patterns of birth asphyxia and trauma over 20 years. Am J Obstet Gynecol 148:490, 1984.

Fenichel GM, Webster DL, Wong WKT. Intracranial hemorrhage in term newborn. Arch Neurol 41:30, 1984.

Friedman EA, Sachtleben MR, Dahrouge D, Neff RK. Long-term effects of labor and delivery on offspring: A matched-pair analysis. Am J Obstet Gynecol 150:941, 1984.

O'Driscoll K, Meagher D, MacDonald D, Geoghegan F. Traumatic intracranial haemorrhage in firstborn infants and delivery with obstetric forceps. Br J Obstet Gynaecol 88:577, 1981.

DELIVERY ANTICIPATED

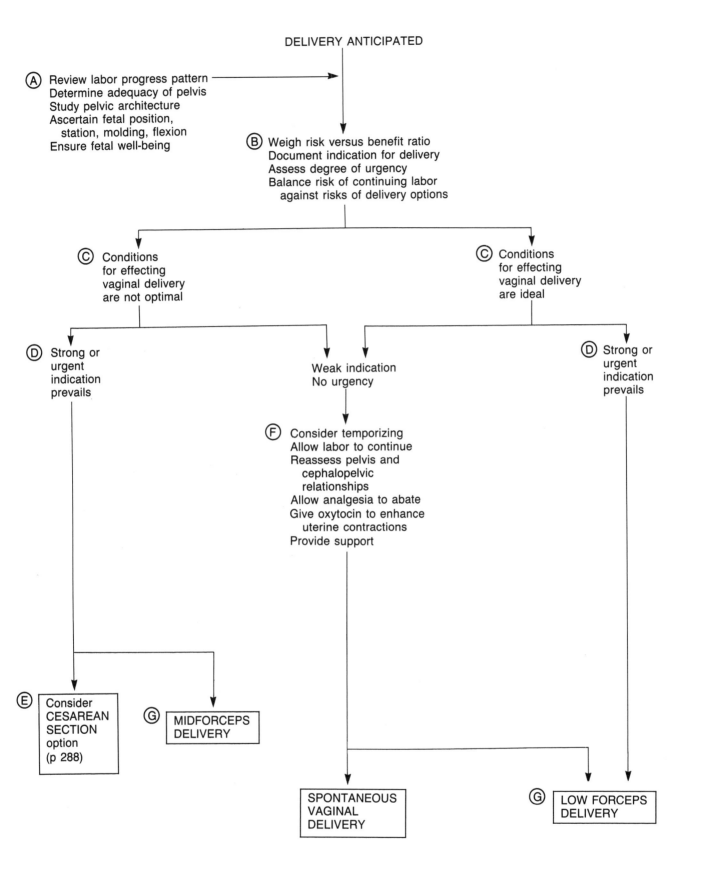

Ⓐ Review labor progress pattern
Determine adequacy of pelvis
Study pelvic architecture
Ascertain fetal position,
    station, molding, flexion
Ensure fetal well-being

Ⓑ Weigh risk versus benefit ratio
Document indication for delivery
Assess degree of urgency
Balance risk of continuing labor
    against risks of delivery options

Ⓒ Conditions
for effecting
vaginal delivery
are not optimal

Ⓒ Conditions
for effecting
vaginal delivery
are ideal

Ⓓ Strong or
urgent
indication
prevails

Weak indication
No urgency

Ⓓ Strong or
urgent
indication
prevails

Ⓕ Consider temporizing
Allow labor to continue
Reassess pelvis and
    cephalopelvic
    relationships
Allow analgesia to abate
Give oxytocin to enhance
    uterine contractions
Provide support

Ⓔ Consider
CESAREAN
SECTION
option
(p 288)

Ⓖ MIDFORCEPS
DELIVERY

SPONTANEOUS
VAGINAL
DELIVERY

Ⓖ LOW FORCEPS
DELIVERY

285

FORCEPS DELIVERY

Emanuel A. Friedman, M.D., Sc.D.

A. Before undertaking a forceps delivery, one must weigh the risks against the benefits (p 284) and then provide objective justification in the form of a compelling indication to counterbalance any potential hazard. Similarly, the procedure being considered should be clearly preferable to alternative options, including allowing the labor to proceed expectantly or with uterotonic stimulation or concluding it by cesarean section. Be especially mindful of any contraindications. Assess fetal and maternal well-being and ensure the availability of adequate anesthesia services for the procedure or any complications that may ensue. Obtain informed consent before proceeding (p 300).

B. Contraindications should be carefully reviewed to be sure that none prevail. Unless the obstetrician has the necessary experience and skill, it is not prudent to undertake a forceps operation without suitable supervision and guidance. One must be reasonably certain that there is no cephalopelvic disproportion; because an antecedent protraction or arrest disorder of labor (pp 238, 240) may reflect unsuspected disproportion, the burden of proof rests on the operator to rule it out in as definitive a manner as possible before subjecting the mother and fetus to the trauma that might result from a forceps procedure under these circumstances. Forceps cannot be safely applied if the cervix is not fully dilated and retracted and the fetal head is not deeply engaged. Be aware that determination of the fetal station by vaginal palpation may be misleading (that is, more cephalad than it appears) if the fetal head is markedly molded or deflexed, such as occurs with a persistent occiput posterior presentation (p 212).

C. Certain prerequisites must be met for a forceps delivery in addition to a skilled operator, appropriate anesthesia, and an adequate pelvis (both to accommodate the fetus and to permit the procedure to be accomplished without inflicting damage). Forceps are designed to be applied only to the fetal head; therefore, a cephalic presentation must be assured. Moreover, it is essential that the presentation (vertex, sincipital, brow, face) and position (e.g., left occiput anterior, right mentum posterior) be known with precision and certainty. In addition to a fully dilated cervix, forceps require ruptured membranes and an emptied bladder and rectum.

D. Forceps can be categorized as classic and special varieties. The several hundred eponymic types of classic forceps are simply variants of the Simpson or Elliot forceps (Fig. 1). The Simpson forceps have separated shanks, which yield a tapered cephalic curve; this best fits an elongated, molded fetal head. By contrast, the Elliot forceps have overlapping shanks, producing a more rounded cephalic curve, optimally suited for the unmolded head. Special forceps were engineered for specific uses. The Kielland forceps, which have essentially no pelvic curve, are intended for corrective rotation of the fetal head in an occiput posterior or transverse arrest in an anthropoid pelvis. The Barton forceps, with congruent pelvic and cephalic curves, are used only for transverse arrest in a platypelloid (flat) pelvis. Because significant hazards have been found to be associated with these special forceps, they are much less often used today than in the past.

E. Correct application is most important for forceps use. Poor application enhances risk. The forceps blades must anchor below the zygoma so that forces are transmitted to the base of the skull. To verify this, check to ensure that the shanks are perpendicular to the sagittal suture, the lambdoidal sutures are 1 cm anterior and equidistant, and the space under the heel of the blade accommodates just a fingertip. Apply traction only if application is verified, providing vector force in the proper axial direction according to the station of the fetal head.

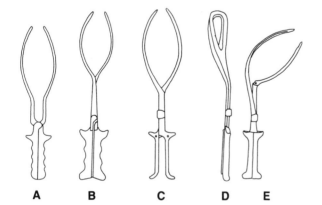

Figure 1 Commonly used forceps types. *A*, Simpson; *B*, Tucker-McLane (Elliot variant); *C* and *D*, Kielland; *E*, Barton.

References

Cyr RM, Usher RH, McLean FH. Changing patterns of birth asphyxia and trauma over 20 years. Am J Obstet Gynecol 148:490, 1984.

O'Driscoll K, Meagher D, MacDonald D, Geoghegan F. Traumatic intracranial haemorrhage in firstborn infants and delivery with obstetric forceps. Br J Obstet Gynaecol 88:577, 1981.

Richardson DA. Evans MI, Cibils LA. Midforceps delivery: A critical review. Am J Obstet Gynecol 145:621, 1983.

FORCEPS DELIVERY CONTEMPLATED

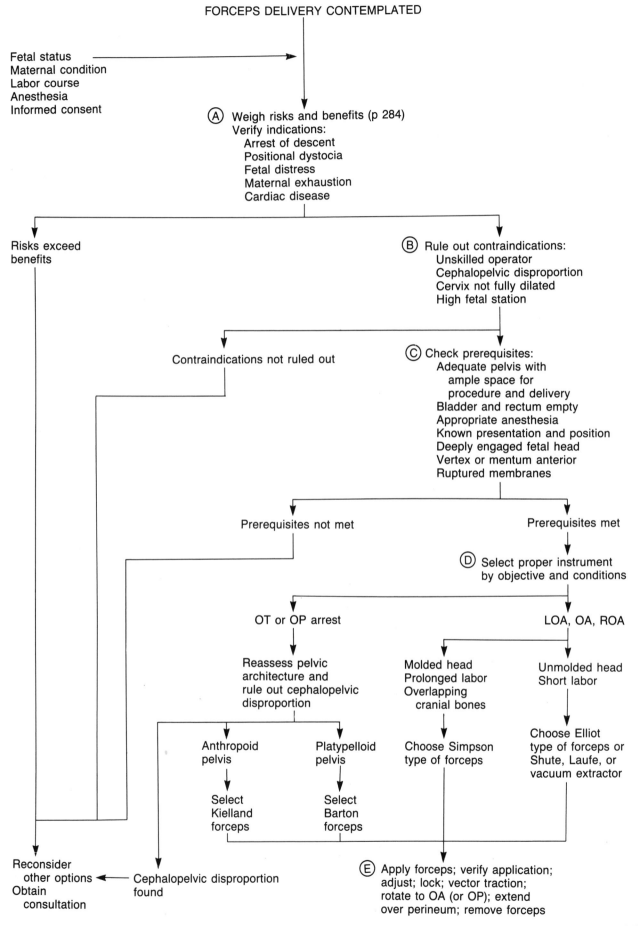

Fetal status
Maternal condition
Labor course
Anesthesia
Informed consent

Ⓐ Weigh risks and benefits (p 284)
Verify indications:
   Arrest of descent
   Positional dystocia
   Fetal distress
   Maternal exhaustion
   Cardiac disease

Risks exceed
benefits

Ⓑ Rule out contraindications:
   Unskilled operator
   Cephalopelvic disproportion
   Cervix not fully dilated
   High fetal station

Contraindications not ruled out

Ⓒ Check prerequisites:
   Adequate pelvis with
     ample space for
     procedure and delivery
   Bladder and rectum empty
   Appropriate anesthesia
   Known presentation and position
   Deeply engaged fetal head
   Vertex or mentum anterior
   Ruptured membranes

Prerequisites not met

Prerequisites met

Ⓓ Select proper instrument
by objective and conditions

OT or OP arrest

LOA, OA, ROA

Reassess pelvic
architecture and
rule out cephalopelvic
disproportion

Molded head
Prolonged labor
Overlapping
cranial bones

Unmolded head
Short labor

Anthropoid
pelvis

Platypelloid
pelvis

Choose Simpson
type of forceps

Choose Elliot
type of forceps or
Shute, Laufe, or
vacuum extractor

Select
Kielland
forceps

Select
Barton
forceps

Reconsider
   other options
Obtain
   consultation

Cephalopelvic disproportion
found

Ⓔ Apply forceps; verify application;
adjust; lock; vector traction;
rotate to OA (or OP); extend
over perineum; remove forceps

OPTIONS IN CESAREAN SECTION

Louis Burke, M.D.

A. Weighing risk-benefit relationships when considering cesarean section can be very complex. Bear in mind that cesarean section is a major surgical procedure carrying a significant risk. It cannot be undertaken without fully documented indications and justification that it is preferable to other options, including expectancy. If feasible, try to inform the patient adequately, and take all appropriate measures to ensure that she is in optimal condition. This includes a detailed preoperative evaluation, including a medical history, physical examination, and laboratory evaluation, as appropriate for any major surgery or anesthesia. If the patient's condition warrants, renal, cardiac, and pulmonary function tests may be necessary.

B. Informed consent is essential, regardless of the emergency that prevails, although the thoroughness of the interview may have to be modified or limited by time constraints. The patient must be counseled to understand the rationale, risks, and alternatives. Only if this is done can one be assured that the consent is meaningful or valid. This can be accomplished in most cases while the operating room team is being mobilized and the preanesthetic evaluation is being done. If the patient has been sedated or the emergency is grave, it is prudent to inform her partner (or the hospital administration) and to provide full details for her as soon postoperatively as feasible.

C. The precept of "once a cesarean, always a cesarean" is no longer accepted (p 292). At least half the women who have undergone a cesarean section should be able to deliver vaginally in a subsequent pregnancy. To ensure safety, select patients carefully, inform them conscientiously and reassuringly, and provide needed resources for dealing with complications. If problems arise during the trial of labor, one can proceed with cesarean section. Although uterine rupture is exceedingly rare, it is nonetheless a potentially catastrophic risk. Therefore it is inappropriate to consider such labor trials in obstetrical units that are not fully prepared with immediately available on-site surgical facilities and personnel. This interdiction applies especially to free-standing birthing units and home births. Oxytocin stimulation is not contraindicated, although it must be used with great care to avoid uterine hyperstimulation; invoking it to correct an arrested labor, which can be associated with cephalopelvic disproportion, may be especially

hazardous, however. The incidence of success in vaginal delivery following previous cesarean section may be increased somewhat by careful and judicious use of oxytocin.

D. Maternal morbidity is commonly associated with cesarean section when done in patients who are in labor. Prophylactic antibiotic therapy has been shown to reduce the frequency and severity of postoperative infections, especially if instituted several hours prior to surgery and continued for 24 hours afterwards. Elective repeat cesarean section, which carries a relatively low morbidity incidence, does not appear to be benefited by antibiotic prophylaxis.

E. Selecting abdominal and uterine incisions depends on a number of factors (p 290), primarily speed and space requirements. A vertical midline suprapubic incision is preferred when an emergency exists or a large exposure is needed. A Pfannenstiel incision takes longer and may give limited access, but it heals better and is cosmetically preferable. The common low transverse elliptical uterine incision has the advantages of less bleeding, ease of repair, reduced postoperative adhesions, and fewer subsequent ruptures; however, bladder injury and lateral extension into uterine vessels can occur. The classic incision, which is quick but yields more hemorrhage and subsequent rupture, is still used when indicated. Extraperitoneal cesarean section is seldom undertaken any longer, even for a grossly infected uterus.

References

Dilts PV. How can we decrease the incidence of cesarean section? Contemp Ob Gyn 18:19, 1981.
Flamm BL, Dunnett C, Fischermann E, Quilligan EJ. Vaginal delivery following cesarean section: Use of oxytocin augmentation and epidural anesthesia with internal tocodynamic and internal fetal monitoring. Am J Obstet Gynecol 148:759, 1984.
Martins MC, Mayen S, Gelfand M. Cesarean section recent trends. Can J Surg 25:85, 1982.
Pauerstein CJ. Labor after cesarean section: From precept to practice. J Reprod Med 26:409, 1981.
Paul RH, Phelan JP, Yeh S. Trial of labor in the patient with prior cesarean birth. Am J Obstet Gynecol 151:297, 1985.

CESAREAN SECTION CONTEMPLATED

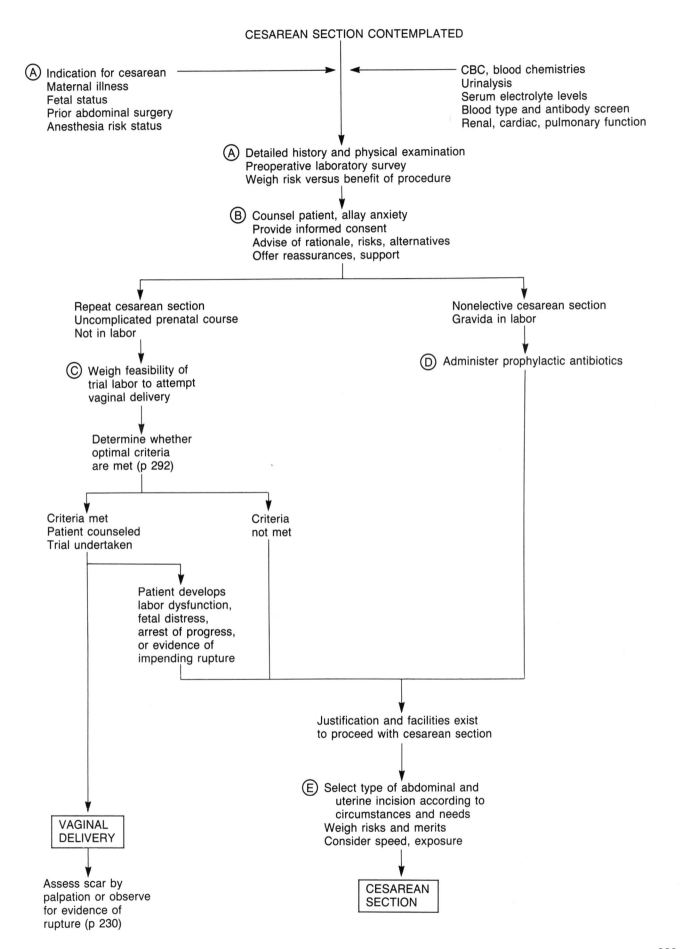

Ⓐ Indication for cesarean
Maternal illness
Fetal status
Prior abdominal surgery
Anesthesia risk status

CBC, blood chemistries
Urinalysis
Serum electrolyte levels
Blood type and antibody screen
Renal, cardiac, pulmonary function

Ⓐ Detailed history and physical examination
Preoperative laboratory survey
Weigh risk versus benefit of procedure

Ⓑ Counsel patient, allay anxiety
Provide informed consent
Advise of rationale, risks, alternatives
Offer reassurances, support

Repeat cesarean section
Uncomplicated prenatal course
Not in labor

Nonelective cesarean section
Gravida in labor

Ⓒ Weigh feasibility of
trial labor to attempt
vaginal delivery

Ⓓ Administer prophylactic antibiotics

Determine whether
optimal criteria
are met (p 292)

Criteria met
Patient counseled
Trial undertaken

Criteria
not met

Patient develops
labor dysfunction,
fetal distress,
arrest of progress,
or evidence of
impending rupture

Justification and facilities exist
to proceed with cesarean section

Ⓔ Select type of abdominal and
uterine incision according to
circumstances and needs
Weigh risks and merits
Consider speed, exposure

VAGINAL
DELIVERY

CESAREAN
SECTION

Assess scar by
palpation or observe
for evidence of
rupture (p 230)

CESAREAN SECTION DELIVERY

Henry Kapholz, M.D.

A. Carefully weigh indications and risks (p 288). Except for rare situations in which minutes might make a real difference in outcome, review rationale, risks, and other options with the patient beforehand to obtain a fully informed consent (p 300). Before undertaking an elective cesarean section, fetal maturity must be assured. Good dating (p 8) is based on the known milestones (last menstrual period, heart tones, and quickening) or early pregnancy ultrasonography. Failing this, carry out an amniocentesis for pulmonary maturity testing (p 64).

B. The choice of anesthesia (p 188) depends on a number of considerations, including available skills, the patient's prior experience and reactions, her general medical status, the degree of urgency to proceed, and the presence of a full stomach. Emergency cesarean section requires general anesthesia to expedite the procedure, to provide maximum maternal oxygenation, and to control blood pressure and hemodynamics. Keep the gravida in the left lateral tilt position to avert supine hypotension. Most cesarean sections without urgent indications can be achieved with conduction anesthesia; if it wears off, local infiltration may be effective, taking care to avoid toxic levels of the drug. Prophylactic doses of antibiotics reduce infectious morbidity postoperatively if cesarean section is done in the course of labor.

C. The choice of abdominal incision (Fig. 1) depends somewhat on the speed of entry required, transverse incisions taking more time for dissection. Other considerations include abdominal scars, special need for room to extract the fetus, and the anticipated uterine incision. A planned classic uterine incision calls for a vertical abdominal incision. A Pfannenstiel incision is stronger, does not eviscerate, and is more comfortable and cosmetic, but it may limit space and exposure. It can be expanded if necessary by cutting the rectus muscles partially or completely to convert it to a Maylard incision. Use a vertical incision for very obese patients unless the panniculus can be elevated (cephalad) easily.

D. A low transverse (low cervical, low flap, Kerr) uterine incision is preferred under most circumstances. It incises the thin fibrous portion of the lower uterine segment and yields minimal blood loss and good healing; it can be covered by the bladder flap. Avoid lateral extension into the uterine vessels by curving it well up. The classic incision is reserved for cases in which the lower segment is not distended and thinned, for transverse lie with the back down, or for anteriorly implanted placenta previa. Consider a low vertical (Kroenig) incision if the lower segment is well developed but extension of the incision is likely. For repeat cesarean sections, try to use the same incision site as before to avoid avascularity and poor healing where scars cross.

E. If the head is very low in the pelvis, especially after a failed trial of labor, it may be difficult to disimpact it without trauma. Transvaginal elevation of the head by a trained individual, cupping the flat of the hand to distribute pressure on the skull, is done under these circumstances preferably before the uterus in incised. Alternatively a pair of small obstetrical forceps may be used.

F. If bleeding is excessive, consider internal iliac artery ligation, particularly if a uterine extension or rupture is found. If the lower segment is so thin as to be irreparable, proceed to hysterectomy. If possible, intraoperative informed consent should be obtained; since this is not always feasible, the possibility must be raised beforehand as part of preoperative counseling. Retention sutures or a Smead-Jones closure should be used when risk factors exist for wound disruption, such as infection.

References

Araujo JG, Oliveira FC. The place of caesarean section and choice of method. Clin Obstet Gynaecol 9:757, 1982.

Chestnut DH, Eden RD, Gall SA, Parker RT. Peripartum hysterectomy: A review of cesarean and postpartum hysterectomy. Obstet Gynecol 65:365, 1985.

Danforth DN. Cesarean section. JAMA 253:811, 1985.

Gross TL. Operative considerations in the obese pregnant patient. Clin Perinatol 10:411, 1983.

Hirsch HA. Prophylactic antibiotics in obstetrics and gynecology. Am J Med 78:170, 1985.

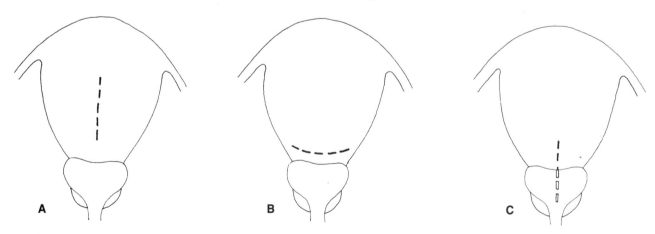

Figure 1 Cesarean section incisions. *A*, classic; *B*, low transverse (low flap cervical) or Kerr; *C*, low vertical or Kroenig.

CONSIDERATION OF CESAREAN SECTION

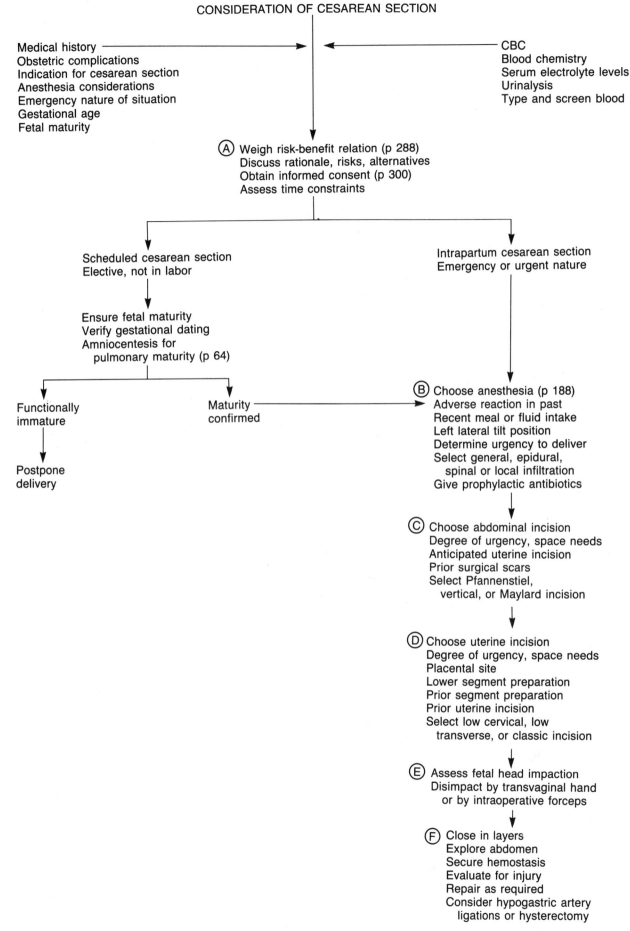

Medical history
Obstetric complications
Indication for cesarean section
Anesthesia considerations
Emergency nature of situation
Gestational age
Fetal maturity

CBC
Blood chemistry
Serum electrolyte levels
Urinalysis
Type and screen blood

Ⓐ Weigh risk-benefit relation (p 288)
Discuss rationale, risks, alternatives
Obtain informed consent (p 300)
Assess time constraints

Scheduled cesarean section
Elective, not in labor

Intrapartum cesarean section
Emergency or urgent nature

Ensure fetal maturity
Verify gestational dating
Amniocentesis for
    pulmonary maturity (p 64)

Functionally
immature

Maturity
confirmed

Postpone
delivery

Ⓑ Choose anesthesia (p 188)
Adverse reaction in past
Recent meal or fluid intake
Left lateral tilt position
Determine urgency to deliver
Select general, epidural,
    spinal or local infiltration
Give prophylactic antibiotics

Ⓒ Choose abdominal incision
Degree of urgency, space needs
Anticipated uterine incision
Prior surgical scars
Select Pfannenstiel,
    vertical, or Maylard incision

Ⓓ Choose uterine incision
Degree of urgency, space needs
Placental site
Lower segment preparation
Prior segment preparation
Prior uterine incision
Select low cervical, low
    transverse, or classic incision

Ⓔ Assess fetal head impaction
Disimpact by transvaginal hand
    or by intraoperative forceps

Ⓕ Close in layers
Explore abdomen
Secure hemostasis
Evaluate for injury
Repair as required
Consider hypogastric artery
    ligations or hysterectomy

PREVIOUS CESAREAN SECTION

David B. Acker, M.D.

A. Each case is evaluated for possible vaginal delivery on its own merits. This applies to women who have not delivered vaginally as well as to those in whom prior cesarean was done because of cephalopelvic disproportion. Written documentation should be obtained about the indication for the previous cesarean, the type of incision, and any obstetrical or operative complications that occurred. Confirm the gestational age by ultrasonographic evaluation in early pregnancy.

B. Ensure that vaginal birth after cesarean section can be safely offered to the patient on the basis of an adequate blood bank, anesthesia, and obstetrical and emergency operating room facilities.

C. A repeat cesarean section is indicated if the prior uterine incision was vertical. The safety of vaginal birth after more than two cesarean sections via Kerr incisions or by unknown types of incision is dubious; repeat cesarean section is, therefore, a prudent choice.

D. The patient's preference for either route of delivery must be respected. The gravida also should be granted the privilege of changing her mind. Economic pressure is growing as a deciding factor, but thus far the patient generally has the option to choose.

E. External cephalic version in a patient with a uterine scar is hazardous. After 38 weeks' gestational age, the chance of spontaneous version is only 2 to 5 percent.

F. If the uterine size, gestational dates, and results of ultrasonographic examination are consistent and confirmatory and uterine growth has continued normally, a repeat cesarean section can be scheduled after completion of the 38th week. If these criteria are not met, one should first confirm fetal lung maturity (p 66); alternatively, await the onset of labor. Delivery before the onset of labor is preferred for those with a prior vertical incision. Ultrasonography in late pregnancy can alert the obstetrician to the presence of placenta previa (p 88). If it is present, appropriate anticipatory preparation should be made for postpartum hemorrhage.

G. It is essential for an obstetrician who is capable of handling all intrapartum emergencies to be present whenever a patient is undergoing a trial of labor after a prior cesarean section. The continuous presence of an anesthesiologist is also optimal but not mandatory; nonetheless, he should be rapidly available if an emergency should arise. Although one should try to minimize the amount of analgesia, epidural anesthesia is not contraindicated in these cases.

H. If labor is clearly indicated and conditions are optimal for the induction of labor (p 182), oxytocin may be cautiously administered. Continuous, close monitoring of the maternal and fetal status, uterine contractility, and labor course is essential.

I. If there is any substantive delay in the delivery of the placenta, suspect placenta accreta (p 90). In the absence of retained placenta or postpartum hemorrhage, there is no necessity to explore the lower uterine segment manually after vaginal delivery. The examination itself may cause damage.

References

Flamm BL, Dunnett C, Fischermann E, Quilligan EJ. Vaginal delivery following cesarean section: Use of oxytocin augmentation and epidural anesthesia with internal tocodynamic and internal fetal monitoring. Am J Obstet Gynecol 148:759, 1984.

Horenstein JM, Phalen JP. Previous cesarean section: Risks and benefits of oxytocin usage in a trial of labor. Am J Obstet Gynecol 151:564, 1985.

Paul RH, Phalen JP, Yeh S. Trial of labor in a patient with a prior cesarean birth. Am J Obstet Gynecol 151:297, 1985.

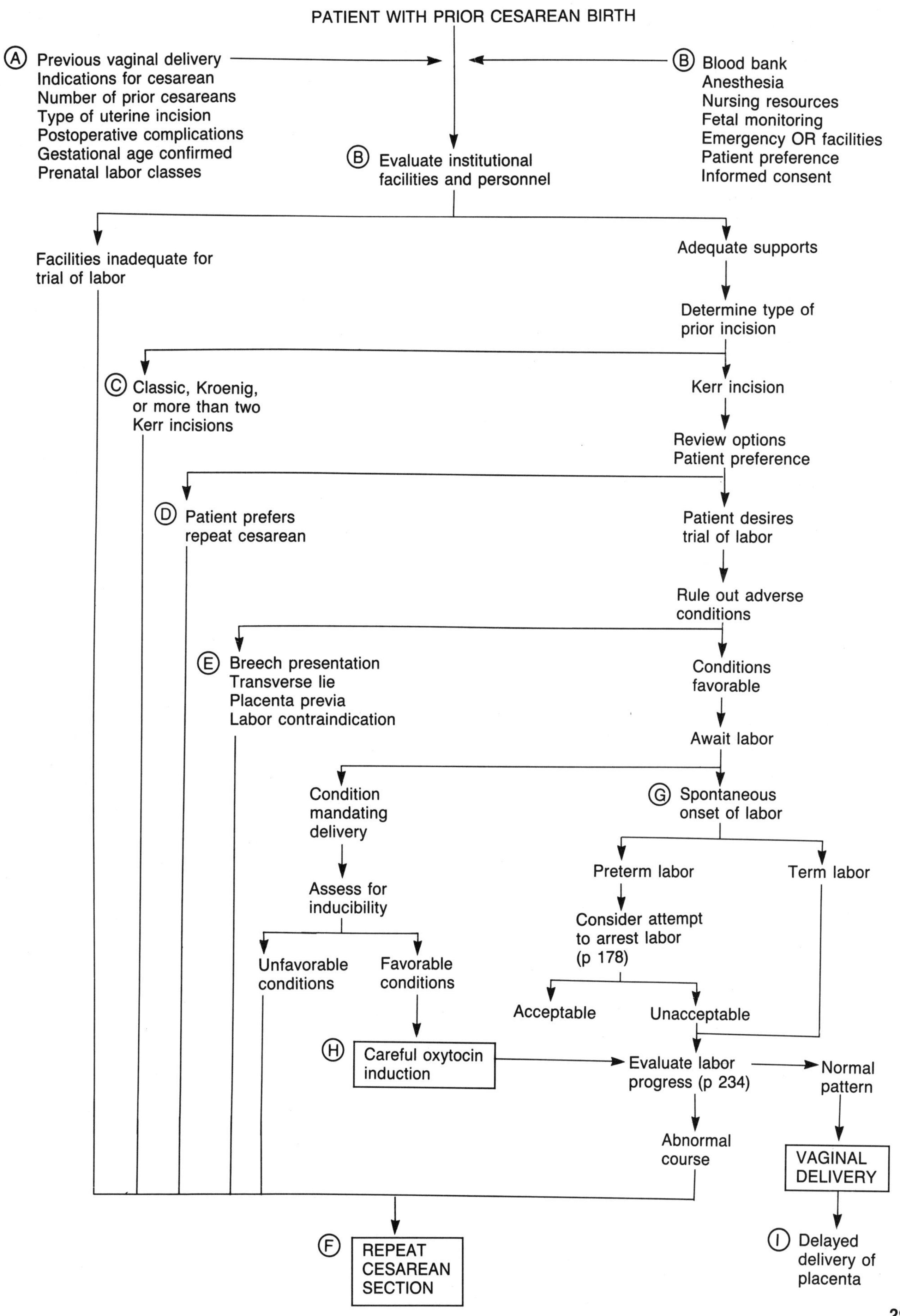

PATIENT WITH PRIOR CESAREAN BIRTH

(A) Previous vaginal delivery
Indications for cesarean
Number of prior cesareans
Type of uterine incision
Postoperative complications
Gestational age confirmed
Prenatal labor classes

(B) Blood bank
Anesthesia
Nursing resources
Fetal monitoring
Emergency OR facilities
Patient preference
Informed consent

(B) Evaluate institutional
facilities and personnel

Facilities inadequate for
trial of labor

Adequate supports

Determine type of
prior incision

(C) Classic, Kroenig,
or more than two
Kerr incisions

Kerr incision

Review options
Patient preference

(D) Patient prefers
repeat cesarean

Patient desires
trial of labor

Rule out adverse
conditions

(E) Breech presentation
Transverse lie
Placenta previa
Labor contraindication

Conditions
favorable

Await labor

Condition
mandating
delivery

(G) Spontaneous
onset of labor

Preterm labor

Term labor

Assess for
inducibility

Consider attempt
to arrest labor
(p 178)

Unfavorable
conditions

Favorable
conditions

Acceptable

Unacceptable

(H) Careful oxytocin
induction

Evaluate labor
progress (p 234)

Normal
pattern

Abnormal
course

VAGINAL
DELIVERY

(F) REPEAT
CESAREAN
SECTION

(I) Delayed
delivery of
placenta

293

CONTRACEPTION

Johanna F. Perlmutter, M.D.

A. Although amenorrhea is common in lactating mothers, ovulation and menstruation can occur unpredictably. It is a widespread misconception that lactation protects against pregnancy. A contraceptive method is needed, but few options are available. Birth control pills may reduce milk production, and natural methods (see F) are ineffective with erratic menstruation. Thus, only barrier methods apply. Defer diaphragm use until after involution to ensure proper fit. This leaves only condoms for the first six weeks or so after delivery.

B. The time it takes after delivery for menstruation to resume is highly variable. The first period usually occurs six to eight weeks post partum, but with lactation it may not start for three to four months. Condoms are recommended for patients who begin intercourse prior to the six week postpartum visit.

C. Birth control pills can be initiated for the non-nursing woman as early as five days post partum, but they are not without risk. If the use of pills is begun before the first menstrual bleeding, contraceptive protection is unreliable. They also can mask manifestations of Sheehan's syndrome. They make it difficult to differentiate pill related breakthrough bleeding from pregnancy related problems, such as retained secundines (p 264). Rule out early pregnancy before starting pills to avoid potentially teratogenic effects on the developing fetus (p 56). Heavy vaginal bleeding or persistent spotting necessitates curettage.

D. Intrauterine devices (IUD) are effective for contraception, but their association with pelvic inflammatory disease and infertility must be carefully explained to the patient. The only IUD currently available in the United States is the Progestasert, containing progesterone. Theoretically the amount of progesterone absorbed from this device should not interfere with lactation. It may be inserted at any time after complete uterine involution. With subinvolution or endometritis, it is advisable to wait for complete resolution because poor IUD placement, sepsis, heavy vaginal bleeding, and perforation are more apt to occur. Avoid IUD use in the lactating woman because uterine hyperinvolution occurs with lactation, making the uterine cavity too small to accommodate the IUD and risking perforation, expulsion, and pregnancy.

E. The most common time for spontaneous expulsion of an IUD is in the first 24 hours after insertion or at the first menstrual period. If inserted soon after delivery, it should be placed high in the uterine cavity. Check to ensure that the device is still in place at six weeks or after the first menstrual period, and look for evidence of infection.

F. Rhythm methods use ovulation timing as the basis for contraception by assuming fertility at midcycle (or 14 days prior to the next period) and avoiding coitus for several days before and after. Even under the most ideal circumstances, such natural methods yield frequent pregnancies. They are especially ineffective after delivery before normal menstrual rhythmicity is re-established. Basal body temperature and cervical mucus changes are somewhat better indices, but they require long periods of abstention for security.

G. Use of the diaphragm as an effective barrier method has to be postponed until the uterus has fully involuted and all genital tissues have returned to normal. Spatial relationships of the cervix and vagina, vaginal tone, and perineal muscle integrity must be restored in order for a diaphragm to fit properly and to retain its functional value over a long period of time.

H. Because the contraceptive sponge does not require fitting, it can be used in the woman whose anatomy has not returned to the prepregnant state. It should not be used during menstruation. Its contraceptive efficacy, however, is clearly less than that of birth control pills, the IUD, or other barrier methods.

References

Debrovner CH, Winikoff B. Trends in postpartum contraceptive choice. Obstet Gynecol 63:65, 1984.

Forrest JD, Henshaw SK. What U.S. women think and do about contraception. Fam Plann Perspect 15:157, 1983.

Mills A. Barrier contraception. Clin Obstet Gynaecol 11:641, 1984.

Wade ME, McCarthy P, Braunstein GD, et al. A randomized prospective study of the use-effectiveness of two methods of natural family planning. Am J Obstet Gynecol 141:368, 1981.

CONSIDERATION OF CONTRACEPTION

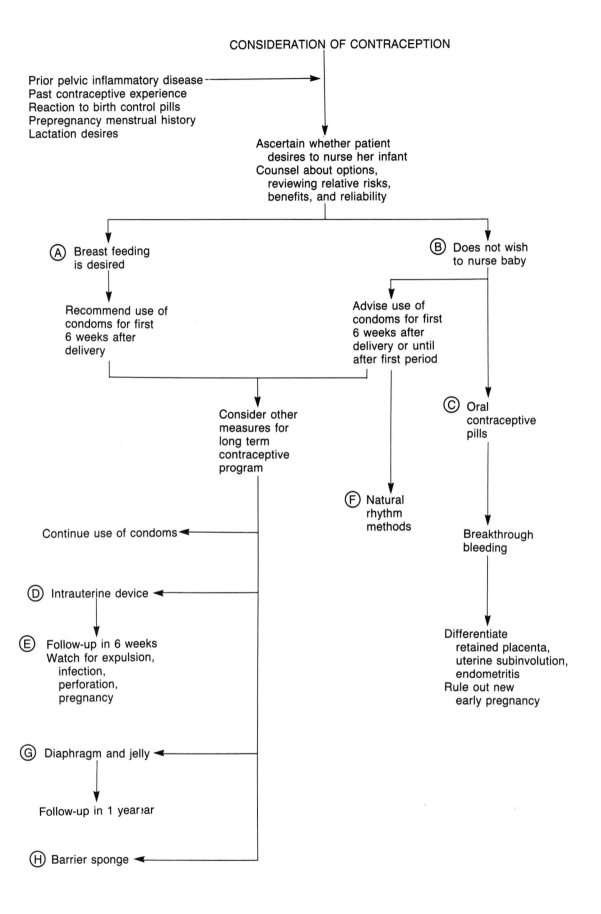

Prior pelvic inflammatory disease
Past contraceptive experience
Reaction to birth control pills
Prepregnancy menstrual history
Lactation desires

Ascertain whether patient
desires to nurse her infant
Counsel about options,
reviewing relative risks,
benefits, and reliability

(A) Breast feeding
is desired

(B) Does not wish
to nurse baby

Recommend use of
condoms for first
6 weeks after
delivery

Advise use of
condoms for first
6 weeks after
delivery or until
after first period

(C) Oral
contraceptive
pills

Consider other
measures for
long term
contraceptive
program

(F) Natural
rhythm
methods

Breakthrough
bleeding

Continue use of condoms

(D) Intrauterine device

Differentiate
retained placenta,
uterine subinvolution,
endometritis
Rule out new
early pregnancy

(E) Follow-up in 6 weeks
Watch for expulsion,
infection,
perforation,
pregnancy

(G) Diaphragm and jelly

Follow-up in 1 year

(H) Barrier sponge

PRESTERILIZATION COUNSELING

Max Borten, M.D.

A. Before proceeding with any surgical procedure that will produce permanent sterilization, it is essential to obtain information about the patient, including her reasons for and concerns about the decision to be sterilized. Arbitrary prerequisites or restrictions for determining suitability based on age and parity have been eliminated. Nonetheless it is prudent to probe into the patient's attitudes, moral and theological background, emotional and mental status, and obstetrical history and contraceptive practices. No description of a sterilization procedure can be considered complete without a comprehensive discussion of alternative methods of contraception.

B. Discretion should be used in suggesting, recommending, or approving sterilization for young women of low parity, women in unstable relationships, or women complaining of abnormal libido or sexual dissatisfaction, or in undertaking the procedure in combination with abortion or another surgical procedure for convenience. Psychosocial evaluation (p 30) is therefore most important. The patients likely to express later regrets about sterilization are those undergoing the operation at the time of cesarean section or immediately post partum. A history of psychiatric illness is not by itself a contraindication for sterilization, but a more thorough evaluation is in order in such a case. Patients with severe personality disorders are more likely than others to be dissatisfied or have adverse emotional effects following the operation. Similarly, women with sexual dysfunction have a poor prognosis; sterilization is an unacceptable treatment for this condition. Communication, collaboration, and coordination among the gynecologist, psychiatrist, and social worker are extremely important.

C. Only a small proportion of sterilized women express any regrets about the operation, and most are delighted at the freedom it provides from fear of conception and inconveniences of contraception. The younger the patient, the lower the parity, and the less complete her understanding of the irreversibility of the procedure, the greater the risk of future emotional problems. If such difficulties develop, they are likely to appear within the first two years after the operation. Do not proceed with a sterilization procedure until you are sure that the patient has a full understanding that the operation is definitive and irreversible. Some mistakenly believe that it can be easily reversed; they must be given realistic data about the surgical success of tubal reanastomosis. An ill advised or incompletely counseled patient is most likely to regret her decision in the future.

D. Evaluation of the couple as a unit is desirable. All available methods must be explained and considered before a decision is made. Vasectomy is a simpler and safer surgical procedure than tubal sterilization. It is usually performed on an outpatient basis and carries the lowest risk when performed under local anesthesia. Concerns about its long term safety have now been dispelled. Successful reversal of vasectomy remains controversial, but here again patients must be made to realize that the procedure is essentially permanent.

E. Ensure that the woman (preferably the couple) understands not only the technical aspects of the surgical procedure but also the nature and consequences of sterilization. Failure rates must be fully discussed. Document details of the information provided. Although reversibility ought to be a consideration for the surgeon in selecting the type of procedure, it should never be a decisive factor in the patient's mind. If the woman is uncertain about her potential desire for reversal, additional counseling is indicated before proceeding. Assess the need for psychiatric or social service consultations. In the meantime, provide contraceptive information and therapy.

References

Goldacre MJ, Holford TR, Vessey MP. Cardiovascular disease and vasectomy: Findings from two epidemiologic studies. N Engl J Med 308:805, 1983.

Gonzales BL. Counseling for sterilization. J Reprod Med 26:538, 1981.

Lindenmayer JP, Steinberg MD, Bjork DA, Pardes H. Psychiatric aspects of voluntary sterilization in young, childless women. J Reprod Med 19:87, 1977.

REQUEST FOR STERILIZATION

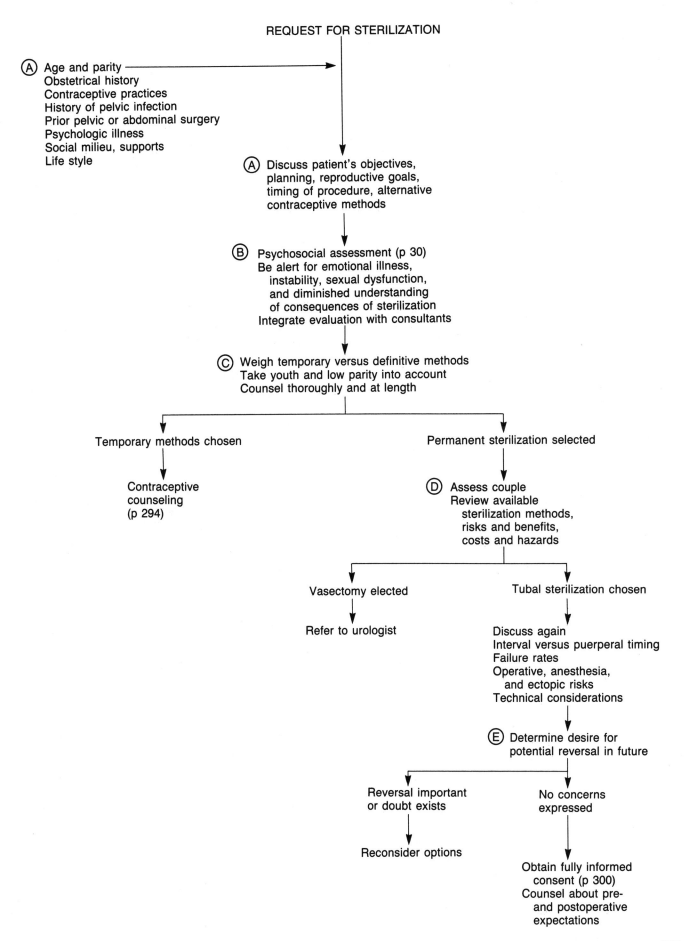

Ⓐ Age and parity
Obstetrical history
Contraceptive practices
History of pelvic infection
Prior pelvic or abdominal surgery
Psychologic illness
Social milieu, supports
Life style

Ⓐ Discuss patient's objectives,
planning, reproductive goals,
timing of procedure, alternative
contraceptive methods

Ⓑ Psychosocial assessment (p 30)
Be alert for emotional illness,
instability, sexual dysfunction,
and diminished understanding
of consequences of sterilization
Integrate evaluation with consultants

Ⓒ Weigh temporary versus definitive methods
Take youth and low parity into account
Counsel thoroughly and at length

Temporary methods chosen

Contraceptive
counseling
(p 294)

Permanent sterilization selected

Ⓓ Assess couple
Review available
sterilization methods,
risks and benefits,
costs and hazards

Vasectomy elected

Refer to urologist

Tubal sterilization chosen

Discuss again
Interval versus puerperal timing
Failure rates
Operative, anesthesia,
and ectopic risks
Technical considerations

Ⓔ Determine desire for
potential reversal in future

Reversal important
or doubt exists

Reconsider options

No concerns
expressed

Obtain fully informed
consent (p 300)
Counsel about pre-
and postoperative
expectations

STERILIZATION

Max Borten, M.D.

A. Voluntary sterilization is currently the leading family planning method around the world. One should not undertake permanent sterilization before evaluating the patient's psychosocial background (p 30) and supports. Review all contraceptive alternatives regardless of age and parity, but especially if the patient is young and of low parity. It is important to emphasize that sterilization is irreversible. The patient should be disabused of the false impression held by many regarding the ease and effectiveness of tubal reanastomosis. Full disclosure and discussion of all options enable the patient to make an intelligent and informed decision. Allow at least 72 hours to pass before proceeding with the operation to give the patient an adequate opportunity to weigh her decision carefully.

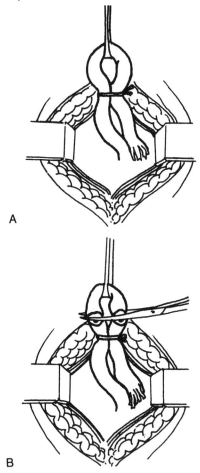

Figure 1 Modified Pomeroy tubal ligation. *A,* midportion of tube is grasped and ligated once with absorbable suture; *B,* the loop of tube above the ligature is resected.

B. The fallopian tubes may be inaccessible to closed trans-endoscopic surgery if extensive adhesions are present. These may result from prior pelvic or abdominal surgery, especially if complicated by postoperative infection, as well as severe or recurrent salpingitis or inflammatory bowel disease. Similarly, if the intestines are adherent to the anterior abdominal wall, the bowel is thereby exposed to the risk of perforation. Prior pelvic surgery or infection contraindicates endoscopic sterilization. An open laparoscopic technique reduces the risks involved in the blind insertion of the insufflating needle and the laparoscopic trocar. Individualize for each patient when selecting the most appropriate procedure.

C. Pregnancy occurring after a sterilization procedure is a serious complication with social, medical, and legal implications. When reviewing the relative risks of sterilization with the patient, include the possibility of contraceptive failure and the real hazard of ectopic pregnancy. A failed procedure may be the result of technical shortcomings (luteal phase pregnancy or misidentification of pelvic structures) or a true method failure (tuboperitoneal fistula or spontaneous tubal reanastomosis).

D. Sterilization procedures are most often done within the first few days post partum. Nevertheless interval procedures tend to be technically easier, with fewer failures, and can be accomplished on an outpatient basis under local anesthesia. The option should be offered to the recently delivered patient. It is important to weigh the risk considerations in each case in order to ensure the best results rather than to compromise principles in order to undertake a standardized endoscopic procedure or to proceed when it is convenient rather than when it is optimal.

E. Knowledge about the various methods by which tubal occlusion can be achieved enables the operator to select the most appropriate method for a particular patient. Furthermore, the surgeon's ability to carry out sterilization procedures in a variety of different ways proves useful if complications arise with the first method selected. An endoscopic procedure offers the opportunity to explore the surrounding abdominopelvic structures visually; it thus permits one to recognize otherwise undisclosed concomitant abnormalities. Operative endoscopic procedures may be used for sterilizing the recently pregnant woman, although laparotomy through a small transverse elliptical subumbilical incision is commonly done and generally proves just as cosmetically acceptable. Of the several types of surgical techniques, the modified Pomeroy method (simple ligation and resection of a midsegment loop of both tubes) is popular (Fig. 1).

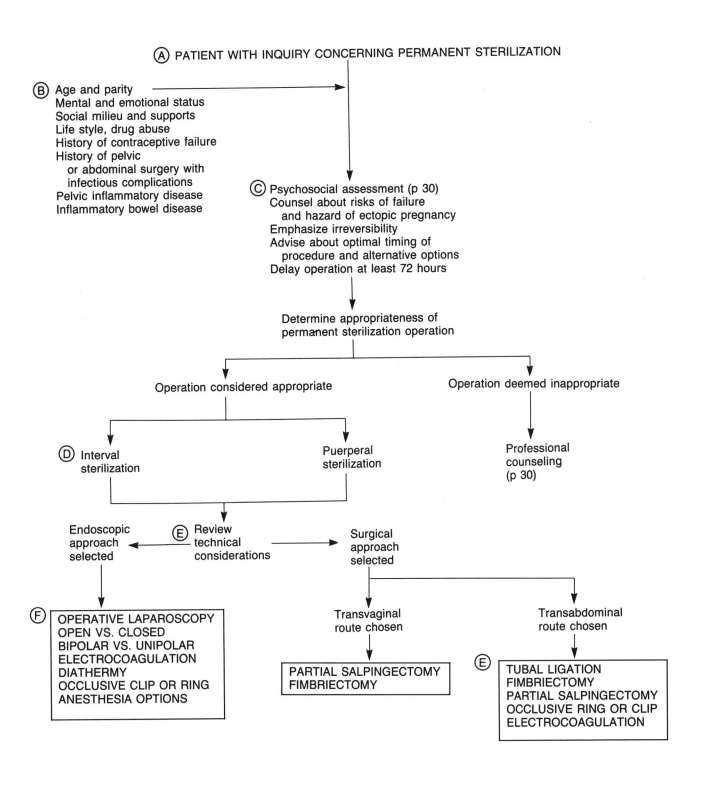

Ⓐ PATIENT WITH INQUIRY CONCERNING PERMANENT STERILIZATION

Ⓑ Age and parity
Mental and emotional status
Social milieu and supports
Life style, drug abuse
History of contraceptive failure
History of pelvic
    or abdominal surgery with
    infectious complications
Pelvic inflammatory disease
Inflammatory bowel disease

Ⓒ Psychosocial assessment (p 30)
Counsel about risks of failure
    and hazard of ectopic pregnancy
Emphasize irreversibility
Advise about optimal timing of
    procedure and alternative options
Delay operation at least 72 hours

Determine appropriateness of
permanent sterilization operation

Operation considered appropriate

Operation deemed inappropriate

Ⓓ Interval
sterilization

Puerperal
sterilization

Professional
counseling
(p 30)

Endoscopic
approach
selected

Ⓔ Review
technical
considerations

Surgical
approach
selected

Ⓕ OPERATIVE LAPAROSCOPY
OPEN VS. CLOSED
BIPOLAR VS. UNIPOLAR
ELECTROCOAGULATION
DIATHERMY
OCCLUSIVE CLIP OR RING
ANESTHESIA OPTIONS

Transvaginal
route chosen

Transabdominal
route chosen

PARTIAL SALPINGECTOMY
FIMBRIECTOMY

Ⓔ TUBAL LIGATION
FIMBRIECTOMY
PARTIAL SALPINGECTOMY
OCCLUSIVE RING OR CLIP
ELECTROCOAGULATION

F. Sterilization is most often accomplished by means of closed laparoscopy. Open laparoscopy is reserved mainly for cases in which extensive adhesions can be anticipated (see B). Unipolar electrocoagulation may be complicated by spark gaps with resulting potentially serious bowel burns. Electrical injuries are rare with bipolar instruments. The procedure involves coagulating three adjacent sites; it is unnecessary to divide the tube in addition. Silicone rings and occlusive clips also can be used for this purpose.

References

Borten M. Laparoscopic Complications: Prevention and Management. Toronto: B. C. Decker, 1986.

Brenner WE. Evaluation of contemporary female sterilization methods. J Reprod Med 26:430, 1981.

Cunanan RG, Courey NG, Lippes J. Complications of tubal sterilization. Obstet Gynecol 55:501, 1980.

Soderstrom RM. Sterilization failures and their causes. Am J Obstet Gynecol 152:395, 1985.

INFORMED CONSENT

Max Borten, M.D.

A. Ordinarily a surgical procedure cannot be done without the patient's consent. Implementing a diagnostic or therapeutic operation without appropriate informed consent risks liability for medical negligence or battery. Negligence consists of the failure to conduct oneself as a reasonably prudent person (physician) would in the same or similar circumstances. Battery connotes unauthorized touching of another's body.

B. In an emergency, consent may be implied to exist from the circumstances. The law infers consent if the patient's life is at stake and if it is just not practicable to obtain consent from some authorized person other than the patient. Similarly, an emergency may justify extending the surgery beyond that consented to, as is the case when taking care of unpredictable complications arising during surgery. Whenever it is not feasible to obtain informed consent prior to surgery, it is advisable to request the patient to execute an emergency care acknowledgment soon after she regains consciousness.

C. The nature of the condition requiring treatment must be explained to the patient in plain language. Both common and serious (even if infrequent) operative risks and complications should be described as well as the likelihood of success or failure (see E). At present, disclosure is not limited merely to the material risks associated with the procedure, but must include a description of alternative options with their comparative benefits and risks. The prognosis, in the event that the condition goes untreated, must also be included.

D. A physician is obligated to have the knowledge expected of a reasonably well trained and knowledgeable physician practicing under like circumstances. Failure of a physician to meet the standard of required knowledge imposes liability based on that shortcoming rather than on the failure to disclose. Ignorance of the potential risks associated with a procedure does not relieve the physician from an obligation to inform the patient adequately.

E. The extent of the risks that should be disclosed to the patient remains controversial. A physician need not disclose every risk that could occur if in his judgment such disclosure may have a harmful effect on the patient's wellbeing. This is known as a privilege to withhold disclosure and is subordinate to the duty to disclose. In the absence of such privilege to disclose, any risk that is material to the procedure to be undertaken must be disclosed to the patient. A risk is deemed material if a reasonable person would be likely to attach significance to it in deciding whether to proceed with the proposed therapy. A physician is not privileged to withhold disclosure whenever the existence of a risk may cause a patient to refuse therapy even though the physician believes that it is for the patient's own good.

F. In the absence of informed consent, the privilege to extend a surgical procedure is generally justified if the condition encountered could not reasonably have been diagnosed prior to surgery, the same operative field is used, sound medical practice dictates it, neither the patient nor a surrogate is immediately available to give the necessary consent, and it was not expressly proscribed by the patient.

G. Clear documentation of the informed consent process is essential. Do not depend on a signed preprinted operative consent form. The validity of a general authorization permitting the physician to exercise his judgment has been rejected for cases with no emergency requiring immediate action to preserve the patient's life or health. A generalized form may be too vague and ambiguous to be considered valid. Be specific. State in the medical record that the patient is aware of her condition, is fully informed about the procedure, and above all understands the risks and possible complications of the planned surgery. The note must also indicate that the patient understands what she has been told and agrees to the treatment as outlined.

References

Fineberg KS, Peters JD, Willson JR, Kroll DA. Obstetrics/Gynecology and the Law. Ann Arbor: Health Administration Press, 1984.

Keeton WP, Dobbs DB, Keeton RE, Owen DG. Prosser and Keeton on the Law of Torts. St. Paul, Minnesota West Publishing Co., 1984.

King JH. The Law of Medical Malpractice in a Nutshell. St. Paul: West Publishing Co., 1977.

Rozovsky FA. Consent to Treatment: A Practical Guide. Boston: Little, Brown, 1984.

Waltz JR, Inbau FE. Medical Jurisprudence. New York: Macmillan, 1971.

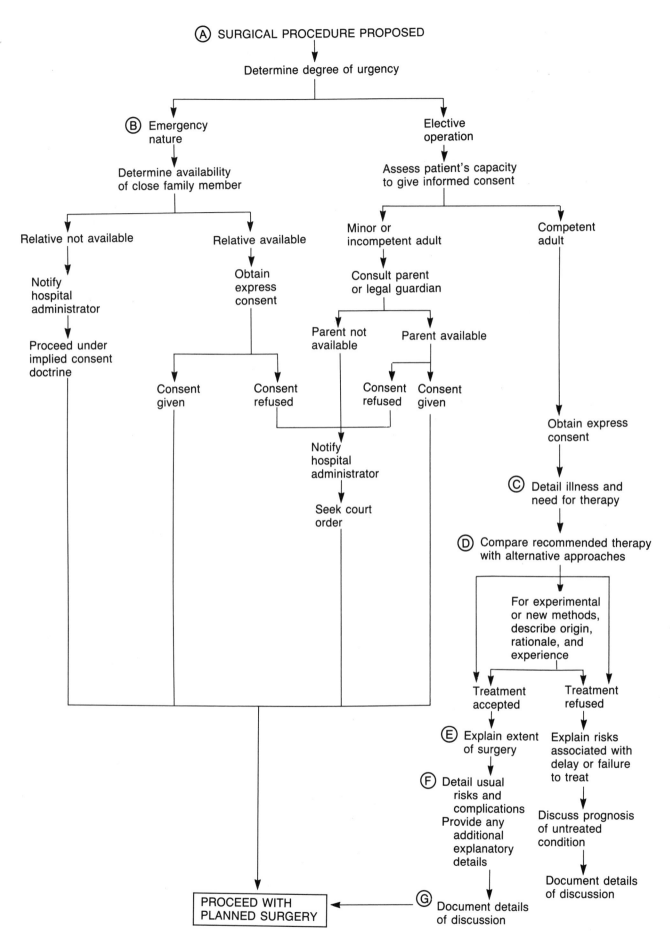

PREVENTIVE RISK

Max Borten, M.D.

A. Complications occurring intra-operatively or postoperatively are understood to be acceptable risks for most surgical procedures. Detailed discussion with the patient in advance and proper documentation of her condition, the available options for management, and their relative risks and benefits are in order. Further open discussion and full disclosure of the complication are also essential after the fact, keeping good records of all events, therapy, consultations, and talks with the patient and her family. Failure to maintain complete, accurate, and timely records can have particularly untoward effects for the responsible physician and supporting staff in the event of a malpractice litigation. Absence of appropriate entries in the medical chart (or the inclusion of inaccurate information) may lead to an adverse legal outcome.

B. Documentation and analysis of the patient's condition are good medical practice. A poorly maintained record may give credibility to an otherwise unmeritorious malpractice claim. An illegible record may preclude adequate evaluation of the care provided. Each entry into the medical record must be dated, timed, and signed or initialed. Record relevant facts promptly and accurately. Delaying an entry risks incompleteness or inaccuracy owing to impaired memory and increases the chance of error. Avoid vague and ambiguous statements that may suggest poor or superficial care. Detailed progress notes indicate that the physician's duty of care is being fulfilled. In teaching hospitals it is equally imperative for supervising physicians to read, correct, and countersign notes written by residents and students to show their responsibility for and approval of the care being rendered.

C. Document your reasons for requesting a consultation. Specify whether a consultant is being called in for evaluation, recommendation, or treatment; if all are applicable, so state. Whenever feasible, introduce the consultant to the patient and be present during the consultation; it helps relieve the patient's anxiety. Above all, keep the patient fully informed about what has taken place and provide her with the reasons for involving other physicians in her care.

D. Unless the consulting physician undertakes care of the patient, it is prudent for the primary physician to discuss the results of the examination and the recommendations advanced by the consultant with the patient. Minimize the number of individuals reviewing the management plan with her to avoid confusion. It is not mandatory to make use of the consultant's recommendation. In the event that one decides not to follow the consultant's suggestions, however, it is essential to substantiate the reasons for the plan of management elected.

E. Document your plan of management in writing. Use objective rather than subjective observations. Include reasons supporting the need for laboratory tests. Elaborate on your thought process. As a rule, a physician cannot be held liable for an honest error in judgment if in the exercise of such medical judgment, he has utilized proper and adequate diagnostic methods.

F. When producing a discharge summary, it is important to be objective. The summary should be confined to a factual and straightforward account of the events that transpired during the course of the hospital stay. Only information included in the medical record should be utilized. Opinions must be avoided to prevent their being perceived as self-serving with counterproductive results.

References

Southwick AF. The Law of Hospital and Health Care Administration. Ann Arbor: Health Administration Press, 1978.

Waltz JR, Inbau FE. Medical Jurisprudence. New York: Macmillan, 1971.

OCCURRENCE OF COMPLICATION

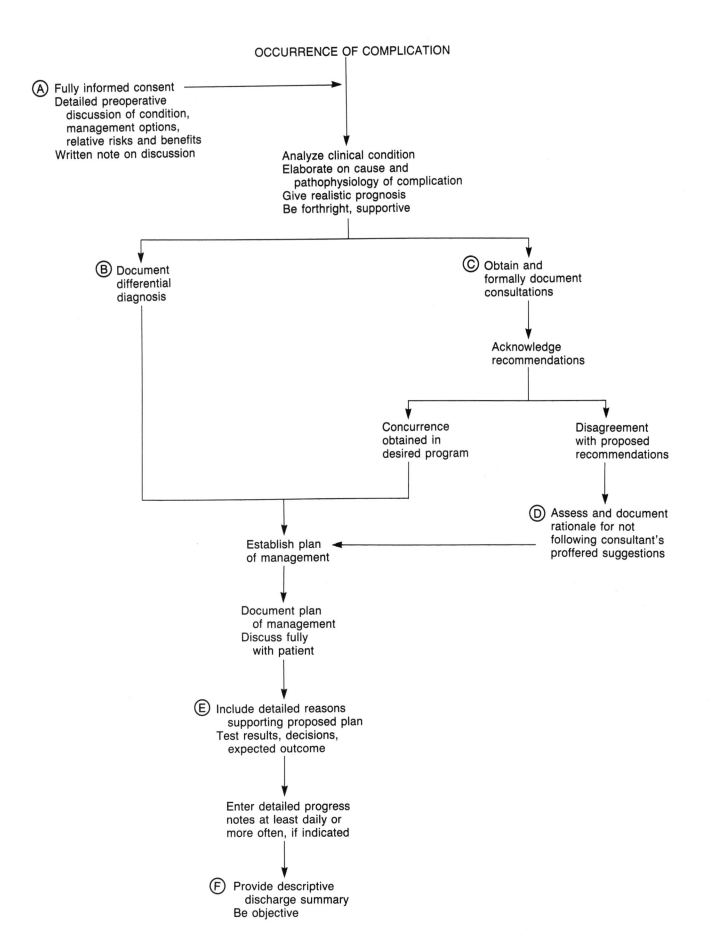

Ⓐ Fully informed consent
   Detailed preoperative
     discussion of condition,
     management options,
     relative risks and benefits
   Written note on discussion

Analyze clinical condition
Elaborate on cause and
  pathophysiology of complication
Give realistic prognosis
Be forthright, supportive

Ⓑ Document
   differential
   diagnosis

Ⓒ Obtain and
   formally document
   consultations

Acknowledge
recommendations

Concurrence
obtained in
desired program

Disagreement
with proposed
recommendations

Ⓓ Assess and document
   rationale for not
   following consultant's
   proffered suggestions

Establish plan
of management

Document plan
of management
Discuss fully
with patient

Ⓔ Include detailed reasons
   supporting proposed plan
   Test results, decisions,
   expected outcome

Enter detailed progress
notes at least daily or
more often, if indicated

Ⓕ Provide descriptive
   discharge summary
   Be objective

RECORD REQUEST PROCEDURE

Max Borten, M.D.

A. Ordinarily a physican receives information relating to a patient's health in a confidential capacity. The patient has the privilege of refusing to disclose and of preventing another from disclosing confidential communications between herself and her physician. A patient's claim of privilege and confidentiality is considered to be waived when the patient puts her medical condition in issue by filing suit. Thus, the physician is allowed to discuss the patient's care and treatment with his defense counsel without the patient's written authorization. For a patient to prevail in a lawsuit for unauthorized disclosure of information, she must show that actual injury or damage was caused by the alleged breach of confidentiality. Thus, there is little risk in sharing patient information with other physicians who have been asked to consult about a patient's condition. However, this should not be interpreted as giving license for discussion of the events of the case insofar as they pertain to any pending claim (see F).

B. In general, a physician cannot lawfully disclose information obtained in the course of a professional doctor-patient relationship without the patient's consent. An exception is made when the physician recognizes a serious danger to the patient or to others. When faced with a request for medical records or a request to disclose patient information, insist on obtaining the patient's written consent for disclosure. If the patient's consent cannot be obtained and time permits, seek a court order allowing disclosure.

C. The physician is the owner of the patient's medical record and has absolute rights to its possession. Nonetheless he has the duty to permit inspection of such medical records. Such duty evolves from the fiduciary nature of the physician-patient relationship under which physicians must reveal to patients that which they should know in their best interests. In some states a patient or authorized representative has by statute the right of access to such records; in others only the patient's attorney has the right to see the records and the patient must show good cause to obtain such a privilege. Refusal to allow the patient's attorney (with appropriate authorization) access to the patient's records may give rise to a charge of fraudulent concealment.

D. Payment of the malpractice insurance premium entitles the physician to obtain appropriate and adequate defense counsel. Such a right is not limited to judicial proceedings, but also includes review and advice concerning potential legal claims. Communicate freely with your risk management officer and legal counsel. Such discussions, prepared in anticipation of litigation, are generally considered a privileged component of the attorney-client relationship. They are thus held to be confidential.

E. After receiving a request for a patient's records, segregate the office and hospital chart and financial information and lock them away securely. This will prevent anyone, including office personnel, from making changes. Avoid making additional entries, since they are generally interpreted as self-serving. Do not make corrections or alterations. A medical record that has been tampered with makes a malpractice case virtually indefensible, regardless of the circumstances. If additional information concerning the patient is recalled, consult your legal counsel as to the appropriate manner for handling and documenting those facts.

F. Avoid the tendency to discuss the case with colleagues or paramedical personnel. This temptation, albeit quite understandable, may lead to counterproductive dissemination of undesirable information. Do not discuss any aspects of the claim with anybody except your legal counsel. Refer all further communications concerning the case to your attorney. Under no circumstances contact the patient or her attorney to discuss events surrounding the claim.

References

Fineberg KS, Peters JD, Willson JR, Kroll DA. Obstetrics/Gynecology and the Law. Ann Arbor: Health Administration Press, 1984.

Holder AR. Medical Malpractice Law. New York: John Wiley & Sons, 1978.

Southwick AF. The Law of Hospital and Health Care Administration. Ann Arbor: Health Administration Press, 1978.

Wadlington W, Waltz JR, Dworkin RB. Law and Medicine: Cases and Materials. Mineola, New York: Foundation Press, 1980.

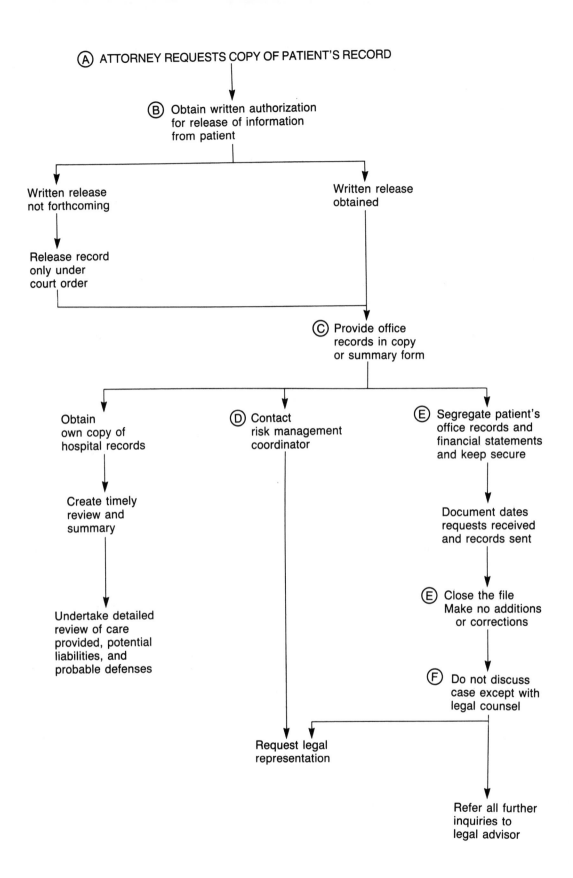

Ⓐ ATTORNEY REQUESTS COPY OF PATIENT'S RECORD

Ⓑ Obtain written authorization for release of information from patient

Written release not forthcoming

Release record only under court order

Written release obtained

Ⓒ Provide office records in copy or summary form

Obtain own copy of hospital records

Create timely review and summary

Undertake detailed review of care provided, potential liabilities, and probable defenses

Ⓓ Contact risk management coordinator

Request legal representation

Ⓔ Segregate patient's office records and financial statements and keep secure

Document dates requests received and records sent

Ⓔ Close the file Make no additions or corrections

Ⓕ Do not discuss case except with legal counsel

Refer all further inquiries to legal advisor

NEGLIGENCE

Max Borten, M.D.

A. Before a breach of duty can be established, the plaintiff (patient) must first establish that the defendant (doctor or hospital) owed her a duty of care. The law does not impose upon individuals the duty to render aid to a person who is ill or in peril. If a formal doctor-patient relationship exists, however, the physician is then under a duty to act as required by the clinical circumstances. At the same time, he has accepted the responsibility not to act in a negligent or reckless manner.

B. The standard of care may vary among jurisdictions. In a few states a "same or similar community standard" is still effective. All other states, by contrast, have adopted the principle that a general or nationwide standard applies for all cases. Thus, a physician offering services as a specialist is held to the standard of care and skill of the average professional practicing the specialty anywhere. This single nationwide standard takes into account advances within the profession that have been widely accepted and generally incorporated into practice.

C. Under the doctrine of *res ipsa loquitur*, the harm suffered by the plaintiff may be inferred to have been caused by negligence of the defendant based on circumstantial evidence. This doctrine is utilized when (a) the event does not ordinarily occur in the absence of negligence; (b) all contributory causes, including conduct of the plaintiff or third parties, are eliminated by the evidence; and (c) the alleged negligence is encompassed within the scope of the defendant's duty to the plaintiff. When this principle is invoked, the burden of proof shifts to the defendant to establish his lack of culpability.

D. The plaintiff must establish that the defendant's conduct— that is, his action or failure to act—was actually connected to the harm produced. The defendant's conduct is not considered to be the cause of plaintiff's harm if that damage would have occurred anyway, regardless of the action taken by the defendant. This is known as the "but for test" or the "sine qua non rule." The ques-

tion is not whether similar harm would have occurred if the defendant had not acted negligently, but whether the "same harm" would have occurred.

E. If an actual cause-effect relation has been established between the defendant's conduct and the adverse outcome for the plaintiff, the defendant's act must be shown to be the proximate cause of the harm to the plaintiff. This is known as legal cause. The defendant's liability is confined to the resulting harm that was a foreseeable consequence of his unreasonable (that is, negligent) act. The defendant may also be held liable for any harm that follows in unbroken sequence from his negligent act if the defendant should have been able to anticipate that the negligence would be compounded by the ensuing negligence of a third party.

F. Contributory negligence and assumption of risk by the plaintiff are substantive defenses in response to a negligence action. In a majority of states some form of comparative negligence has been adopted. As a consequence the plaintiff is allowed to recover damages reduced by the percentage of negligence attributable to her. This effectively abolishes the doctrine formally invoked to the effect that the plaintiff's contributory negligence operates as an absolute bar to her ability to recover for damages.

References

Fineberg KS, Peters JD, Willson JR, Kroll DA. Obstetrics/Gynecology and the Law. Ann Arbor: Health Administration Press, 1984.

Keeton WP, Dobbs DB, Keeton RE, Owen DG. Prosser and Keeton on the Law of Torts. St. Paul, Minnesota: West Publishing Co., 1984.

King JH. The Law of Medical Malpractice in a Nutshell. St. Paul, Minnesota: West Publishing Co., 1977.

Waltz JR, Inbau FE. Medical Jurisprudence. New York: Macmillan, 1971.

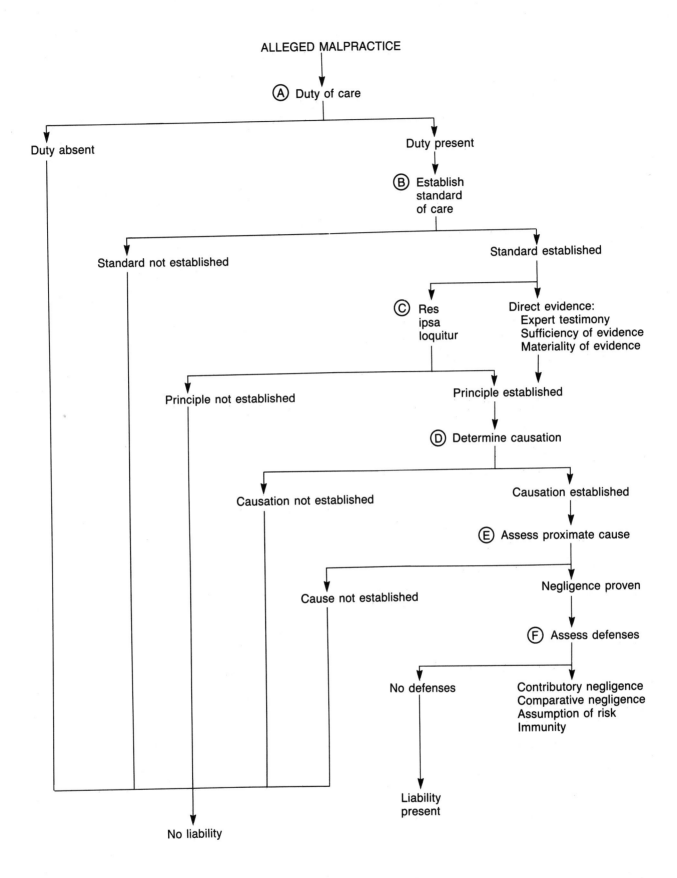

ALLEGED MALPRACTICE

(A) Duty of care

Duty absent

Duty present

(B) Establish standard of care

Standard not established

Standard established

(C) Res ipsa loquitur

Direct evidence:
Expert testimony
Sufficiency of evidence
Materiality of evidence

Principle not established

Principle established

(D) Determine causation

Causation not established

Causation established

(E) Assess proximate cause

Cause not established

Negligence proven

(F) Assess defenses

No defenses

Contributory negligence
Comparative negligence
Assumption of risk
Immunity

No liability

Liability present

toxoplasmosis, 152, 216
viral infection, 151, 152, 216, 217
weight gain, 14, 15, 217
Hydrocephalus, 78
diagnosis, 218, 219
intrauterine shunt, 80, 81
management, 218, 219
recurrence risk, 218
toxoplasmosis, 152
Hydronephrosis
fetal, 80, 81
maternal, 100
Hydrops fetalis
erythroblastosis fetalis, 138
nonimmune, 140, 141
post-term pregnancy, 184
Rh sensitization, 138
Hyperalimentation, 14, 84, 85
Hyperemesis gravidarum, 84, 85
differential diagnosis, 84, 144, 145, 146, 147
incidence, 84
maternal weight, 14
molar pregnancy, 82, 83
Hypertension, chronic
abruptio placentae, 92
collagen disease, 143
diagnosis, 98, 99
elderly gravida, 20, 21
fetal death, 6
fetal growth, 66
history, 10
induction of labor, 182, 183
management, 98, 99
molar pregnancy, 82
premature birth, 174, 176
risk factors, 98, 99
tocolytic agent, 178
uteroplacental insufficiency, 184
Hyperthermia, 16
Hypervitaminosis, 12, 13
Hypoalbuminemia, 12
Hypogastric artery ligation, *See* Internal iliac artery ligation
Hysterectomy
abscess, 258
atony, uterine, 254, 255
cervical cancer, 163
cesarean section, 290, 291
hemorrhage, postpartum, 272, 273
molar pregnancy, 83
placenta accreta, 90, 91
rupture, uterine, 230, 231
Hysterosalpingography, 52, 53
Hysterotomy, 226

I

Immune globulin, 68, 69, 108, 138, 139, 152
Immunosuppressive therapy, 102, 103, 108, 142, 143, 156, 162
Inborn error of metabolism, 74, 75, 81
Incompetent cervix, 16, 17, 50, 52, 53, 56, 174, 176, 177, 220
Induction of labor
amnionitis, 172, 173
Bishop score, 182, 183
bronchial asthma, 136, 137
cardiac disease, 104, 105
diabetes mellitus, 96, 97
failure, 182
fetal jeopardy, 64
growth retardation, 68

indications, 182, 183
macrosomia, fetal, 224, 225
placenta previa, 89
post-term pregnancy 184, 185
pregnancy induced hypertension, 86, 87
premature rupture of membranes, 171
prerequisites, 182
priming, 182, 183
renal transplant, 103
risk, 182, 183
selection criteria, 182, 183
sickle cell disease, 106, 107
staged, 182
technique, 182
Inflammatory bowel disease, 84, 145, 146, 147, 148, 149, 299
Influenza, 150, 151
Informed consent, 180, 181, 205, 230, 288, 290, 296, 297, 298, 300, 301, 303
Internal iliac artery ligation
atony, uterine, 254, 255
cesarean section, 290, 291
coaguloapathy, 114
delivery trauma, 252, 253
hemorrhage, postpartum, 272, 273, 274, 275
placenta accreta, 90
rupture, uterine, 230, 231
Interstitial pregnancy, 54
Intrauterine device, 36, 38, 39
Intrauterine growth retardation, *See* Growth retardation, fetal
Intubation, endotracheal, 262
Inversion, uterine, 252, 253, 270, 271
In vitro fertilization, 28, 29, 220, 221
Iodine, 12
radioisotopic, 62, 116
Iron, *See also* Anemia
adolescent, 18, 19
bowel dysfunction, 128
deficiency, 12, 13
multiple pregnancy, 220, 221
prophylaxis, 112
sickle cell disease, 106, 107
supplement, 12, 13, 106, 107, 112
Ischiorectal fossa, 274
Isoniazid, 134, 135
Isoproterenol, 130

J

Jaundice, maternal, 145, 151

K

Karyotype, fetal cell
alpha fetoprotein, 76, 77
dead fetus, 226, 227
elderly gravida, 20
genetic screening, 74, 75, 78, 79, 80
hydrocephalus, 218, 219
teratogen, 58, 59
Kell antibody, 140
Kerr incision, 290
Ketonuria, 84, 85
Kick count, 184, 185. *See also* Movement, fetal
Kielland forceps 284, 286, 287
Kleihauer-Betke test 94, 138
Kristeller expression
See Fundal pressure
Kroenig incision, 290

Kyphoscoliosis, 25, 126, 127, 128

L

Labor, *See also* Descent, fetal; Dilation, cervical; Induction of labor
amnionitis, 172, 173
arrest disorder, 234, 235, 240
assessing progression, 234, 235
atony, uterine, 254, 255
breech presentation, 204, 205
brow presentation, 208, 209
contractile pattern, 168, 169, 172, 234, 245
delivery trauma, 252, 253
face presentation, 206, 207
failure to progress, 242, 243
false, 236, 237, 246, 247
fever, 232, 233
forceps choice, 284
graph, 234, 235, 242
macrosomia, fetal, 224, 225, 244, 245
nursing role, 168, 169
occiput posterior, 212, 213
phases, 234, 235
post-cesarean, 288, 289
precipitate, 249, 252, 253
prolonged latent phase, 234, 235, 236
protraction disorder, 234, 235, 238
puerperal morbidity, 258, 259
second stage, 244, 245
shoulder dystocia 250, 251
tetany, uterine, 249
trial, 230, 240, 288, 289
tumultuous, 133, 249, 252, 268
Laceration, 226, 232, 252, 253, 254, 272, 273
Lactation, *See also* Breast
advantages, 276
contraception, 294, 295
contraindication, 276, 277
disorder, 278, 279
drug use, 276, 278
engorgement, 278, 279
fissure, 278, 279, 280, 281
galactocele, 278, 279
myasthenia gravis, 120
preparation, 276, 277, 278
pulmonary embolism, 130
pump, 276, 277, 278, 279
suppression, 276, 277, 279
Laminaria, 44, 226
Laparoscopy
ectopic pregnancy, 54, 55
intrauterine device, 38
oocyte aspiration, 28
septic abortion, 36, 37
sterilization, 298, 299
Laparotomy
abdominal mass, 148, 149
abscess, 258
acute surgical abdomen, 144, 145
atony, uterine, 254, 255
cervical cancer, 163
delivery trauma, 252, 253
hemorrhage, postpartum, 272, 273, 274, 275
intrauterine device, 38
molar pregnancy, 83
placenta accreta, 90, 91
rupture, uterine, 230, 231
septic abortion, 36, 37
sterilization, 298, 299
Laryngeal papilloma, 156